ISBN 978-0-259-46289-7
PIBN 10818140

THE

ILLUSTRATED BOOK OF
CANARIES AND CAGE-BIRDS,

BRITISH AND FOREIGN.

BY

W. A. BLAKSTON, W. SWAYSLAND,

AND

AUGUST F. WIENER, F.Z.S.

CASSELL, PETTER, GALPIN & CO.:

LONDON, PARIS & NEW YORK.

PREFACE.

No apology need be made for presenting to the public a work profusely illustrated by coloured plates, concerning so attractive a subject as Cage-Birds. The subject itself will interest thousands, while none is better adapted for pictorial treatment; and it is the sincere wish of all who have contributed the text, that what they have written may be the means not only of increasing the popularity of the fascinating creatures described, but of contributing to their health and comfort.

Each main division of the work has been committed to authority peculiarly qualified to deal with it. Mr. W. A. Blakston's knowledge of Canaries is well known, and will be found fully attested by the pages from his pen. Mr. W. Swaysland has long been recognised as an authority upon British Cage-Birds, and his concise directions for their treatment will be found to embody all that is practically necessary. And concerning the attractive section of Foreign Birds, the publishers have been peculiarly fortunate in obtaining the aid of a gentleman—Mr. August F. Wiener—one of the highest authorities in all Europe as regards length and variety of experience, combined with sound scientific knowledge. The full list of synonyms in this section will, it is hoped, give greater facility than has yet been offered in English works for the ready identification of varieties, and thus advance the popularity of many attractive birds as yet very little known.

The selection of subjects for illustration in the latter portion of the work, it need hardly be said, has been a task of peculiar difficulty; and the publishers owe many acknowledgments, not only to the talented artist who for a considerable period devoted his whole time to the task, but to the owners who so kindly placed valuable specimens before his pencil. Besides those mentioned in this way in the text, special acknowledgments are due to Mr. Joseph F. Hills and Mr. W. Swaysland, for the loan of many British birds

CONTENTS.

CANARIES.

BRITISH BIRDS.

FOREIGN BIRDS.

LIST OF ILLUSTRATIONS.

COLOURED PLATES.

DRAWINGS ON WOOD.

THE ILLUSTRATED BOOK OF
CANARIES AND CAGE-BIRDS.

CHAPTER I.

INTRODUCTORY AND HISTORICAL.

THE longing for something to protect and care for is one of the strongest feelings implanted within us, and one outcome of it is the desire to keep animals under our control, which in its due place is, undoubtedly, one of our healthiest instincts. From what it arises, other than being a wise gift, we will not stay to inquire; but that the desire does exist, in a greater or less degree, in all of us, and that in many it is a strongly-marked peculiarity, few will venture to deny. It is true that the lower animals are all placed in subjection to man; but the disposition to which we refer is not one born of any desire to subdue or destroy, being rather the offspring of some tenderer chord in our nature which impels us to make friends of them, to break down some of the barriers which separate us, to study their habits and attend to their wants, subordinating the whole to their and our advantage. We know that man is in a certain degree a predatory animal, and that an element in our character, different from the higher trait to which we have referred, enters into the case of those who indulge in what, for want of a better word, is known as sport; but even in the field something very like an intimate friendship and intelligent confidence is cemented between us and animals which are made to subserve the pursuit of what is, possibly, a legitimate end, though sensitive minds may question its morality.

A feeling akin to this predatory disposition may be seen in the eagerness with which some village urchin expends his energies in the construction of snares, or the primitive brick-trap—that most picturesque of all traps—or steals stealthily along through copse or by hedgerow, armed with crossbow or other clumsy contrivance of home manufacture, knowing no fatigue and despising every obstacle, happy if only by the exercise of patience and skill he can compass the death or capture of even one small bird. To him, the advent of winter, with its frost and snow and long dark nights, means the arrival of his sporting season, when, impelled by hunger, his "game" leaves its usual haunts and seeks the homestead by day, or affords him by night all the excitement and glories of netting the sheltered sides of stacks, the overhanging eaves of barns, and the still richer preserves of ivy-clad walls. But the lad has a warm corner in his heart for all that. The friendly robin, enticed by crumbs, takes its morning meal at his window, and is allowed to come and go, hopping in and out from under the treacherous stable-sieve, delicately poised over the baited spot to which he wishes to lure other birds, and is a privileged visitor. The half-frozen thrush, captured in the snow on one of the lad's hunting expeditions, or some wounded sufferer with broken wing, appeals to his sympathies, is cared for, tenderly nursed, and, though a captive, becomes a pet. The young rabbits, taken from their downy bed—a short burrow in some fallow—find a home in his hutch, and when grown—well, the lad has not the heart to kill them, and so sets them at liberty, himself scarcely less happy than they. The nest of young birds, long marked down and daily visited with furtive steps lest other watchful eyes should discover them, carefully carried home in his cap, become objects of extreme solicitude, and are, possibly, actually killed with kindness. A strange medley is the lad—a compound of thought and thoughtlessness, but good at the core. Nothing which appeals trustingly to his better nature appeals in vain; and so it is, we believe, that this desire to have something to love and care for overcomes the other and lower tendency. It grows with our growth and strengthens with our strength, and when satisfied, teaches many a lesson of abnegation of self.

The love of pets insensibly leads us to the study of Nature—

——" An effect
Whose cause is God"—

even though very partially and without turning up the ground to any great depth. The volume lies open before us replete with interest, and the study is alike absorbing whether the subject be our own wonderful anatomy or the structure of a mollusc; the oak which has seen the summers and winters of a century or the fungus which springs up in a few hours. Cage-birds are on our particular leaf of this inexhaustible volume, and we propose to look at them from a homely point of view—homely in every sense of the word. This will not be an abstruse work, but one in which the every-day life and management of the most popular and attractive cage-birds will be exhaustively treated. It is not intended for the naturalist or the ornithologist proper, though even they may, perhaps, dip into its pages and learn something—for we are ever learning—of the domestic habits and economy of some feathered favourite; but it is intended as a practical guide, a *vade mecum* for all who take an interest in rearing and tending cage-birds, whether native, or coming to us from far-off climes with stories of tropical splendours.

One of our specialities is the Canary, the home-bird of England, and one more generally met with than any other. Other song-birds, each with its own peculiar attraction, are found in many homes; but the Canary, most probably from his attractive appearance and friendly ways, is the bird of the people. Still, among popular favourites, there is the linnet in his tiny cage, hanging outside the attic casement of some toiling artisan who sees but little blue sky except over tiled roofs and smoky chimney-tops, ever on the move and singing the day through of breezy hill-sides and blooming whin bushes; or the skylark on his fresh sod, bought with hard-earned penny, carolling of green fields, new-mown hay, and skies all sun; the blackbird or thrush, in quaint wicker cage, chanting rich bursts of delicious music, wakening echoes of bygone days and carrying the listener back to some low-roofed, thatched cottage, with porch overgrown with woodbine, reminding him of early hopes and loves, and ambitions now tempered by stern necessities and manhood's cares, every gush of melody flooding his heart like refrains of angels' songs, and whispering perhaps of loved ones left behind sleeping peacefully under a little green mound in a far-off village churchyard.

But these birds are not every one's property. Early associations and early surroundings have a great deal to do with developing a liking in any direction. Born in a woodland district, native woodland songsters are the early friends and companions of one; while others, and they are by far the greater number, unacquainted with these rustic beauties, make friends with the bird within reach of all, and instal the Canary as favourite at home. And well he adapts himself to any circumstances. It matters not whether he be in a gilded cage in a drawing-room, tended by gentle hands, singing finished melodies acquired under expensive masters, or rolling out his own noisy, rollicking, untutored ditty in a cottage; he is equally at home. Cheerful and sprightly, companionable and docile, varied and beautiful in plumage, easily kept and easily bred, it is not to be wondered at that he is such a favourite; not the least of his many virtues being his strongly-marked social disposition and domestic proclivities.

The way in which a pair of Canaries set up housekeeping and order their household, is enough in itself to give the bird a strong claim on our sympathies. Other birds will, under favourable conditions, occasionally breed in confinement; but the hero of the first portion of our volume has, for generations, established himself in our families as one of us, and regardless of prying eyes or inquisitive curiosity, builds his little homestead and treats us to all the interesting details of bird-life which can be seen nowhere else but in his little establishment. There is a strange fascination in a bird's nest, and few there are who cannot recollect with what emotions of delight and wonder they made their first discovery of the family chimney-corner of even the humble hedge-sparrow with its treasure of little blue eggs, carefully concealed in a quiet nook in the garden; and who that has them has not lifted his children, one by one, to peer quietly through the gently-parted leaves, and take stealthy glances at the little freehold? Who will say they were not wiser and better for each visit? If there be living poetry in songs without words, where look for tenderer sentiment, purer rhythm, or sweeter cadence? It is not often that with all our care and watching we are able to observe the whole of the daily routine of such a little household, or to learn how, without design or copy and without ever having seen a model, a bird constructs its nest after an unvarying pattern peculiar to its kind. It is one of the mysteries of creation; and creation is full of these, though some are of such every-day occurrence that we cease to regard them as such. But our friend the Canary brings much of this home to us, and shows us, with scarcely any reserve, how the thing is done, busying about all day long, doing and undoing in a perpetual bustle yet with wonderful method, till the work is turned out in inimitable style. A breeding-cage is an ornament to any house, and almost any room in it.

It is not astonishing, then, that the demand for these birds is immense, the breeding and rearing of them forming no inconsiderable item in the minor industries of the country. The number of amateur breeders who adopt one or more of the many varieties of the Canary as their speciality, and make the development of its beauties their study, is very large, as the index of the catalogue of any public exhibition can attest; but the number produced in this way is but small compared with the continuous stream poured into the London market by those who make a business of it. The city of Norwich, with the surrounding villages and hamlets, counts its breeders by the thousand; while in Coventry, Derby, Northampton, Nottingham, and other towns in the midland district where labour is of a sedentary character, as well as in many towns in Yorkshire and Lancashire, the Canary is the poor man's savings-bank; the family pig where sanitary laws forbid the erection of a stye. In almost every house where the click of the shuttle is heard, the music of the sewing-machine or other adjunct to home industry, there, above all other sounds, rises the cheerful but noisy music of the bird-room; for small though the cottage be, the birds must have their share of it.

The young ones, as soon as they can take care of themselves, are sold by the score indiscriminately, or by the pair; the proceeds materially helping to fill the stocking-foot which provides for a rain-day or the claims of Christmas. There are no breeding establishments in this country where the work is carried on largely as a business pure and simple. It is one of those things which, perhaps, presents no better balance-sheet than does a small poultry establishment maintained expressly for a supply of eggs. Half the profit consists in the pleasure; and the other half from money which might go in more questionable ways being saved in small sums, by every investment in seed or other necessary, and returned in the lump just at a time when it is useful. The occasional self-denial called into operation to minister to the wants of creatures not able to provide for themselves, and the lessons of kindness thus taught, must also be written down on the credit side of the account. Few hobbies pay, except in the hands of larger capitalists than the breeder of Canaries for the London market, but it is from these cottage homes that the main supply of song-birds is drawn. The higher class birds among the more valuable varieties hardly come under this category, our remarks applying, generally, to the Canary *vulgaris*.

Of comparatively recent admission into the ranks of domesticated birds, the Canary has, under man's care and skill, within little more than a couple of centuries branched off into a number of distinct varieties, differing in colour and form so widely from the original stock, that it is difficult to realise the fact that they proceed, one and all, from the same origin, and are simply divergences from one common type. The majority of them have existed for many years, but how they arose we know not. It is easy to guess at the mode in which some of them have been obtained, but when one comes to experiment in the way of crossing, it will be found that the results are generally very far from what was anticipated; and the tendency to fly back, as it were, to the early forms is manifested so strongly, especially in those breeds which are the farthest from the original type, that the hopes and wishes of the breeder to produce some fresh intermediate form are generally set at nought. As an illustration of this may be instanced the fact that the variety known as the London Fancy, one of the oldest and purest branches of the family tree, when crossed with other Canaries, loses immediately its characteristic markings; and at present there is nothing whatever to show a tendency in any variety to retain permanently its peculiar characteristics without careful supervision.

Our bird, then, has a history, and one of ancient date too. There is a charm in its antiquity which smacks strongly of respectability. There is probably little doubt that the species came originally from the islands whose name it bears: at the present day, however, it is found in a wild state in other localities, the majority of the wild Canaries which come to England being captured in the island of St. Helena; it is found also in Madeira, and, we believe, also in parts of Africa. We have not had any opportunities of comparing specimens from these different localities, so that we cannot speak positively as to their being identical; but the bird is so easily acclimatised in any temperate or sub-tropical region, and has been so largely captured and exported from the islands in which it is now found, that we doubt not it is thriving in many other spots to which it has been introduced.

Its first appearance in Europe seems to have been about the beginning of the sixteenth century, in consequence of the loss of a vessel containing numbers of these little birds as merchandise near the island of Elba, where they were set at liberty. After a time, however, they were recaptured, and in this way were introduced as song-birds into Italy. The Germans then appear to have soon taken them up, bred them largely in confinement, and exported them to other countries. The story is simple enough and quite within the bounds of probability, though, unfortunately, we have no corroborative testimony in the published results of any Board of Trade inquiry of the day; and the name of the vessel, with other important particulars, lies buried in the Mediterranean. But we accept it as true, and as affording an easy solution of a question more or less shrouded in mist. Great changes can be brought about in a century, and still greater in two centuries; and things must have progressed very favourably in the Canary way in the early history of the bird, for we find in "The Gentleman's Recreation," an old work on "Hunting, Hawking, Fowling, and Fishing," published in 1677, that at that date the Canaries in England were generally imported from Germany and were of a green colour. There were also Germans living in London who made a business of breeding Canaries, as was practised in their own country.

It appears, however, that it was subsequent to this time that the different and distinct varieties of the bird arose, though doubtless the foundation-stone of many a structure was already laid; for within fifty years after, we hear again of there being numerous varieties cultivated in Paris, comprising many distinct colours, though most of these so-called varieties can only have been pied birds differently marked. We are obliged to take giant strides over wide areas, since, unfortunately, the links are wanting which might serve to connect the chain in anything like continuity; and travelling onwards we find that about a century ago at least one fixed and distinct variety had its home in London, with its established Society of breeders governed by well-digested laws. That end of the cable we can moor ourselves to confidently; and assuming that the other end is lost at the bottom of the sea in the neighbourhood of Elba, we are content to allow it to remain there in the face of the difficulties which attend our endeavours to pick it up and identify it.

But what do we find the bird to-day? We have variations in shape and plumage as marked as anything existing in the poultry or pigeon world, to each of which sections of the feathered creation the same general principles of development we have briefly referred to apply. It is this variation, with its endless ramifications, which renders the Canary an object of attraction to those who merge its naturally engaging ways in other considerations, and makes it an object worthy the attention of the naturalist as well as the fancier. Radiating from one common centre, the castaways at Elba, are not less than ten separate and distinct varieties, each having strongly-marked and fixed characteristics. These are the Norwich, the Cinnamon, the London Fancy, the Lizard, the Belgian, the Scotch Fancy, the Yorkshire, the Crested, the Green, and the German; and each of these *varieties* is subdivided into many *classes*. It is a desire to produce each in its kind in perfection that has led to the present extensive system of scientific breeding, and our object is to assist by an intelligent enunciation of simple principles, and detailed account of actual practice. As time has sped on, so has the desire for obtaining information, even of matters respecting which it might at one day have been thought all knowledge could be enclosed in a nut-shell; and the stream of intelligent appreciation of many apparent trifles has worked out for itself a channel broad and deep.

We say apparent trifles; but the smallest work of creative power is not a trifle, nor are they triflers who give a careful attention to the many seeming insignificant works of nature with which we are surrounded. He is not a trifler who makes the "short-lived insect of a day" a life-long study, nor he who can find food for thought in contemplation of the lowest form of animal organism; any more than he who makes the study of the higher works of creation his constant occupation. Nor is he a trifler who can read a page of the world's history in a fragment of rock cropping up by the roadside, speaking to him with a tongue that cannot lie of that long ago beginning when this planet of ours was created; any more than he who extracts from the bowels of the earth the treasures warehoused there for ages. Nor is he a trifler who carefully gathers the wild flowers in the hedgerow or the grasses of our fields, or notes forms of vegetable existence where the uneducated eye can detect nothing; any more than he who cultivates broad acres, or who brings the flowers and fruits of the tropics under control in our latitudes. Neither is he a trifler who, from among the endless resources at the command of any thinker who goes through the world with his eyes open, selects for his special study the feathered portion of creation; nor when, among other marvels of instinctive work, he finds his attention arrested by a simple little bird's nest, is he any more a trifler than the men whose constructive genius designed the temples of old Egypt, who built the hoary Pyramids, who carved the solid mountains of the Nile into edifices of colossal proportions, or those who raised, brick by brick from their foundations, the more florid but less imposing structures of modern times. There is a time for everything, even for trifles, if such there be. Our trifle is the Canary of to-day—the fancier's Canary—and we propose to deal with him by describing minutely his distinctive features; showing how to breed him, feed him, moult him, develop his beauties, improve his shape and feather, wash him, dry him, send him to the show; how to get him there, what to do with him when he is there, and how to get him home again; how to bear success, how to use defeat, how to help each other, and so help ourselves.

CHAPTER II.

THE OUT-DOOR AVIARY.

THERE are two methods of breeding Canaries, either of which has its own peculiar merits, though the objects desired by each are as widely different as are the results. The one is the aviary plan, and the other by isolation of varieties and classes in separate cages. The former may be said to be most suitable for general purposes, and the latter, it is obvious, is that from which special results are to be gained; and the two must be considered from different points of view. The aviary method is best adapted for those who have no definite purpose, other than the pleasure derivable from general observation—a pleasure of the highest order, though confined, in a considerable degree, to the simple lover of Nature who takes her as she is, regarding all her manifestations with a delight into which no question of how or why intrudes. To such, the aviary opens up a new world of interest, peopled with forms whose outer adornment is of less moment than the beauties of their inner life. These equally charm the fancier, who nevertheless is more exacting in his demands in other respects. His admiration of the general economy of the aviary is not lessened if to it he unites other aims, and seeks to clothe its tenants in higher forms of beauty. It may be, and probably is the case, that any one ruling passion has a tendency to crowd out others; but there is no reason why one healthy feeling should absorb more than its due share of attention, and we fail to discover any reason why the true naturalist and the genuine fancier should not be merged into one in following up two branches of the same stream.

We have said that each of the methods of breeding indicated has its advantages and disadvantages. We may sum up the advantages of the aviary system briefly, by saying that it involves only a small amount of care and attention, the birds being left pretty much to take care of themselves, to choose their own mates, and make their little world inside the wires as much as possible like that outside. This putting the reins of power into their own hands removes all the responsibility from the observer, who has nothing to do but to watch the goings on of the little republic; which will develop, among much that is beautiful, certain forms of government and divers communist principles which the conservative fancier considers subversive of all order.

Among these disadvantages is indiscriminate pairing, rendering it impossible to breed any distinct variety, though this may not be a disadvantage to those who, so long as they breed *something* and have the pleasure of seeing it reared, don't care what that something may be. It would perhaps be scarcely fair to charge the Canary with habitually pairing with more than one mate; indeed, the idea is foreign to the natural habits and instincts of the Finch family in a wild state. Half the poetry attaching to the mere name of nest seems to consist in the halo of quiet and purity which surrounds it, hidden with such care from the world. Still there are now and then evidences of a contrary state of things even among wild birds, and no doubt the commotion which sometimes takes place in the ivy is nothing more than a noisy public meeting to take into consideration the desirability of turning out of the community some ill-conducted member. The occasional capture of a hybrid, too, is evidence of an alliance having taken place between members of different families. These, however, are manifestly exceptions. The wild bird in her beautiful little home demands all her mate's care and attention, and receives it. He spends his entire day in ministering to her wants, and is not more exclusively devoted to her in all his delicate attentions than is she to the precious treasures nestled so closely to her breast. But in the aviary things are different. Although preserving many natural instincts almost unimpaired, the Canary has had some of them modified, or even materially affected, by generations of domestication. Notwithstanding he may, in the early spring, select some one particular bird, and subsequently matters may be arranged to the entire satisfaction of both, he no sooner sees her comfortably settled down on her nest than he finds—though he does not forsake his mate—the atmosphere in which he lives, with all its surroundings, tends to draw away his attention in fresh directions. This is all very pretty and all very well for those who only wish to study bird-life generally, and to keep the aviary well stocked; but it is, for obvious reasons, not the fancier's way of going to work. We must, however, say, for the credit of the sex, that such an erratic disposition is not shared in by the hens: as a rule they remain true to their first selection, till a lengthened separation and entire seclusion wean them from their first mate.

Another exemplification of the tendency towards complete domestication is seen in the fact of all nests becoming common property. The birds seem to want a *place* in which to lay, and nothing more, and select their favourite nest much in the same way as domestic poultry do. All are at one time or another affected by the desire to set up house for themselves, and go about it very energetically, evidently impressed with the importance of having, according to bird building-society maxims, a roof-tree of their own. This once done, and the instinct satisfied, nothing further seems to be desired. There is no idea of privacy, nor the slightest regard for property rights. Two or three, or as many hens as can possibly find a resting-place, may be seen occupying the same nest and even sitting on each other's backs, anywhere and anyhow, so long as they can only find some means of squeezing in, like hens in a poultry-yard, taking possession of the same eggs, too anxious to cover them to think of quarrelling. The young even become common property, and we have frequently seen two hens, one on either side of a nest, assisting the cock bird in feeding a family which could certainly be in no way related to one of them, and which she had taken no part in hatching.

The same misadventures, resulting from attempting to confine nature within fixed bounds, attend the aviary as wait on the cage. The love of animals for their young needs no telling, and the *simile* of a hen gathering her chickens under her wings has been used through all time as an illustration of devoted affection. But in our attempts to tether nature within a circle of our own inscribing, we meet at all points evidences of our ignorance; and a quiet "Thus far shalt thou go and no farther" is one of the lessons we have to learn when we try to investigate some of the unhealthy conditions inseparable from confinement. We never in our younger days, when bird-nesting was an institution with us, remember discovering a nest of young birds neglected or forsaken by their parents. From the moment when they leave the shell till some time after they leave the nest, wild birds are the constant care of their parents; but with the Canary the case is too often the reverse; "Died from exposure and insufficient nourishment," or some such unnatural cause, being the verdict on only too many entire families. These matters will be treated more fully under their proper heading, but are mentioned here incidentally as attaching, generally, to this portion of our subject.

To those, however, who may still prefer the aviary to the cage, there remains the choice of an out-door or an in-door arrangement. The former we know must be, in many residences, and particularly in large towns, out of the question; but where facilities for its erection exist, an out-door aviary is, we think, for general purposes the more desirable of the two. As to whether the Canary can, under reasonable conditions, stand or withstand extremes of temperature, there is not the slightest doubt. He is one of the most easily acclimatised birds we have, and there is no difficulty in housing him so that he shall care nothing for either winter or summer.

MR. STEPHENSON'S OUT-DOOR AVIARY.

We will not undertake to say what might or might not be accomplished in this way very far north, or in situations exposed to long-prevailing east winds; but we repeat that, under reasonable conditions, or even under circumstances which might, until tried, be thought too adverse, the question of being able to establish an out-door aviary and keep Canaries in it throughout the year, need not cause the slightest apprehension as to its perfect practicability. Indeed, we are of opinion that it is *the* method of keeping any number together indiscriminately, and that birds once acclimatised are as proof against the attacks of the weather as our native tribes. And when we say out-door we mean out-door—an exposed structure, with no covering but a roof sufficient to keep out the rain, and with any sort of contrivance to fasten up on the weather side during the storms of winter, when birds at liberty would betake themselves to some such shelter.

An aviary of this kind may be seen in the grounds of Mr. John George Stephenson, at Bishop's Cleeve, near Cheltenham, of which we give an illustration, kindly furnished by his own pencil. It is simply a large cage, with the ordinary perch arrangements, and nothing more, in the interior. One of the sides, if we remember rightly, is boarded, inasmuch as it includes the door, but the rest are wired. It has a thatched roof, and, being intended to be ornamental as well as useful, has a little rustic finish about it which, bear in mind, in no way affects the principle involved in its construction. The only natural shelter it has is a high hedge of box, but on the side from which the severest storms in winter may be expected, it is protected with matting or some similar covering, more for the purpose of preventing the snow drifting in and covering the food on the ground than for any other reason; for, the roof being conical and furnished with perches, the Canaries naturally retreat to its shelter in stormy weather. During severe frosts the ice in the drinking vessels has to be broken repeatedly. Here live some score or two of Canaries in the most robust health, setting at defiance the heats of summer and the snows of winter, innocent of asthma and pulmonary phthisis, and other complaints to which the Canary is heir. We have seen them in this home in the height of the breeding season busily engaged in domestic duties; not omitting, among other peculiarities, to sit three-deep on a nest; and we have seen them on a frosty December morning, when we left our footprints in the rime on the lawn as we made our way towards them attracted by their song. Never did they at any time appear to suffer more inconvenience from the cold than their friends at liberty outside; indeed, we question much if they were not better off. Wild birds do frequently suffer greatly, both from cold and deprivation, during a severe winter, and present a huddled-up appearance with their feathers all the wrong way. They sit about in a listless, apathetic sort of way, and early in the afternoon betake themselves to the shelter of thick hedges or the lee side of stacks, and many situations in which, under other circumstances, they would not be found. Occasionally they die from cold and hunger combined; but the Canary in his shelter, well provisioned, rides out the gale, welcoming every gleam of sunshine with a burst of song, and chanting Christmas carols while our native songsters, half frozen, are engaged in begging crumbs at our windows, and the cage-birds in-doors, unused to extremes, are silent and moping. To all who desire an all-the-year-round pleasure, and have the facility of carrying it out, we say, set up an out-door aviary, and stock it mainly with Canaries, whatever other suitable tenants you may choose to add.

CHAPTER III.

THE IN-DOOR AVIARY.

THE in-door aviary, though intended for a similar purpose to that described in the last chapter, is from the nature of things of a somewhat different description. Its occupants are, by force of circumstances, not so robust and hardy as those more exposed, and require just so much the more consideration as regards their comfort and well-being. We will suppose an empty room or small conservatory to be devoted to the purpose. To begin with, it should have a warm aspect and be well protected from draughts, and, if a conservatory or similar glass erection, must be well shaded from the strong sunlight, avoiding as far as possible all extremes, remembering that under a more pampered system the birds will lead a more artificial existence and be more liable to feel the injurious effects of external influences. The most important consideration of all is to effect a thorough ventilation with a complete exclusion of draughts, which cause the deaths of more Canaries than many people imagine. Too much attention cannot be paid to this, and our instructions on this point are most emphatic. A bird which can be acclimatised to almost any extent can be killed in twenty-four hours in a draughty room.

Having selected a suitable room, proceed to furnish it by placing in it a number of "Christmas trees"—small firs of various sizes—which, if obtained at a nursery, can be lifted in the autumn, and will, if carefully raised and well potted, live the year through, by which time they will be about done for; as apart from the unfavourable circumstances in which they are placed, so far from their making any growth, the birds will make sad havoc with them. In selecting them, choose substantial plants with flat, spreading branches, and arrange them tastefully on such stands as can be extemporised for the purpose, singly or in clumps, filling up corners—arranging them, in fact, in any way and every way—in doing which there is scope for the exercise of much taste. Avoid, however, placing them so that any part of the room cannot be got at if desired; for old birds as well as young are apt to flutter away into inaccessible corners, and make no effort to release themselves from positions not dangerous in themselves, but from which they seem to think escape hopeless. For instance, if a bird, when frightened, should happen to flutter about and scramble between, say, a box containing a tree and the wall, the chances are that it would remain there and die without ever trying to get free again; and this sort of contingency must be guarded against as far as possible. These are simple matters, but the result of experience shows them to be important. Nothing jars more unpleasantly on a sensitive mind than to find that any creature under our care has suffered from circumstances which we might have prevented by the exercise of a little forethought; and one such death in the little household is quite enough to leave behind it unpleasant memories which detract greatly from our pleasures.

One would think that, to use a common expression, birds would "have more sense" than to behave so foolishly; but it is not exactly the want of what we call sense which induces such misfortunes. The bird from some cause or other becomes frightened, or perhaps it leaves its nest before it is able to take care of itself, and naturally betakes itself to the quietest corner it can find, where, removed from observation, it remains till the little heart ceases to beat. The most unaccountable accidents from the most improbable causes will happen at the best of times, and it certainly behoves us to use every precaution against them. There is no excuse for leaving water-jugs and similar traps standing about. The bird has no intention of committing suicide, yet it finds its way into the jug and cannot find its way out. These and many other misadventures have happened in our experience, and we are anxious to save others the pain and vexation we have felt.

HIGHEST TYPE OF IN-DOOR AVIARY.

In addition to the trees or shrubs, a few fantastically-shaped branches (from which all loose bark must be removed, for reasons which will hereafter appear) may be arranged in rustic fashion, and any old gnarled stumps or roots may be utilised in a similar way. The branches are not intended for nesting-places, but only as perches. Nothing is more out of character in a room such as we are describing than long, straight perches; but a substitute must be provided. Canaries are not always on the wing, but will not often visit the floor, except to feed or on other matters of business. The trees themselves are not suitable for perching on, unless any should have fairly substantial branches, and therefore some comfortable resting-places must be provided. The birds will soon find these out for themselves, and the object of using the branches we refer to is that the whole may look as natural and attractive as possible. If, in place of such an arrangement, one or more long perches be used, the result will be that the birds will generally be seen sitting in a row, in not very picturesque fashion, on the topmost bar, to which they will also immediately retreat when any one enters the room. To obviate this, all natural ledges, such as the tops of architraves over doors and windows, must be rendered untenable, and more tempting places offered. The birds will most certainly please themselves in their selection of favourite resting-places, and the thing is to make their choice comfortable for them and pleasing to our own taste. It takes a great many birds to fill a small room, and a place may appear tenantless while a score or two of birds are perched up aloft somewhere out of sight.

Virgin cork, in various shapes, may also be used, but a strict watch must be kept for insects, and, upon their appearance, the pieces infested should be immersed in boiling water in the wash-house copper. Should any of these smaller arrangements be taken up for nesting purposes and be found to harbour insects, give them a touch of oil on the places affected. The danger of harbouring parasites is the only objection to the use of cork and similar material, though the risk is exceedingly small in a room where there is good ventilation. Ordinary nesting-boxes are out of place in a well-furnished aviary, though they might be cast in a rustic mould. The birds will select their own nesting-places in which to build, and not a little amusement will be derived from noticing the impossible corners some will fix on. The slightest projection will suffice for one, and it will spend a great amount of time and labour in constructing its nest under circumstances of self-imposed difficulty. Not unfrequently, some place will be chosen on which it may seem almost impossible a nest could rest; but you will find that the Canary is not a bad architect, and generally turns out to be the best judge of a site. Domestication, however, has impaired this wonderful instinctive faculty, and it will be seen that some will make attempts which turn out perfectly futile, while others will commence to build on a foundation manifestly sandy, in which case it may be well to supply a nest-box, if the bird has shown a determination to settle in that spot and no other. Constant ministration to its daily wants seems to have affected the bird's self-reliance; and though it is well to leave well alone, it is equally well to maintain a careful watch. Draw a line between watchfulness and inquisitive interference, and there will be little fear for the results.

Furnish a good supply of nesting material, such as fibrous roots, where they can be obtained; long, fine, dry grass from the hedge-side; hay; plenty of moss, and, if it can be had, the coarser kind of lichen; also soft cow-hair, which can be had from any tan-yard, and is always kept in stock at the better class of bird-shops: a supply of soft feathers will also be appreciated, as will, also, some rabbit-down. The hair and these latter materials are best packed in small nets, and suspended in positions where the birds can get a good pull at them; if allowed to lie about, the finer stuff will nearly all be wasted. These are the materials which ought to be supplied, but there are some which ought *not* to be admitted on any account—such as cotton, wool, or other long, tough stuff, which can become entangled in the feet. Wool becomes twisted round the feet in a most dangerous way, and, as it cannot be so readily perceived in a room as in a small cage, a bird may suffer exceedingly, and even lose its toes, before the cause of the misfortune be discovered.

To complete the furnishing we might add a small rustic chair, placed in the most retired corner, in which the observer can sit quietly and watch the busy world at work around him, to do which, the only requirement really necessary is that you *do* sit quietly, when it matters not if you have a nest within a foot of your elbow, or even built on the back of your chair; things will go on just as unconcernedly in your presence as in your absence. On one branch may be noticed two birds going through a few preliminary evolutions, advancing, retiring, chattering, and finishing up with a quarrel on the *iræ amantium* principle. Observe, also, what a complete master of his art is this descendant of the shipwrecked unfortunates at Elba. He has in his veins the same hot blood, and has no equal at "delutherin'," unless it may be the goldfinch on the other side, bowing and scraping and spreading out his coat-tails like the dandy he is, while he talks treason to that demure little hen, which we have reason to think is already affianced to one of her own race. Under cover of the bush in the corner sit another couple, whispering the most affectionate soft-nothings, and talking over the eligibility of one or two building sites at their disposal. Immediately above them another pair is hard at work putting the finishing touches to a cottage *ornée* of which the foundations were laid only yesterday, and which must be completed without delay: it is a case of emergency, and will be required in the morning. Within reach of the hand sits a hen on five eggs, "due" in the course of a few hours; and while we watch her bright eye and admire the constancy with which she has attended to the first part of her matronly duties, her mate flies up to make anxious inquiries and give her a mouthful of food. Perched on a piece of root, in a position from which it seems as if a breath would dislodge the entire fabric, is another nest, above the top of which are just visible half a dozen gaping mouths which the attentive parents are filling with dainty morsels prior to their being tucked in for an hour's nap. And here are four more which, though hatched only three weeks ago, are almost as large as their parents, and fit into their warm bed like the pieces in a Chinese puzzle. Look which way we will, we continually find something fresh to attract the attention and interest the mind, and the aviary is voted the best room in the house.

A few items, all important in their way, have to be included in our inventory. The floor should be strewed with clean sand, and a supply of old lime rubbish will be found conducive to the general health of the birds, as well as furnishing a necessary element in the formation of egg-shell. This need not be crushed so small as to become dust; that will accumulate quickly enough without any assistance; but if pieces of a crumbly nature are accessible by the birds, they will not fail to avail themselves of it, and with beneficial results. This should be renewed at very short intervals; indeed, every morning is not too often. When the birds have picked it over and it begins to get soiled, it may still serve as covering for the floor, but nothing more, being virtually dirt. In sweeping it up there is no occasion to flourish a long-handled brush and create as much terror as possible, but do it gently and quietly, and the birds will take no notice of either brush or sweeper; it will soon be seen that the morning's supply of sand will be as eagerly looked for as a supply of fresh food, and every bird in the room will be down on the floor in a moment to turn over the fresh stuff and take in a supply with which to assist his little mill to grind its seed.

In country places, where they can easily be obtained, thin sods will be a great acquisition, and almost every part of them will be turned to some good purpose. All work and no play does not suit a Canary any more than the youth in the legendary poem, who is reported to have been made very dull by the process; and birds are as fond of amusing themselves as other animals. Nothing entertains them more than giving them something of this kind to pick and pull to pieces, which they will do with many a resolute tug; and it is this attention to *little* wants, which may not perhaps be absolute necessaries, that goes to make up the sum of their happiness.

The subject of feeding will afford matter for special consideration. It is no part of the fitting-up of an aviary, though the receptacles for food and water, we think, have to do with it. We do not advise scattering much seed on the floor, as a great portion of it would by that means be wasted: Canaries don't scratch and search for their food like the *gallinæ*, or feast till the dish is empty and then pick the bones. Throw a handful of corn to poultry among loose gravel, and not a single grain will be allowed to hide itself; but the natural habits and instincts of the Canary don't lead it to search in this way, and unless the quantity of seed thrown down be very trifling, it will only be trodden in and hidden under the sand, to be swept up next morning. And remember, the value of a fresh sprinkling of new, sweet stuff is much greater than the saving effected by allowing it to remain till any seed it may contain is eaten up. All other seed must be

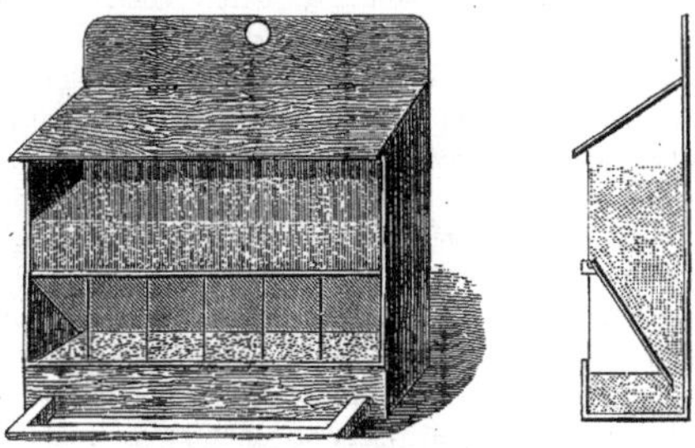

FIG. 1.—SELF-SUPPLYING HOPPER.

given in self-supplying hoppers, by which plan there will always be food at command, and the waste reduced to a minimum. What is scattered from the hopper falls in one place, and may be collected and sifted without so much probability of its being crushed and trodden into the floor. All our sweepings go to the poultry; but the fact of having poultry to pick over waste food is no reason why food should be wasted. We give a handy form of self-supplying seed-hopper in Fig. 1. The top part of the front is of glass, so that the state of the supply can always be seen.

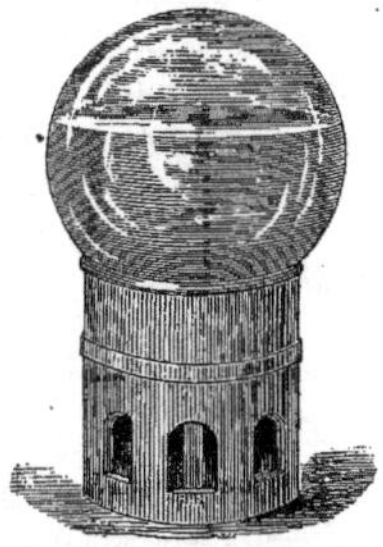

FIG. 2.—LARGE FOUNTAIN.

Water, plenty of it, fresh and clear, is best supplied from a large fountain, a drawing of which appears in Fig. 2. It is simply a glass globe with a long neck inverted in an earthenware pot open at the top, and furnished near the bottom with apertures, the lower edges of which are slightly higher than the bottom of the glass neck. Smaller editions may be placed on suitable brackets, the only thing required being that there shall be some kind of perch or other resting-place, from which the birds can have free access to the water-holes. And let it be borne in mind that though a bird's instinct leads it to build its nest, to look for food and water, and to be in many respects a very inquisitive character, it has no intuition which teaches it that water exists for it, not in brooks or pools, but in a glass globe inverted in an earthenware pot which may look to the bird as much like an engine of war as anything else. Many Canaries, when changed from one cage to another and required to put their heads through a hole into a formidable-looking covered-in vessel in search of what they had been accustomed to find in an open trough, have never found their water, and have died before the matter could be remedied. It is therefore necessary, in using covered-in vessels in the aviary, to see that young birds and new-comers find their way to them: a "general management" hint, but not out of place.

A bath is the last requisite, and nothing is more suitable for the purpose than a large shallow dish, which should be introduced every day for an hour or two. If this be done before sweeping-up time, there will not be much dust. There is no danger in leaving a bath in the room constantly, provided the water be not more than one or two inches deep; but not much is gained by it, because unless nearly all the birds bathe at the same time, those which are not in the humour to do so while the water is clean will not bathe after it has become dirtied. Familiarity with the bath also seems to do away with the desire to use it; whereas, if it be introduced only for a short time during the day, the birds splash into it "head over ears" almost before it can be placed on the ground, the washing, drying, clear-starching, and ironing occupying them a full hour or more.

The in-door aviary may be carried out to the utmost extent of elegance and elaboration. What it may be made is suggested by the sketch on page 12. But even in such an ornithological paradise, the essential matters to be attended to will be just the same and no more, than such as have already been mentioned.

Such we take to be the leading features of the aviary system; which, it will be manifest, can never become the fancier's *modus operandi* so much as a means of general interest and source of pleasure, derivable from general observation rather than the carrying out of any specific system of breeding with the object of bringing about definite results. It has been our aim to present it in this light, as being its true sphere; feeling assured that those who make it their world will discover in it many beauties we have failed to point out, and will find it insensibly becoming peopled with creations of which they once knew nothing, with which they can hold converse and enter into companionship, and find their own world of observation considerably enlarged by taking even this small peep into one portion of the vast domain open to the inquirer who, at every step, recognises the evidences of a Wisdom "past finding out."

CHAPTER IV.

THE BREEDING-ROOM.

A FANCIER'S Canary-room should be selected with some amount of care. Any room will not do, though too frequently any room *has* to do, on the "Hobson's choice" principle. The birds have to spend their lives in it, and it is only a question of common sense to insist that the conditions under which they live shall be as favourable as possible. We say "as possible," because a fancier cannot always have everything exactly as he may wish, but is obliged to make the best of things as he finds them; not a bad plan in other matters besides the selection of a Canary-room. It is not every house in which there is a spare room, or in which the spare room is the most suitable for the purpose; but endeavour to secure one which has the full benefit of the morning sun, without, however, being exposed to the mid-day heat, which renders the atmosphere of any bird-room very uncomfortable. No one ever questions the fact that it is the early bird that catches the worm; though, in inculcating the moral lessons deducible from this particular phase of animal life, the unhappy fate of the worm has been held up as a warning to early risers. Birds are, however, the most practical exponents of the "early to bed and early to rise" principle we know of, and it is therefore not well to place them under circumstances which, to a great extent, subvert this order of things. The first streak of daylight sees them on the move, and long before the close of day their heads are tucked under their wings. Their day is not our day, but we are very apt to forget it. The value of the early sunshine to them is incalculable, enabling them to begin work at a time in accordance with their natural instincts, not the least important part of which is to attend to the wants of their young, who fully enter into the spirit of the early worm theory. Canaries will also make a longer season in a room where they are not done up by the heat, which seems to fag them out and throw them into moult before the proper season. With muling stock—*i.e.*, hens kept exclusively for breeding Goldfinch and other hybrids—this is a matter of the utmost importance, as their season does not begin till the Canary season is half spent, and the value of late nests will be sufficiently apparent. A cool room virtually prolongs a season, and the difference between losing a nest and gaining an extra one amounts to two, which is a valuable consideration.

Avoid a room abutting on to the house, in the way so many of the kitchens, with a room overhead, are built in the yards of small tenements now-a-days. These rooms have generally very thin walls, and have at least two sides exposed, making them miserably cold in winter and as hot in summer. The temperature out-of-doors is much more equable than in a place of this kind, and, as we have shown, birds can stand that without inconvenience; but sudden alternations are most injurious, and to these they are sure to be subject in a room such as we have referred to. We have more than one such in mind while penning these lines, and have not known a really good season's work to have been carried out in any of them; and knowing how sensitive the Canary is to sudden and frequent changes of temperature, we attribute the want of success as much to this cause as to any other. It is a cause, too, which affects the bird most at a time when it is least able to bear up against it; and that is during the breeding season, when the hens, at least, are not in a normal condition as regards health, but are more or less affected by the state of body natural to the period of incubation. Recollect that each pair of birds is boxed up in a house of about eighteen inches frontage and not a foot in depth, and that some cages are placed where the occupants seldom get a gleam of sunshine, while others have no protection from the scorching rays of a summer's sun. They have to make the best of their position, and have not the opportunities for exercise which aviary tenants have—they cannot plume themselves in a warm corner nor retreat into the shade, but are entirely dependent upon the care and forethought of others for their comfort as well as for the necessaries of their mere existence.

Attention to these things constitutes the difference between a well-ordered room and one which, from floor to ceiling, shows at all points indications of a want of thought. This question of aspect and general suitability is one on which we feel perfectly satisfied more depends than many imagine, and is probably the key to the solution of the question of varying success. It takes so little to throw the entire machinery out of gear, that he acts wisely who makes the most searching inquiry into the simple business of why and because, for the because never exists without the why. The most careful calculations are, however, frequently upset in a way that is most puzzling, and which seems to set all rule and method at defiance, while the most complete success sometimes waits on the most unlikely efforts. But exceptional cases of either kind afford no reason why any departure should be made from the simple sanitary laws which rule equally in the bird-room as in any other department of the homestead.

All we have previously advanced on the subject of draughts and ventilation applies to the breeding-room; and we may here indicate some arrangements which will be found useful. Something will depend on the room itself. If it be an attic with an ordinary lift-up skylight, bear in mind that few of these windows shut close, even if well made; they are constructed to exclude rain, but are very draughty contrivances, and the ledge on which the frame rests ought to be covered with thin felt, or some such yielding substance, to ensure a close fit; and more especially during the blustering winter months. The aperture should be covered with wirework, through which the lever used to raise the window can act, and it can then be elevated or depressed at pleasure, while the wired frame can present an effectual bar to the escape of any birds which may find their way out of their cages through a door being left open (which *will* happen sometimes), and also prove equally effective in preventing the ingress of any marauding cat that may be making a voyage of discovery on the tiles. For a similar reason, if there be a fire-place in the room—one of the best ventilators—it should also be wired over; for where the chimney-pots are of primitive construction, or where there are none at all, cats not unfrequently gain access by the chimney. It is not to be supposed that birds make a practice of escaping from their cages, or that cats always select the chimney as the most convenient entrance; but either has only to happen once in the face of an open window or an open fire-place to entail serious loss.

In the case of an ordinary window a wire covering is still indispensable, and a perforated zinc contrivance, six or eight inches deep, may be adapted to the top for use when the state of the weather might render it unadvisable to allow it to be opened without some protection. A similar contrivance in the door or in the wall above it, and as near the ceiling as possible, will assist in keeping up a supply of fresh air, and any trouble or expense incurred in doing the work thoroughly will repay itself in the health and comfort of the stock.

Being so near the roof, it might be imagined that an attic would be either uncomfortably warm or correspondingly cold; but the best breeding-room we ever had was what Johnson defines to be "the *topmost* room of the house," although he gives the meaning of cock-loft to be "the room *above* the garret:" perhaps the current of air in the cock-loft acts as a gulf stream to the attic—a sort of atmospheric fly-wheel.

No breeding-room can be said to be complete without some kind of heating apparatus. To this it is probable some may demur, but we can only say in reply that those are fortunate who can do without it. Such a variety of circumstances combine to make the usage of one district different from that of another, that the "custom of the port," with its statistical results, must not be accepted as a standard rule calculated to produce the like elsewhere. Difference in latitude and variation in other physical relations make just all the difference between the natural productions of any two places, and a certain amount of artificial treatment must be resorted to in order to bring them on a par. We do not say that Canaries would feel the rigour of an ordinary English winter more in one part of the country than in another, but the critical time is when Nature begins to wake up from her winter's sleep. In some places she seems to slumber with one eye open, and in others to relapse into a state of such insensibility as if there would be no awakening. In the one instance she is quick in answering to the call, and balmy airs soon arouse her from temporary inactivity: in the other, pulse is almost dead and circulation is induced only by long and gradual effort.

So with occupants of our bird-rooms, who are soon affected by external influences; their awakening in-doors is simultaneous with that out-of-doors, and every swelling bud or early spring flower is but the indicator of a corresponding spring-time in bird-life. Where the one is late in being roused into life, so is the other; and we hear in some places of pairing, nesting, breeding, and all the excitement attending it, weeks, aye, almost months before those in a less favoured district dare even think of making any preparations for the campaign, lest too much haste might result in disaster. To obviate the evils arising from this, prudence would suggest that where a reasonably early start is contemplated, something should be done to assist in maintaining an equable temperature, so that breeding operations may be followed out independently of the weather. The way in which Canaries are affected by climatic alternations will be pointed out in our chapters on general management; our object here is to explain a simple way of warming the breeding-room, by which means the dangers attendant on early nests may be averted, and other disagreeables which wait on a late spring considerably ameliorated. This last is the true object of artificial heating; not to force birds out of season, but to make the most of them in season —to combat adverse circumstances by means the most nearly approximating to those employed by Nature.

Years have passed since we first drew attention to a simple little gas-stove in use in our own breeding-room, which did its work so well and so cheaply that we thought we could recommend nothing more suitable for the purpose; and we still think it as handy and effective a contrivance as more expensive and complicated apparatus. But gas is not at command everywhere, though the march of civilisation has made the conventional lamp-post almost as necessary a part of an English landscape as a row of telegraph-posts, or the martial helmet and awe-inspiring buttons of the member of the county force who turns up in the most secluded and romantic spots. Our Transatlantic cousins, however, have supplied us with a new source of light and heat, which has been applied in ways once never dreamt of; and the paraffin oil pump is almost as common an ornament in the village grocer's store as the beer-engine with its array of bulbous porcelain handles in the bar of the public-house. The simple contrivance we are about to describe is worked almost as effectively with the aid of a small paraffin lamp as with gas. Small stoves, in which paraffin, or petroleum, or shale oil in some form is the combustible employed, are to be purchased in endless variety, and will doubtless perform all asserted of them; but we have not tried any of them. Our own apparatus we have tested thoroughly, and can confidently recommend. It consists simply of a cylinder of ordinary sheet iron, about eighteen inches in height and eight in diameter, enclosed at the top, and notched round the bottom with a few deep scallops affording ingress for a supply of air. Stand this machine on end, like an inverted overgrown saucepan, on a plate of iron or even on the bare floor in any convenient corner of the room, and underneath it place the lamp, or convey through one of the apertures an ordinary bat's-wing gas-burner. In the side, an inch or two from the top, insert a pipe of the same material or of zinc or tin, which, in carrying off the heated air and the deleterious products of combustion, plays a most important part in the heating economy of this most unpretentious-looking affair.

The only condition absolutely necessary for the effective working of the stove is that the chimney be conveyed into some vacant space entirely free from draught, as any downward puff will extinguish the flame. In the case of a lamp, this will be accompanied by no other inconvenience than the failure of the heat; but if with gas, consequences will be more serious. The possibility of such a mishap can easily be averted, and the whole thing be made to work without a hitch of any kind. It may require a little trouble and a little contrivance at first to arrange the chimney so that *nothing* affects it; but the after-results are so satisfactory that to ensure them no trouble can be considered as such. It must not be merely half done, for although the chimney may be so placed that the nearest approach to extinguishing the flame is an occasional downward puff which disturbs it momentarily, yet this puff forces out into the room a portion of foul air which ought to travel another road and which becomes objectionable. When freedom from annoyance of this kind has once been secured, not the slightest apprehension need be felt on the score of injurious effects upon the birds. We say this advisedly, and as the result of years of experience and years of observation in the breeding-rooms of others where this little machine is considered a great boon; for in this, as in other vital questions, we wish it to be understood that the expression of our opinion is based as far as possible on our own experience, and as little as possible on hearsay, however reliable.

The entire cost of our own stove, with several feet of chimney and short lead from nearest gas-pipe, burner, and fixing, was considerably under a sovereign. This was ten years ago, and it is doing duty yet. We repeat, because it is important and the key to success, that the one condition necessary is positive immunity from down-draughts. We first set it up in an attic, carrying the chimney across the room horizontally, and then at right angles through the ceiling into the roof; but we found that during some winds this arrangement entailed on us the necessity of creeping up-stairs at all hours of the night, in a costume more light and airy than was consistent with comfort, to peep through the keyhole in order to ascertain if all was going on right. But our roof was none of the best, and the east winds making a practice of getting in to play practical jokes with our chimney, our constant visits threatened to land us in a state of chronic rheumatism. A smoky chimney and another domestic calamity we won't mention are proverbial; and though the one helped to produce the other, we ultimately came off master of the situation by inserting the end of the chimney in an inverted box. The wind couldn't get in, but the hot air managed to get out, and we slept undisturbed.

The length of the chimney is immaterial, but the longer the pipe the greater will be the surface from which the heat is distributed. It will be a matter of astonishment to observe how much heat can be generated by a very small flame: it will seldom be found necessary to turn on the full power even during the day, when the pressure on the mains in large towns is always reduced and the supply is proportionately feeble. It is well to place a basin of water on the top to counteract by evaporation any dryness in the air.

Such is our idea of the things to be borne in mind in selecting a good breeding-room, and we have but one more precautionary measure to refer to, and that is with reference to the exclusion of mice, which can make themselves troublesome in various ways if they once gain access to the room. There is no such effective mouse-trap as a cat, but the cat is not wanted in the very place where the mice are; if it clears the lower part of the house it does its duty very well, but it would never do to have it hunting about in the neighbourhood of the bird-room. The most effectual way of excluding mice is to nail strips of tin, bent at a right angle, on the floor and against the skirting-board. Perseverance and good teeth will find a road through anything else, and it requires but a small hole to admit a regiment in single file. See that the bottom of the door is protected by a similar contrivance. Should there be no skirting-board, as is sometimes the case in old rooms, a stout strip of wood must be nailed to the floor close to the wall, and a sharp look-out kept for holes that they may be stopped up at once with Paris plaster or cement. Any holes in the floor itself must be covered with tin, or a pair of sharp eyes will shortly pop up and take stock of the premises, and a colony of eyes quickly follow. If, however, from one cause or another, such as gaining an entrance by some means not suspected, mice do fairly take possession of the room, summary ejection of the whole fraternity is better and more easy of accomplishment than tedious operations with traps. Poisoning can be done without any risk of unpleasant results from the mice dying in their holes, for if one or two should do so their bodies are only very small. If the floor be well swept for two or three nights in succession and baited with a small heap of oatmeal, which must ultimately be mixed with some vermin poison, the entire colony can be cleared out without any trouble in one or two nights, when mice and poison should be buried. But if poisoning be objected to, examine the room for holes and stop up all but one. On going into the room at night with a light, the mice will at once make for this one loophole of escape, which can be closed before even one has time to reach it; for unless the cages are so placed that the mice cannot by any possible means get into them, they will be found banqueting in the seed-hoppers in numbers far exceeding what might be anticipated. If a large box have been previously placed on the vacant side of the room, about an inch from the wall, every marauder will run behind it. There need be no hurry to bring about the *dénouement*, and every long tail must be beaten out of cover; not one will attempt to leave the shelter of the box. A gentle squeeze, and that batch can be swept up, the box replaced, the hole unstopped, and the operation repeated in an hour. There will soon be no mice to squeeze. It is wholesale slaughter, but death is instantaneous and merciful. Dirty cages, filthy little tracks in their frequented runs, soiled seed, and perhaps a dead bird or two, are sufficient incentives to a massacre which need never occur again if the proper precautions are then taken to prevent the ingress of these pests, whose instincts naturally lead them to such a haven of plenty in the way of seed and other delicacies, for which the *mus domesticus* has a strong predilection.

We have referred to the cat as an effective mouse-trap. Some persons succeed in training their cats in such a way that they are allowed free access to the bird-room, and never seem to dream of meddling with the birds; indeed, not a few turn puss into the room every night to mount guard and protect the cages from the inroads of mice; and where the cat has been brought up to the work from kittenhood, it is astonishing how faithfully it will discharge its trust under great temptation to do wrong. We cannot but think the practice is fraught with great danger, and do not consider that a breeding-room containing valuable stock is the right place in which to commence "happy family" experiments. We say so in justice to the claims of the birds, which have no right to be exposed to such a risk. We know many very reliable animals of this kind; but our experience of cats is that they are cats, and that, under favourable conditions, the cat nature will assert itself. It only has to do so *once* to entail disastrous consequences, and we think that the chance of that once should not be allowed. Granted that puss sits down to watch her favourite hole from which she has bagged many a mouse, and watches it as only a cat can; but a slight flutter in one of the cages breaks the stillness of the room, and she is there in a moment, and that unfortunate bird is either "killed fatally dead" or frightened to death, and the cat's appetite being whetted, she makes a complete job of the work before she tires of the amusement of putting her velvet paws through the wires. We have known it to be the case in more than one instance, and think that shutting a cat in a room among birds is like smoking a pipe beside a keg of gunpowder with the head out: but one single spark is wanted to do all the mischief. "A place

MR. YOUNG'S BREEDING-ROOM.

for everything, and everything in its place," is the motto of a well-ordered room; and the place for the cat is on the outside of the door.

We have spoken of mice only, as they are the most common depredators, and are *certain* to be attracted to a bird-room. But in country districts, where other kinds of vermin not unfrequently visit the homestead, the greatest care should be taken to exclude those known to be of a most cruel and bloodthirsty disposition. Visitors of this description are unknown in towns, but in the country, in old buildings in which the walls are none of the soundest, a weasel or stoat may easily secrete himself and play havoc. These gentlemen can squeeze through an opening something smaller than a crack; indeed, the how, when, and where of their ingress is often a mystery, and where such are known to exist they must be guarded against with extreme watchfulness. We need only refer to a disastrous loss sustained by Mr. J. Yallop, of Cossey, near Norwich, when a stoat which obtained admission to his bird-room destroyed between sixty and seventy valuable birds, to show the necessity of vigilance in this direction. The lessons of such a catastrophe should not be lost upon thoughtful fanciers, who should ever study to reduce the *possibility* of an accident within the narrowest limits.

We give a sketch of a breeding-room in which we have spent many a pleasant hour, and which some of our readers at least will not fail to recognise. It is from the hand of an artist better up in Canary-breeding than in the laws of perspective or of light and shadow, and we regret that our "B" pencil is not sufficiently versed in figure-drawing to place in the vacant chair the worthy owner of the establishment, Mr. John Young, Monkwearmouth, Sunderland. It will be seen there is but one chair, the orthodox seats in a bird-room being inverted show-cages or packing-boxes, one of which stands under the window. The closet at the right hand is a moulting-place, which in the winter season also does duty as a large flight, in which breeding stock of all kinds is turned loose during the quiet period of the year when they have nothing to do but to lay up strength for the next season's campaign. The cage is a large thirty-two couple castle in two sections, and is very complete in every respect. In the centre of the room is the gas-stove, before described, with basin of water on top, and chimney carried in a horizontal direction into the chimney of the fire-place. When we say that a single bat's-wing burner in this stove is amply sufficient to keep up a "comfortable" temperature, we need add nothing further as to its efficiency. At the end of the room opposite the fire are other cages, and a general repository for necessaries; but as we don't know how to sketch things standing behind our back, we are unable to give them or the ventilator in the ceiling, without which sanitary arrangement no room can be said to be complete.

CHAPTER V.

CAGES AND CAGE-MAKING.

It is quite possible to go to an extreme; to build with such strict regard to the line and plummet and to conduct our little establishment with such painful order and regularity, as seriously to interfere with the comfort of the objects under our charge. We have a wholesome aversion to the whole family of anti-macassars, and they are a large tribe. Yet we do not wish to be understood as objecting to a well-ordered breeding-room—anything but that; it is only French polish and a sort of clock-work mechanism which admits of no deviation from a set line that we object to when they obtrude themselves to the exclusion of the comfort and well-being of the birds. "Anything will do for a cage." No, anything will *not* do for a cage. The anything-will-do system is bad from end to end, and is born of a careless slovenliness which goes about with holes in its stockings. There is a fitness in things, and a harmony which satisfies the judgment and pleases the eye as much as Dutch gold and stucco are repellant to it. If there be one place more than another in which we like to see handsome cages, it is in a working-man's cottage. They help to cover his walls and represent something, amply repaying the pains bestowed in making them and in keeping them clean. A canny wife, a few bonny bairns, a clean hearth, a four-post bed, a chest of drawers, an eight-day clock, a muling hen or two, a dog and a cat, and what more can a working-man want in this vale of tears?

In fitting up a breeding-room with cages, space can sometimes be economised by utilising recesses. We refer to this as belonging to the sphere of "contrivances;" and we are told that a good contriver is better than he that hath a large appetite. Recesses are also sometimes available in rooms other than those set apart for birds, and may even be the *only* available space at command. They are easily adapted to, or rather converted into cages, with little trouble and not much expense. We must assume that there is no paper on the wall; if there be, it can readily be removed by wetting it, and the plaster laid bare. No better natural sides and back for a breeding-cage can be devised than a dry wall. Set off with a square the exact places to be occupied by the shelving, which should be eighteen inches apart and made of half-inch ordinary yellow pine, the freer from coarse knots the better. If the recess be reasonably square, the shelves can be fitted in tightly without injuring the wall in any way beyond the driving in of a few nails to support them or to fix small ledges on which the ends may rest. Each shelf must, in any case, be bevelled off to the exact angle of the particular niche into which it is intended it should slide, and must be flush with the wall all round, and especially at the back. Any spaces which occur between the shelf and the wall, be they ever so small, must be filled in with thin plaster of Paris, for the same reason that cage-bottoms must be made flush with the back and sides of the cage—viz., to prevent dry sand from running through, and also to prevent insects from harbouring in them. This is, perhaps, the most difficult part of the business, but it is of the utmost importance that it should be attended to. However deep the recess may be, it is not advisable that the shelving be more than about twelve inches from back to front; but if it be not very deep, and it is wished to bring the cage fronts out in the same line as the jamb of the chimney which usually forms the recess, an inch or two is not of so much consequence as disturbing the uniformity desired; but we do not advocate deep cages. If there be width enough, the space at command may be divided into two or three compartments by permanent partitions or by slides, and the whole will then represent a large cage without fronts; and here we will leave it, to enter on the subject of cage-making proper.

Different towns and different schools of fanciers affect different breeding appliances. Custom and long usage determine many fashions, quite irrespective of their suitability. The ancient, heavy, cumbersome, two-wheeled, four-horse plough still reigns in many parts of Kent, and probably elsewhere; while in the north a light, effective machine, which a man might almost swing over his shoulder, is used. Each has its merits and demerits, and nobody will dispute either. In Scotland—and thousands of Canaries are bred beyond the Tweed—open-wire cages are used; while a few miles south of the old Roman wall such a thing is unknown. The "London" cage, the ordinary sale article of wire-workers and cage-makers, of which we give an illustration, is a useful

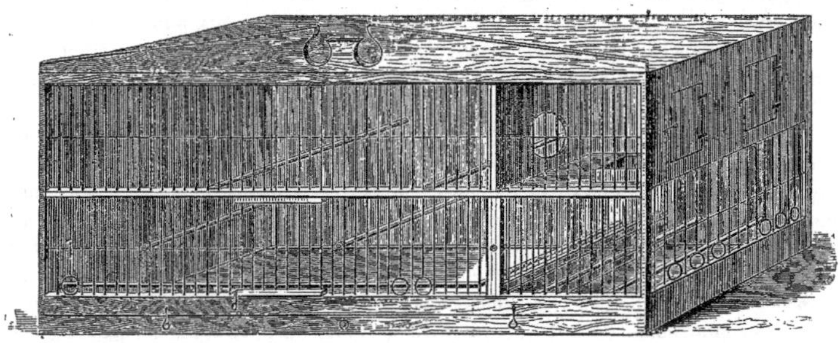

FIG. 3.—THE LONDON CAGE.

thing in its way, and, as generally turned out of the maker's hands, is not an unsuitable ornament to the breakfast-room or study. Our sketch is made from memory, and may not perhaps be quite so elegant as the manufactured article, but the arrangements of the cage are the same. It is an open-wire cage, made in either one or two compartments, and consists of the usual living-room, two nesting-places, and a small nursery, all under one roof. On the shelf of the nesting-place (which can be secluded from the living-room by a falling door, not visible in the sketch) is seen a box, in which the hen constructs her nest. This can be suspended against the back of the little closet if required, and we think it is best so. In place of this box, a basket (Fig. 17) is sometimes let into the shelf like a hand-basin. The doors at the end afford facilities for getting at the interior for examination of nests, cleaning, &c., and the second nesting-place furnishes the hen with another breeding-room in case she should wish to build again before the young ones are old enough to turn out into the nursery below, which is separated from the larger portion of the cage—the living-room —by a wire partition made to slide in and out at pleasure. The nursery may also have a front-door of its own, making it an independent tenement. This we think desirable, and, where such a cage is being made to order, should advise its not being overlooked. It may also be fitted in front with a small drawer of wood or earthenware to contain soft food for the young beaks, and should be liberally supplied with seed and water holes at the end. Two perches running from front to back, about two inches from the wire slide on one side and the wire-holes on the other, will be all

4

the perching-room required, and will enable the occupants to be fed through the wires or to help themselves through the holes. The cage in the illustration was not drawn to scale, but is intended to represent one about three feet long, of which the nursery division is nine inches, height eighteen inches, and width from back to front not exceeding a foot. It is a handy little affair, but the breeder who puts up many pairs looks on it as a toy. A toy it is, but a complete one; and the beginner who wishes to commence in a modest way with not more than one or two pairs, might do worse than purchase this cage, with which he will be able to master the art of creeping before learning to walk.

But the cage we recommend is one with top, back, and sides of wood, the front only being wired, a business-like-looking article, not got up for show, but for work. It can be made in one, two, three, four, or any number of compartments; though we don't advise an arrangement of odd numbers, for reasons which will shortly appear. A single cage—that is, a cage of one compartment and intended for the use of one pair of birds only—is known as a single-couple cage; one with two compartments is called a two-couple cage, and so on; and in describing cages we shall adopt these terms. A "stack" of cages is simply a multiplication of compartments, built either in one piece or in sections; though when built in one piece it is more generally spoken of as an eight or sixteen-couple cage, as the case may be, according to the number of pairs it is intended to accommodate, and is understood to be one piece of furniture.

The advantage of such a cage consists in the economising of material in its construction, the top of one compartment serving as the bottom of another, and the same with the sides; but the disadvantage is the possibility of its becoming like Robinson Crusoe's boat. We always make our own cages, and on one occasion, in the fulness of our zeal, entered on a twenty-couple arrangement, which in the course of time we finished. It is not much to the point, but when we say we don't intend to make *another* twenty-couple, it may, perhaps, convey a moral. We did just manage to get it out of the room in which it was built, though how it was got up two pairs of stairs into our bird-room we don't know, but we soon after received a bill for painting the walls. A year or two afterwards we lent it to a friend who had just built himself a new house, and it was set up in its new home before the hand-rails had been fitted to the staircases. At the close of the season it came home sawn up into sections: he couldn't get it out of the window nor down the stairs, and there was no alternative but to run the saw through it. Since then we have avoided such unwieldy articles.

Cages of somewhat smaller dimensions, say not exceeding four compartments, are very handy, and are as easily moved about for the purposes of cleaning or for arranging in order as are two-couple cages. We only propose to describe the latter, leaving it to the fancier to cut his coat according to his cloth in the matter of multiplication. If it be desired to cover the entire side of a room, we should recommend a stack built up of twos or fours; while if it be wished to fill up some corner or limited area, it may be advisable to build a six for the special purpose, or just such a combination of twos as may suit. Or a breeder may wish to begin in a modest way with a limited number of pairs, and have a desire to make his cage in one piece, even if it be a little over the most handy size; then let him make his cage to suit his requirements; but when all is done it resolves itself into our original proposition, that all cages, whether in stacks or one piece, are best made in combinations of twos, separate or united. Why not in threes? Simply because it is not so easy in a combination of odd numbers to place the seed and water vessels so satisfactorily as in an arrangement of twos, one drawback being that unless the water-tin of the centre compartment be hung close to the seed-hopper, giving the whole a lop-sided appearance, it can only be hung on the centre door; and there is, therefore, a possibility, which never ought to arise, of omitting to replace it on closing the door—an omission which need occur once to bring about a deal of mischief. The simple shutting of the door carries with it the idea of an act completed, and even with the water-tin hanging close by and staring you in the face, the chances are that once in a way it is not replaced. In the case of a centre door working on hinges, the fastening

FIG. 4.—BREEDING-CAGES.

ought always to be the hooks of the water-tin—the door cannot then be fastened except by replacing the tin.

We will now proceed to construct our cage, which, to begin with, is nothing more than a box three feet long, eighteen inches high, and ten inches deep, made of clean yellow pine about three-eighths of an inch thick, neatly and securely put together, every joint fitting as closely as good workmanship can ensure. These dimensions give a *square* frontage to each compartment, which is, perhaps, not the most pleasing to the eye; but if it be wished to alter it, let it be in the direction of the length, which may be extended an inch or two. This is divided into two compartments by a central partition, which can either be the entire height of the cage or only half the height, the upper half sliding in and out in a groove. The only advantage gained by this is that when the breeding season is over the slide can be withdrawn and the two compartments thrown into one; if an entire partition be used it must have an aperture in the centre, about three inches square, which can be opened or closed at pleasure by means of a door suspended on a screw, and which serves as a mode of communication between the two compartments. In place of this aperture a small slide is sometimes used, the various arrangements being shown in the illustration; but these and other minor fittings are entirely matters of taste. For our own part we object to sliding partitions as involving so much more work in making the cage, which is a consideration when a man is his own joiner and cabinet-maker. Our liking has always been to have everything as plain as possible, and to have no sort of complications about a cage when a simpler appliance would answer the same purpose. We mention these things, however, at this stage of our work, because these details must be decided on before the front is made. And while the box is still open and in this crude shape, we may as well direct attention to the fact that if a half-partition and large slide be used, the lower groove in which the slide works will have to be gouged out on the top edge of the partition, and the upper groove will have to be made in the same way on the lower edge of a piece of wood nailed to the inside of the cage at the top. But we think this all means extra work, finished with a precision the amateur joiner may not find it easy to acquire all at once. He has to choose, therefore, between an entire partition with a central aperture or small sliding-door, or a half-partition with a large slide. The entire partition, with central aperture, is the easiest to make, and we are inclined to think will be found the simplest and also the best arrangement.

In the drawing which we furnish of a breeding-cage, it is divided into three sections, each intended to illustrate one or other of the various modes of construction we have described. The bottom section represents the unfinished cage, with wooden cross-bar and wooden framed door pierced ready for wiring. It also shows a fixed partition with central aperture, on the further side of which is supposed to be the small door hanging on a screw, and turned up out of sight to allow of communication between the two compartments. The method of fixing the door is also shown, though it can be seen more clearly in the larger illustration to be given presently.

The middle section shows a wired front, which can either be made a fixture by being inserted in the woodwork, and so becoming part and parcel of the whole, or it can be made in one piece, and attached by small staples. This latter method, however, is almost beyond the scope of amateur wire-working. The doors swing on a stout upright wire. The upper portion of the partition forms a slide which, when withdrawn, turns the cage into a "flight" or "fly-cage."

The upper section illustrates a fixed wired front; sliding, self-closing doors; and a movable partition. The precise construction of the door will be more clearly indicated in an enlarged cut.

Our box now requires a front, and here again we inculcate the principle that simplicity is the first law in cage-making. There are three kinds of fronts which the cage-maker can choose from: wire fronts, which are best made by practical wire-workers and are the most expensive; wired wooden frames, which it requires some little skill to turn out neatly; and a front which is really *not* a front, but which is formed by wiring the front of the box itself—a thing any amateur can do, and do well, with the exercise of not half the care and skill required in making a wired frame. The only advantage to be gained by the use of a movable front is that it can be entirely removed for the purpose of thorough-cleaning the inside of the cage—an operation that can be performed just as well through a properly-constructed door. The disadvantage of a framed front is that, unless it fits absolutely close all over, it affords a harbour for insects between it and the edges of the box. It will be inferred that we advocate the permanent front. We do decidedly, and set about making it in this way:—Plane up three pieces of clean stuff, free from knots, the precise length of the box from outer edge to outer edge, and of the exact thickness: two of them must be an inch and a half wide, and the other three-eighths, which will make it exactly square. These are for the top cross-piece, the bottom cross-piece, and the middle cross-bar. Fit the top cross-piece immediately under the top of the box, cutting slots in the sides and centre partition to receive it. Be careful not to make the slots too wide or too deep: it is easy to take off a shaving, but not so easy to put one on, and these cross-pieces and bar must fit close and tight, and be flush with the front edge. Fix the bottom piece in the same manner one inch from the bottom of the front. This will leave a space of fourteen inches between the two. Now let in the cross-bar neatly, and exactly square, six inches above the bottom piece, and having ascertained that everything fits just as it should, and that there is nothing which requires altering in any way, take out these three pieces, and having marked off on one of them with a pair of compasses the position of the wire-

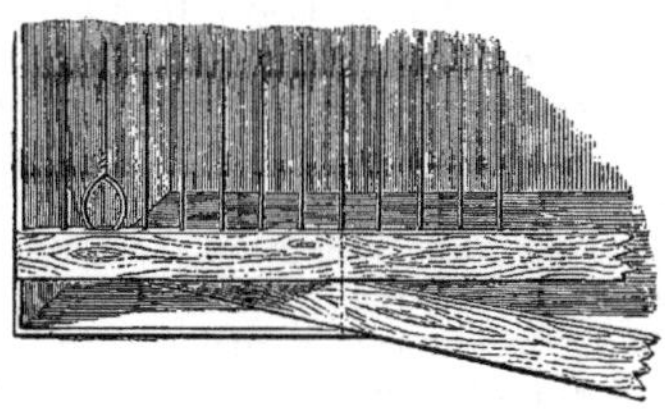

FIG. 5.—TURN-RAIL.

holes half an inch apart from centre to centre, clamp the three tightly together, and mark them across with a pencil and square, drawing the line through each point with the greatest care, for on this depends the accuracy of the wiring. Nothing looks more unbusiness-like than a badly-wired cage, and the operation is really so simple that there is no excuse for doing it otherwise than with the greatest exactness and regularity. Having set off the spaces, run a line down the centre from end to end, and prick the wire-holes on the cross-lines at the intersecting points, using for the purpose a bradawl one size smaller than No. 16 or No. 17 galvanised wire, and either shortened to half an inch in length or loaded with pieces of leather till but that portion of the length remains. This ensures the holes being of uniform depth, and they can then be pierced with a single thrust, without any boring or twisting motion of the pricker. Any one can prick a hole, but to bore it perpendicularly is another matter; and it must be remembered that, in pricking the middle cross-piece, the awl must be kept perfectly upright, or the wires will enter the upper surface apparently in the right direction and come out on the lower in another, when it will be found that the more they are coaxed the more they won't go where they are wanted. But a little care will prevent any irregularity of this kind. In pricking the holes in the bottom cross-piece, it is best not to make any in the middle, on the portion over which the door will stand. It may seem unnecessary to call attention to such a trifling matter, but unnecessary holes are the very places in which insects take up their abode; and in case of the Canary parasite, to which we shall by-and-by have to refer, getting into the cage, these unnecessary holes will all be found crammed with them. It is therefore wise to leave no holes to be crammed. The value of this advice will be appreciated by those who know what pests these parasites are.

Having bored the cross-pieces, replace them, and fix with one or two inch brads, and the cage is ready for wiring.

But the open space of one inch at the bottom—what is to be done with that? Fit into it, on each side of the partition, a piece of wood of the same thickness as the cross-piece; turn the cage upside down and prick a hole through the bottom, through this piece of wood and into the cross-piece above, about three inches from the end nearest the partition. Run a piece of stout wire right through, and the "turn-rail" will revolve on it, affording an opening through which the cage can be cleaned out by means of a small scraper, made by hammering the end of an iron rod perfectly flat and bending it at right angles; turn the other end into an eye, and let it have its special nail to hang on. Many cages are made without this contrivance, in which case all the dirt has to be lifted out with the hand—not the most desirable nor the most effective way of going to work. In place of this turn-rail, a false bottom or tray is sometimes used; but we are full against false bottoms, as being cumbersome, very heavy, liable to warp, and of no practical value whatever. If they be ever so well made the birds will always scratch the sand over the edges, in spite of any beading which may be put round, and after the false bottom has been withdrawn a scraper has still to be used to clear underneath, to allow of the tray being put in again. If this be not done, the sand will either gather at the back or the tray will push it before it into a heap, and the consequence is the concern won't shut up close. The turn-rail obviates all this inconvenience, and has always been a special fancy of ours, as being easily made, in no way interfering with the appearance of the cage, and a most efficient means to a necessary end.

It will be seen that the space to be wired is just fourteen inches high, and to make strong work of it each wire should be inserted at least a quarter of an inch into the wood; they must, therefore, be cut not less than from fourteen and a half to fourteen and three-quarters long. It is best to order the number required from a wire-worker, who will cut and straighten them for a mere trifle. The wire is partially straightened when drawn from the coil by passing it between a simple arrangement of iron pegs; but each piece has still a curve, and to make it absolutely straight is an art acquired only by long practice, and is accomplished by pressure between the finger and thumb. To straighten the hundred and fifty wires required for our cage is the work of only a few minutes for the man who has done the same with as many thousands; and when done they *are* straight, which is more than we would care to vouch for if manipulated by unskilled fingers. In addition to this small bundle of wires it will be necessary to have a piece of No. 14 thickness for a strengthening cross-wire, a few yards of thin binding wire (technically "lapping" wire), and a pair of cutting pliers.

The actual operation of wiring is exceedingly simple. Pass the wire downwards through the middle cross-bar; it ought not to slip through, but should require gently pulling with the pliers, by means of which, being held near the end, it must be inserted in its proper hole and pushed down to the bottom, or till the other end is clear of the lower edge of the top cross-piece: this allows of the wire being inserted in the top hole without bending it, for though it has a certain amount of elasticity, it is best not to have to try it too much in that direction. It will be obvious that this is our reason for directing the holes to be pierced half an inch in depth. The strengthening cross-wire must be run through behind the wires, midway between the cross-bar and the top; but before securing the wires to it we must direct attention to the seed and water holes.

We were almost on the point of building our house without any windows—the door will come presently—but it will be as well to say here that in wiring above the door the wires must come through the cross-piece to the under-side, so as to fill up the holes. It might be urged that it would be as well not to pierce through the cross-bar at this particular place; but by carrying the wires through it materially strengthens the work at a weak spot, at the same time the bar need not be pricked *quite* through if care be used with the awl. Any little precaution of this kind could be better carried out in making one cage than in making a set; our usual plan is to plane up a clean piece of stuff, and having measured off as many bars as the width will allow, and set off the marks for the holes with a square, to prick the entire piece before cutting it up. We have then several lengths all pierced with exactness, and then it matters not where it is cut, or into how many long or short lengths, for the tops and bottoms of doors or other purposes, the holes will always be found to correspond and make true work. The same way with other cross-pieces; clamp as many together as can be managed, and mark them off for pricking on one scale, and

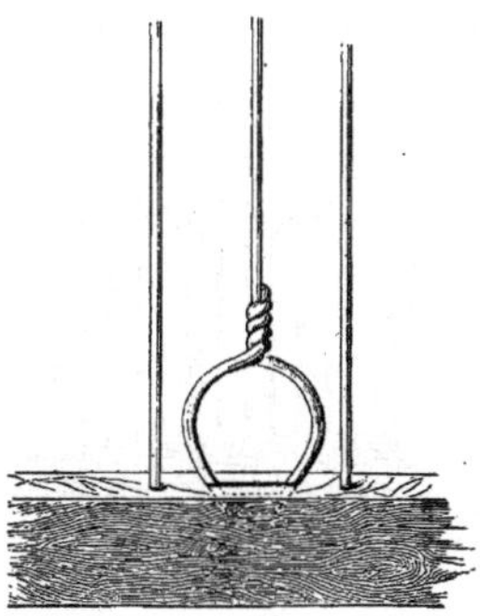

FIG. 6.—SEED AND WATER HOLES.

then there is never any risk of top and bottom holes not corresponding, or the wiring getting out of the perpendicular.

The wires for the seed and water holes must be cut a few inches longer than the others, and three will be required for each compartment, one for water and two for seed. They are easily twisted into shape by bending round a piece of hard wood; we use a ruler of lignum vitæ rather less than an inch in diameter. The most approved twist is shown in the illustration. To secure them in their places it is only necessary to hammer out the lower edge of the loop on any smooth solid surface (nothing better than that useful domestic appliance, a *flat-iron*), when it can be made sufficiently sharp to easily bury itself in the soft wood and remain securely fixed. The water-hole wire should be inserted about the third or fourth from the side, and the seed-hole wires should occupy the third and fifth places next the partition, according to the length of the seed-hopper intended to be used, which, as will be presently explained, should cover both sets of seed-holes on either side of the partition.

We must delay binding the strengthening cross-wire until our door is hung—and the door is a most important part of a cage. A great deal of work has to be done through the open door, which must be large enough to admit the hand easily, and, if needs be, a jar containing a bunch of chickweed or groundsel, or other green food, without being obliged to turn it so much on one side as to spill half the water it may hold. To harmonise with the cage our door must have a wooden frame; indeed, no other description of door would work well under a wooden cross-bar. It is, however, very simple in construction. It cannot be higher than the six inches allowed for it, and the only question is as to the width. Assuming the compartment to be eighteen inches wide, it will give us thirty-six wires, according to our plan of spacing out. The third part of that is twelve, so that if we leave the middle twelve holes in the bottom unwired, it will require a door just six inches square to fit exactly. The use of our lengths of pierced cross-bars will now be apparent. We have nothing to do but to cut off two pieces, each containing twelve holes, allowing very nearly the whole half-inch before the first hole and behind the last—that is to say, we must not cut the length off directly through the first hole and through the twelfth, but before and behind them—we want twelve clear holes, and a small piece over at each end. Place these two pieces face to face, and it will be seen the holes correspond exactly—one is the top of the door and the other the bottom. The side-pieces are of the same dimensions with respect to thickness (but, of course, are not cut from pierced lengths), and must be cut of the precise length

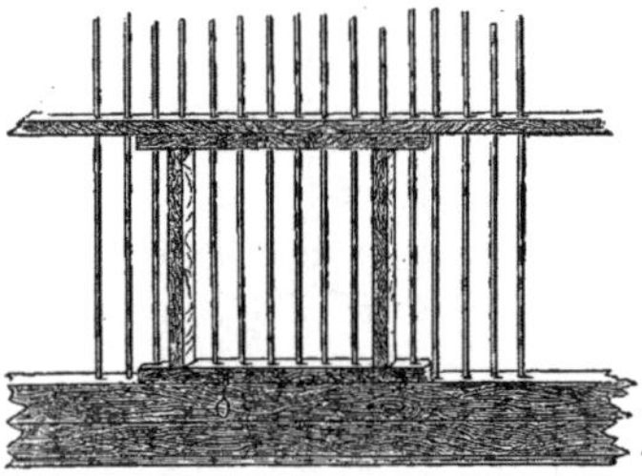

FIG. 7.—WOODEN DOOR.

required. Place one of them fair under the second hole of the top piece, and a single brad driven through the hole will fix it in its place; do the same with the other, placing it under the eleventh or last hole but one; turn it up and put the bottom piece on in the same way, and the door-frame is complete. Wire it, and it only then remains to hang it, which is done by unshipping the twelfth long wire on the right-hand side of the cage, and, after placing the door so that the twelfth hole of the door-frame is under the twelfth hole of the main middle cross-bar, replacing the long wire, on which the door will swing as on a hinge. Notch off the inside of the top and bottom pieces of the door-frame at the other end, so that when it shuts it may catch against the twelfth wire on the left-hand side, and the door when closed will fit flush with the front. The whole thing will take scarcely more time to do than it has taken us to write the details, and when a set of cages is being made of uniform dimensions and uniform scale of wiring, a dozen, twenty, any number of doors can be put together by cutting up the pierced lengths, without any necessity for measurement, and with the certainty of any one door exactly fitting any one cage, whether made specially for it or not. If one should happen to be a shade tight, the slightest tap under the middle cross-piece will give it liberty; or if it should be too slack, a downward tap between the wires will improve matters without putting the bar out of square in a way to offend the eye.

There is another description of door which requires still less making. It is shaped like a block letter **T**, with a foot the same width as the head, and is simply a skeleton-door with an upright in the centre instead of on each side, wired and hung in the same way as that we have been describing.

A third is made by cutting the bottom of it out of the bottom cross-piece, thus causing it to open level with the cage-bottom, and doing away with the necessity for a turn-rail or other contrivance to facilitate cleaning out. This is a useful door, but, to make a good job of it, requires to be hung with hinges on a separate frame, which gives it rather a heavy appearance.

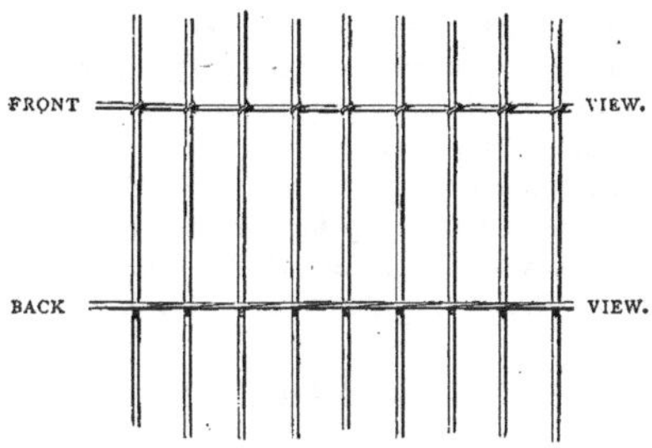

FIG. 8.—MODE OF WIRING.

The fastening of the door comes last. Small buttons or hasps look very neat, but we use no other than a piece of wire run through the bottom of the door-frame and bent downwards at right angles an inch on each side; it requires to be turned up to open the door, but falls of itself, and is entirely self-acting.

We might write a chapter on doors, but verbal descriptions of the simplest contrivances are not always very clear. We trust that a glance at the illustrations will render plain anything we may have failed to explain very lucidly.

FIG. 9.—CANARY'S FOOT AND PERCH.

The finishing operation of the whole is binding the wires to the strengthening cross-wire with the thin lapping material before mentioned in our inventory of necessaries. We give an illustration of the orthodox twist which tightens the whole, and makes it impossible to displace any wire or widen the space between them so as to permit the escape of a bird.

The perches, instead of being about the diameter of a lead-pencil, as is too frequently the case, should be nearly twice that diameter, oval in section, and placed with the broad side uppermost. Notice the formation of a Canary's foot, and the reason will be evident. They should rest on the cross-bar, and project an inch or two, so as to allow of their being drawn out at pleasure for being cleaned, &c.; and if a stock be kept ready, with a brad filed up to a sharp point inserted in one end, they will often be handy to push in here and there in various positions as occasion may require. A perch may also be put lengthways, to enable the birds to get at the seed and water easily.

Such is our cage. We have been minute in our description of it, because we think that many may wish to try their hand at cage-making. The lathe and the bench are now-a-days common accessories to a country-house, and we find many seeking recreation in pursuits which entail a large amount of what is neither more nor less than hard work. But the old saying, that what is one man's meat is another man's poison, can be translated in various ways. Sedentary occupations find relief in severe exercise; and the city man, who has been boxed up in his office all day, regards it as a positive treat to turn up his shirt-sleeves and have a turn at his bench, or a spell in his garden for hours after his gardener has pulled off his boots, smoked his nightly churchwarden, and retired to bed thoroughly tired out with precisely the same work. We have

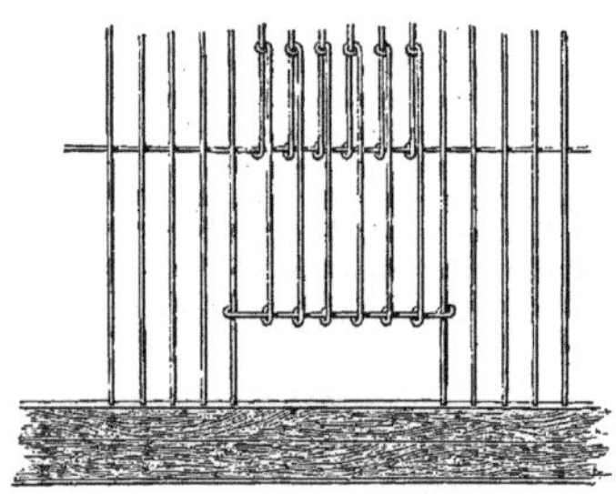

FIG. 10.—SLIDING DOOR.

not aimed at making this part of our subject a treatise on joinery, and have studiously avoided technicalities in a description we wish to give in terms as plain and homely as possible. To us, half the fun consists in being our own designer, architect, and builder. The appliances for the carrying out of our hobby are few and simple, and when we require any we just turn to and make them; and we wish to show others how to do the same, if their inclination tends in the same direction.

Before dismissing the subject of cage-making, we must refer briefly to one other method of wiring, simply because it involves the use of an excellent description of self-closing door, very much in use, both in breeding and exhibition cages. We have before stated that wire fronts, made in the piece, are best left to a practical wire-worker, though there is no reason why a fancier may not unite that art to his other accomplishments, or even wield the soldering iron and become his own plumber. The method of wiring, however, to which we now refer needs no practical hand, and consists in substituting, in place of the wooden cross-bar, a cross piece of stout wire, to which the upright wires must be bound in the manner previously indicated. The door, a pattern of which we show in our illustration, can then be made to slide up and down, and if carefully put together is a most effective self-closing arrangement, which, with its extreme lightness, constitute its chief excellence. Even if it should not slide or fall freely, but have to be pulled down, it has the merit of not being able to swing open; for we have known birds play with the internal fastenings of doors and inadvertently open them. A reference to the cut will show the construction and working better than any verbal description, but it will be seen that after making the eyes to the several wires (which is done with a pair of pointed pliers) and bending them over at right angles, they must be kept in the same straight line while being turned up at the bottom and pinched on to the frame on which the entire fabric works, or the door will not slide at all, or only with difficulty. Success depends entirely on true work. And further, the upper strengthening cross-wire must be placed sufficiently high to admit of the door travelling, or the consequences will be obvious. A sliding door, let it be observed, is not a necessity; an ordinary swing door can be made, but nothing is gained by it, and it requires some amount of skill and practice to turn out one which has not the trade-mark, "home-made," stamped on every wire.

Some, to whom the construction of a breeding-cage is no novelty, will perhaps observe that we have made no reference to egg-drawers and a few *et cæteras*, which sometimes are united to it. We prefer to supply them by inside attachments, though we by no means object to their being made fixtures. One way is as handy as the other. We always like to see the front

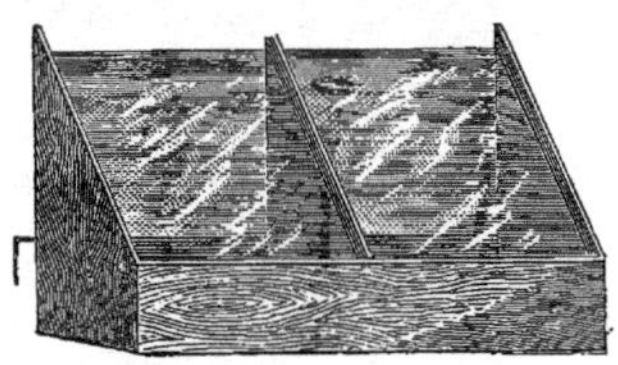

FIG. 11.—SEED-HOPPER.

of a cage cut up as little as possible, though sundry useful contrivances, such as neat earthenware egg-drawers, can be inserted in the front, and are very convenient for general purposes. Experience will suggest many things of this kind, which it is quite unnecessary to enter into here, their adoption or rejection being matters of taste and ingenuity.

Two appliances only are now necessary to make our cage tenantable—the seed-hopper and water-vessels, of which we give illustrations. It is not necessary to furnish any specific dimensions for a hopper, but when we say that it must be made long enough to cover both sets of seed-holes, it will be obvious that to fit our cage and system of wiring, it will require to be six inches in length. The depth is immaterial, but from an inch to an inch and a half is ample, with a width of say two inches. There is nothing gained by increasing these dimensions, except that the hopper requires more seed to fill it. It makes no difference in the consumption. There is a fashion in hoppers as in many other things, the front being sometimes carried round in a curve, or cut off at an acute angle; that in our illustration is, we think, as easy to make and looks as well as any. The two sloping ends are grooved for the reception of a piece of glass or perforated zinc, which prevents the birds throwing out the seed—a thing they will do apparently in sport, or in wanton waste, whenever a fresh supply is given, And very clever they are in doing it; just one sharp peck of the beak, and away goes the seed in all directions. It is well also to have an inside partition in these double hoppers, when used to supply seed to two compartments, in each of which there is a cock: it prevents any fighting through the seed-holes.

The old-fashioned seed-drawer, with the holes inside the cage, is now almost exploded. As a plan of supplying food, it may be as good as any other, but the trouble of making and fixing the inside box, coupled with the facilities it affords for harbouring insects, and the difficulty of getting at them, have caused the hopper to supersede it. Some old-fashioned fanciers, however, have a liking for old-fashioned contrivances; and to those who desire to follow in their wake, it will be a sufficient guide in constructing such a drawer if we say that, for our cage, it would

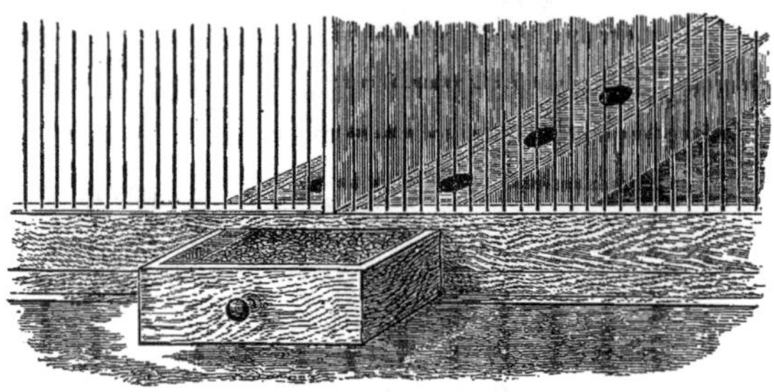

FIG. 12.—SEED-DRAWER.

require to be of double the width, and that the partition of the cage would have to rest on the box into which the drawer slides. The drawers will then be accessible from the two sets of holes on either side of the partition. We can only add in its favour, that the pulling out of a little seed-drawer and blowing off the chaff seems somehow to be mixed up with our very earliest recollections, and we feel some sort of regret in discarding an old friend.

In the matter of water-vessels there is an endless variety of pattern and material. We

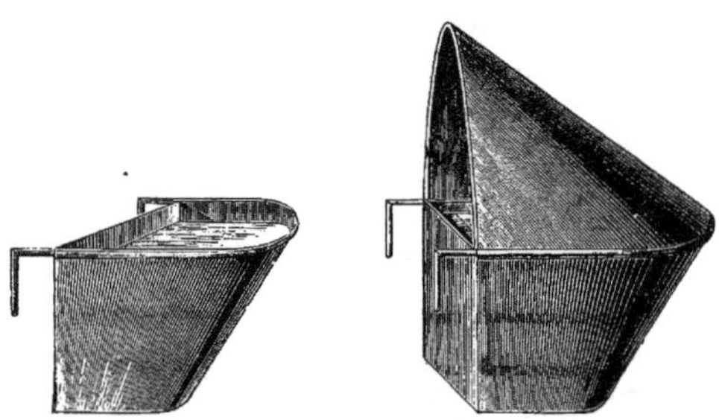

FIG. 13.—WATER-TINS.

will not undertake to recommend one as being superior to another, but we generally use the ordinary open hook-on tin usually kept in stock by dealers in cages and cage-fittings. They are cheap and, when well made, last a long time. They have the advantage of being easily stowed away one within the other, and are not so easily broken as glass or earthenware vessels. They are, however, when slop-made, apt to leak, and share in common with all open vessels the disadvantage of becoming receptacles for any loose material, such as nesting stuff or particles of food which the birds may throw about, and in hot weather require frequent replenishing to prevent the water becoming offensive and consequently unwholesome. Sometimes they are made with a conical cover, but we do not like covers we cannot see through; the tin might leak dry, or might even be overlooked and not filled, and then the birds suffer or die from thirst.

In the list of open water-vessels will also be found the glass and earthenware cups, which require to be suspended in wire loops. These have the great merit of being very cleanly, but are easily broken. No two of the glass ones are exactly the same size, and each must be fitted in its own particular loop, which is a source of a good deal of confusion in a large room where there are a great many cages. The earthenware cups are preferable in this respect, but most of them are ornamented in such a vulgar style that there is no doing with them at any price. Their proper place is among illuminated glass rolling-pins, china spaniels with red spots, presents "from Margate," and other atrocities. There is room for Ruskin even in the bird-room. The covered-in round-topped glass bottles, used for both seed and water in song-cages, we have a great objection to. They

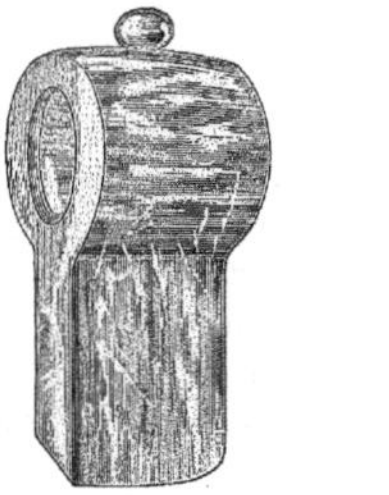

FIG. 14.—GLASS WATER VESSEL.

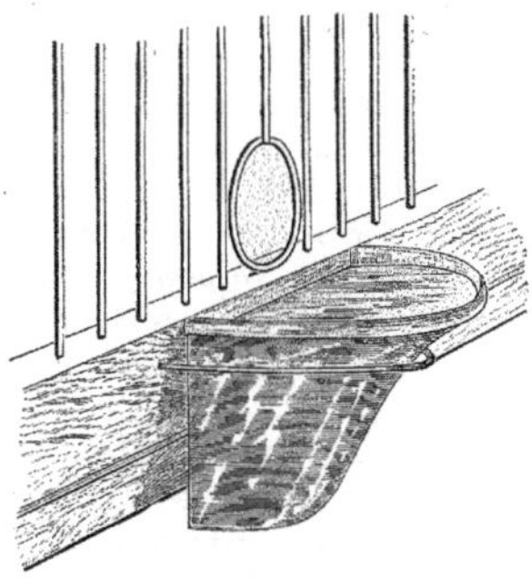

FIG. 15.—SEED OR WATER GLASS.

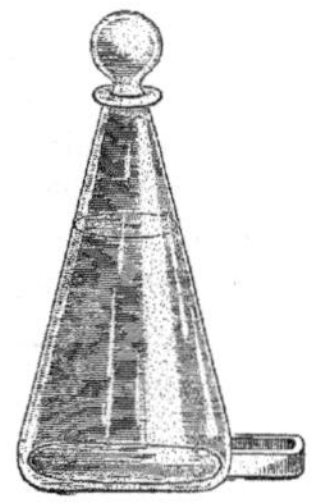

FIG. 16.—CONICAL FOUNTAIN.

require to be fitted with such care, with the mouth of the bottle exactly opposite to the wire-hole, that very little will sometimes displace them; and it has seldom been our lot to visit a show where these dangerous things are frequently used by exhibitors who do not understand their business, without finding some bird suffering from not being able to get at its seed or water; and a pitiable sight it is to see the poor thing standing mutely appealing to some passer-by to put its food within reach. We always feel disposed to smash them—accidentally.

The well-known conical glass fountain, with projecting lip, is a rather expensive but admirable reservoir, furnishing a continued supply of clean water; and if the wire-hole be placed above the cross-bar and adjacent to one of the perches, so that egg and other soft food which is soon decomposed is not apt to be thrown into the mouth, we know of no better water-vessel than this, especially for use in rooms where the attention is limited to a morning and evening visit. They will hold a supply to last for days, and require nothing more than an occasional shake, to discharge any foreign matter and clear the mouth. They may require a little attention during the very hot summer weather, as all water-vessels do, but used in conjunction with roomy seed-hoppers, they are valuable time-savers the year round to the breeder whose spare minutes are few.

CHAPTER VI.

NEST-BOXES AND OTHER APPLIANCES.

In following out the plan of our work, we purpose dealing with the appliances belonging to the bird-room as occasions for their use may present themselves. We shall do this with the view of not tiring the reader with too much dry, but necessary detail all in one place. We have built our cage and fitted it with the three absolute necessaries, and now proceed to hang it up or place it against the wall in some way. There are more ways than one. Perhaps, instead of a single cage, it may be a four or six-couple, and it may be proposed to stand it on a small table, with drawers for seed and tins, and all kinds of neat little arrangements. It is difficult to disabuse any one of the idea that such things are dangerous articles in the bird-room. We do not object to them in the breakfast-room or library, or in any room into which the idea of furniture enters as an element—and we have seen very handsome mahogany-fronted cages designed for this purpose—but table-legs in a bird-room are so suggestive of staircases for mice. If the cage be large and cannot safely be suspended, but must be propped up in some way, make the supports as few as possible; and plant on the top of each support an *inverted meat-tin*, how to get over which is a problem on which the minds of ingenious mice have hitherto been much exercised without arriving at any satisfactory conclusion. The most convenient plan is to hang the two-couple cages against the wall, almost as closely as if built in a stack. There had better be a small space left between each, if it can be done; because, if insects should get into them, they will lodge permanently between the top of one cage and the bottom of the next, if the one is used as a support for the other. Further, it will be found that it is better to suspend the cages on nails passing through holes in the inside, than through metal eyes attached to the outside, as the nails of one cage in the latter case interfere with the hanging of another. Occasionally the way in which a wall is built entirely precludes the adoption of this system of hanging, and the bottom row has to carry the entire superstructure, but it can generally be managed on a brick partition by pricking for the joints, and each cage hung literally on its own hook, not less than from two to three feet from the floor. The wisdom of adopting uniformity in size and arrangement of parts will now be apparent to the fancier as he sits down to take stock of his work: seed-hoppers will be seen to be in rows, one above the other, and the same with the water-tins, and apart from the pleasing effect to the eye, the convenience of the whole will manifest itself to him in many ways, the value of which he will fully recognise.

We might have referred at an earlier stage of the proceedings to the whitewashing which the cages must undergo, but as it requires to be done twice in the year, viz., at the commencement and close of each breeding season, and has then to be managed through the door, we have completed our cage before mentioning it. The brush which has done duty for ourselves for a good many years is a common paint-brush of medium size, with the handle shortened to three or four inches. Mix ordinary whiting to the consistency of thick cream with thin flour-and-water paste. If the whiting be first mixed into a paste, and the liquid be added when boiling, it will work up into a very smooth compound, which can be laid on with a finish almost equal to paint, and, when dry will not rub off. If used too thin, the marks of the brush are left behind, but it is surprising how smoothly the stuff will work from the brush if concocted as we have directed. It is a usual practice with some breeders, before coating a new cage, to thoroughly anoint every joint and crack with a preparation of corrosive sublimate, with the view of making them untenantable for insects; but if the whitewash be well worked into every crevice, and any flaws or defects in the wood be filled up with plaster of Paris, we do not well see how the insects can manage to get in. Such precautionary measures, however, cost but little trouble, and if supplemented by a dressing of varnish before whitewashing, the chances are still further diminished. Top, bottom, back, sides, inside the front cross-pieces, everywhere must come under the brush; and in repeating the operation on old cages, be careful to knock off any loose flakes of whiting, and if there be any dry sand in the corner of the cage, let the brush take it up, and work it well into the corners like so much concrete. All this means nothing more than an injunction to do the work thoroughly, and finish it off smoothly and neatly. We have said nothing about painting the outside, but the front should have a coat of sizing, followed by one of black paint, and then finish off with one or two coats of black varnish.

Nest-boxes play an important part in the economy of the breeding-cage, and the contrivances and arrangements for the same vary much in actual practice. The perforated shelf and basket-work nest, which is sometimes used instead of the nest-box, in the little closet of what we call the "London" cage, and which is not confined to it alone, is so foreign to everything we have been accustomed to that we can offer no practical opinion on its merits. For our own part, we should hesitate before we used a nest of either wicker-work, chip, or any similar material, simply on the ground that every crevice would appear to us to be an advertisement of "Apartments to let," and an invitation to the first stray parasite to wander no further, but to take up his abode in such a cleverly-contrived playground.

We have several times referred to this possibility of "insects" becoming a nuisance, but would like to have kept it out of sight as long as possible. It *will* have to be explained sooner or later, and we may as well out with it at once and be done with it. Perhaps it will be policy also to represent the case as being much worse than it really is, and then the beginner will be agreeably surprised if he finds things not so bad as he expected. The Canary is liable, under certain circumstances, to become infested with parasites much in the same way as other animals are similarly plagued, not even excepting the genus *homo*. The preventive in each case is the same, viz., cleanliness and fresh air, and that is the beginning and the end of the dreadful story. But lest any may find themselves beset by an army of these pests, we give a little further account of them, and show how to deal with them. Without entering into any philosophical disquisition as to what the little parasite is, it will be sufficient to say that if a sharp look-out be kept on the ends of the perches next the back of the cage, the places where these rest on the cross-bar, the tops of the doors where they touch the bar, the inside of nest-boxes at the back, or any similar hiding-hole where the insects may be expected to congregate, a white floury substance will sometimes be found there; and if it be examined closely, it will be found to be replete with life, and will, if disturbed, move about in precisely the same way as the mites in cheese. It is, in fact, a colony of mites, using the word to signify a very small insect, and not as a strictly correct scientific term.

That this peculiar organism is born of the Canary there can be not the slightest doubt, since the presence of the bird is a necessary condition of its existence, or at all events, of its production; but how generated it is not in our power to say. We only know that the fact stands and that it is a very disagreeable fact. Now, if these small settlements be left undisturbed, the inhabitants will increase and multiply at a rate which leaves black beetles and cockroaches far behind in the race for life. In the early stage of their existence they are white, but when they reach maturity they become of a bright red colour, and develop into most active little insects. If the cages be examined by candle-light, they will be observed running over the birds in great numbers with extraordinary speed, disappearing beneath the feathers in a twinkling; and it is only reasonable to infer that their red colour is caused by their being inflated with the blood of the birds on which they are supposed to feed. They are essentially nocturnal animals, and only display this lightning-like agility when running about on the feathers of the birds; for if a nest of them be disturbed during the day, they certainly do run off in all directions, but only in a comparatively sluggish way, and are easily killed. It will be admitted that these insects are most undesirable tenants for a breeding-cage; though while fully admitting they cannot fail to be troublesome and irritating to the birds, we are by no means prepared to go so far as to support the assertion sometimes made, that they suck the blood from the young ones, and cause their death by literally draining them. We can call to mind several nests of exceptionally strong birds which, when we had occasion to remove them into more commodious lodgings, we found had been reared over a perfect ant-hill of insects lining the under part of the nest in a moving mass, in numbers one would have thought sufficient to have effected a massacre of the innocents in a single night. Nor are we, on the other hand, prepared to support the theory of many old breeders that birds are never so strong and healthy as when infested with these insects, and who regard them as positive indications of robust health. Candour, however, compels us to state that, though we would rather be without them if only on the ground of cleanliness and apparent comfort of the bird, and would, and do always, use every precaution to prevent their appearance, we have never been able to trace any evil results to their presence, even when under a visitation almost as severe in its way as that experienced by Pharaoh of old. We have sometimes almost been inclined to question whether the blood they contain (we suppose it *is* blood) is really obtained from the birds, and we will give our reasons. In our breeding-room we had a chair which once had a back, but the top of it having come to grief in a collision in the nursery while doing duty as a stage-coach, we confiscated it, and having mended it by a transverse lashing of stout cord, appropriated it to our special use. It stood in a corner most remote from our cages, several feet from the nearest, and yet we found the parts where the cord was bound round the broken back completely infested with Canary parasites, apparently as full of blood as their relatives in the cages. Now, if this were the blood of the birds, the insects must have travelled every night in a train across the floor like a regiment of ants, up the wall, and into a cage; have feasted on some victim; and have returned to their quarters by the morning. We can readily account for their presence in the chair, but we are at a loss for a theory to account for the presence of the "blood." One or two stray travellers could easily plant the colony, but an old well-seasoned piece of beech will not yield blood, even to the most persistent suction. We state the fact as it occurred, and we drew attention to it some years ago in illustration of the way in which such insects could people the most unlikely places. We do not say that the insects do not suck the birds, but in the face of our own observations, we scarcely think it necessarily follows that because they are seen at nights running about on the birds, and are full of a red fluid, that such *must* be the case, any more than the fact of the saddle being found under the sick man's bed was conclusive evidence that the patient had eaten the horse.

We return to the discovery of the floury substance referred to just now, and remark that this is the time to nip the affair in the bud. Had a still sharper look-out been kept, and a visit paid to the cages every night by candle-light, it is more than probable that the one or two first comers who caused the mischief would have been detected and put out of the way. As it is, if clean perches be supplied and the dusty spots anointed with a drop of oil, the danger is over at once. It will be seen now why we have been so very particular over cracks and crannies. It is only because that the smaller the crevice, the greater the likelihood of its becoming occupied. A loose flake of whitewash is a certain cover, while unused wire-holes and similar minute recesses are preserves which should be regularly beaten. One thing is certain, the insects must go *somewhere*, and it is as well to know where they *do* go; hence some breeders prefer to keep open one crack that they may know where to find them, when short work is made of them by drawing the blade of a knife through it. In a sound cage, however, the places we have indicated are about the only places accessible, and a daily examination will do the rest. Should the floury appearance show itself on the outside of the cage, round bad joints, or in similar places, there is nothing better than to pass the varnish-brush over it, on the "catch 'em alive" principle.

It will be seen that this nuisance is preventible by the exercise of reasonable care. It is only by neglect of ordinary precautions that it attains formidable dimensions, but if a cage should be found to be infested, it is best to remove it and give it a thorough drenching and scalding. Then dress the joints and cracks with a solution of bichloride of mercury, which can

FIG. 17.—BASKET NEST.

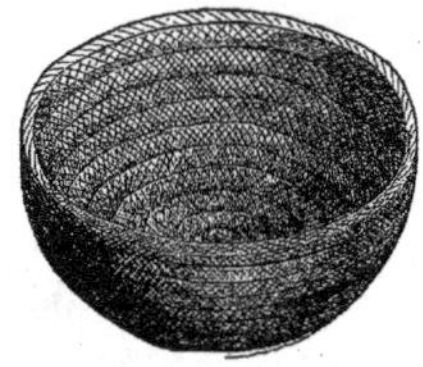

FIG. 18.—MANILLA CORD NEST.

be obtained at any chemist's, and varnish afresh. One word of caution: old rickety cages should not be allowed in the breeding-room, as it is almost next to impossible to keep them clean: burn them.

These remarks have followed on our referring to basket-work nests, and we think that the reason of our objection to them is patent. And yet they are used, and very extensively too. On the face of it, it would seem the very sort of building-place one would suggest for a bird, enabling it to construct its nest under very favourable conditions. And no doubt it is a comfortable foundation on which to build; we admit it all, but the basket can become infested before it is possible to discover it, and therefore we reluctantly discard it, as offering facilities we would rather not allow. A friend of ours uses them, but first soaks them in petroleum, and with satisfactory results: if the reader means to use them, we advise him to do the same. Another friend of ours has not a nest in his room of any other description than a simple cup, formed by stitching stout Manilla cord into the necessary form, which is afterwards lined with flannel. If insects appear, the nest is thrown into boiling water, and subsequently dried in an oven. He is a most successful breeder, and naturally clings tenaciously to the particular contrivance which has carried him through many seasons; but it seems to us a very ordinary sort of makeshift. In some of the pit districts in the North, nothing will go down but a leathern box, circular and flat-bottomed; and no arguments can shake a belief in a lining of *candle-wicks*. This kind of thing, however, is most prevalent in districts which once were remote from any town, and in which very primitive arrangements have held their ground in spite of modern improvements. Strange it is how long people will adhere to early teachings in the face of a better creed. The use of candle-wicks is almost universal in the pit villages, and doubtless arose from the facility with which the material is obtained, and the difficulty of getting anything more suitable. The material referred to is nothing more than the accumulated savings of the spare piece of wick which is left when a common tallow candle is cut from its place in a bunch; and many a Mule that has "caught the judge's eye" at the Crystal Palace was nursed in a pitman's cottage on a bed of candle-wicks.

In Norwich, the city of canary-breeders, a wooden box, shaped something like a kitchen soap-box, is considered the correct thing, and scarcely anything but dried moss is supplied for nesting material; yet who shall say that the Norwich men are not successful breeders? We believe the same fashion obtains throughout the midland districts. The fact is, it is only necessary to furnish the hen with some niche, and she will soon occupy it, failing which she

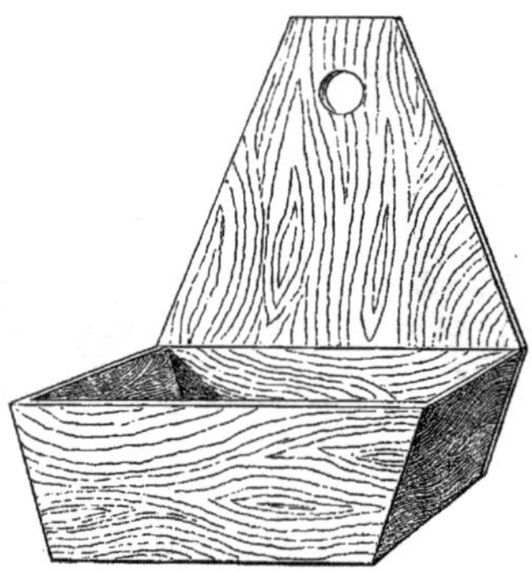

FIG 19.—NORWICH NEST-BOX.

will take possession of the egg-drawer, or even deposit nesting-stuff in the seed-hopper, or in the corner of the cage-bottom. She must build.

We have briefly specified our objections to the nest-boxes we have described. Possibly none of them are very serious. We do not wish to take a one-sided view of any question, but desire to put it as fairly as possible; and it may be that our views are just as much biassed as those of our neighbours, for it is not easy to divest the mind of the influences of early associations. Our own earliest recollections of breeding are connected with a nest-box (by which we mean any receptacle supplied to the hen for the purpose of building in), which divides its allegiance with the Norwich nest. It is after all only a question of suitability of material, though the one we are about to describe has advantages not shared by any other. It is made either of tin or earthenware—we give illustrations, however, of all. The tin nest to which we have been accustomed consists of a cup with perforated zinc bottom, for purposes of ventilation, attached to an upright back, precisely similar in construction to the old-fashioned sconces in vogue before the days of gas, which, containing a spluttering candle, were hung against the wall to render the darkness visible. It is suspended against the back of the cage, on a strong flat-headed tack or nail, driven in at a very acute angle, the hole in the tin being shaped like an inverted keyhole, through the enlarged eye of which the head of the nail passes, the narrow cut allowing the tin to fall on the shank, when the inclined position of the nail will generally afford sufficient grip to prevent the nest being pulled out one side by the bird. This will constantly happen if the tin be suspended on a screw, as there is then nothing but the friction of the nest against the back of the cage to prevent its oscillating freely on the rounded edge, unless the head of the screw be sent well home so as to bite the edges of the slit, in which case it sometimes bites too much, and it is not easy to lift the nest off and on. Sometimes, in place of a cup, there is only a bare framework, in which the nest proper is placed. These tins are usually made of three sizes, ranging from three to four inches in diameter, and even larger; the larger sizes being intended for the reception of extra large nests of young birds, should the smaller ones be found too small for their accommodation; for, be it remembered, tin is not so yielding as the sides of a naturally-built nest. These are lined with soft felt, procurable at any saddler's, of which there are two kinds, white and brown. The white is the softer material of the two, and is a trifle more

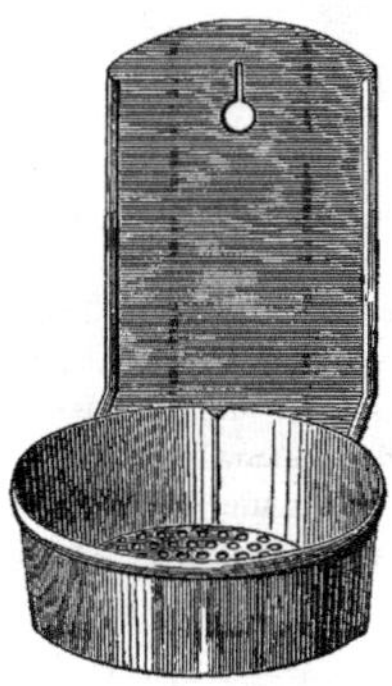

FIG. 20.—TIN NEST.

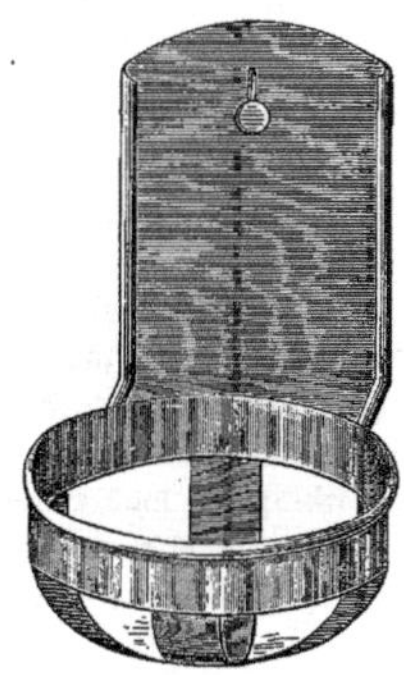

FIG. 21.—TIN FRAME ONLY.

expensive than the brown, which is harder and much tougher—an excellent quality, by the way, for some birds never leave it alone, even while sitting, but peck away at it till the bottom of the nest is completely perforated. The tougher kind is also to be had black; the texture of the material is the same. We have no choice as to selection, but the white looks cleanest, and has a comfortable appearance about it suggestive of warmth. Cut the felt into circular pieces, according to the size of the tins, remembering that the diameter of the felt must be much greater than that of the tin, to allow of its being pressed into the cup, flush with the top edge. Each piece must then be split into two, tearing it open like a muffin. It will be found that the white will split easily, but the brown requires a good pull. In order to fit it into the tins, a deep angular-shaped piece must be cut out of the edge; don't cut it too large at first, but if the felt will not fit smoothly without any ridges, enlarge the notch till the desired shape is obtained, and then cut the remainder to pattern. We have always found one deep notch to be amply sufficient, the stuff being very easily worked into shape in the tins, where it must be secured by a few stitches of stout thread passed through the perforated zinc bottom, and secured firmly too, as the hens will pull away at it in a resolute manner, sometimes biting through the thread and turning the bed out on to the floor. Our reason for making only one notch is that there is only one rent to close, and the less chance for insects finding their way into the stuff. Having cut a lot of these felts, thread them on fine strings, according to the size, and hang them up for use. They will all be wanted before the season is over. Clean nests mean healthy birds, while dirt and filth engender discomfort and disease.

The earthenware nest-box to which we referred is, we think, comparatively local in its habitat. We do not remember to have seen them elsewhere than in our own town, Sunderland,

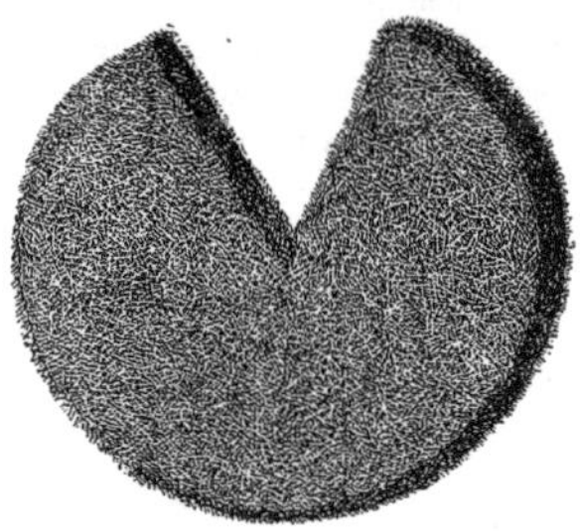

FIG. 22.—FELT LINING.

where they are made in considerable numbers in the potteries on the Wear. They are much used by the breeders of the district, and have in many rooms entirely displaced the tin arrangement, which is also indigenous to the North. They are made of glazed or unglazed earthenware, but the latter is the most commonly used. Lined with white felt, which is easily attached with some thin plaster of Paris, nothing can look cleaner, and no insects can get underneath the lining, which is a point of consequence; for if these creatures be only half as tormenting as a common flea, it is

FIG. 23.—EARTHENWARE NEST.

not a very pleasant reflection to know that there are a thousand only waiting for the candle to be put out.

The wooden box requires no lining at the hands of the fancier. A more skilful architect than he will weave her own felt, and furnish it in a way compared with which all other attempts are but the most clumsy bungling. We are quite prepared for the statement that years of domestication have done their work in impairing the architectural skill of the Canary, and that it is necessary for their comfort to assist them in this respect. It may be so; and yet if the offspring of a wild bird, which never saw a nest built in its life, can construct its own habitation, why should not the offspring of a tame one, which in its turn never saw one built, be able to do the same thing? The fact is, many of the finches build very slovenly nests as compared with other birds, and birds of the same family vary much in the display of a knowledge of the art of nidification, as every school-boy knows. The character of the nest is there, but the finish is frequently wanting. And so it is with our caged Canaries. One will do its work in the most masterly way and turn out its nest with exquisite finish, while another will content itself with a mere apology, scarcely worth the name. No two build their nests exactly alike: one makes the most perfect cup, so deep that you wonder how she will manage to sit in it without turning up her tail like a fantail pigeon; another fills up her box, leaving barely the slightest depression in which to deposit her eggs; another makes an oval cavity; and another invariably selects the corner of her box, leaving the wood exposed on two sides, much in the same way as we sometimes find a wild bird's nest built against a branch, part of which positively forms a portion of the inside of it. And these birds always do the same thing, if they build half-a-dozen times in the season, and yet somehow always manage to take care of their eggs and their young ones if left alone. Perhaps, with all our consideration and well-meant endeavours to assist them, they know as much about it as we do, and, it may be, a little more. We always begin the season by supplying fully as many boxes as tins; there is a charm in the eagerness with which birds go to work early in

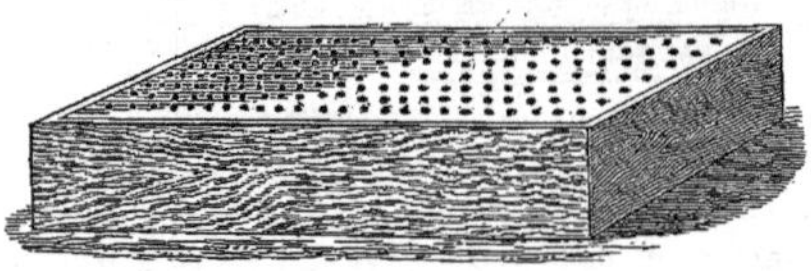

FIG. 24.—EGG-SIEVE.

the season which we can never resist, and it is not until the fun begins to get fast and furious, when one nest of young birds begins to tread on the heels of another, that, to save time, and also because our boxes may begin to get foul, we discard them in favour of the ready-made article. Even then we invariably supply moss and soft doe-hair, and leave the hen to fill up her tin to her own liking, which she will very quickly do.

We have digressed a little, and allowed ourselves to trespass slightly on what is strictly in the province of "general management;" but we have found it difficult to say all we wished about the various kinds of nesting apparatus without doing so in some degree, in support of what we may have had to advance in favour of any particular form or otherwise.

We find, on referring to our inventory, that there are not many appliances left to describe; and we may as well dispose of the most important of those which remain, and then dismiss this portion of our subject. It is well not to have anything to make or to get at a time when it is wanted for use—a fact, the truth of which we all of us experience at some time in our lives, and of which we have now and again been reminded in a practical sort of way, by the furnishing of a mysterious square basket, in connection with the illuminating of a lace-edged bag of bran with hieroglyphics, beautifully rendered in pins' heads, intended to convey the sentiment of a welcome to some expected stranger.

The egg-sieve, or egg-box, as it is sometimes called, is a requisite, in daily use. It consists of a wooden frame about three inches high and eight or ten inches square, with a top of perforated zinc, through which hard-boiled eggs are squeezed by pressure with the blade of a dinner-knife, which is another small *et cætera* to be remembered when the fancier is quietly confiscating such articles as may be likely to prove useful in his room. It is a most simple and effective contrivance for accomplishing the purpose desired, doing more thoroughly in a few seconds what could scarcely be done in half-an-hour under the old system of chopping, though the egg when thus manipulated is still always spoken of as "chopped" when referring to it in the dietary. The adjunct to the

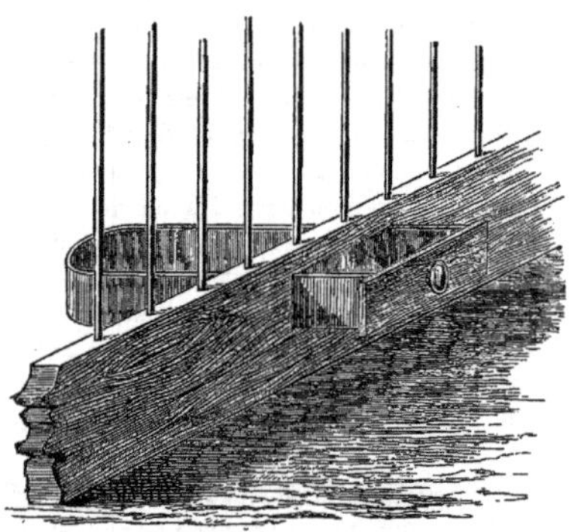

FIG. 25.—EGG-DRAWER.

egg-sieve is a board to place underneath, on which to receive what is passed through it for the purpose of mixing—one clamped at each end to prevent warping will be found most serviceable. A rolling-pin of hard wood is also necessary for crushing biscuit, hemp-seed, or other hard food, as is also a small mill—an ordinary coffee-mill—for grinding seed for young birds.

Egg-troughs must be liberally provided. Even if there be small egg-drawers in the cage-front, there will be constant use for the troughs, in one way or another. They are best made

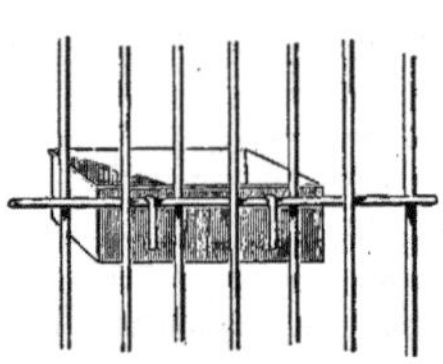

FIG. 26.—EGG-TIN IN PLACE.

FIG. 27.—EGG-TROUGH.

rather shallow, much more so than water-tins, and larger in area; this is rendered necessary by the use to which they are applied, as soft food is very apt to ferment and turn sour when supplied in deep vessels. They are generally made of tin, square or semi-circular according to fancy, with hooks, by which they can be attached to the cross-bar or to temporary cross-wires interwoven wherever required. As good a plan as any is to weave a wire transversely at the bottom of the door, and hang the principal egg-trough on it; it can then be withdrawn on opening the door, and hooked on and off without putting the hand inside the cage. We attach no importance to this, however, for the birds soon become so tame as not to take the least notice of any such intrusion. There are very neat egg-troughs made of earthenware, with holes in the sides for the insertion of wire hooks (see Fig. 27); but we are not aware whether they are generally sold in the trade or are made to order: we think there is nothing to equal them in point of cleanliness.

The bath-cage is a *sine qua non*, and can be purchased in a variety of shapes. It is practically a small cage, the bottom of which forms a trough about two inches deep, and may be had either in the form of a zinc trough wired over, or with a wooden bottom containing a zinc or earthenware basin, and wired in the form of a cage, with one side entirely open. Two strong hooks in front serve to attach it to the open doorway, but as the weight of the water it contains is considerable, it is advisable to further support it by a hooked wire attached to the top of the bath and the cross-wire of the cage. Several of these bath-cages will be required, according to the size of the establishment; for birds have their own ideas as to when is the right time of the day for a wash. The replenishing of the water-tins is generally the signal for a dip, while the water is

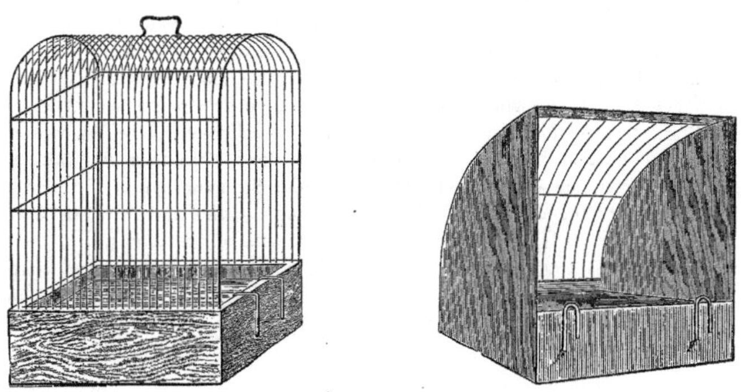

FIG. 28.—BATH-CAGES.

clean; and the Canary can manage a very fair shampoo through his water-hole. A thorough wash is another thing, and it frequently happens that when one wishes them to wash they will take no notice of the bath; but at length, after a few preliminary sprinklings, in goes one bird with a splash, and then out pops every head through its water-hole, and there is a general commotion in the cages. This is washing-time, and the advantage of having several baths at hand to indulge them while they are in the humour will be seen as soon as they are suspended from the doorways.

Nursery-cages, the use of which will be afterwards explained, must not be overlooked. These can be bought much cheaper and better than they can be made. The cheap rate at which small cages can be manufactured is owing to its being a home industry, in which the work of many little hands is turned to account. Those we use as nurseries can be bought at about nine shillings a dozen, and are nine inches square, with light wooden frames; top, sides, and front of wire, and back of wood. This same description of cage is made a size smaller, and proportionately cheaper. They contain a fixed, open seed-trough, and require no other fitting but a water-tin. A stock of these is most useful, as apart from their adaptation for nursery purposes they are always handy for the reception of single birds, spare cocks, invalids, &c., which speedily grow in a large breeding-room. A few single cages more or less are never in the way, and cannot well be dispensed with.

Canisters for different kinds of seed, and a fine sieve for cleaning it, will also find a place in a well-ordered room; but where the requirements of a large establishment demand that seed should be bought by the bushel, or even by the sack, such things as canisters are, of course, out of the question. Seed should always be sifted before being supplied to the birds, and the contents of the hoppers should also be sifted at intervals, as a quantity of dirt finds its way into them.

A judicious manager will gradually confiscate such articles as a water-can, a galvanised pail, a brush and dust-pan, a scuttle, and other useful articles which he may find about the house, and carefully lock them up in his bird-room to prevent their being again "lost" or mislaid. He will find a use for all of them. If he be wise he will also have a small lock-up store-chest, in which he will from time to time stow away such small gallipots as he may find in his predatory inroads on the housekeeping department; they will be required to hold small bunches of green food, and will never be missed till preserving-time comes round, when he will, under any circumstances, have a small rate levied on him for replenishing the domestic store-closet. If a stout little table, with a nest of drawers, and a comfortable chair have been quietly carried up-stairs, there remains nothing for the fancier to do but to lock his bird-room door and put the key in his pocket, and, calling his household together, proceed to the enactment of the most stringent laws with regard to the pains and penalties which will follow any attempt to pry into the secrets of his *sanctum sanctorum*. It will be well for him to remember that he will have to be his own servant and charwoman, and will have to practise carrying his scuttle down-stairs in a way calculated not to disturb the amicable relations existing between himself and the guardians of the neutral territory through which he has to travel. There is an art in filling a scuttle and an art in carrying it, and our practical experience leads us to suggest, in the interests of domestic peace, the wisdom of studying both. Bird-seed and chaff have a natural affinity for stair-carpets, and have a way of their own of working into them in defiance of any combination of bristles with which we are acquainted; and Paterfamilias will soon see the value of our hints and the desirability of carefully effacing all signs of his trail.

CHAPTER VII.

PAIRING AND SITTING.

OUR cages furnished with a good covering of sand mixed with a little lime-rubbish, and our seed and water vessels filled, they are ready for the reception of the stock. Of the different Varieties and the method of breeding them with a view to producing each in perfection, we shall treat *in extenso* by-and-by. We purpose devoting this and the succeeding chapters to the subject of General Management and the discussion of the best means to employ in Breeding, Rearing, Feeding, Moulting, and preparing for Exhibition.

The first question that suggests itself is as to the selection of breeding-stock. We do not mean as regards quality, or the best variety for a beginner to make a start with. One kind is no more difficult to manage than another, and good birds eat no more seed than bad ones. It is only too easy, even when at the top of the ladder, to make a false step and slide down to the bottom; but next to impossible to begin at the bottom and reach the top if the bars be rotten; and we therefore urge the *fancier* to buy the very best his means will permit of his doing. The only question we shall enter into in this place, in speaking of the selection of stock, is as regards age, and we shall dismiss it summarily by saying it is perfectly immaterial. Secure good birds, but never mind the age if they are only healthy. A Canary at twelve months old, notwithstanding it still carries a portion of its nest-feathers, viz., wings and tail, may still be said to be matured, and displays all its natural instincts. The cock birds look out eagerly for mates, and the hens are equally anxious for the duties of maternity, and, if left to themselves, would lay nests of unfertile eggs and sit on them till hope died out with declining health and strength. We have never found that age added one iota to their experience, or that youth was connected with any lack of knowledge. The exercise of maternal duties is the outcome of natural instincts, native and deep-rooted, and as strongly developed and true in their action when the first nestling emerges from its shell as when great-grandchildren are performing like duties. We have heard various theories on this subject of age, but do not consider any of them worth a second thought.

The time of the year at which the birds should be put together varies according to circumstances, as we briefly indicated in a previous chapter. There is nothing in the whole round of Canary-breeding that requires such a cool head and the capacity for resisting temptation as the itching desire every one has in the early spring for making a beginning. We are not free from it ourselves, and do not know any one who is. The symptoms are pretty much the same in every case, and generally show themselves on a sunny day after a short country walk. Perhaps we have picked a sprig or two of chickweed or groundsel, and have given our birds a taste all round, and next day find some of the hens carrying the bare stalks and roots about the cage. It seems to have infused fresh life into the whole room and into ourselves also. The weather continues open, and we take another stroll to gather fresh moss. We are as restless as the birds and must be doing something: we cannot help it. The smell of newly-turned earth in a ploughed field through which we have to pass only aggravates our complaint, while the early spring song of the thrush or blackbird tells us that "the time of the singing of birds is come, and the voice of the turtle is heard in the land." But one swallow never made a summer, and several fine days do not make spring. The return of inclement weather produces a reaction in ourselves and in the birds too, and we feel glad that we proceeded no farther than a general furbishing-up of cages and examination of *matérie..* "More haste, less speed," should be written over every bird-room door. We have known breeders lose half their hens by disregarding this precept; deaths from inflammation of the egg-passage, and consequent "egg-binding," being the penalty for rousing the birds into action before the dreary days of winter were fairly past. Our rule is never to put our birds up till they can see to feed at six o'clock in the morning. They retire to roost early in the day, and during the early part of the season the long nights should be made no longer than necessary. From six till six is a long fast, even supposing the young ones go to sleep on full crops. The policy of waiting till the spring is fairly advanced will therefore be obvious, and the rule we have laid down will be seen to be based on common sense.

Where a number of birds have been living together through the winter, hens in one cage and cocks in another, they should be looked over early in the spring, and those intended for breeding purposes set apart and kept as quiet and free from excitement as possible, and fed on nothing but plain diet, such as canary-seed and summer rape. The cocks will gradually be growing "fresh," and will require to be caged off into separate compartments, though when they have been "flighted" in company for a lengthened period, they will remain good friends till one or more of them begin to come into high condition and full song, when the troublesome ones, at least, must be taken out, or constant skirmishes will ensue. But we will assume that things have gone on in an orderly fashion, and that no jealousies have sprung up, and the breeder finds himself landed into March with a nice stock of healthy birds. We should advise him at once to put a match to his gas-stove, for, at the best, March is but a blustering month, and April is not to be relied upon. East winds continue to harass us, and even winter does not depart without a struggle, firing a few parting shots at intervals and dying hard. Suspend a nesting-box at the back of each compartment between the two perches, the bottom of the nest being about on a level with them, with something like about an inch to spare on each side, which will allow the birds good standing-room when engaged in feeding. But this is not very material, as the birds can, and will, stand on the nest-edge as often as on the perch when so engaged; indeed, some breeders never place their perches on the cross-bar, but support one on the upper cross-wire and the other below the middle cross-bar, on a small transverse wire between the door-frame and the side, obliging the birds to fly up to the nest whenever they have any business to transact there. All these perch arrangements, however, are entirely matters of taste, for it really signifies but little whether Canaries take their everlasting hop, hop, treadmill-exercise on the level or with a rise and fall. If the nest-box be lined with felt, nothing else in the way of nesting material need be supplied at the commencement; but if it be a box-nest, a little moss—not much—must be stuffed between the wires for the hen to play with. Few breeders who use felt nests supply any building material whatever, and in this case a first-size nest—a No. 1—is best; for although a hen will gather her eggs under her in a large nest as well as a small one, she has a forlorn look squatted at the bottom of one that is two or three sizes too large for her, and which she would fill up to suit her own ideas of comfort if material were furnished her. For this reason we recommend using medium-sized tins and supplying nesting-stuff—but not yet.

Having furnished the lodgings thus far, put a pair of birds into each compartment. We need scarcely say that by a "pair" is always meant a cock and hen. Our instructions on this point must necessarily be understood to be general in their application: what kind of cock, and what kind of hen, manifestly belonging to another part of our subject. There is not the slightest necessity for any previous acquaintance, and as for putting the cock in one cage and the hen in another and allowing them to scrape acquaintance through the wires—the thing, in a large establishment, would be practically impossible. We have read somewhere that the cock should be placed face to the wall, opposite his hen, in a cage with a wooden back, having a circular hole in it just large enough to allow of his putting his head through, when he will commence his love-making across the room, and must be conducted in the most gradual way to his hen, until she is made acquainted with his entire personal appearance, from his head to his tail. We really have not patience to comment on such nonsense: it is simply the veriest twaddle. The probability is that when the birds are first put together they will quarrel, but it is not always the case. It arises from the fact that the cock bird is always the first to make advances towards a more intimate acquaintance, and the hen, as is fit and proper, with becoming modesty repels them. If he be a bird who has spent his winter wisely in studying bird-nature in the large flight-cage, he will commence by admiring the nest and giving his opinion on things in general, and will coax his hen with presents of dainty morsels and a display of polite gallantry; but if he begins at once to be too familiar, and the first song he sings is "Oh! name the day, the happy day," she will thrash him, or try to do so. But it is the same old, old story over again, and we all know how it ends. In a few days they will have settled matters to their mutual satisfaction, and then begins the serious business of life. It is not, however, *always* so. Some hens take a settled aversion to a particular cock and will *never* pair with him; but these viragoes are very rare, and though they may succeed in knocking all the nonsense out of one cock, they generally meet their match in the end. And there are exceptionally badly-behaved cocks, though the cases on either side are so seldom met with, that the fact of their existence is no reason why valuable time should be cut to waste in pairing a lot of birds by rule. Still, we have known cocks that would literally scalp their hens, and we once had a Lizard hen that half-murdered her mate, and would have finished him if we had not interfered. She used to drive him under the egg-trough, on which she would sit like a cat watching a mouse, and say, as plainly as she could say it, "If you put your head out, I'll have you as sure as you are a Lizard;" and she did "have" him frequently, by stooping from the perch and picking him up by the top of the head and swinging him backwards and forwards underneath. But ninety-nine per cent. of Canaries pair as naturally as possible, and the breeder will not have long to wait before he begins to see evident signs of their having come to the determination to go through life hand in hand, for better or for worse—for better, let him hope; and a fancier should have hope prominently developed in his cerebral economy.

The first indication of the birds having come to an understanding is the cock feeding his mate. The Canary belongs to a class of birds which feed from the crop. We should have mentioned that, as soon as the birds are put together, they must be supplied with a mixture of chopped egg and bread-crumbs, or egg and crushed biscuit, with just a little crushed hemp-seed mixed with it as a stimulating diet. The cock will, in reply to the invitation of the hen, which is made by a rapid fluttering of the wings, accompanied by a low twittering, constantly feed her by disgorging the contents of his crop; and if, in addition to the soft food, a little chickweed, groundsel, watercress, or lettuce be furnished, or, failing this, a small piece of the tender heart of a cabbage, he will be all the more assiduous in his endeavours to keep her constantly supplied with food. Meanwhile she will begin to show signs of a desire to build. If she have only a felt nest, she will pull and tug at it the day through, constantly getting into it and "scuffling" with her feet and wings in her endeavours to adapt it for use. Now is the time to supply nesting-stuff in the shape of moss and soft hair, but only very sparingly, because till she begins to build in real earnest, she will only waste the stuff to an unlimited extent. So long as there is any hair or moss between the wires, so long will she continue to pull at it, carry it to her nest, throw it out again, and scatter it about in the cage-bottom; and it is astonishing to see how evenly the stuff will be distributed, so much so, that it can all be taken up in the hand in one piece. To allow this is to countenance sheer waste, for this stuff, when once soiled, will never be used for its intended purpose. It seems as though, for a time, her object were nothing but amusement, and a small piece will answer the purpose as well as a bunch; indeed, a single feather will occupy her constant attention, and this she will carry backwards and forwards to her nest all day long. Something of the kind she *must* have, or she will purloin a feather from the cock's tail or disfigure him by plucking him whenever she can get a sly pull. Some hens are very ill-mannered in this respect, and every breeder can tell an amusing story of ill-usage of this description. When it is seen, however, that she is really beginning to construct her nest, remove all soiled stuff and give a fresh supply, and the fancier will be rewarded in the course of a few hours by a wonderful display of skill. She takes a mouthful of moss, pulling it from the bunch a sprig at a time, hops away to her nest, pops it in, and then pops herself in on it, with a quiet pantomimic expression that seems to say, "There is no deception, I assure you. I take this small piece of moss and drop it into my nest, so; then in I drop, so; three turns and a scuffle, and where is it now?—the quickness of the foot deceives the eye. Now I take a small piece of hair, so, and I drop *it* in—there's no deception; three more turns and another scuffle. Now take a peep; you see I have woven a piece of tapestry. Richard! a mouthful of egg, if you please, and don't forget a bit of hemp-seed this time." And so the work goes on, the cock occasionally popping up to see how it is progressing and looking very wise over it, till at length the little nest—we cannot use a prettier word—is completed and lined out daintily with the snowy-white hair, encircled by a fringe of curly moss, behind which the little hen settles herself down full of happy pride, her shining black eyes glistening with love, while her mate bursts into song, answered in a chorus which makes the room echo, by half-a-dozen friends, who also are having a house-warming.

There will not be much alteration in the position of affairs for a day or two, but by that time the hen will have become more sedate and matronly, and indications of the little event which is shortly to come off will be manifest; indeed, what may be expected in the morning can generally be foretold with tolerable certainty the night before. The situation is not now entirely free from danger, and the first duty of a breeder on visiting his room in the morning is to notice whether all his hens which ought to have laid have done so, or if any are making heavy weather of it. Some phenomena, however, occasionally present themselves, startling in appearance, but which need not cause serious apprehension. It will sometimes happen that the day before a hen lays she will be seen in the morning in the most complete health, going about just as usual, her feathers close and compact, wings tucked up, and showing nothing to indicate the presence of any disarrangement whatever; but in the afternoon she will be found apparently about to go home. She seeks a corner of the cage, panting violently, and squats on the ground with wings outstretched, feathers all ruffled, head thrown back, eyes closed, in a state of the most entire prostration, the picture of complete misery. A more pitiable object cannot well be conceived. She seems to have lost the use of all her bodily powers, and if taken in the hand, offers no resistance; indeed, she is too ill to think of it. When replaced in the cage, she scuffles away to her corner, and appears to wish for nothing but to be left alone in quietness to die. You think she might be warmer in her nest, and gently place her there; but it is no use; she tumbles out, or, rather, hops out, falling heavily, and shuffles away to her comfortless corner again. There you leave her and begin to mourn over hopes apparently nipped in the bud. You cannot rest at night for thinking about her, and go up-stairs to see if she is dead or alive. Somehow she has managed to scramble into her nest, which is to her a sick-bed in real earnest. We will not enter into any discussion as to the cause of all this fuss. A probable cause will suggest itself, and as in similar cases of an equally interesting character, we can only say—"My dear, I'm afraid you'll have to be worse before you're better." Do not interfere with the bird, and Nature will do all that is necessary. Next morning, instead of finding her a subject for a *post mortem*, you will find an egg in the nest, and the little hen going about her business quite at her ease.

But if she should *not* have laid her egg, something will have to be done. That something is so very simple, and so efficacious when it is done, that any one can manage it, and nobody should hesitate about trying. Take the hen gently in the left hand, with her head towards the little finger and the tail projecting between the thumb and first finger, and hold her in this position over the steam of boiling water in a narrow-necked jug. Just lift her tail, and allow it to rest on the edge of the jug, and expose the vent freely to the action of the steam. Let her have a good vapour-bath, and then with a bluntly-pointed little stick drop one or two drops of sweet oil on the vent. Do not endeavour to insert it; the parts are too small and will be too much inflamed to allow anything of that kind. The oil will find its way and do its work speedily. Gently replace the hen in the nest, and the egg will soon be laid, even if it be not dropped in the jug. Some cases, however, will prove very obstinate; for some there is no relief, and death inevitably follows. In such case, a *post mortem* carefully made will reveal the internal economy, and explain the difficulties of the position. Heat is an important element in bringing obstinate cases to a successful issue, and when things look bad, the hen should be wrapped in warm flannel and placed near the fire or on a wire-frame over a jug or basin of hot water. *Early* attention also is of the utmost importance, as every minute increases the difficulty and lessens the chances of success. Remember that the egg must on no account be broken, or the consequences will immediately be fatal. The ultimate saving of the egg, also, is a matter of no moment compared with saving the life of the bird, and she should not be placed in her nest too soon, simply with that object in view.

One lesson to be learned from this not unfrequent episode in bird-life is the importance of an early visit to the bird-room. Canaries soon get to know those who have charge of them, and will not be at all put out by a quiet visit, when a glance round will show whether things are going on all right in every cage. We say a *quiet* visit, and is it necessary to point out the importance of entering the bird-room quietly? As regards a clumsy, noisy manner of opening and shutting doors, some persons have a gift that way; but if that gift be practised on the bird-room door, the consequences will be "claw-holed" eggs. Quiet, and the entire absence of everything like fluster, are essentials demanded of visitors. Gesticulation may be the soul of oratory, but we object to having our birds pointed at with an umbrella.

The removal of the eggs as laid is a practice on which there is some difference of opinion. Our own mind has long been fully made up on the matter, and our advice is to do so invariably; but on the other hand, the substitution of ivory eggs or similar artificial contrivances is simply child's play. The only argument we have ever heard adduced in favour of allowing eggs to remain is that those of wild birds remain untouched till the full complement has been laid. But there is not the slightest analogy between the two cases. The wild bird does not become broody until she has laid her complement, and consequently does not even remain near her nest; and we do not think any school-boy ever found one or two or even three eggs in a nest which should on the average contain four, from which he had occasion to disturb the parent bird. But a Canary confined in a box eighteen inches square can scarcely be said to be in a natural state; indeed, some of her after proceedings would almost support the theory that her nature has been modified by circumstances to an extent we are loth to acknowledge. From not being allowed to lose sight of her nest and eggs, she has every inducement to sit, and will frequently become really broody and begin to sit with the first egg. The chances of her wishing to do so are increased on the appearance of the second, and if she should really begin to sit in earnest, the result is simply that the young ones are hatched at intervals instead of simultaneously, the elder rapidly outgrow the younger and literally smother and starve them, because the rule of feeding in the nest is that the largest hatchway secures most cargo. We are aware that some breeders who never interfere with the eggs assert that it makes no difference in the time of hatching. This we do not admit, and are perfectly satisfied that where such may have been the case it has resulted from the hen *not* having begun to sit as was supposed. We do not call sitting for an hour, or two hours, and then coming off the nest for as long a time, *sitting*, any more than playing with building-stuff is *building;* and it is only when this fast-and-loose, on-and-off sort of sitting has been indulged in and has been mistaken for genuine business that the hatching has been simultaneous, and the possible evil results have been averred to be a myth. No one who practises the let-alone system can say that simultaneous hatching is

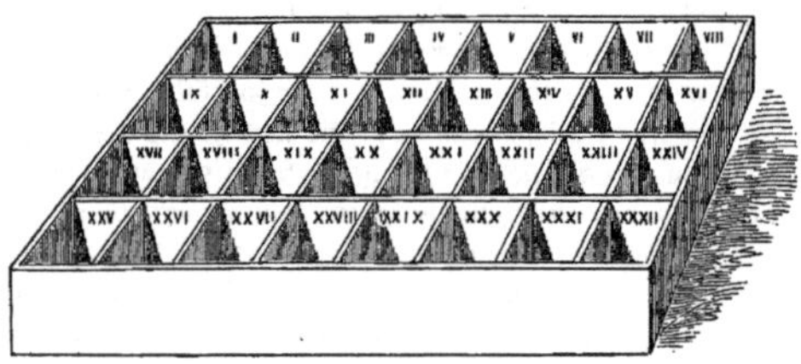

FIG 29.—TRAY FOR STORING EGGS

the general rule; and that is just our point. We fully admit that it may, and does sometimes occur, under the conditions and circumstances we have described; but it ought *always* to happen, and that can only be ensured by removing the eggs, and then setting the hen as we would a broody fowl.

Our mode of procedure is this: we number or letter all our cages, and have a shallow tray divided into compartments, like a seedman's box, lettered in a corresponding way and filled with bran, hair, rabbit's down, or any similar material. As the eggs are laid we transfer them to the tray, and indicate the fact by a chalk-mark on the front of the cage. We keep a stock-book as well, but we post it from our chalk-marks, in which we believe most devoutly. The stock-book is for detailed items, but the chalk-marks show the whole state of affairs at once in a thoroughly practical way which we will explain. We will suppose the fancier going into his room between eight and nine o'clock in the morning, by which time his hens will all have laid. If he have any method in him, he will begin at the beginning and go steadily through. The information given by the marks on a few cages will suffice to explain what we wish. Here is a cage without a mark. The hen was expected to lay this morning, and has done so; we put the egg in its place in the tray and chalk the cage. Here is one with a single mark, or two marks, as the case may be; that means we may look for more eggs, which we do, and add a mark to those already on the cage. We pass on to a third, the chalks, bear in mind, telling us at a glance, without any reference to a book or comparison between it and the tray, just where we have to look, and what we may expect to find when we do look. In the next cage, which has two marks, we anticipate finding the third egg, but we don't. We know from the marks that it *ought* to be there, and that it is *not;* so we add a cross or a cipher, or some such distinguishing mark, which tells us the hen has missed a day, and if the third egg be not there to-morrow we shall not sit her on the two she has laid, but give one to each of two hens on the other side, whose marks indicate that they are likely to stop at three, which experience has shown to be about the worst number of eggs a hen can sit on: a good nest of three is rare; there is, somehow, sure to be one weakly bird among them. This is amply sufficient to explain our system of marking, so far as regards the point of practice we are detailing. We remove the eggs, then, one by one, till there are three in the tray, and on the evening of the third day we replace them. The hen then goes on to her nest at night, lays her fourth egg in the morning, and at once commences to sit so closely that the date of hatching may be reckoned from that fourth morning with certainty. The reason why we replace three eggs, and date from the fourth, is because, though five is a common number, and six not unusual, four is an average nest. If a fifth egg be laid it must take its chance; but the fancier soon gets to know the peculiarities of his hens in this respect, and acts accordingly. Before setting the hen we generally make it a rule to clean out the cage, or at any rate to give it a rough scrape and supply some fresh sand, for it will be a fortnight before it can again be disturbed, beyond removing any excreta which may accumulate during incubation. We should have remarked, in speaking of the sand required for the cages, that it should *be* sand—gritty sand, and not earthy matter, capable of being compressed into small lumps. All birds are not alike, but some are apt to get very dirty feet; and if the sand be of a binding nature, they will be continually gathering it up in a ball under their toes, which will eventually grow so large as to inconvenience the bird seriously, and must be removed. It is easily managed by moistening the ball with water, but no rough usage must be attempted. See also that the claws are cleaned at the same time, for it is more than likely that each will have a small tip of dirt attached to it, and when such is the case, it is evident a hen cannot have much command over them, and is very likely to injure her eggs in consequence.

We advise continuing the egg-food while the hen is sitting, giving a moderate quantity, of which the cock will take care that she gets her full share; fresh green food should also be supplied daily. The hen will leave her nest occasionally to feed, but after cracking a few grains of seed will return, knowing that the cock will attend to all her wants, a duty in which he never fails; indeed, during the whole period of incubation, his life is one incessant round of attentions to his mate. During fine weather the luxury of a bath may also be indulged in, and though the hen may sometimes appear to remain off her nest while pluming herself longer than prudence might suggest, we have never known any but good results attend a free use of the bath.

There is a marked difference in the temperament and disposition of hens and their deportment during the time they are sitting. Some, nothing seems to disturb; they are like broody fowls, and, if at any time an inspection of the nest may be necessary, require to be lifted off by putting the finger under the breast, and even then will often do no more than stand up or at the most hop on to the nearest perch and wait the first moment to settle down again on the precious eggs. Others appear to be sulky, and if disturbed will not return to the nest so long as any one remains in the room, or most certainly so long as they are watched. They will sit on the edge of the nest, in the very act of hopping into it, but as rigid as if stuffed, and not a hair's breadth will they budge. Turn your back for a moment or leave the room, and, quick as thought, they are on the eggs. Others are restless and fidgety, especially if the cock has been removed, and are everlastingly leaving the nest without any apparent reason, really seeming to spend as much time in looking out of the windows as in domestic duties. The remedy in this case is to draw down the blinds, by tacking a sheet of brown paper in front of the cage. Many breeders make a practice of doing this in every instance, to ensure complete privacy, and it is by no means a bad plan, especially when the arrangement of the cages is such that the birds in some of the compartments can see those in others. Besides, it is enough to make any hen feel uncomfortable to be compelled to witness the disgraceful spectacle of her mate sitting with his arm round another hen's waist, vowing the same eternal fidelity which he swore to her not ten days before.

Such, we think, are the principal features to be noticed during incubation, which we will assume has gone on for five or six days. At the expiration of this period the eggs may be examined, to see how many are fertile, for it sometimes so happens that it may be found necessary, with a view to saving time or obtaining a final nest late in the season, to combine two nests, due at the same date, into one. A practised eye can detect at a glance what eggs are "full" and what are not, without taking them in the hand; but if they be held up to the light the fertile eggs will be found to be one-half opaque, or rapidly becoming so, the dividing line being drawn diagonally. A day later, and, in a strong light, the network of blood-vessels can be distinctly traced spreading over the inner surface of the shell; and a day later still the fertile egg becomes entirely opaque, while the unimpregnated ones remain perfectly transparent. An "empty" egg in a nest of four or five should not be removed, as the young ones, when hatched, will cluster over it, and it serves as a support for them; fragile as it is, they will not break it, though it be allowed to remain till they are full-grown.

But the fancier must not, even at this advanced stage, begin to practise that simple elementary arithmetical process which, experience has shown, frequently results in erroneous conclusions; he must wait patiently till the morning of the thirteenth day, before which arrives he may have learnt a practical application of another wise saw—"Many a slip——" We all know the rest and have often experienced it—the proverb is stale, but very true. A man, to become a successful Canary-breeder, must have the property of patience strongly woven in his composition, and will be all the more likely to train on if he have one or two strains of Job blood in his veins. The principal dangers to be apprehended in the later stages of incubation are the misfortune of the hen forsaking her eggs, or the young birds dying in the shell—"going back," as it is called. The former may arise from the sitting-fever subsiding, which may be occasioned by a sudden change in the weather—such as the advent of a second winter, or any marked fall in the temperature, which affects the sitting hens to a considerable degree. They do not like the long, cold nights, and this is when the value of the gas-stove will be seen. Similar causes may have a fatal effect on the young ones in the shell, but most probably the decline in the natural heat of the hen's body has most to do with it. It is the steady decline, the gradual dying out of the fire at a time when the flame ought to be kept up, that does the mischief. Young birds, when within a day or two of hatching, can survive several hours of exposure, and if the eggs be found to be quite cold they should still be persevered with. We are assuming an instance, not of gradual decline, but of accidental exposure, say, from a hen having been inadvertently shut off from her nest. In such cases we never give up till, from the lapse of time, we are satisfied of the futility of prolonged effort. We knew, on one occasion, of a hen having been shut off into the next compartment, where she remained all night and well into the next morning before the mistake was discovered, and yet every egg hatched; and we feel sure that many breeders could tell of similar occurrences.

The Canary sits thirteen days, and hatches almost to the hour with commendable punctuality. But if—we are never done with but's and if's—the eggs do not "chip" at the time expected, and are yet evidently "full," on no account interfere with them—about the most insane thing a breeder can do. We could never understand what could possibly induce a person to do such a thing. To break a shell is to kill the young bird, if alive, to a certainty, and the breeder is not any the better off for indulging his impatient curiosity, except as the knowledge he has obtained about that one egg may make him still more curious as to the others. Note that the first nests in the season are nearly always a day late in chipping, and very frequently as much as two or three days, probably arising from the hen not having got the steam up to high pressure when commencing to sit; the exercise of a little extra patience at this time is imperative.

CHAPTER VIII.

HATCHING AND REARING.

IN anticipation of the thirteenth morning ushering in the event so much desired, it will be well to see that the egg-tin is cleaned out over-night and replenished with a little fresh food, in which the yolk of the egg must predominate, and when the breeder looks into the cage in the morning he will probably see half a shell in the bottom and will hear a little chirp. Under ordinary circumstances he will not think of disturbing the hen, but we will excuse him if, on this occasion, he takes a peep. In the bottom of the nest he will see a bunch of something which looks like a cluster of hairy caterpillars, and as he is sure, instinctively, to give a little chirp on his own account, he will see the bunch open itself out, and untwist four little heads on four long necks out of a knot in the middle, which will raise themselves up and open out four little hatchways. And if he looks further he will probably see that each little neck has a yellow spot on the side of it, which spot is egg, and shows that already, almost before the down on the caterpillars is dried, the hen has given them their first meal—a good omen for the future. He can also indulge in a little speculation if he chooses; and if he notes that the down on one caterpillar is dark, it will develop into a green bird. If the parents are, say, crested Canaries, and he sees that another caterpillar has a dark crown, it will turn out, in all probability, a dark-crested bird. Having noticed which, he had better put the nest back and go to his own breakfast a happy man, though if he sits down quietly for five minutes he will probably see the hen rise gently in her nest, and, without leaving it, go round the little circle and give each a meal with the most tender care, and after performing other little offices most curious and singular, tuck them in and make them comfortable for a nap.

One would naturally imagine that the hen having sat so long and so patiently, and having brought everything to such a successful issue, her maternal instincts would be so much the more quickened, and that she would at once become the exemplification of that love to which such a touching reference is made in the sublime language of the Old Book. But such is not the case, and the time of real anxiety is now only beginning. Her care for her young during the first few hours of their lives is no guarantee that it will be continued. It is a very disagreeable truth, but it is only too true. If all should go on well, the young birds will grow under the eye almost hourly, and the next morning will find them nearly double the size, plump and fat, and like little balls of down. But it may be that the mother will positively refuse to feed them at all, or only at such long intervals and in such a half-and-half sort of way, that the experienced breeder can tell at the end of a day or two what are the future prospects of the nest. If in place of full crops, plump breasts, and heavy abdomen, he finds every feature dwarfed, it is then time for him to step in and assist by artificial feeding, in the hope that the want of attention on the part of the mother—which can only result from unhealthy action of some kind or other beyond our ken—will presently give place, under healthier conditions, to the exercise of the constant attention on which depends the well-being of the nest. Understand that our rule is, in dealing with our breeding-hens, to leave well alone, and to content ourselves with the best they feel inclined to do, if that best be only a reasonable display of care sufficient to keep things moving. But for young birds to stand still is for them to retrograde, and we generally find ourselves every morning not "doing something in a temporary way with a tea-pot," but with a hard-boiled egg in one hand and a little flat spatula of a stick in the other. And our mode of procedure is this:—We cut a hard-boiled egg in halves, and having moistened the yolk with saliva, we visit every nest, particularly the doubtful ones, and where we find any empty crops we scrape up some egg with our little spatula, making it very moist, not much thicker than cream in fact, and give the young birds a good feed. There is no difficulty in making young Canaries open their mouths; it is almost the first thing they do in this world, and they never seem to forget the way; the difficulty is to fill them fast enough. We never interfere with any birds till they are twenty-four hours old, because the yolk absorbed into the stomach is sufficient to sustain them for that time, and we like to give the hen a fair chance of feeding for herself; but after that time the very youngest birds can be fed in this way, and, if attended to at intervals, can frequently be kept going till the hen takes the work in hand. It will be seen that the breeder who has the opportunity of visiting his birds frequently has a great advantage in being able to do so. The man of business is perhaps compelled to leave them from morning till evening, or, at the most, is able to snatch a few minutes in the middle of the day. But in most households there is some person who can be trusted to attend to these matters, and when once it is taken in hand, the interest felt in the little things, dependent on our attention for their lives, grows immensely, and no bird will be allowed to die without a struggle having been made to save it.

We have referred to this possible difficulty arising thus early, because it requires to be met at the outset, and is one of the first disappointments the fancier may have to encounter. When all is plain sailing, the business of the bird-room will run on wheels, despite indifferent management or even positive neglect; the birds will take the reins in their own hands, and astonish even the most sanguine breeder by the way in which they will work out the problem we are endeavouring to show him the way to solve. There are so many phases in Canary life, as seen in the nursery, that it is almost impossible to arrange the various pictures in a very methodical manner, and our plan will be to present them as we think it probable they may pass before the breeder's observation in some cage or other in his room. So far as we have gone we have only dealt with the nest in its very earliest stage, pointing out the dangers which beset it, and indicating the best methods of tiding them over. The fancier will have noticed by this time that the cock can always be depended on as a feeder; we *never* knew one, young or old, which was not reliable in this respect. He knows as well as possible when things are not going on properly, and when he flies up to the nest with his crop full of food, he will stand on the edge and say, as plainly as a Canary can say it, "You know you are not doing your duty; those young ones under you are starving, and you know it. No, it's not a bit of use your fluttering in that way; I don't intend to give you another mouthful. If you don't mean to feed, just turn out, and I will do it, but don't sit there in that unnatural way, starving the family, or there will be a coroner's inquest shortly." And then he looks round and round the nest so wistfully, the very picture of affection and loving attention, twittering and doing all he can to induce some youngster to pop its head out. Presently one pops up from behind, and in a moment the cock has him, and stuffs him as quickly as possible, knowing the value of every moment. And this he will do all day as patiently as possible, though every visit to the nest generally ends in his ultimately giving the hen a great portion of the meal intended for the young ones. Perhaps he does so in the hope that she will disgorge some of it; but that hope is too often disappointed.

We will not make the picture more dismal than there is occasion for, but suppose that the hen is a model mother, and that from the first she settles down to her work in that earnest way the breeder likes to see. The egg-trough in that cage will require filling two or three times a day, for fresh-and-fresh is the rule, and fresh dainties will often induce a hen to feed when nothing else will. And before examining into the contents of the egg-trough we will just say that, in addition to all other, an unlimited supply of green food is necessary. This we give in one of the gallipots, putting in a substantial bunch of chickweed and groundsel, young and tender, as well as watercresses and lettuce. Fresh-and-fresh is again imperatively the rule here, or the water in the pot will soon become offensive. The quantity of this sort of stuff consumed in a day is enormous.

As regards the composition of the egg-food, there are almost as many recipes as there are breeding-rooms. The staple commodity is hard-boiled egg, with the addition of bread-crumbs, dry, or soaked and squeezed dry; milk-biscuit, water-biscuit, sweet-biscuit, stale sponge-cake, or other kind of farinaceous food, mixing in the beginning in the proportion of bulk for bulk, and decreasing the quantity of egg somewhat as the birds become older. We have tried them all, and have also fed largely on egg and crushed hemp-seed with better results than from either. The fact is that each is good, but every breeder naturally, and wisely too, recommends the particular mixture he has found produce the best results. So much, however, depends on the birds themselves that it is unfair to condemn one food or praise another unduly, when it is quite probable the experience of some other breeder is at direct variance with our own as regards the effect of using some particular diet. What succeeds in one bird-room is certain failure in another, and what one swears by another proclaims to be poison. The same remarks hold good with respect to green food. One gives chickweed and nothing else, avoiding groundsel above all things, and can tell you stories by the yard how it killed a lot of young birds. Another will walk miles to find a few plants of groundsel, and will pass acres of chickweed as worthless. One eschews lettuce, and gives dandelion, and each gives a satisfactory reason why. A *reason*, even if a poor one, entitles any statement to respect, but dogmatic assertion should never be listened to. We ourselves recommend finely-crushed hemp-seed as having been a good servant to us, while another fancier will say it is the forbidden fruit, the unclean thing, the abomination of abominations, and he would not have a grain in his room; his diet is egg and ——, it matters not what; we may have tried the mixture, and our birds would not look at it. Our advice is to use any or all of the mixtures we have mentioned, and, in addition, to add a pinch of maw-seed (poppy) or a little summer rape well scalded; but whatever is used, let it be fresh and sweet, and when one diet is found to be working well, go on with it, and make hay while the sun shines. Our experience has ever been that when birds mean feeding they will feed with anything; and that when they do not intend to feed, nothing will tempt them to do so freely—in short, it is a question of the health of the hen rather than biscuit *v.* hemp-seed. Sanguine men and born theorists will say all this indicates defective knowledge and wrong treatment. Men of our acquaintance, thinking men, who dislike groping in the dark and search deeply for the how and why, have said so; but our reply has always been, "Go on long enough, and your turn of bad luck will come." And it always does. The whole question finds a solution in the fact that the Canary is neither wild nor tame; we do our best to reconcile the two conditions, and sometimes succeed and sometimes—*do not;* the one perhaps as frequently as the other, as a comparison between the number of eggs hatched and the statistics contained in the Canary bills of mortality will show.

But everything has gone on swimmingly, and we have been voted a croaker by the reader—too fond of looking on the dark side of the picture. The birds are now four or five days old, and are as fat as moles. On looking at them in the morning, the breeder finds the down all gone or tangled and matted with moisture. This is the first indication of the hen having begun to "sweat" them, as it is not very elegantly called in the vernacular of the fancy, which she does by sitting on them very closely, seldom leaving the nest even for a few moments. This, of course, means two most unpleasant prospects—viz., starvation and suffocation. We know of no effectual cure for this "sweating," certainly not at the time we are penning these lines, though the result of some experiments making in that direction may yet appear in due course. We have seen all manner of cures prescribed, even to the extent of rigging up a contrivance which obliges her to "sit" *standing*, but we cannot call to mind an instance of a cure. We have washed the breast of the hen in salt and water, have ducked her in a pail, and have done perhaps some silly things in our vexation, but with no other result except that the hen continued to "sweat," and so did we. This ailment, however, is sometimes not of long duration, and the ill effects may then be combated successfully by removing the cock, and thus obliging the hen to leave her nest to feed, or else starve. This, at all events, affords the young ones an opportunity of getting partly dried, besides relieving them from the suffocating pressure of the hen; and to induce her to come off as often as possible, it is well to put the cock in an adjoining compartment, if there be one vacant, or into one of the spare nursery-cages we have described, and suspend it against the front of the cage in which the hen is sitting. The consequence will be that he will incessantly call her to come to feed through the wires—an invitation to which she will frequently respond; and the chances are that, on returning to her nest, she will sometimes be inclined to feed the young ones, whose importunity it is not easy to withstand, and so this unpleasant feature is occasionally so far ameliorated as to allow of the nest being saved. A hen *can* at any time bring up her nest without assistance from the cock, and this plan of separating the parent birds is frequently resorted to in the case of an indifferent feeder, with a view to compelling her to work harder. There is always a hopeful chance of saving a nest if the fancier only has the time to devote to the room, because so long as the hen will keep the young ones warm, the cock will always feed them, if the hen be driven off the nest to give him the opportunity. But should a hen forsake her nest altogether, there is nothing left but to break up the establishment, and distribute the young ones among the charitably-disposed occupants of other cages, who will take kindly to the foundlings.

This general uncertainty as to feeding, it will at once be inferred, is the great drawback to success, and in the case of valuable birds it is not advisable to make success entirely dependent upon such a contingency. It will be found most useful to put up a few pairs of the commoner kinds of Canaries, in the hope that among them may be found a few good feeders, whose services will then prove invaluable. The commoner the birds for this purpose, the less reluctance is felt in destroying their eggs, and sometimes, unavoidably, their offspring, to make way for those of greater value. No breeding-room should be without a number of these "feeders," who certainly earn their hay and corn in the important work they discharge.

Surely we are out of danger now, if by one means or another we have got our young birds up to eight or nine days old? The risk certainly lessens every day, but a strange mortality attacks birds sometimes at this age, just when they are going to begin to cut their teeth, or, rather, form their feathers. We can do nothing further than mention what *may* occur, and what has occurred under our observation more than once. We will suppose there to have been positively no drawback, and that the young birds are even exceptionally fine and strong; yet, just at this age, a sickly, jaundiced colour comes over the flesh, and nest after nest will die, plump and fat, and with their crops quite full. We are apt to say they have died from surfeit; but up to within a few hours of death every function has been healthy and the digestive powers unimpaired, and we are rather disposed to think the cause lies in another direction, probably in that we hinted at—some obstruction in the feather-forming functions which at this time are called into action. It arises from no neglect or outward cause, but is evidently an infant ailment, for which we can prescribe no remedy, for the simple reason we know nothing definite of the disease.

It may be said that we have presented the life of the young Canary as consisting of a series of struggles against adverse circumstances. We are glad if our object has been so clearly understood: that is just what it is. We have before said it is easy to sail with the tide, and any one can float down with the stream. The difficulty is to steer clear of the rocks and shoals, and we know there are plenty of them. We have endeavoured to point them out distinctly with all their bearings, and we mistake greatly if the experienced fancier does not recognise them as places where he has either come to grief, or escaped shipwreck by a good look-out and careful navigation. There may be other dangers ahead, but we will not now anticipate them and meet trouble half-way. We must, however, call attention to a very common accident which will happen in some nests. It is that of the young ones being thrown out by the hen in hopping out. It is well, when this occurs, to examine her claws, and if they are very long, just to shorten them with sharp scissors, taking care not to cut so close as to induce bleeding. Some hens are naturally clumsy, habitually doing this sort of thing, and should be furnished with a deeper nest than ordinary. It is quite possible, when not suspecting such a mishap, that the young thing in the cage-bottom may be overlooked; but with a knowledge of these and like contingencies, the breeder gets into the habit of keeping a sharp look-out. This accident generally occurs when the birds are very young, and consequently additionally liable to suffer from exposure; but so long as there is a spark of life left in the little naked thing, there is every chance of recovering it, which can be speedily effected by breathing on it. As soon as it begins to move, pop it under the hen, and it will soon be all right again. It is worthy of note that, kind and attentive as is the cock while the newly-hatched birds are in the nest, he seems to forget all his duty to the sprawling thing on the ground. Perhaps it represents to him in that position something to play with and something to eat, for he will frequently bite off the extremities, the toes, tips of the wings, and the little beak. We have known this occur in the nest; there is something very repulsive in such cannibalism, and one can really scarcely feel kindly disposed to a bird after such a display.

We have done our best in suggesting the various means to be employed to keep things in a healthy state and prevent mishaps, but there is a point beyond which we cannot go, even with the exercise of all the skill we can command, and a not very extended experience will soon indicate that line to the breeder. It then becomes a mercy to destroy such young ones as we know we cannot possibly save. It seems cruel to kill a little, blind, helpless fledgling, but it is more cruel to allow it to linger on in weakness, till the end we can foresee comes. It destroys the pleasure we derive from keeping animals to rear sickly, puny specimens. Our utmost energies should always be given towards alleviating sickness when it overtakes anything in our charge, but the same wisdom which dictates the policy of destroying the weakly young of rabbits, dogs, or any other animal we desire to rear in the beauty of its strength, will tell us when it will be a kindness to put a whole nest out of the way, if we can see no reasonable chance of rearing it. It is one of the disagreeables of the position, but we must accept it, and, by prompt action, make it as little painful as possible.

And what is the sum of all we have advanced? Is it that the bird-room, instead of being the pleasant place we described it, is nothing better than an hospital, and the occupation of Canary-breeding one in which half the pleasure is lost in trouble and vexation? Not a bit of it. Disappointment lurks at the bottom of our best pleasures, and vanity and vexation of spirit have ever been found to wait on many legitimate enterprises. Difficulty and opposition act as a stimulus to endeavour, and it is best to know we have these things to grapple with. The Canary-room is a little world of itself, and we can no more expect to find it free from cares and ills than the great outside world, in which we have to take things as we find them, and do our best to make as much sunshine as possible. Despite all the misadventures to which we have called attention, it is just as likely the breeder may go through a season without troubles as with them, and we now return to our nests as though there were no such things as failures in eggs, or failures in hens, or failures in anything. Nothing seems to come amiss to our birds : they are all feeding well, and several nests contain four and five young ones which are rapidly feathering. At this period of their growth it will be of advantage to notice the principal portions of the body on which the feathers grow. It does not follow that, because a bird is covered with feathers, the covering sprouts from every part of the surface of the body, and such will be seen not to be the case ; a bit of knowledge to be turned to account when we come to speak of washing for exhibition. Briefly, a strip of feathers will be observed to run down the back of the neck, which, with two broad bands, one on each side of the breast, and two smaller ones on the back, will be found to be the principal plantations from which will eventually depend feathers covering otherwise bare places. This is the time, too, when the fancier is able to note whether his expected clear birds are going to be disfigured with dark feathers, or his dark ones with clear feathers ; for every individual feather is discernible, and in nearly every variety, and every class of that variety, the future character of the bird is to be read at this early period of its life with tolerable certainty. Nothing further need engross the attention of the breeder for another week or fortnight, except to see the birds grow and feather ; and by comparison between a nest that is doing well, or better than well, and one which, though safe, is not quite up to the mark, he will be able to learn, better than any words can describe, the difference between the results of *good* feeding and attention not so constant—a difference so marked that those who may think this portion of our subject tedious will, when they come to see the importance of it, wish we had even gone more minutely into it, giving every possible aspect of the case, seeing that on it depends, in the first place, the very existence of the bird, and, subsequently, its growth to mediocrity or advance to high excellence.

It is at this early stage of growth, before the young bird has any idea of using its wings beyond a continuous flap, flap, while being fed, though it has a very good idea of a clumsy scramble, that the nest should be examined for insects, and, if any be found, at once condemned, and a clean one substituted. There is no occasion to study how to make it a fac-simile of the old one, because there is always a strong family likeness between one tin nest lined with felt and another—a thing about which, however, the Canary never troubles herself. Remember that an instinct in the first instance led her to find a place in which to lay, and guided her in adapting it to her purpose ; but having laid her eggs and hatched her young, her affection for them is paramount, and she will cling to them wherever she finds them, in whatever sort of nest they may be. Should a wooden nest-box be found infested, and it be wished to replace it by an imitation of a natural nest, the best plan is to shape it with moss inside the box, then line with a little hair, and finish off by working the cap of the nest by pressure with a hard-boiled egg, twisting it round and round till the nest is shaped—a plan some breeders adopt in the outset. Mark that the hen won't destroy such a nest ; if she were wishing to build, she would soon put it to rights ; but when her object is to lay, or having laid, to sit ; or having hatched, to feed, she accepts each position in the full exercise of the reigning instinctive faculty of the hour.

Having furnished a clean nest, which will be none the worse for being a size larger than the original, the young ones must not again be interfered with ; and not only so, but must be kept quiet, for if they are once frightened from the nest it is very difficult to make them take to it again. There is, of course, no danger of this occurring now, but a week hence such a thing might easily happen. A breeder is always very glad when his young ones are strong enough to leave the nest, and is glad to see them go, but he is always desirous to keep them there as long as possible, snug and comfortable, and well cared for. Extreme care is necessary at the last, when a startled sort of restlessness pervades the nest. So long as they squat and keep their heads well down, there is not much to fear; but as soon as one youngster, more venturesome than the rest, lifts up his head and turns himself round, you may look out for a jump. When one goes they had better all go, for they will still stick to each other a little longer, and, acting in concert, may even determine to return to the nest at night. But a single young one, if he persists in refusing to return to the bosom of his family, fares rather ill the first day or two of his liberty, and it is best to take every precaution to prevent premature flight,

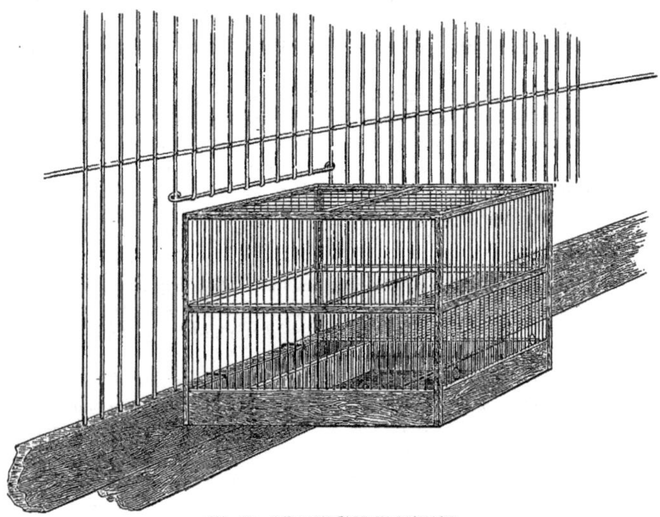

FIG. 30.—NURSERY-CAGE IN POSITION.

which ought not to take place till the birds are nearly three weeks old, by which time they will be almost as large as their parents.

We are exceedingly loth to hint at the possibility of any more misfortunes, but by the time the young ones have reached this age it is more than probable the hen will begin to show indications of wishing to sit again—an event which can scarcely be looked on in the light of a misfortune, but which requires nicely managing. Sometimes she will lay in her old nest, depositing her eggs among the young birds, who will not injure them, although there may be as many as twenty-four or thirty sharp little claws in the nest. Under any circumstances it is advisable to supply her with a second nesting-box, which may be suspended on the side of the cage, opposite the partition door, or if there be room at the back it can be placed there, bearing in mind that as the perches are all movable, they can be removed at will to suit the new arrangement, or additional ones brought into use. It may be that the building fever may not be very strong, and the hen may be contented to take such accommodation as is offered, but a small portion of new, clear stuff should invariably be furnished, as its presence may be the means of giving her employment at a time when she is apt to illustrate the truth of the aphorism that somebody makes it his business to find mischief for idle hands. With her new nest and fresh moss, she may forget that the silky feathers of her young brood make capital nest-linings; but if this once occurs to her, she will commence to pluck them in the most remorseless way, and then there remains nothing but to remove the young birds and the cock into another cage, where he will continue to feed them. This is the use of a "nursery" cage; into which the young ones can be placed alone, and the whole hooked on to the open doorway, when the old birds will feed through the wires, which must be sufficiently far apart to allow of the birds getting their heads through without their bodies following. It is a most objectionable plan to widen a few spaces for this purpose, since it will be plain that to open out one space is to contract the next; and also, if two wires be pulled apart at the bottom, they will still be close at the top, and the hole thus made is nothing better than a trap in which the bird is invited to put its head, with the certainty of being strangled if it should happen to move it up, and be caught and held by the neck in the narrower part. The arrangement of the front perch in the bottom of a cage of this kind must be such that when the young ones are sitting on it they will be just out of the reach of the hen, or whenever she finds one of them sufficiently near she will have a few feathers. The breeder will at once recognise the necessity of keeping a sharp look-out for small feathers in the new nest, for this disposition to pluck becomes, apart from the pain and inconvenience to the young birds, a positive calamity in the case of birds in which it is imperative that the original wing and tail feathers should remain intact. It will be seen, when we come to treat of varieties, that there are at least two in which this is one of the show conditions, and it is not pleasant to find one's prospects in this direction clouded so early. And this "show" view of the question extends still further. Not to mention the discomfort which must be felt when deprived of their natural covering, and the injurious effects of the drain on the system which one would imagine must exist consequent on the growth of a second crop of feathers at a time when the vital energies should be directed to maturing growth in other directions, this plucking is a most unfortunate thing, because when the natural moult begins, the crop of new feathers which will have already appeared on the plucked places will be a different shade of colour from that produced under the system of feeding adopted during the moult, which affects only those feathers in which the blood is circulating. If the plucking have been very slight, and the number of new feathers only trifling, we should no more hesitate to pull them out again than we should to pull out the grey hairs from our head. But if the plucking have been, such as we have too frequently seen it, thorough and entire, leaving the bird positively naked, to attempt to remove a second growth would be virtually to pluck the bird alive—a piece of cruelty nothing could justify. This disposition to pluck is, perhaps, one of the most vexing incidents of the breeding-room. We spoke of it as commencing at a comparatively matured age; but it is sometimes begun when the birds are very young, and not sufficiently fledged to be left all night without the protecting covering of the mother's wing, and is then very distressing and painful to witness. In these cases a deal can be done by wrapping the nest in flannel at night, and placing it in a covered basket —a good plan also to adopt in the case of forsaken nestlings for which no foster-mother can be found. The nursery-cage system will, however, answer well in the majority of instances, and if the cock can only get at them by day, through the wires or by any other means, he will keep at it like a Trojan, to all appearances liking the job. Worth his weight in gold is a good cock. Turn him into a "flight" with the young birds, and he will keep his eye on them, and will always "ken his ain bairns." It is very amusing to see the performance when the cock has been away for a while, and the young are hungry. They pounce upon him in a body, and drive him into a corner, or perhaps he retreats thither on strategic grounds, and ensconced there, supported on his tail on strictly scientific principles, taking care to keep his centre of gravity well within his base, he dispenses his charities to the clamorous applicants, giving each his fair share, and never, under any circumstances, losing his temper.

Nor is this mischievous practice of plucking confined to the hen, but is frequently indulged in by the young birds among themselves in the flight-cage, where it takes, if possible, a worse form, inasmuch as they do not content themselves with plucking the small feathers, for which they have no use, but make the strong quills of the wings and tail the object of their attack. Any one whose acquaintance with feathers has been of even the most superficial character will have noticed that when the stronger quills are growing they are full of liquid, and if accidentally drawn, the blood follows in considerable quantity. When the quill becomes matured, this ceases to be the case. It is when the young birds are first turned into the flight, and before the wings and tail and stronger feathers of the tail-coverts are grown, that the persecution is carried on; and the mode of action is beautifully simple. You observe a bird quietly seated at the end of a perch, close to the back of the cage; he is a bird of a retiring disposition and meditative turn of mind, is very young, and the proprietor of about one inch of tail. Some of his companions are older, and versed in the ways of a wicked world by at least fourteen days more experience. One of them sidles up to him in an insinuating sort of way, betokening mischief, and looks him over in an impertinent manner. He is a bird of delicate tastes, has a sweet tooth, and knows what is nice; and will, if he goes on at his present rate, probably be soon a candidate for the sick ward. The way in which he puts his head down and peers under and over little Verdant Green's tail is the embodiment of cool impudence; and before you can see how the thing is done, out comes a juicy feather, which he turns over in his mouth like a choice cigar, evidently with a keen relish, and having finished it, marks his man down in a remote corner and repeats the operation. The appearance of the latest arrival's tail naturally attracts a considerable amount of attention, and the force of bad example is quickly apparent. There were but twelve feathers in the inch of tail to begin with, and as there are now two missing from one side, some friend commences on the other side to restore the balance; and as birds don't usually do things by halves, they soon finish him up entirely, stripping him bare, literally not leaving him a feather to fly with—a most pitiable spectacle, bleeding profusely from every wound. This is not in the slightest degree over-drawn, and it does not take long either to bring about the catastrophe. When a bird begins to be so maltreated, it must be removed at once, for its feathers will *never* be permitted to grow. It will live in a state of chronic nakedness, absolutely more bare than when, scarcely a month before, it issued from its shell. Nothing, we may add, tends to check this so much as keeping large pots of chickweed as full of seed as it can be gathered, little *trees* of groundsel, and shepherd's purse in the cage; but it is a nasty infectious trick, and only too common.

This digression on plucking has thrown us out of our track a little, but remembering that our hen going to nest for her second "round" was the occasion of it, brings us to our starting-point again. As at the close of autumn the seasons appear to overlap each other, and the gardener in the pursuit of his calling seems to wish to do two things at the same time, and occupy the same piece of ground with two crops, so we seem to want to do two things at the same time in our cage. We want the hen to be attending to one brood and laying the foundation for a second; and we want the cock also to be in two places at once—that is, with the young nest as well as with the hen. The only way is to effect a compromise, by running him in to his hen for a short time night and morning; when she has laid her third egg he can be removed altogether and put in constant charge of the young birds, which, by the time the hen is ready to hatch, will be quite able to do without him altogether.

We think this is the proper place for a few hints on the common, and sometimes necessary, plan of running one cock to two hens. To do this in the most effective way, a cage of special construction is required; and as it forms in itself a complete apparatus, we append an illustration. The dimensions are four feet in length, with a depth of ten inches, as usual, and the height three feet. It consists of a roomy flight-cage, with three boxes on the top, the centre one being twelve inches, and the others eighteen inches wide. The front of the cage, in the cut, is framed of wood to screw on, the flight having a wooden cross-bar and wooden framed door, and the top compartments a wire cross-bar and wire swing-doors opening in the usual way. The open spaces in the partitions are for slides, of which two sets will be required: one of wood for closing all communication, and the other of wire in a wooden frame, the use of which will

FIG. 31.—CAGE FOR BREEDING TWO HENS.

presently be apparent. In the illustration the slides are made short, but they can be carried back the whole depth of the cage if thought desirable, and then, by removing them after the close of the breeding season, a second "flight" is obtained. In each of the larger compartments put a hen, and in the centre one the cock. Now shut off one of the hens entirely out of sight with a wooden slide, and pass the cock through to the other. They can be permitted the run of both compartments if it be wished, but nothing will be gained by it except that they will be constantly travelling to and fro, as if unable to decide which is the more fitting residence. Fit up the hen's cage with all breeding requisites, and allow the pair to remain together till the hen lays her complement of eggs. The cock may now be turned in to the other hen, and the first be entirely shut off by means of the slide. This might have been done with perfect safety when the hen laid her first egg, as the experience of most breeders goes to show that the whole will have been impregnated; but it is as well to allow her to settle down. By the time the second hen has squared accounts with the cock for his desertion after the short flirtation through the wire slide while he was in the middle cage, and has either received him at once with open arms, or pegged him well all over the cage, has made it up again, and is comfortably settled on a nest of eggs, the first will be thinking of chipping. The cock can now either be returned to cage No. 1, or confined in the middle box till it is seen how the hen feeds. All that has been previously written will now apply to the future management. The cock may either be allowed to take part in feeding, or not; if the hen feeds badly, run in the wire slide, and it need not again be explained how the arrangement will work. He will be equally ready for any other emergency, and can be run in, first to one and then to the other, to assist in feeding, and will eventually take charge of one or both nests in the centre cage, from which they will in due time be transferred to the larger flight below, and the business begun again *de novo*. This method of working may have suggested itself if the reader has carefully read our previous instructions; but we give it in detail, because it is a useful plan when there is but one cock of any particular variety and it is desired to make the most of him. We have mentioned two hens only, but he may be paired with several, by simply running him through a set of cages night and morning. When this is done he should not be called upon to take any part in rearing the young, except his co-operation should be required for carrying out any of the little schemes for assisting hens which have been before referred to.

From the time that the young Canary leaves the nest, it makes rapid strides towards independence. It must of necessity spend some days in a nursery-cage before being turned into the flight to shift for itself, as it has to pass through a sort of intermediate stage, and undergo what is equivalent to a weaning process. To carry this out the utility of spare cages, in which groups of young birds, equally advanced, can be placed, will be obvious. Hitherto their food has consisted entirely of the egg-mixture, which must still be continued, though the quantity of egg must be gradually decreased, the object to be attained being to get the birds on hard seed as speedily as possible. As soon as they are on the perch they will begin to pick at the soft food, though at first they will not be able to attend entirely to their own wants, hence the value of the nurseries attached to the breeding-cages. It is not, however, desirable to keep them in leading-strings a day longer than necessary, while at the same time they must not be allowed to starve. If the seed-trough of the nursery be supplied with such egg-food as they can manage to eat, they will make a very respectable attempt; but after a while comes the noisy chirping and begging. If not attended to they soon feel the ill effects of neglect, and ruffle up their feathers in a way indicative of much discomfort. Just in proportion as they have still the craving to be fed will they evince but small desire to assist themselves; and when once they feel the pinch and begin to clamour, they will refuse to help themselves. Hunger at this stage of their lives *will not drive them to search for food*, but to beg for it; and the demand must be satisfied. By degrees, and rapid degrees, they clamour less and help themselves more, and every hour then makes the matter easier; but up to the last, no young bird must be allowed to cry for food without the cock being at once permitted to give it a meal. When its hunger is satisfied, it is much more likely to visit the egg-food than before; and the philosophy of the whole thing consists simply in the bird being ultimately able of itself to keep its appetite in check, and hence it cries no more. But remember that so long as it does cry, it must have that cry attended to in the way Nature intended it should be, the cry being indicative of a still existing necessity. The whole process does not last long, and the visits of the faithful cock will soon be few and far between. It will be seen that we have all along been supposing a nest to have been removed from the breeding-cage at a comparatively early age, in consequence of apprehended ill-treatment; but this is not the invariable rule by any means. The hen, as frequently as not, goes to nest quietly, and the cock has then nothing to do but to continue his attentions to the young ones in the original cage; indeed, it is a very general practice to allow one nest to remain with the parents till the second is on the eve of hatching. This is the way to make fine birds; they never want for a moment, and never seem to feel the isolation which attends their being put on the other side of the front door, while poor old paterfamilias tells them as he drops the portcullis, "You see there is a second family coming on, and you really must turn out; if you require anything, come to me and I will supply you; but you must do your best to shift for yourselves entirely as soon as possible." Canary life has its parallels.

We have found it of great advantage to supply birds in the intermediate stage with ground seed. Canary-seed is, of course, the staff of life; but a variety of other seeds can be used with benefit. The coffee-mill will come into use now; it can be set to grind fine, or merely to crush, doing, in fact, little else than crack the husk—a feat the young bird cannot as yet accomplish for itself, or only with some difficulty. A mixture of canary, groats, a little millet, linseed, and even a pinch of hemp-seed, can all be passed through the mill, and put inside the cage. One lesson at a time is sufficient; and until they learn to eat their seed they should not have to go far to find it. A week of this kind of treatment will go a long way towards maturing the birds; and if a little whole seed be added, and it is seen that they can hull it without much trouble, it is time to be thinking of transferring them to the large flight-cage, where they will have more room for exercise.

Before taking this final step the breeder will have to mark the different nests, so that each bird can be recognised at a future day. This is absolutely necessary in a room in which breeding means something more than putting up so many pairs of birds every year without any regard to their parentage, and with no more definite end in view than producing as many young ones as possible. Such is not what a fancier means by breeding. He will have been endeavouring to build with material of which he knows something, and in that endeavour has not been groping in the dark and trusting to chance. He has been keeping before him one object, and all his work tends in that direction. He has planned to produce certain results, now and in the future, and these results must be chronicled in some way to guide him in his work. Here are several birds which, to any one else but himself, simply mean Canaries. They are very much alike, so much so that he can scarcely tell one from the other; but to him each represents some link in a chain he is forging, some stone dressed and carved into shape, and destined to fill a particular niche in the little edifice he has designed; and each should be duly marked and numbered, so that when required it can at once be put in its proper place and to its proper use. They are more than this: they represent certain elements evolved from raw material he has been passing through the crucible, and are intended to be combined with other elements, also duly labelled and marked with sundry hieroglyphics—indicating their character, whence sprung, and what capable of effecting. There should be no confusion and no mistakes; nothing left to memory, but every bird's pedigree and age registered on the bird itself by a simple system of notching the inside web of the wing-feathers, which in no way interferes with the appearance of the bird, and is not discernible until the wing is examined in the hand. With two wings at disposal, and not less than, say, ten feathers in each to mark on, the breeder requires nothing more than a sharp pair of small scissors to enable him, with the exercise of a little ingenuity, to contrive a set of notches representing numbers corresponding with the number of the cages, and to indicate also the fact of the bird having belonged to the first, second, third, or fourth nest, thus giving its age to a week. The notched wing becomes, in fact, the private index to the stock-book.

The larger and more roomy the flight-cages are, the better it is for the birds. Here they do their growing, and for the first eight weeks of their lives they ought to have nothing else to think about. Every condition which can possibly conduce to this end must be complied with. Overcrowding must be avoided, and ample perch accommodation provided. It is the want of this that frequently leads to quarrelling and mischief. Birds like their own particular corners and places to sit and roost in, and commence early in life the business of elbowing their neighbours who get in their way. When there is space at command, a portion of the bird-room may be partitioned off for a large flight, and enclosed with wire netting. Such a place requires no description, as it must be left entirely to circumstances; but a little ingenuity, a few strips of wood, and a few yards of fine galvanised netting, mixed up judiciously, ought to do a great deal. Keep the flight, whether large or small, scrupulously clean; arrange the perches so that when roosting the birds cannot soil each other; give plenty of good sound seed, whole and crushed; plenty of seedy green food, including bunches of the smaller plantain which ripens its short heads (the "soldiers and sailors" with which children play) in June, and contains a quantity of seed nearly as large in the grain as canary; clean sand and clean drinking water, with the addition of a bath every morning; do not give much soft food, and scatter what is given rather than allow it to stand and become sour, and everything will have been done to promote a hardy constitution and robust growth. The self-supplying seed-hopper and water fountain (Figs. 1 and 2) are the suitable furnishing for a flight-cage.

We wish we could at once go to the next part of our subject without a "but." The flight-cage, however, is often the scene of a malady which carries off many young birds. It is not our intention in this place to enter on the subject of diseases, but we refer to this particular form as belonging to management and rearing. During the earlier part of their existence young birds spend a good deal of time in sleep; but a healthy sleep must not be mistaken for unhealthy listlessness, and when one is observed to sit thick and lumpy, with its feathers at all ruffled up, it should at once be caught and examined by blowing up the feathers of the breast and lower part of the body, when, in place of a plump breast, there will most probably be found indications of wasting, and more or less of inflammation about the abdomen, arising from the presence of unwholesome and undigested food, causing general disarrangement of the system. This may have been induced, in the first place, by the bird eating stale green food or sour egg-mixture, or from partaking too freely of such delicacies as may have been introduced into the flight from time to time. And it means "going home" speedily, if some prompt remedial measures are not applied. We are almost as much opposed to the use of purgatives as we were once an advocate for them; but we have found one or two drops of castor oil, administered by dropping it into the throat from the point of a stick, will empty the bowels quickly; and by putting the invalid on crushed seed, and keeping it in a warm place, we have saved many a one. We have also been very successful in similar cases by following this treatment by doses of cod-liver oil, which can be easily given by removing the water-tin for an hour or two, and returning it floated with the oil. As a general precautionary measure we may say that, in our opinion, the principal ailments of young birds arise from disarrangement of the digestive organs and inflammation, and that careful attention to dieting, and keeping the invalid near the fire, will do as much as anything to restore health. Heat is indispensable, and it is astonishing to what an extent sick birds are benefited by it.

CHAPTER IX.

MOULTING: THE CANARY'S PLUMAGE.

THE next great event in the life of a young Canary is its first moult, indications of which begin to present themselves when about two months old, though, no doubt, preparations have been going on unseen for some time. In adult birds moulting commences about the month of July; but the time varies greatly according to circumstances, the whole period extending over the next three months. With the decline of vigour the moulting begins; indeed, the latter is always accepted as an index of the former, and the breeder notes the presence of a few feathers in the bottom of his cages as sure indications of the beginning of the end of his breeding season. We are referring now entirely to adult birds, and may say here that the first sign of incipient moult—the shedding of one or two quill feathers—is to be regarded as the signal to discontinue breeding with such birds as show it. They may not at first manifest any disposition to give up the duties of domestic life, but desire is sure to fail as the drain on the system consequent on moulting progresses; and even if it be found that the hen is sitting on "full" eggs at the time when the moult begins, it is best to remove them at once and not allow her to exhaust herself in endeavouring to discharge two duties at once. The chances are greatly against a hen's sitting even her thirteen days; and it is certainly too much to expect that, with failing energies and a constitutional sickness coming on, she will continue for a still longer period to perform duties which are born of a physical condition altogether different from that incident to the moulting period. The cocks are, however, generally the first to succumb, in which case few or none of the late eggs will be found to be fertile.

We cannot do better now than take this opportunity of dismissing our breeding stock for a while, and leave them to moult and recruit their exhausted energies in their winter quarters, which we prepare for them by opening all partition-doors and drawing out all slides, and after giving the cages a thorough autumn whitewashing, turn them, as far as such arrangements will permit, into flights. Now will be the time to go over the old stock, with a view to putting aside for further use such as have answered our expectations by accomplishing fair results, and putting into the sale-cage those we intend to dispose of; and having done this roughly, by making a comprehensive selection which will bear further thinning out, the old hens may all be run together, and will require no further attention beyond a supply of good nourishing food and an occasional bath on sunny days. We do not advocate the indiscriminate use of the bath during moulting, but an occasional dip is beneficial. Such hens as possess show properties, and are wanted for exhibition, must be caged off separately, not necessarily singly, to be put through the mill on the special diet which we shall treat of presently. The same with the cocks: many of these may have show properties of a permanent character, and may be required to travel the circuit again. To do them justice they ought to be put into separate cages, but the remainder will do well enough in a roomy flight; and as the blood in their veins is not so hot now as it was in the spring, they will soon be tired of quarrelling, if they only have plenty of room to get out of each other's way.

The young birds will also require to be drafted over, and most probably a selection of hens made from them; and the question at once arises, How are they to be distinguished from the cocks? If the fancier has been in the habit of spending much time among his birds, the greater part of them will have declared themselves; for the cocks begin to sing in their way at a month old, and some precocious youngsters even earlier. But he must learn to distinguish them by other signs. In some varieties the plumage is a slight guide; and in the case of moulted birds, of any variety, the brilliancy of the plumage alone is an almost unerring indication. But it is one of those things which can only be learned by experience. Where there is a marked difference in form and structural points, or in the general character of the plumage, verbal description becomes easy, and a novice can readily learn from it. For example, we think that any one who can write his own language could not fail to describe the difference between a cock and hen in game fowls, so that a child could not possibly mistake the one for the other. It is not so, however, with some birds, and the best judges are liable to be deceived in certain instances. The difference between the appearance of the sexes in some varieties of the Canary is so slight, that although an experienced eye can detect it, it is not easy to define clearly in what that difference consists. All knowledge of this kind is comparative; and if we say, speaking of any one feature, that in the cock it is found larger or broader, or differs in any other respect from the corresponding feature in the hen, we do not see how that conveys any very definite idea, if the same property, as it exists in the hen, has no place in the mind of the person we are endeavouring to teach. We are aware that when two objects are placed before the eye, a comparison between relative properties can then be instituted; but what we mean is, that it is only by long acquaintance that the abstract idea of what is the ruling form can be so impressed on the mind that we are able to recognise it at a glance, without having some other form placed before us at the same time to enable us to arrive at a conclusion by actual comparison. If we say of a Canary that the cock is more sprightly and vivacious than the hen, we must have a correct idea of the native sprightliness or vivacity of either before we can recognise the bird by it, and hence draw a deduction. For this reason we feel that the best description we can give will necessarily be obscure to the general reader in the absence of living specimens to illustrate it, while the breeder himself will at first, perhaps, fail to discover some of the more subtle distinctions.

There will not be found much difference in regard to the colour of the nest-feathers of the young birds of either sex in the flight, though the cock-birds generally show best in this respect, and especially the Yellows, where the brighter shade of colour is more discernible than among the Buffs; the use of which two terms is almost landing us in another digression, which we will avoid by a simple general statement, that with the exception of one or two varieties of Canaries in which the colour is certainly not that which a novice would call yellow or canary colour, or anything like it—with these exceptions every bird in the flight, whether clear in colour or variegated with green or a shade of green, will be found to be in its body-colour what we will, for the sake of simplicity, call either yellow or white; not exactly, perhaps, but sufficiently so to meet our description. The yellower birds are what are technically known as "Yellows," and the whiter ones as "Buffs;" and we say, in resuming the thread of our description, that though there is a difference in the colour of the sexes even in their nest-feathers, it is not so easily seen in the Buffs or whiter birds as among the Yellows, and is not at any time a good criterion as to sex at this stage of their growth. And as we are verging somewhat on the domain of feathers, we may add that the colour of any bird in its nest-plumage is not always a guarantee of its future excellence, any more than the absence of colour indicates a permanent want. No fancier who knows what moulting means ever thinks of disposing of young unmoulted stock, lest by any means he might unawares dispose of a gem in the rough. We discard the colour test, then, as being unsatisfactory, and observe that shape, style, carriage, action, and voice are the most reliable data. The cock is, as a rule, larger and more massive than the hen, is bolder and more energetic in his movements, and, in the flight, bustles about in a commanding sort of way as if anxious to impress the looker-on with the idea that he is the superior animal. Put him in a cage alone for a few minutes, and his carriage is bold and defiant, his chirp clear and ringing, his action quick and decisive and full of fire. The hen is, on the contrary, smaller and more delicately built, is shorter and more chubby, has a neater head and a softer and quieter eye, is less demonstrative in her movements, and, when put into a cage alone, hops backwards and forwards in a quiet way with a soft, plaintive chirp. The cock, under similar circumstances, seems to pull himself together, tightens his feathers, and stretches himself out, while the hen is still all over the same hen: she doesn't seem to know why she has been thus isolated, and her demeanour is melancholy rather than fiery and rebellious. Many fanciers of our acquaintance can tell a hen immediately by her hop and soft "cheep," or failing that, by her head and eye. We might add that the head of the cock is longer and looks narrower, and experienced breeders can tell the sex of birds in the nest at a glance by this token alone. Possibly much of this may seem to the uninitiated to point to distinctions without a difference; but, as we stated at the outset, some of the distinctions *are* subtle, and such as only experience and accurate observation can determine. They exist, however, and to the educated eye are palpable enough, and in mastering them lies the difference between judge and no judge.

In the case of adult birds a mistake need scarcely ever be made, especially in the spring, or when the birds are in condition, as an examination of the vent will quickly decide the question; that of the hen being small, and in the same straight line with the body, while that of the male bird is more prominently developed.

There is an art, too, in catching and holding a bird when any examination is required. Nothing, we are told, should be done in a hurry except catching fleas; and in catching a bird there should be no hurry or fluster, but a sharp, decisive pounce, and when you have him be sure you keep him. To examine either back or breast, lay it in the palm of the hand, with the thumb across the neck: it cannot escape; and if two be held in this manner it is the best way, and, indeed, the only way, to arrive at a correct estimate of the relative colours. To hold a bird securely without ruffling the plumage, take the tips of the wings and the root of the tail between the thumb and fingers, in which position he is powerless to escape.

There is no way of determining the true age of a Canary; but after the first year the scales on the legs become larger and coarser, and a year-old specimen of any variety which does not carry signs of its age in its plumage can generally be told in this way, though some birds would puzzle the best judges. Year-old birds do not, however, usually "make up" so well as young ones, and frequently indicate the fact by the condition of their plumage, which the experienced judge can generally observe. It is not easy to define clearly in what the difference actually consists, but, the legs being all alike, we think a judge could still pick out the two or three matured specimens in a group of twenty, and feel pretty sure he had hit the right nail on the head in every instance.

We now retrace our steps, and return to the subject-matter of this chapter—viz., moulting. We have preferred to explore some of the small by-paths as we have come to them, knowing that when followed to their termination we should have to turn back, and there was no chance of our losing ourselves or coming out upon the main stream lower down, and leaving some portion of it behind unexamined. We think the questions we have just discussed would be most likely to arise in the mind of the fancier at this stage of his experience, and have, therefore, endeavoured to dispose of them in furtherance of our plan, rather than leave a number of miscellaneous items for after discussion.

The phenomenon of moulting is a wonderful provision of Nature, common to all animals whose outer covering consists of hair, feathers, or other analogous forms. The bare mention of this fact seems to open out at once a wide field for thought, upon which, however, we must not venture to trespass one inch. We use the word in its generally accepted significance, as referring to the annual shedding of the feathers of birds, which, besides being of use as an outer covering, are destined for other purposes, for the accomplishment of which they require to be kept in a state of constant repair and efficiency. As a livery, only one suit is allowed in the year, and this is apt to get much injured by wear and tear as well as in the broils and vicissitudes through which it has to pass. Some parts of it will bear patching and repairing; but as it gets old and worn out there appears to be a limit even to this, and the wearer has often to go in rags and tatters, with portions of his body uncovered. One condition on which the new livery is granted is that the old one shall be entirely cast away; and in the exercise of much kindness and wisdom it is supplied just at the time when it is most required. We naturally inquire, What is this covering formed of, what its constituent elements, and what its component parts? Mudie, in his "British Birds," says that "the feathers of birds, the coverings of the featherless parts, and even the beaks and claws, are all, chemically speaking, formed of nearly the same materials; and nearly the same with the hair and cuticle of all animals, and even with the epidermis which covers living shells. This material is coagulated albumen, or nearly the same substance as white of egg when consolidated by heat, in which state it better resists the action of water than almost any other flexible substance. This substance is, especially in the upper or more coloured and glossy part of the feathers, combined with oils and metallic substances in very minute proportions; but in the down and light-coloured feathers it is nearly pure." And further, in giving definitions of the component parts, he refers to the "*ear-coverts*, which consist of certain soft feathers covering the external organ of hearing. The *scapulars*, or feathers which cover the shoulders and shoulder-bones, and the places where the *humeri*, or first bones of the wing, answering to the bones of the human arm above the elbow, are articulated. They unite without much distinction with the common feathers of the back, and along with those of the wings and the sides. The scapular feathers serve only as a clothing to the parts they cover, but they form a thick and comparatively downy covering, which, while it admits of easy motion, preserves the important joints which it covers from the changes of the weather. The *bastard wing*, consisting of a greater or smaller number of feathers, bearing some resemblance to the quills of the true wing. They grow from a little bone which is united to the third joint of the wing. The *lesser wing-coverts*, which are the first part of the plumage of the wings, and which in all birds take the form of definite and firm feathers. There are generally several rows of them; and there are the *under-coverts* which answer to them, and line the under or inner side of the wings; but these are more slender and downy in their consistence, and, generally speaking, have less colour. The *greater wing-coverts*, which lie under the lesser ones, and are still larger and stronger, stretching a considerable way over the quills or flying feathers, and being supports to these for a greater part of their length than the lesser coverts. They are also much stronger in proportion to the coverts which answer to them on the under sides of the wings. The *primaries*, or principal quills, which form the termination of the wings, and are the strongest feathers in the bird. They rise from the hand, or that portion of the wings which is below the wrist-joint, and which, though it sometimes contains three distinct bones in its length, is frequently called the first bone of the wing. These feathers are numbered in order; the outer one, or that which is foremost in the expanded, or lowest in the closed wing, is the first. The *secondaries*, or second quills of the wing, arising from that part of the wing which is commonly called the second bone, and which answers to the forearm in man. They come from it towards the wrist-joint, and admit of a folding of the wing between them and the primaries, when the wing is closed. When the wing is open they sometimes appear a combination of the same curve with the primaries, 'as is the case in the wing of the Canary,' and at other times they form a distinct curve of their own. And the *tertiaries*, or third quills of the wing, arising chiefly from the same bones as the secondaries, but nearer to the elbow-joint."

"From the manner in which the several coverts support each other, and the quills, the wing is a finer combination of lightness, strength, elasticity, and stiffness than could be produced by any other means. These coverts support and admit of motion upon each other, not unlike that which takes place in a coach-spring."

Continuing the description of the remaining portion of the feathers, we have the "*Rump-feathers* and *upper tail-coverts*, the first being a continuation of the covering of the back, and the second the support of the tail-feathers on the upper side, being strong in proportion as the tail-feathers are adapted for action in flying; the *vent-feathers* and *under tail-coverts*, which cover the hinder part of the bird; and lastly the *tail-feathers*, which require no reference."

"The other feathers are to be considered rather as the clothing of the bird than as active instruments in its flight. These ordinary feathers are imbricated—that is, placed one over the edges of two—as slates are in covering a roof. The lines in which the several rows of feathers are placed form very curious curves, and their shafts diverge or converge so naturally, and with such perfect agreement, to the surface they cover, that no line of separation can be traced."

We have given these definitions and interesting descriptions in full, and would strongly advise the fancier, who has not already done so, to familiarise himself with them, and, by comparing them with the features presented by his own specimens, verify their accuracy; feeling satisfied that the little scrap of knowledge thus gained will prove of service by-and-by, and enable him to follow closely descriptions in which the use of recognised nomenclature may be adopted. Our book is essentially homely, and we have no intention of taking a very scientific view of any question, but it is as well to call things by their right names, and to know what is meant when we use them.

We have already briefly pointed out at the commencement of this chapter that no special treatment is necessary in general moulting. It is a provision of Nature; and though instances will occur in every breeding-room in which the functions are impeded, and the operation retarded and sometimes altogether checked, yet these cases are not frequent enough to justify us in characterising the moult as being such a critical period in a bird's history as to cause any serious apprehension as to the result. Birds previously healthy will, it is true, sometimes die at this time, but the percentage of deaths is very small; and although the moulting season may claim a few victims, and may be, in the case of ailing birds, the last straw which breaks the camel's back, we do not think that the number of deaths in previously healthy subjects is greater than those which can be directly traced to other causes. Personally, we never experienced the least difficulty in carrying our birds through this period of their lives; and we are of opinion that the idea of deaths is about the last which enters the mind of the experienced breeder when he finds it time to take his young stock in hand. Beyond doubt there must be a strain on the system to produce the plumage, but it is all perfectly in obedience to settled laws, and Nature does not call on the bird for the effort without furnishing the munitions of war in abundant supply, and doing her best to maintain the healthy conditions necessary for the successful carrying out of the work. It is sometimes spoken of as the moulting "sickness," but we think the term misapplied; for the disposition to incubate and perform other duties is just as much a sickness, inasmuch as the bird requires to be in an abnormal state of body at the time. By sickness, we usually understand a disarrangement of certain functions; but we do not consider the phenomenon results from any such cause, but is a most perfect and healthy recognition of certain laws in the animal economy.

We furnish an illustration of the interior of Messrs. Mackley Brothers' moulting-room at Norwich—the most complete thing of its kind in the country. The "room" is a detached house in Mr. Jacob Mackley's garden, at Upper Hellesdon, on the outskirts of the city, and is a wooden erection about twelve feet high, standing on six substantial posts about two feet six inches from

MESSRS. MACKLEYS' MOULTING-ROOM.

the ground. It is weather-boarded on the outside with one-and-a-quarter-inch stuff, and the space between that and the three-quarter-inch boards with which the inside is lined is filled with sawdust, which acts as a non-conductor. It is warmed by hot-water pipes, and the perforated covering seen at the bottom is contrived so as to admit fresh air from outside as well as the heated air from the pipes. The entrance consists of double doors, the rule being to close the outer before opening that immediately leading into the room, in case any birds should have escaped from their cages. It is lighted from the roof, and is well ventilated by means of six patent contrivances, and lighted by gas, the foul air being carried off by a four-inch pipe through the roof, which is tiled. There are 248 cage-compartments, separated by sliding partitions, the number of wires used being about 5,000, which means pricking 15,000 holes. Each compartment is the same size, and each front slips and unslips by a very simple arrangement of small brass buttons. The doors are all framed, and swing on beads, so as to afford no hiding-place for parasites between the door-frames and the cross-bars, and each fastens with a neat brass button. The seed-hoppers are all made of one pattern, and fit any set of holes. The water-vessels are of glass, and the egg-tins, which also have brass fronts, all draw out.

The building is thoroughly cleaned out at the commencement of the moulting season in the following manner:—The birds being first removed into another room, each front is unslipped, and every compartment is well scraped—top, sides, and bottom—removing as much whitewash as possible. The fronts are then placed inside, each in its own place, and every aperture being closed, the place is well "stoved" by burning a quantity of sulphur—a process that is twice repeated. The cages are next washed with dilute carbolic acid from top to bottom, and afterwards lime-washed twice. Then all glasses, egg-tins, and hoppers are laid in soda and water, together with the fronts, the wires of which, when dried, are coated with Japan black. The hoppers and outside woodwork are then re-varnished, the sides lime-washed and painted black on the outer ends, egg-tins and brasswork polished, fronts fastened in their places, and all is ready for the reception of the stock to be moulted. When the room is in full operation there have been as many as 1,200 birds in it at one time, but we should scarcely imagine they were *all* being fed on "KN," though we have ourselves had many an energetic sneeze while inspecting stock being put through the mill in this refinery. Twenty cages *per diem* are cleaned out and sanded, so that the entire room is gone through once in a fortnight; cleanliness being one of the leading principles in the government of this interesting establishment.

A special department of moulting—that known as "The Cayenne Process"—is worth a separate chapter.

CHAPTER X.

MOULTING ON CAYENNE.

WE propose now to consider the question of moulting from a point of view which clothes it with a profounder interest than that felt by the fancier when regarding it as a simple, natural phenomenon common to bird-life. He divides the whole Canary family into three principal groups, comprising the colour section; those having distinctive plumage; and the birds of shape and position. With the first of these, moulting has everything to do; and the specific treatment and special dieting practised while the operation is going on, with a view to inducing the development of colour, has ever occupied the closest attention of those breeders who have made the colour section their speciality; and such are by far the larger number of the body comprising the great world of the Fancy. The problem of what is colour, how produced, and how affected? is one which breeders have long tried to work out, each in his own way, according to his own theory, with varying success. That some Canaries have the native property of developing it to a greater extent than others, is patent. We know why some violets are blue, and why some are not blue; why grass is green, and how it is that flowers are painted with parti-coloured tints. And there must be a reason why some birds are decked with all the colours of the rainbow; some law which governs the change in the hues of the summer and winter plumage of certain of our native birds, as well as the more strongly-marked changes in those coming to us from tropical climes. What colour really is, what its chemical constituents, can all be clearly defined; but how, when fed from the same fountain, we find it existing in so many separate hues in one and the same member, a single feather to wit, is a mystery seemingly as incomprehensible as some of the higher mysteries which man, in the plenitude of his wisdom (?), refuses to believe, in the face of the most positive evidences of their existence, simply because his mind cannot fathom them.

This, however, is not a treatise on the mysteries of creation, but on the more practical matter of moulting Canaries. A thoughtful consideration of the fact that in the earliest stage of their growth the feathers of the Canary, as of all other birds, are *not* feathers, but simply little tubes in which the blood circulates, and which eventually develop into what we call feathers, the web of which is nothing more than an expansion and minute ramification of the material of which the whole is composed, led to the supposition that the colouring matter must be manufactured in, and deposited by, the blood; and various theories were propounded and methods devised for bringing about this result. The fact that certain food is known to have the direct effect of colouring the fat, and even the bones of animals, seemed to support the theory; and the notion of feeding the feather from its birth, and while in embryo before its birth, took a strong hold on the minds of breeders, though the idea was but very imperfectly developed, and, we should imagine, in many cases worked out in a very clumsy way, and without any clear perception of the principle involved. Anything "yellow" that the bird would eat was supplied to it; no matter what it was, or whether it was a substance the bird could digest and assimilate: so long as it was yellow, that was sufficient; and we have heard of the most extraordinary compounds having been administered in the shape of pills, powders, draughts, anything and everything, any way and every way, no matter what or how, if colour might only be born of it.

From among this diversity of modes of feeding and widely varied practice, however, one truth was eliminated, and it became no secret that certain food *would* affect colour in a sensible degree. Each breeder, with the most commendable selfishness, kept his particular nostrum a profound secret, but the existence of the fact was demonstrated over and over again by fanciers buying high-coloured specimens, and utterly failing to moult them with anything like the same results. Certain towns with their schools of breeders apparently had the game in their own hands, and the secret, such it was, was jealously guarded for years. The difference between the colour of a bird moulted on ordinary diet and one fed on *extra*-ordinary diet was not so marked at the period to which we refer as it is in the present day, simply because the agents employed were not so powerful in their action as those now in use; but it was sufficient to give the feeder an advantage over the breeder—an advantage he has ever held when both have started in the race on the same terms as regards the quality of the birds.

From what we have said it will be gathered that the verb "to moult" is both neuter and active, and that we use it in the latter sense as signifying the indirect doing of something on the part of the breeder, rather than expressing an action entirely confined to the bird. It includes in it the idea of feeding by rule; and we are quite prepared to be met at the outset with the question, Is feeding, then, the whole secret of colour in the colour section of the Canary family? We are very much inclined to answer that question by another and say, Why not? And we might ask one or two more questions and say, What *is* the natural colour of the Canary? Is not the assumption of the fact that the colour in which it usually appears is its natural or proper colour, rather an arbitrary assumption? If various descriptions of vegetable food, all of which it might find in a state of nature, and which it eats with avidity, affect its colour in as many degrees, who shall say that any one shade of colour is *the* colour, and that all other shades are improper and unnatural because novel and comparatively unusual? Is not the word "unnatural" wrongly applied? For how can anything be un-natural which is in direct accordance with Nature? If any description of food be literally un-natural, it is the *artificial* food which the bird could not find in a natural state; for Canaries do not gather hard-boiled eggs among the seeds and fruits of the earth, nor do they find port wine in the brooks and pools by the wayside. Our idea of un-natural food would be the mixing up of some diet the bird nauseated and forcing it down its throat. The results produced might be strictly in harmony with natural laws, just as natural results follow a dose of strychnine. Remember that the Canary has been a domesticated bird for centuries, is dependent upon us for everything, and has no chance of showing us, by any voluntary act of its own, what it would eat, drink, and avoid, if it had the opportunity for unlimited selection. For generations we have followed the traditions of our forefathers, and have acted as if we believed that canary-seed alone was created for the Canary, and the Canary for canary-seed, and that to supply it with anything else of which it is fond, and which does it good, is—the meaningless term over again—unnatural. Unusual, we admit, but most certainly not unnatural. Suppose a Canary to have escaped into a conservatory, and to be observed feasting on some berries growing there in profusion, acrid and poisonous to ourselves, but of marked benefit to the bird, improving its health, and by the action of certain properties inherent in them, beautifying its plumage—what lunatic would call such food unnatural, and such results unnatural, because, among other reasons, these berries happened not to agree with ourselves? The force of this and previous arguments will be seen presently.

Our original proposition we put in the form of the question, whether feeding is the secret of colour? We now answer, Yes; and we have anticipated some of the objections which might arise by asking the questions above propounded—questions which we think require no reply. It is altogether foreign to the question to stay now to inquire *how* the colour is affected;

indeed, no philosophical reason has yet been assigned, though no doubt it will ultimately be shown to result from the deposition of colouring matter in the cellular tissue through the action of the blood. It is perfectly immaterial whether it be brought about in this way, or whether it be due to the development of colour native to the bird, though latent, by calling into vigorous exercise existing functions. So long as the agent employed is no more than the active principle of a natural diet, the process is strictly natural from beginning to end, and is not to be condemned as unnatural simply because it is the development of a phenomenon which has been hidden from our view by force of circumstances for centuries.

We said that the use of *something* to produce colour became a common practice with all breeders, and among the many somethings were included marigold flowers, strong solution of saffron, cochineal, port wine, beetroot, mustard-seed, and other comestibles, the principle feature of which, it is evident, was the possession of colour. But the entire exhibition world was destined to be revolutionised by one important discovery which was made in 1871. In the search after the philosopher's stone an explorer "struck ile." We have read how some of the Australian settlers stared at each other in speechless amazement when, after washing their first pan, they found the little shining lumps of gold in the bottom; and though, to any one not in the great Fancy, it may seem absurd to draw any comparison between the two events, we don't know which of the discoverers felt the greater delight, for each had found gold. To whom belongs the honour of the discovery we refer to we are not in a position to say, no one, to our knowledge, having set up his claim; but the fact came out in this way. Towards the close of the moulting season of 1871, rumours were rife in the Midland districts that in the neighbourhood of Sutton-in-Ashfield some extraordinary birds had been bred—for candour obliges us to state that for a long time the superior quality of these birds was asserted to belong to the breed or strain which it was alleged the discoverer of the grand secret had in his possession. Had it been openly stated that a new "feed" had been discovered, it is very probable that that fact would have been accepted more willingly than the assertion that the breeder had hit on a superior combination of blood, which story was altogether discredited, and the new birds were received with the gravest suspicion on some hands, and avowed unbelief as to their genuineness on the part of others. Some of the best breeders of the day examined them; and though all known tests failed to show that the colour was due to any outward application, yet one mysterious fact stared them in the face—the birds were *two colours!* An explanation of the fact that the colour was owing to the feed, and not to the strain, would still have cleared up this difficulty, which is now understood and will be explained presently; but this valuable strain (?) would then have lost its market value; and as the colour section had always ruled in the market according to the depth and purity of the colour of its representatives, and such colour had always commanded its price as representing breed or strain, a fiction of which the many outside the feeding circle we have before mentioned had been the victims for years, we can scarcely be surprised at the discoverer of a new feed endeavouring to make his market in the same way. This may all seem very naughty, and convey the idea of a lax sort of morality, but it is nevertheless true. We ourselves, and a large circle of friends, had been breeding colour-birds for years, and this was at a time, bear in mind, when Canary shows were not reported, and when the Canary had no literature of its own, and we had never heard of feeding as influencing colour. We well remember the knock-down blow we received when a fancier in a high position, whose *status* in life and official position—for he was a magistrate—forbade the idea of anything but the exercise of any but the most honourable conduct, telling us to give up trying to breed colour-birds, as the secret lay in the feeding and not in the breeding. In the present existing state of things, when the doings in the Canary world are chronicled weekly with as much accuracy as the rise and fall of the money market, it would be next to impossible for intelligent men to grope in the dark as we did; but we are giving a true account of Canary society as we found it ten years ago, when some who ought to have known better persistently followed out the questionable policy of preaching *breed*, all the while taking infinite pains to conceal the necessary adjunct, *feed*. The line of policy, therefore, adopted by the discoverer of the new thing, the miraculous feed, was only an extension of the system of morality in which he had been educated. By ignoring the existence of the true agent, however, it will be seen that he laid himself open to the suspicion of foul play, which was strengthened by the then remarkable feature of his birds being, as we have already said, two colours—not two shades of one and the same colour, mark, but, as was asserted, two distinct colours, viz., yellow and a shade of green, which it was at once affirmed was the consequence of unskilful *dyeing*. And really it looked funny. Fanciers who knew that the best show-birds were the exceptional specimens selected from large numbers, and who were content to produce one or two in a season, would not have it at any price that a dozen could come out of one breeding-room, and from the same pair of birds in one year, much less five or six stars out of one nest, as was alleged of these extraordinary specimens. But the existence of the two colours on the same bird was the pill no one would swallow, and the assumed evidence of fraud. Every breeder, however, now knows that this appearance arose simply from the presence of feathers which had grown before the birds had been put on the colour-producing diet, which, even in the very best specimens, appear absolutely *green* beside the rich, ruddy orange now so common. But our friend in Sutton-in-Ashfield kept his own counsel, and was content to sit and grin and bear the sneers of a virtuous world, strong in his own integrity. We have said this occurred in 1871; but we have reason to believe that birds fed in this way had been exhibited one or two years in succession at one of our largest shows, and had been disqualified on the ground of being artificially coloured by means of outward applications, and that the original discoverer still pocketed the opprobrium and bided his time.

Our own introduction to these birds was at Cheltenham, where we were judging the same year. At that time their fame had not reached us, but one or two of them were sent to Cheltenham, and one we well remember, a Heavily Variegated Buff bird, beat a large class. We were attracted by its extraordinarily rich colour, which fairly took away our breath; but an examination showed us sure indications of its genuineness, and we gave our award unhesitatingly. Shortly afterwards a show was held at which we were solicited to exhibit. The usual clause in the rules that "all specimens shall be *bonâ fide* the property of the exhibitor," was purposely expunged, and a silver cup held out as an inducement for large entries; and six of the now notorious Sutton-in-Ashfield birds appeared in the catalogue in our name. Some of our best friends, and one in particular whose name will appear presently—a gentleman who subsequently became the champion of the new school, and who, with us, fought its battle and won—severely censured us for having anything to do with these dangerous birds. The judges, however, were satisfied with them, and they were duly gazetted winners. Then came the *dénouement*. The committee, in the fulness of their zeal, tested (?) them in a way perfectly unjustifiable, literally scrubbing off the web of the feathers in one bird's tail, and leaving it with twelve almost naked quills; and shortly after charged us formally with having exhibited painted birds, at the same time producing, as evidence, a handkerchief which was alleged to be stained with the colouring matter from this mutilated tail. It is not necessary to refer to the amusing incidents of the protest, but the following copy of a certificate we obtained from an analytical chemist to whose examination we submitted the birds will speak for itself:—

[Copy.]

226, High Street, Sunderland.

There is not the least trace of a pigment or foreign colouring matter of any kind on any of the feathers I took from the birds numbered respectively 1, 2, and 3.

John J. Nicholson, F.C.S.

This portion of our subject has had rather a personal character, but we have detailed it as an historical fact, and as furnishing the first published account of the first chemical test to which these birds were publicly submitted, and their satisfactory passage through the ordeal.

We next find these same birds figuring at the Crystal Palace Show, in February, 1872, by which time our mutilated friend had grown a new tail, which every one said had been painted for the occasion; and though he was passed over as a suspicious character, some of his companions went through their examination and obtained the diploma of V.H.C., which is perhaps a rather significant comment on the knowledge of that day. The year 1872 died out, and the memory of these ill-fated birds died with it, till February 1873 again brought round the Crystal Palace Show, when to the astonishment of everybody, Mr. Edward Bemrose of Derby, one of the keenest fanciers of the day, and a man on whom no one could lay the finger of suspicion, but who was the very friend to whom we have referred as censuring us for having "anything to do with these dangerous birds," brought out two specimens of the same school, which he asserted on his word of honour as a gentleman he had moulted himself in his own house, and which owed their extraordinary colour to nothing but the peculiar diet on which they had been fed. Despite Mr. Bemrose's dignified asseverations, however, he left the Palace Show under the imputation of being in league with the naughty men of Sutton-in-Ashfield; but not before he had delivered himself of a promise, which he fulfilled almost to the letter, that next season he would bring out, not two, but a string of birds which he would send to every show in England, and with which he would take every prize, from Whitby in September, round to the Palace Show again in 1874, and that when he had thus vindicated his character he would give the secret to the world.

And he kept that promise. Next season he was invincible, and the exhibitors in the Colour section of the Canary family lay under his feet. Some accepted their defeat like men, and others writhed and wriggled like worms. In some directions confidence began to grow, while the now historical birds fearlessly travelled the country. In others the opposition was bitter, and every means that blind prejudice or petty interest could devise was called into operation in the endeavour to injure their reputation. But the climax was reached at the great Norwich Show, held in St. Andrew's Hall in October of the same year 1873, on which occasion several of the Norwich breeders protested in a body against the genuineness of a consignment of these birds, which, under our own judging, had taken almost every prize within their reach. From among a large number seven were selected for analysis, of the result of which we append a copy. It was our lot to be connected with similar birds on their *first* examination by a qualified analyst, and we were officially concerned in them in our capacity of judge on this the *last* ordeal they were ever to undergo, and which established their reputation on a basis nothing could ever afterwards shake.

County Analyst's Office,
Eastern Counties' Laboratory, Norwich, October 17th, 1873.

Certificate of Analysis

Of Seven Canaries.
From the Bird Show in St. Andrew's Hall, Norwich.
Mark. $\frac{70}{5}$ $\frac{112}{7}$ $\frac{28}{2}$ $\frac{40}{3}$ $\frac{54}{4}$ $\frac{88}{6}$ $\frac{13}{1}$

I hereby certify that, in the presence of the Chairman of Committee and other representative persons, I have examined these birds with a view to ascertain the presence of artificial colouring matter upon their plumage.

My opinion is that no artificial colour has been used. (Signed) Francis Sutton.

Shortly after this the secret began to ooze out, and the first use made of it by some who had been loudest in their denunciation of the new school of birds was to *sell* it, which was not discovered until one, smarter than his fellows, boasted of having netted £50 by the *sale* of a *gift*.

This coming to our knowledge, we put Mr. Bemrose in possession of the fact, and on Dec. 11, 1873, he published in the *Journal of Horticulture* the grand secret of the extraordinary colour of the birds which had so completely demoralised the whole Canary world; and when he stated that the agent employed was nothing more than CAYENNE PEPPER, we must say in justice to the Fancy that half of them didn't believe him. But in searching after hidden things how frequently does it happen that we place our hands near them, or even on them, and yet don't know it; and it was almost too much for fallen humanity to be asked to believe that in the cruet which stands *next* to the mustard which some of them had been using every day, lay the solution of the whole mystery. The wonder is that it had never been discovered before, for cayenne pepper had long been prescribed as a comforting spice, and it is probable that administering it in excess first led to a knowledge of its remarkable properties. There is also not the slightest doubt that it had long been used in very small quantities simply as a condiment, and that it then produced effects which were not attributed to it, but to some other vehicle in use at the same time. Years ago we were recommended to use a patent pungent condiment as being an excellent agent in conditioning certain birds; and though we have not analysed it, we think there is every reason to believe that it contains the pepper in a large proportion, and that the effect attributed to it as a whole was, in the main, traceable to the presence of cayenne in its composition.

Such is the history of the early struggles attending the introduction of the capsicum into the bird-room. We do not intend to pursue it farther, but the bare statement that cayenne pepper is the principal ingredient in moulting-mixture would not have satisfied any reader who, for the first time, became acquainted with the fact that food influenced colour. Our object has also been to show that although the Canary in its usual garb is very pretty, yet it has ever been the study and aim of breeders to improve its colour by adventitious aids; and that the best specimens in exhibition ever owed their superior finish and polish to a system of feeding long kept secret, and only exploded and blown to the winds by the discovery of which we have given the history. During the two or three years this has been in practice it is only natural that the peculiar characteristic of the capsicum should occasionally have caused some speculation as to whether its pungent heat is not distressing to the birds; but the fact that they eat it greedily and in large quantities without suffering the slightest apparent inconvenience would seem to answer the question satisfactorily. Collateral proofs, also, are not wanting that some varieties of birds, though not belonging to our family, are inordinately fond of the capsicum. We may mention one instance which came under our own observarion. A cockatoo of ours escaped, and was captured in a conservatory where it had lived over again an hour of its old sub-tropical existence. We expressed our regret at the circumstance, fearing it might have done some injury, but were glad to know it had done no mischief, though the gardener expressed his opinion that "the bird had a queer taste," for it had "*stripped all the capsicums of their ripe pods*."

We have introduced the question of the influence of food upon colour in this place as forming part of the practical business of moulting, though it is evident its application will lie chiefly in the direction of those classes we have indicated as forming what we have described as the Colour section. Our reference to them has been necessarily somewhat vague, since we have not as yet minutely described any particular variety, and do not presuppose any knowledge of them. We will, however, exhaust the subject so far as its general principles and practice will carry us, reserving any remarks upon special treatment till the occasion offers to present them.

We return to our flight-cage, where our birds are about eight weeks old, by which time it will be necessary to put those intended for a "hot" moult on "feed." If there be a sufficient number of breeding-compartments at liberty, clean and whitewash thoroughly, and put two or three birds into each. The work can be done as efficiently by utilising them as by using a set of small moulting-cages: a cage is but a cage after all. Specially-contrived cages for certain kinds of birds will be described in their proper place. Some breeders, however, like to have a stack of small moulting-boxes about eight inches square, which can be built in sections to suit the size of the room and the space on the walls they are required to cover, and we must say they have a very business-like look, and occupy comparatively small space, considering the number of birds they will accommodate. Such a stack, for instance, about six feet square, and built in three sections, would afford cage-room for no less than ninety. Previous instructions will suggest the way in which it should be built. Supposing it to be ten compartments wide, each cage will have its own turn-rail, and one bottom cross-piece will run across the entire width; no top cross-piece is required, as the bottom of one cage forms the top of another, and the wires can be inserted in it. A T-framed door, which is easily made, is all that is required, with one wire-hole on each side. One perch, for there will not be room for two, must be put in the middle from side to side (not from back to front), and one in front to enable the bird to get at its food without standing on the bottom of the cage, for the turn-rail and cross-piece should be made not less than one and two inches high respectively. During the moult the bird prefers quiet, and is happy enough on its perch; and we don't want to throw more light into the bottom of the cage than there is any occasion for, as we wish the bird to remain up aloft, and not to grub about and get dirty. The number of little hoppers required for such a cage is the most tiresome part of the work to the amateur builder, but by cutting them out all at the same time the work is much less tedious than might be imagined. The only extra fitting required is an egg-tin, to hook on to the bottom of the door on the inside; a wire woven transversely will be required to hang the tin on, so as to allow it to work clear of everything in opening and shutting the door, and if the T-framed door be used, remember to prick a hole through the T to receive the wire. We said, in giving our dimensions, *about* eight inches square. This will give a five-inch door; for it must be remembered a door is required for other purposes than to get the bird in and out: it has to admit a hand and a little whitewash brush. If required, the cage can be made to consist of a nest of "pigeon-holes," with a framed front to take off and on for the purpose of cleaning; but all these arrangements depend on the amount of trouble or expense the fancier is willing to incur. We can only add that such a cage, neatly made and carefully wired, fitted up uniformly with little hoppers and water-tins, painted black and well varnished, with each box containing a bird undergoing the process of transmutation (for it is little else), is a sight a breeder may be proud of when he lifts up the clean sheet (with which it ought to be covered while the birds are moulting) for some brother fancier to gauge his prospects for the incoming season.

Before finally putting the birds into their moulting quarters, whether into a clean flight to moult a number together, or into smaller cages in smaller numbers, or into single boxes, we must say that at the head of the Colour section stands the Norwich Canary; and we take that bird to illustrate our mode of going to work. It is, in fact, *the* colour bird. Two others of the family have also the power to develop colour in a remarkable degree—viz., the Lizard and London Fancy. The Lizard is, probably, at least its equal in this respect, while the London Fancy is, by its admirers, considered its superior. But each of these has *other* properties which rule above colour in them, and which are their strong points, while in the Norwich Canary colour is all in all, the bird being literally all colour. The remaining members of the family, Cinnamons excepted, although they have colour, yet have so little of it that other properties altogether rule in their case, and it is usual to give them nothing beyond a general moult. Experiments tried on them have shown that they have not the power of depositing colouring matter to any extent; and such being the case, some *other* strongly marked peculiarity has been seized hold of and cultivated, and colour has been left alone. The leading idea throughout is to cultivate to its extreme development the strongest native property, and, in the instances to which we refer, something else is that native property, not colour. True, they are sometimes "fed," but the machinery for assimilating and depositing is not there, and they can do so little that they are just as far behind in the colour race at the finish as they were at the start. Some people consider they *ought* to colour, and that it is very wicked of them not to do so when so much good stuff has been given them; but we cannot turn Nature out of her course, even to oblige the ignorance which affirms that a bird without the necessary machinery can, by means of the capsicum, be turned into one which has it. When will such ignorance learn to comprehend the simple physiological fact, that the difference lies between an economy which can grasp and appropriate, and one which can not any more than the Ethiopian can change his skin or the leopard his spots? We have heard the question asked with wonder and amazement, as if it were a mystery past human comprehension, Why is it that in the same nest, all fed on the same diet, one bird out of three or four will sometimes be found to show no colour? *Why?* simply because the machinery is defective, and the bird would have exhibited the same deficiency and in precisely the same degree on whatever feed. Viewed in this light, colour is nothing more than the manifestation of certain physiological functions which we can search for and *test* by the use of particular food. The deposition of colour is the result of possessing these functions and having them in healthy working order, and by supplying food from which colour can be secreted, we ascertain what birds have and what have not the capacity of doing that, the manifestation of which constitutes their distinctive character in a fancier's eye; and the capsicum, instead of being the paint which has to hide all defects, the cloak to cover a multitude of sins, really becomes the most reliable guide we have, indicating the character of the birds submitted to its test, and showing pretty clearly the direction in which we should look in selecting breeding stock likely to carry out to a practical issue the theory of like producing like.

We take our representative bird, then, to illustrate the business of moulting, and we note, first, that we put it on "feed" thus early at the age of seven or eight weeks, because it is necessary that the colour process should be commenced while the feathers are yet in embryo. And what is "feed?" We have no doubt that half-a-dozen breeders would give as many different recipes, but the active agent in all of them would be cayenne pepper, which can be mixed with chopped egg and sweet biscuit, or crumbs, or any of the soft food compositions which birds are fond of. Or it may be furnished in the form of "cake," in which eggs, flour, and sugar, or any similar sponge-cake foundation, is made the medium of holding a quantity of pepper in the proportion of almost bulk for bulk. That there are other foods in use, or adjuncts to the ordinary cayenne food, we know; and the Fancy still has its little secrets which may or may not be of value, that are likely to remain secrets. This keep-what-you-have-and-get-all-you-can disposition is not found in a true fancier, and when evidences of its presence crop up to the surface they generally indicate an auriferous formation. It may stimulate emulation, of a kind, to measure off its results with a rule on which the chief marks are 20s., 10s., 5s., at short intervals, but such emulation never gives anything to the world except for value received. The thoughtful breeder will have to investigate the relation between cause and effect for himself. Great discoveries have been made by chance, but research tells in the long-run and is the source of pleasure which can neither be bought nor sold.

The present system of feeding may be yet only in its infancy, but the rule seems to be to get the brightest pepper, and to get the birds to eat as much of it as possible; both of which things can be overdone. It has not yet been conclusively proved that the brightest or reddest cayenne produces the best results, or whether the seed or the pod plays the most prominent part in the business—probably each does its share. And as regards obliging the birds to consume the cayenne in excess, that, we think, will ultimately be shown to be un-natural, strictly so, engendering waste and impeding the healthy action of the various organs. It does not follow that because the bird is fond of the capsicum, and eats it greedily, that it can live on it, any more than we ourselves could live and thrive upon mustard, horseradish, and pickles, without a reasonable share of beef. We have seen very poor results obtained from over-feeding, and we have seen most satisfactory ones from the use of barely a tithe of the cayenne wasted in the other case. A judicious use of the food is becoming more common every day, though, unfortunately, the mistaken reticence before referred to makes the progress of knowledge, as gleaned from published experience, very slow. We recommend, to begin with, one chopped egg, with its equal bulk of sweet biscuit, mixed with a heaped-up tea-spoonful of cayenne. The quantity can be increased or lessened as the birds seem to do well on it, and it can be increased almost *ad infinitum* in some instances, as there is no mistake about the birds being fond of it. Give seed very sparingly so long as the birds continue to thrive on the soft food. The experience of a season will do more towards teaching a fancier the actual routine of this part of his business than a volume of instruction. We have explained what we believe to be the principle involved, and it is for the fancier to regulate the heat of his fire as he finds his birds require it.

We note, in the next place, that by a provision of Nature the Canary does not shed its eighteen flight-feathers nor the twelve tail-quills till it is a year old—that is, till its second moult; and it must be evident, therefore, that our moulting-feed can have no effect on these feathers, since they are already quite matured. They are, at any time, the whitest feathers in the bird, having only a faint tinge of colour on the outer edge of the web, occasionally barely perceptible, and when the smaller body-feathers have all been renewed under the most favourable circumstances, these original "nest-feathers" will look to be of a yellowish-green in comparison with the golden glory of the new ones. This difference in colour was not so marked in the olden time; but even then breeders, in their endeavour to make the most of the bird, were accustomed to pull out the flights and tails of their young birds before placing them in their moulting-cages, in order that they might be put on an equality with the rest, and have the opportunity of growing them of a deeper colour. There are many operations performed on animals under subjection to man which, to the superficial observer, savour of cruelty, but which are, really, acts of kindness, rendered necessary by the circumstances in which they are placed. We have not the slightest intention of entering on this question, though our idea of what is included in the notion of subjection is very broad. It comprehends, however, not the vestige of an idea of abuse of power for selfish ends, and we fail to find any justification in our own mind for certain operations which, doubtless originating in abuse, not use, of power without any *necessary* end in view, have come, in the course of time, to be regarded by sensibilities blunted by frequent contact with questionable practices as things not worth a thought. It is just this very want of thought that keeps them alive. We quite recognise the wisdom which, by momentary or, at the most, short-lived pain, can secure permanent immunity from trouble; but we must have an end worthy of the means—not a mere whim or fancy or subservience to a prevailing fashion, but an imperative necessity. We must therefore frankly admit that, although a keen fancier, rigid and exacting in our demands, we cannot conscientiously say we see any necessity to disarrange the provisions of Nature to such an extent as to pull out these thirty-six feathers in a bird's wing to satisfy our eye in the matter of uniformity of colour. We as candidly admit that we have "tailed and flighted" many a score without a thought; but sitting down quietly, as we do now, to supply what we think is an existing want in our Canary literature, and to look at every feature of our subject from as intelligent and philosophical a point as we can, we feel that we should not be true to ourselves if we placed it on record that tailing and flighting, as understood by the Fancy, is a means justified by the end sought. It is with a settled conviction that we pen this, so much so that we scarcely like to advance anything in palliation of the practice lest we should find ourselves fencing with a subject on which our mind is fully made up. But there is just one feature in the case to which we feel bound to refer. The same authority we quoted in giving the definitions of the various feathers says—"The feathers of birds, while they remain perfect and firm in their connection, are really parts of a living animal, and as such they must be regarded as organs of feeling. They do not, probably, in themselves feel pain, but they are in intimate connection with parts which do. The epidermis in no animal appears to feel pain, even in those parts of the animal which are regarded as being more immediately the organs of sensation; but they very speedily transmit impressions to the parts that do feel." A good deal seems to depend, then, on the feathers being "perfect and firm in their connection," and the experience of every breeder will point to the fact that very frequently they are *not* so. The entire nest-tail, for instance, is no sooner fully matured than it requires some care to prevent its being knocked out by the bird fluttering about in its cage, and the occurrence of the tail coming out in the hand when a bird is caught is so frequent as to cause no surprise. This seems to suggest anything but the idea of "firm connection;" and whether it be that from confinement and non-exposure to the effects of a free atmosphere the tail-feathers become prematurely matured, or that the ground in which they are planted is less tenacious than the more muscular covering of the framework of the wing in which the flights are placed, there is no getting away from the fact that the tail is so easily dislodged that, in the case of the two varieties in which the presence of the nest-tail is an indispensable show condition, prudence suggests not only that they should not be handled, but that specially-contrived cages should be furnished them to reduce the probability of an accident to the tail to a minimum. We do not mean to say that the tail is always in this loose state, but when we find it so we believe we cause the bird not the least pain, but do it a positive service, by pulling it all out. We say "pulling" it out, but we might have said, blowing it out; for in such case a puff will scatter it, and it requires more care to keep it in than trouble to pull it out. This, however, does not apply to the wings, in which we find the quill-feathers more securely fixed, as they have a much heavier share of work to perform than the appliance rigged aft, and there is no denying that it *does* take a little jerk to pull *them* out. We cannot tell what is the amount of pain inflicted, but surely there must be some—possibly in some cases less than others—for even flight-feathers are apt to come out in a most provoking way when they are not wanted, as the experience of an hour's washing of dirty birds will confirm. Yet if we take a score of young birds two months old, we don't think there would be a loose wing-feather found in the lot. The pain of extraction may be much, or it may be as imperceptible as that occasioned by pulling out a hair, and the statements of those who talk of quivering flesh and broken bones are met by dispassioned counter-statements that the operation is perfectly safe, and the pain, if any, instantaneous. But the way we wish to put the case is this: we cannot think that the end to be accomplished is such as to demand that it shall be done on the ground of necessity, and as there is a doubt in the case as to the amount of pain inflicted and the extent of its duration, we do not think it right that, practically, it should become imperative on a fancier to do that which he seriously objects to from the highest motives. We do not hold with a spurious sensitiveness which, while it bores the ears of its children, faints at the idea of taking an inch off a lap-dog puppy's tail; but we have no right to pooh-pooh the feeling which says, Show me a necessity and I will comply with it, but I decline to inflict probable pain which is needless. Admitting that the pain is only momentary, and that if the operation be performed skilfully it may be hardly perceptible, and, further, that it may be reduced to almost *nil* by being done at intervals, still we think the position is scarcely tenable on strictly natural grounds, and on that, if on no other, we think the opponents of the practice have the best of the argument, and ought not to be submitted to such an alternative as being virtually driven from the show-field as the penalty for the exercise of faithful devotion to principle. In the case of broken or frayed feathers, however, we think the bird is as much benefited by their removal as inconvenienced by the operation, and all that is necessary is to hold that portion of the wing from which the injured feather springs firmly between the finger and thumb, and then the smarter the twitch, the less will be the pain. A few of the small body-feathers can be pulled out in the same manner, and they are really so small in the quill that the probable pain is not worth a moment's consideration.

The first place on which the new feathers will be observed is on the breast, where a rapid growth takes place, the feathers on the longitudinal strips on either side quickly expanding and covering the whole, giving the breeder a fair opportunity of judging as to the future character of his bird. Very unlikely-looking specimens in the flight-cage may, perhaps, bid fair to become gems. Any such should be removed at once into single cages; indeed, it is this early promise which eventually settles what are to remain to be moulted in company and what are to receive a special preparation; for we have already said that the nest-feathers are not a sure criterion of future merit. The back next begins to throw out its new covering; but the breeder will notice that there is a vast difference in the rate at which the work progresses in different birds. Some seem to go into it with a will, and there is a simultaneous casting of the whole plumage: others are very lazy over it, and, in some cases, the moult is lingering and protracted in a most tedious manner. Our experience has always been that a rapid moult is best in every way, and we believe this opinion is shared by the entire Fancy, not more for the sake of the bird than for the character of the results, which are always more satisfactory. We cannot help the "why?" coming in on the presentation of any natural phenomenon, and we think the "because" which answers it in this case is, that the same amount of vital force which enables the bird to throw off its old feathers enables it to produce its new ones with corresponding vigour; or, inverting the reason, we would say that it is the speedy production of the new growth that displaces the old; and where we find healthy action at work in one direction, it is only natural to infer it is going on in others, and vigorous growth is therefore accompanied by vigorous feather-action of every kind. A lack of ability to produce new feather will, in the same way, be attended by corresponding inability to carry on the other part of the work, and a slow moult, therefore, generally means deficient colour. We may extend this yet a step further, and say that in cases in which birds are late in going into moult, or show signs of not being able to moult at all, it is no cruelty to pull out a considerable portion of the feathers, and by thus compelling a growth do our best to set the machine in motion, in the hope that when once set going it may gather impetus and finish a work it had not the power to begin. The bird *has* to moult or die, and desperate diseases require desperate cures. If we had a bird which, after going so far, seemed to have no power to go farther, leaving the head, the last portion to cast its feathers, unfinished, we should, in the absence of any knowledge how to restore the vital energy, at once pluck the head and remove the obstruction. It is no use to talk of cruelty; it would be cruelty not to do it. It might be a clumsy, mechanical way of getting over the difficulty, but if we did not know how to set the pushing part of the machinery at work from the inside, we should try the pulling plan from the outside.

The importance of keeping up the moulting action will be obvious. Heat is a powerful agent in assisting it, and the gas-stove should be kept in full operation at high pressure. Colds and chills at this time are more than usually fatal in their effects, and additional precautions must be used to ward off their attacks, as the bird is now in a state which renders it very sensitive. As a precautionary measure it is well to cover the front of the cage with a substantial screen, and particularly at nights, when it must be remembered the bird has to sleep with a short allowance of clothes. A covering also serves to keep the new plumage from being soiled by dust or smoke, which will find its way into rooms in towns, despite every effort to exclude it. What may be the chemical effect of light upon the colour we cannot explain, but we have always found our birds do better when covered up than when exposed. Nothing can exceed the spotless beauty of a bird when fresh moulted, before anything can have affected the bloom on its feathers; and for this, if for no other reason, we recommend covering up and perfect quiet, that the bird may literally have nothing to do but to moult. The addition of a blade or two of saffron in the water is considered to have a beneficial effect in assisting the casting of the feathers; indeed, we have known a very strong solution to be used throughout the whole time, but we do not understand its action. We think it quite possible there may be many things of use in facilitating this, as well as of service in assisting the deposition of colour by acting as precipitants. Sugar given in excess is said to act in this way; and in searching for agents of this nature their chemical or physical action is what has to be considered, and this it is which should lead us to something more than a superficial inquiry into the true character of every feature in connection with this page of bird-life.

Some breeders make a point of covering the cage-bottom with chaff or some similar clean material, with the object of raising no dust or dirt of any kind to soil the feathers; but we cannot see the wisdom of depriving the bird of the sand or grit necessary for the trituration of its food. This should, however, be as clean as possible, and as free from earthy matter as it can be had. Where fresh sea-sand can be obtained there is literally no dirt, but other kinds should be washed and dried when extreme care is intended to be exercised.

We spoke of the head as being the last part to cast its feathers. The whole process occupies about a couple of months, and frequently a considerable portion of the whole time is taken up by the head and neck. So long as a single pin-feather is visible protruding through the others, so long is the process going on, and so long must the cayenne food be continued. Even when the bird appears "fine," if it be caught and "blown" it will be seen that there are still an astonishing number of young feathers enveloped in their little sheaths not yet expanded. This formation can be most clearly seen on the head of a crested Canary; and we have known exhibitors open them one by one with a sharp penknife and blow them out on the eve of a show, so as to produce a respectable crest. As the work of reproduction approaches completion, the bird begins to regain its sprightliness, and its appetite, which will have been rather fastidious, will return and demand a supply of substantial food. The more dainty regimen must now be gradually discontinued till the bird is once more on its hard seed; and what cayenne it still has should be given in the form of cake, or, if mixed with soft food, only at longer intervals. The metamorphosis the bird has undergone will be seen to be truly wonderful. Wherever there exists a tiny pigment cell there will the subtle action of the blood have conveyed its complement of colouring matter, while the theory that the leg-scales and other featherless parts are composed of the same material as the feather and are physiologically but cell developments, will receive verification from the evidences they will present of being also receptacles of the pigment matter which, for the last two months, has been playing such an important part in the moult.

Little remains to be said under the head of general management; but the gems of the season should now be transferred to separate cages, because as they continue to freshen and come into song they will turn jealous and pugnacious. The moulting-boxes will be full small for the purpose, but so long as the birds continue to do well in them and do not destroy their plumage, leave well alone, and allow them to remain. There cannot, however, be separate accommodation for every bird, and, after the best have been drafted off, the remainder can go into winter quarters—the cocks, half-a-dozen or more, in roomy flights or in the double breeding-compartments, and the hens in numbers to suit the cage-room at command.

Vincent Brooks Day & Son Lith.

NORWICH CANARIES.

CLEAR YELLOW. (CAYENNE-FED.)

EVENLY-MARKED BUFF. (CAYENNE-FED.)

CLEAR YELLOW. (NATURAL COLOUR.)

[illegible]

[illegible]

[illegible]

CHAPTER XI.

THE NORWICH CANARY.

WE now turn from these details of general management to a description of the different varieties of the Canary and the classes into which they are divided, with specific instructions as to the method of breeding them, and such further remarks on management as may be special in their application. We propose to arrange them in three sections, each based on some distinguishing feature. This, we think, is the most natural course to follow, and we accordingly divide them into (*a*) Colour Birds; (*b*) Distinctive Plumage Birds; (*c*) Shape and Position Birds. At the head of the colour group stands the NORWICH Canary, perhaps the most general favourite of the entire tribe, and certainly the most extensively bred, being the embodiment of the popular idea of the bird, and the fountain from whence spring three-fourths of the drawing-room cage-birds in the country. It is easily recognised as a brilliantly-illuminated edition of the every-day Yellow Canary. It takes its name from the city in which it has for generations been cultivated, and where it doubtless built up for itself a character so decided as to cause it in early times to be recognised as possessing features sufficiently distinctive to identify it with the name of the place in which it had become localised, and as distinguishing it from other varieties already established. It is more than probable that the cultivation of this bird as a speciality began in the latter quarter of the sixteenth century, when the Flemish, driven from their country by the persecutions of the Spanish under the Duke of Alva, took refuge in our "right little, tight little island," indirectly repaying us for the protection afforded them by the impetus they gave to some of our manufactures. A great number of these refugees settled in the county of Norfolk, where they found congenial employment in the woollen manufacturies which had been originally established at Worsted by their kinsmen more than four centuries before, under the fostering care of the first Henry, just in the same way as the silk-weavers, driven from France by the revocation of the Edict of Nantes in 1685, found their way to London, and, by their skill, gave an impulse to our silk trade. Canary-breeding, we know, had by this time spread through a great part of Germany, and was extensively engaged in in the Netherlands; and it is only natural to suppose that the refugees, in escaping with their little all to find a new home, would not leave behind them all their home associations and pleasures, but would carry with them their tastes and likings for natural pursuits, which could not fail to commend themselves to, and spread rapidly among, the population round about them. From that day to this—for the introduction of steam-power into many of our manufactures is only comparatively an event of the day before yesterday—the nature of the occupation and the character of the inhabitants has changed but little; and though the iron horse now waits at the pit's mouth, ready to run his heavy load across streams bridged for his convenience, over valleys filled up to make him a highway, and through hills levelled or pierced to remove every obstruction from his path on the iron road, and deposits it by thousands of tons where the noise of machinery, replete with life and giant power, has displaced the modest loom and the music of the shuttle, still in many a rose-covered cottage by the road-side may still be heard the quiet click, click, of the primitive machine, which yet has a poetry of its own, and in which some most exquisite textile fabrics are still woven by delicate fingers that know no other handicraft. It is not to be wondered at that such sedentary employment, carried on, too, under the domestic roof, should have a tendency to induce a love of quiet home-pleasures; and it is under such favourable auspices as these that the Norwich Canary has for so many years been nurtured, till its fame has spread far and wide, and other towns vie with the old cathedral city in producing the most perfect specimens.

In size the bird is about that of a—Canary! We never measured one, nor did we ever have any tangible idea conveyed to our mind by any figures indicating such measurements. We do not mean that if we read that such and such a bird measures a foot in length from the tip of his beak to the tip of his tail we do not know the difference between that and six inches, but a description we quote—"the Canary is about the size of a linnet, being five inches in length; of which the tail measures two and a quarter; the beak is five lines in length . . . the legs . . . eight lines high"—though it may be strictly correct, conveys no more appreciable idea to us than if we were told it was a medium-sized bird, rather smaller than a sparrow, or about the stamp of the generality of Canaries we see in song-cages. We find it difficult to confine ourselves to any set formula or conventional mode of description. It is a plump, chubby bird, as opposed to length and slimness; stoutly built, and of bold carriage; quick and active in its movements, and lusty in its song, and, when at rest, stands at an angle of about forty degrees, measured from a base line drawn from the tip of the tail. The head should be broad across the skull, and inclined to be flat rather than high and round. A bird with a small, narrow head shows to poor advantage and has a peculiar expression when facing you, giving one the idea of being out of drawing. The richest colour, too, is found on the crown, and the larger the surface, the better the effect. No idea of coarseness should attach to it, but neatness and elegance and delicate feathering should be its characteristics; coarse feathering and overhanging eyebrows indicate a cross in the direction of size, not bred out. The eye is dark, full, bright, and sparkling; the beak a clear pinkish-white, and free from discoloration, though the whole or half of the upper mandible is sometimes dark. This is no disqualification, but *cæteris paribus*, the clear beak would win. We are speaking now of the "Clear" bird, which is one in which the whole of the feathers are entirely free from any dark marks whatever. The discoloured mandible is indicative of hidden marking somewhere or other, which should be searched for, for reasons which will presently be explained. The neck is inclined to be short, the under part forming, in profile, a perfect line of beauty with the breast, which should be broad and full, and feathered as smoothly as it is possible to conceive. Any departure from either of these properties is a defect of some moment. The back is broad, and rises very slightly immediately after the junction with the neck, forming a very delicate curve, and must show most compact feathering without the slightest disposition to open in the middle, which is not an uncommon feature in some varieties. Between the shoulders it is slightly convexed. Look at the bird which way you will, its outlines present a series of subtle curves of singular beauty—a feature common to all birds, in fact, the presence of a hard line being nowhere to be found. The wings must be carried firmly closed, without a symptom of drooping, and tucked in close to the body, the flights matching feather for feather on the back, the primaries meeting in a point over the rump-feathers without overlapping each other. The closer the flights are packed, the better will the colour of the wing show itself, as only the extreme outer edge of each feather is tinged, and close lamination is necessary to maintain the continuity. The same holds good with the arrangement of the larger coverts and the small feathers of the bastard wing, any slovenliness here interfering most materially with the compact appearance indispensable for the uniform distribution of colour throughout the entire member. The shoulders should be well covered by the scapular-feathers and show no projection of any kind, the feathering throughout the whole of this part being of the closest possible character, compactness and perfect imbrication being the most necessary conditions for the exhibition of colour. The rump-feathers are the finest and most silky in quality in the entire bird, and as they merge in the upper tail-coverts become longer and narrower, the greater portion of their length being clothed with snowy white flossy under-flue. Any coarseness here, or in the vent-feathers and under tail-coverts, is a blemish interfering with the gradual tapering which constitutes what is known in the Fancy as a neat "waist," and is one of the properties it is necessary to breed out of any cross which may have been made with a view to obtain size, which it usually accompanies. It is the presence or absence of this coarseness and want of general compactness which indicates the possession or lack of "quality"—a term almost undefinable, and applied to individual parts or to a balance of good properties considered as a whole. The shape of the individual tail-feathers—*i.e.*, narrow at their base and slightly increasing in width in the direction of their length, the outer ones being the longest, and each of the six on either side gradually decreasing in length—will, of itself, determine the correct shape of the tail, which cannot better be described than by comparing it with a closed fan, narrow at the junction with the body, and slightly, but very slightly, radiating, the lengths and arrangement of the feathers causing a V-shaped indentation at the extremity. Here, as in the wing, carriage is everything, the closed fan showing the gilt edges as one feather but when partially spread spoiling the effect.

The only remaining parts of the body covered with feather growth are the thighs, which should be well covered with silky flue right down to the hocks. The legs, which Nature generally makes of a proportionate length, should be free from malformation or defects of any kind, even to the toes and claws. It is scarcely necessary to mention a matter of this kind; and the points, as described in several printed standards, "toes and nails entire and not twisted awry," always seem to us like superfluous definitions. Malformations are malformations wherever we find them, and it seems absurd to point them out as things not to be desired in a perfect specimen.

In summing up the whole under the head of general appearance, we should say the Norwich Canary is a jolly, comfortable sort of bird, rather than one of the extreme graceful school, and that the hens are inclined to *embonpoint* rather than belonging to the family of *Sylphidæ*. It is not a large bird, though size has its value when combined with colour and quality displayed in excess—a combination very rare. Size has its proper value in every variety, but where it is not *the* property it has had to give way before the particular feature sought; and where that feature is found to develop itself prominently in any specimens, they are sure to be selected for future breeding operations, whatever other minor properties, even though they may be desirable ones, are absent; and hence size has, no doubt, been over and over again relinquished in favour of the two *sine qua non* properties mentioned above. It is a fact that the gems of the variety are almost invariably of a medium size, and there seems to be a point beyond which it appears impossible to go in attempting to unite the three. Still, some breeders have made strenuous efforts to do so, though with only partial success, and have only desisted when they found that their birds, though grand and imposing, were palpably deficient in the more valuable points. Other things being equal, the larger of two birds wins; but in the struggle for size, it is evident the chances of other things being *un*-equal are greatly increased. This view of the question will hardly admit of the supposition that size is a property which has been lost and might be regained, since it rather goes to show that the extreme development of colour and quality of feather have only been brought about by a compulsory relinquishing of size, which experience has shown to be incompatible with their existence. If it could be found co-existent with them, it would be of great value; but where it is evident it has been imported at the expense of leading features, it is altogether ignored.

In these general remarks on conformation we have been obliged to mix up the question of feather to some extent, but it must have a place to itself, as forming one of the most important features in this variety. The texture of the material cannot be too fine and silky, nor can the feathers be too short and compact. Nothing can atone for coarseness, for which there is no excuse in the eyes of a Norwich breeder. We say "nothing," for not even colour itself can compensate for a marked deficiency in close, soft feathering. Notwithstanding colour is the first thing looked for, and is supposed to be the beginning and the end of the bird, "all over, underneath, in the middle, outside, overhead, on top, on all sides, and at both ends," it cannot stand unsupported on the show-bench, but must have feather to sustain it. No true fancier of the variety but would accept an average display of colour combined with high quality, in preference to simply excess of colour without it, or with only a moderate share of it. When the two are presented in this way, it is not easy to arrive at a correct estimate of their combined values by the application of a numerical scale, because the sum of the two values is really increased by an indeterminate number representing the effect of the combination. For instance, supposing two birds to score 20 and 30 points respectively under the head of colour, and 20 and 10 respectively for quality of feather; then the value of the first would appear to be $20 + 20 = 40$, and that of the second, $30 + 10 = 40$; but in reality the value of the first would be 40 + an indefinite number expressing the value of the effect of such a balance of power, and that of the second, 40 − a discount for loss of effect occasioned by such disparity in the proportions of the combining parts, assuming, of course, the relative stand and values of the two properties to be equal.

We have left the property of colour to the last, because a great deal is involved in it, and before proceeding to treat of it in detail it will be sufficient here to say that the principal characteristic of the bird is the capacity it has to develop colour, as will have been gathered from what has been previously advanced. A long-continued application of the principles of selection has doubtless fixed this feature. The ultimate colour of all "clear" Canaries is what is generally understood by the word "yellow." But there are many shades of this colour, and it ranges from pale lemon to the deep hue of a Seville orange. Well then, the Norwich bird is the Seville orange among a basket of lemons—the difference in colour is quite as decided; and if a further illustration be necessary, we think we could not make a happier comparison than by reference to the difference between the rich chrome of the dark African Marigold and the pale lemon-coloured flower of the same variety. We have endeavoured to describe its shape and its feather, and these two illustrations will serve to give a general idea of its colour, which is measured for depth and purity. The idea, however, is but general, and we will now go into details.

The entire Canary family is divided into two colour-classes, Yellow and Buff, which are synonymous with the terms Jonque and Mealy; but inasmuch as these terms do not express the real colour, they must be regarded as purely technical. For example, we speak of a Yellow Green or a Buff Green, a Yellow Cinnamon or a Buff Cinnamon, when it is patent neither of these colours can be yellow or buff in reality; and the words, therefore, taken in their general application, are technicalities. The explanation is simple. Whatever be the body-colour of a Canary, whether it be literally yellow, or green, or cinnamon; or whether it be in a Lizard, or even a dark Self-coloured Canary hybrid, it has two forms in which it manifests itself. One is bright and, for want of a better word, we will say luminous, polished and glittering; the other, dull and flat, and is by comparison what frosted silver or dead gold is to the burnished metal. The first is the yellow form, and the other the buff; and one or the other presents itself in every Canary or Canary hybrid. In speaking of the Norwich Canary, the terms Jonque and Mealy are generally adopted, and are both expressive of the general character indicated. The word Jonque is originally pure

French, and may be taken to signify jonquil-coloured, which speaks for itself; Mealy requires no comment.

Having thus cleared the way, we will endeavour to show how the Clear Jonque Norwich Canary to which we have alluded has been produced, and, from our investigation of the subject, deduce the laws which govern the recognised system of classification and the nomenclature adopted with regard to it. We remark, in the first place, that the fountain of colour in the entire variety is the original green. And this word "green" requires some explanation, for after all it may turn out not to be green. That it is a form of green we think is admitted on all hands; and the fact that the corresponding type in some other varieties is green, pure and simple, seems to support the idea. The one green, however, does not eventually resolve itself into the same form of yellow as the other: from the pure green we get lemon-yellow, and from the Norwich green we get jonque, or orange. The foundation colour of our bird is of a rich bronzy tone, so much so that whenever a bird of this type comes into competition with a pure green in a *bonâ fide* Green class it is invariably passed over as *not* being green. Then what is it? It has always seemed to us to be no inapt comparison when we say it resembles a piece of gamboge, or some of the deep yellows in an artist's colour-box. Outwardly it shows but little indication of the delicate tints lurking within, but can be diluted and toned down to almost any shade. So with our bird: we have every gradation of tint, from the semi-opaque bronzy specimen down to pure jonque, which we can further tone down to a pale straw; and in the so-called pure green, which we have admitted to be so as much for the sake of argument and illustration as anything, we find the same diluting process possible, with this difference, that it ends in a lemon-yellow with a decided green tinge, capable again of being toned down to a greenish-white.

These Self-coloured Norwich Greens (we will adhere to the name) having a disposition to break or sport, advantage is taken of this, and it is cultivated to its ultimate issue. The first step in the direction of albinism gives us the "Heavily Variegated" class, as it is called in show language, or the "Broken Greens" of the breeding-room, and is generally understood to include those birds which, although showing a fair amount of light colour, still carry a preponderance of the original green in irregular blotches or patches, one condition being usually insisted on—viz., that the bird shall not have a clean breast, in which case it is said to be "Lightly Variegated." These distinctions are not recognised by some schools of breeders, but they are important as indicating two separate and distinct bars of the colour-ladder. In public shows they are seldom or ever acknowledged, but are united under the comprehensive term "Variegated;" but in clubs where the members understand their business and have an annual exhibition among the members for the purpose of comparing notes, it is usual to keep every link in the colour-chain separate. A Lightly Variegated bird, in addition to a clean breast, must still be more or less marked on the back or neck, either or both, independently of carrying the green on the wings—a feature common to both classes; in short, it must have "foul" or body-marks. From this brief outline it will be seen that the difference between "Heavily" and "Lightly" variegated is entirely a question of degree, the conditions being the existence of body-marks, and the dividing line the presence or absence of a clean breast. The most advanced form of light variegation is when the entire bird, including wings and tail, is perfectly clean with the exception of a few dark feathers interspersed here and there, or in the form of a grizzly patch on the head, neck, or back; such feathers usually being not dark from the quill to the end of the web, but grey or grizzly, showing a tendency to an entire fading out of the native green. These are known as "Ticked" birds.

One feature in connection with the Variegated birds, and more particularly the Heavily Variegated portion, must be noticed as bearing on our gradation of colour theory, and showing that the Jonque really seems to be one form of what we have designated Green. It is the fact that in some parts of the bird the gradation is so delicate that the edge of the green merges in that of the jonque, and it cannot be discerned where the one leaves off and the other begins. This is most noticeable in the region of the "waist," among the soft, silky feathers of the sides and vent, where some of the richest combinations of hues are to be found. We do not yet know what is the precise character of the pigment matter in the cells of the feather formation, but we must observe, as having much to do with the colour question generally, that the Greens are the strongest as regards colour, and have the greatest power of developing or depositing it—a physiological property that breeders are not slow to acknowledge and avail themselves of, by having frequent recourse to the Green as a source from whence to derive fresh vigour and colour-producing power. The first remove from the green always produces the strongest jonque wherever the jonque shows itself; and so it is throughout the whole scale—so long as there is the vestige of a green feather, or even the dark under-flue attaching to it, it is the evidence of a colour-producing power the Clear bird has not. Remember that the direction in which the breeder travels is *from* dark *to* light, and a clear bird once produced is the culminating point. Continue the diluting process, and colour recedes; and we must go to our colour-box for a fresh supply. This is the enunciation of a recognised principle in breeding to which we shall hereafter refer.

We resume our classification, and remark that the introduction and maintaining of the Green element have produced Pied birds, and this immediately opens up a field for the fancier, in the form of a desire to fix this Pied character in certain directions and render it permanent—a task of great difficulty. It is easy to account for this if we regard the Pied or Variegated bird as being in a transition state, somewhere on its journey from a dark self-colour, with feathers dark in stalk, flue, and web, towards the *ultima thule* of the fancier—the Clear bird, with spotless feather and snowy white under-flue. Any exactness or regularity of marking which may appear can, therefore, only be regarded as a fleeting beauty, difficult to arrest and invest with the character of perpetuity. It is by no means an hereditary quality, and the aphorism "Like produces like" is here applicable only to a very limited extent. Well-marked birds are so exceptional that the element of chance should enter largely into the theories for producing them; and we think that nothing shows the utter fallaciousness of such theories so much as the fact that the end to which they profess to open out a royal road is not reached by travelling in it. There is a class of men, however, who are always doing wonders. Breeding birds marked feather for feather with mathematical exactness is child's play to them; only the disappointing part of the business is that the world never sees them—they invariably *die in the nest.*.

What constitutes a "Marked" bird, and what is the difference between it and a "Variegated" bird? It is manifest that any Pied Canary is Variegated, and therefore what is known as a "Marked" bird is as much a Variegated bird as any other. The literal meaning must, it is evident, be discarded at once, and the terms regarded as technicalities, viewed in which light the matter is simple enough. There are certain places on the body of a bird in which the original dark colour seems to love to linger. In some places we often wish it would *not* stay, and vexing is the pertinacity with which it maintains its hold. But the last resting-place seems to be on the eyes, the wings, and each side of the tail. These marks most frequently appear in company with many others, but they are *there;* and as the objectionable patches or blotches disappear, either by careful breeding or in obedience to chance, the eye, wing, and tail marks remain. These, and *these only*, are technically *marks*, and a bird is two, four, or six-marked, according as he possesses each or every pair. Such a bird is a "Marked" bird proper, and any bird which is marked in any *other* place than those indicated is a "Variegated" bird, even though it possess, in addition to its splashes and blotches, any or all of the marks the locality of which we have described, and which are the acknowledged standard "marks" recognised as such by the Fancy. A mark on the top of the head, however regular in its formation, or on the back (and some saddles are most exquisite in shape and characteristic pencilling of each individual feather), is not a "mark" proper; and hence it may be accepted as an axiom that a "Marked" bird must have a clean run, over and under, from the beak to the tail. And since dark feathers on each side of the tail constitute "marks," and further, since there are twelve feathers in the tail, it might be demonstrated from these premises that an entirely dark tail is a "marked" tail. But, if admitted, it would be of no value, because such marking is invariably accompanied by so much of a detractive character that the value of the whole would be subtractive instead of positive; indeed, it is by common consent tacitly agreed that a dark tail constitutes "variegation," and not "marking," because the absence of light feathers in the middle destroys the idea of a clean run from stem to stern, with the marking on each side. When the clean run is obstructed, above or below, the marking ceases and becomes variegation, and this criterion applies as much to the head as to the tail.

It will be plain that "marking" is a question of *locality*, and that there are but six places in which marks can possibly exist: elsewhere they are not marks. The perfection of marking consists in evenness and exactness—two separate and distinct things, though the latter idea is included in the former. Nothing is more common than to hear that a certain bird is not evenly marked, because one wing or one eye mark is heavier than the other; but if it be marked on *each* wing or *each* eye, it is evenly marked, although the marking may be so irregular and badly balanced as to lay but small claim to be called exact. To be exact, the marks should correspond in shape and feather, one side of the bird being the counterpart of the other. It may seem unnecessary to have to explain this, but, simple as the thing is, a misapprehension as to the meaning of the terms gives rise to more misunderstanding than almost anything in connection with Canary-showing. Uneven marking should define itself; but that there may be no mistake, we say that a bird with only one eye or one wing or one side of the tail marked, is unevenly marked; or, to put the definition in a concise form, any one of the three marks not being repeated on the other side constitutes the bird unevenly marked. Such birds are not technically "Variegated," because there is the absence of the necessary body-marks; but inasmuch as they cannot win in a class in which the desideratum is evenness, they are allowed to be shown in the "Variegated" class by sinking the technical character of their markings and considering them as of no value, and thus allowing them to compete with the irregularly-pied birds, whose variegations also are of no value, on the common ground of colour, quality, condition, and all other good properties except marking. This grouping, though sometimes convenient, is not defensible on any other ground except convenience, not always the safest foundation on which to build; and a very little inquiry into the character of the special feature of each of these two classes will show the truth of our position. The birds are representatives of different classes, to begin with, and have been bred with different objects in view. The one must be considered as approximating closely to that standard of excellence which consists in the entire absence of body-marks and the retention of those representing evenness and exactness, to retain and fix which has been *the* aim of all others, in the prosecution of which the production of colour has had to give way, as being only secondary. The other represents a class in which marking or variegation of any kind is valueless, as such, and only exists as evidence of an admixture of the native green element essential to the development of colour. The result of mixing up these unlike things in one competition is that the Unevenly-marked bird has no chance of winning on a colour basis in what is essentially a colour class—a thing which ought not to be; while if it should happen to win by sheer force of sympathy, on account of its being so nearly but not quite perfect, then an injustice is done to the Variegated birds, to whom such approach to perfection of marking is of no value whatever. It may be *convenient*, as we said, to adopt such a system of grouping, and, considering the comprehensive character of the class, to give and take a little on both sides; but in investigating the principles of correct classification we must have something more definite than convenience to guide us.

We do not suppose that a minutely ramified arrangement could generally be adopted under ordinary circumstances, but we wish to exhibit the true principle of classification, so that it may be extended or contracted in the right direction. And with respect to these Unevenly-marked birds, our contention is, that inasmuch as the breeder has aimed at getting "marks" at all hazards—with colour, if possible, but without it rather than lose the marking—it naturally follows that it is not in this section that we must look for the richest colour; and it is, therefore, hard for these birds to be called upon to sacrifice what they have gained at great trouble, and be measured by a property their opponents have been bred for alone and possess in excess. The simplest way would be to give them a place by themselves, or, in the event of such an extension being considered impracticable, to group them with the Evenly-marked birds in one section under the comprehensive name "Marked." They would then, at least, have the opportunity of competing on the merits of their distinctive feature. There naturally arises the question, Would you then give a prize to an *un*-evenly marked bird over an *evenly*-marked one? It would depend entirely on the quality of the marking. There is a description of marking to which we shall presently allude, which is next to worthless. We will assume we have before us a class of "Marked" birds, which will, therefore, contain Marked birds only, but marked in every degree of evenness and exactness, as well as all degrees of unevenness. The *best*-marked would then win; and we put the case of an unevenly-marked specimen being found among them to inquire into his chances. Given a bird with exact wings and one beautifully-pencilled eye, and another with two respectable wings, one good eye, and, on the other side of the head, a mere blotch, which happens to include the eye; given, also, that the first is superior in colour and quality, in our opinion it is the better bird, and should win. In all shows the percentage of really exquisitely-marked birds is small, and among the so-called Evenly-marked ones are always to be found many which it requires a great exercise of charity to recognise as such. They may just come within the pale of the law, and, being there, claim the rights and privileges of citizens of the district. But they are worthless members of society; even the very qualities upon which they base their claim to notice are of negative value; there is an absence of good breeding about them, and all they can do is to flaunt their credentials in the face of birds which, slightly defective, are yet in other respects superior, and which, after allowing a liberal discount for the defect (*blemish* there is none), could, in our way of thinking, win easily.

Before going on to say in what consists good marking, we must draw attention to the thighs of the bird. The covering here is so scant that no decided character can be given to any marking existing there. When it is present it is generally in the form of dark flue which shows itself upon any movement of the bird. It always has a negative rather than a positive value, and more frequently turns the scale against a competing specimen than places any points to its credit. The presence of dark feathers in the tail also is frequently accompanied by more or less of dark colour in the rump-feathers; this is not considered as a body-mark, and a consequent disqualification in a "Marked" class, but simply counts against the bird according to its extent.

The mark most difficult to obtain good is that on the eye, where it only too frequently assumes the character of a mere blotch or patch. There is a wide difference between a clumsy patch which happens to enclose the eye within its limits, and the delicately-pencilled spectacle-mark which gives such a distinctive style to the head of an Evenly-marked Canary. Sometimes a mark is found immediately in front of the eye, extending no farther. When this is the case it is, in the majority of instances, clear and decided, though only small; but such a mark is, in our estimation, of infinitely greater value than one of the blotch type. Sometimes the front of the eye is clear, and the marking runs off from behind it; this is also a good mark when clear and decided. But the perfection of marking should commence in the front of the eye, and passing above and beneath with a clearly-defined edge, continue its course in the same curve as the outline of the head, and run away to a point. This gives us a short rounded mark in the front and a long pointed one behind. Such pencilling can occasionally be met with as perfect as if put on with a brush; but the general form is by no means so regular, and perfection is so rare that any decent approach to it is valuable. There should be no break in it, and no disposition to enlarge into a cheek-mark, any tendency in that direction detracting much from its merit. Neither should it reach so far above the eye as to threaten the crown; but whatever the character of the mark, clear outline is absolutely imperative. We do not object to a heavy mark, if it be only decided and have no tendency to the posterior enlargement we have referred to as constituting a cheek-mark. Equally objectionable is anterior enlargement; which, when it reaches the beak and begins to creep up the skull, ceases to be a "mark." It sometimes happens also that the mark runs round in the direction of the back of the skull; this also is objectionable, and of little worth.

The wing-marking should be confined to the flights, and there is no fixed limit to the number constituting a show-wing; it is all a matter of taste, and the value of an exact wing is too great to afford room for disputing as to the extent of the marking. Some fanciers like the entire half of the wing dark; but we think seven feathers the extreme limit for beauty, and *prefer* only four, especially in a Jonque. We need scarcely say they must be the inner feathers and must form a perfect V, the point of each feather meeting its fellow, and the lighter brownish colour of the outside edge matching exactly with the corresponding bar on either wing. Slovenly carriage is fatal to a telling display, and the heavier the marking, the worse such carriage makes it look. Though we say the dark feathers should be confined to the flights, many wings we have taken notes of have had the corresponding coverts dark also; indeed, it is sometimes astonishing, on expanding a wing for the purpose of counting the feathers, to find how large a portion of it is dark. But this is not of so much importance except in close competition, in which the nearest approach to exactness must win, other points being equal. The worst blemishes are the presence of occasional light feathers among the dark ones, and the opposite; and also an obstinate very black feather, which sometimes grows in the most provoking way among the bastard quills. Dark feathers will also frequently appear among the smaller coverts, the first row often being wholly dark, and though these are hidden by the scapulars when the bird is at rest, they show themselves when the wing is raised, and the bird is said to have black "butts."

A dark feather on either side of the tail is an addition to the markings, but a questionable advantage to a Norwich bird, because it is so frequently accompanied by dark flue at the base that what is gained one way is lost another. A bird with a marked tail and clear flue would beat one with a clear tail; but the difficulty is to get the gain without its equivalent loss. And when, in addition to this, we consider that the dark tail-feather is scarcely visible unless the bird be examined for it, so much so that its existence is not unfrequently overlooked and would sometimes not even be suspected but for the tell-tale dark flue, its value as a show point cannot be much. The most that is seen of it at any time is the extreme outside edge, and unless there be a sufficient number on each side to give a decided character to the marking, we look upon it as worthless.

The highest point of development attainable by the Norwich Canary is the "Clear" bird, which, as its name implies, should present a uniform clear colour throughout. Not the slightest tinge should be observable in a single feather, nor should the under-flue of its spotless golden plumage show any trace of its native black. This is not insisted on by all breeders, but the possession of dark colour *anywhere* is here a most dangerous property, since it is seldom entirely confined to those places where it is entirely hidden, but is apt to develop itself in certain feathers, which, though they do not take a more substantial form than mere down, are very liable to carry at their extremities the colour of the dark under-flue, the slightest indications of which, in a severe competition, would disqualify a bird. The most usual place in which it crops up to the surface is on the downy covering of the thighs, which are sometimes "smoky," and sometimes of a brown or bronzy colour, indicative of the fact that the native green still lurks within, and is doing the work of depositing colour in a way the absolutely Clear bird cannot. The question as to what *is* a Clear bird is generally answered by the definition, One which *shows* no green; and it is probable that it will remain there, in the face of certain difficulties in carrying it any farther. But we think the definition is open to objection, and serious objection too. We have shown how the native green is the fountain of colour, and how it has the capacity for developing it; and the object in breeding from dark to clear is to maintain that capacity to as full an extent as possible, and, at the same time, eradicate all trace of the original colour. We have also said that so long as there is a vestige of a green feather remaining, the colour-work goes on with greater energy; and it is only fair to consider whether the presence of dark under-flue in any quantity is not indicative of a considerable amount of the green element still at work, and whether such a bird really has bid good-bye to the green, and is perfectly clear. We do not desire to take a one-sided view of the question, and are quite prepared for the inquiry, If a bird *shows no green*, where else can it be put, except among the Clears, or the externally clear, since every other bird *does* show it? But the plan of combating objections by asking questions is generally open to being itself met in the same way; and we would reply by asking, If birds with dark under-flue are stronger colour-producers by virtue of that taint, are not the absolutely clear practically as much at a disadvantage in being brought into competition with them, as they would be if made to enter the lists with the *bonâ fide* Ticked birds, which are considered the first remove from Clear, and have one leg already inside the door? Difficulties always commence when we hesitate about drawing a clearly-defined boundary-line. When we have marked out our ground, we have nothing to do but to drive in our stakes and go ahead with our fence on the line; but if we begin to diverge here and there to include something without our circle, we at once lay the foundation of trouble. Now, it is not the breeding up to almost but not quite clear that is difficult, but it is the putting the finishing touches to the work and turning out perfection, without a taint of imperfection, that shows the master-workman; and we have seen really clear gems, clear throughout, with snowy-white silky flue, that it would be a sin to put into competition with birds blowing black all over. And here we draw our line, and define "Clear" to mean not having the remotest tinge of dark colour in quill, flue, or feather; birds from which every trace of the green has been eliminated; which have a clear, silky, snowy-white under-flue, and show by it that they have arrived at the goal. There is not a fancier who has ever exhibited a high-class *bonâ fide* Clear of his own breeding that would not object to be beaten by a bird with dark flue; and doing as you would be done by is not a bad plan to follow, even in digesting a simple question in Canary classification.

We have no desire to turn the dark-flue birds out of their companionship with the Clears

NORWICH CANARIES.

VARIEGATED YELLOW. CLEAR BUFF.

frequently only the delicate flue of the silky, downy covering of the thighs that is dark; and so long as the thighs remain in good repair, and the bird sits still, the discoloration is not perceptible without looking twice at it. But the bird flies up against the wires and uncovers his thighs, and then it is plain enough: the colour is *there*, and the bird owes his deep jonque to it, and is *not* clear, and his grizzled thighs are as much ticked as is the head or neck of the bird in the next class, which may blow almost perfectly clear, and have not more than half-a-dozen grey feathers in it. Birds of this kind are all on an equality: they are in one and the same stage in the march towards *freedom from the trace of green*, which, so long as they have it, groups them in one class. Our arrangement of the whole in order of colour-gradation is—first, Green; second, Variegated; third, Clear. Subdividing them further for the purpose of more detailed classification, and arranging them again in complete order, we have—(*a*) Green, (*b*) Heavily Variegated, (*c*) Lightly Variegated, (*d*) Evenly-marked, (*e*) Unevenly-marked, (*f*) Ticked, (*g*) Clear. This is the extreme extension, and includes every form. The classes which may be called on a common footing are (*b*) and (*c*), which contain practically the same [illegible] in the amount of variegation. Classes (*d*) and (*e*) can [illegible] shown. It is also usual to group (*b*), (*c*), and (*f*) into one, [illegible]; but we have endeavoured to show that there is a closer affinity between (*f*) and (*g*) than between any other, and that (*f*) should [illegible] on the top bar but one.

We supplement these notes on classification based on the natural gradations in colour, by a few remarks on the difference between the Jonque and Mealy bird. We think there is no occasion to say further of the Jonque other than that it is of a pure bright hue, with all the colour on the surface, like an exquisite orange satin. The Mealy bird is of the same hue, but the colour does not appear to glisten on the surface; it is still a ruddy orange satin, and sometimes ruddier even than the Jonque, but the satin is covered with a delicate white gossamer veil by which its gloss is clouded, though rendered, if possible, more beautiful by the veil thrown over it. The colour is softened in places where the lace covering seems to lie in thicker folds, but a movement of the bird brings a fresh gleam of light to play on its beautiful dress, and from under the silvery cloud shines out the golden yellow. The word "Mealy" is very expressive of the appearance of the bird, though the idea is not very poetical: we have seen Norwich Canaries which appeared almost as if the white bloom on them would come off in the hand like that of some

without finding a place for them, and we submit that their proper place is in the *bonâ fide* "Ticked" division, which we define to mean *not* lightly "variegated," in the sense in which we have explained the latter, but simply as having grey or grizzled feathers or dark flue. Nineteen out of every twenty of them *are* ticked, for a "smoky" thigh and dark flue are first cousins. It is frequently only the delicate flue of the silky, downy covering of the thighs that is dark; and so long as the thighs remain in good repair, and the bird sits still, the discoloration is not perceptible without looking twice at it. But the bird flies up against the wires and uncovers his thighs, and then it is plain enough: the colour is *there*, and the bird owes his deep jonque to it, and is *not* clear, and his grizzled thighs are as much ticked as is the head or neck of the bird in the next class, which may blow almost perfectly clear, and have not more than half-a-dozen grey feathers in it. Birds of this kind are all on an equality: they are in one and the same stage in the march towards *freedom from the trace of green*, which, so long as they have it, groups them in one class. Our arrangement of the whole in order of colour-gradation is—first, Green; second, Variegated; third, Clear. Subdividing them further for the purpose of more detailed classification, and arranging them again in complete order, we have—(*a*) Green, (*b*) Heavily Variegated, (*c*) Lightly Variegated, (*d*) Evenly-marked, (*e*) Unevenly-marked, (*f*) Ticked, (*g*) Clear. This is the extreme extension, and includes every form. The classes which may be united on a common footing are (*b*) and (*c*), which contain practically the same birds, differing only in the amount of variegation. Classes (*d*) and (*e*) can also be united under the inclusive term "Marked," as we have shown. It is also usual to group (*b*), (*c*), and (*f*) into one, as representing more or less variegation; but we have endeavoured to show that there is a closer affinity between (*f*) and (*g*) than between any other, and that (*f*) should be used as an adjunct to (*g*) for the reception of birds perched on the top bar but one.

We supplement these notes on classification based on the natural gradations in colour, by a few remarks on the difference between the Jonque and Mealy bird. We think there is no occasion to say further of the Jonque other than that it is of a pure bright hue, with all the colour on the surface, like an exquisite orange satin. The Mealy bird is of the same hue, but the colour does not appear to glisten on the surface; it is still a ruddy orange satin, and sometimes ruddier even than the Jonque, but the satin is covered with a delicate white gossamer veil by which its gloss is clouded, though rendered, if possible, more beautiful by the veil thrown over it. The colour is softened in places where the lace covering seems to lie in thicker folds, but a movement of the bird brings a fresh gleam of light to play on its beautiful dress, and from under the silvery cloud shines out the golden yellow. The word "Mealy" is very expressive of the appearance of the bird, though the idea is not very poetical: we have seen Norwich Canaries which appeared almost as if the white bloom on them would come off in the hand like that of some fruits. This silvery frosting is occasioned by the extreme edge of the feathers being fringed with a margin of white, and the effect produced is greater or less as it is presented in places where the growth is dense or otherwise. The feathering on the Buff birds is much denser than in the Jonques, the under-flue being very thick and long, as the fancier will be able to observe when he makes his first essay in washing. Altogether the Buff bird is built on a larger and stouter scale, and is in every respect the more lusty bird of the two. Every fancier has his own particular liking, and ours is for the perfection of development in a Mealy bird.

Such is the Norwich Canary, of which we have endeavoured to furnish as complete a description as possible. Before entering on the question of how to breed them we will devote the next chapter to a description of an offshoot from this variety, which, during the last few years, has become almost as popular as the parent stock.

CHAPTER XII.

THE CRESTED NORWICH.

THE "Crested" Norwich takes its name from the topping or crest which adorns its head. The name by which it was known in olden times, and is still sometimes called, even in the city of Norwich itself, is the "Turncrown," but the word is now nearly exploded. It was originally used to denote any kind of crested Canary, and not the Norwich variety in particular; for the turncrown, topping, or crest is a feature of old date, and is common enough among the German song-birds. It is a most striking feature, which, when well developed, cannot fail to impress with its imposing appearance, and is just one of those things we should naturally expect would catch the eye of a fancier when in, perhaps, but an imperfect form, and on which he would expend some pains to build it up to his ideal standard; and we might search far for a better illustration of the fancier's work, as distinct from that of the naturalist. The crest, once permanently fixed and decided in its character, would soon attract attention and be transplanted or grafted into more than one variety, prominent among which stands the Norwich, on which it has been so carefully worked, and so long cultivated, as to have become an established, recognised variety. We also find the crest existing elsewhere under its old name of "Coppy;" and though of late years communication between remote places has opened up fresh fields for the breeder and induced an influx of foreign blood into different varieties for one purpose or another, and the Coppy has travelled from Manchester to Norwich, we do not in any way regard it as the plant from which the original scions were taken; for both it and the Norwich Turncrown must have flourished coincidently for a long period while the existence of each was scarcely known to the other. The bird of the present day is more of a made-up type than the old Norwich Turncrown, which is seldom seen now. It is not so very many years ago since some very beautiful crested birds used to be bred in the old city, and though they did not show a great deal of colour, still they were essentially true to the type in shape and feather. It is this absence of colour that may have led to the supposition that these old Turncrowns were of inferior blood, or were some common strain, which, rejoicing in a good crest, was used as a means of producing crest-formation among the higher class of birds; but it is more than probable that the old crest-breeders were obliged to relinquish colour in following up good strains, and that although there frequently is such a disparity between the colour of the Plain-headed and the Crested strains, they may, after all, be not so distantly related as we have imagined, and the crest or turncrown may have been a native feature.

Of late years a great effort has been made to improve the style of these birds by importing good crest from any and every available source, the object being, after having bred *in* the crest, to breed *out* all those points in which the offspring differ from the high-bred Norwich stem upon which the crest is grafted; and in doing this considerable judgment and care are required to ensure success. A really high-class specimen—*i.e.*, one showing high Norwich properties and at the same time a good crest—is the exception to the rule, as it appears to be a work of infinite labour to maintain an even balance of crest and colour properties. The desire for size and good shape of crest presents a temptation to cross in with almost any description of bird having these qualities in excess, and a natural consequence is a wide departure from the ancient form. In the city of Norwich itself, however, the breeders still work closely up to their standard, making great sacrifices in the direction of size of crest in their determination to maintain the character of the bird; and if their crests are wanting in size, nowhere are such close and compact heads to be met with. If anything, they have gone too far, having bred in-and-in from perfection till retrogression has set in and necessitated the importation of new crested blood. There is a medium in all things, and it may be that in our exacting demands for colour we have induced breeders to move on in that direction at a pace incompatible with safe progress, and in insisting upon "Norwich" properties accompanying the name when affixed to the word "Crested," we may have been spoiling a beautiful family instead of improving it, because, from the very character of the feathering of the Norwich Canary, there is a bound beyond which it cannot pass in crest-development. A recognition of this fact has made it an open question whether the Norwich is the best parent stem on which to work the crest, or whether it would not be well to permit some departure from that severe type which demands a quality of feathering at variance with the requisites for a full crest. There is a tendency in this direction, but unfortunately it has gone to the opposite extreme and placed on the show-bench a style of bird so opposite to anything that crest-breeders have been accustomed to, that the innovation cannot be regarded as the most desirable type—certainly not in its present immature form. Crest without any quality of feather is quite as objectionable as fine feather and poor crest: what is required is a blending of the two in a bird which could still bear the honoured name, as it would still carry the impress of the family features. We shall be able to refer to this again when we come to speak of breeding crests. Our object now is to describe the bird which the breeder has hitherto tried to produce, viz., a highly-developed Norwich with a crest; and in referring to it as representing the bird whose name heads this chapter, we have only to say that all the properties which become the Norwich Canary should be found in the Crested variety of the same family in as great a degree as possible, always remembering there *must* be good crest, which is a top-knot of feathers radiating from a common centre on the crown, and falling evenly over the head in every direction. In shape it should approach, as nearly as possible, a circular form, though such are comparatively rare, the more general shape being an approximation to an ellipse. In size it should extend in front over the greater portion of the beak, the circumference passing round to the back of the head in the plane of the eyes, which should be almost, if not entirely, hidden, giving the bird an arch expression. Assuming reasonable compactness—by which we mean the absence of coarseness and irregularity—the most important features in a crest are its size and shape: colour is a second consideration. Size is mainly dependent upon the length of the feather; shape upon its distribution. The width and general contour of the skull have also something to do with it. A small crest will make any head look mean and spare, but a small head can carry a large crest, and show it to perfection, too, if the feather and form be there. It does *not* require an extra area of skull to hold the foundation of a well-feathered crest; but if the feathers be individually not much larger than the petals of a daisy, as is the case in many of the Norwich crests, the case is different. The most beautiful forms which have appeared during the last ten years have all been of the long, wide, flat, silky-feather type, a description of feather entirely different from that we have indicated as characteristic of a Norwich head, in which extreme shortness prevails. The shape is dependent on two things —a small centre, and the position of that centre, which should be sufficiently remote from the base of the beak to ensure a good frontage of regularly-radiating, long feathers, known technically as a good "entrance." It will be plain that, in the case of a crest at all elliptical in form, the farther the centre of the ellipse is from the base of the beak so will its value increase. Nothing will compensate for a bad entrance: any defect there is fatal. The back of the crest is also a very important part of it. If a young dark-crested bird be examined in the nest before there are any indications of feathers, there will be observed at the back of the skull a light, crescent-shaped mark, the rest of the crown being covered with black skin, indicative of the future colour of the feathers. On this light-coloured spot feathers never grow, and if the head be examined as the young quills present themselves, it will be seen that they sprout from every portion of the surface except this, which remains permanently bare. We have heard breeders remark that such and such a crest was a good one, only the bird had knocked out a portion of the feathers from the back in putting its head through the water-hole. It is simply a popular fallacy: there never were any feathers to knock out. The larger this pale spot, the greater the probability of an inferior back to the crest, which ought to cover this naked place entirely, and can only do so by a proper disposition of the feathers. Having only a small vacancy constitutes what is known as being well "filled in" behind, and is more frequently the case in Buff birds than in Yellow, in which the feather is comparatively so scanty as to cause this openness to be very discernible. A really good crest on a Jonque is exceedingly rare, and we never yet saw one made up of the daisy-petal type of feather worth looking at; an entirely different formation here is imperatively necessary, or the vacancy behind becomes a positive eyesore. We do not, as a rule, care to make any prominent mention of negative points, particularly when they assume the character of the malformations referred to in speaking of the toes and claws; but as there are so many *pros* and *cons* in a crest, and as a really good one is not seen every day, reference to a few of the common defects may assist in making clearer a description which, except to the initiated, must be somewhat obscure. A good crest, then, should not stand up in the front, and, if a dark one, should show no light feathers over the beak. This is a common defect in short-feathered crests. The Canary has the power of setting up the feathers on his crown, and some "daisy" crests, as they are termed, though extremely neat, are so short in feather that they can be fairly stood on end, displaying any defects underneath in a most provoking way. The light feathers we refer to form no part of the crest, but are a sort of protection to the nostrils which lie at the base of the beak, and when displayed under the front of the crest are considered very objectionable; but it will be evident that a bird with a good frontage cannot display them, as it cannot lift up the weeping feathers in the same way as it can the shorter ones. A good crest should not be narrow or pointed in front, but every part of its circumference should be, as far as possible, equidistant from its centre. The idea of an oval-shaped crest is not intended to convey the notion of a narrow front, only that its length exceeds its width: the front must still be circular without any clipping away of corners. Neither should a good crest be "tucked in" at the sides, by which is meant having the outer edges broken or pinched-in behind the eyes, giving the crest the appearance of being formed of two parts. It should not have any split or opening in the front, nor should the "centre" assume the shape of a line dividing one side from the other, nor should it be a point from which diverge two lines or partings in a backward direction right and left, destroying the appearance of perfect radiation. Nor should it be without *any* centre, and simply a heavy tuft of feathers falling smoothly over from back to front; nor should it be a mop. Neither should it be flat and exhibit no texture or feathery appearance, as if pressed out with an iron, which it will be observed is the exact converse of falling over the head in a drooping form. It should not be wider at the back than in the front; nor should it be tilted up at the back, and carried as if there were a danger of its sliding off; nor should it be shaped like an escutcheon, nor be square at the back, nor have dexter and sinister corners twisted up as if having been put into curl-papers, all of which ideas convey the notion of angularity and a plane superficies rather than that of an elegant convexity, and are simply the negative forms of the positive properties we have indicated. The edges must not be ragged, as is often the case when it is composed of pointed feathers, giving it a slovenly appearance as if combed out into hair; but the imbrication must be complete and the outline as clearly defined as the small arcs of the extremities of the feathers of the outer edge of the circle will permit. It must not be thin and sparse, but dense and full of feather, and as like the "*rose*" *of a Trumpeter pigeon* as anything we know—which, if we had said it before, might have saved us a few pages of description.

The classification of the Crested birds is based on similar principles to that of the Plain-headed section, but the order is inverted. We have the three main divisions—Dark Self-coloured, Variegated, and Clear, with subdivisions corresponding, though not exactly agreeing with them in every detail. Every bird in the Plainhead section has its counterpart in the Crests, as will be seen by the following comparison of parallels, in which we arrange the birds according to their value, assuming that the crest itself in each case is of equal merit:—

PLAINHEADS.	CRESTS.
(*a*) Evenly-marked.	(*a*) Evenly-marked Crested.
(*b*) Lightly Variegated.	(*b*) Clear body with Dark Crest.
(*c*) Unevenly-marked.	(*c*) Unevenly-marked Crested.
(*d*) Heavily Variegated.	(*d*) Variegated Crested.
(*e*) Ticked.	(*e*) Grey Crested.
(*f*) Green.	(*f*) Self-coloured Green Crested.
(*g*) Clear.	(*g*) Clear Crested.

We will compare their relative values, where necessary, as we describe their respective points. And first we remark that it is entirely a matter of taste or opinion as to which of the first two takes precedence, as both are singularly beautiful; but as it is more difficult to produce a pair of exact wings than to breed a clear body, the order in which we have placed them is that generally accepted. Groups (*c*) and (*d*) are, in most schedules, united into one under the head "Variegated Crested." Also (*b*), (*e*), and (*g*) are similarly grouped under the head of "Clear body with Green, Grey, or Clear Crest," and rank in value in the order named. The Self-coloured Greens are seldom provided for in any schedule, and generally drift away into the well-known refuge for the destitute, the "Any other Variety or Class not previously mentioned."

The Evenly-marked bird must have no mark of any kind whatever on the head, eye-marks *not* being recognised as "marks" among the Crests, as they are apt to assume the objectionable character of cheek-marks. The crest, of course, is dark, and should stand out, clearly defined, in bold relief against the golden ground-colour of the body, though there are rare instances of marked wings and *bonâ fide* grey or grizzled crest, in which case the birds are admitted in class (*a*) by virtue of their wing-marks, the deficiency of colour in the crest being weighed against their winning points. Any marking on the back of the neck, also, is very objectionable and counts against the bird according to its extent. It is, however, a very common blemish and one very difficult to get rid of, being usually present with Crests having no decided character at the back, where it acts as a cloak to hide defects which would show prominently on a lighter ground. It forms no part of the crest, and is nothing more than a foul blotch, sometimes rendered less obnoxious by being bounded by a tolerably regular line. No argument can elevate it to the dignity of a mark, or show that it is a desirable adjunct, its chief use being to spoil the appearance of a symmetrical crest or deceive the eye as to the demerits of a bad one.

The colour of the crest depends a good deal on the strain of blood in the bird, and this also affects its shape and general character in no slight degree. If high Norwich properties reign, the colour will be bronzy-green and the feathering short; while an admixture with some of the more open-feathered varieties will give a darker or blacker green cast to the crest, and the longer feathering we have described. But, whatever the particular shade, it should be bright and glossy, and not dull.

The rules for the wing and tail marks are the same as for the Plainheads, and here the worthless tail-feather can work a deal of mischief. We admit that it is quite illogical to attempt to show that an unevenly-marked tail is no blemish in an Evenly-marked class which insists upon the correct thing in tails; but with the leading feature, the crest, exhibited in perfection, and the most striking marking, viz., that on the wings, also exact, and the body spotless and free from the suspicion of the smallest tick, it has always seemed to us such a pity to have to hold the bird up above the level of the eye, and turn it this way and that way in search of feathers which, when present, are of so trifling a value. We really think that if a Bill were to be brought in for the "abolition of certain grievances in respect to the tails of Evenly-marked Crested Canaries," we should vote for its first reading, if only that its merits might be ventilated by discussion—all of which we know is very inconsistent and heterodox, and calculated to upset a system of Canary government which has lasted for years.

Body-colour, as the family is at present constituted, must be good, with feather replete with the pregnant attribute of "quality." The colour of the legs and feet is practically of no value: it inclines to dark, but is never very decided or uniform.

The Dark-crested Clear-bodied birds are equally as beautiful as the class we have just left. The one ranks before the other in the fancier's estimation only for the reasons we gave. The difficulty of producing the exact wings, we admit, but we are not inclined to grant that difficulty of attainment is a correct standard by which to measure beauty. What is difficult of attainment is usually most valued, and on this ground we are disposed to give in to the claims of the Marked bird; but our own speciality is pure, unbroken colour in the body, with dark crest. The contrast seems to us to be more marked than when the surface is broken by the mosaic-work on the back, beautiful as it is. The general properties are the same as before, but a display of superior body-feather qualities is tacitly required, and is generally present. It has no special marking to attract and satisfy by the way in which it fulfils the fancier's demands, nor anything to balance defects in colour, for the eye has no V to rest on with complacency while it forgets that the pattern is worked on a dull ground. There is but one idea presented, and that is purity and uniformity of colour; and the golden birds with the black top-knots generally carry the sway with those who look at them simply as pictures. Perhaps it is that the clear body looks more Canary-like and familiar; but we think that among those who do not regard the birds as the embodiment of fanciers' fancies, the choice falls where we say. These two are the real show-birds of the family, each representing a perfection of its kind.

Any description of the birds comprising the next two classes, (*c*) and (*d*), is unnecessary, beyond saying that, for reasons which we will presently adduce, their marking and variegation are, under ordinary circumstances, of no value whatever. We pass on to class (*e*), Grey-crested, a most important class in the breeding-room, as will be seen in its place, and a not less important one in the show-room. A good grey crest is very pretty, although it has no recognised value from a colour point of view: we mean that it matters not how grey or grizzly it may be, or how little so;

Vincent, Brooks Day & Son Lith

NORWICH CANARIES.

EVENLY MARKED CRESTED YELLOW (CAYENNE-FED.)

GREY CRESTED BUFF. (CAYENNE FED.)

that is no element in its value, and, consequently, the bird is not bred as a variety. A grey crest is neither dark nor clear, but is composed of a mixture of dark and light feathers, or of feathers having a dark midrib and light edge, which, in a Buff bird, has a very pleasing effect. However, its colour is of no worth, from a show point of view, though we think it worth describing. It is rather remarkable the majority of Grey-crested Canaries are buff, and it is equally remarkable that, as a class they contain among them a greater number of good "all round" crests than almost any other. Extraordinary merit is, perhaps, not met with among them, and we do not remember ever seeing such a development of feather in a grey crest as is not common among some schools of dark Greens; but for fair average quality and a little bit extra, commend us to the Grey-crested Norwich bird. There is nothing extraordinary about it to call for special description, and when we add that it has a clean body, and also most generally "blows" clear in the flue, it will be seen that it is very nearly allied to the last on our list, the Clear-crested bird, which is seldom found having any merit at all, though we see no reason why a Clear-crested strain having good crest properties should not be more cultivated. Shape and feather and every requisite could be had as well in the Clear bird as in any other, but the want of contrast in colour is doubtless the cause of no decided steps having been taken in this direction. In the giant family of the Coppy, a clear crest is the highest point of perfection, [illegible] the best specimens of this breed can have any doubt as to [illegible] now and then really beautiful examples of [illegible], and we think there is a fair field for the exercise of the breeder's skill waiting to be cultivated.

We have left the Self-coloured Green standing out [illegible] in assigning him his true place. [illegible] which is, as will now be thoroughly understood, the first remove from the Green. The self-coloured bird is a most valuable acquisition to the breeding-room, even if his sober appearance renders him not the most attractive member of the show-bench. In him slumber a host of good properties; and when mated, as we shall presently advise, he becomes the foundation of the excellencies of which the bird at the head of our list is the topmost stone. But he is not an exhibition bird, and unless possessing superlative merit in crest (for nothing else can serve him), generally remains where many other sober folks whose gifts don't consist of good looks and attractive dress are constrained to stay—at home.

Throughout the whole of these classes the prominent idea is crest, and after connecting it with the two forms with which we first coupled it, the fancier entirely ignores the value of such marking as remains. He groups the classes (c) and (d) into one, and sees merit in them only in so far as it is connected with crest development. With a fancier's innate love for [illegible] he cannot but accord to it its value when of the right kind, but would rather combine still further and unite the two Marked and the Variegated, than subtract one iota from their crest-growth by recognising any body-marks in them as superior to it. His creed is crest and marking if possible, but the former at any cost. He does not assign to these minor points the value they enjoy when separated from crest, but accepts their perfect development, when they fall to his lot, rather as fortunate adjuncts.

that is no element in its value, and, consequently, the bird is not bred as a variety. A grey crest is neither dark nor clear, but is composed of a mixture of dark and light feathers, or of feathers having a dark midrib and light edge, which, in a Buff bird, has a very pleasing effect. However, its colour is of no worth, from a show point of view, though we think it worth describing. It is rather remarkable the majority of Grey-crested Canaries are buff, and it is equally remarkable that, as a class, they contain among them a greater number of good "all round" crests than almost any other. Extraordinary merit is, perhaps, not met with among them, and we do not remember ever seeing such a development of feather in a grey crest as is not common among some schools of dark Greens; but for fair average quality and a little bit extra, commend us to the Grey-crested Norwich bird. There is nothing extraordinary about it to call for special description, and when we add that it has a clean body, and also most generally "blows" clear in the flue, it will be seen that it is very nearly allied to the last on our list, the Clear-crested bird, which is seldom found having any merit at all, though we see no reason why a Clear-crested strain having good crest properties should not be more cultivated. Shape and feather and every requisite could be had as well in the Clear bird as in any other, but the want of contrast in colour is doubtless the cause of no decided steps having been taken in this direction. In the giant family of the Coppy, a clear crest is the highest point of perfection, and no one who has seen the best specimens of this breed can have any doubt as to the air of refinement the clear crest gives. There are now and then really beautiful examples of birds of this kind seen among the Norwich crests, and we think there is a fair field for the exercise of the breeder's skill waiting to be cultivated.

We have left the Self-coloured Green standing out in the cold, because we have a difficulty in assigning him his true place. Probably it is strictly immediately behind the Heavily Variegated, which is, as will now be thoroughly understood, the first remove from the Green. The self-coloured bird is a most valuable acquisition in the breeding-room, even if his sober appearance renders him not the most attractive member of the show-bench. In him slumber a host of good properties; and when mated, as we shall presently advise, he becomes the foundation of the excellencies of which the bird at the head of our list is the topmost stone. But he is not an exhibition bird, and unless possessing superlative merit in crest (for nothing else can serve him), generally remains where many other sober folks whose gifts don't consist of good looks and attractive dress are constrained to stay—at home.

Throughout the whole of these classes the prominent idea is crest, and after connecting it with the two forms with which we first coupled it, the fancier entirely ignores the value of such marking as remains. He groups the classes (*c*) and (*d*) into one, and sees merit in them only in so far as it is connected with crest development. With a fancier's innate love for marking, he cannot but accord to it its value when of the right kind, but would rather combine still further and unite the two Marked and the Variegated, than subtract one iota from their crest-worth by recognising any body-marks in them as superior to it. His creed is crest *and* marking, if possible, but the former at any cost. He does not assign to these minor points the values they carry when separate from crest, but accepts their perfect development, when they fall to his lot, rather as fortunate adjuncts than the results of systematic breeding. Superior crest formation is so rare that he cannot afford to risk the loss of one important structural point in an endeavour to fix some other foreign to it. Marking is not his *summum bonum*, and he does not care to arrange his classes to meet its varied claims after the demands of one perfect form have been satisfied. If crest and marking went hand in hand, each progressing towards perfection equally with the other, the case would be different; but they do not: it is therefore needless to elaborate an extended classification, based on any erroneous assumption that they do so. The frequent awarding of "extra" prizes, however, in the grouped classes, and especially in the clear-bodied division, indicates the fact that the ordinary first, second, and third barely meet the case, and shows that various forms of merit are recognised as being good of their kind. Still it is not probable that, even in the very largest shows, it will ever be considered necessary to extend the provision for the Crested Norwich beyond four classes, arranged on the following principle:—We first separate them into (*a*) Variegated; (*b*) Clear-bodied; and then break up these two into four, viz.—(*a*) Evenly-marked Crested; (*b*) Unevenly-marked and Variegated Crested; (*c*) Clear body with Dark Crest; (*d*) Clear body with Grey or Clear Crest; leaving the Self-coloured Green to find its way to any haven of rest where modest worth is appreciated.

The general plan we have adopted in following out the prescribed outline of this work has led us at times to diverge somewhat from the strict line of our march—as, for instance, in what we have just written, which, perhaps, really belongs to the subject of classification rather than to simple description. But we have found this to some extent unavoidable, and have not hesitated to digress a little, especially when the digression has helped to throw a light on the subject under consideration. It is, however, our intention to pick up all these threads at a more advanced stage of our work, and unite them; and these hints on classification based on natural forms will assist the reader by-and-by, when we come to treat of compiling prize-lists, a short summary of or reference to leading features being all that will then be required to enable any one who has followed us through our work to recognise at a glance the basis of arrangement and the reasons for its adoption. The show prize-list is, in fact, a map of the entire subject, and our desire is to treat of each separate portion in such a way that, when completed, the fancier will have no difficulty in tracing out the extreme boundary of any section, or in cutting it up into such divisions or subdivisions as will enable him to put his dissected map together either in small pieces or larger. Our main desire is not to leave any piece out, and so have a hole in the middle of our map.

CHAPTER XIII.

BREEDING NORWICH CANARIES.

In commencing to breed with a view to producing the highest class of Norwich Canaries, we cannot too distinctly impress upon the mind of the beginner the importance of having a clear notion of what he intends doing, and of following out some definite plan. Desultory breeding is not breeding, but only an amusement that frequently goes by that name. We think we can best explain our meaning by quoting from some articles on "Pedigree Breeding" which appeared in the editorial columns of the *Live Stock Journal and Fancier's Gazette* from the pen of the greatest authority of the day; and our advice to every breeder is to study the whole series most carefully. The papers open with reference to the popular idea of a "strain," and show what it is not and what it is. They go on to enunciate the theory—not a mere theory, but the fact—that "resemblances have a more or less strong tendency to be transmitted to posterity;" and reasoning from the fact that "in numerous cases in which no resemblance can be traced in children to the immediate parents, a startling resemblance can be traced to the grandparents, or even to ancestors still further back," infer that "these resemblances are so transmitted beyond the next immediate step in the pedigree," and lay down as a sort of starting-point the principle that "it is nearly certain that every feature has a tendency to repeat itself, and would do so more or less were it not modified or counteracted by other tendencies." We should like to have quoted the papers in their entirety, but must content ourselves with selecting the leading features in as succinct order as we can, without breaking up a connected line of argument. The writer goes on to say that "scientific breeding consists in throwing the strength of *all* these tendencies into one definite channel—the causing the tendency of the great-grandparents and the grandparents, as well as of the immediate parents to transmit peculiarities to their descendants, to combine towards one object." Then, taking as an illustration the appearance of a *fifth toe* in one or two chickens, in a variety in which that peculiarity does not naturally exist, but which might have arisen from some remote taint, it is shown what might be done by breeding from one of these chickens. "If one of these chickens be bred from, it is probable that a few of her progeny, but still few, will also show this fifth toe; the greater part, however, reverting to what we may call the usual type of the yard. If we mate this hen to a cock showing the tendency in the same way, the number of five-toed progeny will be somewhat increased; but still, supposing there is no appreciable taint in the yard, they will not be many, and the *four-toed* chickens they produced will have little tendency to breed birds with five toes. But now suppose we select from the chickens produced from these two five-toed parents a pair also five-toed, and breed *them* together. We shall now find the tendency vastly increased—so much so, that very likely a full half of the produce will be five-toed, and even those which are not will show an evident tendency to breed five-toed birds. We have accumulated into one direction—that of producing five toes—the transmitted powers of *two generations*—parents and grandparents. If we breed from this third generation again, still selecting five-toed individuals, the tendency to produce the peculiarity will be increased enormously, and in a generation or two more, a bird *not* five-toed will be as rare as the five-toed specimens originally were. We have now what is called a *strain*, so far as regards this one point of five toes; that is, we have produced a race of birds which we can *depend upon* with almost absolute certainty to produce nothing but five-toed birds. . . . . The first pair have scarcely any tendency that can be relied upon to produce the desired five toes; the other pair can be depended upon as regards nearly every one. The first pair presents nothing to a breeder save the foundation upon which he may, by care and perseverance, found a structure hereafter; the other represents work fully done, and a 'strain' which, as regards the one point we have considered, is perfected and established, and only needs ordinary care to preserve in the same perfection for an unlimited length of time.

"We have selected one feature as an example; but to any other the same reasoning would apply. Single or double combs in fowls; colour or carriage of tail, or of ears, or of any other point in a dog; speed or endurance in a horse"—*marking, crest, spangling*, or other feature in a Canary—"all are subject to the same laws, and can be 'fixed' in the same manner. But it will readily occur to most of our readers that every animal is bred for *many* points, and not solely for *one*, such as we have been considering, and that here the difficulty in breeding successfully begins, and the inexperienced breeder usually finds that, as he attempts to deal with any one point, he is very apt to deteriorate in some other previously attained.

"The chief reason of this is, that the *faults* as well as the good points of any parent tend to be perpetuated. When, therefore, it is considered that it is almost impossible to tell *when* all tendency to revert to the features of any particular animal in a pedigree shall for practical purposes be lost, the complication of the problem becomes apparent. At each step in the process of breeding towards some given point, the parents have to be chosen in reference to it; and in each such case the parents introduce tendencies to produce other points which are *not* wanted. Nay, not only do they introduce tendencies which can be known or surmised, but it will be evident at once that unless their own pedigree and course of breeding are known for generations back, they must introduce tendencies which, not appearing in themselves, are *not* known. When, therefore, we consider the changeful and capricious manner in which most amateurs—in the first instance at all events—conduct their breeding, we shall cease to wonder at the anomalous nature of the results they often obtain."

Continuing the theme, and still drawing his illustrations from his poultry-yard, the following graphic description of a mode of breeding too common in the Canary Fancy is much to the point:—"The first year he breeds, while various faults can be easily enough found amongst his various chickens, he finds probably some one fault peculiarly general: it may be want of leg-feather, or streakiness, or light breast in his pullets—let us suppose that it is want of leg-feather. To correct this he next season buys, or selects from his own stock, a hocked bird. This time he gets plenty of feather, but if his pencilling was good before it is very likely worse now. So for next season he selects a bird with beautiful dark but speckled breast, and splendid hackles, and he finds his pencilling somewhat improved (though not so much as he hoped), but very likely his cockerels are now very light on the breast, and ten to one the old fault of want of feather re-appears. He thinks now that what he wants is a fine jet-black-breasted cock, and he gets one just to suit, when some of his cockerels are splendid in colour: but perhaps the father was coarse in the comb, and so all the chickens are, and very probably the pencilling of nearly all his pullets is quite dull and cloudy, those which are not being nearly white-breasted. We think this is a pretty fair picture of average breeding. Such a plan necessarily fails in producing uniformity, simply because *no* point is bred for long and persistently enough to fix it at all. Each time a fault is attempted to be corrected some influence upon that fault is really exerted; and, if followed up, the ground might be secured; but very little really is gained for the first year or two, and by *dropping the next link in the succession* all, or nearly all, is lost again. Some breeders never get beyond this, but retire from breeding in despair before they have learnt that better things are possible, and how they are to be achieved."

The question of *in-and-in-breeding* next follows, and we are told that "in accumulating all the tendencies to transmission into the desired channel, and taking care that no step gained is *lost* by dropping any subsequent link in the succession, we are confronted almost at once by two difficulties. The first is that it is impossible to follow out such a methodical system without very considerable in-breeding. It is always found, practically, that a man who is buying stock constantly to cross with can never breed well; and the considerations we have briefly sketched explain the reason why. He is constantly introducing into his strain tendencies which he knows little of; which he can, therefore, take no account of, and which crop out in the most unexpected manner. Hence very much harm to good breeding, as regards true show or 'fancy' points, has been done by the stress laid in some works upon the necessity for constantly importing 'fresh blood.' The successful exhibitor—or, at least, no one such who *breeds* the specimens with which he wins—ever acts upon such a system, but depends chiefly upon successive generations of his own stock. But, on the other hand, it is soon found that this course, too, has its limits, and is bounded by the physical weakness and deterioration which result from too close breeding of the same strain."

An important principle is next enunciated—viz., that the "amount of difficulty *varies* a great deal with the object in view," and is followed by another axiomatic statement, that in qualities of a *constitutional* character "the physical degeneracy caused by close breeding is almost always entirely removed by *one* thorough cross; but in a race of fowls or pigeons"—or canaries—"which are bred for some pattern of feather, or other purely 'fancy' points, such a cross with alien stock is inadmissible. In this case the cross at once *destroys* all the creature is bred for, the feather or other point being at once lost. Hence, in producing such properties, close breeding can never be carried so far as to produce evils of this class, but must be modified so as to prevent them. And this brings us to our second difficulty, which is closely related to, if not identical with, the consideration of developing not one only but *all* the various points which the breeder or fancier has in view."

In combating this difficulty the mode of procedure indicated is so literally true a picture of certain difficulties in Canary-breeding that we simply substitute Canary points for poultry points, and again quote this authority, to whom we think the entire feather-world is indebted for the most masterly *multum-in-parvo* treatise extant:—"We would provide at the very outset two, and, if possible, more pairs of birds, in order to avoid any necessity for a cross until the new strain was *thoroughly* established. This is all-important to every one who means to have any strain or stock of his own, not only for the general reasons already given, but to avoid the danger of dropping, *unknown*, the 'link in succession' which we have seen to be so important. Thus, supposing we are at any particular time paying great attention to a good crest in the Norwich, and some evident fault in another point to have appeared in the season's breeding. To correct this fault a cross with another family is, perhaps, necessary; and though such a bird may be selected from a strange room with an exquisite crest, from which it is supposed the course of breeding for crest is not interrupted while correcting the other fault, it may just as likely be the case that he is the *only* good-crested bird in a room of inferior-crested ones, and in that case he spoils all. More even than this. There is a tendency in all animals, as Mr. Darwin has clearly shown, to revert or 'throw back' to *long-lost* characters, and this tendency is developed by *crossing*. Supposing, then, two strains of Crested Norwich to have been carefully bred, but one to have been bred first for feather and afterwards for crest, while the other was bred first for crest and afterwards for feather: the result of crossing two such strains would be many young birds which 'threw back' to the first or faulty points of *both*. Hence it is important that the cross should not only be good and carefully bred, but the produce of a *similar course* of breeding to the birds with which it is crossed; and we need not point out that the only *sure way* of securing this is for the same breeder to have bred both, when he can tell pretty nearly the latent tendencies of each. It is in this way, also, that we secure the advantages of an intelligent plan, or a definite object steadily pursued without the evils of in-breeding. If three strains have been started from three nearly-allied and similar pairs of birds, and the same plan of breeding pursued with all, the advantages of a cross can be had for many generations, without its evils, by keeping a record of pedigrees in any simple manner. Where another must breed together brother and sister, or else resort to a foreign cross, a breeder thus armed can take a bird out of one of his other families, which in the course of breeding has arrived at precisely the same point, and will produce similar effects, yet with nearly all the advantages of a cross.'

In following out these extracts from "Pedigree Breeding" to their conclusion, as indicating the general principles on which the breeder should act, we take as the illustration for the final quotation the Lizard Canary, as best exemplifying the admirable instructions therein given for "commencing any strain or race in which *fancy* points are the chief object sought." The fancy point in this case is distinctive character or marking in individual feathers, and is nearly on a par with that assumed as the object sought by the writer in treating of the "practical details of founding a new strain of Dark Brahmas." Substituting the Lizard for the Brahma, the *modus operandi* is nearly identical—the principle involved, and that is what we are here considering, absolutely so; and we will suppose the object desired is to found a strain of well-spangled Lizards. "We would provide, then, for breeding, several hens perfectly spangled. If we could only afford a couple of such birds, we would rather have them than a dozen even only a little worse in this quality, since every shade *now* saves much trouble afterwards. We wish especially to show the folly of this far too common plan, which stands in the way of success with scores of amateurs. Supposing the cock to be a well-bred bird, it is very likely he may 'throw' some well-spangled young ones from these poor birds; and many people think this is a gain. To a certain extent, and in a certain sense, it is; but from a breeder's point of view it is a serious loss of time and ground gained, and 'puts back' the strain, since if these birds in turn are bred from they '*throw*' *back to the poor parent*. Of course the cocks will also be selected with all practical care. From such pairs, breeding *only* from well-spangled birds, there will be the very first season some equally well-spangled young hens. If the proportion is good, it shows that the cocks, too, are of good breeding quality, and have 'hit' well with the strain of the hens, in which case they should be kept. And so the first season's breeding comes to an end.

"From the produce, in due time, a few birds should be selected—still choosing the best spangled. Next to this choose for caps, and, so far as can be done, also form and other good properties. Having selected the hens, there are various ways of mating them. They may be put with (1) their own father—and if he has proved of sterling quality, and suits them fairly in other respects, this can be done; (2) one of the other cocks—and if he has bred really well, this is a good plan; or (3) a young cock from one of the other nests. If there are enough, *all* these plans should be adopted, and thus several pairs mated up for next year, which will supply crosses enough to go on for a long while without injury.

"Next year's breeding will show a *marked advance*, the proportion of well-spangled birds being very good; so good, that out of them, if ordinary judgment has been employed, we can now have little difficulty in finding the few we want to breed which are also good in caps and other matters. And here will be seen the advantage of the plan we have insisted on, of fixing upon the one *most* important point, whatever that may be, and *never* dropping it. If this plan has been followed, it will be found that we have now—imperfectly, it is true, but still to a very great extent—made it *certain* already in our new 'strain,' and can, to a moderate degree, without dropping it, already begin to select our birds for other points as well. The next season the proportion of finely-spangled birds will be very large indeed (we will suppose *only* the perfectly-spangled to be bred from), and there will probably be no difficulty whatever in selecting those which show also other points required."

In summing up the whole, the writer concludes with the following, which every Canary-breeder should learn by heart:—

"Every variety has *some* point or points which demand long breeding and patience to acquire, and on these should attention *first* be fixed and kept there, gradually giving attention to others, *not by turns*, but just as fast, and no faster, than the increased number of birds (good in the first point, and therefore admissible to breed from) enables selection for the second and subsequent points to be made. One thing, however, is obvious. The best birds, *from the breeding point of view*, must never be sold, but kept for the breeding-room; for a man cannot reasonably be expected to make any marked progress who is constantly selling what represents nearly all the ground he has gained."

We have quoted largely, and are much indebted to Mr. Wright for permission to handle his material as we have; but the principles laid down are so sound, so clearly enunciated, so practically demonstrated, and the conclusions to be arrived at are so manifestly within reach, that we think the instructions given cannot be too widely disseminated and commended to the thoughtful consideration of breeders who use their brains. For our own part we think we have acted wisely in borrowing, rather than in trusting ourselves to handle this part of our subject clumsily.

The first thing to be mentioned in connection with breeding Norwich or any other variety of Canary is that, in pairing, the general rule is to put a Yellow and a Buff together. It is immaterial which sex is the one colour or the other; but, except under special circumstances, the arrangement must be as we have said. The first object is to ensure the production of good feather; the Buff supplying the close, compact element, and the Yellow the silkiness of texture and the colour. There is no rule that has not its exception, nor are there wanting occasions when this order of things is not adhered to; but it is only departed from when specific results are desired. It may be, perhaps, that some particular strain, good in all other points, has, from some necessary line of procedure in breeding, become too thinly feathered or the contrary, in which case it may be advisable to pair two Buffs or two Yellows to counteract this tendency in either direction; and it may even be found necessary to continue such treatment for one or two generations, till the required texture has been obtained. There may be other causes for such pairing—as, for instance, to avoid too close consanguinity; but it must be understood that the rule, as applied to *feather*, is, pairing two Yellows induces thinness, and pairing two Buffs has just the contrary effect; and we do not wish to apply it, at present, in any other direction. It will be seen that there is here scope for the exercise of a considerable amount of skill on the part of the breeder, who, in the pursuit of the many points of excellence recognised by fanciers of this variety, must maintain, from end to end, fine quality of feather. It is in this respect that Canary-breeding differs so materially from poultry-breeding. We have two distinct descriptions of feather, which we are bound to mingle; to maintain, as it were, both *surface* and *grain* of the page to be printed; and this it is which renders our work doubly difficult. We have the same ends in view as regards the production of certain fancy points in feather, but we have to work with these two distinct qualities of material, which we cannot always get. The one object we may be keeping steadily in view may be rapidly assuming its required proportions; but we require, from the time of laying the foundation-stone, that the same property which we are seeking to develop shall be present in the *two* birds we pair. This it may not be so difficult to find, but these birds must, as a rule, be one *buff* and the other *yellow*, and we have no guarantee that we shall find such in the nests we have reared with such strict regard to the development of the fancy points sought. We have to search for these points in two different *forms* of birds, and we have no rule by which we can determine the way to produce these two forms with anything like certainty. The success of our operations may depend upon an even balancing power in the direction of Buffs and Yellows throughout our nests; but the result of the season's breeding may show such a marked difference in their respective numbers as to puzzle us how to pair them the next season without imminent risk of injury to feather, which, in the Canary, is a serious matter, because many of the fancy points sought depend upon that display of feather caused by the union of Jonque and Mealy, which would be ruined by compulsory pairing in any other way. The balance is, we admit, pretty evenly maintained; but, from the nature of things, it is plain where the difficulty lies, and it is one which is at the root of much of the want of success of some breeders who will import fresh blood, Jonque or Mealy, at any time to stop a gap.

The pairing of Jonque and Mealy also affects colour most materially. The Jonque is undoubtedly the fountain of colour, for though good Buffs frequently display it in great purity, yet the tendency of an ordinary Buff is in the opposite direction. This is sometimes a reason for pairing two Jonques, the philosophy of the thing being nothing more than a concentration into one channel of the power to produce yellow. Occasionally it is found necessary to do this, owing to some peculiar feature in the colour of the feather, arising from too much concentration of Buff blood at some previous stage, through which the brilliancy of the yellow has been clouded by a decided leaning towards the semi-opacity of the duller shade. Its lustre must not be dimmed by the suspicion of even a fringe of meal, and in such a case the pairing of "double Jonques" (*i.e.*, the offspring of two Yellows) showing this extra proportion of Buff blood would probably restore the balance of power; or two Buffs bred from loosely-feathered, high-coloured Jonques, similarly paired, would have the same effect. Breeders frequently wander some distance from the beaten path of recognised custom in endeavouring to bring about certain results; and only experience dictates when to stop, and what use to make of the material obtained, which is, in many instances, very valuable, from the fact of its containing a concentrated potency tolerably certain in its action.

These observations apply simply to the general way in which colour can be affected by systematic pairing. The whole thing lies in a nutshell, so far as concerns the simple principles involved. The Jonque bird represents brilliant colour, the Mealy bird subdued colour; the former fine, delicate feathering, the latter excess of feather. The elements in each case are simple, requiring nothing more than the exercise of the most ordinary common sense to control them, their mixture being almost mechanical in its action. These remarks are strictly general in their bearing; and when we refer to the pairing of two Yellows or two Buffs, or the uniting of these opposites, the question of the *degree* of colour in either is not taken into account in laying down a rule applicable not only to the Norwich variety, but to the whole family, and which is intended to do nothing more than indicate what is required in the first place, whatever may be the quality of the birds so put up for breeding, whether as regards colour, distinctive plumage, shape, size, or any other feature. The distinctions which are peculiar to Buff and Yellow birds respectively are, possibly, entirely the result of selection in breeding, and are not native to birds in a wild state. They are, therefore, properties which can be retained or lost, improved and made thoroughly distinct in character, or allowed to deteriorate by neglect.

The necessity which exists for working with two sets of birds, if we may so express it, may make the work of breeding sometimes rather complicated; but the pairing of the two produces each in its beauty, and even here the principles of pedigree breeding can assist a thoughtful breeder in directing the course of the channel in which he may wish any stream to flow.

We will assume that to produce Clear Norwich birds is the aim of the breeder, and the question is how to do it? Pair Clear birds in the way we have mentioned, and Clear offspring will be the result. There may, perhaps, be one here and there not quite clear, but the tendency is decided, and the direction of each succeeding season will be towards perfect and complete uniformity of colour if everything of a contrary character be excluded. But, with this plan, depth of colour will certainly decline. This then, evidently, is not what we want to be at, and the inference is plain that we have begun at the wrong end. We have selected parents in which are concentrated the tendencies of generations of families all bred and selected for the one purpose of getting rid of the native green, which is, perhaps, only one form of the paler colour we call yellow; and we have been pushing this tendency still farther, and paling our birds still more. In fact, we have begun just where we ought to have left off; our colours have been carefully blended and toned down till the required shade has been obtained, and to maintain this we cannot dilute further without loss, which must be replenished from some source or other. We will go to the fountain for it, and remark that it may be laid down as a maxim worth remembering that a breeder of high-class Norwich should never be without a good Green bird in his room: not a dull, flat, smoky-looking Buff, but a brilliant Jonque Green, in itself a beautiful bird, which we will for our present purpose consider in its character of a colour-fountain. We do not say to beginners, commence with Greens and plod on patiently till they break; that might never be, though never is a long time: but it would certainly be a tedious process, and more especially if the Greens come from a fixed strain not much given to sporting. This is where, even at the very outset, it is desirable that something should be known of the constituent elements of the material with which it is proposed to work. A good Green will often be thrown by parents themselves very lightly variegated, and well advanced in the journey up the hill Difficulty. It is natural that such a bird should occasionally present itself, as the eradication of the dark self-colour is not accomplished without an effort and a struggle on both sides; and such are valued accordingly as they emanate from a branch of a family more or less remote from a known starting-point. Greens bred immediately from Greens may, as we have indicated, be reluctant to produce anything else, and may hesitate before they unlock the door of the warehouse containing their wealth of colour; but a Green thrown by comparatively light parents is, in most cases, almost running over with colour, which seems only seeking an outlet to diffuse itself through many channels, all of which it will tinge with something of its own brilliancy. Mixed with itself it probably would have a tendency to become more fixed, but poured out upon the rich yellow or equally rich buff of a Clear strain, it adds to their lustre, and infuses fresh, vigorous, colour-blood. This is called "taking a dip into the Greens," and the benefits to be derived are in proportion as we dip into the *right kind* of green at the *right time* and in the *right way*.

Now every breeder, if he have any claim whatever to the title, knows when he has this sort of stuff in his possession. He is bound to know, because he has ground his paints in his own mill and mixed them on his own palette; and this is what we mean when we say that every bird in a breeder's room ought to represent in a breeder's eye something more than it would to a casual observer. He knows what it is made of and what it holds, as plainly as if it were a glass phial duly labelled with the registered strength of its contents. It is to an intelligent man of this kind that we should apply for our first pair of birds, and, whatever else we got, we would take care that at any rate we did our best to be supplied with tubes from which pure colour could be extracted by careful manipulation, rather than with empty ones which had been squeezed dry. One of the best birds of this kind we ever saw was a Clear Jonque exhibited by Mr. Edward Bemrose, of Derby, some years ago; it was in the last show held in the Tropical Department at the Crystal Palace, and was claimed by Mr. John Young, of Sunderland. In those days we, perhaps, didn't know so much about Greens as we do now, but we had a glimmering of the truth. This bird was paired with a Clear Buff hen, as was then our wont in our endeavours to produce high-class Clears; but the produce was a marked preponderance of Heavily-variegated birds. Among the offspring were one or two Clears, which were fully up to the standard of the day, and, notably, a Buff, which has been gathered to his fathers only recently. The hens were, most of them, very heavily marked, some of them being only slightly broken, but all could be relied upon for producing first-class Clears when mated with Clear cocks; and one cock, a Variegated Yellow, was equally reliable for producing pure Clears when paired with Clear hens. Clears from this strain were also pretty sure to throw one or two birds more or less marked, the balance of Green blood being such that by careful mating, so as not to harp too long on one string, it could be diverted into certain channels with a degree of certainty we never knew surpassed by any strain which came under our observation. The immense number of birds of the variegated form which find their way into our exhibitions cannot be accounted for by any supposition that they are bred in that direction from any desire to produce the infinite variety of marking which we find in them, for the sake of any value which may attach to them on account of such irregular variegation. They are in reality the exhibition of so many intermediate links in the long chain, the value of each link being in exact proportion to its known tendency towards progression or retrogression; and all goes to prove the existence of a recognised system by which the peerless beauty of the Clear bird is developed.

It is important, then, in selecting breeding-stock, that the Variegated birds chosen should be taken from the upper branches of the tree and not from too near the root; and so long as they are of known pedigree and can be relied on not to play unaccountable pranks as regards colour, it is not of much moment on which side, male or female, the green is found present or latent—for it is possible that it may not always be present, though very near the surface. Some breeders prefer to pair Variegated cocks with Clear hens, and others the reverse; but in actual practice it is found necessary to mate them, not as one would wish, but as they are to be obtained; for with all the care in the world they cannot be bred to order, and the breeder who wishes to work with his own stuff must take it as he finds it and overcome difficulties as best he can. Bear in mind that the danger of introducing fresh blood into any known strain consists in the risk arising from the admixture of blood of which the constituent parts are not known; and a careful breeder, who may find himself short of Clear or Variegated cocks or hens, may have some of his carefully-arranged measures completely upset by the introduction of a foreign cross which appears to be what it is not, viz., an established Clear, when it may in reality be nothing more than the chance issue of an obstinate dark strain. We do not say that this risk is very great, for good Clears are not so easily bred as to be the frequent produce of dark pairs; but we do say that indiscriminate buying or claiming birds of unknown pedigree at our shows is not free from risk, and is not the road to success or to the sure accomplishment of such results as might be wished for.

In this selection and gradual building up, as it were, of reliable breeding-stock, it has been the custom of some of our oldest breeders to introduce certain crosses with other varieties, and chiefly with the Lizard. This would seem at the outset to strike immediately at the root of the theory of "pure" breed of any kind; but fanciers generally know how extremely difficult it is to maintain what is understood by purity of breed, or to refute the truth which seems to speak out occasionally in the persons of their different specialities, hinting at a remote impurity, imported for useful ends, which has not quite died out. That, we take it, is the purest breed in which the most desirable properties are most securely rooted and perpetuate themselves with the most constant fixity; and we might almost go so far as to say that, in some fancies, the demand for ultra-excellence has induced systems of breeding which would make a reversion to some of the "old," "original," "pure" (?) types anything but satisfactory, few of them having reached our day without having been vastly improved upon and materially altered, to their manifest advantage, despite the teaching of an obstructive old-fogeydom, itself a genuine specimen of a pure race very tenacious of life.

The cross with the Lizard is one from which we think good results have frequently been obtained; for, apart from this bird possessing the colour elements in an eminent degree, its shape and texture of feather harmonise well with those of the Norwich. It is, however, chiefly on the former grounds that an occasional cross is made; but now that colour can be drawn in such a degree from Nepaul, it is to be feared that, for a time at least, a few sound breeding usages will be neglected. We must not overlook the fact that the true object of breeding is to produce a bird *capable* of performing great things in this way, and that therein lie the elements of strength. No plan more surely fatal to future prospects can possibly be followed than a persistent endeavour to make feeding supersede careful breeding.

The first nests from a Lizard cross will be, for the most part, more or less pied, showing in a marked way a combination of the distinctive features of each variety; but by judicious mating of these Pied birds with others from Clear strains—selecting for the purpose those most lightly variegated—the dark markings will soon vanish, and Clear birds of good feather and rich colour appear. Very beautiful birds will occasionally be produced just as the last vestiges of the Lizard are taking flight, the spangling of this bird lingering in a soft, hazy indistinctness on the saddle and about the neck, while a closer examination of the bird will probably disclose some traces of the dark stems of the larger feathers, accompanied by a grizzly appearance on the coat, the whole having a faint, undecided character about it suggestive of its inability to stand before the continued infusion of Clear blood. It will also be found that a few of the Pied birds may probably be marked with some degree of exactness; but this must be regarded as nothing more than a fleeting beauty, because, owing to the tendency the Lizard has to become paler and paler on each successive moult, these dark markings, being of Lizard creation, are as likely as not to fade into grey at the first shedding, if not to disappear altogether, in which respect they differ from the permanent markings derived from a dip into the Greens, which will repeat themselves year after year.

This intermixture with the Lizard is by no means general, nor is it now, probably, so common as it was a few years ago; indeed, there are many breeding-rooms in Norwich in which a Lizard never was seen, though the strain of "fancy" hens, as they are called—that is, hens containing Lizard blood—is much prized throughout the city. Nor is the free use of the Green so much in vogue in some breeding-centres as in others, but this element cannot be dispensed with for any length of time in a room in which breeding is carried on upon anything like a sound basis. The results of different systems are apparent to an educated eye, and it is not so difficult as might be imagined to pick out at a large show the representatives of various schools, in which subtle distinctions in form, size, texture of feather, and tone of colour, presence or absence of meal, and other points, indicate the distinguishing features of known strains.

While enunciating the theory of the intimate connection between the Clear Yellow and the Self-coloured Green, we do not mean to say that very pleasing results may not be obtained from mating Clear pairs, especially such as are nearly allied to the Greens. Very beautiful birds are bred in this way, birds which, for the spotless purity of their plumage and other good points, cannot be excelled; and those who do not aim at ultra-excellence will doubtless derive more pleasure from rearing nests of lovely Clear birds of average quality, than from making a science of breeding and pursuing a system which, though it ensures some prizes, turns up many blanks. Our object throughout will be to show how the very highest excellence is to be obtained; but we do not, at the same time, wish to disparage the efforts of those who may be content with lesser achievements satisfactory in themselves and replete with pleasures of their own. We have endeavoured to show whence the source of the natural high orange colour, how developed, and how maintained; and the gist of our theory being that it is but one form of the normal green plumage arrested at a certain stage of its decadence, when it is in its greatest beauty, it will be manifest that the art of maintaining it at this point consists in a careful selection and pairing of birds showing the least tendency towards retrogression, and checking any disposition towards decline of colour, when it sets in unmistakably, by such a use of the stronger element as we have indicated. There is no set rule how to pair birds; the experience of the breeding-room and knowledge of the stock must be the guide; and whether it be Clear with Clear, Clear with Variegated, or even double Variegated, there should be a reason for each system of pairs, an accurate noting of results, a weeding out of such birds as show no progress in the direction desired, and a steady perseverance with such as promise favourably.

We have just now used the expression "average quality," and we wish it to be taken literally. In our opinion anything above the average of the present day is exceptional in its character, so high is the standard and so closely is it bred up to. To reach this mark requires care and something more systematic than hit-or-miss breeding, but is not difficult: to get beyond it is not at the command of even the most thoughtful breeder every season. No one should be discouraged because the sensational birds of the year are not in his nests; they are like the proverbial angels' visits. The truth of this must be patent if we consider how many thousands of breeders there are in the country, and what an enormous number of this one variety must be produced annually. The points of excellence being comparatively few, and culminating in the great property, colour, the severe nature of the race and the desperate struggle for supremacy will be evident, and while numbers of birds reach a respectable mediocrity, few will make any marked advance beyond it; fewer still will be able to compete in the lists and receive honourable mention, and a still smaller portion of the vast army will reach that extraordinary height of perfection which classes them among the champions of their year. But that this distinction is within the reach of all must be the fact, only the field is so immensely large that the probability of producing *the* star of the year is the more remote. To keep well up in the front rank should, however, be the aim of every fancier, to whom accomplished results, though not of the highest character, are always sources of genuine satisfaction. The breeder who is able to produce Clear Norwich Canaries good enough to stand the ordeal of critical examination at our public competitions, and make their way into the "honourable mention" list, must have done a great thing and have passed many a hundred in the race, even though he may not be gazetted as first prizeman of his year.

CHAPTER XIV.

BREEDING MARKED NORWICH.

It was scarcely to be expected that the disposition to sport or break into varied forms of marking should not have arrested the fancier's attention, and that some particular form should not have been fixed on as being the most beautiful as well as the most difficult to obtain. This has been the case with the Evenly-marked birds of the Norwich variety, the points of which we described in our remarks on classification. Our object now is to endeavour to show how to produce them; and we think that the last four words will excite the interest of some breeders as much or more than as many folios may others. How to breed Evenly-marked birds. A few considerations will show that there is a great deal attached to the how, and that it does not resolve itself into such a simple matter as many may have imagined who have embarked in the pursuit and found the object desired apparently unattainable, a kind of *ignis fatuus* luring them on to perpetual disappointment and despair. If those who contemplate entering this field would just consider what it is they are going to do, the probability is that they would exercise greater caution in taking the first steps, would make each step secure before they took a second, and, recognising the difficulties of the way, would be less sanguine as to immediate results but more hopeful as to ultimate success. We are afraid we shall offer a rude shock to the ideas of some of our readers when we say that we know of no established strain of Evenly-marked Norwich Canaries, and unhesitatingly affirm our opinion that, so far from its being a fixed "variety," it has in this day, 1877, *no cxistence* beyond the few-and-far-between specimens which make their way into our shows; and how few, and how far between, and how far remote some at least are from being what they are represented to be, those only know who have frequent opportunity of examination. We can assure our readers that the small number which do appear in the category "Evenly-marked" will bear a liberal discounting, even though it cast a reflection on the exhibition morality of the day. The truth is not always pleasant, but we should only mislead if we said other than that, in the Norwich variety, even-marking is exceptionally rare, is not the permanent feature of an established strain, and that the breeder must not for one moment expect to pair these birds, in the belief that like will produce like—an excellent maxim in its way, but one which every one who has tried to breed Evenly-marked Norwich Canaries will say has little or no existence in his experience. Let the breeder rather enter on his task with the idea that he is going to make an attempt to arrest a very erratic beauty —one seldom found, and, when found, requiring very careful handling, despite which it is as likely as not to make its escape temporarily, if not altogether. And what is this beauty? In itself it is nothing extraordinary, being simply the dark pencilling encircling the eye, a description of marking common to many foreign finches, and which we think is perhaps the counterpart of a somewhat similar feature native to the wild Canary. This may or may not be so, but it is worthy of note that when the domesticated bird has lost every other trace of dark plumage, here it seems frequently to linger, as if it were hard to entirely eradicate this old family mark.

These eye-stripes are referred to in the Editor's Introduction to the "Book of Birds" from the text of Dr. Brehm, "There are many birds which have stripes of variously coloured feathers situated above, before, and behind the eye; while others sometimes occur at the base of the lower mandible. To all these distinct names have been appropriated. A *superciliary* stripe is situated *above* the eye, occupying a position analogous to that of the human eyebrow. An ordinary eye-stripe is either *anterior*, *posterior*, or *entire*. It is called *anterior* when it only occupies the space between the eye and the bill; *posterior* when it commences behind the eye and advances or unites with the ear-feathers; and *entire* when it is both posterior and anterior. A *maxillary* stripe commences at the base of the under mandible and descends on the sides of the neck." We referred, on page 99, to that form of marking which is considered by the fancier to be the correct thing, and which may be seen in the coloured plates, and also to other forms not so highly prized, all of which find their counterparts in the description given above, and which a reference to the subjoined cuts will make sufficiently plain. In Figs. 32 and 33 the anterior and posterior stripes will be recognised, and in Fig. 34 will be noticed a combination of the anterior and superciliary marks, the latter, when it occurs really as a mark and not in an exaggerated form,

Fig. 32.

Fig. 33.

Fig. 34.

Fig. 35.

Fig. 36.

being usually very clearly defined in outline. Figs. 35 and 36 represent enlarged forms of anterior and posterior marking, the latter not only advancing towards but uniting with the ear-feathers, where it loses its character and eventually breaks into an objectionable patch, which sometimes almost breaks the heart of the fancier.

To fix this feature with exactness is the object in view. And is this all? No; there is a corresponding exactness in the marking of the flight-feathers to be secured; but this is not a matter of so much difficulty, the wings appearing to be much more tractable and open to impression than the much-coveted eye-mark of the fancier. Whether or not our theory as to the probable origin of this mark be correct is, perhaps, not much to our present purpose, but we might say further in its support that this particular form of eye-mark, a long streak from front to back, frequently appears with more or less regularity of form in the most heavily and irregularly variegated birds, which have *never in any way been bred with a view to its production*, and it will also occasionally appear in lighter strains in which, if any attempt has been made, it has been in the direction of *entire obliteration*. The fact, also, that there is no fixed strain of Evenly-marked Norwich, and that they are to a very great extent chance productions—nuggets laid bare with the stroke of the pick while delving for other treasures—is evident from the statistics of our largest shows. Take the Crystal Palace exhibition, for instance, and it will be seen that there were in 1877 two hundred and forty-three Clear and Variegated birds staged as against forty-eight Evenly-marked, many of which had only very slight claims to the title, while some did not belong to the class at all; and of this small number only thirteen hailed from the city of Norwich itself, which perhaps contains more breeders of the variety bearing its name than all the towns in England put together, and annually sends to the different markets its thousands of Canaries. Breeders and dealers alike know the value of an Evenly-marked bird too well to allow it to slip through their fingers, and we can only infer that among the hundreds of scores which pass through their hands, not one of which is disposed of without a careful examination if it show even an approximation to a fancier's ideal of perfection, about ·001 of the whole will express the average rate of production of Evenly-marked specimens. We do not mean to say that this is the case everywhere. The bird has of late years grown much in popular favour, and a few breeders have given it their special attention, and have, by care in the selection of their breeding-stock, endeavoured to concentrate in one focus the desired tendency whenever observed, though we do not think the results are as yet so fixed in their character as to warrant our saying that any reliable strain has been established. We do not say this with the intention of disparaging the character of any strain which may be more or less certain in its action, but to disabuse the minds of our readers of the idea that when they see an Evenly-marked Norwich Canary it is the representative of a fixed and distinct variety, and that they have nothing to do but to pair such birds to reproduce them. That this is a widely-extended belief we know, and one which, indulged in, leads only to disappointment. Better by far acknowledge the difficulty, face it, and endeavour to overcome it, and found your own strain of Evenly-marked birds—a thing which *has* been done with great success in another variety, to which we shall refer in its place.

In enunciating a few general principles which must be observed in trying to produce these beautiful birds we must direct the attention of the breeder to the fact that there are some things he wants and must have, and other things he does not want and must endeavour to eradicate. He wants chiefly well-formed and decided eye-marks. Every fancier knows the value of these, though it would be equally correct to say he does *not* know their value, for their worth cannot be over-estimated. He also wants lightly and exactly-marked wings, and he knows he can breed a hundred good wings for one good eye. If we add a correspondingly exact marking in the tail to the extent of a feather on each side, which, by the way, the bird is as well without, we have indicated the necessaries. Then he does *not* want and must not, on any account, have any body-marks, which are the great bugbear to be exorcised. The great difficulty, indeed *the* difficulty, will be in making a beginning, because, select what stock you may and let it look ever so promising, the probability is that unless it really have been bred for some length of time with due regard to the principles of selection and rejection, the offspring will show surprisingly little of the points desired. In commencing, therefore, the first thing we should insist on is that the birds chosen should be entirely free from body-marks of any kind, because when it is remembered how intimately these are connected with irregular variegation, liable at any time to make its appearance in the most provoking way, it will be plain that any trace of this should be studiously eschewed. The accompaniments of this sort of thing, also, and the indications of its presence not far beneath the surface, such as any considerable amount of dark flue, dark legs, or dark beak, must be considered as dangerous concomitants to an otherwise promising-looking bird, and will represent shoals and quicksands the dangers of which will be patent to those who have read carefully our remarks on development of clear colour from the normal green. Fully satisfied as we are, both from practical experience and extensive observation, that our theory on this point is correct and based on sound premises, we should select birds which, as regards the body, fulfilled all the requirements of Clear birds, although the *bonâ fide* marking on them was not strictly even, but was really marking, as technically understood, and nothing more—that is to say, we should not hesitate to breed from birds having nothing further than one good eye-mark, or good eyes and only one wing, or any similar defective arrangement of the feathers we do want, provided only there were the entire absence of those we do not want. Birds having eye-marks only, or wing-marks unsupported, we should regard as valuable material so long as they were clear in the body; and even these will, when paired together or with absolute Clears, throw quite sufficient irregularly-pied birds to severely try the patience of the most patient breeder. We need scarcely say that birds showing all the desired points in a high degree of perfection would of course be valuable allies, but it may be accepted as a fact that the greater the amount of the marking, the greater the risk of reverting to the variegated form; and we know that this risk is so great that we would, in beginning, *prefer* breeding from the lesser degree of marking and take our chance of getting it reproduced in an improved form, to breeding from birds in which the heavier marking would be almost certain to land us in a wilderness of blotches and irregular patches. Unevenly-marked birds such as we have referred to are not difficult to find. They frequently occur in large stocks, and, not being exhibition birds, are not generally much valued, and the breeder who is on the look-out for them will be able, in the course of a season, to pick up many such. These opportunities should not be neglected, always having due regard to the quality or character of the marking, and not gathering up indiscriminate rubbish, but neat birds, free from objectionable features and showing some one desirable point clearly developed.

This, we think, will show the description of raw material we should select, and our reasons for so doing; and any one who has rushed into breeding Marked birds in a blind faith in the like-producing-like creed will admit that we have not one whit exaggerated its difficulties nor made one mole-hill into a mountain. We know only too well what it means and how it is usually set about; and though a slice of luck may occasionally accompany a turn of the wheel of fortune, or nearly the whole hand turn up trumps, yet we know how hit-or-miss breeding ends in the long-run.

This carefully-selected stock will require equally careful pairing; and in doing so we should, at starting, make colour a secondary consideration—that is, we should not for one moment allow any rule as to pairing Jonque and Mealy, or *vice versâ*, to interfere with our main object, which is marking. If we found the necessary combinations existing in the opposite forms of colour, well and good, but we should not be diverted from our purpose for the sake of keeping up perfection of colour or feather. We fully recognise the truth that "extremes are dangerous," and would certainly do our utmost to maintain these desirable requisites; but marking we want, and marking we must have—note particularly the "must"—with colour, if possible, but marking at all events. And bearing in mind that while we are endeavouring, by mating marks, to concentrate in one channel the tendency to produce them, as we are, at the same time, concentrating two forms of development of native green, we should be very careful to avoid pairing two Heavily-marked birds, lest the combination of two streams of Green blood should cause an overflow on the body: we would mate a Heavily-marked hen with a Clear cock, and the opposite. Here we could mate Jonque and Mealy, and maintain feather. Very lightly marked birds we would pair; but not if both had dark legs, or we should not be astonished to find a speedy reversion to heavy variegation. Birds with eye-marks only we would couple, or we would pair eye-marks with wings. An odd wing is very apt to be repeated, but knowing how certainly heavy wings will produce what we don't want, we would prefer one wing, if containing only three or four dark feathers, and run the chance of getting a neat V. We should not be disappointed if we obtained a lot of odd wings, provided they were neat; on the contrary, we should be pleased, as it would indicate some tendency towards fixity, and we would wait patiently for duplicate marks. We should never expect to produce accurate marking in any quantity, and should be more than satisfied if we simply held our ground. To do that would be virtually to advance, for one step made good means protecting our rear, and security from retrogression.

Fig. 37 represents an expanded wing, in which it will be observed that the six inner flights alone are dark, the larger and smaller coverts, as well as the bastard flights attached to the thumb, all being clear. This may be accepted as a perfect wing from a fancier's point of view. There are one or two features in the formation of the wing worthy of note. When expanded to its full extent it will be seen that the marginal outline formed by the extremities of the feathers is practically a straight line: the stalk or midrib of the outer flights is close to the outer edge of the feather, and the ends of these feathers are pointed; but as we proceed towards the inner portion of the wing the midrib is found nearer and nearer the centre of the web, the dark feathers are fringed with a lighter margin, and the extremities alter in shape from pointed to round, becoming

Fig. 37.

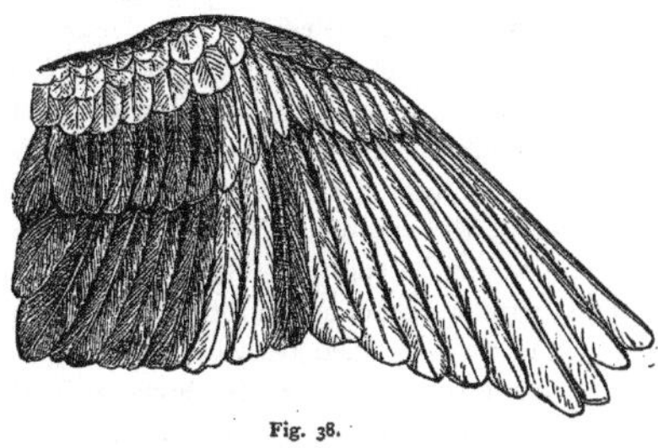

Fig. 38.

squarer and squarer in each succeeding feather till the tip is merely rounded off at the corners, the inner flights or concluding portion of the secondary feathers, however, again becoming more ovate and less substantial in their structure. When the wing is folded and at rest the marginal line is entirely changed, being almost as irregular as is that of the human hand when the fingers are extended and consequently at rest. Close the hand as when in the act of grasping, and the tips of the fingers will be found to be as much in a straight line as is the margin of the wing when in action. It is not in our present domain to examine into the cause of this peculiar construction of the wing, but if the thoughtful fancier will examine for himself he will find that a Canary's wing can teach wonderful lessons, and this slight digression will not have been without its value if lead to a study of higher things than even fanciers' fancies.

Fig. 38 represents a type of wing to which we made reference on page 99. We insert the cut here to show the breeder in one view *several* defects he will be sure to produce either separately or combined. There is the otherwise perfect wing, but that the larger coverts corresponding to the dark flights are dark also. Note, this is not exactly a blemish, but the wing is better without them, for we have just shown how apt the green is to *run over*, and the next step would probably be a few green feathers in the margin of the saddle. There is also the *mixed* wing, an unfortunate white feather intruding itself among the dark ones, or *vice versâ*. Observe, also, that the bastard quills are dark, and that the first row of small coverts is also dark—serious blemishes which it must be sought to eliminate.

The breeder will have to content himself with very slow progress, and even approximations to what he desires must be accepted and made the most of. Where we found that any particular pairing had the direct effect of fixing the point aimed at, we should again pair the birds so bred, either among themselves, by selecting cocks and hens from the same nest, or with their own father or mother, or with others from nests in which similar results had been obtained, and so endeavour still further to unite the various streams and concentrate the same tendencies in one channel. This would, it is obvious, necessitate some departure from the regular beaten tracks of every-day practice, but it must not be forgotten that the object desired lies wide of the line of ordinary sailing, and must be followed through such channels as lead to it. The ship will occasionally make heavy weather and be blown off the land apparently right out of her course, or drifted hither and thither by undercurrents not laid down in the chart; but the breeder must not be discouraged by anything of this kind. The knowledge of the existence of difficulties only acts as an incentive to exertion to a disciplined mind; and now that we have pointed them out, we hope that many a fancier will endeavour to overcome them by thoughtful care, and that some who have spent much time and money and patience in trying to build with useless materials upon a sandy foundation will follow our advice and make their own bricks, and become their own architect and builder. If batch after batch of bricks come out of the kiln worthless, try a fresh seam of clay.

We prefaced our remarks on this subject by saying that the chief difficulty lay in the *beginning*, and it will be seen that it is so, our contention being to show that it arises from the uncertain character of the raw material we have recommended as the nucleus of a stud. The question naturally arises, Could no other more reliable base be chosen than the pure-bred Norwich Canary, with its predilection for sporting in all conceivable forms of variegation? Could we not graft on to the rich Clear Norwich, from which the green has been eliminated, the even marking of a variety not so much given to throwing Pied offspring? We have been shown that this erratic character of Norwich variegation is at the root of the difficulty, almost defying control; and could we not, therefore, temporarily sacrifice some family trait—colour, shape, anything in fact—if by so doing we can introduce, from some other source, fixity of marking, and then rely upon the potency of the Norwich blood to recover, gradually and cautiously, the sacrificed features? We think so, and would go for marking to the *Yorkshire* variety. This is not the place to describe minutely its leading characteristics, which will be gone into in detail when we come to treat fully of this Canary; but it will answer our purpose now sufficiently if we say that it is not one of the colour birds, but has been for generations bred for shape and marking only; and, as a natural consequence, and a living demonstration of our theory of development of colour, heavy, irregular variegation, the companion of colour, is seldom found in it in excess; the birds which comprise the "Ticked and Variegated" classes of Yorkshires at our shows being either merely slightly ticked, or else *well-marked*, and showing evidence of careful breeding in this direction, though slightly variegated by having trifling body-marks, which, as we explained in our chapter on technicalities, is the boundary-line between marking proper and variegation. This is the variety to which we referred in the early part of the chapter, as containing an established fixed strain of Evenly-marked birds, and we propose to utilise it for our purpose. We need not refer again to the general routine to be observed in following up this cross, from which, we may add, we have seen some excellent results. The principle is the same, though the difficulties to be overcome may be of a different character, and the reader will have followed us to little purpose if he is not able to apply our general principles to special circumstances. We do not think it matters much whether Marked Yorkshires be hens, or whether the marking be put in from the cock's side, nor has our own practice or observation enabled us to afford any reliable statistical information as to the preponderance of Marked birds, or otherwise, which may be expected from either method of pairing. The object is to use the best-marked birds which can be got, irrespective of sex, coupling them in every case with the best Clear Norwich types at command. The shape will be the point most affected at first, the Yorkshire being a long, erect Canary, inclined to be slim and taper in form, as opposed to the chubby Norwich bird; and this has to be counteracted

ORNITHOLOGICAL REGIONS OF THE BODY OF A SMALL BIRD.

1. Upper Mandible.
2. Lower Mandible.
3. Nostrils.
4. Ridge, or Culmen.
5. Commissure, or cutting edges of the Mandibles.
6. Apex, or point of the Beak.
7. The Chin.
8. Upper Throat.
9. Keel, or Gonys.
10. } Coloured Bands, usually called
11. } Bridles and Stripes.
12. The Forehead.
13. The Gape, or Rictus.
14. Space around the Eye.
15. Lower Throat.
16. Superciliary Region.
17. Crown, Summit, or Vertex.
18. Hind Head, or Occipital Region.
19. The Nape, or Nucha.
20. The Ear, or Ear-feathers.
21. The Throat.
22. The Breast.
23. The Neck above, or Upper Neck.
24. The Back, or Mantle.
25. Scapular Wing-covers.
26. Lower Back, or Tergum.
27. The Shoulder.
28. Body, or Lower Breast.
29. The Belly.
30. The Vent.
31. The Tail-feathers.
32. The Under Tail covers.
33. Spurious Quills.
34. Secondary Quills, or Secondaries.
35. Primary Quills, or Primaries.
36. The Shoulder Margin.
37. Wing-covers.
38. Under-surface or Under-part of the Body.
39. The Tarsus, or Leg.
40. The Front Toes.
41. The Hinder Toe, or Hallux.
42. Upper Tail-covers.

by judicious selection and pairing of the offspring, never forgetting that whatever else has to be relinquished for a time, exact marking is what is wanted and must be maintained at all hazards. Colour, also, will pale, but as the rich hue of the Norwich will accompany each step in its return to its normal shape, this property may be left to assert itself by its own native potency. We recommend this cross with established Marked Yorkshire blood with great confidence, and need scarcely remind the breeder that, in selecting birds for the purpose, he need not go to the extreme type of Yorkshire shape for the material he requires. There are plenty of very neat hens to be met with at our shows, which, though exact in marking, are perhaps too small, or in other ways come short of the demands of the fancier of this variety, but are admirably suited for our purpose, the only necessary condition required of them being that the marking shall have become so far a permanent feature as to give fair promise of its being repeated in the cross. the nature of the work to be effected and the probability of the steps in the process being more or less intricate, alike suggesting the wisdom of having to deal with as few conflicting elements at one time as possible. But we will not depart from the original proposition we gave as the enunciation of our problem—marking we want, and marking we must have; and whatever be the difficulties in the shape of foreign elements, we must breed them out one by one so far as we can, and consider ourselves very fortunate if we secure our point even at some sacrifice of minor properties. The position, briefly summarised, is this: technical marking when accompanied by variegation is valueless, but, owing to the constitution of our bird, it is only with extreme difficulty that the two can be separated, and the percentage of success is so small as almost to amount to *nil.* We have exhibited as one solution of the difficulty a process, which may be more or less tedious, by which order may be evolved out of this chaos, the continually disturbing element being the latent tendency towards irregular variegation; and we have shown another solution in which the chief opposing force is difference in form. As in most struggles, so in this: the tougher the work the more brilliant the victory. The former plan, when successful, produces the most perfect birds at all points; the latter, just in proportion as it may be easier, gives us specimens in which, perhaps, the fastidious eye of a fancier can detect, not positive blemishes, but a possible trace of some foreign family likeness in connection with the required feature now beautifully grafted on the parent stock. Either plan has its advantages, and each affords ample scope for the ability of the breeder.

We furnish on the preceding page an illustration of the ornithological regions of the body of a small bird, for explanation both of what has been advanced, and also for future general reference. It is from "Brehm."

Vincent Brooks Day & Son Lith

NORWICH CANARIES.

DARK-CRESTED BUFF. (CAYENNE-FED.)

VARIEGATED CRESTED YELLOW (CAYENNE-FED.)

VARIEGATED CRESTED BUFF. (CAYENNE FED.)

CHAPTER XV.

BREEDING CRESTED NORWICH.

OUR pathway here is somewhat clearer and freer from difficulties than we found it in our last chapter. The reader will, however, think we have only a very moderate estimate of his mental calibre if we again preface our observations on breeding this, the last of the many branches of the Norwich family, by saying he must first have a definite notion of what he is really going to do. To breed Crested Norwich birds, to be sure! Just so; but then there are so many forms of Crested Canaries which lay claim to this title that it is not easy to say which are legitimate representatives and which among them hold their position only upon sufferance. In all the other ramifications of this great Norwich tree a most rigidly exacting demand is made for a display of the leading characteristics of the family, little or no departure from them being permitted; and in no variety is less latitude allowed than in this, when it comes to anything like competition between specimens boasting blue blood. Although some profess to fail to discover anything but a vulgar beauty in the orange livery, yet no outline must be more carefully chiselled, no clothing cut with greater care or woven with material of finer texture, while the slightest suspicion of tell-tale features indicating descent, however remote, from some foreign race, is sufficient to remove the possessor beyond the pale of respectable society, and is an effectual bar to his introduction among the upper ten of a community as exclusive in its way as any section of the Canary world.

But the Crested variety (which term we think we might qualify by the addition of the word Modern) being a made-up one, an acknowledged combination of Norwich and crest, obtained from some source or other—indeed, from any source, provided only that the crest be worth grafting—it is not to be expected that among the varied forms included in it there will be found the presence of Norwich properties in excess; and, taking the class right through, considerable deviation from the Plainheaded type will frequently be discernible. These deviations are all evidences of various methods of breeding pushed on in one direction or another in search of the one feature without which the bird is valueless, much fresh ground having been broken up in this way of late years with very pleasing results. We cannot refrain from remarking, in passing, that if as much energy were bestowed on the birds forming the subject of our last chapter, we should see the fruits in the shape of marking of a more fixed kind, accompanied by even less objectionable features than we find among the Crests, inasmuch as the sources from which marking is to be obtained are more in unison with the general character of the Norwich bird than are some of the rougher elements too frequently the accompaniments of good crest development. We feel quite sure that in the course of a few years the standard of these birds will be much raised: the tendency is in that direction, every season showing a great improvement in the quality of the bird and a corresponding advance in the quality of the crest—two things which it is exceedingly difficult to advance at one and the same time, because, as will have been seen by those who have carefully studied our remarks on the Crested variety in Chapter XII., good crest and high Norwich properties are the results of different forms of feather, the difficulty being to combine them in such an harmonious way that, while endeavouring to secure the one, we do not lose the other. We will proceed to show the best methods to be pursued, and in doing so we recommend crest-breeding as one of the most interesting branches in connection with the Canary fancy. It is a wide field, every possible form in which the Plainhead appears having its counterpart in the Crested family, so that a bird of this description needs but to possess the credentials of a good crest to be able to find its way into one of the many classes provided at our shows. It is the leading feature, and is so highly valued that, after exhausting every usual arrangement for the reception of recognised forms, it is not unusual to provide yet *another* class, in which "crest alone" is all that is asked for, and reigns supreme over shape, feather, marking, colour, or any other point otherwise considered of very great importance. From this it will be seen that the crest-breeder need never despair or relax in his efforts for want of encouragement, or because he may be afraid of producing birds for which he will find "no class" in our schedules. An exceptional crest always has a class, even if it be relegated to the "Any other Variety." Superlative merit will always enable it to pull through in the hands of a judge who understands what crest-breeding is; and such a bird will always command a high price, even though it have no other redeeming feature to commend it to notice.

The first general rule to be observed in pairing birds for crest-breeding is to mate a Crest with a Plainhead, and this rule is so general as to be almost invariable. The reason for this is somewhat obvious, if we bear in mind that a Canary's crest is not a high spherical tuft, but a flat, fimbriated arrangement of the feathers on the top of the skull, which, radiating from a centre, would have their character entirely altered if any approach to a high tuft were to take place. We have seen indications of this tufted form, and a crest without a centre is not so uncommon an occurrence as to excite much surprise. Tuft-crests, if we may coin the word to describe these occasional departures from the regular form, seem to present no methodical arrangement of the feathers, which themselves are different in character from those found in a radiated crest, being much shorter and apparently but a slightly enlarged form of the ordinary feathers on the crown, increased in number, and, to use a homely but expressive phrase, "combed the wrong way." Such tuft-crests are generally very dense and more like rough mats than anything else; and it has been found that pairing two Crests ultimately leads to the production of similar forms in which *excess* of feather, without any regard to arrangement, takes the place of the radiated type so dear to the fancier's eye. At the same time, this does not always follow as an immediate and direct result; and the general rule we have given is occasionally departed from, as all rules are under exceptional circumstances, when it is found desirable to pair with a view to obtaining excess of crest-feather at the risk of sacrifice of form and radiation, which are not always, as a necessary consequence, affected by a *first* double cross. Much depends upon the character of the two crests so paired, and some of the most effective forms which have ever appeared on the show-bench have resulted from a happy hit in this direction. In a general way, however, what is gained in feather is lost in symmetry, which requires to be afterwards developed by systematic mating of Plainheads.

For, besides such direct "hits" and crests of approved type, there will be some objectionable forms which it is not desirable to perpetuate. We have already referred to some of these on page 104, but it may be well to show them more particularly. Fig. 39 shows good front, but defective arrangement in the rear, where two ugly partings destroy the uniformity of the radiation—a not uncommon defect. Fig. 40 illustrates the "split" crest, in which the absence of any defined centre affects the character of the front very materially; it will be noticed, in fact, that there is *no* centre. A split seems to be the first attempt at radiation, and its presence appears to indicate a reversion to some form we certainly do not want: moreover, this fault is extremely difficult to breed out. Fig. 41 also represents good front, but broken or "tucked in" at the sides—a defect sometimes noticeable in the original Coppy. Fig. 42 is not sufficiently filled in behind, and is also badly carried, being too much tilted up. Fig. 43 delineates neat feathering, but bad shape, being too narrow in front and too square behind, with the objectionable corners described in our list of forms to be avoided. Fig. 44 represents a decent crest spoiled by a dark patch at the back of the neck, in which the crest-feathers merge and lose their outline: there is nothing to complain of in the way of shape, but a clear body is not in any respect improved by such a mark.

We give no credence to vague assertions that the produce of two Crests will be more or less bald on the pate, sometimes even to complete nudity. We never found such a thing happen in our own breeding experience, nor have we, in response to inquiries most carefully instituted, ever succeeded in finding either such a specimen or any person who could afford reliable information as to such a thing having occurred. We have bred Plainheads often enough from two Crests—a thing easily accounted for on the hypothesis that the recognised form of crest has much of the Plainhead element in it, and we have seen more or less disturbance of the usual type, but never anything

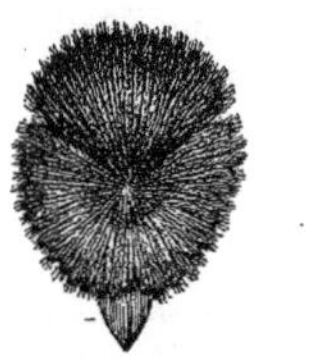

Fig. 39.

Fig. 40.

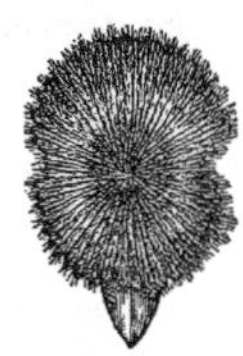

Fig. 41.

Fig. 42.

Fig. 43.

Fig. 44.

remotely approaching baldness—in fact, always the reverse. And further, among the thousands of crests we have seen in our day, good, bad, and indifferent—and many very indifferent—of all conceivable styles, and bred, doubtless, in all sorts of ways, from Crest and Plainhead, and, for want of better knowledge, frequently enough from repeated successions of double Crests, we do not remember ever seeing a head *so* bald as to lead us for a moment to infer that it arose from any such method of pairing as we refer to. This belief, which has gained considerable credence, we are fully satisfied is a complete myth; and we unhesitatingly affirm that to pair two Crests is a sure way to obtain, not baldness, but excess of feather, which can afterwards be regulated and brought into shape.

We are dealing now only with general principles, and say, as a second thing to be observed, that whereas, in breeding Plainheads, two Yellows are sometimes paired to obtain colour even at a probable sacrifice of feather, so, in breeding crest, double Buffs are paired to get feather at the expense of colour, and the latter practice is by no means as exceptional as the former. It is next to impossible to breed a heavy crest from a thinly-feathered bird, and the nature of the work to be accomplished will therefore suggest a reason for frequent departure from the line of procedure usually adopted in breeding Plainheads. What is wanted is crest, bear in mind; and since we *must* have crest, just as we *must* elsewhere have marking or any other leading feature, we must furnish the elements at all hazards. Once obtained, it then rests with the breeder to restore and maintain a balance of other properties by the exercise of skill in his art.

Commending the consideration of these three first principles, we will call them, of crest-breeding to the reader, we must at the outset caution him against the mistake of supposing that he has nothing else to do but to go to the Crystal Palace Show, open his purse-strings, and at once commence to breed Crests of merit equal, or anything like equal, to those he has purchased. We wish we could show in more emphatic terms than those at our command how this is the rock on which so many come to grief. Every one who can afford it naturally purchases the best stock he can, and wisely so; but our advice would be not always to buy the specimens most perfect at all points, unless for exhibition purposes, but rather to invest in such as show extreme development of the one point desired, remembering that our rule is a sound one—when a cultivated ideal reaches its zenith it must be maintained, or it will assuredly decline, and the fire slowly burn itself out unless fed with necessary fuel.

We will follow the same plan, then, that we adopted in our chapters on Plainhead breeding, and show how to lead up *ab initio* to a satisfactory issue, rather than recommend playing with ready-made birds—a course which would, in a season or two, confirm the soundness of our position in a way the experience of many can endorse. We have already shown that the crest can hardly be considered as native to the variety unless the old Norwich "Turncrown" be accepted as the original type—a fact which the existence of crests among the Continental song-birds, the probable founders of the family now so extensively domiciled amongst us, perhaps goes to support; and also that the present popular style of crest seems to point to its having been obtained elsewhere than from the neat head-gear of the ancient Flemish bird. We shall go at once to a bird differing from the Norwich Canary in many essential particulars: we refer to the Lancashire, or, as it is generally called, Manchester Coppy; and the verdict so frequently returned, in brief but concise terms, by many a jury who "sit upon" the merits of modern Norwich crests—viz., "Coppy-bred"—is sufficient evidence that we are not far out in our latitude in determining the geographical position of the pit from whence they were quarried. These mines have been more extensively worked of late years than in the olden time, for the Crested bird of ten years ago is not the bird of to-day by a long way. We shall not describe the Coppy in more detail than we did the Yorkshire; but when we say that it is a giant, stands very erect, is inclined to be coarse in feather, is clear in colour, and has very little of it, it will be seen that we enumerate a list of properties we wish to have as little to do with as possible. Its crest, however, which is either clear or grey as regards colour, for size, shape, and every desirable property, stands alone, and this we want to obtain as much of as we can; so we know our work, and must be prepared to thread a few somewhat intricate mazes in following up our object. We have an infallible rule for finding our way into or out of any maze or labyrinth, and no complication of sinuous paths ever yet caused us to lose our way. It is this: *keep the right hand to the wall,* and you will make your way to the centre at the first attempt. Try it. And in crest-breeding keep your right hand to the wall; never take it away, never lose sight of crest; and though you may have to travel some distance, sometimes being apparently near the centre, and then obliged to turn away, yet keep the hand to the wall, and you *must* land.

In selecting our Coppy let it be chosen for crest properties entirely; but if the bird show less size, less roughness of feather, and less Coppy points generally than are cultivated by the fancier of this variety, it will be so much the better for our purpose and we shall have the less foreign matter to eliminate. It is not practically of any moment whether the bird be cock or hen; but the advantage of working from a cock consists in being able to run him with several hens, and so secure at once a greater number of "first crosses" from which to make selections for future operations in pedigree-breeding, according to the principles enunciated in previous chapters. It is also immaterial whether it be Yellow or Buff, though we should prefer the latter if it be a hen, as it would probably show less coarseness. It will at the same time, however, be very material that the law of pairing Yellow and Buff be observed as far as possible, as the surplusage of feather will continually require toning down. The next thing to remember is that the Norwich Plainhead birds should, if procurable, be what are called Crested-bred—that is, the Plainhead offspring from Crested nests—by which we do not mean the issue of double Crests, but of birds paired for crest-breeding in the ordinary way, which it will be found will always throw a fair average of Plainheads as well as Crests. It is not imperatively necessary that they be so bred; but one of the simplest deductions from the principles of pedigree-breeding will suggest the inference that such birds must contain a latent tendency towards crest, which is further shown in some by the character of the feathering on the top of the head and the overhanging eyebrows, giving the bird a rather sulky kind of expression altogether different from that of the highly-bred genuine Plainhead. These and similar indications of Crest blood, subtle in their character and not easily described, but which the observant breeder soon learns to recognise, all have their due weight in guiding the fancier in making a judicious selection. But whatever be their parentage, it will be advisable to select birds of some size and with broad skulls, and, having these properties, to get combined with them the highest type of Norwich properties, as shown in colour and fine feather. It may be suggested that we already have size on the other side: true, it is size of its kind, but we do not wish to perpetuate it in that form, and therefore select our Norwich birds with size and the distinctive shape of *their* kind, in the hope that these features may play their part in moulding the offspring; and this is specially desirable if our Norwich birds be the hens.

Another important matter remains for consideration. We said that the Coppy is clear in colour: practically it is so, and as such we must here treat it. This will not satisfy the Norwich breeder, who wants the contrast of clear body and dark green crest, or clear body with dark wings and crest, in quest of which typical forms of ideal beauty he creates variegation *ad infinitum*, for every shade of which we have said there is a place on the show-bench if only good crest accompany it. This is introduced, in the first place, in a very simple way; but when once the green is brought into play, the reader need not be told that a very intractable element is infused, requiring all the skill of the thoughtful breeder to control it, despite which it will, with its native impatience, occasionally break away just when it is wanted to stand still. But before we go any further, we think this is a suitable place to remark that if the breeder do not care to embark on the troubled waters of variegation, there is open to him a vast area in which there are few or no settlers, and which scarcely requires more than simply breaking up to yield, we were going to say, a spontaneous harvest. We refer to breeding entirely Clear-crested Norwich, which at this day have virtually no representatives. We have a vivid recollection of some lovely birds of this description exhibited a few years ago, and think that a high-class Clear Yellow or Buff with a clear crest up to the standard of the day, and shown in spotless bloom, would be a class of bird worth breeding, and one which could not fail to commend itself to the refined tastes of many who visit our shows in search of a household pet. Every possible form in which the Plainhead Norwich Canary can be produced has its counterpart in the Crested section, *except* the Clear bird. We admit the beauty of the contrast between the green and gold of the Clear body and Dark Crest, but we think the entirely Clear bird would possess a beauty of its own of a very chaste order. We have no Clear-crested bird except the gigantic Coppy; and it has frequently occurred to us that the work of bringing out such fair birds as we have described is one in which our lady-fanciers would take an especial interest. There is a beauty in the unsullied loveliness of the Clear bird that renders it at all times a favourite with the softer sex, and we commend this bird to their special care. To breed such would be comparatively easy, for nothing would be required but Clear birds on both sides, sufficient brilliancy of colour being maintained by a careful infusion of the best Clear non-crested blood.

Reverting now to the thread of our subject, we remark that any amount of variegation can be introduced into Crested stock by pairing a Clear and a Variegated bird together. Perhaps we shall make this plainer if we put our proposition in the form of a question we have frequently been asked: "How can we breed Dark Crests?" We reply that if one of the parents be Variegated there will be a full average of Dark Crests in every nest, on which fact we base our final general rule, that if our Coppy be a Buff cock, he must be paired with Variegated, or, as they are known in the Fancy, broken Green hens; if he be a Yellow cock, the hens must be similar in character, but Buff; and if we elect to breed with a Coppy hen, our cock must be a Variegated Yellow or Buff, as the case may demand. There need be no apprehension as to the chances of procuring Dark Crests, for every bird, if it be in the slightest degree marked and have a crest, will have a dark crest, than which there is nothing easier to breed. We say every bird, because practically it is so; and we do not remember having seen but two which, having dark wings or variegation of any kind, had other than a dark crest: the two in question were what is called Grey Crested. This result may be accepted as invariable. It only remains to do our best to develop from the variegation, generally, such forms of marking as we have described under that head.

The first cross from the Coppy will present, as regards shape and general conformation, a strong resemblance to the Lancashire bird, with considerable improvement in feather, though these will be birds in which, notwithstanding they may bear something of the Norwich impress, coarse feather will be exhibited to a great degree. Although this extreme roughness is in itself most undesirable, yet it has its value, because where it exists there is frequently a corresponding growth of crest and a marked enlargement of the individual feathers of which it is composed—a most valuable property, and one which every endeavour should be made to maintain. We might indicate many forms which will probably be found in the first nests, but they may be summed up in two—refined Coppies and coarse nondescript Norwich, Crests and Plainheads of both varieties. Occasionally there will be a direct "hit" in the shape of a mammoth edition of a Crested Norwich: several such have appeared of late years and travelled the show circuits in a series of triumphs. The appearance of a bird of this character on the stage, one in which, possibly, very great merit is found in many leading features, has rather a tendency to demoralise the taste for more refined specimens. Such birds are very difficult to pass in a show in a class in which the Coppy element crops up in many forms and in a greater or less degree. With commanding size, not more of the tell-tale Coppy contour than is shown in a somewhat erect attitude, with average display of feather properties, and, above all, a large, well-formed crest, he becomes a formidable competitor by the side of a more genuine example of Norwich blood, although every breeder of the variety knows that he is not an improved Norwich, if we may use the term "improved" to mean carefully reared on a Norwich substratum, so much as a chance offshoot from the imported Coppy. The most noted of these birds have, however, appeared in the irregularly Variegated section, in which stock birds and those in an intermediate state of development are usually shown, and have been tolerated on account of their *embarras de richesse*, rather than accepted as types of the finished specimen.

It will be observed that we make no mention of any other features but such as may be supposed to be included in the general idea of form and feather when we separate the produce of our early nests. We shall consider colour and marking by themselves, because, though every point will ultimately require to be bred coincidently, we do not wish at this stage to make anything indistinct by treating of too much at once. Of the two classes of birds produced, we will deal first with what we have called the refined Coppies, which for future operations will not prove of so much value as the coarser, which in general character lean towards the Norwich. The majority of these finer birds will be found to have neatness of crest rather than size; and it is not of so much consequence to cultivate the first as the last: neatness is certain to come ultimately with fine feather, and, if aimed at too soon, will eventually result in permanent loss of size, which is just exactly what we don't want. Therefore leave these very neat Crests alone, unless they have more than average size, in which case, if cocks, they will prove valuable mates either for Crested-bred hens of a fresh Norwich strain, or for some of the coarser-feathered Plainhead hens from one or other of the nests which show that the potency of Norwich blood has asserted itself in the direction of shape. If they be hens, they will prove perhaps more valuable still to pair with Crested-bred Norwich cocks from a fresh strain, or selected as before, which will in all probability land the breeder a long way on his journey; for it does not require *many* crosses to produce a fair bird, in which the redeeming feature of an extra good crest atones for minor deficiencies.

The real strength of the cross will, however, be found in the birds showing a departure from the Coppy shape, even though it should be connected with more coarseness than the breeder may care to see. Still, as good crest cannot emanate but from plenty of feather, we must put up with the surplus, if only it brings with it what we want, and by careful mating endeavour to get rid of it as best we can. To this end pair the best cocks with fine-feathered, Crested-bred Norwich hens, still having regard to size, and always endeavouring to select such hens as show good colour points and general neatness, without any suspicion of being puny. Handsome Crested birds are sometimes bred small; but a decrease in size will come quickly enough by the constant infusion of Norwich blood, without being courted too soon by breeding with hens which, however beautiful, are small. It may be taken as one fixed point in the modern Crested Norwich that it is a larger bird than the Plainhead—that is, than the very best of the class—which are only of medium size; and nothing of the natural beauty of the bird will be lost by breeding it up to a standard rather in advance of the average size of the non-crested variety. We do not think that, as a general thing, the fine, short, compact, silky-feathered bird in which the souls of the veterans among Norwich fanciers do delight themselves can be bred with the large weeping crest now so much in vogue, and which has established itself as a practical expression of opinion, on the part of the Fancy, that crest in the Crested variety shall be the leading feature. We must admit we have a great admiration for the tenacity with which the old Norwich breeder clings to his bird, scorning all innovation and refusing to sacrifice an iota of the treasured "quality" he has been breeding for all his life even for a form of crest admittedly superior to the average standard of the olden time. Talk to him of size of crest, and he has you at once on the fundamental articles of his creed—colour and quality; and when he produces a bird, some exquisite specimen of his skill as a breeder, you feel you are preaching almost a heresy when you hint at the possibility of its being improved on. We must, however, march with the times. The fact is that this beautiful bird is in a transition state, the infusion of Coppy blood having so far altered its character that it has not yet had time to settle down in its new shape in a highly-finished form. The best breeders have gradually adopted the new style; and though many repudiate the idea of a Coppy cross, and really never had one in their possession, yet any one who knows the influence of a good sire in any department of live-stock breeding can easily understand how, by "picking up" a good stock bird here and there, and importing fresh strains of Crest blood, the Coppy element, unwittingly introduced, has been largely diffused, impressing its stamp in ever-widening circles, till we find its imprint clearly defined on the head of the highest types of the variety—viz., in the Clear body with Dark Crest, and the Evenly-marked and Crested, the most perfect forms in which the bird appears.

We have not thought it necessary to follow out to its extreme issue the system of pairing we have recommended as a means to secure crest, since it involves nothing more than the application of the principles of selection and concentration, which are the same in their action whatever may be the points to be seized on or rejected. The materials we proposed to deal with were an imported necessary accompanied by an undesirable feature, to which the former is, nevertheless, to a considerable degree, indebted for its full development, but which is foreign to the character of the stock on which we propose to graft the scion; and herein consists the difficulty. It is manifest that some sacrifice must be made on one side or the other, or on both; but without carrying the figure further, we say that the mode of procedure to be followed is, briefly, in the first place to reject those birds which show no marked character either way, and then to select from the rest those in which crest has been stamped with the least loss of character consistent with the greatest amount of gain in improved condition of body-feather. Systematic pairing of these birds among themselves, or with approved strains, will accomplish all that can be desired. Out of the varied produce will occasionally spring a specimen apparently far in advance of his fellows; but the breeder must not come to the conclusion that the three points—crest, feather, and shape—are fixed until he sees them repeated, not in isolated cases, but with sufficient frequency to warrant him looking in some particular direction for some special feature, and finding it produced. As the distinctive features of each bird become gradually merged in the new type, quite as much attention will be required to maintain the ground gained as has been expended in making it, and any tendency towards decline must be met by the introduction of a fresh supply of the failing element. The breeder who has worked with several pairs, and has noted carefully the character of his stock, knows exactly where to lay his hand on what he requires. Here he notices a falling away in crest, and mates with it a rather coarse Plainhead. It scarcely looks like the sort of bird we would like to cross with a fine strain, but he knows it was the only rough one out of a fine nest, and can do wonders in resuscitating crest without affecting body-feather. And here is a rather persistent coarseness, at which he fires a shot by pairing with an exquisitely neat bird, and so on, doing nothing without a reason, adding crest, reducing coarseness, adding feather, or performing any other necessary step by the aid of material of which he knows the composition and the certainty of its action.

We shall conclude our remarks on this most popular class of Canary by a few hints as to how to breed for marking. It is much easier to produce this in the Crested than in the ordinary Plainhead classes, less being demanded, and what is required being more easily controlled. The only two points are a dark crest and even marking on the wings, the dark crest appearing either by itself or in connection with the wing marking. We have said how the same marking that stamps the wing also stamps the crest, and it only remains to show the best means to adopt to secure one or both. The bare mention of the word marking must suggest to the reader the prospect of some difficulty in its treatment; but when it is remembered that we only seek to fix it in one place, and that place the easiest, the difficulty will diminish or die away altogether, the large number of specimens constantly in exhibition, all of them being good representatives of the kind of marking required, showing that, so far as the marking is concerned, its production is an every-day occurrence. Still, if there be a difficulty, we may as well face it; but it will be necessary only to mention the cause to enable the breeder to cope with it. It arises from the previously-explained erratic character of variegation generally, which, when once introduced, is apt to try hard to have its own way, playing hide and seek, and turning up in places where its company is not wanted.

We will take the two which rank highest in the Crested scale, the intermediate forms being born of these spontaneously—too much so sometimes—and requiring no effort of any kind to produce them. It is of no consequence which we place first, but the Evenly-marked Crested is usually considered to occupy the foremost position, being the more difficult to breed. To obtain these birds, the Green element is required on one side only, and in selecting the Crested parent we would as soon choose a Grey, or even a Clear, Crest as any other, though good examples of the latter are seldom seen, and pair it with hens neatly and exactly marked on the wings. We should not, unless under special circumstances, select birds marked on the eyes, because any such marking on the face of a Crested bird is fatal to its reputation. This is all that is required, and the produce will most probably consist of (*a*) Grey Crests which, of course, will be Clear-bodied; (*b*) Dark Crests, also Clear-bodied; (*c*) Variegated Crested, with perhaps (*d*) a good Evenly-marked bird among them, and generally (*e*) a few Plainheads, Clear or otherwise—not all in one nest, certainly, but the birds we have described will constitute the average results of such a mode of pairing, always bearing in mind the difference between average results such as may be expected under ordinary conditions, and special results from known constituent elements existing on or underneath the surface, the above being the answer we should give to an unconditional question, What should I obtain from a Grey Crest and an Evenly-marked bird? Much the same results would follow the pairing of an Evenly-marked Crested and a Clear bird, though there might not be so many Grey Crests, the darker form being likely to repeat itself. In both, however, we should expect to find a full average of *respectable wings*, the point we wish to secure. There also might, and probably would be, if the original marking were light, consisting of, say, not more than about four dark feathers in each wing, one or two birds marked only on one wing—a useful form, but given to be rather obstinate. Analysing these nests, we should take care of all the Grey Crests worthy of the name: they are special favourites of ours and are useful in many ways; moreover, among any number of Crests of all kinds, there will be found a higher average of quality among the Greys than among the darker ones, though the paler colour may not show off the shape to such advantage. These Greys we should pair with the marked Plainheads, sailing as close to the wind as possible in the matter of selecting the nearest approach to even and exact marking, our object being to put in crest without offering any temptation to run to irregular variegation. Suitable mates would probably be found among the Crested-bred young ones, in which case we should prefer pairing the offspring of these various hens by the same cock to bringing in any fresh blood at this early stage; and if the sexes have been reversed in one or two of the original pairs—viz., by pairing a wing-marked cock with a Grey-crested hen—there will be material sufficient for any combination. The Clear-bodied Dark-crested we should pair with Clear Plainheads to reproduce the same class of bird, or with wing-marked birds to procure that form. The Variegated Crested and Evenly-marked Crested can be paired with Clear Plainheads in a similar manner; but we have such a wholesome dread of variegation breaking loose and running riot that we should not venture to couple two wing-marked birds unless the marking were of the lightest possible description and the body perfectly clear, showing little dark underflue. This dark underflue is a capital guide: wherever it is found lurking, it only waits the first opportunity to come to the surface, which it will do with the slightest encouragement. The one-winged birds may be paired with comparative safety, and, in the case of reverse wings, with advantage.

It is now time to take leave of the Norwich Canary. While endeavouring to indicate the principal steps to be taken in breeding this bird, we have aimed at treating the subject exhaustively without being tedious; but the breeder will discover as he goes on that there are many little by-paths, each with its own peculiar belongings, that we have not explored, in which he will be able to wander with great pleasure, and will find that the general principles we have enunciated will throw ample light on his path, and enable him to make his way with as much of certainty as attaches to a pursuit in which there is a great deal of speculative uncertainty, an element in which perhaps consists much of its charm. And yet there is not so much uncertainty but that a careful study of the catechism of "Why and Because" will assist him in arriving at a more satisfactory solution of many a knotty question than can be effected by a blind-man's-buff plan of breeding. On sundry points we may have been somewhat prolix, but this being so popular a Canary we have made use of it to illustrate certain items of general application to which we shall not again have to refer.

We append a series of Scales, in which we have endeavoured to express the approximate and relative values of the leading features in numerical terms. This is not an easy thing to do, and, when done, is but the expression of an opinion. While seeking to omit nothing of importance, we have not made these scales so full of detail as to be practically unmanageable when applied to the purpose of critical judging. It might be urged that 10 points out of 100 is too much to assign to the vague property of "Condition," which is no positive part of any bird; but health, cleanness, and soundness of feather are such essentials on the show-bench that no scale of show-points would be of use unless the value of this item were expressed in the terms at which it is assessed by every practical judge.

SCALES OF POINTS FOR JUDGING NORWICH CANARIES.

CLEAR YELLOW.

Points of Merit.

	Maximum.	
COLOUR—Depth and purity ...	30	
Brilliancy ...	5	
Uniform distribution on both body and wings ...	5	
Whiteness of underflue ...	5	
		45
FEATHER—Body-feathers: for compactness ...	10	
Wings: for compactness and carriage ...	5	
Tail: for ditto ...	5	
		20
SHAPE—Head and neck: for neatness ...	5	
Back: for width ...	5	
Breast: for fulness ...	5	
		15
SIZE ...		5
BEAK, LEGS AND FEET—For clear colour and freedom from blemish ...		5
CONDITION—Health, cleanness, and sound feather		10
Total ...		100

Negative Properties.

A Clear Yellow Norwich Canary should not appear dull in colour, however deep the tone may be, nor show any signs of meal on the back or breast, nor be patchy, nor white on the outside edge of the flights or wing-coverts, nor show dark underflue or discoloured thighs. It should not be loose or coarse in body-feather, nor carry its wings loosely or crossed at the tips, nor spread its tail like a fan. It should not have a coarse head nor overhanging eyebrows, nor be long and narrow. It should not show any discoloration on either mandible or on the legs, and should never be shown dirty or with broken feathers.

CLEAR BUFF.

Points of Merit.

The points, positive and negative, of a Clear Buff are virtually of the same relative values, but in place of "Brilliancy" and "Uniform distribution" of body-colour, we should substitute "Meal," and allow the 10 points to indicate its value when found in perfection as to quantity and harmonious frosting.

Negative Properties.

A Clear Buff Norwich Canary should not be deficient in Meal, nor look like a bad Yellow, nor be unevenly frosted, nor show any indications before referred to as foreign to Clear birds. It should not be coarse, shaggy, or open-feathered, or other than as if cut out of boxwood. It should not be narrow in the skull, nor in the slightest degree puny in build.

VARIEGATED.

(*a*) EVENLY-MARKED.

Points of Merit.

	Maximum.	
MARKING—Eyes: for neatness and regularity of outline—Anterior mark, 10; Posterior, 10; Entire	25	
Wings: for exactness, decreasing in value as the marking extends beyond the secondary flights or encroaches on the wing-coverts	15	
Tail: if not accompanied by discoloured tail-coverts—for exactness	5	
	—	45
SADDLE—For width and clear margin		5
COLOUR—For depth and purity of body-colour		15
FEATHER—For compactness of body-feather and carriage of wings and tail		15
SIZE AND SHAPE		10
CONDITION		10
Total		100

Negative Properties.

An Evenly-marked Norwich Canary should not have broken or ragged eye-marks or irregular patches on the side of the head, nor marks running towards the top or front of the head over the beak, nor should it have a cap, however symmetrical. It should not show any light flight-feathers mixed with the dark, nor any marking on the greater or lesser wing-coverts, nor on the still smaller coverts fringing the upper margin of the wing, which, when the bird is at rest, are hidden by the scapulars, nor should the feathers of the bastard wing be dark. It should not show any dark feathers on the margin of the saddle where the feathers merge with those of the wing-coverts, nor any discoloration in the upper or lower tail-coverts, nor should there be any mark whatever to interfere with a "clean run" above and below from the beak to the tail.

(*b*) TICKED.

The *bonâ fide* Ticked birds are judged for precisely the same features as the Clears, with the exception that the unavoidable presence of dark underflue entails no subtractive value, the points which would otherwise be allotted to white flue and clear beak and legs being distributed between the two all-important features, viz., colour and quality of feather, the scale of points being as under:—

	Maximum.	
COLOUR—Depth and purity	35	
Brilliancy	5	
Uniform distribution on body and wings	5	
	—	45
FEATHER—Body-feathers: for compactness	15	
Wings: for compactness and carriage	5	
Tail: for ditto	5	
	—	25
SHAPE		15
SIZE		5
CONDITION		10
Total		100

This scale is still further simplified when applied to the Lightly and Heavily-variegated birds, the property of "Uniform distribution of colour on body and wings" not being referable to birds which are more likely to have dark wings than light. The five points allotted to this property can therefore be added to the first item, and the assessment made as under:—

(*c*) VARIEGATED PROPER.

	Maximum.	
MARKING—Of whatever character	*nil.*	
COLOUR—Depth and purity	40	
Brilliancy	5	
	—	45
BALANCE—Distributed as before		55
Total		100

CRESTED.

(*a*) CLEAR BODY WITH CREST OF ANY COLOUR.

	Maximum.	
SHAPE of crest, depending on—		
Form of individual feathers : ovate	5	
Fall of feathers : radiating and drooping	5	
Position and size of centre	5	
Front of crest : broad and round	5	
Back of crest : well filled-in	5	
SIZE of crest : length of feather and area	10	
DENSITY of crest : quantity of feather	5	
COLOUR of crest : dark, to be preferred	5	
		45
COLOUR of Bird : depth and purity		20
FEATHER—Compactness of body-feather and carriage of wings and tail		15
SIZE AND SHAPE		10
CONDITION		10
Total		100

(*b*) EVENLY-MARKED CRESTED.

	Maximum.
CREST (deducting colour-points from foregoing scale)	40
MARKING—Exactness of wing-marking	10
SADDLE—Width and clear margin	5
BODY-COLOUR—Depth and purity	15
FEATHER—Compactness of body-feather and carriage of wings and tail	10
SIZE AND SHAPE	10
CONDITION	10
Total	100

It is scarcely necessary to fix any scale for judging the VARIEGATED CRESTED birds. It will have been gathered from our detailed description of them that in their case the crest is virtually the entire bird if expressed in numerical values. But inasmuch as it may be desirable to set some limit to coarseness of feather and other objectionable features which have crept in with the crest, we give the following values to certain necessary points and apportion the balance to the crest :—

(*c*) VARIEGATED CRESTED.

	Maximum.
BODY-COLOUR—Depth and brilliancy	10
FEATHER—Compactness of body-feather and carriage of wings and tail	15
SIZE AND SHAPE	5
CONDITION	10
CREST	60
Total	100

We have not referred to the negative or adverse properties of Crested birds in any of the foregoing scales, the most objectionable types of crest having been described and illustrated by cuts.

CINNAMON CANARIES.
NORWICH TYPE.
BUFF YELLOW.

CHAPTER XVI.

THE CINNAMON CANARY.

OUR language is not very fruitful in words having their meaning stamped on the surface, thanks to the ups and downs of its early history and the quantity of foreign material imported, to the intense gratification of philologists and the unmeasured disgust of school-boys, whose introduction to roots and crude forms is not always connected with associations of the most pleasant character. But the name of the Canary at the head of this chapter surely tells its own story. It is the colour of, and takes its name from, the ordinary cinnamon of commerce. This name, however, is of comparatively recent date, though now generally accepted and firmly established. The original Cinnamon bird was a sober, quiet, unpretentious-looking Canary, and in the olden time was more generally known as the Dun; and as the meaning of the word "dun" in our "Walker" is "of a dun colour," we must leave it there as expressing in very intelligible terms a correct idea of what the colour really is. Many of the old school still call the bird by this name, and in some few schedules the nomenclature Cinnamon Dun is adopted, though we do not consider the name a happy one. The old name was certainly more appropriate as regards the old style of bird than the modern one, and it may be that with an improvement and alteration in the colour the name has gradually altered, and as the quiet dun has given place to the richer and warmer cinnamon, so has the one name displaced the other. The Yellow Cinnamon of old times (remember that the technical terms Yellow and Buff run through the whole Canary family) was a bird in which the prevailing pale brown, such as it was, was tinged with a greenish-yellow—or perhaps yellowish-green would convey a better idea—and the more general or "level" this pale dun tone, and the more evenly distributed, the better the bird. In Buffs, the dun was more decided, more true to name and character, singularly soft and mellow in tone and covered with a delicious bloom; in fact, the whole bird had more of the dove-colour about it than anything we can compare it with, and we are not surprised at the name Dun being given at a period of its history when possibly it more correctly indicated its colour than the modern title.

We have heard it said that by breeding from Greens, selecting those with the brownest tinge and following up the work closely, the result will be Cinnamons, and have also read some account of work carried out in this way, the end of which was alleged to have been the advent of Cinnamons; but we entirely discard all such theories: no combination will produce them. Forty years ago we, in the exercise of a very simple faith, planted some field daisies and primroses with the roots uppermost in the confident anticipation of their growing into double daisies and polyanthuses. The one result is as possible as the other. We should be sorry to dispute the fact of Cinnamons having been born from a pair of Greens, but there was gold in the crucible to begin with: Cinnamon blood lurked in the veins of the Green to a certainty.

What may have been the origin of this Canary, as a variety, we can only surmise; but that it is a distinct variety, its peculiar characteristics not common to other Canaries, and certain native properties not elsewhere discoverable and which seem to cling to it in spite of the endless crosses to which it has been subjected, abundantly testify. Most prominent among these is the ***pink eye,*** which no other Canary, not having Cinnamon blood in its veins, possesses. That the bird is traceable to the common stock we must take for granted, and we think its distinctive plumage is referable to the peculiarity many wild birds possess of assuming a cinnamon garb. This is by no means a feature of rare occurrence with many of our indigenous birds, such as the jackdaw, starling, blackbird, goldfinch, greenfinch, redpoll, skylark, sandmartin, and others; and this colour may have been prized and perpetuated in the case of this Canary by the selection of those bearing it. We take it that this conjecture has a sound basis, referable as it is to a well-authenticated natural phenomenon. The variety, when fixed, having probably little to recommend it beyond the unobtrusive singularity of its originally homely plumage, would not become a very popular favourite, and so would remain comparatively unrecognised and thrown into the shade by the more strikingly beautiful varieties which engrossed the attention of the fanciers of a century ago. Indeed, the bird appears to have been regarded with disfavour rather than otherwise. In a very old book lying before us, containing a deal of sound information on Canary matters, but which unfortunately has neither back nor title-page (and we are not sufficiently versed in bibliography to fix its date), it is said, in a very quaint phraseology, in speaking of the different varieties and referring particularly to the *pink eye*, the hall-mark of the Cinnamon :—

> "Some are all Yellow, which are Cocks,
> Some the Colour of Buff, & some of an Ash Colour.
> Some have Red Eyes, & the Cocks of this Sort
> Sing as well as Others, but the Hens are good for
> Nothing at all, being always Dim Sighted, and can
> not See to Feed their Young Ones (if Ever they
> Should have Any) and so Starve the Whole Nest."

Brehm also says, "such as have red eyes are weak;" and Bechstein speaks of Canaries which "have often red eyes and are not strong." True, neither Brehm nor Bechstein refer the red eye directly to the Cinnamon; but we know that none other has it, for although in some instances not a trace of a single cinnamon-coloured feather is to be found in certain pink-eyed birds, yet they are to all intents and purposes Cinnamon in character, having all the peculiar traits found only in the family. There seems to be some doubt also as to what was meant by Ash-coloured Canaries, though we take it to mean Dove-coloured. Hervieux, in his work translated and published in London in 1718, speaks of "Ash-colour Canary-birds with red eyes," and also "Buff-colour Canary-birds with red eyes," though he afterwards connects the red eye with almost every form of colour in the most perplexing way, which would lead one to suppose that the Cinnamon must have been crossed more extensively a century and a half ago than now. Brent, in his little treatise, refers to this vague definition of colours and says, "The principal difference consists in the names given to the colours. For instance, what the translator of Hervieux, 1718, calls Ash-colour, P. Boswell names Flaxen, and Buff is designated Yellow *dun* colour; thus rendering the obscurity of the first translator doubly confounded." Sufficient, however, is adduced to show that the red-eyed Canaries of the olden time bore a bad character for stamina, rightly or wrongly, and hence, probably, the bird which we imagine to have been the Cinnamon and nothing else did not rank high in the fancier's estimation.

But what do we find the bird to-day? We have three types varying as widely as the three stems on which the pink-eyed bird has been grafted—viz., the Norwich Cinnamon, the Yorkshire Cinnamon, and the Belgian Cinnamon; some fanciers inverting the order in which the two words stand, the last-mentioned being, in fact, almost always spoken of as the Cinnamon Belgian. It is our province here to describe the first of these three forms, belonging as it now does pre-eminently to the Colour section of the family—a section we purpose exhausting before dealing with birds of shape or position or distinctive plumage. We have, certainly, referred to the distinctive plumage of this bird, but have done so more with the intention of calling attention to one peculiarity, viz., its colour, than with any idea of classing it with those having many peculiarities, each in itself a feature of consequence. It was open to us to have ignored the bird altogether as a separate variety (for it is now very seldom found pure and free from some cross, unless it be in the pit districts in the North, where, next to a mule-breeding strain of hens, the "Dun" is still the bird of birds), and to have referred only to the effects of crossing it with such pure tribes as we may from time to time treat of; but we prefer to give it the place we consider it deserves, and discuss both its general character, and, so far as we can without departing from our plan of arrangement, the effect produced upon it by being crossed with other varieties, as well as the effect it produces upon them.

Considering it, then, as a colour-bird, we accept the modern Norwich type as a much improved form of the old bird. It is not so very many years ago since it was comparatively rare, and the winning strain was supposed to be in very few hands. How the colour had been so intensified was a matter of some speculation, but the great family resemblance the new bird bore to the Norwich variety, and the unmistakable stamp of the Variegated birds, soon indicated the fountain from whence came the hot blood. The Variegated Cinnamon of that day was essentially a bird of shape and markings, until some of the southern breeders, by sending *their* notion of a Variegated bird northwards, opened the eyes of the admirers of colour to the fact that there were other valuable crosses besides birds of the Position school. Many of the Heavily-variegated birds exhibited were hens, and, being claimed or sold into the North, soon told a tale which, in the course of a few years, has produced the remarkable Cinnamon of to-day, capable of developing almost as much colour as the Norwich bird itself. Every one who is learned in Canary lore will remember the consternation caused in the ranks of the Cinnamon breeders—a consternation almost amounting to demoralisation—when Mr. Bemrose added to his then mysteries the still greater mystery of two or three Cinnamons which put competition at defiance. Great discoveries have been made by accident or while in quest of something other than the thing found, and it may be that it was when in search of variegation the new vein of colour was struck. In describing it we say, first, that in size and shape it is almost the counterpart of the Canary with which it has been so systematically allied, though there is more than the average disparity between the size of the Buff and Yellow birds, the former being, as a rule, much the larger, and carrying its size without the corresponding increase in coarseness of feather which would be looked for in any other fine-feather variety. The colour of a highly-improved specimen is, in the Jonque, a brilliant chocolate, the deepest shade being found on the top of the head, where it is sometimes of a blackish-brown. There is some very pretty pencilling on the cheeks, and the back, like that of a Green Canary, has always more or less of a striped appearance, owing to the saddle-feathers being much darker near the midrib than on the margin. Excess of this marking is considered a defect, and a uniform distribution of the chocolate, forming what is known as a "level" back, is one of the strong points of a show-bird, though it is extremely difficult to get the brilliant colour without the pencilling. The throat and breast should show none of this, as any one who has paid attention to the character of the breast-feather of most Self-coloured Canaries will understand. It is here, perhaps, that the purest and brightest shade of colour is to be found, the whole surface of the breast being unsullied by a single streak, and being free from the comparative dulness caused by the darker midribs of the saddle. Here, too, the rich Norwich blood seems pent up, inducing a ruddy glow startling in its warmth when compared with the quiet old-fashioned vest of but a few years ago. Where the breast-feathers merge with those of the side, it is not unusual to find in the very best specimens indications of stripes more or less decided in their pencilling; and where this is the case it is invariably connected with rich warm colouring throughout the region of the waist. When they are not present their absence is a tolerably reliable indication of the desire of the Norwich blood to break bounds and tinge the waist with a lighter but very brilliant colour, which, though not always discernible, is but one remove from yellow proper, and is as prejudicial to the winning chances of a Cinnamon as a yellow waist is to a Green Yorkshire. A Cinnamon, in fact, however rich in Norwich blood, must be true in colour whatever the depth of shade. It must also be bright and glossy: mere depth of colour counts but little in the show-room if it be dull and unpolished, requiring burnishing to bring out its true quality, and a good judge will allow a balance of points in favour of shining silk as against a rusty coffee-coloured suit. The feathers of the wings and tail are paler on the broader web than the rest of the bird, but the outer margin is full of colour, and on its development and a good carriage depend much of the effect to be derived from equal distribution. The underflue is dark; beak clear, and legs and feet usually so, but sometimes inclined to be dark. The thighs, we have omitted to mention, should be well clothed, and the colour of the livery well maintained. All that has been said of the Norwich Canary with regard to texture and compactness of feather attaches to the Cinnamon with equal force as a necessary condition for an effective display of colour.

The Buff bird differs from the Yellow with respect to colour more directly than does the corresponding form in the Norwich. In the highest types of the latter the body-colour of the Buff is, where most exposed, and even under the gossamer frosting, equally as rosy as the purest Jonque; but in the Cinnamon it is duller and of a different cast, even in the old, unmixed—we were going to say unadulterated—strain, being softer and greyer, and showing little real chocolate or cinnamon; the entire bird, and more especially the hens, being shrouded in a most delicate dove-colour, so quiet as at one time to have obtained for these birds the name of Quakers. But, in mixing with the gay company of a world of vanity and vexation of spirit, and feasting on its dainty meats, it has shown itself not averse to marching with the times and throwing off its quaint attire, and appears now in a vestment which perfectly bewildered the Fancy when the cayenne regimen first developed its latent beauty. We do not wish to convey the idea that the Buff Cinnamon is not cinnamon-coloured, but simply to call attention to the fact that, whereas in the improved Jonque the bird is in every part some shade or other of the rich cinnamon, in the improved "fed" Buff the intensified colour is accompanied by a ruddy glow which is not so plainly a chocolate as some of the corresponding enriched portions of the Jonque. This is most noticeable on the breast, which, in the Buff, is remarkably fiery, contrasting strongly with the polished walnut hue of the breast of the Jonque when placed side by side. On the top of the head, too, this is observable, despite the intensely deep brown, and also on the scapular feathers, where the play of colour, assisted by the meal, is very pleasing. This feature is, doubtless, an immediate result of the strong infusion of Norwich blood. Any disposition to run light in colour in the waist or in the region of the vent or under tail-coverts is, as in the Jonque, a weak point, and a single *bonâ fide* light feather—*i.e.*, white in the shaft, flue, and web—is a fatal defect in either form of bird. The level back which, in the Buff, shows less of the streaky marking before referred to, and also the closest feathering, are indispensables.

In order to explain the classification of Cinnamons it is necessary that we should assume that the old form, the veritable Dun, is, for all practical purposes, *non est*, having been entirely supplanted by the type of bird we have described in detail, but which is a creation of only very recent date, though now so firmly established and so universally recognised as *the* bird, that no other form is tolerated in the show-room; and a fancier of the variety, in referring to it by its generic name, has no other ideal in his mind, albeit the very bird he accepts as a type of the purest form is only one of the many crosses which have resulted from grafting Cinnamon scions on other stocks; and no flower of the show-room has been worked on so many bottoms. But, colour being the primary feature, it will at once be understood why, in the pursuit of a fancier's fancy, that stem should be selected in which flowed the strongest sap. Unlike the dark Self-coloured Green Norwich, with its inborn disposition to sport and change to brilliant yellow, the Cinnamon is born a Cinnamon, and, like the members of the estimable society whose name it once bore, its children follow in the footsteps of their fathers, dressing in the same quiet garb with but slight variation. There is occasionally found, even in the oldest and, therefore, we infer, purest strains most remote from foreign taint, some slight tendency to break into a colour which, so far as it may be regarded worthy to be called colour, is little more than a greenish-white, and, having nothing special to recommend it, has never been deemed worth cultivation. To check such disposition, indeed, has ever been the object of the Cinnamon breeder: to produce whole, sound colour is his aim, and light feathers are as much his *bête noire* as is the obnoxious tick vexatious to the Norwich breeder. The infusion of Norwich blood, however, renders this not always a matter so easy of accomplishment as in the days of really pure Cinnamons, when the only departures from the self-coloured form—which, bear in mind, was not crossed in any way for colour purposes—were to be found in the variegated offshoots of crosses made for other purposes. But now we have not only the rich whole-coloured bird known as Clear which, it need scarcely be explained, must here be regarded as a technical term meaning clear from light or non-cinnamon-coloured feathers, but we also have the variegated *colour-offshoots* thrown off in working upwards from the Norwich cross. This gives us, therefore, the key to a natural classification of what we call the modern Cinnamon, which is, (*a*) Clear, (*b*) Variegated, always recollecting that the Clear bird is the self-coloured form and that the order of progression is from light or parti-coloured up to dark, the two birds we have described being the representatives of Class (*a*). It must also not be forgotten that the original Cinnamon which we have assumed to be defunct—practically, it is so—we are regarding only as a base, having indelible traits, on which have been reared three superstructures, and that we are dealing with the first of the three, the Norwich Cinnamon or Cinnamon Norwich, as representing the bird from a colour point of view in harmony with our original plan of arranging the Canary family in groups.

We will dismiss Class (*a*), then, without further remark, and proceed to the Variegated, or Class (*b*), which is subdivided into *Variegated* proper and *Evenly-marked*, the first including every possible pied form, not being evenly-marked, from the bird which has but one light feather in it down to that having but one cinnamon-coloured feather. Between these two extremes it is obvious there exists every degree of variegation, its extent counting for nothing, though, as in the Norwich, the greater the quantity of clean feathers and the less the green, the nearer is perfection; so, in the Cinnamon, the larger the distribution of cinnamon colour and the fewer the light or white feathers, the nearer the bird is to the goal. In judging a class, however, in which the definition "Variegated" is meant to convey nothing further than its purely technical meaning and no idea whatever of marking, the amount of variegation is not of so much value as the quality of the colour which rules paramount. Slight ticks in an otherwise whole-coloured bird are easy to detect, a frequent form being a very small patch on the back of the head, one of the many trials which sorely exercise the minds of some fanciers. The safest way to inspect such birds is with the hands deep down in the trousers pocket; for, if handled, these foul feathers are so apt to—for want of a better word we will say apt to come out. Canary and cage-bird morality, let us say here, even if it be scarcely the right place, to its credit be it written, is governed by no fast and loose policy. We don't say its laws are never broken by the unscrupulous; but nothing is allowed, or recognised, or understood, in the sense of "they all do it," to make a bird *appear* what it *is not;* and the wretched sophistry which argues that a bird must be good to begin with, to bear "making"—the fertile cause of deception and fraud among poultry and pigeon fanciers—has no rest for the sole of its foot in the Canary and cage-bird show-room. Some reader may ask, smiling, "How about Cayenne feeding?" To answer the question is, perhaps, to admit its reasonableness: our reply is, that it neither adds to nor substracts from, *mechanically*, but develops *naturally*, and shows what a bird *is*.

Concluding our remarks on Variegation, we observe that another common and very vexatious form is the presence of a white feather in the wings or tail—a defect which, as an item of breeding information, it is much more difficult to eliminate than mere body ticks.

The Evenly-marked birds are judged in precisely the same way as in the Norwich variety, due regard being had for the richness of the Cinnamon marking, and extreme care being required to detect any small ticks, which are not so discernible on the deep orange ground as are the green feathers in other varieties.

Evenly-marked Cinnamons of the Norwich type are as yet entirely in their infancy, and we do not remember ever having seen a class set apart for them; indeed, we question whether there are enough birds of the kind in the country to make a respectable show, even if Yellows and Buffs were grouped, those claiming to be evenly-marked being found either in the comprehensive Variegated division or among the evenly-marked specimens exhibited as such without regard to their being Colour, Shape, or Position birds. This is one of the anomalies of our cut-and-dried system of show-classification, and yet, at the same time, an arrangement which can scarcely be prevented when it is remembered that there are not *many* of either of the three types, and that, until each is more extensively bred, financial considerations compel them to be so grouped and judged for one common property, viz., even-marking, although each has a separate and distinct property, apart from the marking, for which it has been especially bred. The bringing of birds having dissimilar properties into competition in the same class is defensible only as a matter of policy. It is an Incontrovertible axiom that it is impossible to compare unlike things. We may compare colour with colour, size with size, shape with shape, position with position, or any like with its equivalent; but when we endeavour to institute a comparison between colour and shape, or any other dissimilars, we attempt an impossibility, and the result is an absurdity out of which springs as much unpleasantness as is possible to be born of such a Babel of confusion of ideas.

The few Evenly-marked Norwich Cinnamons which have from time to time appeared, doubtless, to a great extent chance productions, have been birds possessed of beauty enough, one would have thought, to fire the enthusiasm of the most unimpressible fancier; but the bird has as yet failed to take any great hold of the show world, and up to the present time we have seen but little indication of its occupying the prominent position it might. With all the lustrous beauty of the clear plumage of the Norwich bird, it has a softness and delicacy peculiarly its own. Granted that the contrast between green and gold is more striking than between chocolate and gold, and that the dark pencilling of a Norwich eye is more effective than the softer auburn; but it is in the quiet, soft expression that the beauty consists. The marked Buffs have a chaste refinement about them that cannot be gainsaid. Whether it arise from the admixture of the Cinnamon blood, bringing with it a softness and peculiar tone in the colour of the clear portion of the plumage, or from some other cause, we know not; but there is that about the texture and colour of the Buff which is found nowhere else, and this beautiful quality is so patent that even in the case of an almost perfectly clear pink-eyed bird, or one having so few cinnamon feathers that they require to be sought for to satisfy one as to their existence, there is no difficulty in at once determining from the very "something" which surrounds it that the bird is Cinnamon-bred, and a fancier has seldom to appeal to the pink eye to confirm his opinion, so clearly is the character of the bird stamped upon it.

In addition to these standard classes there is the Crested Cinnamon, in which every class of Norwich crest, as previously detailed, has its counterpart. Very few, however, are bred; and on one or two occasions only, within our knowledge, has even as much as a solitary class for the entire variety been provided at any show; the present place of one of our prettiest Canaries being that home for the houseless, in which *new* varieties of sterling merit are perhaps not so often recognised as are the representative specimens of standard forms, which, for want of a class being provided, are, for the occasion, sent into the "Any other Variety." A few very fair specimens, chiefly Buffs, have made their appearance during the last few years, but nothing possessing more than average merit; the principal defects being, apart from want of that striking crest development which can only result from continued careful pedigree-breeding, want of purity in body-colour, and also lack of depth of colour and consequent failure of contrast between the colour of the cinnamon crest and the clear body-feathers, in which must consist much of the beauty of the bird. We do not think that the endeavour to produce this bird in perfection has ever been very persistently followed out, but we are fully satisfied that one gem has but to appear to set the Fancy in a blaze, and create as widely-spread a taste for Crested Cinnamons in every form as for Crested Norwich. From the nature of things, we know that high-class Crested Yellows of any variety must always be rare, but with Buffs the case is different; and we think that a rich clear-bodied Buff with well-formed cinnamon crest, or a bird with good cinnamon wings and crest, is one worth trying for, and deserving of a leading position in our schedules.

Our description of the Cinnamon as a member of the Colour section must here cease. We shall have to refer to it again when we come to speak about one or two varieties with which it has been crossed for other than colour purposes, here only asking our readers to keep in mind our line of arrangement—viz., to consider the bird, first, *per se*, and then to treat of the use made of it. Its connection with the Norwich variety, with the effects produced, and the intimate mutual relations existing between the two, we have exhausted, and shall devote the next chapter to the subject of breeding the modern Cinnamon, with some remarks on sundry peculiar features attaching thereto.

CHAPTER XVII.

BREEDING CINNAMON CANARIES.

NOTE that we say breeding, not producing—a distinction with a wide difference. How originally produced we have endeavoured to investigate; how to breed we will show. In the whole round of Canary-breeding there is not a bird subject to such remarkable peculiarities as the Cinnamon, in whose blood abides an influence so subtle as to make itself felt in a very astonishing way. Were it not that these peculiarities are certain in their action and invariable, they would prove as perplexing to the breeder as their cause is puzzling. Instead of proceeding to enumerate them in detail, we will begin by putting a case to which probably many a fancier will find a parallel in his own experience. We will assume that a breeder of the variety, roused to enthusiasm by the rich colour of specimens he may have seen in the show-room, and having heard of the potency of a Norwich cross, has determined to import that blood as a means of bringing his birds up to the standard of the day. He doesn't believe in working with ready-made stuff, but prefers to mix his own paint; and what more natural than that he should procure one or two of the richest Jonque Norwich cocks he can find to pair with his Cinnamon hens? He has gone on long enough pairing Cinnamon with Cinnamon, and has bred birds beautiful enough in themselves and apparently able to cope with anything he remembers to have seen, but has found himself a long way from the front when his pet specimens have been compared with the celebrities of the year. The Norwich blood is to perform the necessary transmutation, and his very best hens are paired as we have described. His first nests rather surprise him: the young ones are nearly all Greens or broken Greens, but never a Cinnamon has he. These Norwich cocks must have been bred from a very strong Green strain surely? Try again. And he does try again, with the same result, and again without producing a single cinnamon feather. The season is fast waning, and his room is full of Greens, and many of them only very indifferent in colour, but his Cinnamons are still *in nubibus*. All this comes, he thinks, from having neglected the advice given in a previous chapter about ascertaining the pedigree of the birds before introducing a cross; because it *must* be the new cocks. He puzzles his brain over it till he can think of nothing else, and becomes a silent man. The wife of his bosom, from whom he has never concealed anything since they twain became one, begins to be uneasy, and wonders whether he has been accepting a little bill. It isn't often she goes into his bird-room; but she did yesterday, and there lay his diary full of mysterious memoranda and a note about something "falling due" in a few days. The little affair, when due, brings with it only a repetition of his disappointment. He has another Yellow bird, however, a Norwich bird, or at any rate he bought it for such, and he resolves to try what it will do, and pairs it with one of his Cinnamon hens. Hope has nearly died out of his breast, and he awaits the "chipping" of this nest with some anxiety, but to his great delight finds there are at least two or three pink-eyed young ones, which, while they puzzle him the more, lead to mutual explanations and restored domestic confidence. The solution of the enigma is very simple. Cinnamon blood cannot be introduced with direct results, *except from the male side;* or, to use a

CINNAMON CANARIES.

EVENLY MARKED CRESTED BUFF. NORWICH TYPE.

EVENLY MARKED YELLOW YORKSHIRE TYPE.

simile we have frequently adopted, no scion whatever can be grafted on a Cinnamon stock, but the Cinnamon can be worked on any bottom. If a cock Canary, not being a Cinnamon or crossed from the variety, be paired with a Cinnamon hen, the produce will not show the pink eye or any cinnamon feathers, but will consist of Self-coloured Greens, cocks and hens, and Variegated Greens. If, however, we invert the order of things, and infuse the Cinnamon blood by mating a Cinnamon cock with, say, a Norwich hen, we obtain altogether different results. The progeny will, for the most part, consist of Self-coloured and Variegated Cinnamons, with an occasional Green or Green-marked bird, and with this strange result also, that all the Cinnamons, Clear or Variegated, will be hens. This is a fact not generally known, but our own experience has shown it to *be* a fact, while inquiry on every side has never in any one instance led to a knowledge of any other result. Some breeders will only declare positively as to the Yellow Variegated, but our experience is that every bird which shows one cinnamon feather will be a hen. Among our northern breeders, who above all things delight in a good "Dun-marked" bird, the Green and Green-marked birds from this cross are not, for ordinary breeding purposes, recognised as Greens proper, however brilliant they may be, but as bred from or "off" the Duns, and, when their pedigree is known, are much valued for the results to be obtained from them. Paired with Clear birds of any variety, they will throw both Green-marked and Cinnamon-marked, as well as pink-eyed clear-bodied offspring, which last are Cinnamon in their acts and deeds. While penning these lines a friend writes to us from Darlington: "I have bred this season from a Green-marked cock, the son of a Cinnamon, which I have paired with two well-bred Norwich hens having no trace of Cinnamon blood in them, and have got both pink-eyed Clears and Cinnamon-marked produce."

To any one not acquainted with their peculiarities, it might seem strange to find Cinnamons preponderating in a nest bred from, apparently, common Greens. But it is so very frequently, and some admirers of the variety obtain their Evenly-marked Cinnamons from these Variegated Cinnamon-bred Greens. Many of them, indeed, will throw decently-marked young ones with such certainty as to be almost as valuable in their way as are the "muling" hens which produce the wonderful hybrids, so mathematically exact in their marking, between the Goldfinch and Canary; some of the very best and most reliable of these muling hens being, in fact, full of Cinnamon blood, which, when united with any other, seems to have the property of appearing either in the green or cinnamon form in the eye-stripes, and other regions where native marking is probably latent. We did not refer to this in our remarks on breeding Evenly-marked Norwich, simply because we did not wish, in that place, to suggest a Cinnamon cross for that purpose; preferring rather to deal with the peculiarity here in the character of a property of this variety, which, beyond any doubt, will be developed to an extent hitherto not dreamt of when the breeding of Marked Cinnamons of the Norwich type, persistently followed up, will throw the *Green-marked* birds so produced into the Norwich classes, just as the *Green-marked Cinnamon-bred* birds of the Yorkshire type are thrown into the Yorkshire classes—many of the best Evenly-marked examples of which are greatly indebted to Cinnamon blood for the accurate pencilling of their beautiful eye-stripes. A fancier in the South commissioned us last spring to procure him two or three Evenly-marked Yorkshires, for the purpose of mating them with Norwich hens, with the object of building up a marked strain. We claimed three Buffs exhibited at a northern show by the most successful man of the day and the holder of the largest stud of these birds, and, anxious to know the result of the cross, arranged for information being sent us. We may say that these birds were marked almost as perfectly as if painted. In due time the promised information came: "One of the three *hens* you sent is a *cock*. I have paired him with a Clear Norwich hen of my own breeding, Clear-bred for two generations, at least; but the result has completely puzzled me. My young

Marked Norwich are Marked *Cinnamons!*" The inference is plain: the Evenly-marked Yorkshire was "off the Duns."

We have said that the pink-eyed Clear-bodied birds also are Cinnamon in their functions. We knew a dealer who was in the habit of making rather extensive purchases of Norwich birds from an exhibitor in the South, who, at that time, had also one of the best strains of Cinnamons in exhibition. Our friend, the dealer, not having disposed of all his stock, put up his surplus pairs in the spring, mating a Clear Yellow *Norwich* (?) cock with a Buff hen of the same variety. The result was, that in every nest there were some fine *Cinnamons;* and an inspection showed the *Norwich* cock to be *pink-eyed.*

The information given above with regard to Marked Yorkshires, so far as it throws any light on the subject of producing marked birds in *any* variety, may be taken as general in its application. We have referred to it in this place as being pertinent to the solution of the case we stated at the beginning of this chapter.

The principle involved in breeding colour-Cinnamons is easy of deduction from what we have advanced, and is analogous to that on which the production of Clear Norwich Canaries is based, in so far as it consists in improving colour by the infusion of a foreign element, every trace of which ultimately requires to be eliminated, leaving only its active agency behind. In the Norwich, we operate on the Clear plumage by infusing the strong Green; and in the Cinnamon, we work in the same way by adding the Clear element in various stages of its development, striving in each case to maintain the plumage operated on intact, and changed only in regard to the brilliancy and depth of its colour. The two processes may appear to be the reverse of each other in their practical operation, but they are nearly identical in principle.

To breed Clear or whole-coloured Cinnamons, pair the purest and richest-coloured Selfs. The improved bird has not been manufactured sufficiently long to have had time to retrograde, and it will require a few years of Clear pairing to materially affect the quality. The bird is, in fact, full to the brim and running over with colour-blood, as the constant recurrence of light ticks and pied forms attests. We mention this plan first for the encouragement of those who, altogether inexperienced in Canary-breeding, may see difficulties in our exhaustive details which, possibly, may debar them from commencing with a variety requiring so much building up and maintaining in a high degree of excellence. All varieties require this building up: in it consists the art of breeding; but we think this string can sustain its present tension long enough for the amateur to acquire some proficiency before it will require tuning afresh. In pairing Yellow cocks with Buff hens, select, if possible, male birds having some size: such are not always procurable, as the tendency of the richest-coloured Jonques is to run small. We only mention this as a disposition it is desirable to keep in check, but do not advise sacrificing any material point in doing so. Remember that the true Norwich is *not* a large bird; but remember, also, that the Jonque Cinnamon cock need not be allowed to become even smaller. Bear in mind, also, that size and colour are difficult to bring out in the same bird, and, therefore, be cautious. We deem it well to refer to this in all its bearings, inasmuch as the acknowledged want of size in Jonques is so far admitted by the Fancy as to warrant large birds of high-class "all round" properties occupying leading positions in the most severe competition. In mating the other way there will be no difficulty as regards the size of the cock, the Buffs having, by some means or other, managed to carry a full share of colour with size; the Buff Cinnamon cock being, perhaps, the most evenly-balanced bird in this respect in the whole show-room. But be careful in the selection of a Yellow hen, many of which, though very dark, are singularly dull in tone, and lack the lustre which gives finish to a bird when in high condition.

Such hens are generally very compact, and we would sooner pair them with Jonques than with Buffs, which in some feather points they resemble. Choose a hen which, if not so brown, is brighter and purer in colour, and in every instance, male or female, Yellow or Buff, avoid birds having a greenish tinge, often betokening a common extraction.

The first and simplest cross to restore declining colour is with the richest Self-coloured Green Norwich hen; and we would not in this instance insist on the rule for mating Jonque and Mealy being carried out, preferring rather to use a compact Yellow cock. This cross, being less likely to sport than any other, will give least trouble, and is one to be recommended if there be any tendency on the Cinnamon side to throw occasional white feathers. From this cross will come some improved whole-coloured Cinnamons direct, while such Greens as may be produced will be invaluable colour-fountains. Not one should be sold till tested, for a Green cock from this cross may, when paired with a Cinnamon hen, throw Cinnamons of the purest water; and if one or two foundation pairs have been mated as directed, the Green cocks from the one when paired with the Green hens from the other *may* also produce a preponderance of Cinnamons, which are certain to be of high character. Where a breeder is working with but one or two pairs there is not scope for much interbreeding of this kind, but if the same cock be mated with two or three hens, Yellows and Buffs, it will be plain that from the offspring two or three threads can be twisted into one, and desirable forms concentrated, at the same time that the admixture of Yellow and Buff will afford material for keeping up the texture of the feather. It is unnecessary that we again enunciate the general principles which should guide the intelligent breeder in gathering up his threads. Concentration into one channel is the leading idea. All that is requisite is to have shown how to spin the threads out of a peculiar material.

To detail the working of a cross in which the vehicle for introducing colour is a Variegated hen would be merely to repeat the instructions given in Chapter XIII. on breeding Clear Norwich from the Variegated form. It might be asked, Why make use of Variegated birds and court difficulties, when the same result may be obtained from Selfs with less trouble? We do not say the same results, or rather such good results, *will* follow the cross with the Green, as will eventuate from pairing with a rich Jonque Variegated hen having the pure yellow well developed. The Green cross will make a marked improvement, but an infusion of brighter blood from a Variegated or Clear spring will do still more in producing a brighter and warmer hue. This cross will also furnish the breeder with several classes of birds, all of which are valuable for different purposes. There will probably be Clear Cinnamons, at once, which will show the highest and purest form of colour, and which may be mated with the original strain without more ado. It must not be expected that such mating will produce nests entirely free from blemish, because the Clear Norwich blood is very near the surface, and will, in all probability, bubble up; but it is a very safe cross, and one from which very little trouble may be expected. Then there will be others in all degrees of variegation, heavy and light, which will require dealing with according to the extent and quality of the cinnamon marking. Some may be merely ticked, some have nothing more than pied wings or tail, and others may be irregularly splashed. For every one there will be a place. Some may be Green or broken Green: these also can all be treated as Cinnamons, and worked accordingly. But some will probably show very fair *marking*, either cinnamon or green, and one or two may be clear from cinnamon-coloured feathers entirely, but yet have the *pink eye*, which, we may remark, can be discerned by the merest novice directly the young birds leave the shell, and is the distinguishing mark by which the breeder can determine at once the character of a mixed nest in which he anticipates finding Cinnamons. The existence of this pink eye does not appear to be so known as it should be, as the infallible tell-tale of Cinnamon blood; and many instances have come under our observation of persons having pink-eyed birds without having the slightest idea of their descent; any knowledge of the fact being further kept out of view owing to many of these birds having been bred for one purpose or another perfectly clear, without as much as a single cinnamon feather being discerned in them, and having thus passed from hand to hand till they have come into the possession of persons who were quite unacquainted with their character, and, not suspecting it, have mated them with birds of other breeds, with some of the perplexing results we have referred to. Young birds of this class, when feathered, it will be well to mark by a distinguishing notch on one of the flight-feathers, or in some similar way, to ensure identification at a future day. The value of those found to have good technical marking, or even a decent approach to it, cannot be over-estimated. We have in them the starting-point of a *marked* strain, and there are many ways of pairing, a few of which only need to be suggested in order to indicate the direction in which the work can be carried out. The Cinnamon-marked birds, *being all hens,* may be mated with Clear-bodied pink-eyed cocks, with the tolerable certainty of having marking of some kind reproduced. The Green-marked cocks might also be similarly mated with these hens, and by that means would be concentrated in one channel two like tendencies, even at the risk of producing a heavy form of marking, or a leaning towards irregular variegation through the infusion of two streams of Cinnamon blood. Or these valuable Green-marked cocks might be paired with Clear hens of a fresh Norwich strain, with a reasonable expectation of throwing lightly-marked Cinnamons or a further supply of pink-eyed Clears, both cocks and hens, to be made use of in the almost endless ways in which the principles of pedigree-breeding can be brought to bear on this remarkable Canary.

We do not think it necessary to devote a separate chapter to the subject of breeding Crested Cinnamons in all its detail, because the line of operation can be deduced from our foregoing observations; the chief point for consideration here being how to introduce the crest in the first instance—this, of course, implying the assumption that the breeder has no Crested Cinnamon of any kind at command. The most direct method, it is obvious, will be to import it through the hen, since in that way the object sought is obtained at once. It is not material what class of hen we select, but we should prefer a Grey-crested or a Clear-bodied Dark-crested Norwich. Hens of this description, paired with a rich Jonque Cinnamon cock, would produce—what? In accordance with the law of Cinnamon first-cross we should expect to find Greens, Cinnamons, Variegated birds of either kind, and also Clears with pink eyes, the nests containing, as a natural consequence, both Crests and Plainheads. Of these the Cinnamon-marked Crested birds must, at least, be hens, whatever the amount of their variegation, be it merely a few cinnamon feathers mixed in the crest or a more widely-distributed form of variegation. And the Green-marked Crested will be—what? Cinnamon-bred, of course; the cocks being a medium through which cinnamon crest can be planted on any variety, just as the corresponding form in the Plainhead can produce cinnamon marking. Similar forms of feather will also be found among the Plainheads, and there will also probably be the pink-eyed Clear body. What are we to do with these varied products? If we have put up several pairs, or have mated the same Jonque Cinnamon to two or three hens, we shall have material at command to carry out our pedigree-breeding efficiently, without forming a series of alliances too far within the prescribed bounds of consanguinity; though, in commencing, we should mate irrespective of such laws if any two streams ran in the direction wished, only too glad to unite them in one. Take the Green-marked cocks first, Crested or Plainhead: a Crested bird we would pair with a lightly Cinnamon-marked hen, and expect to find among the produce Variegated Crested Cinnamons of either sex, more or less evenly-marked according to the marking of the parents; a Plainhead we would mate up with a Clear-bodied Cinnamon-crested hen, and expect them to produce the same as the previous pair with probably lighter marking; we would also pair a Green-marked Crested bird with a Clear Norwich hen, and a Green-marked Plainhead with a Crested Norwich hen, and look for similar results, with the addition of more Green-marked and pink-eyed Clears, in all of which we should expect to find increased depth of colour. So far we have worked only with the produce of the pairs put up for crest-breeding, but in any room in which the breeding of colour-Cinnamons has been carried on there will be Plainhead cocks and hens in every stage of development, both Buff and Yellow, with which suitable mating can be effected when once the crest has been introduced and developed in the cinnamon form.

We need not pursue this further. There are many forms in which the results of crossing in the way we have endeavoured to explain will show themselves, to which we think it unnecessary to refer. The presence of any such form will at once suggest to the breeder a method of dealing with it in accordance with the laws which regulate Cinnamon-breeding, and the law of common sense which directs all breeding operations, apart from special considerations arising from peculiar conditions. There is one feature, however, to which we must refer before dismissing the Cinnamon. What is to be done with the house full of Green birds, the produce of the Norwich cock and Cinnamon hens, to which we directed attention at an early part of this chapter? Are they useless for the purpose of Cinnamon-breeding? On the contrary, they are very valuable; but when we left them there was nothing in the breeding-room with which they could be mated with such effect as with some of the birds resulting from the combinations we have suggested. But bearing in mind that Cinnamon blood infused from the male side will assert itself in *any* cross, it will be evident that if the hens, at least, of this batch of Greens, which now contains an addition of strong Norwich blood, be paired with the original Cinnamons, the result will be an improved edition of the bird, deeper in colour and richer in tone, but not so rich and bright as when obtained in the other way. In the same manner, if it be thought advisable, for the sake of some exceptionally superior crest formation, to import that feature through a Norwich cock, it can be done in that way, although the direct result will be, not Crested Cinnamons, but Crested Greens, which can, in the next generation, be made Cinnamon by mating with pure Cinnamon cocks. Birds of singular beauty, however, can be obtained from these Plainhead and Crested Greens, by mating with pink-eyed Clear Yellow or with Variegated Yellow Cinnamon cocks—a plan which must be adopted in the case of the Crested birds if it be desired to breed Variegated or Marked Crested Cinnamons, because the mating of a Self-coloured Crested Green with a pure Cinnamon would produce Self-coloured Crested Cinnamons, though, from the fact of the Green being full of Norwich blood, there might be a few irregular sports. Self-coloured Crested Cinnamons can be more readily obtained in this way, than by following up heavy variegation till light feathers be all eliminated and a perfect self-colour result, though the latter process might produce the more brilliant bird.

We now append Scales for expressing, in a tangible form, the relative values of the principal features. Being so nearly allied to the Norwich, the values of corresponding properties are almost identical, though we have the points given to the white underflue, and to the beak, legs, and feet of the Norwich at our disposal for distribution elsewhere. We introduce the element of richness or warmth of tone more discernible in some of its shades than in the, by comparison, more uni-coloured Norwich. We also use the expression "*transparent* brilliancy," noticeable principally on the breast—an effect we cannot describe in words any more than we can an *atmospheric* effect in a neutral-tinted background, though we recognise its presence when we see it. We also add extra points for size, subject to the explanations given in our notes on that feature.

SCALES OF POINTS FOR JUDGING CINNAMON CANARIES.

CLEAR YELLOW.

Points of Merit.	Maximum.	
COLOUR—Depth and purity	30	
Richness and warmth of tone	5	
Transparent brilliancy	5	
Distribution uniform; back level and free from dark stripes	5	
		45
FEATHER—Body-feather: for compactness ...	10	
Wings: for compactness and carriage	5	
Tail: for ditto	5	
		20
SHAPE—Head and neck: for neatness	5	
Back: for width	5	
Breast: for fulness	5	
		15
SIZE		10
CONDITION—Health and clean sound feather		10
Total		100

Negative Colour Properties.

A Clear Jonque Cinnamon should not show any tinge of green, nor be dull and rusty or semi-opaque, nor should it be patchy in colour or show dark stripes on the back or saddle, nor should there ever be any doubt as to the soundness of the cinnamon colour throughout, or any suspicion of a break.

CLEAR BUFF.

The Feather, Shape, Size, and Condition points admit of no appreciable alteration, unless it be that instead of giving points for "neatness" of head and neck, they may be placed to the credit of "width of skull" combined with neatness and finish, the bird being altogether more massive than the Jonque, and looking very mean when the skull is narrow. The Colour points, however, require some modification, as the mealy character of buff feather is not, in a Cinnamon, so intimately associated with the idea of richness or warmth of tone or transparent brilliancy, as with the notion of a regular distribution of colour as opposed to simply a dark skull, a mealy neck, and a breast showing fair colour only in front, but paling as it recedes towards the under region. We therefore submit the following:—

Points of Merit.	Maximum.	
COLOUR—Depth and purity	30	
Distribution: uniform on head, neck, and breast	10	
Back: level and free from stripes	5	
		45
FEATHER—Body-feather: for compactness ...	10	
Wings: for compactness and carriage	5	
Tail: for ditto	5	
		20
SHAPE—Head: for width of skull and neatness ...	5	
Back: for width	5	
Breast: for fulness	5	
		15
SIZE		10
CONDITION—Health and clean sound feather		10
Total		100

Negative Properties.

A Clear Buff Cinnamon should not show any shade of green, nor have the expanse of colour on neck and breast hidden by meal, nor have dark stripes on the back. It should not be coarse in feather, nor have a slovenly carriage of wings or tail, nor have a narrow skull.

VARIEGATED CINNAMONS.

Here the assessments correspond exactly with those in the Norwich scales, due regard being had to the depth of the cinnamon colour in the Evenly-marked class, as well as to the purity of the clear body-colour. This applies especially to the irregularly-pied birds, in which the 45 points allotted to the items, "depth, purity, and brilliancy," must be understood here to apply to those properties as attaching to the cinnamon colour, which is *here* the *body-colour*, the position of things being inverted.

Only a very slight alteration, also, will be necessary to adapt the foregoing scales to the requirements of the

CRESTED CINNAMONS,

in which, in the CLEAR-BODIED CINNAMON-CRESTED birds, the 5 points for colour allotted to the Crested Norwich in Class (*a*) must here be regarded as the maximum for the purest cinnamon-coloured crest. In the EVENLY-MARKED CRESTED, the Norwich scale measures the bird exactly, noting our observation as to the meaning of depth and purity of body-colour. But in the VARIEGATED CRESTED, in the face of the fact that the crest will have, in the majority of cases, been imported from the Norwich bird, and ought to be transmitted with more general Norwich colour-properties than we can expect to find in some of the rough forms in which the foundation of Norwich crest is occasionally laid, we give more points for body-colour than we have done to the Variegated Crested Norwich bird in Class (*c*), which may be supposed to have perhaps only recently imported its new feature at some expense of its own native colour. This, restored in the Cinnamon, we assess at double value and write it down 20, making the total of the body-points 50, and leaving the balance to the crest.

CHAPTER XVIII.

THE LIZARD CANARY.

We enter now on a description of the birds included in the second of the two groups in which we have arranged the Canary family—viz., those having a Distinctive Plumage, which we define to mean a fixed, distinctive character of feather, as opposed to the one simple notion embodied in the idea of colour. To this group belong the Lizard and London Fancy—tribes most probably intimately related. Which of the two is the elder we will not pretend to determine; and it is by many considered an open question whether the Lizard is an offshoot or a cultivated form of the London Fancy, or whether it is the parent of a bird known to have been in existence at least a century ago, and for which its admirers claim an ancestry exceedingly remote. It is said that the Chinese, in drawing out their chronological tree to show the antiquity of their nation, after descending through many ages, a few more or less being of no moment, arrive at a period concerning which they say that "the English and other barbarians have a tradition that about this time the world was created;" and far back in the olden time, in the early history of the London Fancy, we believe there is to be found in its unpublished archives a similar legend that "about this time common Canaries were introduced into England," which is a sad let-down for the Lizard family, who appear to possess neither a written nor a traditionary history. We propose a compromise in this case, and suggest the possibility of each being as old as the other, though, if we have any leaning, it is in favour of the Lizard, which we think, from sundry features in its character, presents indications in harmony with the laws of development seeming to point to the fact of its being the parent stem rather than an offshoot. We shall not pursue this question further at present, but will enter into it more fully in our remarks on the London Fancy and its probable connection with the bird under review.

We do not know that it is incumbent on us to trace out the origin of every Canary we have to do with, any more than it is necessary to account for each one of our many varieties of pigeons or domestic poultry; and the difficulty is increased when we can find no trace of a history to deal with, but must confine ourselves to speculative theory. Most probably the Lizard was born of a desire to develop to its fullest extent a description of feather-marking more or less common to nearly every dark Self-coloured Canary, and which bears the name of spangling—a form of feather not entirely absent even in some Clear birds, in which it may be traced in a rudimentary shape. This fact alone is evidence of its fixity, while the highest examples of its cultivated development show what it is possible to do in any one direction by careful and long-continued gathering up of impelling forces which, when united, are powerful and constant in their action. This spangled form of feather early attracted attention, and even in its imperfect embryo state seems to have been regarded as a feature worth encouraging. The old volume we have previously quoted from in our notes on the Cinnamon says:—

> "The Fine *Spangled Sort*, commonly called, *French Canary Birds*, and the *Mealy* Ones, are the Best to Breed with, for *Those*, who are very Curious.

Vincent Brooks Day & Son l

LIZARD CANARIES.

GOLDEN SPANGLED. SILVER SPANGLED.

> Because, A *Spangled Cock*, with a *Mealy Hen*, will
> Produce a more *Regular* Spangled Feather, than
> if Cock, and Hen were *Both Spangled*. For *Then*,
> They would Breed too *High* upon the Yellow.
> Because, The Young Ones, *Take* mostly after the
> *Cock Bird* in their Feathers, rather than the *Hen*."

It is quite possible that the term "spangled," as here used, may have a wider and more general significance than when used in the restricted form in which we apply it; but it is evident that spangling of some sort is referred to, even if the meaning be as obscure as that of "ashen-grey" and other forms of colour mentioned by old chroniclers which we do not recognise in any Canary of our day.

The description of feather-marking to which we have referred as being in all probability rudimentary spangling, and common to most dark Selfs, we may describe as consisting of nothing more than a darkening of the web on each side of the mid-rib, edged by a lighter margin, in some instances more decided than in others, but in all cases essentially the same in character. We have seen some horse-shoe saddles on Norwich birds in which we know there was no admixture of Lizard blood, elaborately worked with rudimentary spangling resulting from the presence of feather of this kind; and in the Scotch Fancy, which, of all the varieties in existence, must surely be entirely free from Lizard taint, there is often the same appearance—the ground-colour, the dark centre and the lighter edge; and we are not surprised that the presence of similar feather should have set some of the thinking fanciers of the olden time pondering how, on such a foundation, they could rear the structure we are about to describe—a structure so complete and so elaborately finished in every part, as to have become one of the highest, if not the very highest, triumph of the breeder's skill.

This Canary has been named, we think, from the striking resemblance its glittering plumage bears to the back of its scaly prototype, the comparison being not at all inapt, especially in the case of some of the old-fashioned sort. In size it is rather smaller than the average run of Norwich birds; the Jonques, and more especially the hens, being cast in a decidedly smaller mould. We attribute this, to a great extent, to the fact that there is no cross that can be used for the sake of obtaining size, absolute purity of breed being imperative; and hence there is no wandering away into any by-path in this direction. In shape and general conformation it is precisely similar to the two varieties we have described in our previous chapters, belonging to the chubby school, and in no way claiming to have any connection with Shape or Position birds. Its colour, also, in so far as regards the clearly-defined line between Jonque and Mealy, is as decided as is that of any example of the Colour section, the Jonque form being known as Golden Spangled; and the Mealy or Buff as Silver Spangled, these two names being most appropriate. But here we may at once remark that the Jonque or Golden bird is not really of a yellow or gold colour, but is rather, as regards what is called its body-colour, a rich, dark, bronzy yellow, very difficult to paint in words so as to be recognised, unless we have a familiar acquaintance with the warm tones of some of the rich umbers of the artist's colour-box. The richer, warmer, and purer the tone of this body-colour, the more valuable it is, and in it there should be no admixture of a greenish tinge, unless the bird be throughout of a positive green cast, as is the case with a school of Lizards common in Lancashire; in which case the purer the green, and the more brilliant and glittering, the better for the character of the bird. This last class of Lizard is not so popular a favourite as the former, but it has its followers, and represents a distinct strain, opposed to any idea of an intermediate form which is neither one thing nor another, and is not tolerated. Personally we are very fond of this description of bird; we admire them exceedingly, and have seen among them birds which, when innocent of any adventitious aids to strong colour-development, have seemed to us to be the type which may have suggested the characteristic family name.

The body-colour, or, as it is as frequently called, the ground-colour, can be best gauged by its display on the breast, which is generally a pretty good index of the quality in this respect. It will be obvious to all who have carefully read our remarks on the nature of the colour on the *back* of any dark Self—a Cinnamon for instance—that that is not the best place to look for an exhibition of ground-colour in a mass, the formation of the feathers of the back and the graduated colouring of each being adverse to such display, though the educated eye soon detects the appearance of the true shade in whatever place it appears. On the breast, where there is less of this graduated shading than anywhere, and where what is present does not in any way affect the display as a whole, there is, however, to be seen, delicately traced and softened down into hazy indistinctness, something like rudimentary spangling, which takes a more definite form as it approaches the sides and stretches away towards the region of the waist, where it not unfrequently seems to gather itself up into dark stripes, all of which indicates possession of that species of feather which produces good spangle. In those varieties of the Canary in which a "level" back is a desideratum, it will be seen that the presence of these stripes is not desirable, since they are evidences of a disposition to produce stripes or streaks, of which, remember, spangle is born, but uniform distribution of colour is not. We do not regard this as a show-point, by any means, but we do not consider it in the light of an objectionable feature. A bird appears more highly finished without such stripes, but they are valuable landmarks to a breeder in selecting stock for any special purpose.

So far we have referred to the colour of the Lizard only in general terms, and no further than was necessary in sketching a brief outline of its usual character, without going into minute details of individual parts in which colour, *per se*, plays a less important part than the distinctive character of the feather. The bird, as it at present appears on our canvas, must therefore at this stage be understood to be simply roughed out in the warm ground-colour we have indicated, and we will now proceed to finish it in detail.

Beginning with the head, we remark that it is one of the most important features in a good Lizard, and, while having extreme neatness and finish, must also have good width of skull, in order that it may show to the greatest advantage what is held by many fanciers to be the greatest ornament of the bird, viz., the cap, which in a Golden Lizard is a patch of pure yellow, and in a Silver pure buff, covering the crown. We cannot pass this beautiful feature without some remarks as to its probable origin. We regard it entirely as a cultivated and not a native development. It is the least constant feature in the bird, and is the most difficult point to manage. Sometimes it is present in excess, at others in a very imperfect form, and not unfrequently is entirely wanting. Its erratic character is of itself, to our mind, sufficient evidence of its having been originally merely a chance beauty-spot, captured and made the most of, and its presence is no more astonishing to us than is the white top-knot on a black Poland fowl. Any feature may be made constant by following out the principle of selection, though it may be a work of time and considerable difficulty, the development and improvement of native features being more easy than the cultivation of sports, which are apt to revert to their original form even under the most careful management, their whole existence being a lifelong struggle of nature and art. Now, as to the colour of the cap, it will be sufficient to say that just in proportion to the warmth of the ground-colour will be the richness of the pure colour on the crown, which is no doubt only one form of development of the body-colour. Just as a rich, bronzy, Green Norwich breaks into the purest Jonque, so will the same thing happen in the Lizard, and as a natural consequence the paler the body, the paler will be the cap, and, in the case of a very green body in which warmth of colour is wanting, the cap will be of a shade of lemon instead of rich orange. In shape the cap should approach an oval form, though there are almost as many opinions on this matter as these slightly varied forms, some liking to see it bounded by a straight line at the back, or, as it is called, "cut square," and others perfectly elliptical. Perhaps the best form is what is familiarly termed a "thumb-nail," which may be described as being midway between the two, being, in fact, a "square-cut." cap with the corners rounded off, by which nothing of the width is lost, while there is no harshness of outline. There are really no angles or straight lines in the outline of a bird. What is recognised as an oval cap sometimes appears narrow, and detracts from the positive width of the back of the head, especially if the oval be at all pointed; while the "thumb-nail," which in its most perfect form is bounded in the rear by a curved and not a mathematically straight line, and is in reality one form of ellipse, fills the eye. This cap now occupies that place in our allegiance we were at one time disposed to give to a pure oval. We have given as our idea a civilised example of a "thumb-nail," because there are thumb-nails and there are oyster-shells.

A perfect cap should be bounded by a line commencing at the top of the beak and passing over the top of the eye round to the back of the head in the same plane, and returning in the same way on the other side. It must not come lower than the top of the eye, and the boundary-line at this part should be a hair-line of clearly-defined feathers. The absence of this hair-line is not a fatal blemish, its presence in an unbroken form being comparatively rare. A good type of it may be seen in any of the coloured illustrations. This dark marginal bordering is not formed by a single row of minute feathers, but as frequently as not by the extremities of feathers forming quite a patch over the eye, their base being entirely covered by the lighter feathers of the cap. This formation can be seen if the margin of the cap be raised with the edge of a knife; and it might, perhaps, astonish some who do not look very closely into such matters to see on how small a surface the actual cap frequently grows. The cap of a nestling, when just beginning to sprout, often presents the appearance of a mere streak, and seems to bear no proportion to the amount of dark feathers on either side; but if it be regular in shape—and at this stage of its existence every feather can be seen, and the slightest defect ascertained—there need be no fear as to its ultimately covering its allotted space, and such apparently too wide margin of dark feathers becomes no defect, but develops into the fine hair-line we have referred to as the cap arrives at maturity.

The outline of the cap must be clearly defined and unbroken, and its entire area unsullied by the presence of a single dark feather, which simply means that it must be absolutely clear—a point which cannot be too rigidly adhered to as a standard, though its practical illustration is so exceedingly rare that by common consent the nearest approximation to perfection is usually accepted, notwithstanding there are some fanciers of the variety who will not accept any compromise, maintaining that it is the hard and fast line by which a Lizard shall be qualified or disqualified for the show-stage. The slightest departure from what is understood as a clear cap constitutes it *foul*, and the principal defects to which the cap is subject may be described as (*a*) those affecting its fair surface, and (*b*) marginal blemishes. The whole are included in the idea *foul*, since every imperfect cap, in whatever may consist its imperfection, must be considered foul; but whereas the blemishes which affect the fair surface or area can only arise from the presence of larger or smaller isolated patches of dark feathers in its clear expanse, the marginal blemishes can consist either in an encroachment of the cap on the surrounding dark region, or in a corresponding encroachment of the surrounding dark feathers on the margin of the clear area; any intrusion of the surrounding feathers on the clear surface constituting what has of late years come to be generally recognised as a *broken* cap, and any intrusion of the cap itself on the dark feathers of the neck being called a *run* cap, than which two more suggestive terms could scarcely be used, conveying as they do clearly in the one case the idea of a clear surface broken into or intruded upon by a foreign element, and in the other the idea of that clear surface running over or exceeding its prescribed limits. The idea of *broken*, of course, attaches also to ticks or patches of dark colour remote from the margin, but a *run* cap has but the one meaning we have endeavoured to make plain. In two words, the one is an encroachment *on*, and the other an encroachment *of*, the cap.

That this constant inclination in the direction of irregularity should exist in the Lizard cap we take to be one argument in favour of its being not so much a developed native property as a chance feature requiring constant attention, the large proportion of broken caps as compared with the number of run examples showing a determined tendency to revert to a form in which, probably, the cap would be entirely absent, as is sometimes the case in exceptional specimens even now.

Fig. 45.

We furnish illustrations of the most common forms assumed by defective caps. Fig. 45 represents a decided patch of spangling in the centre, and speaks for itself. It is not always, however, so clearly defined as in the cut, but may assume the character of a minute tick, consisting, in fact, of but a single feather. When such tick is clearly isolated and detached from the surrounding margin, the blemish is more plainly seen, and offends the eye more than would an equally trifling irregularity in the margin, unless it existed immediately over the beak, in which position it destroys the effect of a clear surface as much as if found in the centre. A tick so situated cannot, however, be regarded as a strictly marginal blemish, since there is

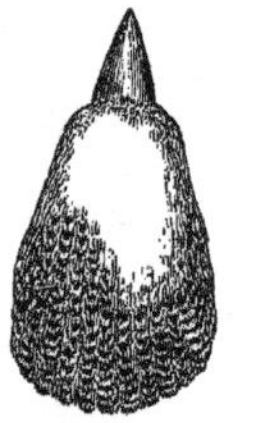

Fig. 46.

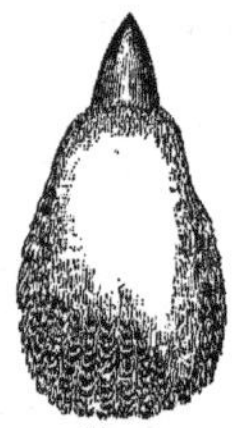

Fig. 47.

no area of feathers between the front of the cap and the beak, and there cannot, therefore, be any intrusion. Dark feathers in this place, therefore, have all the weight of isolated spots; and with respect to such, wherever found or of whatever extent, there is but one law against which there is no appeal: they determine a foul cap. Fig. 46 also represents a form of broken cap unmistakable in its character. This is an intrusion, and something more than a mere marginal irregularity, a great portion of the area of the cap being absorbed by the encroachment of the dark neck-feathers in a solid, unbroken mass. We have given this illustration for a twofold purpose—to exemplify this particular form, and to show clearly the difference between it and Fig. 47, representing a run cap, in which the clear colour is seen running over and down the back of the neck.

The three forms we have described—viz., the greater and lesser isolated blemishes, and the clearly-defined intrusion of the neck-spangles in a connected mass—constitute the three representative examples of the broken-capped bird, the presence of any of the blemishes entailing the penalty of disqualification in ordinary competition. In the case of marginal shortcomings a certain amount of licence is allowed; and in weighing these, their extent as well as locality must be taken into consideration in deciding whether they shall be disqualifications or simply represent subtractive values. Too much dark margin over the eye, for instance, is worse than none at all, and is very apt to assume such proportions as to bring the cap under the category of broken. Another dangerous region is the space between the top of the eye and the beak, margined by the dark feathers of the face. These sometimes rise into the cap, a very slight disarrangement here destroying the perfect oval frontage and condemning the cap. Blemishes at the sides or towards the front are more serious than at the back, where some irregularity of outline is more frequent. A not uncommon defect in the rear is when the corners of a square-cut cap run, one or both of them, slightly into the neck: it may be merely a very faint streak, and scarcely perceptible; but, if even to the extent of only one or two feathers, it is visible, and destroys the finish which should belong to a clean-cut

Fig. 48.

outline. Occasionally the posterior boundary of the thumb-nail is fringy, arising from one or two of the clear feathers projecting beyond the margin; and sometimes an oval cap becomes pointed to an extent which, while what remains of it may be clear, renders it anything but a desirable form.

There is one other blemished type to which we must call attention, being in reality one form of the run cap, but run in a direction different to that indicated in Fig. 47; we refer to what is known as a *bald face*, an example of which is seen in Fig. 48, in which the cap includes not only the eye, but a portion of the cheek. This is a very serious defect, and is frequently accompanied by other departures from soundness of body-colour, of which we shall treat in their proper place. One would imagine that an extension or running of the cap in *any* direction would be equally reprehensible, but practically it is not so. In a mere longitudinal extension the cap is enlarged in a direction in which it *may* travel within certain limits, but the lateral boundaries it cannot pass without trespassing on a region which cannot be said to belong to the crown, and such departure is indicative of a disposition to run riot in a way which belongs not to the good Lizard. This gross form of blemish, a form which seems to brook no control, might perhaps have been classed with departures from sound body-feather; but emanating, as it most frequently does, from the cap, we have preferred to connect it with that feature. Figs. 49 and 50 illustrate two forms which, while perfect in their way, are undesirable shapes. The first represents a short or under-sized cap, and the latter one which droops in the rear, and is, therefore, not on the same plane throughout: of the two, the latter is the least objectionable, provided always that the base be decided in its outline.

We have been thus minute in our detail of every point, good, bad, and indifferent, which belongs to the cap, because it is considered by some of our best breeders to be *the* feature of the bird. We fully recognise its great importance, and when it is found absolutely faultless would be disposed to award it a greater proportionate value than we should to a close approximation to perfection. Shape, size, and colour are frequently presented in the cap in a way leaving little to be desired; but there is generally a something wanting, which, if there, would add an almost indefinite worth to the whole, so difficult to assess in any numerical valuation of individual features. The point in which many otherwise perfect caps fail is in the delicate hair-line above the eye, the "eyebrow," as it is familiarly termed. Sometimes it is present on one side and not on the other, or may appear in a line wanting continuity; but, under any circumstances, the perfection of development is so rare that, as we explained in the preface to our Norwich scales, it can only be represented by some indefinite number representing the value of a well-balanced combined whole.

We now pass on to what, with all respect to the cap, we consider to be the feature of features in a Lizard; viz., its spangling. We hold this opinion without any mental reservation whatever, nor do we think this expression of our faith needs any defence. A Lizard having beautiful

Fig. 49.

Fig. 50.

spangling always has its value, even if the cap be very defective; but let the cap be ever so good and the spangling bad, and it is held in slight estimation. We do not wish to over-estimate the value of the one or disparage that of the other, but we are heretical enough to say that of the two we would prefer to see a well-spangled Lizard without a cap, rather than a good cap without spangle. The one would still be a Lizard, but the other nothing. Our ideal is that even balance is more difficult to obtain than excess of any one property; but if asked what we consider the essential feature of a Lizard, our answer is "Spangle."

And what is spangle? We have in our opening remarks briefly referred to what is probably spangling in its rudimentary form. An examination of a feather taken from the middle of the saddle will show what it is in its developed shape. The flue of each feather—that is, the soft, silky portion next the root of the quill—is entirely blue-black, and we may say here that as a standard point the blacker the flue the better; but as the feather finds its way to daylight, and the flue assumes the character of feather proper, the colour changes, and the centre of the feather becomes of black-brown, margined with a lighter shade, the central colour increasing in depth till it reaches nearly to the extremity of the feather, where it expands into a circular form corresponding with the outline of the feather, and is then as nearly a true black as possible. The marginal edging also assumes a new tone, becoming of the shade we have described as the body-colour, its extreme edge being fringed with a very narrow bordering of a still lighter shade, which in the Golden-spangled bird is the same as the cap, and in the Silver has, in addition to what coloured edge it may possess, an extreme outer verge of white, being, in fact, simply the buff or mealy form of the

Jonque bird, and takes its name from the frosted, silvery appearance this mealy fringe produces. A reference to Fig. 51 will show this formation of the feather and will also explain how one feather overlapping another produces the appearance we term "Spangling;" and will further show, better than we can describe, how, the wider and blacker the expanse of the central dark colouring, the larger and more distinct will be the dark eye forming the nucleus of each individual spangle. This arrangement of colour is seen in every feather, from the small ones at the back of the head, and *on* the head in a broken-capped bird, down to the larger feathers of the saddle; and when it is borne in mind how gradually these increase in size and how regularly they overlap each other, a pretty fair idea may be formed as to what the back of a good Lizard should be like. Commencing immediately at the back of the cap, it should consist of a series of continuous chains of spangles, gradually increasing in distinctness and size. At first the spangles are not distinct, but have more of the appearance of black specks, owing to the disposition of the neck-feathers and the continuous shifting of their position from the motion of the bird; but when the spangling is carried up on the crown, as is seen in a broken cap, it assumes all its regular form, though on a small scale, the peculiar marking of each feather being seen very plainly when one or two have been extracted, thus exposing the dark flue at the base of those which the extracted feathers previously overlapped. We cannot give a more familiar illustration of this than by saying the vacancy is precisely the same as when one or two slates have been removed from a roof.

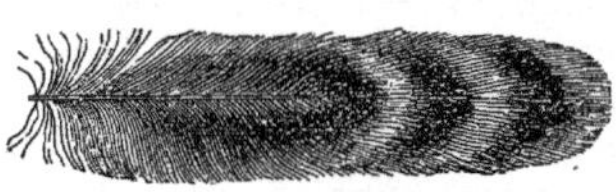

Fig. 51.

Spangled feathers removed from the margin of a cap expose the clear flue of the clear cap-feathers they overlapped, and clear feathers removed from a run margin expose the base of the spangled feathers in the same way, and sometimes tell a tale not much to the credit of a manipulator who may have been trying to give a practical exposition of the truism—

"Things are not what they seem."

We have used the expression "continuous chains." Regular rows of spangling are necessary to form a good back, but they must on no account resolve themselves into mere longitudinal stripes. Each link in the chain must have its clear edging, and each spangle must be as decided as the eyes in a peacock's tail. They must not be thrown on as if indiscriminately and without method, but arranged with the greatest regularity, to which anything approaching open-feathering is directly opposed. The importance of compactness in this respect will be obvious. A bird of slovenly habit simply fails to show its pattern. The back of a Lizard is like an elaborately painted fan on which some geometrical design is drawn. Unless opened out just to the exact degree, the pattern is confusion; but when rightly arranged, is perfect in all its parts. Or it resembles a volume with illuminated edges, which requires the leaves to be so arranged that each shall contribute its tiny portion of the whole with the most minute exactness, but which, when opened too far, throws the entire design into a mist.

And a word as to the decided character of the colour of the spangling, in so far as concerns the difference between the rendering on the backs of Jonque and Mealy—*i.e.*, Gold and Silver birds. The same general properties which belong to these two distinctive forms of colour, where-ever found, must here be marked with the utmost precision. The spangle of the Golden bird must be bright and glittering, without any trace of the mealy edging sometimes seen in doubtful forms of Jonque feather even in Clear Norwich Canaries. Some Golden Lizards do show this, and it is not uncommon to see Jonque hens with a decided silver lacing. Such will always be found to be very close in feather, and to possess, in fact, strongly-marked *buff* proclivities; still they are Jonques, but only indifferent forms, and are valuable as breeding stock, accordingly as they may be known to possess certain traits which may be in the blood but not on the surface, but not representative types of the Golden Lizard. And in the same way a Silver must *be* a Silver, and should exhibit its spangling in connection with every property supposed to attach to the buff form of feather. There is a profusion of wealth in a good specimen. Nothing can exceed the beauty of the spangling with its clear silver edge, while the natural compactness of the plumage exhibits the chains of "moons" in a way not always discoverable in the Jonque. Skilful feeding, too, brings out its colour in a remarkable way, giving the bird an appearance as if warp and woop were of different shades, the plumage in places shining like a shot-silk with every movement of the bird; and the neck with its tiny yet distinct spangling, on which the shape of every feather is as distinctly defined as on the neck of a grey parrot, has no equal in any Canary.

Before dismissing the subject of spangle, we may remark that some old fanciers speak of a tribe of birds which must now be extinct even if it ever existed. We refer to what are occasionally called Blue Lizards, respecting which a fancier, who has been a careful observer and a student of the family history for nearly forty years, writes, "The Blue Lizard of former days I never see now." Whether such a variety was ever recognised we cannot say, but we would suggest that what may at one time have been known as Blue Lizards were probably only Silvers spangled in excess. And this leads us to our closing remark on this feature. Excess of spangling, when it assumes the form of diminutive moons and over-development of lacing, produces a hazy indistinctness technically termed "moss," which is perhaps the most dangerous shape in which it can appear, as any disposition to obliterate the dark eyes of the spangles means doing away with the dark centre in the feather which produces them, and thus destroying the very life of the variety. Write down a "mossy" back as being to spangle what a bald face or other tendency to "running" is to the cap.

The wing of the Lizard plays an important part in its show economy. "Black, home to the quill," is one of the oldest laws of a very old code, and indicates, broadly, what should be the general character of the feather. It is not, however, intended as a rigidly exact definition so much as to convey the idea that black or some form of black is the standard colour, and that white or any tendency thitherward is forbidden. The web and flue should be "black, home to the quill," but the shaft or quill itself is only black for as much of its length as is exposed, its base being nearly as white as that of any ordinary clear flight-feather. A reference to Fig. 52 and the coloured illustration will show that the inner flights in particular are margined with a paler shade of colour (a feature common to all dark wings, whether Green, Cinnamon, or anything else), and the beauty of the wing, so far as this arrangement is concerned, consists in the darkness of the web and stalk and the rich character of this marginal edging, which is more or less brilliant as it is found in the Gold or the Silver form of the bird. Notice, further, that the extreme outside margin of the primary flights or ten outer feathers is also fringed with an edging of colour for some small portion of its length, but it should not extend so far as that part of the feather where the narrow portion of the web is so much narrowed as to cause the stalk to become almost the actual margin; else, when the wing is closed, the effect of these minute edgings of colour being placed side by side will be to give the appearance of a transverse band of light colour extending in the direction of the middle of the wing, just so far into it as the close packing of the primaries will produce it, entirely destroying the effect of what should be a uniformly dark wing. This defect is sometimes very patent, and an examination of the individual feathers of such a wing will show an extended margin of distinctly grey edging which is very objectionable. It should be remembered that it is the broader inner flights—technically, the tertiaries, or tertials—those in which the stalk is found in the middle of the web, which have the wide marginal lacing, and that as the stalk nears the outside the light margin should vanish. We strongly recommend a careful examination of a living wing, closed and expanded, when the distribution and effect of the colour will be plainly discerned.

The larger wing-coverts also have much to do with the make-up of a bird in which every feather has its definite value. Each covert must represent a smaller edition of its corresponding flight, the position and the extent of outer edging displayed demanding the most exact lacing: the innermost are hidden by the marginal feathers of the saddle. With these larger coverts, lacing may almost be said to end and spangling to begin, for the second or smaller coverts with their

FIG. 52.—FOUL WING.

rounded extremities possess something very much resembling the dark terminal eye which determines spangle, albeit the marginal fringe does not assume a silver or a golden colour until we reach the row of feathers next above these, which, however, are not on the wing, but are the outer row of the scapulars overlapping the base of these beautiful second coverts with the most perfect regularity.

It will now be readily seen that our term Distinctive Plumage is not misapplied, since the character of our bird depends, literally, on the distinctive character of each feather, and in no part is distinctive elaboration more imperatively demanded than in the immediate region of the shoulder, where the arrangement of the feathers can be more plainly seen than in the wing of a clear bird, the body-colour of which is white, or at the best a very pale yellow, with only a faint edging of the same colour. In the latter any defect is not so patent, but in the Lizard wing the slightest blemish is palpably evident. On the decided marking of each of the smaller coverts, of which there are several rows, though the first is the most important, depends much of the finish of a good wing, and a well-marked clearly-defined row of "pinion-feathers," as they are frequently called, will always turn the scale in anything like close competition. Where general good properties prevail we may safely look for a good wing, but blemishes are often to be met with of a positive character. A wing may be poor in colour and have only very indifferent edging, but so long as it is a perfect wing its shortcomings are nothing more than negative, and the most that can be counted against them is a subtractive value. But it sometimes happens that an otherwise beautiful wing is spoiled by the presence of one or two (*one* is enough to disqualify under the rigid Lizard law) clear feathers, which, when they occur in the smaller coverts, constitute what is known as a "rose shoulder," "rose wing," or "shell wing" (see Fig. 52). This is a most vexatious and fatal blemish, and a white smaller covert is just exactly one of those feathers which stick to the fingers and are apt to come away quite unintentionally. A white flight-feather will also only too frequently intrude where "black, home to the quill," forbids its presence. Such a feather is fatal to the reputation of any bird, and entails summary disqualification, though if it be not absolutely white, but show some trace of black in stalk or web, it does not actually disqualify, though, however good the bird may be in other respects, it reduces its winning chances to something indefinitely lower than zero. We need scarcely add that if any feathers ought to be blacker than the rest, they are those of the bastard wing.

Travelling to the other end of the bird, we find the tail, the twelve feathers of which must be essentially the same in character as the flights. It must not be spread out like a fan, nor piped, but expanded just enough to show the extreme outer margin of each feather, its base being thatched by the upper coverts, which must show not the slightest approach to coarseness—a defect not for a moment to be tolerated anywhere in a Lizard.

Cap, spangle, wings, and tail: there cannot be much remaining except the beak, legs, and claws, which ought to be as dark as possible, since the clear beak and flesh-coloured legs and claws are indicative of a tendency towards paling in colour. The general appearance of a Lizard is dark, and he belongs to a dark-flue school: light points are, as a matter of contrast, objectionable; as a matter of breeding, still more so. Dark beak, dark legs, and ebony claws are the correct thing in a Lizard: they are his hat, gloves, and boots—things some people don't care about. We do. He should be a perfect gentleman in all the details of dress. There is a fitness in things: sheep-skin kid gloves, sizes too large, and seditious-looking boots spoil the best costume.

CHAPTER XIX.

BREEDING LIZARD CANARIES.

ALTHOUGH it is considered a difficult thing to breed a perfect Lizard, it is not more so than to produce any other bird in perfection. We have before adverted to the fact that average quality, now-a-days, is another name for a high degree of excellence, and that the exceptional birds we now and then see are at no one's command, though they are within the possible reach of every intelligent breeder. We think there is every encouragement for the fancier in commencing to breed this interesting variety, because its leading features may be said to be fixed, and he has not, as in some cases, to deal with properties so fickle and erratic as scarcely to be under any control whatever. He will not find himself pairing Clears and producing Pies; mating marks, and looking in vain for their reproduction; nor will he find any of the many seemingly unaccountable results which follow ploughing in some of the fields of the Canary fancy. If he pair Lizards he will obtain Lizards, capped and spangled, and from any given quantity of genuine material will obtain a greater proportion of satisfactory results than can, perhaps, be arrived at in any other direction, simply because he will find himself working with elements constant in their action. Considering the comparatively small number of Lizard breeders and the few birds bred, we think the per-centage of high-class specimens exhibited is far in excess of those found in any other variety; and to any fancier anxious to commence with a reliable bird which will to an appreciable extent accomplish what is asked of it, and is capable of being bred up to a high state of development through sure channels, we say "go in" for Lizards.

The general principles which should guide the breeder in the selection of his stock, and the philosophy of its subsequent management in dealing with its fancy points, may be gathered from our adaptation of the essay on "Pedigree Breeding" referred to in Chapter XIII., and the importance of *beginning right* will be manifest from the case cited on page 112. "It is the *not* beginning right, this far too common plan, which stands in the way of success with scores of amateurs." Let the selected parents be the most perfect in all points that can be procured, but, above all, let them be from some *reliable strain on both sides.* This is the essence of a successful start. To disregard this salutary advice is to begin in a way which is certain to land the novice in a maze, from which even a practised hand would require all his skill to extricate himself, but in which the amateur would grope about in the dark and inevitably meet with the shipwreck of all his hopes. Even the very best strains require attention to maintain their virtues unimpaired; but so long as a beginner finds he has not retrograded, made no leeway, he knows his whereabouts, and can beat up slowly but surely in the required direction, confident in the strength of his resources; but blown off the land in his first essay, and his supposed good strain put back nobody knows how far or into what impure channels, cap, spangle, colour, and every good property blown to the winds, he votes Lizard-breeding a delusion, and gives up at once. We have said perfect in *all* points, but remember that the most important are spangle and sound body-colour. These *must* be maintained, at the same time that great care is exercised lest there should be deterioration in the cap; and our object here in so emphatically urging the necessity of obtaining stock of established character is, that the beginner may avoid the fatal error of attempting at one step to supply deficiencies in either parent by the infusion of the required element entirely unsupported by such other good properties as may already exist on the side in which there is a deficiency of the element proposed to be supplied. We can, perhaps, make our meaning plainer by supposing a case. The beginner has secured a good bird from a family habitually sound in colour and elaborate in spangle, but it has a poor cap. For a mate he selects a bird of which he knows nothing but that it has a perfect cap—the point he wants—but which is deficient in spangle and colour, and thinks to graft each good property on the other. Such a false step as this may be taken at any period in a breeder's history as well as at the commencement, and *has* frequently been done, to our knowledge, with the most disastrous results, and, in consequence, a little quiet recrimination and covert reflection that the imported cross obtained by a "friendly exchange" was not the "right thing." The result is simply a failure. Our novice finds his colour and spangle utterly demoralised and his caps not much improved. He has, in fact, let slip what he previously held—lost much and gained nothing: lost much, because (see "Pedigree Breeding," Chapter XIII.) he has introduced into his habitually well-spangled strain tendencies he knows nothing of; and gained little or nothing, because his perfect cap may only have been an exceptional head in a poor lot, and the general effect of the influx of "fresh blood" has been the inevitable reversion to long-lost faulty points of both parents. Hence the importance of beginning with birds the produce of similar courses of breeding, and in which the latent tendencies of each is known.

When we were very young, almost in our nest-feathers, and in commencing early the study of Mathematics were floundering about in the then, to us, mysteries of Algebra, a work of Cobbett's, in which the subject was treated of in a series of letters to his son, was put in our hands, and one thing in it we have never forgotten. At the end of each letter occurred an item of instruction of this kind: "Go back to Chapter ——, and study carefully the theories therein enunciated." We say the same in real earnest. Go back to Chapter XIII., and study carefully the theories therein enunciated. Make them part of your morning study and your evening meditations. Commit them to memory, and master their principles thoroughly. Illuminate them on scrolls and hang them in your bedroom—bird-room, we mean; in both, if you like. We thought we knew a great deal, but we didn't know how little we did know till we studied them. They embody the briefest, simplest, and clearest enunciation of the soundest principles of breeding with which we are acquainted.

A few specific directions will now suffice for the breeder's guidance. They must be understood to apply to the nicer distinctions in the mating of approved stock, and must always be considered as subservient to general principles. Pair Gold with Silver always, as a rule. The advisability of exceptional departures from this universal system will occasionally suggest itself to a thoughtful mind in this as in any other variety in which quality of feather and colour are properties involved, though here quality of spangle is also concerned. The gain from mating two Golds may be set down as comprising improvement in colour and in brilliancy of spangle; the loss, falling off in size, want of compactness of feather, and consequent lack of regularity in arrangement of spangle arising from the display of an excess of meal or silvery frosting, causing the bird to be too light, or to have a cloudy, "mossy" back. Birds undecided in the character of their feather should be mated accordingly—*e.g.*, a dull Gold having white marginal fringe, pair with a bright Gold, not with a Silver, which would probably only increase the fault, while there would, on the other hand, most likely be found in such an undecided Gold so much colour, in addition to the close feather indicated by the presence of the mealy fringe, as to warrant the expectation of something more than a mere restoration of balance of power from a feather point of view only.

As far as possible, pair dark birds. Don't break up a pet arrangement to do this, but try to work a breeding system with this as one of its bases. Remember that dark feather means dark spangling, and that the Lizard will deteriorate in this respect quickly enough if encouraged. White beak, white legs, and white claws are frequently followed by white something else. Mate, as near as can be got, with a view to a balance of good properties—a problem not always easy of solution, the practical outcome of the "concentration" theory being that in most good breeding-rooms two strains insensibly grow up, good in most points, but *strong* in *one;* the exceptional bird, the lion of its year, being generally a happy hit in which, by means of two sister strains, good spangle and fair cap have been augmented by union with fair spangle and superlatively good cap. But since experience has shown that the *cap* is the most variable and intractable feature, never hesitate to pair birds, however wanting in this respect, even to the extent of having no cap, if good caps have been bred from the strain. And further, inasmuch as a *bald face,* though connected with the cap, is in reality a defective condition of *body*-feather frequently accompanied by other body blemishes, and is further indicative of a disposition to grow light feathers instead of dark—do not breed from these unless for good reasons.

This leads us to a brief notice of a few things to be avoided or dealt with cautiously; and chief among them is the frequent use of any birds showing white feathers either in the wings or tail. These will occasionally appear even in the best strains, and puzzle the breeder as to whence their origin. We are disposed to regard them, in such cases, as mere sports rather than decided indications of foul blood, and we would not altogether discard an otherwise superior strain simply on account of its now and then producing a pied wing or tail. But we need not say that it would be contrary to the principles of Pedigree Breeding to pair two pied birds unless we wished to follow a suicidal policy with our stock. Counteract the influence and check the sport by mating with the blackest of black wings. Don't try to stamp out *any* defect in a hurry: it cannot be done any more than good properties can be fixed all at once; and take care that in doing this or anything else some other point is not stamped out which ought to be stamped in, or something added which ought to be subtracted. Attention to or neglect of these matters either means breeding or else mere waste of time.

The Lizard possesses its show-plumage for one year only. In its nest-feathers it shows no spangle whatever, but is just like a common Green Canary with a yellow cap, though some indications of its future character may be discerned by a practised eye. The breast of a good Gold nestling is speckled not unlike that of a Skylark, and sundry other small items are so many grounds of hope on which the old breeders, especially in Lancashire, speculate as to the number of copper kettles, the traditionary prize for a good Lizard, likely to depend from the hooks in their kitchen ceilings at the close of the show season. "First-feather"—that is, nest-feather—shows are common in the districts where this bird is bred as a specialty; indeed, every stage of its existence is watched with as much interest as a school-boy bestows on his silkworms during their successive metamorphoses. The changes which take place at the first and second moults are these:—In common with all others of the family, the bird casts its entire suit at the first moult except the flights and tail-feathers, which retain their original dark hue while the body puts on its spangle, and it is then, as we have said, in its show-dress. At the second moult the whole is renewed with a great alteration in character. The body-feathers become much lighter, the delicate marginal fringe turns paler in the Gold and whiter in the Silver, extends further into the web and defaces the clearly-defined eye of the spangle, which itself becomes less distinct as the entire feather loses its original brilliancy, and a general fading results, shared by the stalk or quill also, which, from being black, turns to grey, and "black, home to the quill" no longer represents the new state of things. This takes place with all Lizards, but with some more than others. We have seen some year-old and even older birds of high character very little changed, but all are so far changed as to unfit them for show purposes, while others put on age very rapidly; and this tendency to decline in colour, which increases with each successive moult, is a feature to which we shall have to call attention in our remarks on the London Fancy, with which interesting Canary we have expressed our belief that the Lizard is closely allied. A change, equally striking, also takes place in the flight and tail feathers, which become perfectly white at their tips and not unfrequently for a considerable portion of their length; and this change, it will be obvious, occurring whether the feathers be moulted in the due course of nature or abstracted by accident, the damage to the show prospects of a bird which ought to have its eighteen flights and twelve tail-feathers "black, home to the quill," which may result from its losing any of them and having them replaced by others white-tipped, must at once suggest that extreme care should be taken to prevent any such misadventure during moult. Unfortunately, these members, as we showed in our remarks on "Flighting and Tailing"—an operation from which the Lizard is happily exempt—are only too apt to get injured, especially the tail, and the vicissitudes of a Lizard's youth are a fruitful source of anxiety to the breeder. Supposing him to have left his nest with his full complement or with the loss of only a few small feathers from the back, which are of no moment, because they must ultimately be shed in a few weeks, and to have come unscathed out of the nursery-cage, there is still the ordeal of the "flight-cage" and the prospect of persecution and mischievous plucking by his fellows to be faced; and he is a lucky and generally a plucky Lizard who reaches the mature age of eight weeks in full possession of his entire original wardrobe. To reduce the chances of accident to a minimum, in the first place, *never catch or handle a young Lizard* in any way if it can possibly be avoided. In transferring young stock from one cage to another, do it gently and without any fuss. Place the open doors opposite to each other, and, quietly and patiently, coax the birds to hop from one to the other. Don't hold the second cage in such a way as to expose the hand. The first mental act of a bird on entering a new cage is repentance, and actuated by fear and fright he always makes strong efforts to do himself as much injury as possible in endeavouring to get out again. Much of this may be obviated by having a sliding door in one end of the flight-cage, and keeping a smaller open-wire cage constantly hooked on at the aperture: curiosity will soon induce the young birds to explore the new premises, and there will not be much difficulty in a short time in singling out any bird and caging him. If a bird *must* be handled, as in case of sickness when it may be necessary to administer medicine, don't hold him in the orthodox fashion by the tail and tips of the wings, but lightly grasped in the hand, or the consequence of a sudden flutter may be that he will leave between your finger and thumb, in the shape of his tail-feathers, whatever chance he may have had of adding to your stock of kitchen utensils.

If the cage accommodation be such that all young birds must be transferred to "flights," there to take their chance, let them be as large and roomy as possible—a little room, in fact, such as we described on page 70. We have seen some excellent arrangements of this kind in Mr. C. J. Salt's aviaries at Stapenhill, Burton-on-Trent, where corners of rooms boxed off with a few pieces of upright scantling, across which were tightly tacked lengths of common cheese-cloth, made capital temporary homes for birds likely to have their plumage injured or frayed by contact in clinging to ordinary wirework. We thought the cloth was suggestive of hiding-places for insects; but Mr. Salt assured us that with thorough ventilation and scrupulous cleanliness he was entirely free from any such pests. In such a retreat, young birds gain strength of wing by exercise, and can at any time be caught without risk in a small net and soon rendered quiet and tame in a covered-up cage. One advantage of such a flight-room is that it will hold a great number, and that the occupants can easily keep out of each other's and harm's way. In a smaller flight, the number must be limited, and quarrelsome members must be ejected for obvious reasons. And note that the Lizard is the most pugnacious of the whole Canary family. He is the game-cock of the tribe; and, be it male or female, when a Lizard makes up its mind to quarrel it carries out its intention conscientiously.

We are going into this part of our subject at length, because the greater portion of it applies also to the special management of the London Fancy, the second representative of the Distinctive Plumage class, and will not have to be repeated.

The best plan to adopt with exceptionally promising specimens is to isolate them as early as possible, giving each bird as roomy a compartment as can be spared. This, of course, implies plenty of cage accommodation; but a great deal can be done in this way by extemporising very simple appliances. Boxes of all sorts, shapes, and sizes can be procured at almost any grocer's, these "commercial envelopes" being now got up very neatly and cheaply, much more so than

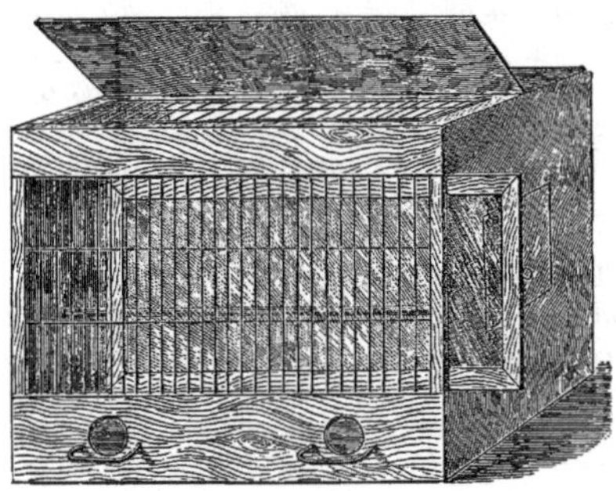

FIG. 53.—MOULTING-CAGE.

could be done by the amateur joiner. Nothing further is wanted in the way of wiring than to stretch tightly across the front a piece of good galvanised wire netting of small mesh, and with a door cut in one end—don't forget the door. Very little ingenuity will suggest the necessary internal arrangements for perches, seed-hoppers, and drinking-vessels. We said *isolate* the best specimens, but under ordinary conditions two or three will not quarrel. It is generally only in larger communities that some seditious fellow disturbs the public peace; lock him up, and quiet is restored. But remember that early isolation is to prevent the *possibility* of such mishap as might at any moment occur in case of a sudden brief disturbance.

There is a very elegant moulting-cage in use among the London Fancy breeders, of which we give an illustration in Fig. 53. It is generally made of mahogany, and is altogether a cage-maker's article. A glance at the cut will show the arrangement. A glass slide, which can be withdrawn at pleasure, serves the double purpose of preventing the bird from injuring its plumage by rough contact with the wire front, and also admits of the bird being more or less "boxed" to hasten the moult by maintaining equable warmth and freedom from draughts, while the cover on the top allows of stealthy peeps to ascertain how the work is progressing without needlessly alarming the bird. Inexpensive adaptations of this cage will also suggest themselves.

The same general treatment as regards diet applies to the Lizard as to the Norwich, but the cayenne system requires some modification. From some cause which we cannot explain, for at present we are to a great extent cognisant only of cause and effect, though we think our theories as to the *rationale* of cayenne feeding as expounded in Chapter X. are near the truth, notwithstanding some links in the chain may be missing, the Lizard does not behave in a uniform way under the cayenne regimen. We know we have capsicums at one end of the system and a blaze of colour at the other, but the food appears to be very uncertain in its action. With only one result we have now to do; the general results have been witnessed for two or three years, and have been considered on the whole eminently satisfactory. We refer to the consequences of extra liberal treatment; under which the plumage of the Lizard sports in a way nothing in the appearance of its nest-feathers would seem to warrant, and which sports or alterations in the character of the second feathers have never been known to occur under any of the old systems of feeding, in which, whatever may have been the constituent elements of any particular breeder's moulting-diet, cayenne pepper certainly never occupied a prominent place.

Mr. T. W. W. Fairbrass, of Canterbury, one of the most successful breeders of this variety, brought about some remarkable results by what proved to be over-dosing. Birds with perfect caps, or so nearly perfect as to be thought by him eligible for the severest competition, and therefore worthy of special care and the daintiest of dainty meats, were found, when moulted, to be foul-marked and "run" into the neck in a most perplexing manner, at the same time that the spangling had lost its distinctness and melted into a complete fog. The latter feature might perhaps be accounted for to some extent in this way: a "mossy" back, particularly in a Golden bird, *would* appear more cloudy and "run" under cayenne diet, inasmuch as the yellower portions of the feather would come out still redder, and so render the whole more hazy and indistinct; but the decided "running" of a previously perfect cap could be attributed only to the agency of the food, though in what way we cannot profess to explain. There is really an art in feeding a Lizard judiciously, much the same as in feeding Cinnamons. Only sufficient should be given to bring out the beauties of the bird in stronger relief, and no more. No judge would allow his eye to be carried away by colour alone; nor, in fact, is the dull brick-red we have observed on some birds by any means the tone a breeder likes to see. Brighten up the cap, by all means, and polish the fringing of the spangles, but do not feed to such an extent as to materially affect the darker plumage, and in so doing utterly destroy the tone of the lighter, and with it the character of the entire bird. This caution, however, applies chiefly to Golden Spangled birds, as the Silvers seem to revel in the warm food, and the more of it they assimilate, the more beautiful they become.

We do not care in a work like this to give more than a passing reference to any of the malpractices in which some exhibitors of the Lizard are adepts, for converting a blemished bird into an apparently perfect one, but which we hope are passing away before increasing light and improved education. We will not say that this Canary is more tampered with than any other in proportion to its many show-points, or that Lizard morality is of a lower order than the average status of that flexible virtue; but we know that ticks are extracted from foul caps, and patches too large for extraction are treated to an application of a solution likely to remove the little difficulty in the way of colour. An irregular margin at the back or a cap inclined to run is "eased a bit" by the scissors, and that trifling objection smoothed over satisfactorily. That homely commodity, candle-snuff, mixed with a little of its native tallow, will do wonders in removing the unpleasant effect of a bald face, a white covert, or an unseemly grizzle in any of the larger feathers, unless the defect be so palpable as to require the offenders to be extracted or cut off close to the stump, in which case high art can introduce others of approved quality into the hollows of the old quills, while a careful use of nitrate of silver can do all that may be necessary to a white beak, legs, or claws, or play its part generally in many ways which commend themselves to an observant mind. We are sorry the list is so long, but as an "artist" remarked to us on one occasion, "a Lizard take a deal of *doing* to put him right—*he do indeed.*"

The classification of Lizards must, it is plain, be restricted, in the first place, to the two forms—Golden Spangled and Silver Spangled, and until very recently no more extended arrangement than that included in this general division was to be found in any schedule. This is not the place to enter into a lengthened discussion of the principles which ought to determine the basis on which exhibition schedules should be formed, either from a general or special point of view. The subject has been well ventilated from time to time in such serials as are devoted to the interests of home pets generally, more exhaustively, perhaps, in the columns of the *Live Stock Journal* than in any other, and has narrowed itself within very prescribed limits embracing the whole of the ground. Briefly, the matter resolves itself into the one question, Shall the basis be provision for *perfection only* and nothing beyond? What may be the subtle distinctions between absolute and approximate perfection we will not stay to consider, but the idea implies *degrees* of perfection; and it is sufficient for our purpose to say that this most common-sense and most reasonable idea was not until late years recognised in dealing with the Lizard, a hard-and-fast line which, though supposed to be drawn with the most rigid severity, was, practically, constantly disregarded, separating the absurdly narrow and frequently spurious area of *perfection* (?) from the broader field of approximate excellence beyond, containing much genuine honest worth. This ridiculous barrier was the *cap.* The cap was the whole Lizard, and the whole Lizard was cap, to exhibit which in its perfect (?) form was the fertile cause of more nefarious manipulation, however ingenious and artistic, than arose out of any other demand of a very exacting code. Breeders might go into ecstacies over their beautiful spangle with its "moons" and "circling" and other vital properties, and glory in their rich bronzy colour and every other item in the inventory of the Lizard wardrobe, giving to each its carefully-measured value, and also to the cap its value, which, by the way, we find in an old scale to have been estimated at less than one-eighth of the whole, and in a more modern one at less than one-fifth, every maximum except that of the cap being subject to a subtractive process clearly implying the idea of graduated excellence; but on a blemish being found in this part, which mysteriously equalled its whole, the entire bird was supposed to vanish, for the cap was the bird. This we submit is an entirely different case to disqualification on account of the presence of white feathers. Certain material is permitted, with which, and with *no other*, the bird is to be built up, and the importation of foreign or deleterious matter is simply an infringement of the primary contract. Use the given material to the best advantage, working to the plan as closely as possible, and let the premiums be awarded to the most successful results according to their degrees of merit, not absolutely disqualifying from competition a mass of substantial and highly-finished work on the ground that some other portion over which the builder has not unreserved control has not been executed with undeviating accuracy.

To Mr. Richard Hawman, of Middlesborough, belongs all the credit of having put a stop to this anomalous state of things, by boldly introducing into the schedules of the Middlesborough Ornithological Society, of which he was President, classes framed for the express purpose of recognising the claims of birds with faulty caps, which, be it remembered, are often of unusual excellence, and infinitely more valuable than many specimens which make their way into the prize-list by virtue of their cap alone. Like many other reforms, this was thought to be very revolutionary, and offering prizes for imperfection could be nothing short of the beginning of the end of the ancient family of Lizards. But it turned out to be nothing of the kind, each succeeding year evidencing, by the marked improvement in the bird, the wisdom of giving premiums not only for examples of perfected development, but also for the best samples of *raw material*, which, to the surprise of many, was found to be frequently invoiced at higher quotations than the finished article.

The adoption of classes for faulty caps would probably never have been suggested had the practical application of any recognised scale of points been permitted by the Fancy, who, while professing to be governed by graduated scales which can only be applied in one way, continued to maintain a dogged allegiance to cap, rendering the use of any scale a farce. Judging was a duty fraught with endless annoyance, as one disappointed exhibitor could take a bold stand on the all-sufficiency of his perfect cap, and another, on being reminded that that feature was not quite perfect, would coolly argue that the defect was "only a trifle," and point to the beauty of his spangle; the difference between standing or falling by the cap varying according to the temperament of the exhibitor, for which there was no provision made in the scale—an absurd state of things from which all are now glad to have been released.

The classification now general in all liberal schedules is—

(*a*) Golden Spangled Lizard.
(*b*) Silver Spangled Lizard.
(*c*) Golden Spangled Lizard with Broken Cap.
(*d*) Silver Spangled Lizard with Broken Cap.

Classes (*a*) and (*b*) require no explanation other than that they are supposed to include the perfect form of bird, or those in which there is no palpable infringement of the laws regulating the formation of cap. To recognise *any* defection from the high standard, however slight, in the face of an arrangement ostensibly formed to meet the difficulties of the case by providing for perfection and imperfection, would seem, at first sight, to be inviting still worse complications; but a few words will explain how the requirements of one division serve as a guide for the other, and clear the way for a satisfactory settlement of a difficulty which never could have been arranged but by admitting that there are *degrees* even of perfection. For the purposes of classification the term "broken" is considered as general in its application and not strictly technical, and in this sense may be taken to include every form of blemished cap. For the sake of simplicity and clearness, however, we think it is not advisable to retain it as a generalised term, inasmuch as it belongs also specially to one of several forms included in the comprehensive idea, and in this way sometimes causes confusion. We suggest the substitution of the term "blemished," which includes in its embrace every possible defect without hinting in the remotest way at the technical name of any. This furnishes us at once with a definition which cannot have two meanings, and does not in any way interfere with existing technicalities. We speak of a cap as "blemished," and the idea of defect at once comes home; and the question follows as naturally as possible—*How* blemished? It is "broken." *Where* is it broken? In the centre, over the beak, over the eye, &c. It is "run." *Where* is it run? At the back, on the neck, over the face, &c.; and we at once get accurate information and clear notions. In the "blemished" classes (*c*) and (*d*), the bird is judged for every good property belonging to the Lizard except the cap, which, whatever be its character, is *entirely ignored.* It matters not, indeed, even if it have no cap. This clears the way at once. Given a bird with fair spangle but nothing extra, an average back but superior cap: we need scarcely say its place is in (*a*) or (*b*). Given a similar bird, a little better in spangle, one a judge would look at twice, but still not a constellated map, and let it be not *quite* so perfect in cap though still good: its place is still in (*a*) or (*b*), because its spangle is not of that ultra-excellence as to give it any chance in a competition where its cap would count *nil*: let it compete with its fellows among nice shades of approximate perfection of cap. Given a third bird, altogether superior in spangle, something exceptional, colour and other points all of a high order, but the cap slightly blemished, sufficiently so, however, to raise a doubt as to whether it would not interfere with its winning chances: this bird represents, practically, the pivot on which the classification turns. Two courses are open for it; either to enter it in (*a*) or (*b*), where its cap will be measured by the degree of its merit and possibly be assessed at a low rate, or to enter it in the "blemished" section (*c*) or (*d*), sinking the cap and competing on the basis of its other commanding features.

The whole matter may be briefly summed up as follows:—Absolute perfection in the cap of a Lizard is so extremely rare that to insist on its invariable presence without the slightest departure therefrom is, practically, to demand what does not exist. To meet this, degrees of perfection must be recognised and judged according to their approximation to the perfect standard. Any Lizard with a blemished cap may decline to compete in Classes (*a*) and (*b*), and claim admission to (*c*) or (*d*); but this involves the *utter and entire renunciation* of the points which represent cap value, to be judged for its *other* standard features *only*.

We close with a Scale of points, in which we endeavour as nearly as we can to express our estimate of the relative values of the many points of this most beautiful example of developed beauties. Many difficulties present themselves in attempting this, one of the most unsatisfactory parts of our task. We have seen but few scales we could not pick to pieces, our own among the number; and for each bird we have compiled at least half-a-dozen, of which no two were alike—a very cheering and consolatory state of things. In every case we try to build up our bird in a mathematical sort of Chinese-puzzle fashion, and there are always one or two pieces which won't fit—square pegs which won't go into round holes. The most carefully-digested arrangement always results in some disproportionate valuation of two or more points, and altering one of them throws the whole machinery out of gear. Roughly, it is generally estimated that the spangle represents one-half of the bird, and the cap the other half, wings and tail a third half, and colour a fourth, with sundry small points remaining, all having their own positive values; so that if we say let l = our Lizard, then spangle = $\frac{l}{2}$, cap = $\frac{l}{2}$, wings and tail = $\frac{l}{2}$, colour = $\frac{l}{2}$, and we have the following interesting equation—

$$\frac{l}{2} + \frac{l}{2} + \frac{l}{2} + \frac{l}{2} + \cdots = l$$
$$\text{or } 4l + \ldots = 2l$$
$$\therefore\ 2l + \ldots = l$$

This is a plain mathematical demonstration that it requires something more than two average Lizards to make one good example, which is a fact; and we cordially commend the study of the above algebraical formula to any one anxious to reduce the bird to a system of figures of which the sum shall be $l = 100$.

We shall frame the following scale in a way differing slightly from our previous plan. Being a Distinctive Plumage bird, we make that our starting-point; and inasmuch as the effective display of one of its features, spangle, is in a great measure dependent on a broad back, and cannot well have much of the attributes of "size and distinctness" without the broad back and compact feather, just as a wide cap cannot be present in the absence of a broad skull, we have eliminated the items "Feather" and "Shape," with their separate properties as set forth in the "Norwich" scales, and have embodied them in the values awarded to spangle and cap respectively, to have which in perfection *implies* the existence of the eliminated items. This we have done to prevent our scale becoming needlessly complex, as the value of the bird can be represented without going so much into detail as to render the scale practically valueless.

SCALE OF POINTS FOR JUDGING LIZARD CANARIES.

Points of Merit.

		Maximum.
SPANGLE—On neck, commencing at the back of the cap in elaborate minuteness, and enlarging on the scapulars	5	
On the back, in longitudinal rows of gradually increasing width: for size, distinctness, brilliancy, and regularity	30	
	—	35
CAP—For clear area, regular outline, width and symmetrical proportions, orbital margin or eyebrow, and colour	...	20
WINGS—Flights and greater coverts: for blackness of quill and web, richness of lacing on inner feathers, and generally compact carriage ...	...	10
TAIL—For blackness of quill and web, and good carriage...	...	5
THROAT AND CHEST—For soundness of colour and show of elaborate rudimentary spangling ...	...	5
COLOUR—For richness and purity	...	10
BEAK, LEGS, FEET, AND CLAWS—For darkness ...	...	5
SIZE	...	5
CONDITION—Health, cleanness, and sound feather	...	5
Total	...	100

NOTE.—We may explain that our reason for reducing the number of points allotted to "Condition" is not that we consider this property, in the abstract, is of less value to the Lizard than to any other bird, nor that we have any difficulty in fitting in the pieces of our puzzle so that our equation shall result in $l = 100$, but because *spotless purity* is not so much required here as in the case of the Norwich bird fresh from the bath. A good Lizard might, with care, and under favourable conditions, go unwashed for a whole season without cap or spangle losing *much* of their lustre; and the ratio of 10 : 5 exhibits, as near as figures can, the relative values of this property, "Condition," in the two birds, at least so far as absolute and spotless cleanness is concerned.

Negative Properties.

A Lizard should not be hazy or indistinct in spangling, nor should its spangles be arranged without regard to regularity, nor should they have small eyes, nor should the terminal edges be of a character inconsistent with the true type of feather of the class to which the bird may belong, nor should any Silver trait whatever be mixed with Gold, or the opposite. It should not have a narrow skull or a narrow cap, nor should the cap be sensibly narrower at the back than the front, nor should the back of it be pointed or extend further than the base of the skull. There should not be the slightest indentation in margin of the cap, nor should it include any portion of the eye or face in its area, which should be neither run, broken, nor fouled by a single speck. A Lizard should not have a pale throat or show a clear spot under the beak, nor have a pale breast. It should not exhibit a grey or a white-tipped feather in wing or tail in its show-dress. It should not show light flue or white skin anywhere except on the crown. It should not show a dirty green cast in its ground-colour, or any shade that is not brilliant and decided in tone. It should not have white beak, legs, feet, or claws. It should not be shown dirty, nor in such loose condition of feather as may militate against the most effective display of every beauty belonging to Distinctive Plumage.

Disqualifications.

A white feather either in the flights or tail; or a clear feather in any other part of the wing or on the body.

The scale for judging the Blemished classes (*c*) and (*d*) is the same as the foregoing, except that the points for cap may be distributed proportionately over spangle and colour.

Vincent Brooks Day & Son. Lith

LONDON FANCY CANARIES.

JONQUE COCK. MEALY HEN.

MEALY NESTLING.

CHAPTER XX.

THE LONDON FANCY CANARY.

IN endeavouring to propound a possible and probably correct theory as to the origin of this remarkable Canary, we must admit at the outset that we have little else than conjecture to guide us in lifting the somewhat obscure veil which shrouds its early history. That it is, as we stated in the opening of the previous chapter, very closely allied to the Lizard there can be little doubt, and we think we shall be able to show how circumstances seem to point to its being an offshoot from, if not really simply nothing more than a modified form of that bird. In so far as regards reliable published historical data, the London Fancy can certainly point to its name in the registers of a century back, and say to any other Canary, "Here is evidence that a hundred years ago *I was*, and that at a time when, in the absence of proof to the contrary, I assume you *were not*." That, however, might arise from the fact of its admirers being better organised and banded together under stringent laws, which have been handed down to us, for the purpose of developing this then *new* fancy from something *older;* and it may be, and probably is, quite true that the London Fancy is the oldest "fancy" development and the first Canary which, singled out from many other varieties, made for itself a name among its nameless contemporaries, who may not have been known by any special designation or distinguished by other than general terms more or less characteristic of some peculiar feature; *e.g.*, "THE Fine *Spangled Sort*, commonly called, *French* Canary Birds . . . . the Best to Breed with, for *Those*, who are very Curious." (See page 154.)

The historical relation between the two may only be very slight, but we think it more than probable that the "fine spangled sort, commonly called French Canary birds," would form part of the *penates* of the Protestant refugees, chiefly silk-weavers and workers of other textile fabrics, who found shelter here from the persecutions in France and the Low Countries a century before we hear of any form of that "fine spangled sort" being known by the special name identifying it with the locality in which it was cultivated; and it is a fact worthy of note that the "fine spangled sort," now known as the Lizard, is now, as then, the pet bird of the same class of handicraftsmen, whether the community be planted in Nottingham, long the centre of the Lizard fancy, or in Lancashire, where certain known strains descend as heirlooms in families.

But, whence evolved, is the problem we have to solve, and, Is the London Fancy originally from the loins of the Lizard? the direct question we have to answer. We are of opinion that it is. The general tendency of the whole domesticated Canary family is to struggle out of darkness into light, and we think it more in accordance with this natural law that the dark, spangled body should develop into a clear form than that the clear should grow dark. This is, in brief, our position, though, as in many other cases of disputed title, we know the difficulty of settling any such question conclusively. It may be said that there is no necessity to raise the question: here is the bird; make the best you can of it, and never mind where it came from. That is all very well; but the two birds are so singularly alike at one period of their lives, so unlike at another, and again, as age creeps on them and they turn their backs on the show-world with all its vanities and go down the hill together, they once more become so much alike that, forgetting the middle period of their lives when, inflated with pride, each scouted the idea of the remotest relationship with the other, they seem willing to say, "We were wonderfully alike in our cradles, and are nearly as much so in our last days, and perhaps, after all, may be of the same family-tree." Says the London Fancy, "Yes; you are from a distant branch of my ancient race." Says the Lizard, "Stuff! my nation was before London Fancies were;" and each, dropping his wings, pipes his death-chant, while breeders wonder whether they *are* related and which is really the foundation stem.

We shall depart somewhat from the plan we have hitherto followed, and begin with the London Fancy in its nest-feathers. We have already intimated that we shall have nothing fresh to offer by way of special instruction as to general management, moulting, &c., and the reader will be able to see as we go on how close is the probable relationship—so close as to invite the strictest investigation in the direction we have indicated, an ultimate opinion on which he will have to form for himself as to whether these two streams ever flowed in one, and, if so, which is the parent river.

The young bird in its nestling stage is so much like a nestling Lizard that the difference between the two could scarcely be distinguished even by the most experienced. It has the clear cap, the same dull greenish-brown body-feather, the black wings and tail, with pretty much the same general character of detail even to the grey margin on the outside of the narrow web of the premier flights, producing the identical effect of the pale transverse band referred to in our notes on the Lizard wing; and this description of the young bird will, apart from its serving to show the resemblance between the two, suffice for our purpose. On its first moult the character of the body-feather entirely changes, the dark nondescript green or brown giving place to a brilliant orange; now, in the most carefully-bred specimens, entirely free from ticks or dark feathers of any kind, but in former years more or less ticked or spangled, the really perfect bird being exceptionally rare. The dark flight-feathers as well as the bastard quills, of course, remain, and with the dark tail form a very beautiful contrast to the rich orange of the body. This change we take to be analogous to that supervening on the first moult of the Lizard, though the resulting effects may have become so widely sundered in the lapse of two centuries as to appear superficially to have no relation. Here, however, is the foundation of a metamorphosis which we think more likely to have progressed in the direction of from dark to light, the line in which it always drifts, than in the opposite way. The Lizard still has, after who knows how many, many years of persistent endeavour to fix and enrich its dark plumage, a latent disposition to pale, every avenue of escape requiring careful watching. The *perfect* development of either the dark spangled coat of the Lizard or the light rich dress of the London Fancy, we can easily understand, is the work of extreme care and systematic breeding, and we do not think that the presence of occasional light ticks in the one or dark ticks in the other proves much for either side, since the argument *pro* and *con* is equally cogent; for if it be urged that the Lizard has a direct disposition to pale, and that there are not wanting instances which could be adduced to show how colour and spangle have vanished very rapidly, and, *ergo*, the London Fancy is the perfect development of this tendency, it might be urged with equal force that since the fault of the London Fancy is a leaning towards ticks and rudimentary spangle, *ergo* the Lizard is the perfected development of this feature. We think that the fountain whence flowed these two streams is more likely to be discovered by following the broader theory that, of two given forms of colour, one dark, but having a tendency to fade, and the other light, with an inclination towards a darker form, the first would descend through a greater space than the second could climb, and would ultimately lose more of its original character and approach more nearly the level of the second than would the second be able to do in an opposite direction by any latent energy. One of the oldest breeders of the variety in the country says:—"I think that it would take a very long time to develop a London Fancy bird from a Lizard, as it took me more than *twenty years* to breed out the spangles on the back which were common with these birds thirty years ago, and I cannot see that any cross with other breeds would help the matter. But, on the other hand, one cannot help fancying that the intermixture of a London Fancy bird with a green, or even a wild bird, might produce something very like a Lizard, though certainly I have found, in making the experiment in certain directions, nothing of the sort was the result."

Following the bird a stage further in its existence, we find that on its second moult it undergoes another change. Its body plumage loses much of its brilliancy, and what ticks or rudimentary spangles may have been present either disappear or become much less distinct. But the great change is in the wings and tail-feathers, which are now replaced by yellow ones in which the shaft alone is dark, giving the bird a grizzly, pencilled appearance. And this is just the case with the Lizard in a corresponding degree. His body does not turn yellow, nor do his strong quills: the bird has been too carefully bred with a view to *maintaining* these in their native strength to suppose this all at once possible, but the *tendency* is there and shows itself in the most decided way. We need not say that the occasional presence of exceptionally strong colour which requires more than one moult to materially affect its tone, proves nothing but the evidence of skill on the part of the breeder to combat a tendency which is known to exist; and which in time always asserts its potency. In the ordinary run of Lizards, however, this decadence sets in steadily on the shedding of the wings for the first time; and we intentionally refrained in our Lizard notes from referring to the *extent* to which this sometimes does take place, in order that we might here apply it to our present purpose. Jonque Lizards, in particular, are frequently seen after one or two moults so entirely changed as to be almost unrecognisable as Lizards: cap, gone altogether, and in its place an irregular patch of colour, including the face and throat, and covering a great portion of the neck; spangle, gone altogether, and resolved into a grizzly form, rendering the back much clearer than we have seen in many a "strong" or heavily ticked London Fancy.

We shall not follow this any further. For the fancier's purpose it is immaterial which was the parent stem, or even whether either is really the foundation of the other, though it is quite within the bounds of probability that in trying to perfect the development of spangle in some ancient type, a form of albinism was detected and encouraged; or that in attempting to found a school which should moult from dark to light, spangle was discovered, and the admirers of each carried out either property to its ultimate issue, fixing and perpetuating it till from one fountain flowed two streams. The streams we have, but the fountain is lost somewhere in that poetical region, the sands of time, in which are buried as many treasures as in the more material but equally greedy sands of the Goodwin. We do not profess to have so far unearthed it as to remove all doubts as to its identity, though we think we have been digging at the right spot; and have only carried on our excavations because we have heard so many inquiries made as to its whereabouts, but have never met with any answer which appeared to us to be based on reasonable premises.

Continuing our description of the bird *per se*, we remark that the body-colour in the nest toilet should be entirely dark, and not show any light or pied patches such as sometimes do appear, but are not considered a favourable feature. The cap or crown ought to be quite clear and free from ticks or foul feathers of any description. These may disappear in the moult, but occasionally are not so easily disposed of. The flights and tail-feathers, we have said, should be black, or as nearly approaching black as possible. A white feather here is a fatal blemish, and at once cancels all hopes of future greatness; but if there be but the faintest trace of grey in any part of it, shaft or web, it does not disqualify. Here the parallel between the show requisites of the London Fancy and Lizard will be seen, and also how identical are the essentials of either bird.

In the adult bird the body-colour is of the richest hue. It is seen in the richest profusion on the crown, as is usual with colour-birds; and in all the old standards, some of which, however, are very hazy and unintelligible, considerable weight is attached to "purity and richness" as displayed in this place. Throughout the entire bird, and notably on the breast, deep golden orange should prevail. We make no separate mention of the Buff form, because we take it that its characteristic features are familiar to the reader and thoroughly understood in every point, and it will be unnecessary to say more than that it exists in the London Fancy, as in other varieties, in all its attractive beauty. If it possess any one feature peculiar to itself, it is a mellowness and absence of the harshness sometimes observable in certain schools of overgrown Norwich, though there is little or no difference between buff in the London Fancy and its development in the purest type of the Norwich bird. In the old days of the plain feeding, this Canary was as deep in colour as anything on the show-stage, and, in a good specimen, was not surpassed by the warmest tones of the best examples of the Norwich variety, with which, indeed, we have known it to be crossed with a view to the improvement of colour, and with the best results. We did not refer to this cross in its place, simply because the bird is so very scarce as seldom or never to be used for the purpose, while its ally and probable blood-relation is occasionally selected with good effect. The authority before quoted, Mr. Brodrick, of Chudleigh, Devon, writes us:—"I almost wondered, when speaking of the use of Lizards in producing high colour in the Norwich birds, that you did not refer to the same use of the London Fancy strain. This I myself believe to be the true origin of good colour. I have tried it often, and can produce *clear* high-coloured birds in the second generation from a London Fancy cock and a clear hen." We insert this here as bearing on the fact of the rich tone of colour we say belongs to this bird, but we cannot endorse the opinion that it is the true origin of good colour in the direction referred to, because hundreds of Norwich breeders have never even seen the bird.

The show plumage of the adult specimen should exhibit no trace of its dusky first-feather garb, though very frequently a decent approximation to this has to suffice. There is an appreciable difference in the quality of birds in this respect, some of the richest forms of colour being very unwilling to part with every dark feather, and, as the variety now stands, the clearest are not always the richest in tone. We think this a natural consequence, and an illustration of our original colour theory, rather than the result of a careless system of breeding, or an evidence of deterioration from the in-breeding to a great extent rendered obligatory by the limited amount of material at command. Referring to this propensity to retain something of its dark feather, Mr. Brodrick says in one of his communications to us:—"When I first obtained them in 1842 there was not a bird to be seen free from ticks or spangles; now numbers of them are quite spotless. I was, unfortunately, obliged last year to introduce fresh blood into my old strain, and that has thrown them somewhat back. Before this was done I bred as many as ninety young birds with only *two foul* feathers amongst them, and the large majority of them quite free from ticks." A valuable testimony to the truth of the principles of pedigree breeding.

The wing and tail feathers of the adult obviously require no further comment, unless it be to note that in a show specimen they are not always found entirely black. This is perhaps only referring to a show-point; but all show-points are based on natural features, their perfect development constituting a perfect show-bird, such as we have attempted to depict so far as we have gone. We have referred to perfection and to approximate perfection in body-feather, and to the same features in the original quills, but what we wish to direct attention to now is not a congenital but an accidental blemish. The presence of lighter or darker quills in the adult may arise from the accidental shedding of the nest growth, in which case the renewed originally grey feather will be verging on white in the web, and only sufficiently grey in the stalk to afford an inferential clue to its former character, while the renewed originally dark quills will be, at the best, but a shabby grey. We point this out, not as part of our work in describing what a show-bird ought to be, but to indicate that the line of demarcation between approximation, however faintly remote, and positive blemish may be defined to consist in congenital defect. Here also the parallel between the London Fancy and Lizard is again apparent.

One wing-feature remains to be noticed, in respect to which an amount of licence is granted which would not be tolerated in the Lizard. Black bastard feathers are imperatively demanded in the latter; but in the London Fancy, although they are considered most desirable and are highly esteemed, they are not included in the category of wing-feathers, numbering eighteen, which must be black, and therefore they may be white. Many otherwise perfect specimens exhibiting this shortcoming—for such we consider it—which have come under our notice have been admitted to honour under the *dictum* of professed London Fancy critics of a stern school, the acknowledged exponents of the code of laws governing this ancient feathered community.

The underflue, a feature of considerable importance, should be black in the Jonque, and blue-black or slaty in the Mealy bird. It has a good deal to do with the body-colour, since it must be remembered it is only the exterior portion of the feather which assumes the golden hue, and the quality of this hue depends much on the quality of that portion of the feather hidden from sight by the imbricated arrangement of the plumage. The more intensely black the flue, the more brilliant will be the marginal edging of gold. This we pointed out, in general terms, in our remarks on the source of colour in the Norwich Canary, where we showed that the Jonque is richer in a variegated bird than in a clear specimen where all trace of black flue has vanished. The same principle applied here suggests the value of the intensely black flue in maintaining a correspondingly rich margin. We say nothing of the *difficulty*—that belongs to the province of breeding.

Beak, legs, feet, and claws should all be dark. An old standard of excellence before us says: "Legs: for blackness;" a more modern one says "*white*." We agree with the old, and entirely dissent from the new. When obtainable, this property is very desirable, but it is not often seen when the body-colour is pure and spotless. In former days, when these birds were always more or less spangled, there was not the same difficulty about the colour of the legs; and these two features go far to exemplify what has been proved to be a chemical truth—that the component parts of the *entire* covering of birds, whether feather or leg-scale, as well as the beak and claws, are identical in their elements. We cannot, in the face of what we take to be physiological truths, recommend that white shall be accepted as the standard in this respect, without at the same time consenting to the sacrifice of brilliant body-colour on the ground of the undesirability of the ticks or spangles which often accompany it. The difficulty of combating an obstinate feature has nothing whatever to do with fixing a standard which, in demanding that the difficulty shall be overcome, demands nothing impossible. Rather let us emulate Mr. Brodrick, who has been at the work thirty-five years, and whom it took *more than twenty* to breed out the objectionable spangle, with the result we have put on record: "I bred as many as ninety young birds, with only *two foul* feathers amongst them, and the large majority of them quite free from ticks." We do not say that in doing this, *something* of the blackness will not be lost: it must be, and will; but we do say, fix the standard as high up as we can reach, and endeavour to maintain it, knowing the advantages accruing therefrom, and not at the lowest possible point, with the certainty of manifold evils following its adoption.

CHAPTER XXI.

BREEDING LONDON FANCY CANARIES.

"THE breed never was popular, and cannot *easily* become so. I doubt whether there are at the present time a hundred London Fancy Canaries in existence." So wrote Mr. Brodrick to us two years ago, since which we have seen no evidences of any increase in popularity; while the same gentleman writes us with reference to the last Crystal Palace Show, "I was sorry to see to what a low ebb these birds had fallen," which is not very consolatory, and does not form a cheery opening to our chapter. That the lane is long which has no turning; that it is always darkest just before dawn; and that when things are at their worst it is a sign they are going to mend, are truisms we hope will have a fulfilment in the history of the London Fancy Canary. It was popular enough in the olden time, which, of course, was a year or two before Mr. Brodrick's long-ago "never," in the days of high, red-tiled roofs, old-fashioned gable-ends, quaint little window-panes, curious sign-boards, cocked hats, periwigs, hair-powder, knee-breeches, buckles, high-heeled shoes, and other fashions which move in cycles, coming in and going out no one knows when or how or at whose bidding; and we shall not think we have written a word too much about this interesting bird—a sort of connecting link between the Fancy of to-day and of two centuries ago—when we can picture to ourselves a little knot of genial souls, substantial citizens may be, seated round a blazing fire in the chimney-corner of some snug hostelry, waited on by a rubicund Boniface, himself one of the guild, discussing over flagons of foaming October the progress they were making in developing their beautiful little bird—if only we succeed in exciting fresh interest and bring it into fashion once more.

That the bird is not popular now arises really from no fault of its own, unless it be that "one season" birds are never likely to become *so* popular as those which continue in good plumage year after year—a remark applying with some force to the Lizard. For this reason, and also on account of the care required to breed it up to the required standard, it will probably ever remain more of a fancier's bird than an every-day production, and always live in somewhat select circles; but that its admirers should be *so* few and its orbit *so* circumscribed can arise from nothing but a misapprehension as to its general character. As regards its beauty, we must admit that during the last year or two it has not gained by comparison with the army of Norwich birds arrayed against it; but it must not be forgotten that those lovely specimens are the selected of thousands, while the few London Fancies brought before the notice of the public at the great shows of the year at the Crystal Palace represent a larger fraction of the whole number of living members of the tribe than many suppose. Nothing in the annals of bird-breeding has any parallel with the energy displayed in developing the Norwich variety, now in the zenith of its fame, while the other is at low-water mark, and comparison between the two is scarcely fair. Under favourable conditions the London Fancy would at least *equal* its popular rival, and we say what it *might* be made, to remove misapprehension as to its native beauty.

Then there is an idea that it is delicate. We say idea, because it is an idea, a mere supposition not endorsed by those who *do* breed the bird, and therefore worthless as an opinion when expressed by those who do *not*. We give another of Mr. Brodrick's items of experience. "As soon as the young birds can feed themselves, I do not reckon on losing more than one in a dozen, and of the older birds (until they are six or seven years old) the annual mortality with me is not above five per cent., and this generally with hens weakened by the breeding season, dying during the subsequent moult. Two pairs gave me fifteen young ones last season, and all are now living." That the bird has been a good deal in-bred, and has, probably, to some extent deteriorated in consequence, it would be idle to deny; but a hearty co-operation on the part of some of the principal breeders has prevented even less of this than might be supposed, and the deterioration is not so serious after all; while the bird has at least this great merit—that, of the one or two hundreds which remain, the pedigree of the greater portion is to a great extent known; and the breeding, though carried on in such narrow limits, is really, by the very force of circumstances, conducted on sounder principles than obtains in some varieties, and no beginner, let him procure his first pair where he may, need start in the dark. There is a widely-spread prejudice against in-breeding, amounting in some instances to a perfect horror, accompanied by an undefinable dread of untold disastrous consequences sure to follow. The bare mention of such a thing is enough to make some breeders' hair stand on end. Inquire of such a one if he ever *tried* it, and you get a very emphatic and deprecatory *no*. Did he ever know any one who did? A less emphatic no, with just a faint glimmering that perhaps, after all, it might not be so bad as supposed. Then *why* does he assume it is so dangerous? Well, it *is*; it *must* be; *everybody* says it is, and—and it *is*; *of course* it is. Instead of being so, it is the first step towards the concentration of latent tendencies, and has laid the foundation of many beautiful forms. It has its limits, we know, and in the case of the London Fancy Canary may have been carried, by the exigencies of the position, further than usual; but the best breeders, reliable, intelligent men, who have made the bird a life study and have moulted from dark to grizzle and from grizzle to grey in the work, assure us the case is greatly exaggerated, and that, from the stock at command, there is ample material with which to build up the bird and rehabilitate it in all its ancient glory.

In selecting stock, the breeder must bear in mind some traits in the bird worth a second thought. It was not always what it is now; and even in this day, small as is the remnant of the race, there is still some diversity of type—a diversity sufficiently marked to show that the close consanguinity supposed to exist throughout the entire tribe is, perhaps, not so close after all. We do not wish to occupy one line more than is necessary on this subject; but what constitutional defect, if any, there may exist has been so exaggerated that we should not be doing our duty to the wonderful little bird, or to the few breeders who still follow its declining fortune with an enduring devotion worthy of the highest praise, if we did not do our best to champion it. We shall make but one other allusion to this, and dismiss it. The case bears on the selection of breeding stock, but will be additionally interesting to those who may regard it from a physiological point of view. On page 111 we quoted an axiomatic statement from Mr. Wright's "Pedigree Breeding" to the effect that in qualities of constitutional character the physical degeneracy caused by close breeding is almost always removed by one thorough cross; but in a race of birds bred for some pattern of feather or other fancy point such a cross with alien stock at once destroyed all the creature is bred for, the feather or other point being at once lost. Now apply this to Mr. Brodrick's statement as to the result of the cross by which his strain was thrown back for years, in the matter of the production of ticks or spangles previously absent; evidencing that the cross was *thorough* and *alien*, and not one of close consanguinity, which must have been the case, from wherever obtained, if the in-breeding had become so complete as to have united the whole tribe in one family.

The difference in type to which we refer consists in the amount of dark feather, or what was formerly known as spangle, present after the first moult, and which varies according to the strain. It appears to have been a standard property in former days, and we find it occupying a place in an old list of show-points, supplemented by an explanatory remark as to its character—viz., for "distinctness." This is fully borne out in old treatises, where the bird is generally referred to by the name of "Spangled Back," or some such synonymous term, supporting Mr. Brodrick's account of the condition in which he found it thirty-five years ago. Brent, in his interesting little book, also refers to this old form and laments its decline. "I am sorry," he says, "to see the fanciers departing from the standard of excellence laid down in their own rules, and losing sight of the ticks or spangles on the back and the dark colour of the legs and down." There has evidently been a radical change in the standard, for what we find to have been, in the earlier times, a point of excellence; we now hear nothing of unless in connection with a desire to *eradicate it;* and when we remember that this spangle consisted of not much more than, at the best, a grizzly plumage caused by the partial retention of the dark stem and a portion of the adjacent web—really only a washed-out form of the original feather, destitute of any marked character, and most probably only the ghost of the expiring embers of real spangle inherited from its ancestor the Lizard (a ghost very hard to lay, and which appears to like to visit its old haunts, uninvited, in a more or less shadowy form)—we cannot be surprised at the eradication of these ticks having been thought desirable. This we take to have been done by system, and not to have resulted from misadventure, and do not regard it in the light of a misfortune to be laid at the door of the scapegoat, abstract in-breeding, which has to bear the weight of no end of shortcomings, real or fancied, of this little-understood bird.

In endeavouring to breed up to the modern standard, the theory of colour-development and sustentation will require to be worked out with care. The clear-bodied bird must be regarded as the perfected development, and the ticked or spangled body as the raw material. To breed the former from the latter would not be a task of very great difficulty if *nothing else* were demanded, especially in the present state of the ticked bird, which is already a long way on its journey. Selection would soon tell its story in a palpable way, and we should have nothing else to advise, as a means to this end, than insisting on a persistent selection of the clearest specimens. The consequence of this, however, would be that the gradual approach to a clear body would be accompanied by gradual loss of colour. And not only this, but inasmuch as brilliant black wings and tail mean rich body-colour, a decline in the latter would mean a falling off in the other most important features. A strain of high-coloured clear-bodied birds might be maintained with a fair degree of excellence for some time by mating the highest-coloured specimens, but the most careful management would not result in much increase of colour, if indeed anything more were effected than simply maintaining it for a while. We mean maintaining it in that rich form which supervenes upon the departure of the last trace of dark feather, for we do not mean to convey the idea that colour in a carefully-bred, slowly but surely built up strain would, if unsupported, at once fade away; but remember that the tendency has been encouraged and is progressive; at each step colour has been supported, and if no longer supported must slide. Mr. Brodrick says, with much point, "There is a top to the ladder, and those near the top are inclined to give you progeny not quite so high up. I would rather breed with a full brother of a first-prize bird, even if not quite perfect, provided only he was not 'foul,' than with the prize bird himself."

The position, then, is this: a clear body has to be *ob*-tained, and at the same time colour has to be *re*-tained, and finally *main*-tained. And what is the material at command? All London Fancy stock may be classed under one or other of two heads—viz., "strong-coloured" and "fine-coloured," or, as the latter are sometimes called, "fine-feathered" birds. The "strong" are those in which there is much grizzled feather and dark flue, and the "fine" or "soft" birds those in which the ticks are pale and indistinct, consisting for the most part of little more than a dark or grey stalk with only an occasional grey tinge on the web. A "soft" bird will also show less dark flue on being blown, and an additional "soft" feature is a white leg. These distinctions, of course, are supposed to be referable to the bird on its first moult only, though the absolute "strength" of any strain is further gauged by the tenacity with which the ticks cling to the feather in subsequent moults. The pairing of Jonque and Mealy, with all its relations to a balance of colour and feather properties, obtains here as with any other variety, while the pairing of two "strong" or two "fine" birds, or "strong" with "fine," properties belonging to Jonque and Mealy alike, is based on precisely the same principles as regulate the pairing of analogous forms in the Norwich. Breeding from two "strong" birds will, as a general rule, result in increased colour, at the probable expense of increase in ticks and kindred features; while mating two "soft" birds will produce contrary effects, remembering that these general results may be materially modified by the action of latent tendencies. It would be perfectly needless to wade through all the details of a system of pairing which has its exact parallel in the method to be adopted in developing a Clear Norwich, already fully explained. A few hints should suffice to show the bearings of the principal landmarks, what channels to pursue and what to avoid. The natural laws governing the whole are identical, whether it be required to develop a light body or a dark, to remove spangle or to perfect it, the difficulty in every case being the intrusion of *other* features *not wanted.* The plan the London Fancy breeder has to follow is obviously the mating of "strong" with "fine" feather, which, without considering *other* features, is essentially pairing for *colour.* Then follows the selection of pairs showing the highest development of what is wanted and the least tendency to what is not wanted, most carefully and scrupulously excluding positive defect. The fountain from whence proceeds colour has to be fed with care, and *never,* except it be from dire necessity, from an *alien source.* A breeder, under favourable circumstances, has usually at command in his own cages a supply of "bottled up" material of which he knows the exact strength, or, more plainly, whether it be progressive or retrogressive in its character. Here are one or two ticked cocks: they scarcely look like the sort of stuff one would like to pair with a clear-bodied hen; they might "put back" the work a little. Not they; the direction of that strain has ever been upward. Here is another—a very "strong" bird, apparently a dangerous one. Not at all; it is perfectly safe and a little gold-mine, being an exceptionally strong bird from a well-established clear strain, and may be relied on to do more good than harm. When this is the case, the breeder knows where to look for colour or any other standard property; but when, from misadventure of any kind, he *must* make a dip into another strain, he should be most careful to ascertain that the imported "fresh blood" has been bred for the purpose required, or he may find that the effect of the alien cross will cover a wider field than he anticipated, and afford him work for years to come in pulling up weeds, the growth of unsuspected seeds long buried, but now brought to the surface.

The points of resemblance between this bird and the Lizard have suggested to some fanciers the possibility of good results following a cross between the two. Brent says:—"I would suggest that, as Lizard and London Fancy are so similar, each might be made useful to improve the other if a very slight cross were introduced. I think that a little of the London Fancy blood thrown into the Lizard would soften its colour and improve its spangling; while a slight dash of the Lizard in the London Fancy birds would strengthen their constitution, bring out the black ticks on back, which seem nearly to have departed, and strengthen the colour generally, so that we should hear fewer complaints of patching or foul-feathered young ones." For the very reasons here adduced, we think the proposed cross about the very worst thing which could possibly be made, as it would simply spoil both and improve neither. To "soften" the colour of the Lizard would be to ruin it, while we are very confident no addition to the perfect development of its spangle could be made by admixture with the hazy uncertain tick of the London Fancy. We need say nothing as to the "bringing out the black ticks on the back" of our bird. It would certainly do *that*, and give the breeder years of work to *get them out again*. A writer of the present day, Mr. R. L. Wallace, falls into the same error. He says:—"Were I a regular breeder of this variety of birds, I would not hesitate to cross them with a Lizard Canary occasionally—say once in five or seven years. If this is not done I am afraid that the days of these lovely gems are numbered, and that they will soon become extinct, for already the in-and-in breeding is telling with painful effect upon their constitutions; in fact, to quote the exact words of an old fancier, who observed to me, in reference to that variety, not long ago—'I would not bother with them; they are all as rotten as blown pears.'" This statement as to the condition of the bird we consider as unsound in its basis as is the assumed condition of the pomological simile. The promised advantage, an improved constitution, is also a myth. Granted, for the sake of argument, a physical degeneracy; and granted, also, that it can be removed by one thorough cross, as laid down in "Pedigree Breeding;" where would the improved constitution be if, at the end of every five or seven years of persistent close in-breeding, which would be the only way to eradicate the Lizard in *that* time, it became necessary to cross again with the Lizard to repair the *again* impaired constitution? Some breeders, when in a strait or for experiment, may have been tempted to cross in the Lizard, but have been sorry enough afterwards and glad to cross it out again. Mr. Brodrick never had any blood other than that of its own kind imported into his birds for five times seven years, except on one occasion, referring to which he says:—"I have not *one* bird this season fit to sit for its portrait, having only bred two birds, mealy cock and hen, of my own pure strain. These are spotless, but not good in colour; the others, a cross from hens of ———'s, are all of them more or less spangled. I rather think he crossed with the Lizard two or three years ago, and the result will be what I should have anticipated—ticked and spangled birds for *many* generations."

Every detail with respect to *moulting* as given in our Lizard notes applies strictly to the London Fancy, every precaution that ingenuity can devise being necessary to prevent any accidental shedding of the flight or tail feathers, the value of which for show purposes is very evident.

The practice of moulting the London Fancy Canary on cayenne diet cannot be said to have become so general as with other varieties. Belonging to a class in which other standard properties besides mere colour have great weight, it is not so dependent on what we may call a forced development of this one property by adventitious aids, as are some of its kindred, to enable them even to qualify for admission in a section in which colour reigns supreme. We do not wish to be misunderstood on this point. Colour is, as we have all along endeavoured to show, one of the gifts profusely lavished on this bird, being, and properly so, one of its standard points; but assuming it to be pure and rich to begin with, the old breeders do not seem to care for the extraordinary increase in depth effected by the modern system of feeding—a depth some of its most critical admirers think interferes with the well-balanced harmony they could discover in the older form of the bird which has satisfied them with its many beauties for so long. Colour is, to the London Fancy, pretty much what it is to the Lizard: in both it is a necessity; but cayenne cannot make a Lizard, and most certainly cannot make a London Fancy. The question of feeding is really in the hands of the breeders; they are the men to say they will or will not adopt it. Among them Mr. Brodrick, and also Mr. James Waller, of London, who will in days to come be remembered as one of those who in troublous times sheltered the bird and protected it from annihilation, have already declared against it. We are not quite sure whether Mr. Brodrick ever did really bow the knee to the great Juggernaut of Nepaul, though Mr. Waller did worship at the shrine for a short season. Both, however, have in spirit expressed their adherence to the creed of the olden time—that no one "be permitted to feed his birds with anything but bread, egg, and Savoy biscuits, all description of seeds, and green meat of every kind. That no marigolds, saffron, or dye of any kind be permitted to be used on any pretence whatever."

Mr. Brodrick, in one of his chatty communications with us, says in reference to this:—"The cayenne feeding has also, I find, done away with all confidence one can feel as to the natural quality of the bird, and I do not now give mine a grain of it; but, of course, where colour is the main point in competition, a non-pepper-fed bird has no chance whatever. The old London Canary fanciers were right in restricting the diet of their show-birds to simple food—not that I consider pepper-feeding otherwise unfair; it simply places an otherwise inferior bird over a better one." And in a recent letter:—"I am quite opposed to the use of pepper with these beautiful birds; by disguising their true natural properties it only leads to incorrect selection for breeding purposes. A hen-bird I obtained last year, highly fed, was on its arrival far deeper in colour than any of my unfed cocks; after the moult it was about the lightest in my room."

We give these expressions of opinion, not so much as bearing on the "KN" question generally, as being the conclusions of a thoughtful mind with respect to a bird which has been made the careful study of a lifetime. That there are two sides to every question we know; and we have given the opinion of an old fancier—an authority—that it may be thought over in connection with the present condition of the bird, in which it is perhaps undesirable that anything should be done which might in the slightest degree disguise any of the nice distinctions which the London Fancy breeder is, as we have said, in the present condition of the bird, bound to take into the most careful consideration in the selection of his stock.

It is not with this variety as with one bred in thousands and exhibited in hundreds, of which it may fairly be assumed that the resulting effect of a uniform system of feeding may be accepted as a reliable basis on which the relative qualities of a number of birds can be accurately estimated, both for exhibition and for future breeding operations.

With this bird, of a few put on "feed," some might accept and others reject the stimulating food; and not having a large number of average results to guide him, the breeder might inadvertently come to an erroneous conclusion as to the intrinsic worth of some one or more of his specimens; for, regarding the development of colour as a test of the completeness of the organisation for producing it, he might attribute its non-appearance to defective machinery, instead of to the fact of the mill really not having ground any corn, and so be entirely misled in his colour schemes, and indirectly led into what Mr. Brodrick describes as "an incorrect selection for breeding purposes." It is from a breeder's point of view only that we wish these observations to be considered. When the bird is bred in numbers, and reliable breeding-stock can be as easily procured as in other varieties, it may serve as an additional impetus to show what *can* be done in the way of colour; but till then, we think respect should be paid to the opinions of men who, acknowledging a gradual decline, affirm they can see signs of a further decline in a system of feeding which has more to do with *showing* than careful *breeding*—the thing wanted for some years to come.

We conclude our notice of this beautiful bird with a Scale of Points. We have not been able to compare it with any recognised standard—indeed, we do not know of the existence of one—but we submit the following as embodying, as nearly as we can express, the ideas of such breeders of the variety as we have had opportunities of communicating with :—

SCALE OF POINTS FOR JUDGING LONDON FANCY CANARIES.

Points of Merit.

	Maximum.
COLOUR—On the body, including the cap or crown: for depth and purity, absolutely clear cap, and freedom from ticks or spangles on back	20
On the wings: for blackness of web and quill of flight-feathers and bastard-feathers	20
On the tail: for the same	10
Underflue: for blackness	5
FEATHER—For fine silky quality and compactness... ...	10
SHAPE—Head, broad and neat; back, for width; breast, for fulness	10
SIZE—For generally robust appearance	10
LEGS AND FEET—For darkness	5
CONDITION—Health, cleanness, and sound feather ...	10
Total	100

Negative Properties.

A London Fancy Canary should on no account show the slightest tick on or about the region of the crown or cap; nor, in the perfectly-developed form of its show-plumage, should it show any dark feather or any feather ticked or grizzled in web or quill on the neck, back, breast, or other part of the body, or any tendency to a ticked or spangled habit of plumage. It should not on any account have a white feather in the wings or tail, either in its nest-feathers or as the result of accidental shedding; nor should any of these strong quills show a grey or grizzled form, or other than a glossy black colour. It should not have white bastard-quills. Neither should it exhibit white underflue or white skin anywhere except on the crown, nor is it desirable that it should have white legs or feet, or similar features belonging to clear-bodied birds of other varieties. It should not have coarse feather, nor a slovenly carriage of wings or tail. It should not have a narrow, mean head, nor be long and narrow in body, nor upright in position, as opposed to the broad-backed, full-breasted, semi-erect type of Canary, nor should it be small or puny in its build. It should not be shown dirty or with broken feathers, or in a way calculated to hide the brilliancy of its clear body or mar the effect of the contrast furnished by its distinctive plumage.

Disqualifications.

The presence of dark feathers on the cap or crown, constituting the bird "foul capped." An *entirely* white feather in wing or tail, *i.e.*, a feather which does not show *some* trace of dark colour either in web or quill.

In this, as in previous scales, we have given only what we consider the leading features of the bird, and have endeavoured to avoid any hair-splitting in our valuations, adopting 5 as our base or unit, and making other values multiples of that number. Nicer distinctions might, perhaps, have been made, but for practical work they will be found included in one or another of our headings. The smaller fractional parts of a workman's rule are not numbered, except in some complicated arrangements; and we have no desire to make our scales so elaborate that those for whom they are intended will run the risk of losing themselves among our figures. We know which side of a two-foot rule is most frequently referred to, and we think that our simple scale will measure any bird with sufficient accuracy if intelligently applied.

CHAPTER XXII.

THE BELGIAN CANARY.

HAVING disposed of those birds whose attractions consist in the beauty of their plumage and the many peculiar features attaching thereto, and which are certainly, with the exception of the last referred to, the most popular varieties with English breeders, we pass to our third group, the birds of Shape and Position, including the Belgian, the Scotch Fancy, the Lancashire Coppy, and the Yorkshire—four most important families, each possessing strongly-marked distinctive features which single it out in an unmistakable way, and give it a separate niche in our portrait gallery.

We commence with the Belgian, a Canary which retains the name of the country where, no doubt, it was originally produced, and where it is to this day an object of the greatest interest; being literally one of its "institutions," and occupying a *status* to which we have no parallel in our Canary world—at any rate, on this side of the Tweed. We are indebted to an esteemed correspondent "over there" for much valuable information about this nationality, for such it is; and we extract the following account of its early history from a mass of original matter in which this remarkable bird is invested with no small degree of romance:—

"Although it may seem, at first sight, to be launching out upon the unstable ocean of improbabilities to claim for this variety of Canary a right to be considered as having arisen out of the history of the country whose name it bears, yet I feel assured it has a certain right to such a claim. In endeavouring to trace back from the bird of to-day, so curiously developed in its structure, to the ordinary form of the species, I think this claim will be recognised. I shall not enter into a long account of the history of Belgium, but simply advert to the fact that when the country was so harassed either by avowed enemies or pretended friends as to have been not inaptly termed 'the cock-pit of Europe,' the people, shut out usually from participation in political affairs, formed themselves into societies called *Gilden*, or, in the Latin of the time, *Gildonia*, for the protection of trade and the extension of commerce. These guilds, as a body, exerted great influence on the affairs of their towns, until the communal authorities in time came to acknowledge them as their chief supporters, and encouraged them even so far as to enrol themselves as members, meeting on a footing of equality, and entering into the aims and affairs of the society with freedom and good-fellowship.

"As time rolled on, and no longer public safety or trade had need of such protection, these societies became more truly social in their aims, in accordance with progress of knowledge and the spirit of the times, having for their object the advancement of art, music, or simply pleasure. 'The customs of the older societies, with all their traditions, are so well preserved, that they exist to this day unchanged, so much so that a musical society intending, perhaps, only to take part in a concert would not think of marching without their standard, and on grand occasions one or two pieces of artillery' ('L'Industrie en Belgique,' p. 47). Thus painting, sculpture, music, ... *bird-catching*, rabbits, pigeons, *canaries*, &c., came to be encouraged, each society having its position in the social scale of the town; having its colours, flags, and motto, which it carries, along with the

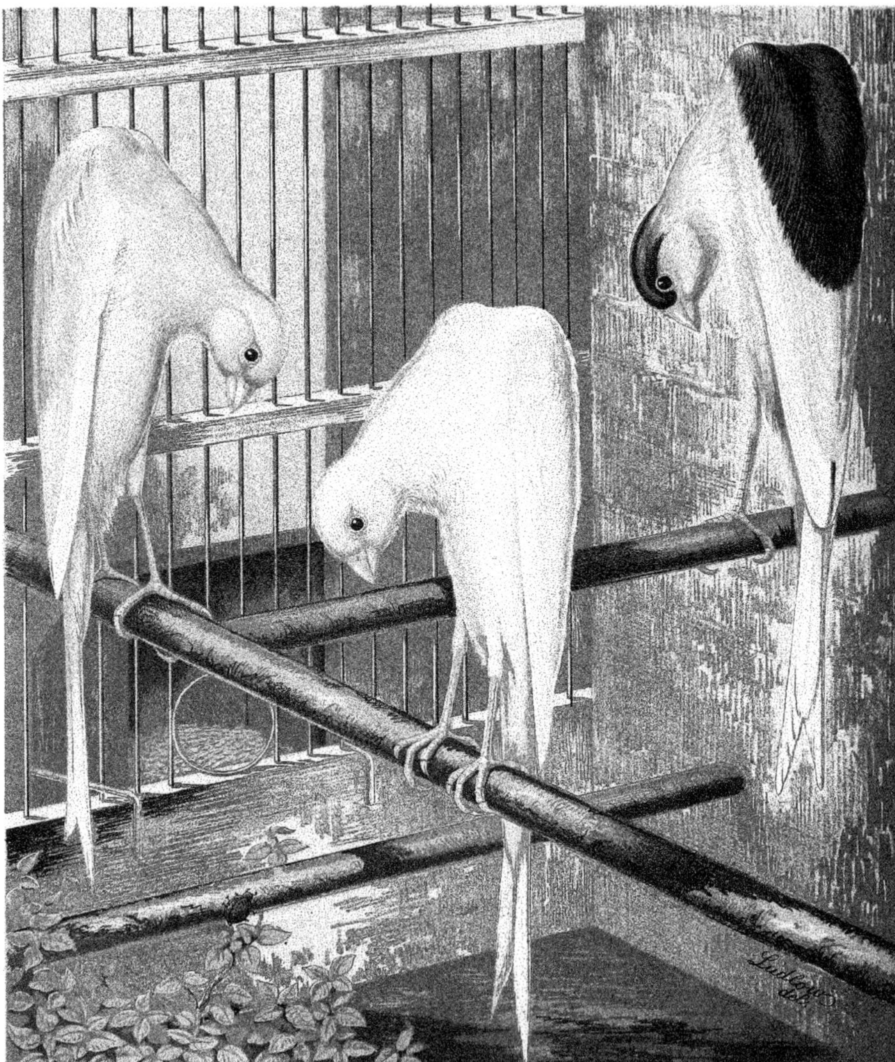

Vincent Brooks, Day & Son, Lith.

BELGIAN CANARIES.

CLEAR YELLOW. VARIEGATED YELLOW.

CLEAR BUFF.

medals or other prizes in
communal *fêtes*, the
learned societies.

"But what bearing
do with its peculiar de

"I would have you
contradistinction to the
that when a society ad
encouragement from the
peculiar form, was not ex
consideration and aim

"How far this
England is matter for
little importance. In the
object of a single mind,
social meetings.

"The precise date
show was held, is I th
anything certain on the
when a large show was
Courtray, which was at
whom I am indebted for
society of Courtray was
passing, that this gent
CAGE-BIRDS, observed
must be inferred that
carried on in vain in

"Whatever uncert
years ago Courtray was
towns followed in this
only."

After this tribute
position among its
description of it.

Shape and Posit
since something more
every case occupied a
described are supposed
feature, if we may use
presenting such a marke
or development from a
a general statement
peculiar or out of the
its companion, Shape,
other considerations

medals or other prizes it has won, at its head when it takes its place in the processions at the communal *fêtes*, the members carrying with equal pride the colours of a Canary or of one of the learned societies.

"But what bearing has this upon the origin of this variety of Canary, or what has this to do with its peculiar development?

"I would have you note *first*, that societies were formed before the Canary was adopted, in contradistinction to the regard for the bird leading to the formation of the society; and, *secondly*, that when a society adopted the Canary, the society was at once countenanced, and received encouragement from the authorities of the town; *thirdly*, the construction, the building up of the peculiar form, was not exclusively confined to any individual case, but was the object of the general consideration and aim of all the members of the society.

"How far this may account for the absence of the diversity of variety which is found in England is matter for conjecture. Although we have one or two other varieties, they are of little importance. In the societies a model was adopted, and to breed to that model was not the object of a single mind, but of united care continually stimulated by public exhibitions, prizes, and social meetings.

"The precise date of the formation of the first Canary society, or the town in which the first show was held, is I think not clearly established; at all events, I have not been able to arrive at anything certain on the point. As far back as I can trace with certainty is about thirty years ago, when a large show was held at Ostend, at which most of the prizes were carried off by the town of Courtray, which was at that time of high repute in Belgium for its Canaries. The gentleman to whom I am indebted for this information was a visitor at that show, and he computed that the society of Courtray was at that time of not less than thirty years' standing; and I may remark, in passing, that this gentleman, on looking at the illustrations of the Scotch Fancy in CANARIES AND CAGE-BIRDS, observed respecting them, 'Ah! those were the birds of that day;' from which it must be inferred that half a century of persistent breeding up to a certain standard has not been carried on in vain in respect to this very remarkable bird.

"Whatever uncertainty may exist on some points, this much may be accepted—that thirty years ago Courtray was first, from a Canary point of view, of all Belgian towns, and that the other towns followed in this order: Brussels, Antwerp, Ghent, and Bruges. This refers to *position* birds only."

After this tribute to its historical importance, who will deny to the bird of Belgium a leading position among its fellows? We will now, according to our usual plan, proceed with a detailed description of it.

Shape and Position—the terms require some explanation when used as technicalities, since something more is implied than is conveyed in the abstract meaning. Hitherto, Shape has in every case occupied a place in our lists of properties which the varieties of Canaries already described are supposed to possess; but only a comparatively *subordinate* one, being an uncultivated feature, if we may use the expression, shared by all without much variation, and in no case presenting such a marked peculiarity as to call for special note, or suggest the idea of improvement or development from a "fancy" point of view. And the same with the idea of Position. Beyond a general statement as to the ordinary posture of any bird, such as semi-erect, implying nothing peculiar or out of the ordinary course, no further idea has been attached to this feature, which, with its companion, Shape, must now be considered as special cultivated developments, before which all other considerations must give way.

We commence our description with Shape, as including that peculiar physical conformation on which possible perfection of Position depends, although the results of that conformation are not at all times presented to the eye in the form of a constant beauty, the bird being able at will to shut itself up, as it were, destroying all its elegant proportions, which are only exhibited in their highest form during periods of nervous excitement. From this it will be seen how much the one property

FIG. 54.—SHAPE AND POSITION.

is dependent on the other, and is interwoven with it to such an extent, indeed, that it becomes difficult to separate the consequence from the cause, since so much of outward shape is gathered from position, and so much of position must depend on anatomical construction. This it is which causes the bird to be regarded essentially as a Position bird, its being able to develop a certain remarkable configuration being dependent on its formation, and the position or posture being demanded as evidence of the formation, just as the formation is studied with a view to its assisting in a display of posture which, resolved into its primary elements, it will be seen is simply shape under another term.

The head of the Belgian is singularly neat, and is an evidence of careful breeding in one direction. To a casual observer, the head of one Canary may appear pretty much like that of another; but the eye of the fancier at once detects a marked difference. It is smaller in the Belgian, in proportion to the size of the bird, than in any other variety—the Scotch Fancy, which is an offshoot from this tribe, only excepted—and is much flatter on the crown, causing the bird to be what is known among fanciers as "snake-headed." The eye, too, is full of softness and intelligence, possibly the result of long-continued effort in the direction of taming or quieting down and subduing native restlessness. There is nothing coarse or vulgar about the member, but an air of patrician refinement extending even to the beak. The neck appears to be formed on a telescopic plan, being capable of a remarkable degree of extension or elongation, of which we shall speak when we put our bird into "position." At present we are supposing our bird to be at rest, or standing "at ease," under no excitement whatever, at which time it is sufficient for our present purpose to say, its attitude is erect, or nearly so—the body assuming nearly the same posture as when "in position," but the head and neck an entirely different one. When "at ease," the head projects from the body at as nearly as possible a right angle, the summit of the crown and the tips of the shoulders being about on the same level, the upper line of the neck being practically concave, though made up of a series of small convexed arcs. The upper line is that which is generally referred to when speaking of length of neck in general terms, because the underneath line has little more of length belonging to it than attaches to the throat, which speedily joins the breast. We refer to this simply as an explanation of what is technically "neck," because parallel lines drawn across the neck at the beginning and end of the throat would easily show how much of the longer upper line really belonged to the outline or domain of shoulder, which extends much further than that point indicated by the tips of the pinions. The shoulders themselves are very high and prominent, and in a good specimen should be broad and massive, the pinions not projecting through the scapular feathers or those at the upper part of the back and leaving a vacancy between, but being well covered by them, thus destroying every appearance of angularity by producing a rounded surface of considerable area, and further by filling in the space between the shoulders to a level with the back, which itself should be long, all of which features are considered strong points in the configuration of a Belgian. A line from the back of the shoulder through to the breast will give the deepest transverse section. The breast itself should be prominent, but not full or broad, and, following a profile line from the bottom of the throat, may be observed to project in a very graceful curve. The wings are long, and cannot be carried in too compact a form. Their apparent length frequently depends on the style in which the bird stands; but in a good specimen they will frequently reach to a point below the junction of the feet with the legs, and consequently below the upper surface of the perch on which the bird may be standing. Some birds, when in the least excited, have a habit of opening out the extremities of the wings and showing the upper tail-coverts; but this is a most undesirable exhibition. The body, from the breast downwards, should gradually taper, the feathers of the vent and lower regions merging in those of the under tail-coverts in a regular way. The tail is long and narrow, and should appear like a continuation of the taper arrangement of the body, rather than of a fish-tail form. The shape and arrangement of the tail-feathers necessitate the formation of a small fork at the extremity, but the more compact the tail, the smaller will be this fork, and the nearer will the tail approach to the standard which requires it to be piped as opposed to expanded. Thighs and legs should be long and straight, the former well covered and hidden for the greater portion of their length in the feathers of the body. Flexed knee-joints present an unsightly appearance as if dislocated, and are to be avoided. It is almost needless to add that the feet and claws should be perfection in their way, and in no way differ from those of other Canaries. The feather throughout should be fine in quality, and compact, though many otherwise beautiful specimens are inclined to be rough, and sometimes very much so, disposing their feathers in such disorderly fashion, as to present a really ludicrous appearance. Shape and Position, however, cover a multitude of sins in a Belgian. Beauty of plumage, we have ever maintained, should play a most important part in the show economy of every bird, and an exaggerated display of coarseness we hold to be a serious drawback even in a "position" bird. Colour is seldom displayed to any great extent, but when present, adds much to the beauty of a fine-feathered specimen.

Such is the Belgian Canary in his formation, the peculiarities of which are not presented to the eye until, in a state of nervous excitement, he braces himself together and shows what the little frame is capable of doing in the way of "Position," much in the same way as the Pouter among pigeons shows himself in his pride. "Position" now becomes the comprehensive property which includes all others as the greater includes the less, since without it minor points cannot be exhibited. We will try and put him on his mettle. On entering a room in which a number of Belgians may be caged singly, or in numbers in flight-cages, we are not at first struck with the peculiar merit of any one specimen. The very best of them, which when put in position may exhibit the most remarkable conformation, is seen hopping in a slovenly manner from one perch to another, or sitting apparently in meditation. His legs are certainly too long, and set too far back. He cannot, when on the bottom of the cage, keep his tail off the ground, and when pecking at a grain of seed stiffens his legs into two splinters, straightens his tail into the same line with the body, like those artistic conceptions on children's toys, and looks eminently uncomfortable. And this is one of those most extraordinary Belgians of which one has heard so much? No wonder his beauties have no charm for the *profanum vulgus*, and well may it require an educated eye to discover them. Wait awhile. He hops on a low perch, and from that to a higher, drops his tail, which was never intended to be dragged about on the ground, pulls himself together a little, stretches an inch or two, and is already not the swan out of water he was a moment ago. You pass him into an open show-cage, and possibly one or two others hop in at the same time. Let them remain; there may be something in them, for surely those ungainly frames and apparently badly-proportioned forms were made for some purpose not yet evident. But we must get them on even terms, for one is standing turned in an opposite direction to the rest. Don't hurry or frighten them in any way. Possibly they may look a little alarmed and not be very steady, or may even heave a little with the excitement, but a few minutes will set them to rights. Our well-bred Belgian is not a bird to be jostled about roughly: he is accustomed to polite society and is not unseemingly boisterous. Hang the cage a little higher, on tbat nail just above the level of the eye in the far corner of the room, where the attention of the birds will not be distracted by the bustle and twitter in the other cages. Don't lift the cage by the top, or the birds will perhaps cower and become more frightened at the novelty of the situation: take it by the bottom and keep the hand out of sight. Surely these cannot be the same birds we saw in the flight? They are already standing in an erect attitude with their legs straightened, their wings tucked up closely, tails so nearly in the same line with the back that a plumb-line would not show much deflection. Some may differ from us in this respect, but we hold that the line from the shoulders to the tip of the tail cannot be too straight, and altogether dissent from opinions which prescribe as the correct line a form having an appreciable curve. On this question we perhaps hold extreme views, but we have been educated in a severe school, and have for years had opportunities for closely examining some of the grandest Continental specimens, in all of which the line of the back is straight, in contradistinction to anything approaching a decided curve or a tendency towards "circling," as it is sometimes termed. A model, cast in bronze, the accredited standard for the year of one of the Flemish societies,* of which an illustration is furnished in Fig. 55, stands before us, and also exhibits the straight back with the tail in a continuous straight line.

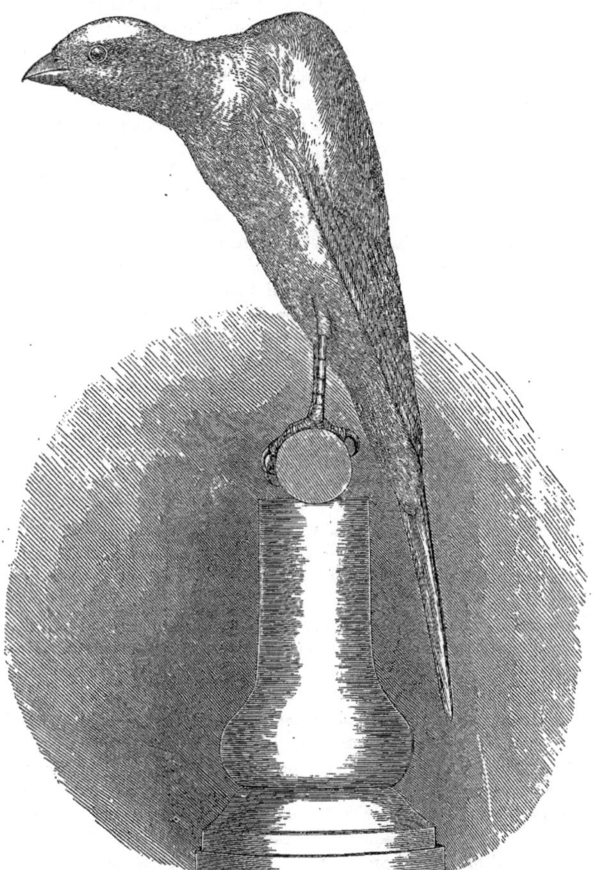

FIG. 55.—BELGIAN BRONZE MODEL.

This formation is not depicted in Fig. 54, which is nevertheless a life-study of a bird which *could* do almost anything in regard to "position."

But our birds are now nicely steadied, and approaching them quietly, first divesting ourselves of our tall hat, an object of dislike to a sensible Belgian—an evidence of its superior intelligence and good taste—we gently scratch the underneath part of the cage with the fingers or a little wand. Sometimes a mere tick or gentle tap will do, and, when it *will* do, the less rubbing, and scrubbing, and chirping, and blowing off the steam, the better. Just a faint tap and a little scratch to attract attention, and they draw themselves up farther and farther till their legs are perfectly straight and rigid, showing a portion of the thigh: a little more and an encouraging chirrup, and the shoulders are raised, higher and higher; and still higher yet, as if the bird were trying to reach a point which, once touched, still cannot be maintained without continued exertion, consisting not in an undignified straining but singularly graceful action. In this straining with the shoulders the head is depressed and the neck stretched to its extreme limit, not with any distressing exertion, but with the most consummate ease and grace; and in that posture it will stand, occasionally turning its head on one side and looking up with a soft pensive glance, with nothing defiant about it, but just simply an air of thorough-bred gentility and quiet dignity. A bird of very strong nerve will sometimes, when apparently doing its utmost and when at its seeming greatest tension, grasp the perch with renewed energy, and, leaning back till its tail is brought under the perch and one would think it would lose its centre of gravity, literally double itself in a way not unlike the picturesque attitude boys assume in playing at leap-frog, till head, neck, and shoulders form an almost unbroken bend. If in this position the tail should be brought into a curve, it is no drawback, but is no improvement on the standard idea of perfection of posture, and a bird which can do all that is asked of it while still maintaining a perfectly erect stand is to be preferred.

And now note the *direction* of the head and beak when the bird is thus extended, as contrasted with their position when it is "at ease." When at rest, that is, when standing in a fairly erect attitude without being in any way excited, at which time we have said the top of the head and the shoulders are about in the same straight line, then, and *only then*, is the head in a horizontal position. The moment the bird begins to extend its neck or to "reach," as it is technically termed, and the head is correspondingly depressed, its direction is altered and it begins to point *downwards*, continuing to do so till, at the extreme point of extension and depression, the previously concave or beautifully hollowed upper line of the neck becomes arched, and the head is bent till the beak points *inwards*, every upward movement of the shoulders being accompanied by a further development of the arch and a more determined tucking-in of the head, as seen in the Variegated Yellow bird in the coloured illustration, which is by no means an exaggerated representation, but rather the contrary.

This is "Position," the credential of a high-class Belgian; an in-born quality which clings to it as long as life lasts. We have seen a bird so prostrated by asthma that it seldom or ever—and, towards the end, never—sat upon the perch, but lay night and day in the bottom of the cage, squatting with wings outstretched, breathing with the rapidity incident to the complaint, and apparently very near its end; yet struggle on to its perch on being asked, and show such position as would scarcely be believed if we were to attempt to describe it. Some who have not made the bird a study talk of "position" being all the result of training; and there is a legend in the traditions of the Fancy that one successful exhibitor wore through the oil-cloth of his bird-room floor and half through the floor itself in one particular spot, by shuffling with his feet on a little sand, in training his birds to get into position. But it is all nonsense. Undoubtedly a bird taken from a flight-cage and placed in an open show-cage for the first time, and asked to do his best at five minutes' notice, will not do so well as one which has frequently been caged and made familiar with the situation. The one is agitated and restless; the other quite cool and equal to the occasion. It is simply a question of tameness or familiarity, and not of training. If it be *in* the bird, like true gentility it will come out; but if it be *not* there, all the training that can be brought to bear will not develop that which does not exist. A high-bred young bird, when sitting on the nest-edge, can be made to show to a surprising degree what promise it has of future greatness, and there can be no "training" here. Only bad birds require much training, and they never pay for the trouble. The best they can do is to make an attempt at standing upright, then twitch their tails and hop up and down like a robin on a spade-handle, then flourish against the sides of the cage, and wind up with a general fluster. Such are not Belgians. They may have neat heads and other respectable properties, but lacking the "guinea stamp," it is no use testing the quality of the metal any further.

On the subject of "training," so far as it is necessary, we shall have something to say in its proper place.

And then there are one or two other types of birds sometimes shown as Belgians. There is one which stands up after a fashion of its own, such as it is, much after the style of an owl, with about the same amount of neck, and, what there is of it, very suggestive of apoplexy. This class of bird often has the merit of close, fine feather—a property always desirable, but which does not constitute "position" nor make a Belgian. And there is a bird a little higher up the ladder. Its strong point is its leg; indeed, it has no other unless it may be a little shoulder. This class of bird is generally very seedy. We don't remember ever seeing one young. It has an air of faded gentility about it, and with its scaly shins, indicative of age, reminds one of some dilapidated old fellow with just a little blue blood in him. Without much persuasion it strikes a favourite attitude something in the way we have seen other bipeds do: left leg bent backwards with the knee well in; right leg with knee projecting and a graceful curve from the hip, with a kind of this-style-all-wool-only-sixteen-shillings sort of expression. Such are not all wool, nor is this "position." There is also the bird of mercurial temperament, which won't stand still without grasping the wires at the side of its cage with one foot. There is also its opposite, the phlegmatic subject, whose mountain of shoulder and fine lines, generally, are enough to drive one crazy, but which won't get up, even in reply to our most persuasive solicitations and a considerable expenditure of finger-nails, maintaining the most provoking indifference and utter disregard for its reputation, a grand specimen of a sublimely lethargic Deutschlander, whose very chirrup, when he so far rouses himself as to give one, seems to savour of obstinacy and contradiction, and spells "*nein;*" not a bad stamp of bird, nevertheless, as he demonstrates after allowing all the honours of the show-room to pass away from him, by rearing himself for a few moments, just long enough to assert himself and vex, by showing he belongs to a class which won't try when wanted or begin to race till past the post. And there is to be met with the bird that is constantly "up," the irrepressible Belgian, full of go if he could only go in decent form; generally an angularly-built, undersized bird with a little breeding cropping through the surface in strange places; smart and clever in some respects, but merely a butcher's pony among high-class company; useful as a hack, and a likely specimen to earn railway expenses and entrance fees at second-rate shows; full of nerve and always willing to do his best, but vulgar withal, and wanting the port and presence, the ease and repose, indicative of high breeding. Not uncommon, also, is the bird which will bear critical dissection tolerably well, and would, measured by a scale of disjointed points, sum up a respectable total, but which spoils all by persistently standing in a posture in which the shoulders are the vertex of an angle formed by the lines of the neck, back, and tail deported in such a manner that they seem to depend like counter-balancing weights, bringing the centre of gravity below the base and causing the bird to poise itself on its straight legs something in the same way in which a coin is balanced on the edge of a knife by inserting it in a cork from which depend two forks. If the line of the back and tail, instead of inclining at forty-five, stood at ninety, it would be a good bird; but we always stop short at the *if* in judging a Belgian and assign the conjunction no value in our scales—in fact, there is no such thing as an *if* in a good Belgian.

We might refer to many other types of this bird, all of which are familiar to fanciers of the variety, in illustration of what is and what is not shape or position, but we will give only one more. It is the lanky, scraggy—we cannot find better adjectives—stilty, acrobatic contortionist, whose every feature is an exaggeration, lacking the harmony which deserves to be perpetuated in marble or bronze. We are reminded the bird has plenty of neck—so has a crane: ditto shoulder, but we see projecting pinions and a "spout" in the back in which we could bury our pencil: ditto legs, but we think of a heron; and so on throughout, its very "position" making its deformity only more deformed.

We do not hesitate to portray this form, even though it somewhat complicates the difficulty of determining which of the two, shape or position, is the more important feature: possibly they are more intimately connected than is generally imagined, being mutually dependent to an extent that renders it difficult to define with positiveness the precise domain of each, and leading to the conclusion that there is more included in the idea of "position" than is understood by the abstract idea of posture. It is, in fact, a comprehensive term implying the notion of being able to exhibit certain developments of shapes or forms of individual parts which do not lie on the surface, and which can only be done by birds having a particular physical conformation. The links are so carefully welded that it is not easy to discover the joint. On one occasion, when we were judging at an exhibition in the North, at which there was a strong muster of Belgians of widely-differing types, our colleague began, as all judges do, by making a preliminary examination of the whole, giving each cage the little scratch which follows as the hand instinctively finds its way under the cage-bottom. After a little observation, and without removing a bird from the stage where it stood not four feet from the ground, he made his selections, and they were just the selections we expected he would make under the circumstances—three neat, but very lively birds of good feather and colour. We made altogether a different selection, taking, to begin with, a somewhat ungainly subject, as it appeared when unroused, but which showed evidences of quality, and we proposed placing our respective selections side by side on the wall for the purpose of comparing notes. At first our colleague objected to this, alleging it was not fair to try them in such a way, and contending that they should be judged where they stood. Of course we could not put up with such nonsense as that; and after a little trouble got our own way so far as to have a few nails put in the wall and the competing birds hung side by side. Then our friend began, and, being a much older man, talked to us with parental earnestness, enumerating all the "points" of a Belgian from the tip of his beak to the tip of his tail; to all of which we listened patiently, and then reminded him he had altogether failed to show that his representative was a true Belgian at all. We contended that the birds must first be put into "position" in order to exhibit their "points," and that then, when fully displayed, a comparison could be instituted. The result was that our quondam undemonstrative selection showed itself to possess an astonishing configuration nothing in its class could approach.

Respecting the origin of this remarkable configuration we have no reliable *data*, but from what was stated in the notes prefacing this chapter respecting the style of bird in vogue a generation back, we think it is only a reasonable deduction to infer that the bird of our day is the result of a carefully-worked-out system of development of some abnormal form which must have been in existence from very early times. It will be seen from our description that it stands alone, differing from every other variety we have hitherto noticed in the important particulars of entire abnegation of every feature held by them in common, and the adoption of characteristic physical traits to which they have not the slightest claim; the wide difference evidencing how remote must have been the time when the cultivation of the abnormal form began. Here we must be content to leave it. An old fancier of the variety, compared with whose oracular deliveries Jack Bunsby's utterances are transparent, once told us, with an air of profound awe, that "they had them in the *Vatican*." We feel that it would be nothing short of sacrilege to think of peering through this delightful cloud of mystery. We are always grateful for information which goes to support a belief that the Canary had once in his day aristocratic surroundings.

Then, as opposed to these forms, all of which show some degree of culture, we have occasionally presented to our notice a bird of an entirely different type which still claims to be called a Belgian, because it hails from Belgium, though it sails under another flag and professes to belong to the "Old Dutch" school—a definition so comprehensive that it may mean a great deal or nothing. What may have been the characteristics of this "Old Dutch" family we will not attempt to determine, but we think that the name covers the whole of the crude forms of a long-ago period when the bird was being first roughed out of raw material. There are several schools of birds in Belgium, differing somewhat in minor points though all tending towards one ideal, but we are not aware that any of the what we may term intermediate forms are recognised as sub-varieties, and the "Old Dutch" now appears to be a haven in which any nondescript pattern finds shelter. It reminds us of the P.M., "peculiar metre," embracing the whole outlying region beyond long, common, and short, in old books of psalmody. The clerk in the quiet little Kentish village in which we went to school used to telegraph to the choir by placing books on his reading desk. One meant L.M., two C.M., and three S.M.; but when he built a complete rockwork of books, and surmounted it by his snuff-box, a circular chest as big as a cheese-plate, we knew it meant P.M., and looked out for something frantic. The "Old Dutch," the P.M. of the Belgian variety, now-a-days seems to contain birds like nothing but themselves, unless it may be that they can many of them compare favourably with the Lancashire Coppy in respect to size. In shape, ungainly to a degree; in position, neither upright nor anything else; in feather, rough, coarse, and disorderly to an extent which cannot be equalled for slovenliness. Cumbersome specimens sometimes appear classed as Belgians at the Crystal Palace shows, which make one wonder whence imported, or by what means so many objectionable features have become concentrated in one bird. An inquiry as to the pedigree of these very unattractive examples usually elicits the response, "Old Dutch;" but such are certainly not the style of bird we would select with a view to utilise any one feature of which they may be possessed. We repeat that we think these are only irregular forms, and that others not quite so declared in their eccentricities, and which we have seen described as existing varieties, are none the less so, and have no recognised *status* among the finished specimens of Continental show-rooms—they are the "hocked" stock of the poultry-yard, and nothing more.

We have made no allusion to colour, other than that it adds to the beauty of a good specimen. In the way in which we understand colour, it has no existence in Belgium, having no more appreciable value there than among the breeders of the Scotch Fancy in our own country. On the face of it, this is attaching but very small worth to a feature that fanciers prize highly in almost every variety; but so it is. Nor is it difficult to account for an indifference which to an English fancier seems surprising. We remember well our own feeling of—we will not call it surprise, but rather describe it as something quite novel to us, when on our first visit to the great annual exhibition at Glasgow, at which, including single birds and pairs, something like a thousand birds of the Scotch Fancy variety competed in the different classes, we found but one idea running through the whole, and that was, in brief, "shape," to the entire exclusion of colour or variegation in plumage in the way in which it is recognised by us; but by the time we had made a critical examination of the exhibits on the standard basis, we discovered there was no room for colour when it was demanded that the eye should be filled by shape. Old likings, however, are not to be thrown aside all at once, and the eye would occasionally rest with pleasure on a specimen in which were united the beauties of shape and colour also; but the leading idea, once grasped, soon shoulders all others out of the way, and we can easily understand how, in the eager pursuit of the one main object, nothing would be allowed to interfere with its absorbing character. When we remember that this development of form alone has been the study of generations, it needs no argument to show that the most plastic materials would be selected from time to time, irrespective of properties which, to the uninitiated, might seem undesirable. To the English fancier, the pale lemon-yellow or the almost colourless buff may appear capable of improvement, and the irregular variegation susceptible of correction and control; but the Belgian breeder sees nothing of this—his ideal is a statuesque model, and he cares not whether it be chiselled out of spotless marble or other material. He shrugs his shoulders as he passes showy-looking birds, contenting himself with the expressive comment, "No position; no position." To him "KN" and "marking" are delusions.

It should be remembered that we are dealing with a Canary perhaps the least popular of any of the varieties which grace our show-stages. We will not stay to ask why a bird which can engross the attention of a whole people, should be looked on with an indifference amounting almost to positive dislike by another nationality having kindred likings; yet so it is, and we find this Canary making but slow headway here. It may be that it is not understood, and it certainly is *not* understood if we may consider the provision made for it in some of our exhibitions as any criterion. This has most materially to do with the point under consideration—viz., Colour—in its relation to the generally-received notion of the bird here as compared with the estimation in which this feature is held in Belgium. In its home, the land of its creation and development, where in all conscience one must give its admirers credit for knowing their bird and its belongings better than we—though we have known egotism go to the length of asserting they do not—there are only the two natural divisions, Yellow and Buff, and *no other*. Our esteemed "Belgian Correspondent" before quoted says:—"There is no reference to *Variegated* birds in any of our prospectuses, and in those I have sent you"—the subject-matter of which we will presently detail—"you have the substance of every one I have met with. I have ascertained that once at Bruges, some years ago, there were two classes given for these birds—one for cocks and the other for hens; but no gentleman with whom I have spoken has heard of any other occasion, although it is *possible* there may have been. Variegated birds are shown in that class to which they belong by virtue of their native body-colour, yellow or buff, as the case may be. I have heard it repeatedly asserted, or hinted at, that Variegated birds are below the average in position qualities; but I assure you it is quite a mistake, the majority of victorious birds during the past show season *not* having been Clears. I say this from observation."

It was perhaps scarcely to be expected that here, where colour and beauty of plumage have ever ruled, the idea of shape and position should at once supplant deeply-rooted notions of what constituted beauty in a Canary; and while the attractions of an ideal which consisted in symmetry of a fascinating character could not be denied, it is not a matter of surprise that its admirers here should have sought to invest it with some of the charms, to them, inseparable from colour and other properties of plumage, hitherto their Alpha and Omega, in which they considered the Position bird wanting. Or it might be that, knowing nothing of its history, or the laws regulating its classification in the country from whence it came, it was inferred that the same distinctions affecting colour and feather which ruled throughout our English varieties were also applicable to this bird; and hence we find that in the earlier days of our public exhibitions it was usual to extend to the Belgian a system of classification similar to that adopted in our Colour sections, in which the highest degree of excellence was represented by the term "Clear." This was carried out so far that within the last few years liberal prize-schedules contained a class for "Crested" Belgians—a bird having really no existence. Personally, however much we may be fascinated by this wonderful bird—and that it is perhaps our specialty of specialties, we admit—and however much we may lose sight of our colour and plumage predilections in admiring it, still we cannot throw them overboard entirely, and with the strong in-bred tastes of an English fancier we should be disposed to maintain the desirability of separating, at least, the heavier forms of irregular variegation from the Clear, or approximately Clear type, drawing the line below "Ticked," clearly understanding that term to mean nothing more than the presence of grey feathers, and *not* the decided patch or blotch of well-defined green, constituting technical variegation—a division which, for colour purposes, we think to be as substantially sound in its basis as the separation of the primary colours, Yellow and Buff. We say for colour purposes, advisedly, because we are quite aware that in *other* respects Yellows and Buffs differ so materially as to render them unfitted for competition in the same class. We will not say that the Belgian breeder does not rise superior to us in his devotion to the *one* object in whose direction all his energies are expended, and to which untiring individual and united action the Position bird of to-day owes its existence; but the English fancier is, in his turn, so firmly wedded to his ideal forms of beauty as found in the varied plumage of his birds, that he seems unwilling any other property should drive it from its place, and will only accept a new type, provided he can make it work harmoniously with his own views. He admires the form of the Belgian bird, and his eye never ceases to be pleased in following its subtle lines; but he has also been educated in the matter of certain forms of plumage, and to disturb these is to disturb the harmony of the whole. Our object now is simply to show that in adopting this system too closely a mistake is made in endeavouring to unite dissimilar things too intimately. Dismissing for a moment the Variegated section, we will only refer to a form of classification often presented to breeders, and be it remembered that the classes in a schedule ought to represent provision for recognised distinct forms. The arrangement to which we now refer is that of providing separate classes for *Clear* and *Ticked* Belgians. It will be only necessary to point out that these are minute distinctions belonging to *colour* properties, and not to *form*, to show that such a basis is not broad enough to meet the requirements of a bird in which *form* is paramount, and is one calculated to have a prejudicial effect from a breeding point of view, since it implies that the Clear type is so manifestly a superior class of bird as to demand for it a place by itself. It is virtually making colour *transcend* form, and the evil is still further increased by sometimes providing classes for Clear birds only, as if the sculptor were required to expend his skill in procuring a clean block, instead of bringing to bear the subtleties of his art on any reasonably sound marble. This absurd state of things we have combated for years, and are glad to find the principle involved is gradually becoming recognised; but instances are not wanting in some Belgian centres in which it has yet to be understood. The very fact of colour being entirely ignored from beginning to end in the production of the bird, does make it seem the most absurd folly to set up one of the nicest distinctions pertaining to colour in its highest form, when the bird finds its way to the show-stage. When defending a principle, we do not think that politic arguments should have much weight, for it is a poor principle which cannot assert itself without being linked with policy; but we may add that the adoption of such a meaningless line of demarcation as that existing between Clear and Ticked, as applied to Belgians, tells prejudicially on our exhibitions by sensibly affecting the number of entries, and further, by opening the door for unscrupulous work, which may be either (*a*) showing very faintly-ticked birds in the Clear class, or (*b*) removing the obnoxious tick, not less an insult to the bird than to morality. The Belgian is, of all Canaries, the one which presents the least opportunity for the exercise of those skilful manipulations which occasionally disgrace an exhibition: nothing can be added to or subtracted from its shape or nervous energy, and it is derogatory to its dignity to ask it to compete on other conditions than those peculiarly its own.

Reverting now for a moment to the Variegated forms, we remark that the bird, never having been bred with any ulterior view to variegation being taken into account in the slightest degree, this property should possess the same value in an English show-room as on the Continent, and that is *nil.* It all comes to the same thing in the end. It is not a plumage bird. Variegation, considered in its proper light as a natural sport or divergence from the dark self-colour, is to the Belgian exactly what it is to the Norwich Canary, a thing of no value in the face of some *higher* property, viz., *colour* in the Norwich, and *form* in the Belgian. In the English Canary it has been systematically reduced within prescribed limits; in the Belgian bird, never. Occasionally a specimen may chance to turn up which happens to be marked in the way we, in England, consider to be the correct thing; but such marking is not the result of systematic breeding in that direction, any more than is the appearance of one such bird among a thousand Scotch Fancies in Glasgow. On an English show-stage, where marking has a value, such a *rara avis* may be an object of attraction, and may be, by some, supposed to be a representative of an established variety; but it is nothing of the kind. The best examples of marking, considered from our English standard, which have ever been exhibited, have all been *imported* birds, and therefore cannot be regarded as representatives of an established variety, since they have merely been the chance productions of a system of breeding, the remotest thought in connection with which would be the idea of attaching a value to such marking and seeking to perpetuate it. It does not follow from this that what we would consider to be an exquisitely marked Belgian cannot be a high-class bird: anything but that. We have occasionally had under our notice well-marked Belgians of the highest quality possible. What we wish to show is that up to the present time the breeding of "Marked" birds, according to the English standard, has not been attempted in Belgium; that Clear and Variegated have not even been separated; that such "Marked" birds as may from time to time have been produced are not valued on account of their markings, but that all *feather* points have had to succumb to the one ruling idea of Shape and Position.

The *possibility* of being able to breed such birds and add them to our list of English varieties as established forms, will occupy our attention in the proper place. Here we have only endeavoured to show in what respect our English notions of the bird agree with those of our Continental neighbours, and in what respect they differ, at the same time trying to show how the popular idea may have received its impress from old associations, from which it is not easy to disconnect it.

The natural consequence resulting from this bird, which is virtually a stranger in a strange land and not *bred* among us as breeders should understand the word, being so affected by its surroundings, is that it occupies a somewhat anomalous position. Even though the occasional grouping of the Clear and Ticked forms has of late put these classes on a more satisfactory footing, yet the heavier forms of variegation still remain to be dealt with in an equally common-sense way, and until they are, the Variegated Belgian cannot be said to receive ordinary fair play at our hands. There are two ideas to be exploded before this can be the case—the one that the Variegated bird is necessarily inferior in "Position" properties; and the other, that mere technical "marking" should outweigh true Belgian conformation and character. Mr. R. L. Wallace, for instance, says:—"It is a well-established fact that the Variegated birds are much inferior in points of merit to the Clear birds. This is somewhat difficult to account for, unless we could believe that the progenitors of the last-named were originally all Clear Yellows and Buffs, and that the Marked variety are the result of a foreign admixture, and that whenever the birds appear in the mixed plumage they inherit more largely the properties of the allied blood. Be this as it may, it is a singular and undoubted truth that the more heavily a Belgian bird is marked, the more deficient he is sure to be in all the essential characteristics which constitute a high-class bird of this variety." We really can *not* believe such nonsense, nor do we think Mr. Wallace would have us believe that the Belgian breeder, who cares neither for colour nor marking, but worships form and posture, would cross clear "Position" blood with some "foreign admixture," an unknown green something which could only affect colour and variegation, about which he cares no more than if they did not exist, with the certainty of losing all he *does* prize. The hypothesis is absurd, and reasoning from it leads to an absurd conclusion. If variegation were such a certain bar to the development of form, it would have been bred out long ago, with other faults, by the simple process of selection; but the fact is that it is nothing of the kind. It is, however, undoubtedly the case that the majority of the Variegated Belgians exhibited *in England* have been inferior to the Clears in respect of "Position" points; but we have not far to look for an explanation of that fact. It consists not in native inferiority, but in the demands of the English standard, which has required *first* marking, and *then* such decent approximation to Belgian form as might accompany it. In another pamphlet, by Mr. Varley, of Nottingham, we find the following:—"Belgian Variegation is a class which should have the underflue blue-black, the exterior feathers of the neck and body entirely clear yellow, or buff, or white. The cap, the belt surrounding each eye, all the lesser and some of the adjoining larger flight-feathers, also the beak, legs, feet, and nails, all black or black-green. The tail, in the Yellow Variegated specimens, should be wholly or principally composed of feathers entirely black or black-green. In the Buff or White variety, the tail may be all buff or white, instead of black or black-green. The markings or variegation should be alike on both sides. *After* having taken cognisance of variegation properties, birds of this class are judged for *figure* by the applicable standard rules for Clear Belgians." It is not our province here to discuss the merits of this description, but we think it explains clearly enough how it comes to pass that Variegated Belgians, in England, are inferior to Clear or Ticked—a fact which has nothing whatever to do with their relative values when compared unfettered by any restrictions.

It only remains for us to arrange as briefly as possible the classification we should suggest as most in unison with the character of the bird and our English tastes, without allowing either to interfere with the other.

Classification of Belgians.

(*a*) Clear and Ticked Yellow Cocks.
(*b*) Clear and Ticked Yellow Hens.
(*c*) Clear and Ticked Buff Cocks.
(*d*) Clear and Ticked Buff Hens.
(*e*) Variegated Yellow Cocks.
(*f*) Variegated Yellow Hens.
(*g*) Variegated Buff Cocks.
(*h*) Variegated Buff Hens.

Here it will be seen we have, for the first time, made separate provision for the sexes—an arrangement not adopted with our English varieties, which, being shown for the beauty of their plumage or some property found in excess in the male bird, as, for instance, size in the Coppy, are not so provided for, very few hens finding their way to the show-stage; the only specimens having any chance of competing successfully with their more showy mates being exceptional examples of Evenly-marked Norwich, Cinnamon, or Yorkshire, or the Crested Norwich, in which a special feature shown in high perfection gives its fortunate possessor a special chance. To these we might add an unusually good Lizard or London Fancy hen, which, however, would require to *be* good to hold its ground in a competition in which the weaker vessel usually gives way with becoming modesty. In this and in other most material points, as we shall presently show, the Continental exhibitions differ from ours, which contain a considerable infusion of the element of spectacular display almost inseparable from the homage paid to plumage. From a breeder's point of view, the addition of classes for hens throughout our varieties would be a matter for congratulation; but as they do not, with the exception of the examples quoted, possess in a prominent manner the qualities demanded in a show-bird, they remain at home. With the bird of Position it is an entirely different matter. Shape and position are not materially affected by sex, the chief difference in the cock-bird consisting in size and a general masculine bearing, which, with some more refined distinctions, afford a satisfactory basis on which to ground the separation of the sexes for show purposes irrespective of the value of the arrangement in its relation to breeding, which is the principal object of a Continental exhibition. At present we cannot regard this bird in any other light than a comparative stranger struggling hard in the hands of a few enthusiastic fanciers to assert its claims to popular notice. It is a sore point with its admirers that our prize-schedules are so circumscribed in their provisions; but it should be borne in mind that the promoters of most of our shows are not men of means, and must cut their coat according to their cloth, a defaulting bird-show being a thing unknown. It is for managers of large gatherings claiming to be national in their character to issue model prize-lists, and so gradually extend this fancy to its proper limits. For such a purpose the foregoing classification is fully adapted, but under ordinary circumstances classes (*a*) and (*b*) are united, as are also (*c*) and (*d*); occasionally the Variegated section is similarly treated, but, more frequently, condensed into one, or, more frequently still, altogether omitted.

It will also be observed that we have made no provision for "Evenly-marked" birds. We have followed this course advisedly, because we maintain that up to the present time such do not exist as a variety either here or in Belgium, and to offer premiums for them in the present state of the Belgian fancy in England would be detrimental to the interests of shape and position. This may appear to be rather arbitrary, but we write in the interest of the bird; and when we say we have known an exhibitor grumble sadly because a nondescript specimen, possessing little else but marking, failed to score in good Belgian company, and afterwards grumble still more because the *same* bird failed to catch the judge's eye in a *Yorkshire* class, we think we have said enough to show the evil of dabbling with this element before English breeders have first learned the alphabet of form and position.

One reason why the merits and capabilities of this extraordinary bird are so little known is that at our exhibitions, where it ought to be seen at its best, adequate provision is scarcely ever made for the purpose. Take the Crystal Palace, for instance, where the cages will be found duly marked 1st, 2nd, 3rd, &c.; but there is no opportunity for examination, and unless any bird should spontaneously make a display of his true form, the admirer of the variety has no chance of gratifying his taste nor the learner of being instructed. If the bird is ever to occupy a high position among us, it must be shown under conditions in harmony with its peculiarities.

CHAPTER XXIII.

CANARY SOCIETIES IN BELGIUM.

We propose now to give some account of the Belgian Canary "at home;" and the following details respecting Continental societies are supplied by our "Special Foreign Correspondent," whom we have before quoted, and who says on this subject:—"The present Society of Antwerp (of which I have just had the honour of being elected a member) was established in 1847, and remains unchanged with the exception of having moved its place of meeting two or three times. The accompanying rules, which I have translated freely, will explain its object."

Rules of the Society of Canaries, known as Posture Birds.

Established in full form at Antwerp in 1847, under the name "Den Arend" (The Eagle).

Article 1.—The society is to take the name of "Den Arend," to have for its object the breeding of Posture Birds, following the model adopted by us, and to improve the "Liefhebberij" (Liefhebber: lover, amateur; from *lief*, love, care, and *hebben*, to have).

Article 2 relates to election of officers and sundry details of internal management not of much interest. We shall only give those rules bearing directly on the subject in hand.

Article 3.—The competition will take place each year on a Sunday in the month of January, to be decided upon by the Committee of Management after careful consideration. Birds eligible to take part in the competition must be young birds hatched the preceding summer. Old birds are distinctly forbidden to enter in the contest. Transgressors breaking this rule shall lose all rights should it be discovered, and in case such should be a winner, the prize shall be given to the bird next following without the transgressor having a right to make any remark respecting it.

Article 4.—Any member taking part in the competition shall take good notice that he is obliged to compete with birds, hatched by him in his own room, and his own property. In case it should be detected that any bird has been borrowed or bought and has won a prize, the successful bird shall be sold in public and the proceeds of the sale given to the society. Also, the member shall be dismissed from the society without being allowed to become again a member until after an interval of three years.

Article 5 relates to the distribution of prizes, and enacts that each member shall be present on that occasion and other meetings or pay a fine of one franc; and the rule following deals with subscriptions and fines.

Article 7.—Every year each member shall have the right to bring four birds to the contest, and to compete in each class. On entrance two francs per bird must be paid. The birds must remain three days in the care of the examiners, and their decisions respecting the examination shall remain irrevocable.

Article 8.—Every year there shall be sixteen silver prizes given, divided into four sections for the birds, as follows:—1. Yellow Cocks; 2. Yellow Hens; 3. Buff Cocks; 4. Buff Hens—in equal divisions as regards money value, and according to the funds. The prizes shall be proportionately divided in each section, commencing at the 1st to the 4th prize.

Article 9.—In case a member unknowingly enters in the contest as a hen a bird which during the time of competition is found to be a cock, he must resign all claim to any prize he has won without demur.

The next two Articles refer to the conduct of meetings, at which a due decorum befitting such an assembly must be observed, any member addressing the meeting without having first obtained the consent of the chairman being fined from one to ten francs, the penalty to be "enforced immediately"—a salutary regulation for the government of all-speak-at-once bodies.

Article 12.—It is forbidden to clip, cut, or in any manner to unnaturally mark the birds. Should any member do so the fine in *Article* 11 will be enforced.

Article 13.—Each member shall have the right to bring birds to the sale should a sale be held, but is strictly forbidden to depreciate the birds of any other member under a penalty of from one to ten francs.

The remaining Articles refer principally to internal details and are exceedingly stringent in their character.

In addition to these rules we also give a copy of the ordinary form of a Belgian prospectus, the equivalent of our "schedule," to which we shall presently have occasion to refer. The classification of birds in each parent society being identical, no reference to any system appears to be deemed necessary in the prospectus.

SOCIETY OF CANARIES UNDER THE MOTTO "YOUNG AND WILLING TO LEARN."

To be held in "De roode Port" Klein Turkeijc, No. 14, *Ghent.*

GENTLEMEN,—In a meeting, the 3rd of June, 1877, we have fixed for a public competition, to be given for "Liefhebbers," who are members of a Canary society in this country, which shall take place the second Sunday in January, 1878.

CONDITIONS.

Article 1.—There shall be a "Prix d'Honneur" given, of the value of thirty francs.

Article 2.—Each "Liefhebber" being a member of a Canary society* shall have the right to enter from one to four birds for competition, the contribution (entrance fee) to be five francs for each competing bird. There shall no birds, on punishment of confiscation, be brought to compete belonging to persons other than those in whose name they have been entered.

Article 3.—Four "experts" shall together judge the birds, and should their opinions be equally divided, a fifth expert alone, to be chosen by the owners of the competing birds, shall, without being spoken to about either the one or the other, decide. The experts shall not be the owners of birds in the contest.

Article 4.—The four societies having the greatest number of entries, but at the least four, shall have the right to elect an expert, but no town shall elect more than two. The fifth expert shall be a stranger to the town.

Article 5.—It is positively forbidden that any bird be brought for competition that is not a young one, that is to say, which has not been hatched during the summer preceding the exhibition. Should other birds be sent for competition, they will be sold for the benefit of the society.

Article 6.—Each year, on the 15th August, the entrance list will be closed. The Committee of the society in each town shall collect the money from their members and hand it over to the Secretary.

Article 7.—The entrance of all additional birds must take place before November 18th in each year. After this date can no birds be entered. The entrance fee of additional birds must be paid on the day of entry.

Article 8.—All competitors are asked to attend the distribution of prizes. Those absent, whose birds have won prizes, will be fined to the extent of a fourth part of the value of the prize. An excuse will be entertained for those absent on account of sickness.

Article 9.—The competing birds must be brought in on the Friday preceding the competition, between 11 a.m. and 4 p.m. The judging will begin on Saturday and end the same day. The distribution of prizes will take place on Sunday at 10 a.m. The birds shall hang for exhibition until 4 p.m. Each "Liefhebber" taking part in the contest shall have the right to hang up three other birds at the exhibition.

Article 10.—All incidents which take place during the competition and exhibition shall be made the subject of a "proces verbal."

Article 11.—The day of the contest is by the rules fixed, and under no condition can be altered. The decision of the judges shall be final. All other affairs which have been overlooked shall be settled by the Committee of Management.

Our Foreign Correspondent continues his interesting explanation of Canary competition in Belgium as follows —:

"The points of contrast between societies here and in England must be kept well in mind, especially the following three: 1. The countenance given to them by the authorities of the towns. 2. There is not that spirit of gain in these contests which is so perceptible in England; for in the majority of cases the value of the prizes lies in a great measure in the honour. 3. The strict rules limiting the number of entries, confining them to young birds, and excluding all not bred by the exhibitor, destroy every possibility of monopoly, the fruitful source of grievance in England. An exhibitor must be a member of a society, with very rare exceptions, and the society of which he is a member feels itself morally responsible for his honesty, and would be the first to discountenance and detect any falling off in this respect. The prizes are provided out of the funds of the society, plus any communal gift, and we know of nothing like holding a show on speculation and then possibly falling short of what was anticipated; but the monthly subscriptions,

* This regulation that competing "Liefhebbers" shall be members of some society appears to be the rule, though in the prospectus of the Society of Fraternization, another Flemish community, the following appears as an addendum to this Article: "Nevertheless, to encourage bird-breeding, persons shall be allowed to take part in the competition who are not members of a society, on condition of paying eleven francs for the first bird entered, and five francs for each following bird."

plus gift, plus entrance fees (which latter item, however, is not depended on), pay for the prizes *first;* then if any money remains to the credit of the society it goes towards the feast, and makes each member's contribution on that important occasion so much the less.

"The society of any town can, if its funds are flourishing, hold such open shows as those of which prospectuses have been given. There are times also when shows are held in the spring, at which older birds are exhibited, but always in pairs for breeding, and the awards go to the best and most uniform pairs adapted for this specific purpose so far as the eye can judge of their suitability.

FIG. 56.—BELGIAN SHOW-CAGE.

"The shows are always held in the 'estaminet' where the society meets, and there is no charge for use of room nor for admission.

"The cages are of a uniform pattern and colour (Fig. 56), and are provided by the society or house.

"The birds are brought in on the Friday, as per rules, in travelling-cages (Fig. 57), or in bags (Fig. 58). The travelling-cage speaks for itself, and is usually a well-made piece of furniture of mahogany, with several perches just sufficiently high to keep the birds clear of the ground. The bag is a circular disc of wood to which a linen top with worked holes is nailed, and an excellent contrivance it is.

"The bird having been brought in, the bringer takes a small slip of paper and writes the name and address of the owner and exhibitor upon it, which, after he has placed the bird in a cage with seed sufficient to last for the next three days, he then places under the drawboard, and immediately a piece of white paper is gummed over the end, so that it is not possible to draw it out again without discovery. The cages are then placed in a private room, where next day the judges visit them: it is *never* judge (singular number), and it usually takes them *the greater part of the day* to go through the four classes, and very often the entire day. I don't know, but I think *you* will agree with me when I say that no one man, however expert a judge he may be, can do full justice to a class (as they are classed here) by simply walking up one side and down another and washing his hands of the whole in half an hour. I say as they are classed *here*, for if an old bird is allowed to compete with a batch of youngsters, all of nearly equal merit, why, the older bird need not usually require long to decide upon. The method adopted by the judges is, first to go through them in a superficial way, placing by themselves those showing decidedly good points. The second division is again gone over to make certain that nothing having merit has been overlooked, and then commences the real sifting process, by which the selected birds are separated and weeded,

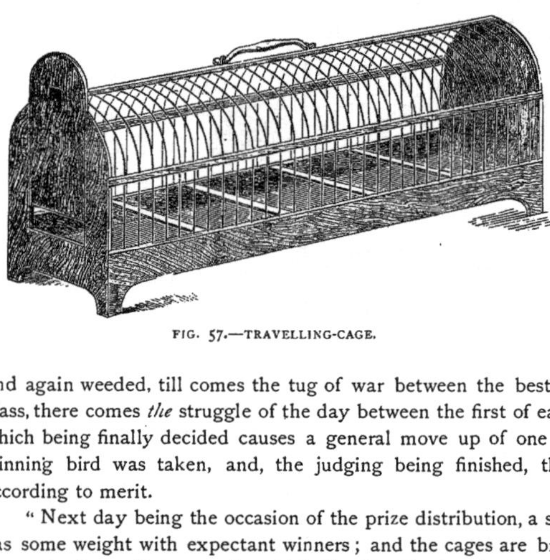

FIG. 57.—TRAVELLING-CAGE.

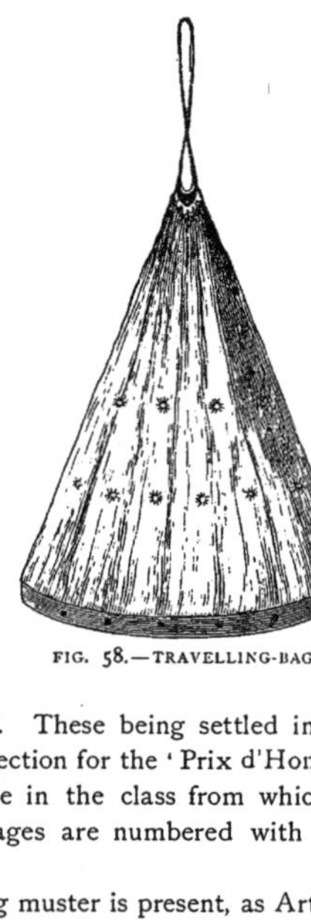

FIG. 58.—TRAVELLING-BAG.

and again weeded, till comes the tug of war between the best four. These being settled in each class, there comes *the* struggle of the day between the first of each section for the 'Prix d'Honneur,' which being finally decided causes a general move up of one place in the class from which the winning bird was taken, and, the judging being finished, the cages are numbered with chalk according to merit.

"Next day being the occasion of the prize distribution, a strong muster is present, as Article 8 has some weight with expectant winners; and the cages are brought in from the judging-room to the general meeting-room, in which the President and other office-bearers are seated at a table. One of the secretaries sees that the cages are numbered and follow in rotation, and after calling out a number and the prize awarded it, hands the cage to another official, who breaks the paper covering the drawboard, draws it out, and taking the paper from underneath, during an interval of intense excitement, in which every one is certain he sees his own bird in the distance, slowly, and with clear intonation suitable to so solemn an occasion, reads the name and address of the happy winner. He, amid clapping of hands and other emphatic demonstrations, moves up to the table and bows to the President; who rises, shakes hands, and congratulates him, after which the address paper is gummed to the cage and the bird hung up for inspection. Thus in like manner all are gone through, the recipients of the prizes being as proud of the honour achieved as are the successful candidates in an examination by a learned society.

"There is not the same strictness about touching the cages as in England, for any one wishing to inspect a bird may take it down for the purpose, and I never saw the licence abused. Nor does the incense from the 'fragrant weed' seem to affect the birds, for frequently it is nearly impossible to see across the room in this country of cheap tobacco.

"From an £ s. d. point of view the winners are often the greatest losers, as a custom strongly savouring of good-fellowship is usual on such occasions; the successful exhibitors providing a certain number of bottles of wine in honour of visitors, and as a *solatium* to less fortunate contestants. Here, again, must not be overlooked the social usages of Belgium; nor this fact, that with very rare exceptions excess is never indulged in, nor are unseemly disputes, which the Articles are specially framed to check.

"An endeavour was made in 1854 to establish a chief society for the country, with Brussels as its centre, called 'The Central Society of Emulation;' but although its aims and purposes were excellent, as established, it lived a very short time—not long enough to gain much sympathy at its death."

Such is an account of the constitution of the Belgian Canary societies and the mode of conducting Continental shows. In whatever respects we note a contrast to our English fashions, we discover at least the elements of genuine earnestness and a healthy emulation in the direction of *breeding*, the thing, of all others, to be thoughtfully studied by every "Liefhebber," whether he be wedded to plumage or the "postuur-vogel." In many ways the show economy of our Belgian neighbours can never become ours, any more than ours can become theirs. There is a vein of nationality permeating the whole, foreign to the genius of our system; but, following the motto of the Society of Ghent, we think each might copy a page from the other with great advantage.

A chapter on breeding the "postuur-vogel," with a few special hints on its management, will close our notice of this Canary.

CHAPTER XXIV.

BREEDING AND MANAGEMENT OF BELGIAN CANARIES.

We all know the importance of catching the hare before proceeding to further operations with it, and the hare has to be caught in this case in one of three ways: through an agent on this side, or on the other, or by being your own agent and going across for it yourself. The bird of high character is not so rare here that it cannot be procured; but it is still, comparatively, so rare that specimens above the average quality always command long prices in private hands, not only on account of their intrinsic worth, but from their value as show-birds. Nearly the whole of the best examples are imported birds, of which a number are every season consigned to English dealers. These consignments contain, like other drafts of live stock from breeding establishments, both good and bad; but if a purchaser places himself in the hands of a respectable dealer he will get value received. In dealers, as in the stock they deal in, there are classes, but we have no patience with the cry that casts a slur on any calling in life. The consignments we have referred to probably do not contain the *best* forms: it is not natural they should, because high-class birds are neither bred in numbers nor disposed of wholesale; but a dealer who understands his business and makes the bird a specialty will always give his agent on the Continent instructions to procure what may be desired. This is, from the nature of things, the ordinary channel through which imported stock is obtained, because it is only under peculiar circumstances, such as when direct communication can be had with the Continent, that the breeder here has the opportunity of availing himself of the means of rapid transit offered by steam communication with ports within easy reach. It is not during the sea passage that there is any risk; the birds are then in comfortable quarters; but it is the difficulty attending a long journey to the coast on the other side, and again on this, which renders importing not always free from considerable anxiety. For those who have the time and means at disposal, and whose biliary secretions are not easily disturbed, there is the pleasure of going over to select for themselves, the best time for which is in the fall of the year before the stocks are much thinned, though it is worth remembering that the *best* are not sold *first*, and any one who has not a wholesale commission on hand will find at all times ample material to choose from. The age of the birds is not very material, though the custom in Belgium is to pair a year-old bird with a first season, *i.e.*, a maiden hen. The main point is to start with good *breeding* stock, which is not always the best *show* stock; and in this respect, till the English breeder really does become a breeder, there will always be some difficulty unless a reliable agent can be found. There is really not a world of risk in the matter, because like has the same tendency to produce like in a Belgian as in any other Canary; but the *extent* of the difficulty and the importance of a good start will be manifest if we at once say that first-class position-birds can no more be bred to pattern in numbers than can first-class Norwich or any other variety. Mediocrity, we have all along shown, is one thing, and exceptional merit, another thing. Touching the question of breeding-stock, our authority before quoted says:—"The majority of show-birds are not breeding-birds. A breeder has a right to expect that if he pairs a cock having six good points with a hen having four, he will have young ones with five good points; but I wonder what are the odds against this being done with birds bought indiscriminately at shows. I have been following my system only five years, and consequently am not able to work with such certainty; to do so, a man must use tools of his own making: it can never be done hap-hazard. Your theory of obtaining a culminating point with colour is equally applicable to position, which is a property that must be bred up to. I do not mean by this that it is impossible to go higher with position-birds than has been already attained, but I do mean that an *extraordinary* show specimen is frequently one which carries, outside, the concentrated good qualities of its parents, while, lying hid, perhaps not far from the surface, are some of the more objectionable features; and this bird, if mated with another exactly similar, will make full amends in the offspring for the abeyance in which these forces have been lying without having lost their desire for expansion. If it were not so, what charm would there be in breeding? To me, none: it would be the simplest child's play."

The whole moral of this is, that endeavour should be made to procure breeding-stock as reliable as possible, and then *pedigree-breeding* begins at once to apply. To furnish any definite rules for guidance in selecting the first pairs is almost impossible, but it will be a wise policy to start with a combination of quality with quantity. So far as is possible, and in the absence of any knowledge of the special character of the birds, let no essential be wanting on either side; but if there should be a lack in any way in either bird, endeavour to obtain that property in excess in the other. It may be well to remember that in following out an ideal perfection of symmetry, a tendency towards a not very massive build has been developed in some Belgians, and occasionally very exquisite form is found in unquestionably undersized birds. We would not recommend pairing two such, but where opportunity occurs for free selection, choose massive proportions in the cock and elegant conformation in the hen. It is only fair to *assume* that the presence of good properties is an indication of their being to a reasonable extent fixed in their character, and the beginner will have to risk something on the truth of the assumption. The results will soon show in what direction declension is apparent, and then is the time when the breeder must exercise his maturer judgment in rectifying defects which may not have appeared on the surface at the start.

The laws affecting the blending of colour and regulating the quality of the feather rule throughout this as in every other variety, yellow and buff being mated according to the established plan, and the contrary. In this respect, the same discretion must be exercised as with plumage-birds, but the paramount claims of form must not be overlooked when departure from the rule appears desirable. Nor must the comparatively little worth of an absolutely clear type of feather be allowed to interfere with judicious mating. It is frequently almost impossible to determine when a bird is clear and when not, so exceedingly faint and indistinct is the grizzly form constituting a tick, often nothing more than the most trifling discoloration of the shaft of some small body-feather. This disposition to assume a ticked form runs through the entire tribe of Clears, and so uncertain is it in its appearance that positively not the slightest attention must be paid to it as a feature in any way affecting the character of breeding-stock.

In accordance with the idea followed out in our classification, we would advise the keeping separate of the Clear or Ticked and the Variegated forms, and would not recommend mating the two unless the breeder should desire to pair with a view to producing Variegated birds. Abundance of birds of the Clear school from which no Variegated offspring will be produced can be had, and ample scope is afforded in that field alone for the skill of the most enthusiastic breeder. But if it be desired to have both forms, pairing Clear with Variegated will produce them, only it must be remembered that the Clears from such a cross, if again mated, could not be depended on to produce Clears. The effect of introducing a Variegated strain is very lasting, and only a breeder who is prepared to forego every colour consideration whatever in pursuit of shape should mix the two. This is, however, a perfectly legitimate field of operation, and is, as we have shown in our remarks on the practice of the Flemish breeders, the only true field as recognised by them.

We promised to say something about the feasibility of breeding Evenly-marked Belgians. Now we do not wish it to be understood that we think this a chimerical idea. In what we have previously said on the subject we merely desired to show that at present they do not exist as a variety, and to point out the rocks and shoals on which it is possible shape and position might be shipwrecked in too hasty a recognition of the value of marking without being accompanied by true Belgian conformation. What has been done with one variety may surely be done with another; and if technical marking has been to a great extent fixed in the Norwich without destroying its character, and still more decidedly in the Yorkshire variety, there is no reason whatever why it should not be done in the Belgian in harmony with our English views of beauty, if at the same time there be a fixed determination that on no pretence whatever shall mere marking outweigh the essentials of a true Belgian, and a resolve that the breeder will not nurse his pet idea to such an extent as to allow it to over-ride common sense and delude him into the belief that he has produced something he has not produced, and that specimens he would fain persuade himself are Belgians are nothing of the kind. Adherence to this principle may bring about a satisfactory result: departure from it can only lead to a disastrous issue.

To breed birds of this description we should advise the selection of the most evenly and accurately pencilled specimens procurable, in which, at the same time, exist the highest Belgian properties. Such, though the children of chance, can be had. We have seen some, but not many. These should be paired with high-class Clears—not with marked birds, or the marking will have a tendency to assume the shape of irregular variegation, as we demonstrated in our earlier theories on the subject. We need not follow the course to be pursued one step further, having detailed it at length in Chapter XIV., but would only impress on the breeder the important fact that he must not forget he is aiming at producing, not a nondescript, but a Belgian, and that his creations must be prepared to meet such a condition as that we suggested for the schedule of the Norwich Show in 1876—viz., "High Belgian properties shall count above any marking, however good, not combined with high quality." With these few hints we close our notes on mating for marks, and mentally throw our oldest shoe after the adventurer about to embark in the enterprise, wishing him good fortune and a niche in the temple of Fame beside Sir John Sebright, Mr. Laverack, and other worthies with whom to plan was to do.

Our remarks on breeding will now be general, and devoid of any application to special forms. We preface them with a few observations on the physical constitution of the bird, which is popularly supposed to be weakly in its character when compared with the robust varieties cultivated among us. Opinions differ as to this, some maintaining that it is delicate and tender to a degree, and others that it is equally hardy. We have seen it under nearly every condition, and might instance examples in support of almost every statement as to its robustness, or the contrary. Our friend's opinion is that "it possesses as good a constitution as any other, but from the very careful breeding it has gone through it has developed a most sensitive organisation. The results of various experiments I have tried with the bird during some years lead me to this conclusion. Two years ago, during the winter, I found that cold did not permanently affect it, even when it was so intense that the water in the fountains was frozen." The way in which some of them knock about the country during the show-season proves they can stand a considerable amount of wear and tear, and though they may not be able to exhibit themselves to perfection in the variable temperature of our show-rooms, that really does not go far in evidence of a generally weakly constitution. On the whole, we think there would be some difficulty in disproving the accuracy of the above opinion, though the variable character of our English climate must be taken into account as a disturbing element materially affecting the question, since the bird can scarcely yet be regarded as thoroughly acclimatised in this country, where we sometimes enjoy the luxury of the four seasons and the wind blowing from every point of the compass in twenty-four hours. Climatic alternations have frequently more to do with physical geography than with latitude and longitude. Fruits will ripen in the north which cannot be brought to perfection in Cornwall, while delicate plants which will not grow at all in northern latitudes will stand a south-west winter unprotected.

The sensitive organisation previously referred to is also sometimes mistaken for physical weakness by the casual observer who is accustomed to the ringing, ear-splitting music of an English bird-room where the occupants are as bold and impudent as sparrows. Says our observant correspondent:—"Our high-bred birds are sensitive to a degree, even to the positive ill-effects of certain colours. One morning, going into my bird-room, having on a red smoking-cap, in passing one of my cages containing a single bird, I noticed it stagger and fall off the perch, and before I could introduce it to an apparatus which has saved the life of many a bird, it was beyond my assistance. In the meantime, an unusual amount of fluttering was going on in my other cages until I bethought me of my offending cap, the removal of which at once caused peace and quietness. Since then I find my training-rods always more effective *when tipped with red sealing-wax.* I have made numerous other experiments with my birds, but the majority of them were not sufficiently pronounced, or were perhaps too much the subject of exceptional conditions to be of much interest, but on the whole they warrant me in arriving at the conclusion that this variety is anything but the weakly-constituted bird it is imagined to be by many: its over-sensitiveness has been mistaken for weakness. In one point only is there, I believe, any weakness to be found more pronounced than in other varieties which I have had to do with, and that is in regard to the legs and feet of young birds, any defect in which, I need not say, is a serious drawback. Let them be startled out of their nests when young, and down to the bottom of the cage they go; and, as any one who has had to do with young birds knows, it is one thing to put them back, and quite another thing to persuade them to stay; but it may be taken as nearly certain that if they do not remain, or great care be not taken of their legs, feet, and claws, deformity or weakness, more or less serious in its character, will ensue, and then good-bye to a firm, easy stand. I have noticed at Ghent, a plan they have well calculated to counteract this misfortune, and it may be a 'wrinkle' for English breeders: it is to cover the bottom of the cage with rye-straw. When the rye is mown in Belgium it is tied up more carefully and in much smaller sheaves than in England, and the flail—for Belgium is still in a primitive state so far as agricultural implements are concerned—is used only to the heads, so that the body of the straw remains unbroken. These straws are cut into lengths to suit the cages, and spread evenly over the bottom, admirably serving the purpose desired, taking the weight off the foot when extended, and giving it a notion of grasping." We think this is not the least valuable "wrinkle" which has come to us from across the "silver streak." It is perhaps, strictly, a "management" item, but we give it as bearing on alleged constitutional weakness, as does also the following.

"Another fallacy is that these birds will not or cannot bring up their own young. I believe this arises out of the desire to get as many eggs as possible from one pair of birds, but nevertheless it is always the custom here to have other hens (Saxons), small German Canaries, put up at the same time, to which the eggs of the Belgians are given. Five years' careful trial of that system convinces me, so far as my management goes, that it is decidedly unprofitable. Of course, more eggs are obtained, but *fertility* and not *number* is the point, not to mention the health of the hen, which is surely of some value, and especially for the second year. I would go no further than to recommend breeders to have a few common hens, in case the parent Belgian should refuse to do as she should. There is no *real* reason why this variety should not be treated precisely the same as any other of the family confined for life in a prison a dozen inches more or less cube. Without one exception in all my birds, the cock has never neglected his duty to his wife and family, while one old fellow, a great favourite, attended to his business so assiduously that he starved himself to death. I dissected him, so I am positive about it.

"Then how comes the notion in England that the breeding of this bird is so difficult? That there is such a notion, I know by letters from various correspondents, who agree in this, however much they differ in anything else. I have already said that all show-birds are not the best breeding-birds, and one cause of want of success arises from the conditions accompanying an order usually being something after this kind—that the bird shall have good shoulders, good neck, good this and good that, but seldom that it shall be such as can be recommended for breeding purposes. It is desired to make something out of the bird, perhaps, by showing—a perfectly legitimate object in its way; but no discount is allowed for the exhaustion, the wear and tear, and the loss of vigour and condition consequent on travelling the English circuit for a long show-season—a line of life our Belgian birds are not accustomed to, and which their highly-sensitive nervous organisation renders them unfitted for when carried to such an extreme as it is with you. There is a limit to showing in its effect upon the health of a bird, and I am satisfied that *over-showing* is a fruitful source of injury to the constitution of even the most robust specimens. There is such a thing as burning both ends of the candle.

"Over-pairing, also, is another evil which is not always estimated at its proper value. The great value of the birds leads to this; but the proverb says that 'much would have more, and reaped nothing.' Mr. £ s. d. is not satisfied with enough, so, if he possess a good Belgian, while his hen is between nests, Mr. Belge must be the father of a few 'improved' Yorkshires; or the Coppies or Plainheads want 'improving,' or a little length and style are wanted elsewhere; and the bird, instead of being kept in clover and maintained in the highest possible condition of vigour, pays a morning and evening visit to half-a-dozen cages, or, at the very least, must have two or even three wives of his own class, and this, mark you, not under carefully-arranged and well-sustained healthy conditions, but after he has spent some months alternating between the excitement of long days in the show-room, and dreary, comfortless nights in the guard's van, jolted about till position and life have both been nearly shaken out of him, while other less valuable birds have been taking their ease and storing up the strength and vigour which lead their unthinking owners to jump to the conclusion that 'common' birds are the best breeders. Well may they be." Another wrinkle. *Verb. sap.*

Our friend's description of a Continental breeding-room is short and to the point:—"A breeding-room in Belgium is usually a cock-loft, or rather a corner of the loft, kept under lock and key, where mystifications are concocted, or supposed to be, such as fiighting and tailing, &c.; and much as I am afraid I shall upset some preconceived idea you may have respecting these halls of mystery, I must in strict regard to truth say that cleanliness is not the most prominent feature, and that the olfactory nerves are apt to assert that there are odours attending Canaries other than agreeable. But there are all descriptions of rooms, and all kinds of ways of managing the birds. Respecting the breeding-cages, their forms are legion: high, low, broad, narrow, shut-up and open all round, with, however, three points of likeness—glass fountains are universal, the seed is always placed inside the cage in some sort of box arrangement, and the nest-boxes are always placed outside. Basket-nests are universally used, and excellently made they are."

This arrangement of the outer nest-box and the insertion of the basket-nest differs from our usual English plan, though it resembles in principle that of the "London" cage, with its little room. In cage-appliances, however, custom goes a long way, and we will not undertake to say that one system of arrangement is superior to another in so far as the successful rearing of young birds is affected by it. The most we can do is to describe the various breeding appliances as we meet with them, leaving it to the practical fancier to adopt them or adhere to his own contrivances. There is scarcely a breeding-room we enter without finding a departure from some detail which, from long acquaintance, appears to us a necessity; but it is proverbial that some workmen manage best with their own tools.

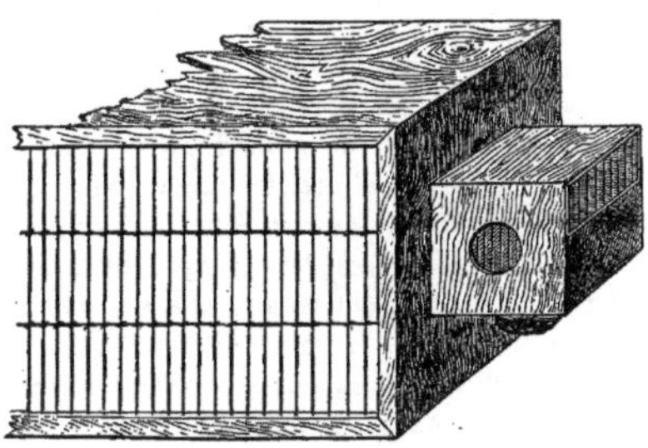

FIG. 59.—BELGIAN BREEDING-CAGE.

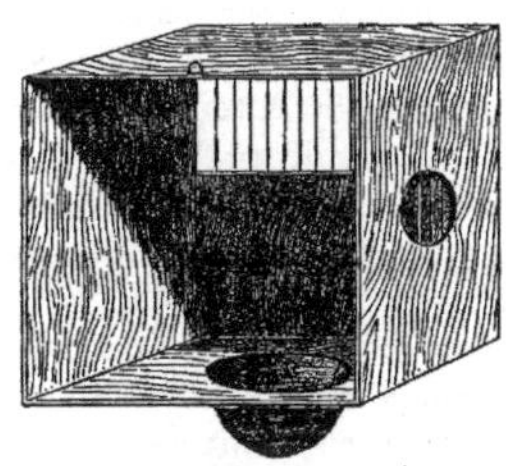

FIG. 60.—NEST-BOX (ENLARGED).

As an illustration of this, though it relates more directly to rearing generally, than to the use of special appliances, our authority says, in a very amusing manner:—"I will give you an instance of peculiar management quite unique in its way. A fancier of my acquaintance, of forty years' standing, during a period of five months in the breeding season neither drinks wine nor any strong drink, and abstains from tobacco, simply, as he says, 'to keep his saliva clean,' as his mouth is then employed for other purposes, chiefly as a mashing-machine in which he prepares all the soft food for his young birds, which he feeds about every quarter of an hour, whether the parents do so or not. Another breaks a piece of hard-boiled egg with his fingers, and throws it down in a lump with a quantum of bread, say every three or four days, and cleans his cages out at intervals of weeks; and yet both have extraordinary good luck at times."

The breeding-cage for Belgians need not differ in any material respect from that in ordinary use for other varieties, except that if it be made a trifle more roomy it will be no disadvantage. There should also be a liberal supply of perches, seed and water and food of every description being placed where it is accessible from a perch rather than from the ground.

Of more importance than the cage is its situation; and we cannot too often repeat the injunction to be careful to avoid draughts as the source of infinite trouble. The temperature of a breeding-room devoted to Belgians should also be a matter for careful arrangement, not with a view to coddling and pampering, but being thoughtful to provide for protection against sudden changes and extremes, from which greater danger is to be apprehended than from a uniformly very low temperature, more care being necessary with imported birds than with home-bred stock, for the reasons previously stated. On no point in connection with Canary-breeding is there greater difference of opinion than on the subject of artificial warmth; but an extensive observation confirms us in our estimate of the importance of being prepared for emergencies, and especially in the case of these birds during the early part of the breeding season, when it is just as much incumbent on the breeder to afford seasonable protection as it is for the gardener to protect his half-hardy plants from unseasonable frost—the one must not be *forced* any more than the other. In judicious management the operator shows his knowledge of his business, and he is a poor gardener who fires his houses to excess.

As regards any special management of the young in the nest, there is not much to note of real consequence. If anything, they are rather more ungainly and clumsy and given to sprawling about than other young birds, and when they reach a size at which it is well to give them a more roomy nest than that in which they were hatched, it should be sufficiently large not to require a second change, and sufficiently deep to prevent any youngster who overbalances himself when standing on his toes to beg from falling out of bed. This could not occur in the case of the Continental nest-box, which, we may remark in passing, appears to us, as the "London" cage also has always done, to suggest the idea of a nest built on the ground, rather than after the custom of finches generally, and further suggests to the practical breeder sundry difficulties in the way of cleanliness which do not occur when the margin of the nest is clear. We apprehend this can be got over by daily attention, as also could a change of nest be managed by substituting a fresh box with a larger basket. Some breeders, however, object to any changes whatever; the fewer the better, perhaps, but sometimes they are necessary. An artificial nest of flannel or felt confined within walls of basket-work, wood, tin, or earthenware, is not so elastic and disposed to accommodate itself to the requirements of a rising family as is one built by the bird itself. The deep, unyielding cup of the nest of the Song Thrush always appears to us to be designed for prospective use.

Young Belgians, at about the half-fledged stage, are rather *hobble-de-hoyish*, all legs, wings, and neck, and swagger and sway about as we have seen in a great, gaunt puppy on long, clumsy legs, apparently belonging to some other dog's body. We miss the chubby plumpness of smaller birds, and when a nest of four or five are standing swaying about with that wide, red fissure at the end of the long neck, every facility should be afforded the hen to feed with comfort. It is not a bad plan to have the perches above the level of the margin of the nest; and it will be found that, in feeding, a hen will at all times prefer this higher stand from which she appears to have greater command than when perched on the nest-edge doing her best to be impartial in her distribution of food. The art of feeding is a natural feminine gift. We have thought so from the time when we discovered how futile were all our efforts to resist the attacks made on us with a spoon containing one or other of those treacle-and-brimstone mixtures which so frequently haunt the spring-time of early youth with their shadow.

From the hour the young birds leave the nest it must be laid down as a rule, not to be departed from except in a case of emergency, that *they must never be handled*. It will be remembered we gave the same injunctions with respect to the Lizard and London Fancy: in those cases it was on account of the risk of injury to the feather; in this, it is undesirable owing to the sensitive character of the bird. Other Canaries do not require to be tamed: the Belgian does. In any other exhibition-bird, so long as it is not wild, sprightliness and vivacity are virtues, and frequent handling for the purpose of critical examination, with occasional "tubbing," soon render the wildest of them reasonably tame, but to nothing like the degree required in a Belgian. All Canaries thoroughly dislike being handled, their repugnance to it being apparently the last vestige of their native character. Isolated cases there are, we know, in which they do not object to be caressed, and even seem to like it; but such training belongs more to the "Happy Family" line of business than the sphere of the fancier. We will not say that Canaries generally, Belgians included, could not be so far tamed as to be caught with comparative ease; but it would be a dull submission to what seemed an inevitable necessity, brought about in the case of the Belgian with considerable risk of life and limb, owing to the sensitive character of the bird and its peculiar conformation. The reaction, also, on being released, with the consequent flutter and agitation, are so entirely opposed to the quiet repose and unruffled deportment demanded in our bird that handling is never for a moment to be thought of; but as the bird, in order to display its beauty, must be quietly separated from possibly a large number in a roomy flight and caged without the least excitement, it is necessary that it should be early trained to come and go by a process least calculated to agitate it, the resulting tameness being something like that of a parrot which will permit any amount of familiarity short of actual bodily handling. The first thing we would advise is attaching to the cage containing the young birds an open-wire cage in the way we described on page 168. If the position of the larger cage is such that the end is not "get-atable," hook the open cage to the doorway, and allow the birds full time to examine it and be accustomed to it. This is the beginning and the end of the difficulty, if any there be, and it is as well to understand what it really is that the bird is required to do. Any one who has had much experience in caging Canaries knows how very unwilling they are to take the little hop from one cage to another. It is nothing but timidity. Even a bird which has been travelling all night in a small box will prefer to squat in a corner where it feels itself safe, to leaving its little prison. Let this natural caution and timidity be overcome by familiarity with the act, and the work is half accomplished before it is even commenced. It is not required to accustom the cattle to being driven from one part of the pasture to another, but to quietly entering the door of the shed or byre, which, if left open all day, they will do of their own accord. A little lad may drive a bullock through the streets, but half-a-dozen butchers cannot induce it to step over the threshold of the stable. And just so with birds. You may drive them about the cage from end to end and get them with their heads set fair for the door through which you wish them to pass, but that is just what they are afraid to do. It is not that they have not intelligence enough to tell them what is wanted, but they have not nerve enough to do it. Then set about the thing intelligently yourself, and leave the bird's intelligence to overcome its timidity. Begin when it is very young, as soon, in fact, as it is strong on the wing, and with a wand sufficiently thin to pass easily between the wires, and long enough to reach every part of the cage, endeavour with the utmost delicacy to direct it where required. Familiarise it with the appearance of the rod, which, it will be remembered, our friend recommends should be tipped with red sealing-wax, and it will soon know no fear, but obey its directions. Let it know no other system from the very first, and implicit obedience will soon follow. The simple act of passing into the open cage will come of itself, and on no account should a bird be forced. The skill and care are required in separating any one bird from the rest, and in delicately handling the rod so as to prevent its rejoining its companions. After a very short time the birds become so accustomed to the wand that its introduction to the cage is a matter of no further concern than as a signal as to who shall be first through the door; and so perfect does the training become that if two or three birds should happen to pass out simultaneously the slightest direction of the rod will send them back at a moment's notice without the least agitation, and when the open cage is removed from the door those left standing ready for a hop will, as often as not, remain in the doorway, never thinking of escaping into the room. We do not put this as an extreme case, but simply to show how different is their action from that of birds unaccustomed to this quiet training, and which, in the fright consequent on being caught by the hand, would be as likely as not to make a dart through any opening. There need be no hurry to close the door on a Belgian. If one should happen to make a voyage of discovery into the room, his agitation at the novelty of the situation will at once be apparent. Whether on the floor, or clinging to the wires of a cage, or on any projection, never attempt to catch it. Approach quietly with an open cage, and it will soon show how thoroughly these birds become the "slaves of the wand."

A bird being thus familiarised with the process of "running" from cage to cage, the most promising specimens should be isolated in cages of a pattern similar to that in which it is intended they shall be exhibited. When he is required to be put on his mettle, a Belgian does not want to have his attention distracted by surroundings to which he is unaccustomed, but should feel thoroughly at home; and the homely-looking four-post-bed-pattern cage shown in Fig. 56, which is from a sketch "taken on the spot," is the orthodox article in which he best puts forth all his beauties. It is of rather primitive construction, and, one would think, might be made a trifle lighter and more elegant; but it reigns throughout Belgium, and has long been identified with the bird. The legs are really so many handles by which the cage is lifted and turned about, for it is against all rule to touch the top of the cage, which has the effect of frightening the bird. A Belgian fancier can almost be told by the way he handles a cage, in doing which there is as much skill shown as in manipulating with a Scotch Fancy. The perch, which is omitted in the sketch, usually rests on the upper framework, throwing the bird well up into the dome, and is of substantial construction, affording the bird a secure stand. In such cages the birds should be hung against the wall of the room and receive daily attention, both to accustom them to frequent handling, and that the development of gradually maturing "position" properties may be noted and encouraged. There is a wide difference in the dispositions and temperament of Belgians, as we showed in our remarks on the various types. Excessive nervous sensibility must be treated with great caution, and a sluggish, lethargic disposition roused to the utmost. Under any circumstances every bird should be encouraged and excited to do its best, for the exhibitor who wishes his birds to acquit themselves satisfactorily in public should familiarise them with show usages at home. A Game fowl or Bantam taken up from a walk and whisked off to a show has small chance against one which has been put through its paces for some time in the home pens, and many an exhibitor who has neglected to continue periodical lessons on deportment and company-manners has had the luxury of seeing himself beaten by, perhaps, inferior birds from the same yard from which his own were taken. And it is just so with Belgian Canaries. And what is all this but "training?" We are quite prepared for the question, and reply that it entirely depends on the meaning attached to the word. If we are to understand it as meaning teaching, in the sense of teaching a trick foreign to natural habits, we say that in this sense the idea of "training" is in no way connected with the exhibition of "position" made by a Belgian, any more than among pigeons it has to do with the expansion of the crop of a Pouter or the proud strut of a Fantail. But if it means the drawing out and cultivation of native features by judicious treatment, we say that the most careful "training" of this kind is the legitimate sphere of the Belgian fancier. Those who think that the performance of the "postuur vogel" is on a *par* with that of the bird which balances itself on a tight-rope, fires a little gun, and wheels his wife in a barrow, should try the experiment with some other variety and see how much "position" can be developed by "training."

Before finally dismissing the subject of position, which crops up in various ways while treating of this interesting bird, we must here give an important item of information, which it will be seen could not have been introduced earlier, inasmuch as it has been supplied by our Belgian friend since the preceding pages have been in type. It is, however, *so* important as bearing on *English* v. *Belgian* ideas touching a vital point, that no further explanation is necessary for introducing it in this place. Our correspondent writes:—

"I must congratulate you on the excellence of the rendering of the bronze model. I cannot, however, say so much respecting the engraving on page 190. I do not think that the *coup d'œil* of an English and a Belgian judge follows quite the same lines. I will give you what I have gathered from our best judges, and also an amusing incident confirming me in my opinion that my view is correct. First, the time of forming the decision of comparison is not at the moment of the acme of stretch when the bird is standing with its head *en bas*, but immediately afterwards, when it has elevated its head and assumed an easier attitude. Second, the object of first and special regard is not precisely the same with us as with you. It is neither shoulders nor back, but what is, in Flemish, expressed in a word 'afgewerk,' the 'working off.' You will notice at once what I mean if you compare the two engravings. The 'afgewerk' of the model is excellent; that of the other figure, at any rate in the position represented, rather inferior. Taking a line diagonally from the extreme shoulder-points to the extreme point of projection of the breast as the base of a triangle, with the commencement of the tail as the apex, the triangle so formed should be isosceles, and the longer the sides and the truer the triangle, the more nearly will the features of the bird appear in harmonious proportion. Proportion and beauty are very closely connected. Any one feature developed in excess becomes deformity, be it shoulder, legs, or what not.

"I visited the last show held at Ghent last year, in company with the members of the Antwerp Society, and on going from place to place continually came across the tracks of an Englishman who was over buying birds. At the distribution of prizes he was pointed out to me, and I spoke to him; and as he had been for a few days entirely dependent on a commissioner for conversation, he appeared relieved to hear himself addressed in English, especially as he much needed an opportunity for discharging a little splenetic humour to rid him of some of the disgust he felt with the breeders of Bruxelles and Ghent. 'Ten years ago, sir, I could come over and buy in a couple of hours such birds as would astonish you now-a-days, sir, at from twenty-five to thirty-five francs each. Now, sir, I've been here and in Brussels four blessed days, and I can't come across a really good bird neither for love nor money.' 'You astonish me,' I said, 'for surely there are enough here to satisfy you at any rate.' 'Sir,' he replied, with such a look and in such a tone, 'there's not *one* really good bird in the room; they are all "wastrels"' (that's Lancashire for something, I don't exactly know what); 'there's not one with any *timber* in it; *timber*, sir, TIMBER is what we want in Lancashire;' and he stretched his arm across my shoulders. Yet that Ghent show was the show of last year, and one of my friends made an offer of one hundred and fifty francs for a buff hen a long way down the prize-list, which was refused.".

We give the above, not with a view to discounting the value of position when the bird is standing with its head *en bas*, but as supporting our contention that there must *first* be position and the "acme of stretch" *before* we can have the "afgewerk," or "working off;" the former, of a necessity, preceding the latter, which, in its turn, determines the time when we can correctly measure the proportions of the bird, the whole showing incontestably the force of our proposition that position and shape are interwoven to such an extent that it becomes difficult to separate the consequence from the cause. The corollary to be deduced is that a satisfactory "afgewerk" can only be expected to supervene upon good position. Fig. 54 is not intended to illustrate "afgewerk" but position, the points in which it is defective having been admitted and explained by us.

No departure from ordinary routine is required in moulting the Belgian, but every care should be taken to encourage and hasten on the work, when once begun, by keeping the birds warm and free from the ill-effects of chills. If we repeated this injunction with every hint we gave on moulting, we should mention it none too often to impress on the breeder the great importance of this salutary caution. Occurring as it does at a season of the year when the least inconvenience or risk to the bird may be anticipated, the chances of any mishap attending the moult are reduced to a minimum, especially in the case of young birds, as the earlier nests, at all events, will commence to shed their feathers before summer has taken its departure; and we would recommend nothing more than keeping the birds covered up in enclosed flights and following the instructions given in Chapter X. The operations of "flighting" and "tailing" have here, certainly, no defence based on any connection they may have with improved colour, because colour is really a matter of small moment; but candour obliges us to admit that tailing is frequently practised with the object of gaining a little additional length. Probably it is the rule rather than the exception—a rule more honoured in the breach than the observance. The growing interest manifested in the consideration of the broad question of "mutilation"—a term scarcely literally applicable in this case except in so far as it is connected with the idea of pain inflicted—in its relation to fashion or necessity, an interest which we take to be one of the healthiest features the love of live stock has induced, and which has narrowed the question between clearly-defined bounds through which there is no loophole of escape, demands that there shall be no fencing or trifling with the matter on the part of those who may be called on to express an opinion; and our adhesion to the simple principle involved, viz., that the infliction of pain is not justifiable unless a direct corresponding advantage can be shown to render it a necessity, constrains us to say that, failing to discover such necessity, we condemn any interference with the tail of a Belgian beyond the removal of broken feathers, the restoration of sound ones being an adequate compensation on the assumption that a perfect tail is not without its uses. The extremely unsatisfactory state of the title-deeds by which a bird holds possession of its tail, we have before commented on; but while this fact *sometimes* reduces the pain of extraction to a point scarcely appreciable, we should be sorry to allow it to be used as a general argument against the principle enunciated, and have no desire to countenance the insertion of the thin end of a wedge which, by expansion, might do great injury and become a dangerous precedent.

Year-old Belgians require more attention during the moult, since the work commences later and is frequently protracted to a tedious length. When such is the case and it extends into a time of the year unfavourable to satisfactory progress, we strongly recommend artificial heat—a condition admitted on all hands to be one of the necessaries for bringing the matter to a successful issue. A Canary is but a Canary, and the physical changes in one variety are essentially the same in all, but the difference between the wholesale moulting of some hundreds of young birds and the attention required in moulting matured specimens of great value, in or out of season as the case may be, is just the difference between a sort of carelessness which leaves things to take their chance and lays the blame of failure on Nature, and a careful watching which, acknowledging that Nature is to some extent interfered with, does what it can to correct irregularities and tide over difficulties not so much the result of a natural as an artificial mode of existence.

Colour, that is, colour in excess, being of no value, none of the means resorted to to develop it in other varieties are necessary here. We have before shown, we believe on sound artistic grounds, that form and colour should not in some cases be brought into juxtaposition, and we do not hold with adding to form anything which has a tendency towards affecting the eye in another direction. We are not going to stay here to argue the question in all its bearings, but simply state the proposition as one which, in the abstract, requires no demonstration. The Belgian is essentially a development of form, and, we think, appears to most advantage when its natural colour is entirely unassisted, any attempt in that direction being nothing more, even considered from a fancy point of view, than an endeavour to connect the bird with a feature entirely foreign to its spirit and genius. To colour a cast of the "Greek Slave" in warm tones never seemed to us to add to its beauty, and vulgarity sometimes reaches its "acme of stretch" in the use of lacquer and Dutch gilt. Cayenne and similar colour-stimulants are therefore out of place in the Belgian moulting-cage, and the diet should be restricted to the usual nourishing elements best calculated to counteract the drain on the system consequent on the rapid growth of new feather.

We conclude our notice of this bird by drawing attention to one or two matters of importance which can be referred to in brief. It will be found that in consequence of its erect attitude, occasional looseness of the bowels—which, by the way, is often chronic—will cause an offensive accumulation of the excreta on the long fluffy feathers in the neighbourhood of the vent, which, besides being very unsightly, is a source of inconvenience to the bird. This can be removed by moistening the hardened excreta in warm water and carefully picking off the softened mass, but we should do this only when the looseness is not chronic. When it is so, the operation would require to be repeated too frequently and at the cost of a good deal of handling, affording only temporary relief. In such case it is better at once to clip the feathers in the region of the vent. The reason is obvious: if clipped, the small stumps will remain and no new growth will follow; but if pulled out, the work will only have to be done over again when the new growth is matured, by which time the accumulation will have become very troublesome, as it is not prudent to meddle with it during the growth of the young feathers at a time when the accidental extraction of one or two would be followed by bleeding. With stock-birds we should always advise cutting away the feathers, but inasmuch as a free use of the scissors would disfigure an exhibition-bird, we should be disposed to resort to washing in preference. We have, however, explained the *rationale* of the matter, and leave it in the hands of the breeder to act as circumstances may require.

Belgians are never "tubbed." Sometimes, when they get *very* dirty, and the tail in particular becomes soiled and perhaps ornamented with a small knob of dirt gathered up from the cage-bottom, the sponge is applied, but anything approaching a thorough wash—the *modus operandi* of which will be detailed in due course—is never attempted. We mean that nothing further than cleansing the tail or the tips of the wings should be done, and this with *water only;* on no account be tempted to use *soap* in giving what is little better than a dry rub. If a bird really must be tubbed, wash it and be done with it, but don't begin to dabble with soap and flannel, giving a touch here and a touch there. A half-washed bird looks worse than if it had never been touched. So far as concerns any risk to the life of the bird, we would not hesitate to wash the most sensitive specimen without the slightest apprehension as to the consequences, but the birds can be kept in fair show condition by the free use of the bath. Repeated drenchings with warm water by means of a fine syringe, allowing the bird to dry itself before a fire, will do much to cleanse the plumage, but it must not be only half done. Dirt is not a show element, and thoroughly dirty birds are apt to be overlooked in a show-room for no other reason than that they suggest the idea of worthlessness, something not worth attending to, and, consequently, not worth much critical examination.

The last trait to be mentioned is that the Belgian has conscientious objections to displaying his merits on an empty stomach, though he is often called on to do so. He is not like a bird which can be inspected as well when busy at his seed-box as at any other time, and so long as he is under examination, which may last for a considerable length of time under the judge in the show-room, and be repeated at short intervals by any visitor desirous of asking him a question, he is practically debarred from getting a bite; and the better the specimen, the greater the probability of his suffering from this cause. It is therefore advisable, when sending valuable specimens from home, to provide them with a supply not only of seed, but also of nourishing "soft" food off which a bird can make a good meal in a short space of time; and this, we advise, should never be neglected. The first thing a Belgian should see when uncovered in a show-room should be a tempting breakfast in the shape of some chopped hard-boiled egg and bread-crumbs or crushed biscuit. If this be supplied over-night, as, of course, must be done before despatching on a journey, the mixture should be *dry*, to prevent the chance of turning sour; but when there is the opportunity of feeding in the early morning, as is frequently permitted as an act of courtesy in the case of these valuable birds, the bread may be first soaked in clean water and then squeezed as dry as possible before mixing with the egg. After a good meal of this description a bird will show much better than when his mind is bent on his seed-box, and will be the better able to stand the fatigue of a long show-day, during which it will be manifest he may have but small chance of getting another substantial feed. It is the neglect of simple precautions such as these which takes so much out of a bird during an extended show-season, when it has sufficient to contend with in the way of ordinary and extraordinary fatigue, without having added to the consequent tax on its energies the evils attendant on irregular feeding.

In conclusion, we feel that we have done but scant justice to a bird, the peculiarities of which are not to be learned in a day. Some of the positions we have taken up we know are not exactly in harmony with the views of English fanciers, but we believe that when the bird comes to be better understood and more extensively bred among us it will be found that what we have advanced is, in the main, in strict accord with the idea of the bird as held by the leading Continental breeders, whose the bird essentially is, and to whose opinions we defer. We think we have told the story before, but the lesson is so fitting that we tell it again and append it as the "moral" of what may have been to some a dry chapter. We once thought we could play Whist; but one night, after making a spectacle of ourselves, a friend tendered us the sage advice to throw overboard all our ideas on the subject, study "Cavendish," and save seven years of our life.

And now for the Scale, touching which we will give our Antwerp "Liefhebber" the honour of almost the last word. "You should have seen," he writes, "the wonder expressed on the face of the gentleman who acts as the principal judge in Antwerp when I showed him a tabulated scale of points. 'Not but,' said he, 'that would do well when the *prix d'honneur* is on the *tapis*, but *how* can you judge PROPORTION?'" That is just the question. How can we judge proportion; the harmony, the intangible something to which we have referred in our remarks on previous scales? We can only shrug our shoulders, elevate our eyebrows, spread out our hands like the wings of a penguin or the "flappers" of a seal *à la* puzzled Flem, look sapient, and set our face to the task, feeling very much the incubus of the *how*.

SCALE OF POINTS FOR JUDGING BELGIAN CANARIES.

Points of Merit.

SHAPE.	Maximum.	
HEAD—Small, neat and flat on the crown ...	3	
NECK—Long and slender, and capable of extension	10	
SHOULDERS—High, broad, massive, well filled-in between the pinions, and presenting a considerable area between the base of the neck and the summit, which should be well rounded	10	
BACK—Long, straight, and well filled	5	
BREAST—Prominent and deep through from the back to the front of the chest	5	
BODY—Long, tapering gradually and evenly towards the waist from a base-line drawn diagonally through the body from the breast to the back to a point between the shoulders	5	
WINGS—Long, compact, and carried close to the body, with the tips meeting evenly	5	
TAIL—Long, narrow, close, and only slightly forked	3	
LEGS—Long and straight, with the thighs well covered	5	
FEATHER—Close and compact, so as not to disturb the outline of the body. Upper and lower tail-coverts dense and compact, forming the vertex of an isosceles triangle of which the sectional diagonal line is the base	3	
SIZE	4	
COLOUR—For purity rather than depth	2	
	—	60
POSITION.		
ATTITUDE—Erect stand, with quiet, easy pose. The line of the back and tail as nearly plumb as possible	6	
LEGS—Straight and rigid	4	
SHOULDERS—Elevated	10	
HEAD—Depressed	10	
NECK—Length of reach and arching...	10	
	—	40
Total		100

Negative Properties.

SHAPE.

A Belgian should not have a large, coarse head, nor a short, thick, straight neck, nor narrow shoulders with the points of the pinions raised so as to cause a cavity between them; nor should the point of deflection formed by the meeting of the lines of the neck and back be sharp or angular. Nor should the line of the back be round, nor should it be hollow or have any sign of a "spout" formed by a continuation of a hollow between the shoulders. Neither should it have a broad, full breast, nor should the body generally be short or chubby. It should not droop its wings, neither should it cross them at the tips. The tail should not be thick or fan-shaped, nor deeply forked. It should not have short legs. The body-feathers should not be open or rough to a degree which interferes with the general neatness of the bird, and it should not be diminutive in size.

POSITION.

A Belgian should not stand with the line of the back and tail forming other than a right angle with the plane of the perch, neither should the line be curved; nor should it be restless and unsteady. It should not stand with its knee-joints projecting forwards till thighs and legs are thrown into a curve, neither should it be cow-hocked or inclined to squat, nor should it refuse to rise to its full height. It should not refuse to elevate its shoulders, nor to depress its head, nor to reach out and arch its neck; nor should it be sluggish or manifest any want of nervous energy in any of its position movements.

The practical application of these scales may require a little explanation, since, on the first glance, it may appear difficult to reconcile the ratio which some of the foregoing assessments bear to each other and to the total. But we think this difficulty will vanish when it is seen that we have, practically, divided the bird into two parts, each maximum being calculated on the ratio it bears to the total in its section. Though these two parts are intimately interwoven with each other, we, at the same time, regard the latter as a consequence of the former; and inasmuch as the perfection of position may be assumed to result from the most symmetrical disposition of the elements of form, we have given such a balance of points to the latter as we think would represent it in a degree from which the best position results might reasonably be expected. Though the ratio between shape and position, as the scales now stand, may be represented by $1\frac{1}{2} : 1$, which may appear to some critics to be giving undue preference to shape, yet a *very trifling* alteration of *minor points* would materially affect it. Deduct, for example, the values of "Feather" and "Colour," which are not *very* important items, and add them to the first two in the "Position" scale, and the ratio becomes as 6 : 5. It might even be equalised without much disturbance, but we should but give an extra shrug when the work was done, and say *cui bono?*

For the sake of convenience we have assumed the element of "Condition" to be uniform. We have not attempted to devise a separate gauge for "afgewerk," as it can be accurately measured by applying any of the values assigned to the elements of shape, which can, in fact, only be properly judged at the time of the "afgewerk."

Our readers will sympathise with us if we say that here we draw a long breath.

Vincent Brooks, Day & Son Lith

SCOTCH FANCY CANARIES.

CLEAR YELLOW HEN. CLEAR BUFF COCK.

CLEAR YELLOW COCK.

CHAPTER XXV.

THE SCOTCH FANCY CANARY.

THIS in every way most remarkable Canary is, as its name suggests, a creation of our neighbours across the Tweed, and is wholly and entirely an exclusive speciality, as is the "postuur vogel" in Belgium, of which bird it is, doubtless, an offshoot, and is, in truth, the "postuur vogel" of Scotland. It is known also as the Glasgow Fancy and Glasgow Don, the Glasgow breeders preferring, we believe, the national name, and only tolerating the other as reflecting some honour on the city as being the head-quarters of the bird. East and south of Edinburgh the name Don is general, and the Glasgow definition "piebald," the equivalent of our "variegated," becomes "flecked," these differences in name and idiom being sufficiently marked to indicate the distribution of the bird geographically—a matter which further affords indirect information to the fancier who recognises under the local difference in nomenclature some variation also in the type of bird, the standard of Glasgow and the western district generally being far in advance of that set up in some other places.

No authentic history of the bird has ever been put in our hands, though the heads of many of the breeders have moulted white, and their memories are rich in stories of the old days from the history of the first pair—the "Girvan" pair we think they were called, from the name of the town where they appeared—down to to-day. So far as we can gather, however, there is nothing directly connecting the bird with historical events, the story of its development being probably of local interest, but the bird itself is an unwritten narrative of deep interest.

Whatever may be the real state of Canary-breeding, in its strict application, in England, the national bird of Scotland is a living evidence of the way in which it is followed up on the other side of the Cheviots. It seems to be with the Scotch a thing not to be spoken of lightly or entered into thoughtlessly; a pursuit to be followed out through any difficulties, and, once taken up, never to be relinquished. A Scotch breeder would think he had not done his duty to his wife and family, or as a citizen, till he had earned a "first and special"—his crown of rejoicing. We say "breeder" and write it with respect, for in Scotland the *breeder* is everything and the *exhibitor* nothing. We don't mean to insinuate that the man of long purse is not as much honoured on yon side the Tweed as on this, or that bawbees are not as much respected for what they can accomplish; but we do say that genuine deference is paid to the man who breeds his birds, and not to the man who buys them, however necessary the one may be to the other; and there are many birds which cannot be bought at any price—they represent something achieved, the result of years of careful breeding, an honour and satisfaction which has not an equivalent value in Scotch notes. We, on this side the Border, have no idea of the absorbing interest manifested by the Scotch fanciers for their bird. We have nothing akin to it, unless, perhaps, it may be found here and there in certain districts in which one bird has become a favourite; as, for instance, in Norwich, whose well-known bird has for generations been the household god of succeeding generations of breeders, who have never forsaken the faith of their fathers, but held on tenaciously to their one idol despite all modern innovations and revolutions. The London Fancy breeders, too, are a small but enthusiastic band of devotees who worship only at one shrine; and others might be mentioned who are not triflers or men who play with their work; but in most cases the thorough-going genuine breeders of any one variety can be summed up with few figures, while the general character of the Fancy here is indicated by a large amount of energy spread over a very wide field. We do not mean to imply that any one man cannot fix upon one object and, by his own individual thought and application of settled principles, develop something like perfection. We see it done every day; but as in Belgium, so in Scotland, the entire community direct their attention to one bird—the enthusiasm which here exists only in individuals, or comparatively small sections, being there so universal that we shall not be considered as reflecting in any way on our English fanciers when we say again we have nothing like it here in the light of a whole Fancy striving after one object.

We are not advocating this exclusiveness, but only stating a fact. Something resolute and determined and grim there certainly is in the earnestness with which the pursuit is followed up, and once in the race there is no such thing as looking back; but we who see many things to charm us in the Canary would prefer to roam more at large, acknowledging beauty wherever we find it, and while giving our due meed of admiration to the one bird of Scotland, cannot abate a fraction of our regard for any one of the many varieties cultivated in our English homes. We are all, however, working for one purpose, are all fanciers and members of one craft. We will agree to believe that there are beauties in every direction, and each, in his own way, does his best to cultivate his special liking, knowing well there is room for all.

In describing the bird which can command the allegiance of a people, we wish to cast no stain on its fair escutcheon, and think it is more in harmony with its character to consider it as a form of the Belgian than as a mixed breed. A very brief description of its distinguishing trait will show the groundwork of our position, one we think we shall have no difficulty in maintaining. We define the Scotch Fancy to be a Belgian built on a curve instead of on the ordinary rectangular scaffolding; a definition quite accurate enough to start with, though we do not wish it to be accepted strictly, and which implies no admixture whatever with foreign blood, but rather a common-sense application of the ordinary principles of selection in a given direction. The bird repeats itself, with never a reversion to any form not essentially Belgian in type, nor is there anything in its conformation, as fixed by the best standards, which it requires any other than Belgian blood to produce; neither is any other ever infused on a decline of any of those requisites which, though they may be *modified forms*, are essentially Belgian, and can only be recruited from a Belgian fountain. The bird can be regarded as belonging to a "mixed" breed only in the sense of mixing fresh Belgian blood with the accepted standard type; and it certainly does not follow that, because some breeders may make a freer use of the Belgian element than others who possibly may work with such care and skill as not to require it, the bird is therefore to be spoken of as of "mixed" blood. Gaps must be repaired and missing links supplied; retrogression must be carefully guarded against and any departure from a fixed standard of beauty at once intercepted, by returning to the source whence derived; but *these* requirements are no evidence of alien blood, and no *other* evidence of alien admixture, however remote, crops up in the best strains. If it be of mixed blood, what are its elements? Belgian and *what?* We know that some of our English fanciers are apt to speak disparagingly of the bird, and assert that it can be knocked together out of next to nothing; but we know of no two varieties we should put together in the expectation of turning out a bird with the many pronounced features of the Scotch Fancy, while on the other hand we find no difficulty in tracing the reflection of every feature, more or less distinctly, in the Belgian bird alone, of which, we repeat, there seems to be external and internal evidence that it is a skilfully modified form, a lineage to be proud of.

We have given the general idea of this Canary in the brief statement that it is practically a curvilinear Belgian: we will endeavour to describe it in detail, merely premising that some of its features are not easily described in words. The head of a good specimen differs from that of the Belgian only in that it is flatter; how much so would scarcely be imagined unless the two were compared side by side. This flatness on the crown adds to the apparent length of the head, and the term "snake-headed" is well applied to the standard type. This may seem but a small point, but we are particular in referring to it as illustrating the extreme care which has been exercised in producing a curve which, continued to the very extremity of the beak, shall not be seriously interfered with by any marked rising of the skull. In local sketches of the bird, in which faithful delineation frequently has to give way before an attempt to depict the ideal, this is generally a most exaggerated feature, but one which, nevertheless, serves to show how the formation we have indicated is prized. A large, coarse head is an abomination in the eyes of Scotch Fancy breeders, who, as a class, can detect very trifling departures from the line and plummet with surprising precision, the result of continued observation. A good head has all that pretty, graceful style of modest carriage and all the delicately soft expression belonging to the Belgian character, with nothing bold or vulgar. The jaunty and more confident bearing of the male bird has no taint of swagger, but speaks the well-bred individual. Before we go further we must remind our readers that our bird belongs to the erect school; but while the Belgian, when excited, throws his shoulders up and his head *down*, the Scotch Fancy holds his head *up* fearlessly. Getting back to the head, then, we remark that it is set on a long neck which should be neither thick nor clumsy, but delicately rounded and of just such a size as shall agree in strict harmony with the well-turned shoulders; and when we call attention to the fact that head, neck, back and tail should form one continuous arc, it will be understood what should be the correct carriage of the neck. In some types in which there is not so great a display of Belgian points as in the more advanced forms, this curve of the neck is very true in its continuation of the arc, but the arc itself is necessarily smaller, owing to the bird being shorter in the neck; while in some of the best examples the very length of the neck, a point insisted on in a high-class bird, prevents the arc being continued with that mathematical exactness observable in the former case. But when to a long neck is united the ability to sustain it in the desired position, there can be no question as to its beauty. It will be inferred that the longer the bird, the greater should be the included arc, and hence the value of a long neck with a long reach as opposed to a shorter development.

The structure of the shoulder is one of the most wonderful features in the bird. The Belgian shoulder, bear in mind, is at all times prominent, and is rendered more so when the bird is put up; but the Scotch Fancy, though possessing the same high shoulder, must exhibit no such prominence, so that the curved line shall not be interfered with to any appreciable extent, and it is surprising how in many instances the slightest projection appears to have been shaved off. We must, however, remark that there is, in some districts, sufficient variation in the fashion as to the correct thing in shoulders as almost to warrant the assertion that there are really two distinct schools of birds. At first sight it does appear so, and it was this to which we referred in our observations on the geographical distribution of this Canary. The difficulty, however, finds a ready solution in the fact that, of late years, there has been a marked advance in the direction of length, now a *sine quâ non*, and this has been obtained in many instances by the direct infusion of Belgian blood, which, it will be plain, must at the same time have caused some departure from the smooth, unbroken curve, with which Belgian shoulder and neck appear incompatible, a decided break, arising from prominence of shoulder, showing from whence the increased length has been derived. Despite this, the shorter-bodied, shorter-necked, and, consequently, smaller birds have had to give way to the more commanding specimens in which shoulder is really a valuable feature, so long as no undue projection causes a break, or any depression of the neck does not destroy the general direction of the curve considered as a whole. At the same time, it would be idle to deny that we have seen birds, aye, standing on the tables in Glasgow and contesting every inch of ground for a place in the prize-list, in which the junction of the neck with the back was decidedly more angular than curvilinear; but whatever the character of the curve at the point of junction, the broad back and massive shoulder of the Belgian must give way to a well-rounded contour and narrow shoulder. Breeding out any objectionable type of shoulder may safely be left in the hands of the men who have already done so much, and who, in determining to press this development of shape to its extreme limit, have not so resolved without first weighing over the difficulties and assuring themselves that the maximum of length can be obtained at the same time that a clean unbroken sweep is maintained. It must not be understood that we wish to imply that this increased length has in *all* cases been obtained direct from the Belgian. The Scotch Fancy is as fixed in its characteristic traits as is any other Canary, and judicious selection and pairing have alone accomplished these results with birds which we have been assured were not assisted in any other way—a statement the accuracy of which we have not the slightest occasion to doubt.

Passing now to the body, we remark that the back, it is obvious, should be long and convexed. The importance of this, it would be superfluous to comment on. The wings should be long, and carried close to the body, exposing plenty of side, which assists materially in defining the contour of the bird. Nothing can compensate for slovenly carriage of wings; it simply destroys the entire fabric. Continuing our outer line—for we shall have to speak of the breast and under portions of the body in referring to the concave sweep of the crescent—we note that, precisely as in the Belgian, the tail, taken in connection with the upper and lower coverts and vent-feathers generally, which play an important part in assisting to form the natural curves of the bird, has the character of a continuation of the body rather than an appendage, and is a most important member of the whole. To begin with, it must be long and compact, proportionably broad at the base and tapering, anything like a fish-tail or an open fan being out of character. It must not be tucked under the perch as though the bird were in a fright, but curved gracefully in the same arc as the line of the body, which, if the bird be of true proportions, will bring it up to the perch and keep it there without the semblance of an effort. This alone, to an eye which can grasp the bird, will often show at a glance the difference between the perfect bird and a half-made-up specimen. The one seems all in one piece; the other as if made in sections, with a tail moving on a hinge: the one is elegance, and the other something else not half so attractive.

Commencing now with the under surface, we note that a line from the throat to the breast, thence to the vent and on to the end of the tail, will form the concave arc of the crescent, of which that portion passing over the breast is the most important. It will be remembered how we showed that a prominent breast was a redeeming feature in the structure of a Belgian; yet here, where we have Belgian formation throughout, we must have no prominence in this region. If one proof were required more than another to show the connection between these two Canaries, we should point to this prominence of the breast, which shows itself in the Scotch Fancy only too frequently to please its admirers. Yet, notwithstanding this, they have succeeded in reducing it within very small limits, and in a really good specimen we look in vain for any sign of prominence, in place of which there is almost a hollow. The rule says it *shall* be hollow; and in the painted standards, which are to be accepted as ideal perfection, the breast is absolutely concave. An approximation to this, however, is more generally the rule; but the demand is, nevertheless, inexorable, and an otherwise good bird is passed over without much compunction if, as the judges remark, it require the spokeshave.

It is not of so much importance that the bird be very fine and slim, though these are strong points, as that it shall be proportionate and shapely. The shape of the body, taking a section cut through the shoulders to the breast, should be round, or nearly so, gradually tapering away in the waist, but not abruptly, which causes the tail to appear as if it were stuck in instead of growing naturally; indeed, as we have shown, the outline is materially affected by the character of the feathering in the neighbourhood of the waist.

The legs should be long and well clothed on the thighs, and the bird must, for reasons hereafter to be mentioned, have as much control over its legs as over its tail. It must not stand so as to expose too much of the nakedness of the thigh—none if possible, for a stripped thigh, even if only "a wee bit streppit," is an eyesore; but it must stand erect, with just as much and no more of the thigh exposed than is feathered. Neither must it stand as if cow-hocked, or as if its legs were not strong enough to sustain its body, but with legs straight and firm, ready for the indispensable "hop," which it must perform *ad lib.* without disturbing or ruffling a feather and without opening its wings to assist it in any way. To "travel" properly the bird must be possessed of two requisites, "nerve" and "action." If the cage be taken in the hands gently and quietly without alarming or in any way disturbing the bird, which we will suppose to be in the attitude of "attention," as seen in the cut on page 235, and if the thumb of the hand, which we will suppose to be elevated against the wires at the end of the cage next the bird, be suddenly depressed, the bird will hop to the other perch and instantly face about and assume its position, continuing to do this almost any number of times at command, showing in its action its true shape and never once attempting to flurry itself. The promptness with which it acts, the liveliness and sprightliness of its motion, and the sharp way in which it whisks itself round into position, determine the merit of the performance. Some will not do this neatly or with spirit, but will either steady themselves at each hop by taking hold of the side of the cage with one foot, or will clap their tails under the perch with an ugly "break" and soon end their performance with a flutter in which all trace of symmetry is completely lost. The female is more lightly built and is less sprightly than the male—so much so that the two are not supposed to be able to compete on equal terms, as we shall presently show when dealing with classification.

Shape and position in the Belgian find their counterpart in "model" and "action" in the Scotch Fancy, which must possess both properties. Model without action cannot win, though, as an authority once told us, "for-r-r-mation is a r-r-recommendation." So important is model that every consideration as to feather is entirely ignored. It matters not one iota how rough and open-feathered a bird be so long as it has "model." The medium-sized birds alone have very compact plumage; with increased size, feather seems to decline. Some of the best specimens are rough and coarse to a degree which, to any one educated in the feather school, is positively ugly. A bird may have its breast-feathers growing in all directions but that in which feathers usually grow; they may turn up like a drake's tail; its thighs may be enveloped in a rough frieze Ulster coat; it may have a bunch of fluffy feathers growing out of its back as big as a respectable cauliflower; and it may have in any place where its presence is most objectionable as much fluff as would fit out a decent Cochin fowl; but if it only have the essentials of "model" and "action" its calling and election are sure. We are not exaggerating one whit. Colour is also not much esteemed, though it might turn the scale in a close competition. All that we have said with reference to exceptional roughness of plumage affecting the general outline of the Belgian applies with equal force here, and we look upon the utter disregard of feather, if it be a fault, as a fault in the right direction in so far as it is a carrying out of one of the principles of pedigree-breeding, if not the whole art, in its entirety. The Scotch certainly have concentrated into one channel one tendency, and have never dropped one link of the chain, but have held on to it with commendable pertinacity. But we cannot help thinking that one of the primary laws which teaches how, when one feature is fixed, gradual attention should be given to others, might be worked out with advantage, and with all deference to devout worship of the crescent, we think that to it might gradually be added feather, and to feather variations in plumage pleasing to the eye. We admit the extraordinary beauty and grace of the Scotch bird; no one can help it; it is the essence of beauty, but we are equally fond of beauty of plumage. Our eye can follow its graceful lines, and fully enter into the grave solemnity of the mathematical truth that if the line of its back includes 180° it is better by 2° than one which includes only 178°, and we can raise something very like enthusiasm at a fine display of nerve and action; we can appreciate neck, and shoulder, and back, and side, and tail; we can tell when there is too much on in front and not enough behind, and we can see the instinctive something which declares the good bird; but coarse feathering is not a beauty with us: it makes a stout bird seem stouter, and in our eye breaks the lines of a bird "licht got up." To our Scotch friends we would say, don't give up any of the beautiful symmetry you have gained, but try and gradually develop *other* points in the bird; don't drop the link, but endeavour to forge another to it.

The system of classification adopted by the Scotch fanciers is in one respect the same in principle as that upon which Belgians are arranged, but is more elaborate in detail when it touches colour distinctions. We say it is the same in principle, because the element of *shape* is the prime agent in determining the first great division, viz., the separation of the sexes, which, it is obvious, results from an admitted disparity between the general proportions of the male and female, and is essentially the kind of arrangement we should expect to find in shows which are not mere spectacular displays. The connection between the two systems, however, may be said to cease at this point, though this point of resemblance runs through both classifications with an unbroken thread. Underlying the subdivisions may be traced some resemblance to our English tastes, though that again is lost sight of when "marking," the apple of an English fancier's eye, is swallowed up in comprehensive variegation. We give the recognised standard forms with such explanatory notes as are necessary:—

SCOTCH FANCY CANARIES.

BUFF PIEBALD. YELLOW PIEBALD.

Classification of Scotch Fancy Canaries.

Cocks.	*Hens.*
(*a*) Clean Yellow.	(*b*) Clean Yellow.
(*c*) Clean Buff.	(*d*) Clean Buff.
(*e*) Foul-feathered Yellow.	(*f*) Foul-feathered Yellow.
(*g*) Foul-feathered Buff.	(*h*) Foul-feathered Buff.
(*i*) Piebald Yellow.	(*j*) Piebald Yellow.
(*k*) Piebald Buff.	(*l*) Piebald Buff.
(*m*) Yellow Green.	(*n*) Yellow Green.
(*o*) Buff Green.	(*p*) Buff Green.

In all, sixteen separate and distinct classes, which, in the Glasgow schedules, are lettered as above.

The "Clean" or, as we are accustomed to call them, "Clear" classes require no remark other than to notice that in adopting the word "Clean" it is not meant to convey a distinction without a difference, but applies to the external feather only, while the English term is understood to refer to every part of the feather, whether stalk, flue, or web, and is essentially an expression pregnant with meaning in its relation to colour. A "Clean" bird need not necessarily be "Clear," and in cases where external purity only is required, without reference to the strength of the outward colour, it is usual to employ the former term as implying freedom from external blemish, rather than the latter, which expresses so much more. We might, perhaps, have more correctly applied the term "Clean" to classes *a*, *b*, *c*, and *d*, in our Belgian classification, but this explanation will serve to show the true meaning of the terms, which, nevertheless, are sometimes inadvertently used to express the same idea.

The "Foul-feathered" birds correspond exactly with our *boná fide* Ticked examples. We retract the exactly: a tick, however small, will qualify, but very lightly-variegated specimens are also admissible, *e.g.*, such as are slightly marked on the wing or head, but are clear of body-marks. This Foul-feathered class appears to us to be nothing more than a connecting link between Clean and Piebald, and we do not see clearly why, if marking counts absolutely nothing, there should be so many distinctions in degree. Why not include the Foul-marked with the Piebald, if "model and action" determine the intrinsic worth? It is not our province in this place to dictate: we only describe things as we find them, but this is our English view. When the Millennium arrives, and Celt, Anglo-Saxon, and Teuton all show on one stage, perhaps some friendly Congress will have settled this and other questions on a mutually satisfactory basis.

The "Piebald" section answers to our Heavily-variegated, but the marking on the saddle should be no more than a horse-shoe. In no class is any provision whatever made for technical marking, a feature as entirely ignored as among Belgians. It will be observed that our Scotch friends do recognise and arrange in a most extended plan every departure from the clean type except technical marking, in which respect they differ as widely from the admirers of form on the Continent, who repudiate all marking, as they do from us in repudiating the one form which we have come to regard as the highest type of beauty. But so it is, and probably the three Canary-breeding nationalities will each ever "gang its ain gait." If we wish to show Evenly-marked Scotch Fancies we shall have them to make, the same as in the Belgians, and from a very scanty supply of material too, since in the Glasgow show of 1876, among no less than two hundred and four Piebald birds of every form, including the Foul-feathered, where "marking" was most likely to be found, only *one* had the slightest pretensions to the property.

We remark, further, with reference to the Variegated groups—that is, the Piebald proper and the Foul-feathered—*any* ground-colour is admissible, by which we mean either Green or Cinnamon, of which, it will be understood, any Piebald form whatever is simply the equivalent of our "broken." Cinnamon, *as* Cinnamon, is valueless in Scotland, and no special provision is made for it as with us. The consequence is that Cinnamon and Green blood is mixed without regard to any consideration apart from "model," and the pedigree of some of the finest specimens bears out all we have advanced elsewhere with respect to the singular potency and striking peculiarity of Cinnamon blood. Many of the Clean birds are pink-eyed; and, indeed, throughout, there are evident signs of a strong admixture of this element, though the bulk of the Piebalds are of Green extraction. Many of the Greens, however, are what practical Cinnamon-breeders will recognise as "from the Duns," as is shown by the frequent appearance of Greens and Cinnamons in the same nest, though no immediate direct admixture of the latter may have been used.

A Green bird in Glasgow is one which has no break in the green on the back—head, neck, and back must be all green: that is sufficient. Few Scotch show-specimens would pass muster in our Green classes where even a slightly run waist would disqualify. The body-colour of these birds—*i.e.*, the green—is, however, of the most brilliant description, and such as would ravish any disciple of the long, straight, Yorkshire Green school.

Such is a description of the different varieties as classed in the leading Scotch schedules, of which that issued by the Glasgow Ornithological Society may be considered the principal. They may vary slightly in some districts, as they may be more or less remote from that centre, but the foregoing will be found to include all the recognised forms under whatever name they may appear, the requirements of shape being such as we have described, subject to any trifling differences which may arise from more or less implicit allegiance to the high modern standard to which breeders generally are directing their attention, and which we have done our best to depict.

CHAPTER XXVI.

BREEDING AND EXHIBITING SCOTCH FANCY CANARIES.

We cannot devote an entire chapter to the subject of breeding these remarkable birds, for there really is not material sufficient for the purpose. It will be evident that the classification adopted is not so much to encourage the production of any one form representing a type of variegation worth special attention, with a view to its perpetuation, as to provide a place for each of the many forms which result from promiscuous pairing when in quest of something considered of more value—viz., model. Some breeders pair systematically for Piebalds, and others for Clean birds; but whatever may be the practice of individual breeders in this respect, it must be obvious that the general principles to be observed in pairing, as detailed in Chapter XIII., will hold good here, the theory of variegation, so far as it can be reduced to system, not requiring fresh elucidation when applied to different varieties. Nor does the introduction of the element of shape call for much remark, because the reader who has followed us carefully through our enunciation of the principles which affect the laws of pedigree-breeding will understand how to apply them in *any* direction. The utmost we can do is to remind the fancier who contemplates giving his attention to Scotch Fancies of the importance of selecting stock in which is found the full development of essential features; and need we point out further the equal importance of commencing with birds in which these leading points have become fixed, and which may be relied on to repeat them with tolerable certainty. Just at the present time there is, beyond doubt, a strong desire to obtain shoulder, and we all know the pleasure in taking "short cuts" to lessen the length of a journey. This is, indeed, the age of short cuts and premature developments. There are no boys, no girls—nothing is born young now-a-days. But the shortest way about is frequently the longest way home, and in taking short cuts we may lose our way. There is no short cut to breeding first-class Scotch Fancies, as many a "frosty pow" can testify, and the theory of reversion to long-lost forms, and many of them very undesirable ones, is sure to find a practical illustration in the experience of those who commence with stock ostensibly good, but really the offspring of a recent cross with the original "postuur-vogel." Let the first pairs, at least, be genuine, thorough, and not dependent on Belgian element, scarcely skin deep, for the much-coveted shoulder and graceful neck. The breeder can then experiment or use approved means to produce desired results with reasonable prospect of success, and can steer a safe course by the landmarks and buoys laid down for his guidance. We should advise the selection of lengthy, nervous birds, even if a trifle ungainly, in preference to the shorter, thick-necked type still struggling for existence, which, however neat in feather and comely in its way, is fully some degrees behind the standard of the day, literally and mathematically, if we may so apply the expression, against which improved and daily improving standard it is folly to run counter. It is much easier to manipulate with properties cultivated to excess than to develop them to the same degree, and it is easier to dispose of a load when you get it to the top of the hill than it is to get it up the incline, down which it will run with wonderful ease if the break be not applied at every stage. Some of the old school of small birds really seem to have run down till they can run no further—till their momentum is expended and they remain motionless and useless. Our advice is to let them remain where they are. For years we have from time to time come across such birds and always find them *in statu quo*, neither better nor worse, but decidedly out of the race. Never think of beginning with such, but get into good company at once and keep there. One of the greatest delusions we know of in connection with bird-breeding is one of the most common—so common that but few fanciers have not had a touch of the complaint at some time or other. You go into a breeding-room and find one or two fair average show-birds, the remains of the past show-season, mated respectably, though cage after cage exhibits entire want of quality but plenty of pairing which must have been done without any settled purpose except to hatch a lot of thorough rubbish to consume seed. You call attention to a *very* ordinary pair, something more than extra shabby, and ask what they were put up for? "Well, they are not of much account, certainly, but I thought they would *do to breed from.*" We have had that answer over and over again. To breed from? To breed *what? Ex nihilo nihil fit.* Canary rearing is very fascinating, very pretty, very innocent, and a source of great pleasure; but going into breeding any high-class birds, especially of the "model and action" school, is quite a different line of art. Every intelligent breeder should admit this at once, and, avoiding defective models, study only the productions of the best masters and work with the very best material.

In selecting stock, let it also be remembered that nervous energy and sensitiveness are traits of *character* not necessarily allied to *form*. They are to a very great extent united in the Scotch bird as one of the results of a judicious commingling of every good property; but the *and* must not be forgotten in mating for model *and* action. The latter exhibits the former to greatest effect, and, other things being equal, we should give preference to vivacious, sprightly birds and good travellers in place of sluggish, lethargic specimens which are as likely as not to transmit their bad as their good properties. "For-r-r-mation is a r-r-recommendation"—a veteran said it: he sits on the left hand in the plate of the "Three Scottish Worthies;" but nerve should be regarded in the light of an hereditary trait to be transmitted with the "for-r-r-mation." A slovenly, shuffling, look-before-you-leap, half-run, half-hop, is not nerve. Avoid such and think of the *and.*

We think it needless to give further cautions beyond observing that a breeder who does not wish to perpetuate defects will not mate them, but will do his best to neutralise them by the best counteracting influences at command, which is just the point where he is required to finesse with extreme care as his strain develops its weak or its strong points. This is, perhaps, a matter for consideration at a more advanced stage than at the outset, but beginning carefully and avoiding the strengthening of any defects will save a world of trouble in the end.

Mating for the different forms of colour as represented in extended classification also requires only a passing note. We have already said that the Scotch classification is the servant of circumstances, an orderly arrangement of forms which continually present themselves and which are not sought to be controlled beyond what can be effected by separating Clean from Piebald in the breeding-room. There are established strains of each, some breeders seeing the perfection of beauty in the Clean bird and others in a "Peebal' Cŏck;" but all this, it will be evident, is only a question of feather distinct from shape, and is subject entirely to the laws affecting variegation which we have fully discussed. It may, perhaps, be remarked that our variegation theories were deduced from a variety bred for colour *only*, but that here we have *another* point to watch—namely, the ever-present item of shape, which might be found to decline in either the Clean or Piebald strain in a breeding-room, and require some admixture of the two to restore it. Contingencies of this kind will not dismay the breeder, since careful selection will soon return either form to its regular channel after such a method of pairing has been found necessary. The inference to be drawn from this is that the breeder who pins his faith to shape *alone*, and follows promiscuous pairing entirely untrammelled by feather considerations, has the widest field in which to work, and the fewest difficulties to encounter. Clean and Piebald are alike the same to him as to the Belgian breeder. He may have more of the one than the other, and a season's breeding may even find him without a representative of some one particular class with which to do battle at some coming meeting of the Clans; but on all sides he has a wealth of shape which he values more than any chance form of feather, a thing he considers as merely the expression of a minor canon of his creed, the fundamental doctrines of which are model and action in whatever garb they may be clothed.

Of the practical management of this variety during the breeding season there is also nothing fresh to say. The custom of the port differs in some trifling details, but it amounts to the same in the end. Our large stacks of breeding-cages are not in vogue, at any rate in the Glasgow circuit. Open wire cages, such as we should at first sight regard as "general purposes" or "flight" cages, each a separate establishment by itself, are in common use; the nesting-place is attached to the outside, and removed at the close of the season, when the cages which, in a well-ordered room, are of uniform pattern are placed side by side, and being generally of superior design and workmanship, look well, and in their light, airy structure harmonise with the character of the bird.

It is a usual custom with many breeders to cut the tails of their breeding-stock. When the show-season is over and the birds are relegated to domestic duties, the steering apparatus, being no longer required to form a part of the elegant model or to act as a rudder when the bird is called on to "'bout ship" and answer its helm with a whisk, is unshipped; not entirely, but is shortened fully half its length. This partial dismantling of the ship, it need scarcely be explained, is not done without obvious reasons, and finds its parallel in many cases in which a feature developed to excess in obedience to the severe standards of fashion becomes, when no longer required for ornament, a positive inconvenience.

No more "training" is required for the Scotch Fancy than for the Belgian. It appears to be born with a full consciousness that the chief business of its life is to hop, and it goes to work at an early age; not with that everlasting, characteristic family jump from the perch to the side of the cage, nor a ceaseless click-clack as regular in its beat and as full of music as the melodious tick of an American clock, but with an easy grace befitting its high breeding it begins to practise the regulation hop of seven inches, the distance between the two perches of a Scotch Fancy show-cage, itself a piece of furniture *sui generis*, of which an illustration is given in Fig. 61. It is oblong in shape, the bottom or body being about 15 inches by 5, and is fitted with a seed-box and false bottom, or draw-board. Some exhibitors content themselves with work of the plainest description, by which we mean the absence of characteristic ornamentation, which is sometimes of the most elaborate description of inlaid work. Next to his birds the Scotch fancier prides himself in his cages, many of them being no mean specimens of cabinet-work. The superstructure is slightly arched in the direction of its length, and is either entirely of wire, or the four uprights are of wood for half their height, into which the wires forming the framework are inserted, the whole combining by means of the most finished workmanship a maximum of strength with the extreme of lightness. A sliding door at the end is the usual arrangement, though some have the ordinary open-and-shut door at the side. The birds are never handled, but are taught to run like Belgians, and in this respect are very tractable and obedient, so that any opening suffices for passing them in and out of their cages. These show-cages are frequently made in pairs, one being a shade smaller than the other, and the top of the larger being contrived so as to lift up like a lid, the smaller is made to slide into it for convenience in packing in boxes, for the Scotch fancier never trusts his fragile, airy temples to the tender mercies of railway officials without a better protection than an ordinary wrapper. Such a pair costs about fifteen shillings. The packing-cases vary in form from cumbersome chests made to hold half-a-dozen, to most elegant boxes, inlaid with various cunning devices, brass-handled, brass-bound, and with the owner's name and superscription emblazoned thereon (see Fig. 61), to hold sets of two or four, two birds being carried in the inner

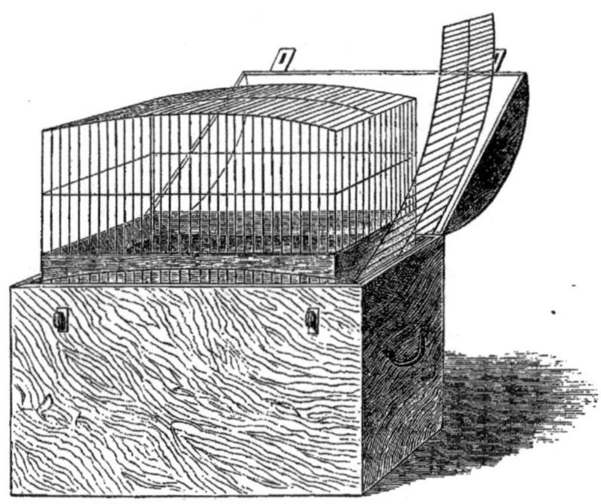

FIG. 61.—SET OF CAGES AND PACKING-CASE.

cage and separated on arriving at their destination. The water-hole is always immediately at the end of one of the perches, which rest on a strengthening cross-piece or stout wire running round the cage. The water-vessels themselves are very suggestive, being invariably small glasses minus the foot. Into such a cage as this the young birds are early taught to run, and the rest is simply a question of taming down native wildness and accustoming them to the necessary handling of the cage which must take place when putting a bird through its drill in the show-room.

Not less interesting than other surroundings of this bird are the public exhibitions, which are held as so many weekly festivals throughout the winter in all the principal towns in the south and south-west of Scotland. As with the Belgian shows, so with the Scotch; we have no parallel to them here. At one of the Glasgow shows we attended there were no less than seven hundred and fifty separate entries of this one variety, and, including "pairs," close on eight hundred and fifty pure Scotch Fancies were exhibited, which certainly indicates an amount of enthusiasm fully bearing out all we have said of the hold this bird has on the people as a national fancy. These were divided among about three hundred exhibitors, which does not give an average of three birds to each. Such a thing as a monster individual entry is a thing unknown, simply because the highest form of model and action is not found wholesale in any one man's hands, but each makes his entry of his one, two, or three champions, and, as may be imagined, the struggle is severe. *Every* bird is a bird of character. The absence of the honorary degrees which figure in our shows is of no moment to the Scotch fancier: if he cannot find his way to a place among the first seven, he cares for no lesser honour. On entering the large Drill Hall in Stirling Road we found the four

JUDGING "SCOTCH FANCY CANARY"—THREE SCOTTISH WORTHIES.

walls of the immense place lined with light, elegant stages, three tiers in height and all backed with green baize, which staging, with the addition of a long double tier in the centre of the area, furnished a length of twelve hundred feet of available space, and we wondered much where all the cages were to come from to fill it. But the early morning brought a busy scene. The three hundred exhibitors poured in in one continued stream, each with his packing-case. Plenty of bustle was there, and the hum of many voices speaking in what, to us, was almost an unknown tongue, but no confusion. Eight long tables, destined for the use of sixteen judges, were formed into a hollow square at the entrance, and each cage, bearing the distinctive letter indicating the class, and also a label on which was inscribed its catalogue number, was handed over the extempore counter and quickly placed on the stage, and very soon every inch of space was occupied. Then commenced the serious business of the day. The eight tables, each furnished with a piece of chalk, were placed opposite certain classes, and then the sixteen judges, chosen eight from Glasgow and eight from other towns, appeared on the scene, each Glasgow judge being paired with a stranger. Nearly every man took off his coat and addressed himself to his work in real earnest. It requires some practice to handle a Scotch Fancy properly, and we could see some very clever jockeyship displayed. The mode of judging is for each man to take a cage, and then, facing each other, each trots his bird out, indulging, the while, in little soliloquies. Then they exchange cages, and the better bird is kept for comparison with the next, every specimen being most critically examined, the best being set aside for a final sifting, sundry hieroglyphics in chalk placed on the cages expressing the merits of each. An enthusiastic committee-man remarked to us that before they were done every man would be "swēatin' an' hauddin' his neebor by the hēad like a hor-rse," which really was the case when each sat down to ride his selection and get the last ounce out in a severe finish, several dead heats having to be "refereed." The work completed, the winning cages were decorated with prize-cards in coloured morocco, on which was emblazoned in gold letters the degree of distinction obtained, while the judges, wearied and exhausted with their exertions, retired to an inner sanctum to recruit their energies with oat-cake and the dews gathered from their native hills, that said to be obtained from the summit of Ben Nevis being most in request.

In attempting to frame a scale of points for judging the Scotch Fancy, we are conscious that we are doing something of which, to the best of our knowledge, Scotch breeders themselves have seen no necessity; at all events, we have not met with any such scale having an authoritative impress. Our intention is simply to give our readers in the usual tabulated form some idea of the relative worth of the parts which make up this interesting whole, attaching to each a value which will leave sufficient margin for a subtractive process, and not rendering complications more complicated in an attempt to draw too nice distinctions. Our first impulse was to make it very short, and include the whole in the two pass-words "model" and "action;" but the former comprehends so much that we have endeavoured to resolve it into its constituent parts. Difficulties lurk beneath each step of the operation, and many of them it is quite useless to combat; but we prefer to indicate broadly the different values rather than to shave off the corners for the purpose of making a neat fit.

It will be seen that in our scale of points we have given what we take to be the leading features of this Canary, and the most common forms in which inferior breeding shows itself. It will also be noticed that we have first furnished the elements of its shape, giving prominence to the four without which the bird could not be constructed even in a very rudimentary form. From that we have proceeded to assess the value of the combined whole as exhibited in elegant contour, and lastly we have determined the value of "action." It is perhaps immaterial whether the item "size" be attached to the first or second part of our scale, but we have preferred to connect it with "model," to which it seems more strictly to appertain, the idea of size embracing the whole bird rather than any individual part. To feather and colour we have apportioned just the value they appear to have in Scotland—viz., *nil;* but in taking leave of this most beautiful creation we commend feather to the consideration of our English breeders, at least, as a feature which seems to us to play an important part in assisting to make or break the fine curves which determine outline.

With these preliminary remarks we proceed to place our Scale of Points for judging Scotch Fancy Canaries before our readers:—

SCALE OF POINTS FOR JUDGING SCOTCH FANCY CANARIES.

Points of Merit.

SHAPE.	Maximum.	
HEAD—Small, neat, and very flat on the crown ...	3	
NECK—Long, thin, and tapering	10	
SHOULDERS—High, narrow, rounded, and well filled-in between the pinions...	10	
BACK—Long, narrow, round, and well filled ...	5	
BREAST—Hollow, and without any prominence ...	10	
SIDE—Long, and well exposed	5	
WINGS—Long, and carried very closely	3	
TAIL—Long, supple, well covered at the base ...	10	
LEGS—Long and straight, without being rigid; thighs well covered; shins set well back ...	4	
	—	60
CONTOUR, OR MODEL.		
ATTITUDE—Erect. Head carried well forward, with neck extended and forming with back and tail—which must be curved under the perch—one continuous arc. Throat, breast, and under surface of the body forming the concave sweep of the crescent; the whole rounded as if turned in a lathe	20	
SIZE	5	
	—	25
ACTION.		
For Nerve, sprightly regulation-hop, and smart recovery	...	15
		—
Total	...	100
		—

Negative Properties.

SHAPE.

A Scotch Fancy should not have a large, coarse head, nor a high skull, nor should it have a short, thick neck; neither should it have broad, angular shoulders, nor show any hollow between the pinions. It should not have a short, broad, or hollow back, neither should it have a prominent, chubby breast, nor should the breast be frilled, nor show any development of feather or similar obstruction to the clear concave sweep from the throat downwards. It should not be short in the side, nor carry its wings so as to hide the side, nor should its wings be short or in any way slovenly in carriage. It should not have a short tail, neither should the tail be straight and inflexible, broad, fan-shaped, or deeply serrated. It should not have short legs.

CONTOUR, OR MODEL.

A Scotch Fancy should not stand "over the perch," nor should it stand rigidly erect, neither should it destroy the curve-line of the body by depressing its head and elevating its shoulders like a Belgian in position. It should not expose its thighs, nor stand with its legs forward, nor with its tail tucked-in under the perch as if attached to a hinge, nor disport itself in a way so as to break the continuity of the convexed outline of the back. It should not be small.

ACTION.

A Scotch Fancy should not be sluggish or listless, nor should it be slovenly or shuffling in its gait, neither should it be fussy or wanting in precision in any of its movements. In its hop it should not make any use of its wings, nor land on the opposite perch as if from a flight; nor should it appear nervous or timid or cling to its perch, leaning back and thrusting its tail underneath as if for a counterpoise. Neither should it hesitate nor steady itself before or after its hop by holding-on to the side of the cage with one foot, nor should it delay a moment in whisking round into position, nor in any of its motions destroy the general outline of its shape.

CHAPTER XXVII.

THE YORKSHIRE CANARY.

IN pursuing the scheme we laid down for the convenient grouping of the various members of the Canary family, we must now deal with the popular representative of the county of three Ridings, a bird belonging essentially to the section now under discussion. It is of ancient date, and has for many generations found a home in Yorkshire, where it is still the bird of the many, being as highly valued and as carefully bred as are other distinctive varieties elsewhere. We will not attempt to gainsay that great alteration in style has taken place of late years with respect to this bird, and possibly the Yorkshire of to-day is not precisely the same bird as the Yorkshire of fifty years ago; but while other varieties to which we have directed attention have been bred, some locally, and others over a wider area, there has always been a bird of eminently distinctive character, a long, slim, straight, erect Canary, identified with the Yorkshire fanciers to such an extent as to be known by the name of the county where it has been cultivated, and which has been handed down to them with its traditions through a long succession of breeders all devoted to its interests. Regarded from this point of view, the Yorkshire has as much right to be considered a pure breed as any other, and no doubt the original strain of birds of which we still hear the old fanciers speak—and some of them can recall the time when the present century was very young—was as free from taint of alien admixture as any of the other varieties whose history we have endeavoured to investigate. Looking at the modern Yorkshire as he stands in the show-cage in 1878, we are constrained to say that we find in him stronger evidence of, not one cross but many, than we do of a carefully worked-out modification or adaptation of one particular form, such as we recognise in the Scotch Fancy in its relation to the Belgian; and in this respect the Yorkshire, or at all events the modern stylish Yorkshire, must be regarded as a somewhat mixed breed, not more so, probably, after all, than sundry other fashionable fancies in which such rapid strides have been made to satisfy the requirements of a fastidious modern standard that much of the original character has been lost amid not a little disputing as to what is the genuine type. We need not point to examples of this; they abound on every hand in every department of live stock. It is in a qualified sense, then, that we use the expression "mixed breed," and do not mean to imply that the Yorkshire Canary can be compounded out of raw material in a year. Too much may have been attempted at once and in too many directions at the same time with the view of improving the bird, which has come to the front with an unmistakable "rush" during the last few years, but it will be found that those who have turned out the best specimens are a class of men who, setting themselves to do a certain thing, carefully think it out and do it, selecting their material, building, shoring and propping up the edifice, leaving nothing wanting and no one point exaggerated at the expense of something else.

If we were required to find a history for this bird we think we should not be far from the truth if we were to say that it probably owes its origin to the fact that in both Lancashire and Yorkshire there have been for no one knows how long two varieties of Canaries of the erect school,

Vincent Brooks Day & Son Lit

YORKSHIRE CANARIES.

CLEAR BUFF GREEN.

Crested and Plainhead, in some respects resembling each other, and in others very dissimilar; and while one set of breeders adopted the one form and cultivated it to an astonishing extent, a second with equal care followed up the other channel and, toning down every asperity, accomplished the object sought: in the one case the majestic Coppy and Plainhead proper resulted, and in the other the refined Yorkshire.

Before proceeding to give a detailed description of the bird, we may state in brief its place in the "Shape" section of the family by comparing it with the Canary we have just dismissed. It is to the Scotch Fancy just what the Scotch bird is to the Belgian. We defined the former to be a curvilinear edition of the latter, and we cannot give a better general idea of the Yorkshire bird than by describing it as a rigidly straight version of the Scotch ideal—the crescent-shaped, nervous bird being replaced by a smart, bold, defiant, upstanding bird, in which the sweeping curves of the former are represented as far as possible by straight lines, taking the expression to refer to their general direction. Shape is its essence. The head should be round, of medium size, and narrow in the skull, without the least suspicion of any of the overhanging eyebrow observable in the Lancashire Plainhead, or indeed in Plainheads of any variety bred for crest. This is one of the most important points; a sour expression, even, not to mention a more serious departure from the neat head imperatively demanded, telling seriously against a bird's reputation. The neck should be long and straight, and not of the short apoplectic model, swelling gradually till it reaches the junction with the shoulders, which must on no account show any prominence whatever, but be covered regularly and evenly by the scapulars—a feature it is not easy to obtain in birds of the erect school, where prominence of shoulder exists as a characteristic trait. Between the neck and the shoulders there must be not the slightest indentation or break of any kind beyond the natural subtle curves of the leading lines. From these beautifully rounded, well-filled-in, narrow shoulders depend long, taper wings, the long flights tucked in closely and stowed away, tip to tip, at the end of a long, narrow back, in which the shadow of a suspicion of a spout would be a fault beyond redemption. A well-filled-in back is a natural consequence of level shoulders, and any hollow or spout becomes an impossibility, the presence of such a defect indicating faulty construction in the shoulder. Continuing the line of the back, the tail must be long, perfectly straight, narrow, flat, and shut up so closely as only to show the mere edge of the outer feathers, and requiring to be opened like a fan before it can be ascertained whether there be any pattern painted on it in the way of dark feathers. If the back of the bird we have been modelling be now tried with a straight-edge before going further, it should show nothing requiring chiselling away, but from the back of the head to the tip of the tail should present, practically, a straight line, which is the line of beauty in a Yorkshire.

Following our usual line of construction, we go to the under surface, and observe that the breast must be narrow and perfectly round, which, taken in conjunction with the narrow shoulders, means small girth, another important point. Broad shoulders mean broad back and large girth, which detract from the apparent length of the bird by throwing it out of drawing. A bulky Yorkshire bird usually has near relations somewhere in Lancashire. From the breast downwards the bird must taper away gradually till it ends in a fine waist, where there must be no loose or fluffy feather, neither must there be on the breast any trace of a frill, the entire feather throughout being of the closest and most compact description possible, in which respect we think no Canary can compare with a first-class Yorkshire, of which we have seen specimens so exquisitely fine in feather that the old simile, "like waxwork," is no inapt illustration. The legs must be straight and long without being stilty, and should support the bird in an attitude as nearly erect as possible.

Attitude is one of the vital points, and one about which no two opinions exist. A bird which has the slightest disposition to stand across the perch is not of any use in a show-cage. Size, also—or, perhaps, it will be better to say length—is a commanding feature; for it will be evident that length without bulk is what is required. It is in this respect chiefly that so much alteration has taken place during the past few years. Not so very long ago there were two schools of fanciers of the variety—those who adhered closely to the original type in all its essentials, but who, in clinging to them, had allowed a manifest deterioration in length and size generally to creep in; and those who, determining to recover these features, plunged rather wildly in the opposite direction, and imported a lot of foreign element which almost threatened to swamp the stylish bird of the olden time. Indeed, there was at one time imminent danger of the massive Lancashire Plainhead supplanting the genuine Yorkshire. Decisive action in the show-room eventually settled the question, and the variety was established on a sounder basis than had existed for years, the importation of the Lancashire and other elements, in which Belgian and Norwich also played no inconsiderable part, not having been without some advantage. The bird was really declining, and required vigorous treatment, though the work of restoration was rather hastily performed. The features now requiring the most careful watching are the various distinctive marks of the different crosses introduced, and are chiefly the imprints of the Belgian and Lancashire blood. From the latter came bulkiness and a certain degree of coarseness of feather and width of skull incompatible with requirements demanding length without thickness, close feather, and a narrow head. To this we might add a tendency, common to the Lancashire bird, to grow a breast-frill on a front which cannot be starched and ironed down with too much care. The first of these bad points, undue size, was to some extent toned down by the Belgian cross, which in its turn left the inevitable system of curved lines, the prominent shoulder, hollow neck, too fine head, and generally nervous temperament not wanted in the Yorkshire. The Norwich was also called into requisition, and to this may be attributed the improvement in colour which has taken place, many specimens now showing the power to develop it in a degree little short of that possessed by the famous colour-bird itself. There is not much fear, however, of colour ever interfering seriously with standard properties, though it will always carry some weight when present in conjunction with them—not otherwise. It will be admitted that there are recognised features which *must* be stamped on certain varieties; they are their sign-manual; they must be there, whatever else be absent, must be first looked for and last lost sight of; and keeping this principle in view, we think that fanciers of this beautiful variety are united in their desire to maintain a high uniform standard, from which there is now as little—perhaps less—departure tolerated than in any variety in exhibition. The champion birds of the day are so uniformly true to one model as to leave no room for doubt that the true character of the Yorkshire is thoroughly understood; though, if we might venture on a caution, we would suggest that there is yet a possibility of coming to grief by overdoing the bird in respect to mere size. It is not a safe policy to leave any boundary-line undefined, and the fence between Yorkshire and Lancashire, once put in repair, should be most scrupulously kept up. By aiming at undue size and ever harping on that one string, the Yorkshire breeder drifts towards the very rock he should seek to avoid. If his bird be a modified form of the Lancashire, then should the distinction be well maintained, since with every addition in the direction of size will return those features originally belonging to it. Let it be remembered that neither bird can take the place of the other under a judge who knows the difference between the two. An indifferent Lancashire is not a Yorkshire, nor *vice versâ*, and a greater folly does not exist than bringing the two so closely into juxtaposition that essentials are lost in the resulting fog.

We shall at once proceed to treat of the classification of this variety, taking the opportunity to add such further remarks as may suggest themselves in the course of our explanatory review of the system adopted, which is as follows:—

Classification of Yorkshire Canaries.

(*a*) Clear Yellow.
(*b*) Clear Buff.
(*c*) Evenly-marked Yellow.
(*d*) Evenly-marked Buff.
(*e*) Ticked and Variegated Yellow.
(*f*) Ticked and Variegated Buff.
(*g*) Green.

With regard to the Clear classes, we have only to remark that shape being the essence of the bird, colour does not count till the standard properties have been carefully weighed, when superior colour would turn the balance. It is a feature, the value of which is steadily on the rise, because it has been shown that it is possible to incorporate it with the essentials of a good bird without interfering with them; and such being the case, there is no valid reason why it should not have its value—its full value, but not *more*. If the admirers of the bird say, One lesson we have learnt from the changes of late years is that colour is within our reach and we mean to have it, we reply, the bird is theirs, and no *ipse dixit* of any judge should stand in the way of the development of the new beauty. The evil to guard against is giving it a fictitious value or permitting it to trench, however slightly, on the domain of shape. In the interest of the bird and a desire to see it ever maintain an unequivocal position in the sphere in which it has moved so long, we urge extreme caution in dealing with this matter, and unhesitatingly express our opinion that good model, though clothed in the palest of lemon-yellow or the whitest buff, should ever stand before the ruddiest jonque in which can be seen the shadow of a defect in symmetry. On this question we wish our opinion to be as pronounced as possible. We do not regard colour as a useless innovation—quite the contrary; but to set colour against form is, in this case, at once to trifle with settled principles and a waste of good cayenne.

Of the remaining classes, (*c*) and (*d*) supply the key to (*e*) and (*f*), which last are intended to include every possible form of variegation not being technical even-marking. Here also—that is, in (*e*) and (*f*)—shape rules over everything, colour seldom intruding itself, except it may be in a close contest between two *bonâ fide* Ticked birds, in which case, other things being equal, it has the power of a casting vote. In this Variegated section, however, another element enters by common consent. Assuming the all-important property of form to be present and to be fairly balanced between any two birds, the nearest approach to even-marking then decides the question. Nor is this an unsound position; neither must it be tested by the law which governs the awards in the corresponding section in the Norwich variety, in which colour is the *summum bonum* of the breeder, and in which variegation is dealt with solely in its relation to colour. In the Yorkshire variety, as we shall show presently, the cultivation of technical marking has been as closely followed up in its place as form has been, and hence the idea of variegation, as used here, is not connected with colour so much as with a special form of marking, the nearest approach to which becomes of value when found united to the indispensable primary qualification of shape. The wording in some schedules is "Ticked and Unevenly-marked," which, accepted literally, has a direct bearing on the perfect form of marking to which we have alluded; but inasmuch as this definition is really restrictive in its meaning when taken literally, we prefer the broader and more comprehensive term "Variegated," which, it will be at once understood, includes in the abstract every other form of variegation not specifically provided for in (*c*) and (*d*); magnificent birds, Unevenly-marked as well as Variegated proper, occasionally presenting themselves for competition, besides others in which *both* forms are combined, and which would virtually be ineligible in a class definitely restricted to uneven marking, if by the latter expression were to be understood simply examples of technical marking in which the reduplication necessary to constitute it, even in character, were wanting. No difficulty whatever is experienced in the practical application of this broader scheme if the principle underlying the whole be understood. In brief, form and approximate excellence in marking will count above equally good form and merely irregular variegation, but *superior form* will count above *anything* in this class.

Classes (*c*) and (*d*) occupy almost a world to themselves. Everything pertaining to the character of an Evenly-marked Canary has been so fully explained in its place that it is unnecessary to make the slightest reference to it here. Suffice it to say that the breeding of these birds has been so long and so systematically carried out in Yorkshire that the variety has become fixed with perhaps as much certainty as can be calculated on in the pursuit of a very erratic property. The length of the bird and the compact carriage of the wings exhibit the extended **V** to perfection, while the glossy black-green of the dark feathers, contrasting strongly with the not very brilliant body-feathers, gives a singular beauty to the markings not so observable in the Norwich, in which the bronzy marks are printed on a ground-colour as brilliant as can be produced. The wing-marking is also much lighter than in the Norwich, and the best examples do not extend beyond four feathers. A Yorkshire breeder's idea of perfection is a six-marked bird—*i.e.*, one marked on each side of the tail, as well as on the eyes and wings—an opinion from which it may be nothing short of treason to dissent, though, personally, we attach but small value to tail-markings, because the neater the tail, the more effectually will it hide its markings from view.

There is one special form in which the Evenly-marked Yorkshire appears to which we must call attention, and that is in connection with the Cinnamon cross. In our description of the Cinnamon we referred to this when speaking of the bird as a pure breed which had been put to various uses for specific purposes, confining our remarks in that place to the use of it in the Colour section, and purposing to touch on the subject again, briefly, in this place. We stated that the original Cinnamon had been grafted on two or three stems for various objects, and we exhausted the subject in relation to one of them, viz., the Colour stem. But the Yorkshire breeder also has been long alive to the use of Cinnamon blood, and has grafted it on his stock, establishing a strain of birds with Cinnamon markings, which, ignoring colour properties, ought to compete, primarily, on the basis of shape, in a separate and distinct school from the Cinnamons of the Colour family. We know that Cinnamons are Cinnamons under whatever flag they muster; but our object is to draw attention to that branch of the family which we will, for distinction, call the Yorkshire Cinnamon, as indicating the nature of the addition to the parent stem. Our notes here will afford the key to our remarks on page 114. The Evenly-marked examples of the Yorkshire Cinnamon are *not* classed as a variety of the Yorkshire, nor are the corresponding specimens in the Norwich Cinnamon classed as a variety of the Norwich, but both are shown under the Cinnamon flag, an incongruous grouping of shape with colour; the remedy for which is either to provide for each a separate class in its own section, or to provide two classes for Evenly-marked Cinnamons in the Cinnamon section, separated on the basis of colour *v.* shape.

Vincent Brooks Day & Son Lith.

YORKSHIRE CANARIES.

EVENLY MARKED YELLOW. (CAYENNE FED.)

CLEAR YELLOW. (CAYENNE FED.)

EVENLY MARKED BUFF. (CAYENNE FED.)

We might even suggest a *third* class, as the cross has been closely followed up with the Belgian, and the strain is by no means uncommon in some localities.

These Evenly-marked Cinnamons of the Yorkshire type are very beautiful, and are in every respect subject to the rules affecting the Green-marked birds, to which they are, in many instances, more closely related than might be supposed.

And lastly there are the Greens, the Grass-Greens, as they are sometimes called, though the name singularly fails to convey a correct idea of the colour, and we shall perhaps not make matters much clearer if we say it is a very green green, and that in the purity of the green and its freedom from any tinge of orange or yellow consists its value. These Greens, which belong exclusively to the North, and certain forms of them to certain districts, almost constitute a separate Colour family, and at one time no schedule issued in the North would have been considered complete without a class for the popular "Green Canary"—a somewhat vague definition, it must be admitted, and attaching it to no particular variety. As regards shape it would have been difficult to assign some of them a definite place, as the fanciers of the colour developed it on any base according to taste, and the bird appeared in all shapes, from indifferent Belgian down to the nondescript type known as "Common," though, in most instances, length, erect stand, smart build, and other characteristics of the Yorkshire indicated, if not the probable source of the main stream, at all events the direction in which it was wished to divert it. Now, the best school of Greens is so thoroughly Yorkshire in its style that no more convenient place can be found for its representatives than among the variety they most closely resemble and with which they are daily becoming more intimately identified. For this reason we have attached this class to the Yorkshire, feeling satisfied it is its proper place, and that, so affiliated, it is more likely to attain a high position than when drifting about homeless and without a parish. It may be urged that this disposal of the bird is somewhat arbitrary, but we think it is not more so than the caprice which kept it so long floating about in the region of no man's land, measured by no shape-standard but such as suited individual cases, while it does away with the anomaly of a colour-bird ostensibly amenable to no law regulating its shape yet practically subservient to as many laws as there are to be found varied tastes. We cannot see our way clear to pronounce it a distinct variety on the ground of its colour, which is simply the basic form of several varieties from which clear plumage has been gradually developed. If we accept that theory as the foundation of its claim, then must we admit Green Scotch Fancies into competition with any Green form simply because they are Green—a most absurd proceeding. More in accordance with the principles of natural arrangement is it to classify under each variety the different forms of colour in which that variety appears, and we think the Yorkshires can safely take under their wing the erect "Grass-Greens," leaving other types to gravitate to their proper level and find a home among their fellows.

The colour-points of a Green Yorkshire are the purity and brilliancy of the green, its uniform distribution, and the absence of black stripes in the feathers of the back. The flights and tail-feathers are a glossy black, edged with a delicate margin of green. Nowhere must there be seen any indications of running or breaking in the colour, which must be throughout characteristic of a genuine dark self. We have made a class for the Yellow Greens only, but there is no bar to exhibiting Buffs; they are, however, usually so dull in colour as to be seldom sufficiently attractive for show purposes.

The principal thing to be kept in view in selecting breeding stock is to secure length, shape, and style without coarseness—features not always procurable on demand, or good Yorkshires, like good anything else, would not be so valuable as they are; and the beginner will probably find that whatever may be the opinion outside as to "anything" passing muster for a Yorkshire, those who understand the bird know when they have the true "anything," and that it has its market value. The extreme of neatness and delicate finish is to be found among the smaller birds of the older *régimé*, but increased size being demanded, it is no use to work entirely with this material if the breeder wishes to rise above the barren honours of V.H.C. cards and get into the foremost rank. Such birds are, nevertheless, very useful, inasmuch as their character is firmly fixed and they will stamp it with more or less accuracy on such material as may be selected with a view to framing a larger model, about which more will be said shortly. Assuming that good material in which no evident departure from standard points is visible is to be had, we should prefer that the cock should show commanding proportions rather than the hen. We do not think that there is any established physiological law knowing no variation which governs this system of pairing, but it is generally found that the male exerts a marked influence in determining the size of the offspring, and we do not care to breed from small cocks in any case in which we desire to maintain or improve size. We should not elect, with a free choice, to breed with small hens, but we would prefer to use a medium-sized hen, perfect in its symmetry, in place of a larger, if we failed to discover the presence of sterling merit. It is a matter in which there may frequently be not much opportunity for choice, but we refer to it both as a question affecting the general principles of breeding and as a caution against being led away in quest of size at the expense of essentials which must be present, whether size accompany them or not. Beyond this there is nothing we can suggest relative to working with pronounced material which will not probably occur spontaneously to the mind of any thoughtful person who makes use of common-sense principles in his breeding-room so far as not to expect to gather grapes of thorns or figs of thistles.

In working with foreign material or such as shows traces of its admixture, care is required. The most common cross, and, in many respects, the most useful when judiciously used, is with inferior forms of the Manchester Plainhead, a bird which we have said bears strong points of resemblance as well as of dissimilarity to the Yorkshire. The kindred features may be briefly summed up under the two ideas of straight build and erect stand. These we want; its other features we do not want. The Plainhead, for example, has been cultivated to a gigantic size, with every feature correspondingly enlarged, and notably the skull, which, in a good specimen, is of extraordinary width. But many of these birds fail to come up to the required standard, and many more are so far down the scale as to be of no value for the particular purpose for which they were bred. They are, in fact, fair examples of the original bird from which most probably sprung the present houses of York and Lancaster, and it is from this source that the breeder can borrow with advantage. Here, the broad skull will probably be wanting; the loose feathering incident to huge size, replaced by a closer plumage; and various other features, valuable to a Plainhead but prejudicial to a Yorkshire, will be found toned down or entirely absent, leaving many Yorkshire essentials at our disposal. From such birds, paired with refined examples of the Yorkshire, the best results may be anticipated, but care must be taken not to select such as show any leaning towards cultivated Plainhead proclivities, the broad skull being the feature of features to be avoided, as it indicates the cultivated Plainhead more than does any other point, and when present there is no knowing how potent may be other adverse influences lurking underneath. This is the only foreign element we should with confidence make use of, and we use the word foreign in a very qualified sense, which, if analysed, would perhaps show that we have adopted a term as inappropriate as if we spoke of the fountain being foreign to the stream.

What to avoid is as necessary to be known as what to eat and drink; and among a class of birds to be avoided, if the breeder does not wish to be continually perplexed with self-imposed difficulties, are those showing Belgian blood. There is no denying that some of those which have appeared of late years are, as Canaries, very beautiful, but the cross is manifestly unsuitable. That the shoulder, hollow neck, and other Belgian traits *can* be bred out in the course of years may be possible, for pedigree-breeding can accomplish almost anything; but by the time shape is restored *in statu quo*, we look in vain for any compensating resulting benefits, while those who go to the posture-bird for help will have to endure a wearisome interregnum, during which their birds are entirely shelved for show purposes, owing to the pertinacious way in which the potency of good Belgian blood will continue to assert itself, the opposite character of the two birds sufficiently indicating the nature of the difficulties to be encountered if the cross be attempted. There is scarcely a single Belgian feature but requires to be entirely eliminated, and we think the prospective advantages are scarcely sufficient to recompense the breeder for fishing so long in troubled waters.

Also avoid, if possible, pairing two birds, however good, which show a frill on the breast. It is a most obstinate feature to get rid of, and nothing should be done calculated to perpetuate it. We know it is sometimes very perplexing to contrive so as to steer clear of the many objectionable traits which occasionally come to the surface, but the fact that they *do* come to the surface should have its full weight when seeking to bury them or cut them up by the root, not forgetting also that the presence of certain weeds frequently indicates the character of the soil and what it will produce. More sometimes lies beneath the frill than meets the eye.

In seeking to breed Marked birds, more trustworthy material is at command than in the Colour section, as we explained when treating of Marked Norwich, and the beginner will find less risk attending the undertaking; indeed, he can scarcely get wrong in selecting his stock, of which there is usually a fair supply little short of show form, even in the selling classes at most north-country shows; the frequency with which birds of this description are so exhibited, as well as the long numbers in which they appear in open competition, being evidence of fixity of type so far as marking is concerned. Nor has marking ever been allowed to interfere with correct form, and in this respect the novice has less to contend with than is sometimes the case with Clear birds. The peculiar results attending the Cinnamon cross must, however, not be lost sight of, and the breeder must not be surprised if, from some of his Green-marked pairs, he obtain a sprinkling of Cinnamon-marked young ones. These he will understand how to manage, if he have carefully read our remarks on the peculiarities of the Cinnamon variety in Chapter XVII. He may or may not get these Cinnamon-marked birds, according as Cinnamon blood is present in the strain or otherwise; but under any circumstances its presence will soon declare itself, and, when so declared, is easily controlled, adding much to the value of a strain at the same time that it increases the field of operation and renders the work even more interesting and to a great extent more certain. And we may observe here, as a corollary to the foregoing, that if it be desired to breed the Cinnamon form of the Marked Yorkshire, Green-marked birds bred from the Cinnamons will produce them in obedience to the physiological peculiarities we have explained, precisely in the same way as the Green-marked birds are obtained from some of the Cinnamons. At the same time, either variety will reproduce itself with certainty if there have been no admixture. In claiming birds at a show at the catalogue price according to the law "therein made and provided," there will always be some amount of uncertainty as to connection with the Cinnamon family; but in purchasing from a breeder, all matters relating to pedigree should be ascertained and the birds paired accordingly, first with regard to producing the required markings, and then with a view to possible and probable results arising from the character of the strain. It will be remembered that we instanced some peculiar results as having occurred within our own knowledge in connection with breeding with Norwich birds in which was a trace of Cinnamon blood. All this applies here, only we think the mixture is more general in the Marked Yorkshire, and hence our calling special attention to it in this place, but beyond that there is no necessity to enlarge on a subject which resolves itself into the application of settled general principles.

As regards feeding this bird for exhibition, by which it will be understood we refer to cayenne-feeding, although the impetus given to colour by the discovery of the potent agent which assists so materially in its development has spread in ever-widening circles till its waves have reached the extreme confines of Canarydom, and colour is, as we have stated, steadily on the rise and will probably some day reach a much higher level in connection with this bird, there has as yet been no clearly pronounced opinion uttered by its patrons. These, most wisely we think, give their allegiance to form, and pause ere they subscribe to a new creed until it can be shown that a substantial advantage has accrued to the bird therefrom, preferring to allow colour, as connected with feeding, to remain entirely a matter of taste for the present. Some exhibitors send out their birds in their native bloom, altogether innocent of any knowledge of stimulants; others in all the blaze of ruddy jonque, assisted by the hidden leaven of Norwich blood; and others, again, with just sufficient burnishing to lead one to infer they had been fed on the crumbs which had fallen from a table spread for the delectation of some cage of "hot" youngsters privileged to feast on spiced meats at the rate of five shillings a pound. We should be glad to see colour advance with form through legitimate channels, keeping respectfully in the rear, for not one hasty step to the front would we sanction, but would watch most jealously the infusion of any ingredient calculated to depose the true genius of the bird from its rightful position and set up a specious substitute in its place. We would not refuse to colour its due weight in the presence of sterling excellence, but we would not allow a pound of the best cayenne to gloss over one single spot.

To exhibit any class of Yorkshire Canary to the best advantage it should never be put in a box-cage—that is, a wooden cage with simply a wired front—however roomy, for in such a contrivance the bird always seems to be afraid to stand up at his full height. For a similar reason the usual living-cages, which, for the sake of comfort and general convenience in the breeding-room, are generally of the box-cage model, should be extra lofty, so as not to induce a slovenly, hesitating carriage, or that standing across the perch which is sometimes the result of want of cage-room as much as of any radical defect in the bird. There is a tradition in the North that the last generation of collier captains were broad-shouldered men of low stature, had parenthetical legs, and were frequently prematurely bald, their longitudinal contraction and lateral extension, &c., being attributed to difficulties in the way of stretching themselves or standing upright in their cabins without rubbing off their hair against the deck-beams and ceiling. We are always reminded of this particular strain of the genus *homo* when we see a fine Yorkshire shut up in a small box, in which it could scarcely stand upright, even if there were no perch. The most effective exhibition-cage is one of wire, about 7 inches by 8, and 17 inches in height, with flat or arched top, according to taste. One perch, resting on the middle strengthening wire which runs round the body of the cage, is sufficient—indeed, position or shape birds, the Scotch Fancy excepted, should never have but one perch. The water-vessel should always be on the outside, but seed can be supplied either by means of a small hopper to hook on the outside, or in a seed-drawer or open box in the inside. For many reasons we prefer either of the latter arrangements, but chiefly because hoppers add to the weight and are inconvenient to pack. Seed should never be strewn on the cage-bottom for any Canary of erect stand, as the tail is apt to become frayed and dirtied while the bird is feeding, and a scrupulously neat toilet is one of the necessaries for success in the show-room.

We conclude our notice of this Canary with Scales for judging the different forms. We have framed them with extreme care, in the hope that they will materially assist in maintaining a correct standard by which to measure a bird hitherto not so generally understood as some which have passed under review.

SCALES OF POINTS FOR JUDGING YORKSHIRE CANARIES.

CLEAR BIRDS.

Points of Merit.	Maximum.	
SHAPE—Head: small and round; skull: narrow...	5	
Neck: moderately long; straight	5	
Shoulders: narrow, rounded, and well filled ...	5	
Back: long, straight, and well filled	5	
Breast: round and smooth; the body, long and gradually tapering to a neat waist	5	
Legs: long, without being stilty; thighs: well clothed	5	
Wings: long, and evenly carried	5	
Tail: long, straight, and closely folded ...	5	
	—	40
SIZE—For length, with corresponding symmetrical proportions	...	15
POSITION AND CARRIAGE—Attitude: erect, with fearless carriage; head, neck, back, and tail in a straight line	...	20
FEATHER—Short, close, and tight	...	10
COLOUR—From pale yellow to orange; underflue white; beak, legs, and feet clear	...	5
CONDITION—Health, cleanness, and sound feather	...	10
		—
Total	...	100

Negative Properties.

A Yorkshire Canary should not have a large, flat, coarse head, nor any overhanging brow indicative of Plainhead extraction; neither should it have a short, thick neck, nor should the neck project after the manner of a Belgian or appear to be set on in any other way than in the line of the body. It should not have broad, square shoulders, neither should the shoulders show the slightest prominence or have any hollow between them. It should not be short in the back or body, neither must the back be hollow, nor curved in the direction of its length. It must not show a prominent breast, nor have any frill or similar arrangement of feathers thereon. It should not have short legs, neither should they be rigid or stilty. It should not have short flights, nor should the wings be carried in a slovenly way or cross each other at the tips, neither should the tail be short or fan-shaped. A good bird should neither be short and squatty, nor large and bulky. It should not stand across the perch; nor, in whatever position it stands, should the line from the back of the head to the tip of the tail be a curve. It should not have loose, fluffy feather, nor should the colour, however pale, be undecided. A clear bird should not have dark underflue, nor should beak, legs, or feet be discoloured, nor should it be shown except in perfect feather and scrupulously clean.

We have again preferred to assign equal values to the various constituents of the principal division, because each is so dependent on the other, and we can see no advantage to be gained from a more elaborate valuation. We have also made no separate provision for Yellow and Buff. Practically, the birds are in every respect, excepting colour, one and the same, and the value we have given to colour will afford ample margin when dealing with either form.

When applied to Evenly-marked birds the scale will require some modification. It is not that shape or position, or any other essential, is not as necessary in a Marked bird as in a Clear one, but Marking being the principal feature, it absorbs the greater part of the value, leaving the remainder to be worked out on a fresh basis with another unit of measurement. The following will, however, meet the requirements of the case:—

EVENLY-MARKED.

Points of Merit.	Maximum.	
MARKING—Eyes: for neatness and regularity of outline, and for distinctness	25	
Wings: for exactness, decreasing in value as the marking extends beyond the secondary flights or encroaches on the larger wing-coverts ...	20	
Tail: for exactness	5	
	—	50
SHAPE AND POSITION—For symmetrical proportion, fair size, and erect carriage	...	30
FEATHER—For compact body-feather, and close carriage of wings and tail	...	10
COLOUR—For pure body-colour and brilliancy of markings	...	5
CONDITION—Specially for sound feather	...	5
Total	...	100

Negative Properties.

An Evenly-marked Yorkshire should not have broken or ragged eye-marks, nor any of the irregular forms not recognised by the laws governing eye-marking, neither should it have a cap, however symmetrical. It should not have a "mixed" wing, nor should any feathers attached to the wing be dark, excepting the flights; and specially, the feathers of the bastard wing should not be dark. It should not show any discoloured feathers on the margin of the saddle or where the feathers merge with those of the wing-coverts, nor any discoloration in the upper or lower tail-coverts, nor should there be any mark whatever to interfere with a clear run, above and below, from the beak to the tail, nor any other violation of the simple law which determines the difference between technical "marking" and variegation.

TICKED AND VARIEGATED.

The scale for Clears applies to the Ticked birds without alteration of any kind, except that the points for colour may all be given to external body-colour, no deductions being necessary for dark underflue or discoloured beak, legs, &c., which, from the nature of things, are as likely to present themselves as not. But with regard to the Variegated birds, since the greater part of them represent failures in the direction of even-marking more or less mixed up with irregular variegation, the latter being a thing of no value in a Yorkshire, while the former represents considerable worth, the scale for judging Evenly-marked birds is applicable in cases in which there is an approximation to respectable marking, such birds being better representatives of the Variegated portion of the class than are the patched or blotched birds, which stand less chance than do the purely Ticked birds of finding their way into the foremost rank, unless they show exceptional merit or are so lightly marked as to afford reasonable grounds for supposing they are slight departures from the Clear form rather than useless offshoots from the cultivated Evenly-marked strain. This, we can see, is open to the objection that the Ticked and the Variegated, though grouped in one section, will be measured, practically, by differently constructed scales, inasmuch as we have said that the Ticked birds are to be judged by the same scale as the Clears, the assessments in which are not identical with those in the Variegated scale; but the mistake, if there be any, consists not so much in the system we have worked out, as in a universally adopted classification which groups unlike things, bred for dissimilar objects, in one class. The logical solution of the difficulty would be to form two classes—(*a*), including the Ticked and such other forms of variegation as could compete on the basis of shape irrespective of marking, and (*b*), such as might expect to compete with reasonable prospect of success on the basis of approximate connection with technical marking, and this is really the true foundation on which the classification of this variety should be built. That which is lawful, however, is not always expedient, and in the practical working of our public exhibitions such an arrangement, probably, could not conveniently be made. Note particularly that if the two classes of birds, though dissimilar, were by common consent to sink their dissimilarity, *i.e.*, variegation, and be measured by their similarity, *i.e.*, shape, the same scale would measure both; as it is, we must work with such tools as we have, though the difficulty is lessened if the principle we laid down in our explanatory notes on the usual classification be recognised, viz., that form and approximate excellence in marking will count above equally good form and merely irregular variegation, but *superior form* will count above *anything* in this class; thus giving an appreciable value to a fair attempt at technical marking in a mixed class, while superior form still remains the standard feature.

GREEN.

Points of Merit.	Maximum.	
COLOUR—Purity and brilliancy	50	
Uniform distribution: back free from dark stripes; breast and under-surface of body even throughout; marginal edging of flights and tail-feathers bright green	10	
		60
SHAPE, SIZE, AND CARRIAGE—For Yorkshire properties generally		20
FEATHER—Short and fine		10
BEAK, LEGS, AND FEET—As dark as possible ...		5
CONDITION—Health, and clean, sound feather ...		5
Total		100

Negative Properties.

A Green Yorkshire should not be of a dull shade of colour, neither should it show any tinge of yellow or bronze, nor should it lack lustre. It should not show dark stripes on the back, nor on the under-surface of the body or in any other place should there be any departure from the genuine character of the pure Green; neither should the marginal edging of the flights or tail be wanting in colour. It should not be small in size, slovenly in carriage, or loose in feather, nor should a good specimen have light-coloured legs.

Disqualification.

The presence of a white feather in any part of the body, or a decided "break" in the colour.

The above scale can be applied to any form whatever in which the Green Canary is found, by substituting for "Size, Shape, and Carriage" the characteristic features of the particular bird with which it is proposed to connect the colour. We have constructed it with colour as its base, and with so large a margin for individual character, in order that it may be so applied.

CHAPTER XXVIII.

THE LANCASHIRE COPPY.

THE last, but certainly not the least, either in size or importance, of the exhibition Canaries which will pass under our review, is the Lancashire Coppy. He comes of a high family and is of good repute, and ever has held and does to this day hold his plumed head far above that of the Chief of any other tribe. What may be the heraldic devices of his family coat of arms we are not able to say; we rather incline to the belief that it has been quartered with that of some other noble family, probably the "Old Dutch," an ancestry sufficiently remote to be very respectable, and shrouded in just enough of fog to render it difficult to clear it up, not an uncommon trait in many pedigrees. The family crest, however, has always been "a shako, *or*," and the motto "*Erant olim gigantes*," the two sufficiently indicating the character of the bird in the olden time, a character its descendants have maintained in its integrity.

The word "Coppy," which signifies a crest or topping, and must not be confounded with copy, is also of ancient extraction, and requires no further explanation, its connection with the bird being plain. The prefix "Lancashire" seemed at one time as if it were on the point of being superseded by "Manchester," the bird having for some years been so described in exhibition schedules. We have used the word superseded, but we are not sure it is appropriate, for we are not aware that the bird was originally known by other than the generic name Coppy without any prefix; but when the word Manchester began to come into general use, the Lancashire breeders of Oldham, Rochdale, Ashton-under-Lyne, and other towns where the bird is extensively and almost exclusively cultivated, feeling jealous of a county honour being, as they contended, bestowed on any one town, even though it were the great Cottonopolis itself (where they maintained the bird was *not* bred in any numbers), entered their protest against the assumption of the title, and making out a good case, secured for the bird the name which is now becoming generally recognised, although it will take some time to obliterate all recollection of the one by which, in the absence of any other of universal adoption, it was rapidly becoming known, and by which it is still called by some of its partisans. The balance of power, however, was with the county; and, on the principle that the many should rule the few in such cases, we adopt the prefix Lancashire, though the other had, in the course of years, grown to be a familiar household word with us.

This Canary is bred chiefly in the busy centres we have just referred to, and also in the surrounding district, where towns numbering thousands of inhabitants extend their borders at such a rapid rate and elbow their neighbours in such a bustling way, that it is not easy to say where one leaves off and another begins. Here, the Coppy reigns conjointly with its companion, the Plainhead, and, though one of the most interesting birds in the whole Canary family and second to none in its individuality, is essentially the most local specialty in the entire fancy, seldom travelling far from home, and still less frequently beyond the bounds of its county, to which fact alone is to be attributed its comparative want of popularity. It is a bird which has hitherto been nursed principally by local working men's clubs, being generally exhibited under the auspices of some local society at the "house" where its meetings are held. These shows are very general in

Vincent Brooks Day & Son Lith

MANCHESTER OR LANCASHIRE COPPIES

GREY COPPY YELLOW COCK. CLEAR BUFF PLAINHEAD HEN.

Lancashire, and the published lists of fixtures for one year, held under the management of the "United Canary-Showers' Association," gives Oldham, Staleybridge, Rochdale, Ashton-under-Lyne, Stockport, Middleton, Todmorden, and Manchester as the towns in which exhibitions are authorised to be held during nine consecutive months, commencing in June for unmoulted or first-feather birds, and in November for moulted specimens, each show being held at a "house," which, with the name of the host, is duly announced. It must not be supposed that this organised system of home-and-home shows is due to any want of a wider spirit of emulation. It is simply an old custom in harmony with the tastes and habits of the members of these clubs to whom these weekly gatherings are fraught with as much interest as if the arena were the All-England platform. Their tendency, however, is to keep the bird confined within narrow limits and is a great bar to increasing its popularity. But though the Lancashire breeder fights in a small ring, he fights none the less determinedly. He is opposed to innovations, and, as an old fancier once remarked of this system of home-shows, "it has done for forty years, and why not till the end of time?" Carried out in this spirit, the effect of home-shows would be that to the end of time this King among Canaries would hold its court in Lancashire and nowhere else; but there are signs that this home exclusiveness will not last another forty years. All-England shows on a large scale are gaining ground in the county, and the bird is gradually coming under the notice of breeders generally. We have reason to believe, also, that there is a strong desire on the part of the thinking portion of its patrons to remove it into a healthier atmosphere than that which has "done for forty years." The home-shows, however, have their good side; they are meetings of *breeders*, as distinguished from mere exhibitors, and they are also the strongholds of the Fancy as at present constituted; "and if they *are* held in the long-room of some 'house' where the landlord adds his five pounds to the prize-money, we must provide something *better* before we find too much fault with the only arrangement the working man is familiar with." So remarked a Coppy breeder and social economist to us.

But our bird is none the less interesting on account of some of its surroundings. We are glad to be able to place to its credit, that rough and horny hands *are* attracted by it rather than by more questionable pursuits. In stature it is the giant of the family, standing almost a full head and shoulders above any of its fellows. Length and massive proportions, a large crest, and a bold, defiant, erect stand are its characteristic traits, of which we will briefly treat in detail, merely premising that the Plainhead is the non-crested form of bird and in no way differs from the Coppy in contour, its head only requiring special description, which we will give at once, as it is the base on which good crested formation is developed. A Plainhead skull, then, should be large, flat, and very broad—a little table-land, in fact; indeed, it cannot have these features too largely developed. Not content with mere width of skull, it should also have heavy, overhanging eyebrows; and in place of the neat, short feather which gives finish to the head of all other Canaries, the presence of a redundant crop, as if with very little encouragement it would grow into crest, is a desirable feature. The expression as the bird peers out from under its drooping brows is stolid and sulky, rather than sprightly, with a seeming consciousness of power and supreme contempt for things mundane. It is withal a phlegmatic bird, and not given to indulging in those hop, step, and jump exercises from which other Canaries derive great apparent satisfaction. Such a skull as we have described is, in the Coppy, thatched with a large crest somewhat differing in shape from what we find in other crested Canaries. It is not in all cases so large as might be expected from the great size of the bird, but is invariably very neat, having a well-placed centre, good circular frontage, and regularly radiating feather. In respect to shape, the difference to which we refer consists in the frequency with which it is found with what fanciers call all front and no back, that is, with a perfect frontage, but showing little or no true crest formation or radiation from the centre in a backward direction, the crest, in many instances, extending no further on each side than serves to form a frontage of half a circle, the hinder portion either being destitute of true radiation, or falling over the back of the skull in such a smooth way as to make it difficult to say whether it consist of true crest-feather or not. This must not be regarded as an exaggerated description, but such a crest contains an exaggerated form of a feature which we have shown in Chapter XII. to be most valuable; we refer to the well-filled nape, so valuable a feature in its place that the Coppy cross is frequently resorted to for no other purpose than to obtain it. The form of crest we have described is, however, in a greater or less degree, so far a representative form, that an approach to it when found in any other crested variety is always described as Coppy-crested, by which is intended to be conveyed the idea of all front and no back, as distinguished from the more perfect form.

There is also a singularly neat description of crest not uncommon even on large birds, though it is most frequently found on small skulls, the small area probably having a good deal to do with it. It consists in a small, round, very flat, very silky-feathered and exquisitely finished little arrangement, reminding us of the flat, narrow brim of a straw hat as much as anything. It is worn very jauntily, slightly elevated behind, just enough to give rather a rakish expression, but always well filled in at the back. In its way it is very pretty, but has to give place to the large, full, drooping coppy, a good example of which is as rare as is the perfect development of any other cultivated feature. The Lancashire birds, nevertheless, show, among any given number, considerably above an average amount of excellence, which is only what might be expected in a variety long bred for this special feature; but the admirer of crested forms, generally, must not labour under the misapprehension that Coppy is a term inseparable from the idea of enormous crest. There is the high average in respect of size and good form, but nothing further; the rest is made up by the size and majestic carriage of the bird. As regards comparative size of crest as seen in exceptional examples of the Coppy and the modern Crested Norwich, there is really nothing to choose between the two, which is also not a matter for surprise, as the latter is undoubtedly indebted to the Lancashire bird for its large dimensions. In the best specimens of either variety the shape of the crest, too, is nearly identical, which, again, does not require much consideration to account for. The monster crests of either are not simply enlarged editions of its ordinary type. Only very few crests would, if indefinitely increased in size, assume the form which common assent has declared to be perfection; it requires a certain description of feather to produce this, and only when it is present, be it in Coppy or Norwich, is this exceptional standard of excellence obtained.

One feature in connection with the Coppy crest is worthy of note, and in this respect it takes the lead of all others, viz., in the average and exceptional superiority of its *yellow* crests. The difficulty of obtaining a good yellow crest in the Norwich is well known, but among the Lancashire birds some astonishing forms of the yellow are to be met with, and are by no means uncommon.

The highest standard of beauty in a Lancashire crest in respect to colour is the Clear form, though the Clears do not usually contain the largest or best crests. These are generally found among the Grey or Ticked Coppies, beyond which slight departure from clear feather the Lancashire bird knows no variegation whatever. We will not stay to inquire why, with all his devotion to crest, the Lancashire breeder yet allows the question of colour to interfere with its production, nor will we speculate as to what might be done in the way of much increased size if dark crests were recognised, further than to remark that the dark crest might be bred without much risk of introducing other variegation, which, of course, would not for one moment be tolerated. While describing things as we find them, we cannot help sometimes looking at them from our own standpoint, but we have no wish to obtrude our ideas or suggestions in an authoritative way. The Coppy belongs to Lancashire, and Lancashire has a right to determine what it will and will not do with its own; indeed, its breeders might say and with much reason, "Please leave our bird alone; we really don't want dark crests, and are sorry we have even so many greys, which we take infinite pains to breed out; you are welcome to the use you have made of our bird in improving your own crests, and are at liberty to produce them in as many shades of colour as you think fit, but we believe in only one." And who shall say nay?

In shape the Coppy is, throughout, massive in its proportions. The neck is moderately long and also straight, but loses something of its apparent length in its stoutness, as the head and crest must not appear as if attached to a mushroom stalk. A long, thin neck is the usual adjunct to a small, neat head, which is the very thing we do not require. The shoulders are broad and well filled, but not in any way prominent. The back is broad, long, and the straighter the better, though the bird is often of such unwieldy proportions, that although a line from the back of the skull to the end of its substantial tail ought to be straight, or as nearly so as can be had, there is frequently a curve, which only extraordinary size can be weighed against. The tendency of all *very* long Canaries is in the direction of a curve, and the Coppy sometimes carries so much material in its construction that it becomes difficult to dispose of it in strict accordance with the plans and specifications laid down for its erection. Average birds, however, and birds *above* the average, especially among the Yellows, are to be found rigidly straight, but some of the huge Buffs really set all rule at defiance. They stand alone; they are like nothing but themselves; they are simply giants, and claim a giant's privilege of being constructed on their own special lines. The breast is very full and prominent; the body long and tapering, and showing plenty of side. The wings, as the general construction of the bird would indicate, are also long, and are not unfrequently, especially in the Buffs, crossed at the tips: this is not to be considered other than as a defect, though the difficulty is how to overcome it when a certain point with respect to size has been passed. The legs are long and strong, with the thighs well feathered and not too much exposed, or what we have elsewhere described as stilty, *i.e.*, straight and rigid. The body-feather ought to be long without being coarse, and there should be plenty of it with a profusion of white flossy underflue. This is to be obtained in reasonable perfection in the Yellows and some of the finer Buffs, but when we get among the Patagonians of the family many of them make their toilet after their own fashion. The most common disarrangement of feather is the presence of the ruffle on the breast, and a general fluffiness about the waist and the larger upper tail-coverts. These are points which would tell against any specimen in close competition, but unusual size and a superior style of coppy will smooth over a vast amount of the slovenliness accompanying abnormal developments. It is a strong point to obtain a high amount of finish in conjunction with a heavy, drooping crest, and true perfection doubtless consists in the harmonious blending of many good properties rather than in the exaggeration of one; but the Coppy is no exception to the rule which assigns high values to ultra-excellence in a cultivated feature, even if accompanied by others not in themselves desirable, though excusable when it is remembered how materially they contribute to the object sought.

Colour, such as it is, seems to be a feature on which some diversity of opinion exists.

The bird is virtually found in but the two clear forms, the Ticked being considered more in the light of an undesirable departure from the standard than a variety to be encouraged; indeed, we have shown that the grey crest is looked upon with a certain degree of disfavour, and is only tolerated because it cannot be entirely eliminated except at a great sacrifice of some of the best types. Taking this view of the matter, it is only reasonable to infer that the Lancashire breeder, while pursuing certain types of form and seeking to present them clothed in a special way, is as much alive to the beauty of his colour as to its spotlessness, and that the same fastidious taste which excludes a tick, however faint, will appreciate such purity of colour as, from the nature of his birds and his mode of breeding, he is able to produce. And it is so. Breeding from Clears for a succession of generations is not the best way to produce colour, and therefore much cannot be expected, but such as it is, it must be good of its kind. Yellows must be Yellows, and Buffs must be Buffs, and the brighter the better, though pale and washed-out to a degree is the best apology for Buff that can be produced. Still, there must be no indecision in either form, no nondescript mealy admixture to destroy the tone of the Yellow, nor any trait, peculiar to yellow feather alone, present in the Buff to cheat the eye into a belief that it is better than it really is. It may be that the Ticked birds play a not unimportant part in keeping up some brightness in the Yellows in accordance with colour-producing laws; but, be that as it may, their colour is frequently not to be despised, and, adding as it materially does to their beauty, is a feature to be maintained and credited with a reasonable value. But having said this much, we are driven back upon the original position that the bird belongs entirely to another school, and we are at once on delicate ground when we essay to temporise with principles. Admitting the force of this, the fact presents itself to us in rather a stubborn way, that when it comes to practical judging, and soundness and purity of colour have been satisfactorily disposed of, the question of richness or depth resolves itself into one of gradually decreasing proportions. In two scales before us, one of them framed or subscribed to by an experienced Lancashire breeder, this property is very differently treated. In the one it is valued at 5 points in 100, and in the Lancashire scale at 3 in 21, or nearly three times as much, which we consider an over-estimated valuation, but one which may have arisen from an imperfect knowledge of the comparative value of figures when used in the construction of scales, since the important properties of "*Good Back and well filled*," and "*Elegance of Shape*," are, in the same scale, assessed at 3 in 21 and 2 in 21 respectively, either being of vastly more value than colour; the latter, in particular, is a very important property, and to place it behind colour is to subvert the legitimate order of things in a serious manner. In a third scale we find "*Length of bird and fulness, the wings not crossing at the tips*," expressed by 1 : 6; and "*Richness of colour throughout*" valued at the same. This last, though purporting to be an approved Lancashire scale, we cannot endorse. If "length of bird and fulness" conveys any meaning whatever, it is the idea of massive proportions, and we cannot accept colour as its equivalent. Our purpose here is to show that in a bird which is *not* a colour-bird we consider purity and decided character, regarded as the boundary-line separating Yellow from Buff—two forms of feather which represent materially different forms of bird—as of more importance than mere depth of shade; while the breeder is justly entitled to a reasonable value for a property obtained under not the most favourable circumstances, but not such a value as tends to place it in a false position.

We proceed to the classification of these birds, which is very simple, and at once suggests itself, being exactly in accord with the colour differences to which we have referred. The

Vincent Brooks, Day & Son, Lit.

MANCHESTER OR LANCASHIRE COPPIES.

CLEAR BUFF COPPY HEN. CLEAR YELLOW PLAINHEAD COCK.

same arrangement is carried out with either variety, Coppies and Plainheads alike, and is as follows:—

Classification of Lancashire Coppies and Plainheads.

(*a*) Clear Yellow.
(*b*) Clear Buff.
(*c*) Marked Yellow.
(*d*) Marked Buff.

Classes (*a*) and (*b*) explain themselves. In (*c*) and (*d*) the term "Marked," which we have taken from the schedules of Oldham show, the largest All-England exhibition in Lancashire, is not to be understood as referring to the description of marking found in other varieties, but simply to the Ticked form of the bird, than which, we have explained, there is no further form of marking. Isolated instances may occasionally present themselves in which the larger quill-feathers are slightly discoloured to the extent of a grizzle, but the marking seldom extends beyond the bounds of legitimate ticking, the slightest indication of which qualifies for admission to the class, just as one foul body-feather disqualifies for competition among the Clears. In both varieties the marking is frequently so very minute and delicate as positively to require some information as to its whereabouts to enable any one to discover it, causing a distinction so nice that if we were to stop for a moment to consider it we should find ourselves questioning its advisability in dealing with a bird in which such tick is of no more consequence than in a Belgian. But Lancashire has so determined it, and to Lancashire the bird belongs; beyond the confines of the county, in shows in which classes have been opened out for the encouragement of the bird, the distinction is never recognised, Clear and Ticked competing on a common footing. At home, however, where the competition is close and severe, the standard classification is rigidly adhered to and is closely followed by all the local clubs. Some Coppies, we may add, are very much marked on the crest, though strictly within the limits of what is known as "grey," *i.e.*, not entirely dark, but with some portions of every feather clear in colour. It is from such, we are of opinion, that *bonâ fide* dark-crested Coppies might be bred, and probably will be, though probably not in Lancashire.

In suggesting hints for breeding these giants of Canarydom successfully, we do not think we have anything to advance which may not be found embodied in our instructions for crest-breeding in Chapter XV., in which the general principles affecting it were fully discussed. There is not, certainly, in respect to Coppy-breeding, so much finessing required to keep up fine feather in conjunction with crest, as with the Norwich, and in this respect the work is, to some extent, more plain and straightforward, as will be evident if the licence allowed to comparative open-feathering, as seen in the difference between the two varieties, be duly considered. The first principle is the same: pair Coppy and Plainhead, and in accordance with the ordinary colour rules. From this union both forms will result, and the rest is entirely a matter of pedigree-breeding and selection. Plainheads, not being generally bred *inter se* to produce Plainheads, but being the non-crested form of the Coppy proper, are, as a rule, obtained from the standard mating of Coppy and Plainhead; but that is no reason why exceptionally superior Plainhead types should not be occasionally paired—a step which may be taken with great advantage, since size and the other attributes of the Plainhead are not confined to the crested bird alone, but are often found in excess in the non-crested, and in such case can be converted to good use with a view to rearing large Plainhead stock for future Coppy operations. While doing this, it must not be forgotten that the ultimate object is the *crested* form, and that therefore Plainhead pairing must not be too persistently followed up, lest the fixing of a *non-crested* form of head lead to a short supply of Coppy forms when such cultivated Plainheads are mated for crest-breeding, all of which, however, is just so much *a b c* application of the elementary principles of pedigree-breeding.

Another matter to which we may advert very briefly is the policy of occasionally pairing two Coppies, and also of occasional departures from mating strictly in obedience to colour rules, *i.e.*, buff with yellow, and the contrary. The latter needs no further remark than that it sometimes becomes necessary, and can be done with manifest benefit. The pairing of two crests is a matter on which much has been said, but little of actual experience detailed. The theory of the thing is fully explained on page 128, and this also is a step in crest-breeding which can be taken with confidence, subject to such subsequent management as we explained in that place.

In respect to sundry details pertaining to the breeding-room something may be said. The size of the birds will suggest the use of commodious cages and roomy nest-boxes; and with all these erect and comparatively loose-feathered Canaries it is advisable to shorten the tail, and also to keep a look-out for soiled or matted feather in the region of the vent. Many breeders make it an invariable custom to clip away the long fluffy feather from this part, and with beneficial effect. It is a common plan, also, in some of the large breeding districts, and one which we believe to be pretty general throughout, to pair one cock with two hens, in separate cages, but not to allow him to assist in the work of rearing the young. We know this to be the practice of several very successful breeders, who maintain, and not without reason, that by adopting this plan his vigour remains unimpaired for a longer period than when he is burdened with family duties, which he is only too assiduous in discharging. It seems at first sight to be "saving at the tap and wasting at the bung," for it must put an additional strain on the hen; but the experience of those who adopt the system appears to be strongly in its favour. Other breeders have all the hen's duty performed by deputy, keeping a supply of reliable nurses, who either sit the nests from the beginning, or, being timed to "chip" coincidently with the Coppy hens, receive the young ones as soon as hatched. This system, also, which appertains to general management, though here we refer to it as special, is open to consideration as to whether the rest so afforded to the Coppy hen is not fully counterbalanced by the additional drain on the system from over egg-producing. Both plans seem to be departures from a natural course of procedure, but we submit them as established customs which the breeder can adopt or reject as his judgment may dictate. From reliable sources we are assured that in the long-run breeding hens suffer less from egg-producing than from the disorders which so frequently attend them during the period of incubation and rearing the young, and at all events are, when released from nursing duties, freed from the distressing symptoms attending "sweating," which at once impairs a hen's health and is almost invariably fatal to the young.

The cage in which a Coppy should be shown differs in no material respect from that used for the Yorkshire, except that it is usual to have the woodwork on which the wire structure is reared made much deeper—not less than three inches at least—and the whole is supported on turned legs about two inches high. Fashion also orders that the seed shall be furnished from the outside, in a hopper accessible through two seed-holes. The top of the cage is never arched, but the wires meet in a wooden knob in the centre, similar to that seen in Fig. 56, to which is attached a stout wire ring, which is of use for other purposes than simply carrying the cage. When being sent to a show, it is usual to put each cage in a bag, and pack them in sets of four, passing a light wooden rod through the rings, to which it is fastened with string. Such a package is light, and requires no additional covering. It is at once seen how fragile is the whole and what are its contents, and the package is less likely to be crushed or turned upside down than one which, however conspicuously labelled, is not at once suggestive of its character.

We conclude with a Scale of Points, which we have worked out in detail, and have endeavoured to give to each item both its relative value in connection with the leading feature of which we think it forms a part, and also, as near as we can estimate, its value when compared with other individual items and as part of the whole.

SCALES OF POINTS FOR JUDGING LANCASHIRE COPPIES.

CLEAR BIRDS.

Points of Merit.	Maximum.	
CREST. SHAPE OF: depending on—		
Form of individual feathers: ovate	5	
Centre: Position of: set far back on the crown. Size of: a point, literally having "position without magnitude"... ...	3	
Radiation: perfect in every direction	5	
Fall of feathers: drooping	4	
Front: broad	4	
Back: well filled...	4	
	—	25
SIZE OF: depending on—		
Length of feather...	10	
Density, or quantity of feather	10	
	—	20
SIZE OF BIRD—Length and generally massive build	...	20
SHAPE OF BIRD—Neck: moderately long, straight	3	
Shoulders: broad, well covered, and well filled	3	
Back: broad, long, straight, and well filled ...	3	
Breast: round, full, and smooth, with body long and tapering	3	
Wings: long and evenly carried; tail, compact	3	
	—	15
FEATHER—Body-feather: dense, with long, silky flue	...	5
ATTITUDE—Erect, easy stand on long, stout legs; head, neck, back, and tail in a straight line...	...	5
COLOUR—For purity and depth: beak, legs, and feet of Clear birds to be free from discoloration ...	...	5
CONDITION—Health, with sound, clean feather ...	...	5
Total	...	100

Negative Properties

The crest of a Lancashire Coppy should not be formed o small daisy-petal feathers, nor of such as are fringy in texture. The "centre" should not be too near the front of the head, nor should it be in the form of a clear, open area, nor as a line or parting in the middle. The crest should not be deficient in true radiation at the back or in any other place, nor should the feathers lie flat on the head or project without drooping, or assume any position other than falling away from the centre. It should not be narrow or short in front, nor should there be a vacancy of any kind at the back. It must not be small or wanting in quantity of feather.

The bird itself must not be other than large and massive in its proportions, and should not have a thin neck, prominent or open shoulders, narrow, hollow back, or narrow, ruffled breast; neither should it be short in the body, nor carry its wings crossed at the tips nor its tail like an open fan. The body-feather should not be loose or disorderly, nor deficient in quantity. The bird should not stand in other than an erect attitude. It should not be undecided in colour, nor should a Clear bird exhibit a single ticked feather in crest or body; neither should it have dark or discoloured beak, legs, or feet, nor be shown other than with perfect feather and in clean condition.

Applied to Plainheads, the above scale requires modifying, the following being what we consider an equable adjustment of values:—

PLAINHEADS.

Points of Merit.	Maximum.
SIZE—For length and massive proportions...	30
SHAPE—For "Coppy" features, 5 points each	25
HEAD—Large, flat, broad, and with overhanging eyebrows	25
BALANCE—For "Coppy" features as before	20
Total	100

Negative Properties.

A Plainhead should not exhibit any feature opposed to the character of a Coppy, and, specially, should not have a small, round, narrow, or contracted style of head, or show any disposition to be slim or puny in its build or curved in the line of its stand.

CHAPTER XXIX.

GOLDFINCH-AND-CANARY MULES.

GOLDFINCH-AND-CANARY MULES, or, as they are generally termed, Goldfinch Mules, are, as the name indicates, the hybrids resulting from pairing the Goldfinch with the Canary; and if we begin by saying that of all varieties of cage-birds these hybrids are among the most beautiful, we shall only be saying what we have said before about something else, and will probably say again when fresh beauties are under consideration. The truth is that every variety is beautiful in its way, and we lessen our enjoyments just in proportion as we narrow our field of observation. A true fancier is a true lover of Nature in all her marvellous works, and is affected none the less by the most insignificant display of her handiwork simply because certain individual forms attract his special attention. Not the least we can say of the curious tribe of birds, the subject of this chapter, is that, apart from their cultivation as cage-birds, they afford an interesting study from a naturalistic point of view.

We shall proceed at once to their classification, and then describe them in detail, merely premising here that they range from the self-coloured Dark bird through the many phases of technical variegation up to the Clean bird, to breed which means immortal fame and Westminster Abbey. For the sake of convenience we shall invert the usual system of arrangement and commence at the base. A clearly-defined distinctive character of feather runs through the whole, separating the two divisions of Jonque and Mealy in the most unmistakable manner, and requiring to be seen but once to be recognised beyond any doubt. Plumage of a nondescript character occasionally appears in some of the advanced variegated forms, but is of rare occurrence, and is disposed of just as is a similar undecided type among Canaries, according as it more nearly approaches one or other of the recognised fixed forms.

CLASSIFICATION OF GOLDFINCH MULES.

(*a*) Dark.
(*b*) Variegated.
(*c*) Evenly-marked.
(*d*) Ticked.
(*e*) Clean.

A few words descriptive of the general contour and such feather-features as are common to all will suffice for the whole, so far as these matters are concerned. In shape a good Goldfinch Mule should resemble the Canary as much as possible, with the exception of the head only, which ought to be long and "snaky," like that of the Finch. There is a great difference in shape even in the heads of Goldfinches, and the practised eye soon learns to single out the long beak and peculiar form of head which give the character to the bird so much prized by fanciers, and it is this formation which should be shared by the Mule. We will not stay to describe the exact difference between the head of the Canary and that of the Goldfinch, but a glance at the coloured illustrations will show that the former is furnished

Vincent B

GOLDFINCH AND CANARY MULE.

DARK MEALY. CINNAM

DARK JONQUE.

with a short, strong beak, while the beak of the latter has a larger base and much greater length, more length, indeed, than many would suppose until made aware of the fact by critical examination. The Goldfinch's beak also is very tapering, ending in so fine a point that unless the bird has the opportunity of grinding it down upon some hard substance, such as a piece of old mortar, it will require to be trimmed occasionally with a pair of scissors. This Goldfinch form of head is indispensable in a good Mule, both on account of the character it stamps on the bird, and also for other valuable Goldfinch properties invariably displayed to greater effect on such a head than on one essentially Canary in its formation. What these properties are we shall presently explain: here it is sufficient to say that a good Mule should carry a Goldfinch-shaped head. The shape of the body and general style of the bird will depend to a very great extent upon the style of hen from which it has been bred, but a long, finely-built, erect bird is at all times to be preferred before a small, chubby, sit-across-the-perch specimen, and size is in all cases a strong point. The only feather-features it is indispensable to possess in *every* case are as much as possible of the Goldfinch blaze or "flourish" on the face, and the bright yellow edging on the outer edge of the flight-feathers. The tail, whether entirely or partially dark, will be found to have the Goldfinch pattern stamped on it. Other features peculiar to certain forms of the bird we shall describe as we come to them.

The Dark self-coloured Mule stands first on our list, and is the form in which ninety-nine out of every hundred appear. Till within the last few years these birds were of no value except for song purposes, for which they were, and still are, in great demand, as the mixture of Goldfinch and Canary notes forms much more pleasing music than the uncultivated roistering of the pure Canary, whose larynx, we think, can turn out more noise than any machine of its size. We may remark, in passing, that Dark hen Mules are entirely worthless; but what becomes of them all is a mystery. Possibly there is a market for them somewhere; and perhaps they may be useful to throw in with large lots when sold by the score, something in the way in which a percentage of bad chestnuts given in with a costermonger's purchase increases the retail value of his investment. Variegated hens are of more or less value according to the beauty of their markings, but they seldom find their way into exhibitions unless of extraordinary merit, and even then are of comparatively little value, owing to the absence of brilliancy of colour and the dash and commanding deportment characteristic of the male bird. As a rule, the satisfaction arising from producing a good hen is more than outweighed by regret that it is but a hen, and the only rent in the cloud is the hope that the Canary which bred it may one day throw as good a cock. But with regard to the Dark birds—the class we have now to deal with—the prizes offered for good specimens at our exhibitions have led to their being bred in a much superior form than was originally found among what was really only the refuse of nests bred for the off-chance of obtaining variegation. The bird is now bred for itself from carefully-selected large hens, and a perfect specimen is of more value than an irregularly-variegated one, though the latter is, perhaps, much rarer; but belonging as it does to a class in which *even-marking* is the desideratum, its *irregular* marking, although a rare commodity, tells against it, and it had better not have been marked at all than badly marked and imperfect in its way, while the Dark self-coloured bird *is* perfect in its way, and, if a good specimen, is a bird of singular beauty. The Jonques are the most taking in appearance, though a high-class Buff is a grand bird, especially if carrying a good face. The Buffs are, however, for the most part, more chubby in shape and deficient in length and style as compared with the Jonques.

A good Dark Jonque should be of a rich, warm bronzy-yellow, or what is known as such among fanciers, though the colour is difficult to describe in familiar terms, deepening into dark shades of rich brown on the top of the head and back, the distribution of this what we may call ground-colour being not unlike that of the Cinnamon in its varying tones. The colour cannot be too glossy or too brilliant, and, under cayenne-feeding, can be wonderfully intensified in birds bred from hens capable of assimilating the stimulating diet. But whatever its character, it is imperative that it shall not be broken by the presence of a single clear feather, however small. The underflue is black, and is generally considered as a test of the character of doubtful feathers, in which, if really clear, the flue will probably be clear also, though it is often exceedingly difficult to determine the question with certainty, and the bird, if in all other respects essentially a Dark Self, takes the benefit of the doubt. The richest display of warm colour is on the breast, and is continued underneath right through to the waist, where, in the highest-coloured examples, it has a tendency to merge itself into yellow. Still, if this yellow shade be compared with the yellow of a Variegated bird, it will scarcely be found to be the same colour, and does not detract from the value of the bird as a Self, being, in fact, a guarantee of high excellence in other respects. It is probably nothing more than an exhibition of the tendency all Canaries, and the Goldfinch also, have to run lighter in colour in the region of the vent, and bears the same relation to the bird, as a whole, as the corresponding paling of colour does in a Self-coloured Green Norwich, a high-bred Cinnamon, or a Yorkshire Green; and the distinction between this and *bonâ fide* breaking will be easily recognised by those who know the difference between the paling of the waist of a pure Yorkshire Green and the breaking into a yellow which is *not* green. Having due regard for the prevailing character of vent-feather, some licence is here allowable, and, we think, on substantial grounds. The most dangerous place for a break is at the back of the head, where, not unfrequently, a few unmistakable ticks spoil the winning chances of a gem if honestly shown. Some Dark Mules will show more of the decided character of the Goldfinch wing than others, but the yellow bars and edging should be as full of colour as the bloom on a whin-bush. The greatest beauty of the bird consists in the blaze or flourish on the face. This, in the Finch, is of a carmine tint bounded by a cleanly-cut line, and covers just so much area that its limits can be seen on a front view. In the Mule, however, its character is entirely altered, the blaze spreading over a larger surface, sometimes far down the throat and over a considerable portion of the breast, where the colour, a fiery red, loses itself among the rich tones with all the delicacy of a carefully-shaded vignette. This effect is much increased by cayenne-feeding, the subtle agent permeating every feather in which the minutest trace of colour can be developed. The colour of the face, and of the bird generally, becomes more brilliant in the spring, as is the case with some of our wild Finches when assuming their nuptial plumage. These are the leading points of a Dark Jonque, and are, as might be presupposed, mainly colour-features. To them we may add commanding size; and it is worthy of note that though large size is not common among *Variegated* Jonques, yet among the Selfs it is the rule rather than the exception, arising from the fact that in breeding Selfs there is no restriction in the selection of muling hens, because *any* hen, from a Lancashire giantess downwards, will throw a Dark Mule, and size is so far under some control; but any hen will *not* throw a Variegated Mule, as we shall presently explain. The most compact form of feather imaginable is also a property, to lack which is to put any otherwise good Mule almost entirely out of court; it is, however, generally ensured by the admixture of the naturally close plumage of the Finch. The same features may be accepted as indicative of the general character of the Dark Buff or Mealy bird, the distinction between the two consisting in the colour, which in the Buff is less brilliant, and if we say *greyer* we shall perhaps include the whole in one word. The face is also more Goldfinch-like in type, the blaze not extending so far nor changing so much in character.

The first departure from the Dark form is the Variegated, in which more or less of clean, if not clear feather, is present, the slightest break rendering a bird eligible for the class. This variegation assumes endless forms, knowing no law, and having no special value in themselves, though some are very pretty. Among these Variegated birds are to be found splendid examples of form, colour, and feather—birds in which every valuable property short of technical marking is displayed in excess. They are judged entirely for their colour, its purity, brilliancy, and extent, and every good quality *except* marking. For a bird to have any chance of winning in this class in good company, it should at least have a clean breast, and if it have, in addition, a clean cap, with simply heavy cheek-marks in place of pencilled eyes, and a dark saddle, it may be regarded as a good average specimen; and, better still, if it have a clean tail, though neither this, nor any other form of irregular variegation, has any value. The whole matter resolves itself into this: a display of clean feather being required, a clean breast is better than a foul one, and a clean cap than a dark skull, and so on, never forgetting that in this class rich colour and fine texture will at any time outweigh more perfect marking, if still imperfect and unsupported by colour and generally superior style. Natural beauty, as distinct from technical display, is the actual standard, and implies some degree of regularity pleasing to the eye, though amenable to no rule. A combination of Goldfinch and Canary traits, sometimes singular in their beauty, also has some weight. For instance, we have seen a clean breast with a clean-cut Cheveral throat—that is, with the blaze lined off from each side of the lower mandible as evenly as is seen in a Cheveral or White-throated Goldfinch. We do not say that these and similar peculiarities come under the head of standard show-points, but they all assist in giving character to a bird measured by no special positive properties other than display of clear colour and disposition to approach something resembling the recognised forms of standard technical marking. These observations apply principally to the heavier types of variegation, for when it comes to a case in which a Mule is almost, but not quite, up to the form demanded by the rules binding on Evenly-marked birds, an average display of colour and general good quality will give it a prominent place in this class, so valuable is approximate excellence in marking when once it passes the line separating it from mere variegation. In this category, also, are placed Unevenly-marked Mules, though free from the blemishes in body-feather which determine variegation as distinct from marking. There is nothing inconsistent in their being so placed, since they meet on a common footing, and are judged, not for their peculiar property, but for the general good qualities shared alike by all. They start from one and the same mark, and run on even terms, which, it will be remembered, is *not* the case in the corresponding grouping of Canaries belonging to the Colour schools.

Condensing this, the rule will be seen to be that this class of Mule is valued, in its darker forms, according to its display of colour and quality, and, in the lighter, for its approach to an approved style of marking. There is yet a third shape in which the *bonâ fide* Variegated bird appears, which belongs to neither of the above forms, and that is when the entire body, wings, and tail are clear, but the bird is disfigured by, not a simple tick, but a distinct patch or blotch of dark colour on the head or neck. Such Mules are difficult to place; but assuming the body-colour and texture of feather to be unimpeachable, the fact of such a display of colour, and approximation to the highest type of all, viz., the clear form, would place it in the highest place, and especially if the patch were of so symmetrical a shape—say an oval cap—as not to offend the eye by its irregularity. The principle involved is that marking is valuable, but the clear form is more so, approximation to either being prized accordingly.

Next come the Evenly-marked birds, and here we find ourselves dealing with a class of Mules about which there is no uncertainty and no twisting any Act of Parliament or adapting the law to meet individual cases. In so far as regards markings, they are judged by the severest standard it is possible to apply, the slightest defect being most jealously weighed in scales of extreme sensibility. It is needless to refer to the different points of excellence in marking, which have been minutely detailed elsewhere, but we may observe that good eye-marks, that is, clearly-defined and neatly-pencilled, are not every-day occurrences among the Jonques, in which a somewhat hazy form has occasionally to pass muster for the more perfect delineation. Among the Buffs, however, this feature is frequently of most singular beauty, being not only accurate in outline, but astonishing in colour, sometimes being found literally as black as jet. Negative properties, such as dark flue in the region of the vent or smoky tail-coverts, tell, every feather of them, against high-class Mules in close competition. So spotless are the best specimens that the faintest suspicion of a tinge, even to the extent of an almost imperceptible brownish cast, in these places is sufficient to entail substantial loss in a carefully-estimated valuation of points, while an amount of discoloration of tail-coverts, which would be tolerated among marked Canaries of the highest character, would almost furnish grounds for disqualification in a Mule contest, and is, as will be understood, the greatest danger a six-marked Mule has to encounter. Apart from this severe standard as applied to marking, the leading points in a Marked Goldfinch Mule are—first, the purity and richness of the body-feather. There must be none of the nondescript character about it we referred to at the outset. Jonque plumage must be glittering and transparent, without a trace of the opacity induced by the presence of meal. Want of character here tells with fatal effect, and is a failing more frequently seen among Jonques than Buffs, where the colour is generally so decided as to leave no room for doubt, a questionable Buff being a rarity. The texture of the feather, too, is a thing by itself. In the finest-feathered Norwich Canary ever fledged there is always perceptible in the body-feather more or less of what we may call grain, but the clear plumage of a Goldfinch Mule is, in comparison, as glossy satin is to the finest ribbed silk: it has no grain, but simply a polished surface, a singularly fine texture which, as we explained, is attributable to the hybrid character of the bird, and which, in its highest form, is the tangible expression of the idea of quality. The wings of both Jonques and Mealies are margined by the pure natural yellow of the Goldfinch wing. This "bloom," as it is termed, adds much to the beauty of the otherwise almost colourless flights of the Buff bird, and is a strong point. The ground-colour of a Buff Mule is a pure dead white, delicately shaded by creamy tones which, under the effects of cayenne-feeding, become richer and warmer, particularly on the breast, where the colour scintillates with great beauty. Both forms of the bird should show as much "blaze" as possible, which should be ruddy and full of "fire." In the Jonque it is generally evenly distributed and delicately shaded off towards the margin, but in the Buff is sometimes found less so, and occasionally in small disconnected patches, possibly more discernible than in the Jonque from the nature of the ground-colour, a ticked form of face having its counterpart in some examples of the Goldfinch itself. These disconnected ruddy feathers must not be confounded with the darker specks occasionally present near the margin of the face, which are in reality *bonâ fide* dark feathers connected with the cheeks, and can be regarded in no

Vincent Brooks, Day & Son, Lith

GOLDFINCH & CANARY MULES.

EVENLY-MARKED BUFF. VARIEGATED YELLOW.

EVENLY-MARKED YELLOW.

other light than as positive blemishes detrimental, but not fatal, to the interests of a Marked bird, though altogether inadmissible in one claiming to be Clear.

Within one step of the perfection reached in the Clear or Clean Mule—we use the terms in this place as synonymous—is the Ticked bird, generally understood to mean, as among Canaries, one without marking of any kind on eyes, wings, or tail, and having no body-marks except an indistinct form of variegation. This is the strict definition; but it is usual to allow a little licence, which we think might be still further extended with advantage to this class, and without infringing on the spirit of the rules governing any other. To convey our meaning in terms as brief and concise as possible, we must explain that the term "Ticked" is usually understood to apply only to body-feather, but really includes two ideas. A bird is said to be "ticked," not only when one or more genuine dark feathers show themselves in such a form as not to constitute a bold patch or blotch on the clear plumage, but also when *any* of its feathers, either body-feather or the large quills, are not more discoloured than arises from a grey or grizzly appearance as distinct from entirely dark stalk and web. The former is strictly a minute form of genuine variegation, but the latter is the true "Ticked" form; and a technically "Ticked" Mule, therefore, may either be one in which the *variegation*, though distinct, is minute, or one in which what would otherwise be technical *marking* is so faint and indistinct as to be entirely devoid of character: hence a clear-bodied bird with wings or tail slightly grizzled is said to be "Ticked," although the original definition would confine ticks within the precincts of body-feather. The corollary is that *any* minute or faint, hazy, indistinct form of variegation whatever, whether found in the domain of variegation proper or marking proper, is, practically, a "Ticked" form. Extending this principle to the one other region in which technical marking exists, viz., about the eyes, we find a home in this class for birds which otherwise are disfranchised and have no sphere in which they can compete on even terms with other birds, conditions we regard as indispensable in every contest. We refer now to such Mules as being in all other respects Clear, yet have an indistinct marking about the *eyes* as undecided and wanting in character as is the grizzled feathering of the *wings* of birds otherwise Clear, but which are by licence eligible for competition in a "Ticked" class. We admit the force of the argument that marks are marks, and that marked birds, good, bad, and indifferent, should be shown together; but our contention is that law is not always equity. Mules are not Canaries, and are not bred according to settled principles which lead up either to colour or marks, and therefore Canary law, as deduced from principles affecting those features, does not apply: they are, so far as we have any control over their production, essentially the result of chance, dropping from the clouds in all shapes in utter disregard of every attempt to mould them after any set pattern; and the general character of any Mule, so far as regards colour, is in no way affected by the character of the marking in which it happens to make its appearance, as is the case with colour-Canaries, some of which, being bred for a set pattern of feather, are willing to sacrifice some other point to obtain it. Mules are subservient to no breeding law, and we therefore classify them irrespective of any connection with it, simply grouping them so that the members of each section may compete in respect of some property they share in common, and not in respect of dissimilar qualifications; and on this ground we urge that the non-representative forms of class (*b*), *i.e.*, the minutely and indistinctly variegated, and the non-representative forms in class (*c*), *i.e.*, those faintly and indistinctly marked by simply grizzled feather, irrespective of any reference to what trifling claims either may have to be connected with the class from which it has been taken, worthless as they are in comparison with the superior properties enjoyed by both, should be united in class (*d*) and judged for general all-round Mule features and approximation to the Clear type class, by which our argument is they can be most equitably measured. We may add that this form of bird is more common among Buffs than Jonques, the only example of the latter in exhibition at the present day being in the possession of Mr. Joseph Stevens, of Middlesborough. This, and another specimen bred by Mr. George Shiel, of Sunderland, a lovely Jonque, absolutely clear with the exception of a slightly grizzled cap, but which never found its way into exhibition, being "born to blush unseen, and waste its sweetness," &c., are nearly all that have come to our knowledge during the last ten years.

Of Clear Mules we have only to remark that they are required to be absolutely spotless in the unsullied beauty of their plumage. But very few visit this earth, and a Clear Jonque is indeed a *rara avis* of which we know no living example. The most noted specimen ever in exhibition was one in the possession of Mr. Edward Bemrose, of Derby, some few years ago, and which subsequently passed into the hands of Mr. Howarth Ashton, of Manchester. Among Buffs, "Snowdrop," "Snowstorm," and "Snowdrift," a group of Peri long since admitted to the Paradise where, doubtless, all good Mules go when done with the vanities of the show-room, and also the peerless "Snowflake," who left a wealth of silver plate behind him, all the property of Mr. John Young, of Sunderland, are among translated celebrities; while "Snowflake II.," belonging to Mr. C. J. Salt, of Burton-on-Trent, and another marvellous unnamed Buff in the possession of Mr. John Brown, jun., of Penrith, are the champions as we write. The points of a Clear Mule, apart from the indispensable spotless plumage, are the richness of the bloom on the wings and the intensity and area of the flourish on the face, great weight being attached to the continuity of the latter feature and its freedom from such defects as are indicated in our notes on the general characteristics of a good face, the nearer absolute perfection is approached the greater being the subtractive value of otherwise comparatively trifling defects. A Clear Mule must have *no* blemish: remember that.

CHAPTER XXX.

MULE-BREEDING.

THE subject of Hybrid-breeding, than which there is no more interesting and fascinating work within the whole range of cage-bird pursuits, is one opening up a wide field of theory, those who have studied it extensively having a mass of curious information to offer on the matter. For our purpose we can take only a very circumscribed view of the subject, our horizon being limited, including, at the most, what is but, to a great extent, a *terra incognita*, while we have no intention of exploring the outlying region beyond in support of any theory which may find a real or supposed solution in some other field of operation. Hybrids are one of those perversions—we use the word for want of a better—of Nature's arrangements which remind us, after taking one step, how futile are our efforts in the direction of new creations; and well it is, no doubt, that they cannot reproduce themselves. Touching this latter point there is some contradictory evidence to be obtained, but in the face of the most trustworthy of it (and the most trustworthy generally has a broken link in the chain) there exists the fact that nowhere do we see living proof of the reproductive power of any hybrid; and in the absence of this evidence we dismiss this portion of our subject in as summary a way as possible, simply adding our own testimony, the result of extensive observation, to the mass of proof demonstrating its general if not absolute impracticability—most certainly in the case of the birds we are describing, although they will manifest the most ardent natural desire, and will build, lay, and sit with commendable perseverance on their tiny eggs, sometimes not much larger than peas.

The great charm of Mule-breeding is its uncertainty, and, apart from the natural difficulties to be overcome, the excitement attendant upon the chance of drawing a rich prize, which is about equal to that enjoyed by a speculator who finds himself the possessor of a ticket in a German lottery, the initial figure of which is a nine followed by at least five digits. Life is proverbially the most uncertain description of property we possess, and yet the duration of that has been calculated from safe premises and made a medium of fair commercial speculation; but no one yet has enunciated a formula expressing the probable chances of breeding a Clear Mule. We know a man who has been trying for a lifetime; he walks with a stick now, and has grandchildren, but never a good Mule. He trudges on his way manfully, careworn and with a disappointed air, certainly, but buoyed up by the ruling passion which this absorbing pursuit engenders. The story of the sporting pitman who, when dying, told his doctor that if they met in the next world and both had wings, he would "flee him a mile, just for a friendly sovereign," is only equalled by that of another who, when bidding his family good-bye, regretted he could not live the summer out, "just to see whether the little Dun hen would breed a Clear Mule."

Before commencing Mule-breeding, a man should be sure he has the right sort of stuff to work with. And first, his own pedigree must be as certain as that of his hens; there must be no doubtful cross in either. If he cannot go back in a direct line to the patriarch whose patience has passed into a proverb, or satisfy himself that that virtue has been a fixed trait in the strain from which he *is* descended, he had better not vex his soul with Mule-breeding. The next indispensable—and it is *the* indispensable of indispensables—is to procure the right class of hens, that is, hens which will throw Pied Mules. If it be wished to breed only Dark birds, *any* description of hen will answer; but the larger, more stylish, and richer in colour the hen, the more likely is it that corresponding good points will be found in the Mules; and note also that yellow hens are to be preferred before buff. We have read recipes for compounding hens for muling purposes, elaborated with extreme care, in which each ingredient is weighed out as carefully as if for making pills; but we regard them as utter nonsense. It is difficult to say what a Canary would be like if compounded of such a heterogenous mixture as we have seen authoritatively recommended, but we do know that it would be most unlike any representative of various muling strains which have come under our observation. And further, if trustworthy hens could be made to order, good Mules would soon become plentiful, whereas we never in all our experience met with a show-bird bred from a hen compounded of mule-breeding-in-six-lessons materials. Many theories have been propounded to explain why certain strains of hens produce Pied Mules, and synthetic analysis has tried to show how such hens can be built up, the prepotency of concentrated tendencies being the principle underlying every process suggested or boldly stated to be infallible. We have always found fallibility—extreme fallibility—to be the strong point of these manufactured "strains." It does not follow that because Mule-breeders never on any account introduce any cross into an approved strain *for fear of altering its character*, in-and-in breeding from a strain of *no character* if carried on for ever will have the opposite effect or do other than fix its negative properties; and though close, persistent inter-breeding *may* result in the production of some mysterious element favourable for the development of the desired idiosyncrasy, we have not met with an instance within the sphere of our observation in which the process has in actual fact been brought to a successful issue.

How muling hens have originated we cannot undertake to explain. Starting with the knowledge that ninety-nine out of a hundred hens will throw only Dark self-coloured Mules, it may be that the singular phenomenon of one throwing Variegated birds may have attracted attention, and, by careful breeding in the same family, a strain may have been established having a tendency to throw Variegated rather than Dark birds. The *rationale* of the matter may form subject for intelligent discussion, but we have now to deal with facts. Such birds exist in various parts of the country, and that is all we know; but of the many breeders we have rubbed shoulders with in our day, we have not met one who ventured to say he had built up his strain out of *nothing* by simply in-breeding. *The tendency must be there to begin with.*

The best muling hens we have here in the North—and we hail from the Wear—are either Clear, with pink eyes (indicating Cinnamon), or Variegated Cinnamons or Variegated Greens bred from Cinnamons of the old-fashioned dove-coloured type. They are not large birds, but, on the contrary, are in many instances very insignificant in size and general appearance, destitute of any pretensions to colour, and, but for the special purpose to which they are applied, valueless as Canaries. They vary, however, in these respects according to the strain. A fundamental rule most scrupulously observed is that no cross of *any* kind, not even of any noted and recognised strain of muling stock, shall ever be allowed to taint the blood, and more than one breeder of our acquaintance has bred in-and-in without a shadow of a cross for thirty years or more. To procure these hens is not easy, nor is it a matter for surprise. The way to measure selfishness is to try on the cap; it will be found a very elastic and accommodating fit. It is not, however, always selfishness which stops the way, so much as the fear of *losing the strain* which makes holders so careful how they part with even a surplus bird. There are among muling men some who would not part with a feather if they thought it was worth anything, just as there are among other breeders men who might possibly be induced to part with something not of much value, but who would not sell anything—feather or information—likely to be of advantage to a neighbour; yet we have generally found among our miners—and they are the men who have the best birds—anything but this short-sighted policy. The birds are to be had, but mostly through private channels; they do not exist in such numbers as to be an article of merchandise to be advertised and puffed and sold by the score, and fortunate is the beginner who can secure one reliable pair. A friend of ours who had bred between seventy and eighty Mules in one season, but all *Dark*, made up his mind to get into a better strain, and it will be admitted there was room for improvement. He knew where the hens were, but how to get at them was the question. Well, he fitted himself out in workman's clothes, and, so disguised, entered the enemy's country. This precaution was necessary, for a long purse is apt to spoil the market, and the fame of a "plucky" buyer soon spreads. He managed to hit on the right spot, and was fortunate enough to secure a cock and two hens at a reasonable price. But there was a hen—a noted hen—the mother of *his* hens, which had produced more than one star, and he cast a longing eye upon it; in fact, he prolonged his stay till the vendor began to be suspicious, and thought something more than met the eye was covered by our friend's war-paint. At last, grown desperate, he made such a bid for the hen that suspicion became certainty, and he was met with the pointed question, "Do they ca' yea Mr. ——?" He returned home without the hen. On another occasion he found his way into the wilds of Northumberland, among the pit districts. The old style of pitman's cottage is a two-roomed house—a living-room, with bed-room overhead under the tiles. This bed-room is got at by means of a cross between a ladder and a staircase, but in our particular instance it was a superior style of cottage with real staircase, flanked on either side with hams and sides of bacon, for pitmen breed something else besides birds. The bed-room is generally the bird-room, and our friend found himself doubled up (for, being six-three, he couldn't stand) close under the tiles, in the presence of hens, every one of which could be warranted to throw a certainty. But there was no doing any business; not a feather could he buy. And there he sat on a low stool, with his head between his knees, like an inverted letter N, looking the picture of misery and disappointment. But his offers to buy had touched the worthy possessor of these hens in a weak point. If there is one thing a pitman admires, it is pluck; and after watching our friend intently for a long while, he said very deliberately and kindly, "Aw like the luik o' ye: thoo shall hev the bawds," and, without more ado, he put the *best* he had in a small store-box or travelling-cage, with the simple comment, "*There!*" Payment was out of the question. "A poond or two is ne way wi' me, mistaw: tak' the bawds an' welcome; they're aall reet in good hands." The only difficulty was to get away without accepting a ham, which *did* come shortly afterwards, and more than one, in a most delightfully mysterious way, with which "Ham Peggoty's" Brazil-nuts left behind "Little Em'ly's" door will bear no comparison. The birds are to be had. Q.E.D.

Having procured an approved pair, the first thing to be done is to breed from them to secure the strain. The early part of the season is occupied, in a Mule-breeder's room, in multiplying stock; and as the muling season does not commence till May, there is plenty of time to secure one or two nests of Canaries. Inter-breeding being the rule, the birds are paired in total disregard of all laws affecting consanguinity. Old birds which may have thrown good muling stock are mated again; hens which in the previous year have distinguished themselves for muling properties, or have shown fair promise, are paired with cocks from the same nest, or, in default of an equal balance of sexes, with their own father, or the nearest relative open for engagement in the matrimonial market, in any way and in every way best calculated to ensure *concentration of the existing tendency* and maintain the strain intact. And, remember, that any hen which will throw a Pied Mule—we don't mean a good one, the question of quality and other matters affecting the character of the Mule being an after-consideration—but a hen that will throw a Pied Mule of *any sort* is not to be despised. It is just this peculiarity, a peculiarity not possessed by one in a thousand, that we require, and, where it is found to *exist*, is the feature to be *cultivated*. Such a bird might appear among Norwich or any variety, and a Mule-breeder would at once look after her brother or some near kinsman, and from *that* beginning, where there *is* something to fix, would be much more likely to build up a muling strain than by commencing with birds of no character, and having no tendency to cultivate, unless it might be in the opposite direction to that required. We refer again thus briefly to the question of founding an independent strain, because it crops up naturally in this place. That the disposition to produce Pied Mules arises from *some* cause is as certain as that all effect results from cause, the question being, what is the cause? An instance, such as we have supposed, has occurred within our knowledge in the case of a well-bred Norwich hen, and it might be urged that the cause was probably inter-breeding, of which the owner might have been ignorant. To this we reply that in no variety is in-and-in breeding carried on so closely or to such an extent as is supposed to induce the state of body necessary for the production of Pied Mules. To do so would be fatal to the well-being of any variety, and we do not suppose that out of a hundred hens, purchased indiscriminately, one would be found to have been so inter-bred as to be half-way on that long journey some theorists tell us they must take, even to become possible Pied Mule breeders.

This preliminary work of multiplying stock is simply a matter of Canary-breeding so far as concerns general management, but is an anxious time for the Mule-breeder, because a bad season may reduce a very valuable stock to a low ebb. Hence the importance of keeping birds in hand; a prudent breeder, when his stock is getting low, even resisting the temptation to take a single nest of Mules from any hen in order that the entire season may be devoted to rearing muling stock for future operations.

The next important step is to procure suitable Goldfinches, in selecting which nearly every one follows a whim or fancy of his own. One looks for a long, slim, snake-headed bird, while another doesn't care how chubby it may be; one must have a full face, while another cares not a straw how defective it may be, and in place of beauty and distinctive character prefers positive defect or an amount of general deficiency indicating some tendency towards albinism. Some pin their faith on Cheverals, and allow nothing to slip through their fingers, from "pea-throats" to the widest and cleanest-cut throats procurable; while others care little what their bird is so long as it is a Goldfinch. Each, no doubt, follows out some path which has, in his experience, led to success, though the how or why of this it is so difficult to reduce within known limits, that there are almost as many theories as to Goldfinch requisites as there are breeders. In two noted breeding-rooms, which have for some years contained very strong muling stocks, and in which have been bred some of the most extraordinary birds of the day, the Finches are almost all Cheverals; and the result of one experiment showed that a hen which, when paired with a Cheveral, threw lightly-variegated birds, produced only dark ones when paired with an ordinary Finch. We do not advance this as being an argument in favour of the Cheveral, but only as a fact to be taken for what it is worth, for many of the best Mules in exhibition have been bred by men who never had a Cheveral in their cages. With Goldfinches, however, "handsome is as handsome does" is the test, and unless it be a "breeding" bird, or one which will mate readily with the Canary, all his beauty counts for nothing. Some will not look at their hen, and these little Josephs, these paragons of ornithological virtue, are worthless in the breeding-cage, as nests of "empty" eggs only too often testify.

It will be inferred from the foregoing that the Finch must always be the male bird. The reason is that from such an alliance there is a greater chance of obtaining Mules resembling the Canary, and also because the Canary hen, being the more domesticated, is likely to prove the more reliable mother; but as a matter of fact the hen Goldfinch will breed readily in confinement mated with a Canary or with her own kind, or even with other Finches; and we have known several nests of Mules obtained in this way, though all were veritable sweeps, not very shapely and not very brilliant, and resembling the Finch too closely to be of much value from a fancier's point of view, however interesting in other respects. The Cinnamon Mule in the coloured illustration was bred from a Cinnamon cock and a Goldfinch hen, and is a *cock*-bird—a result not in harmony with Cinnamon law in Canary-breeding.

It is well, when it can be done, to procure Finches early in the year, so that they may be tamed and thoroughly domesticated by breeding-time—a matter of some consequence. Fresh-caught birds, captured late in the season, will breed readily; but when used for the purpose they are frequently short-lived, and often go off after the first nest. Sound over-year birds which have been moulted in captivity and have proved their ability are much prized; and a breeder who wishes to have more than one string to his bow will generally manage to secure a few reliable birds in the course of a season or two, and very old-fashioned little fellows they become. Some breeders house-moult a few "grey-pates," that is, Goldfinches in their nestling plumage; but mature birds are such a plentiful commodity in the market that a good selection can be made by purchasing, as opportunity presents; an extra Finch or two being very necessary, as they have a little way of their own of making up their minds very quickly when they think of departing for the happy hunting grounds.

Some Finches become "fresh" early in the spring, but it is not desirable, and a breeder likes nothing less than to see a beak turn prematurely white, the sign of fitness for breeding. When such does occur, the bird seldom lives through the year, and no practised hand would give a long figure for a forward bird out of season, though the rule is not infallible. The month of May is quite soon enough for the little fellow to begin to show such signs as are required previous to introducing a Goldfinch to his future spouse. His first work usually is to take stock of the furniture, the nest-box coming for its due share of critical examination. Then he sets to work to clean his feet, selects his own corner on the perch, and calmly waits the course of events; seldom making more advance at first than indulging in a sly snatch at his hen when she comes within reach. To get him into blooming condition he must be fed with stimulating diet—a little egg, maw-seed, summer rape, and hemp-seed, of which he is inordinately fond and will soon learn to take from the finger.

When the last tinge of black has disappeared from his beak and it begins to assume that delicate, transparent pinky-white colour, the admiration of muling men, it is time to think of running him to the hens, which by this time will probably have brought up one or more nests of Canaries. Here we take the opportunity to remark that a belief in the development of possible physiological phenomena as the result of "the influence of previous sires" has its followers among Mule-breeders, and some assert, though we don't know how far supported by proof, that hens previously mated with Canaries are likely to tnrow the lightest Mules. We cannot discuss the theory here, nor indeed have we studied it sufficiently to feel justified in expressing any opinion on the subject, but we have known endless schemes tried, from the application of the "ring-straked" theory, to which we refer reverently, as applied by breeding in cages which with every appliance were coloured perfectly white, down to mating with Clear and Marked Canaries previous to introducing the Finch, and then allowing the Canary cock, the first love, to remain suspended in a small cage in front of the compartment containing the muling hen till after she had laid her complement of eggs to the Goldfinch; but with no satisfactory result. As a practical way of dealing with a hen which refuses to receive attentions from the Goldfinch, but which will "call" in response to the song of her old mate, such an arrangement has manifest advantages, upon which we need not enlarge; but as regards the "previous influence" theory we can say nothing in its favour.

If there be several approved Finches at command, they may be mated up with hens precisely as Canaries, but if not, a good bird in the bloom of high condition may be "run" through almost any number of cages, where he will not fail to leave his mark. He need not, of necessity, be allowed to remain long with his hens. A more tractable bird does not exist, nor one more amenable to social and home influences. If allowed to settle down with his hen he will make the most attentive mate, and at once accept the responsibilities of his position, nursing and feeding in the most exemplary manner. It is well, however, not to tax him in this way, as a hen is well able to attend to the duties demanded by her offspring, and he is more likely to remain in robust health and vigour if not overworked. There is some degree of risk in leaving an untried bird with a hen till she lays, as he may prove to be of an inquisitive turn of mind, and may take it into his head to examine into the contents of the eggs, for which purpose his pointed beak is well adapted; but this mischievous propensity is happily rather the exception than the rule. When such a habit has been acquired there is one simple preventive—*don't allow him the opportunity.* The most inexperienced can soon learn when a hen is on the eve of laying, and removing the Finch is a much simpler and more effective plan than using a "drop-nest"—one with a hole in the bottom, through which the egg falls into a bag or other receptacle containing cotton-wool or down, to prevent injury. These "drop-nests" nevertheless are very useful, and where the time at a breeder's disposal is perhaps limited to an hour's attention in the middle of the day, long after the time when the mischief is done, such self-acting appliances are invaluable for preventing the possibility of any misadventure. A compact, handy arrangement can be secured by fitting an ordinary tin nest into a tin receptacle like a small canister, into which it will slide with sufficient grip to keep the whole in position, the apparatus looking like a flour-dredger with an inverted lid.

The hatching of a nest of Mules is an event of importance, and beginners are often deceived by appearances. All Dark Mules are not born equally dark in skin and down, though they usually are veritable little "niggers," nor are all Variegated Mules born with such decided indications of variegation as are seen in the discoloured skin of young Canaries; but an experienced eye soon detects the unwelcome signs. When one bird is whiter than the rest, paler in the flesh, or shows no visible signs of discoloration, hope runs high; and we have known a powerful magnifying-glass, carefully concealed in some corner lest it should betray unbecoming anxiety, frequently brought into operation. No expected comet was ever searched for more earnestly than are the small specks on the naked wings, which indicate something of future greatness or the opposite, and it is at this stage of growth that rumours of a Clear Mule having been born into the world disturb the horizon in private circles. A promising yearling with a Derby nomination excites scarcely more interest, and he must indeed be a privileged friend of the stable who is allowed just one peep through the magnifier, which, like other magnifiers, only too frequently raises hopes and prospects of future success destined never to ripen into fruition. Fortunate is the man, despite the agony of his bereavement, whose bantling is sweated, smothered, starved, or choked out of existence thus early, before it has lived long enough to destroy all his air-castles, and teach another of the thousand-and-one lessons that appearances are deceitful. You meet your friend in the street, pale, haggard, and worn out with days of anxiety and sleepless nights of weary watching in costume of rheumatic proclivities. It is needless to speculate on the cause; the Mule has gone home. You can only wring his hand in mute sympathy, and leave him to go on his solitary way, feeling thankful to know that in his own pedigree there are two or three good strains of the patriarchal blood, and hoping that the exercise of the virtue inherent in the family will some day meet its reward. It would be worse than unkind not to respond to the heart-broken request to "call and see it," and you go to the house of mourning to find the bird of so much promise stretched out on the window-sill of the bird-room, a cold, clammy little cherub which, had it lived, might have turned out just what it is now, nobody knows what, but quite likely as worthless as its brothers and sisters in the same nest, black as sloes, and refusing to die. It is at this interesting stage of their existence that most Clear (?) Mules *do* die; and well it is that they do, for it keeps alive a hope which would be crushed out of most men if they lived to mock their anticipations. It is a sort of hallucination some men labour under to imagine they have bred Clear Mules without end; and, as is often the case with people who deal largely with the marvellous, the story is told and re-told so frequently that the narrators in course of time come to believe it true, even if no one else does. We are very charitable in our estimate of the *bona fides* of some of the stories we are asked to credit, because the supposition that the young Mules really are as represented arises in a great measure from ignorance as to the correctness of the estimate it is possible to form of the true character of any light Mule in the early stages of its life. Dark Selfs can be recognised early enough, and the broader forms of variegation as soon as the small black specks which subsequently develop into dark feathers appear on the naked wings and elsewhere; a narrow line down the back of the neck, for instance, indicating at the least a dark saddle, if not an entirely dark back; but beyond reading correctly the ultimate character of these clearly-defined indications, the most experienced judge can determine nothing certain of a young bird at the age of ten days or a fortnight. It may be seen that there will be eye-marks of a kind, but whether large, small, distinct, broken-up, or well-pencilled, no one can say. A very foul breast may be foretold sufficiently early to damp the breeder's hopes and put him out of his misery at once; but the smaller and less distinct markings, such as discolorations on the cheeks or neck, are from the very nature of the plumage invisible till the growth is comparatively matured, while a host of defects, which might stamp an apparently Clean bird anything but Clean, may appear in minute but palpable shape long after their existence has been deemed almost an impossibility. The reason of this is because the discoloration of the body-feather altogether differs in character from that of the Canary, where we have only to deal with the presence of the native green, which shows itself in a less subtle form than do some of the more delicate tones in a Hybrid, in which matured feather, in other respects clear, frequently develops a minute edging of darker colour, so minute and delicate as only to be discerned by a practised eye on the clear yellow or snowy white ground, and yet sometimes covering a considerable area, and declaring its character by its connection with a dark underflue. This species of blemish may appear to the uninitiated scarcely worth notice, but in it consists the difference between Clear and not Clear. We have known such discoloration to cover a considerable portion of the neck of an otherwise Clear Mule, and yet to be so faint as only to be discoverable when the bird was rejoicing in the freshness of a recent "tubbing," the slightest soiling being enough to disguise the true nature of the blemish, something like a certain class of light-grounded carpets in which some housekeepers delight, because they never "show the dirt." Where the underflue is dark, such a discoloration is generally permanent; but in the case of grizzled feathers, in which the shaft and web are merely streaked white, the underflue remains clear, and more especially with grizzled wings, the discoloration is apt to become lighter with each successive moult, and sometimes ultimately disappears, to induce which much-coveted result such feathers are persistently plucked as fast as they arrive at maturity, and a really Clear bird is produced in one season. Of the *morale* of this procedure as concerns the comfort of the bird we say nothing; but it is a fact, and is a mode of treatment not confined to Goldfinch or Pied Hybrids generally, but is also practised on Canaries when an objectionable grey feather appears where it is not wanted, and which an experienced eye at once sees is of such a character as to afford reasonable grounds for supposing it will ultimately become Clear. The most remarkable instance of reversion from a Dark to Clear form which has come under our observation was that of Mr. Spence's famous Linnet-and-Canary Mule, a portrait of which appears in our coloured illustration. This bird was originally very much marked on the skull, cheeks, and neck, and was also ticked on the saddle, but in the course of time replaced the whole of these dark feathers with perfectly clear plumage, the eyes and wings alone remaining dark.

There is nothing fresh to offer in the way of general management of young Mules, which in no respect differs from that observed in the rearing of Canaries, cayenne-feeding and every other "move" being applied with telling effect; and as not much is to be gained by flighting and tailing, these practices are not much in vogue, indeed, except for the purpose of adding colour to the bloom on the margin of the wing, nothing is gained by a practice now becoming more honoured in the breach than in the observance.

We pass on to a brief consideration of some other Canary Hybrids, chief among which are Linnet-and-Canary Mules, and we need scarcely say that by Linnet we mean the common Brown Linnet, or Linnet proper. These are bred precisely in the same manner as Goldfinch Mules, the Linnet pairing readily with the Canary under ordinary conditions. The bulk of these Hybrids also are Dark Selfs, bearing a strong resemblance to the parent Finch, and are not, except when the latent Canary elements are brought to the surface under the magic influence of cayenne, particularly showy birds. A "fed" specimen, however, if bred from a colour-hen and possessed of size, is very beautiful, developing in the Jonque form a rich, ruddy umber, its glistening breast showing up the Linnet pencillings in beautiful relief. The usual Pied form is of the irregularly-variegated type, the blotches being patches of Linnet feather. Anything like marking is exceedingly rare, and is seldom found in the shape of decided eye-marks; indeed, we do not remember having met with more than two "four-marked" Linnet Mules in the course of ten years, the general form of the most noted specimens being an approach to Clear, of which there are several now in exhibition. Mr. Stevens's celebrity, which appears in our plate, has only about seven dark feathers visible. It and Mr. Spence's bird have each taken not less than a hundred prizes, and are unique specimens, the equal of which may probably never be seen again. We may add that most of the Variegated Linnet Mules are Buffs; a few Jonques have appeared, but the colour is

Vincent Brooks Day & Son, Lith

LINNET & CANARY MULES.

MR STEVENS'S MULE. DARK MULE. (ORDINARY TYPE)

MR SPENCE'S MULE.

not sufficiently striking to render it valuable except on account of its rarity. The feather of both is very soft and silky, and, like that of most Finch Mules, very compact.

Next to these in interest, both as regards natural beauty and the numbers bred, are the Greenfinch-and-Canary Hybrids, of which any other than a heavily-variegated form is seldom or never seen. The generality are entirely dark, being brilliant editions of the Finch, in which its dusky green plumage is wonderfully brightened and made very transparent, especially in the natural development of the yellow on the wings, which maintains a character so distinctive as to indicate the parentage at a glance. The example in the coloured illustration, also the property of Mr. Stevens, is a faithful delineation of the finest specimen of his day, and but for the distinctive wing and a suggestive hue on the darker parts might be mistaken for a Canary.

The Hybrids produced by the union of the Siskin with the Canary are also pretty birds, mostly resembling enlarged and brilliantly-feathered examples of the Finch. Some few of them are pied to the extent of a few light feathers in the wings and tail, and we have met with a few rare exceptions in which the pied form of plumage has extended in an irregular way to the body. There is probably no reason why a more regular form of marking should not occur both in this and the last-mentioned Mule, if sufficient numbers were bred to embrace the possible chances; but neither is so strikingly beautiful nor so generally attractive as to commend itself to the fancier's attention, and anything like systematic breeding of them has never been followed up. The Siskin itself is an engaging little cage-bird, though we cannot say that the Greenfinch is a very popular favourite: neither holds the same place as a household pet as does the Goldfinch or Linnet, and to this fact, perhaps, as much as to any other, is to be attributed the scarcity of these and other still less interesting Hybrids; since few breeders, except those who take up Hybrid-breeding for its own sake, apart from producing extraordinary specimens for show purposes, would be at the trouble to procure the necessary material, which, in the case of the more popular Finches, is at command in nearly every room. From any view, however, it is a most interesting pursuit, and one in which those who do not take much interest in Canary-breeding will find ample scope for amusement, in addition to the chances of unearthing a valuable nugget.

In addition to the more common Hybrids of which the Canary is one parent, there are the rarer Finch-and-Finch Mules, by which we mean the Hybrids produced by pairing different varieties of our native British Finches. Chief among these stands the Bullfinch-and-Goldfinch Mule, beyond all compare the most beautiful example of the whole class, and also occupying the highest place as an exhibition-bird. It is almost needless to give any description of this lovely bird, in the face of our coloured illustration, which is a singularly happy and life-like delineation of one of the most characteristic specimens which has graced our public exhibitions for some years, and was bred by Mr. J. Drake, Ipswich. An examination of and comparison between the Mule and the parent Finches, as depicted in our illustrations, in which is seen life-like truth without artistic liberty, will show how remarkably the plumage and configuration of each are blended in the progeny. The plate represents the cock-bird; the hens are clad in sober attire, and more closely resemble the female Bullfinch. In size a good specimen is as large as an ordinary English Bullfinch, which it resembles in its quiet demeanour and generally "old-fashioned" deportment, having but little of the restlessness native to many, though not all Goldfinches. Its song is low, very sweet, and continuous, as distinct from a jerky, snatchy style of vocalisation. It is a hardy bird, and content with plain fare, though not averse to dainty meats, among which it regards hemp-seed as a great luxury, and will consume a considerable quantity. Our readers will be glad to know that it is not a very difficult Hybrid to breed. We do not wish to convey that it can be bred as easily as the common Goldfinch-and-Canary Mule, but that the elements of chance and uncertainty do not enter into the case in the manner in which they, to a great extent, bar the way in well-arranged efforts to produce a high-class bird of the latter variety. All Bullfinch-and-Goldfinch Mules are cast in one mould, and the difficulty consists, not in the uncertain character of the birds produced, but in successful management during the breeding-time—a thing no breeder should despair of accomplishing. The female Bullfinch is very easily tamed, and a little attention will soon be repaid by the greatest familiarity, the bird becoming as thoroughly domesticated and reconciled to cage-life as the most exemplary Canary matron in the room. To assist in bringing about this desirable state of things, it is well to procure a few hens in the autumn, when they can be obtained at a cots of a few pence each; but to increase the probability of producing large Mules, we would recommend the use of the imported German birds, which are much larger than our indigenous specimens. No further attention to the hen is requisite during the interregnum than the gentle humouring and coaxing necessary to remove all shyness, and render the presence of its master or mistress an evident pleasure rather than a cause of uneasiness. In the early spring the Goldfinch should be introduced, as much that he may become accustomed to his hen as she to him; and as the season advances, it should be noticed whether they seem to have made up their minds to accept each other for better or for worse. This will be before either bird becomes very demonstrative, and it will only be necessary to observe whether the Goldfinch has determined to be master in his own house, or submits to be hen-pecked: if the latter, remove him, and introduce another known to rule his house with firmness. The most that can be expected in the early part of the season is mutual forbearance, the absence of unseemly quarrels, and no display of cowardice on the part of the Goldfinch. About the end of May the Bullfinch will begin to show signs of a more ardent temperament, and will not repel the advances of almost any mate; and then it is that the advantage of having a Goldfinch who is master of the situation is apparent; for it is amusing, although vexing, to see her behaviour to a Finch who, with a lively recollection of sundry snubbings, is really afraid to look at her, even when, forgetting all that has passed, she is evidently anxious to make up matters and commence housekeeping. The Goldfinch who has been thrashed can't believe her, and the greatest patience in such a case will never be rewarded.

A roomy well-lined nest should be supplied, and also building material, with which the hen will at least amuse herself, if not re-model her nest—a matter of the greatest consequence, since she is apt to lay in the bottom of the cage. The difficulty in breeding with many wild Finches is not in inducing them to lay, but in securing the eggs when they are laid; and hence the importance of doing everything to lead them to construct their own nests—a thing they frequently do not seem to care about in captivity. To prevent any mishap to eggs laid in the cage, or even dropped from the perch, it is well to cover the bottom with bran to the depth of an inch, and if persistently dropped from the perch, to lower it to a height from which no danger from fracture can be anticipated. The number of eggs is uncertain, the natural order of things being occasionally disarranged in a strange way; two or three only being sometimes deposited, while at others a "nest" of five will be laid with regularity, or a considerable number, a dozen or more, at uncertain intervals. These should all be placed under Canaries to be hatched, literally not putting too many in one basket, both on account of the ordinary risks and the extraordinary demands the young birds

Vincent Brooks Day & Son Lith.

GREENFINCH & CANARY MULE.

GOLDFINCH & LINNET MULE

BULLFINCH & GOLDFINCH MULE.

will make upon the feeding capabilities of their foster-parents. The rest is only a question of ordinary management. The following is a brief account of a Mule of this description, which for beauty was second only to the subject of our illustration, and will be read with none the less interest from the fact that it is furnished by the lady who bred it, Mrs. Tallent, of Mettingham, Suffolk. She says:—"The Bullfinch hen was one bought from a poor man in my neighbourhood in the autumn of '76, being a young bird of that year. In the following spring I put her in a cage—an ordinary breeding-cage—with the Goldfinch. I cannot quite remember the date when the first egg was laid, but she laid in all nineteen: on the first occasion six, then eight, then four, and finally one, the last being without any shell. She seemed very ill all the day, and I gave her a drop of castor oil, and late in the evening she laid, but died a few minutes afterwards. She built her own nest in a round zinc nest-box, and usually sat for a day or two. Once she sat for a week, and once for thirteen days, on Canaries' eggs, which would have hatched, but on the last day she refused to sit any longer, so I never knew if she would have brought up any young ones. The Goldfinch was always with her, and never attempted to touch the eggs, which, with the exception of two or three, were all laid in the nest. From the nineteen eggs only five young birds were hatched, of which two died at about three days old. In the same nest with the Mule which I reared were two others, both healthy birds; but at the end of a week, upon examining them, I found one had no eyes, but simply an indentation at the place. This bird I had destroyed. The other lived eight weeks, and died suddenly. All were hatched and reared by Canaries, the food being egg and bread, with the addition of a little hemp-seed. I may add that I removed the Goldfinch on one occasion for a short time, but was obliged to return him, as the hen pined so much that I am sure she would have died if I had not done so."

A Hybrid much more common than the foregoing is the Greenfinch-and-Goldfinch Mule. It is not a very pretty bird, being built more on the lines of the former than the latter, and partaking to a considerable extent of its dull colour, though occasionally a more brilliant example than usual, having a good deal of the Goldfinch character about it, appears on the stage to keep alive an interest in a bird at no time a very popular favourite. We have seen a few specimens of singular beauty, with large Goldfinch blaze, and lustrous plumage different in texture to that of either parent. Its song is full of melody, without being noisy. It is easily bred, the female Greenfinch mating readily and laying a great number of eggs, though much in the irregular fashion of the Bullfinch.

Among other curious Finch-and-Finch Hybrids bred in captivity which have come under our notice is the Goldfinch-and-Linnet Mule, of which the specimen now in the possession of Mr. Jno. Brown, jun., of Penrith, and which figures in our illustration, may be accepted as an exceptionally good type. In his "little ways" he is a Goldfinch all over, and will fight with the finger, and in other respects deport himself like that bird. We have also met with examples of the Bullfinch-and-Linnet, in which the character of each was too plainly stamped to leave any doubt of the parentage. Where it is desired to experiment in the way of Hybrid-breeding with the Linnet for one parent, it should always be the male bird, as but few accredited instances are on record of the female Linnet breeding in captivity, notwithstanding an entire aviary, fitted up with whin-bushes and such cover as the bird delights in, has been placed at its disposal.

Doubtless many other interesting and curious Hybrids might be added to our list, but they scarcely come within our province, especially such as, having been caught in a wild state, afford no further evidence of their supposed parentage than a family likeness.

CHAPTER XXXI.

WASHING AND EXHIBITING CANARIES AND MULES.

(FROM NOTES BY MR. BEXSON AND MR. EVANS.)

WHETHER or not cleanliness be next to godliness in general, it has very much to do with success in exhibiting, and hence most birds have to be washed more or less before being shown. Many a good bird has lost a fair chance because its toilet had not been properly attended to; but none the less the necessity for "tubbing" must be considered an evil. A few country fanciers, who reside in those sweet villages a few of which are still left to old England, are exempt from the necessity, since birds will keep themselves clean enough in pure air if properly attended to. We have seen many Canaries in such places which needed no more than a "blow" or a natural bath to surpass in brightness and bloom all that the best washing could do for those bred—say in Manchester. Most Canaries, however, are town-bred; and such must be washed occasionally to have a chance of success; though one good washing will often suffice for more than one show. The evil of too frequent washing is a kind of giving way of the feathers, which might almost be called a rubbing-out, and which is very apt to display itself about the back of the neck especially. By these or similar signs a bird which has been subjected to much tubbing can often be recognised at good shows. In spite of all this, however, washing being a necessary evil, let us see how it may be made the best of.

We have long ere this hinted at the propriety of engaging the approval and more or less active sympathies of one's "better half" respecting all experiments and adventures in Canarydom; and now that the final stage is approached, this is more than ever necessary, since her own domain is almost necessarily invaded. If breeding, and rearing, and moulting have been successfully surmounted, it will be strange if hopes and sympathies are *not* excited by this time as to the ultimate result; and judicious hints as to a new silk dress in case the long-cherished pets *do* win, may have happy effects. Some such encouragement is indeed sorely needed at this stage; for if the ordeal of washing has to be gone through now for the first time, faith is apt to experience a severe shock during certain stages of the process. First of all, before operations are commenced, if there are children in the house it will generally be best to see them safely to bed. There are some little treasures, born fanciers, who know how to abide still as mice until need arises, when a little hand will pass a warm cloth or other necessary, neither one moment too soon nor too late—no one would think of sending *them* to bed. But average children are sadly in the way, and all the space by the fire is badly wanted. Moreover, washing a small bird requires care, and chatter by no means assists the process. While this is being managed, then, let a good fire, *free from ash and dust*, be made up, and some large vessel full of hot water placed upon the hob so as to keep simmering. Boiling is not necessary, but if many birds are to be done, plenty of hot water will be wanted through the evening. An open wire cage should have previously had a thorough washing for the occasion, to be used as a "drying" cage, and must have the bottom covered over with clean flannel or some handy woollen article; this is placed where a good heat from the fire can reach it. The mistress of the house—previously propitiated as aforesaid, or otherwise—must be asked for a few clean and soft cloths—clean *and* soft, mind. And lastly, you must get from the same or other source three good-sized basins. Heavy washing-basins are very suitable for the purpose, as being less easily overturned; but better than all are the round white pans to be had in some parts of England, the same size at bottom as at top: these, when procurable, are not only impossible to overturn, but without occupying any more room hold double the water, which consequently keeps cleaner and needs less attention.

The first basin or pan should be half filled with water milk-warm, or lukewarm. Dissolve in it a bit of clean soda the size of a nut (much must not be used), and then taking in one hand a piece of good yellow or white soap, and in the other a badger-hair or other *soft* shaving-brush,

Fig. 62.

Fig. 63.

alternately dip in the water and rub over the soap, till you have a basinful of good suds. Half fill the other basins with warm water, full blood-heat, but not more: if you have a thermometer you may keep it at 90°. The soap must also be placed handy; and it is a good plan to *bed* it in the soap-dish with flannel, so that it may not slip about while the brush is passed over it. With these preparations you are ready to begin.

Take your first bird and place it along the palm of the left hand, as in Fig. 62, the head towards the wrist, and the tail projecting between the thumb and forefinger, while the other fingers hold the bird lightly but firmly, the little finger securing the head, and the others the shoulder or side of the wing. It will be readily found that in this position the bird can be held lightly yet with perfect security, and that the position of its body can be changed at convenience, according as the back or sides are being done. Immerse all but just the head in the suds for a few seconds, whilst the lather-brush is being plied with telegraphic speed over the soap; and as soon as a good free lather is obtained in the brush, lift the bird out, remove the thumb or second finger out of the way, and wash well with the brush the lower part of the body, the wings, and tail; always working in the same direction as the feathers lie, and occasionally dipping the parts being washed in the suds. Do this until the dirt seems got out; then hold the bird with forefinger and thumb, and remove the other fingers sufficiently and alternately, like those of a violinist, to give space for the head and shoulders being washed, taking care that the dirt is well removed round the beak: the third finger placed *under* the throat will readily raise the head for that purpose. It is no use attempting to be too particular about the eyes; you had better forget that the bird has any, except that you will of course take care the brush itself does not come against those delicate organs. The soap will, and you cannot help it, so it is no use fretting, and most sensible birds shut their eyes. Being satisfied that the back is clean, turn the bird over in the hand (Fig. 63), with its head coming under the little finger towards the

Fig. 64.

Fig. 65.

wrist as before, and again commence brushing the wings and tail, opening the wings as much as possible. Finish off with the throat and belly.

Should the foregoing method of holding a bird be found awkward or difficult—and different hands seem naturally to fall into different methods—there is another we have seen practised with good results. In this method the head is passed between the thumb and forefinger of the left hand, and the three other fingers spread out so as to support the flights and tail whilst they and the back are washed with the brush (Fig. 64). Then close the last three fingers over the back, and open the thumb and forefinger sufficiently to allow the head and shoulders to undergo the operation; and when it is done, turn the bird over and wash the under part of the tail, the inside of the wings, and the belly, finishing off with the throat and breast. Should this method be pursued, care must be taken not to press the neck-feathers too tightly with the fingers, or they may become "frilled."

So far all is pretty simple. At first one is almost as afraid to handle the Canary as average men are to meddle with a new-born baby: it is hard to avoid a fear that the legs will come off, or something else happen equally dreadful. Once get over this, and you simply have to get the dirt out. There is no danger so far, and no great need for extra caution, or any great particularity as to which way the brush moves: if it move in the *general* direction of the feather, that is enough.

You will of course see there is no particular pressure on any part of the body, on the belly especially. Supposing now that you have the bird clean, squeeze the suds from the brush, and with it *wash* out the soap with the water in the second basin. Finally, holding the patient (which by this time is reduced to comparative tameness) in as perpendicular a position as possible, scoop the water in the third basin over it with the right hand until it is *perfectly* free from soap; after which, draw the flights and tail gently through the fingers to remove as much water as possible before proceeding to the drying stage. If preferred, a sponge may be used for the final rinsing, and the bird may even be dipped and freely moved in the clean warm water—keeping the head out, of course, unless for a moment. Remember, however you do it, that the great point is to get every least particle of soap completely out of the plumage: *any* left in will hinder proportionately a good result.

At this stage a heavy sigh may probably be heard from the "better half," and an anxious face be seen watching the proceedings. Very likely the operator feels badly too, as he beholds the miserable little object he has produced; few men have ever "smole a smile" at this crisis of their first wash. Never mind; but having first "wrung out" the bird with the fingers, as it were (some people draw the wings and tail through the lips instead), take one of the soft cloths, previously *well* warmed at the fire, wrap the bird in it, and "dab" it gently between the hands, until the worst of the wet is soaked up by the cloth. Be especially sure that the water is well absorbed from about the belly, vent, and under the wings. An excellent method of "towelling" for effecting this purpose is to place a second dry and hot cloth *over* the whole left hand; then take the bird by the right hand, with the two first fingers under the belly and the thumb over the root of the tail and ends of the wings, when the patient will open its wings a little at the shoulders. At once you pop in the covered left thumb under one wing (extending between wing and body), and the left second and third fingers (also covered by the warm cloth) under the other wing (see Fig. 65), which will, with a little judicious manipulation, rapidly soak up the wet all along the belly and under the wings. After this the left forefinger, brought up over the right side of the bird's neck, holds it securely while the right hand takes up the loose end of the cloth and wipes over the head, down the back, flights, and tail.

The wet being in the main soaked up, take another piece of hot dry cloth in the right hand and stroke the plumage into position, and place the bird in the drying-cage, pretty near the fire. See especially that the plumage lies right about the back of the neck and rump. The bird may appear half dead, in which case some think it best to hold it quietly in a cloth near the fire till a good pulsation can be felt in the heart again, when they place it in the cage. But very few—not one in hundreds—really do die, and it is as well to place the bird in the warm flannel-lined cage at once, *on its back* on the flannel, with the tail pointing towards the fire. It will generally lie there till the belly is pretty dry, when it will turn over suddenly, and hop either on the perch or the wires of the cage, taking care of itself till the feathers assume their natural appearance. Here a word of caution is necessary. The drying-cage must be very warm, the danger of chill being considerable. On the other hand, if too hot, and especially if the *wires* get hot, such neglect might cause suffering one shudders to contemplate. It is advisable, therefore, for the "better half" to keep turning the cage round to avoid this. A very much better plan is to use a wooden box open one side, and closed in every other part except a small window and the door. The open side should be covered with clean unbleached linen, and the inside lined with clean stuff and supplied with perches. Such a box may be opened to the fire till it is nicely warm, when the linen front, drawn down or shut down, will shade off all fierce glare, yet keep the temperature what is desired. Or a larger cage may be employed, and covered on all sides but that towards the fire, when it will be found that a greater distance may be preserved.

Throughout the washing the heat of the water should be kept up by judicious changes or additions, and it should also be renewed as fast as dirt or soap make it necessary. The cloths should be regularly dried and heated after being wetted, so as to be always ready; and a towel should be kept for the sole purpose of wiping the wet hands before taking up one of them: it is great loss of drying power to wet the cloths with anything but the wet birds. If a bird gets cold and shivers, it should *always* be taken in hand and carefully warmed before being placed in the drying-cage. In conclusion, we may remark that one practical lesson from a good practical washer will be more effectual than a cart-load of instructions; but if it cannot be obtained, it is well to practise on a few common birds before those of value are operated upon. Even a sparrow will answer the purpose.

As the birds get thoroughly dry, they should be gradually moved rather further off from the fire. When there are many, this is generally into another cage; and it need hardly be said that *every* cage into which a washed bird is put should be scrupulously clean. All being washed and cleaned up, it is best to draw a linen cloth over the cage and leave them for the night. In the morning, if time can be allowed, it is a good plan to put a flannel over the bottom of their cage and

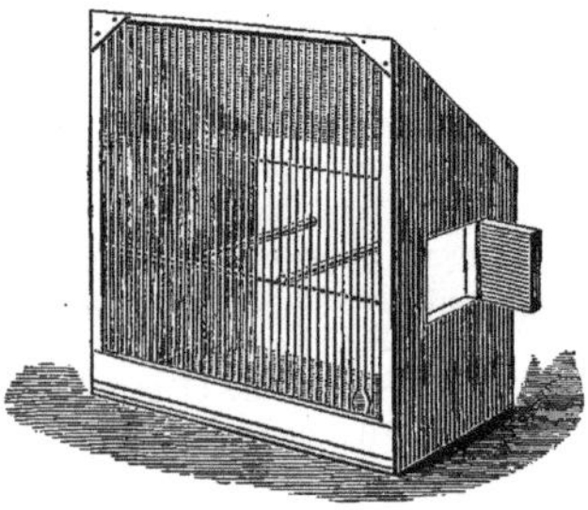

Fig. 66.

Fig. 67.

give them a natural bath, which is the surest and best way of getting the feathers quite right and restoring the natural bloom, always rather lost by washing. If, however, there is not time, or the birds will not bathe, the mouth is filled with *cold* water and "blown" or squirted in a spray through the compressed lips till they are again wringing wet. Perhaps a hollow tooth may raise objections to this process; if so, a spray-producer or fumigator, which may be purchased at any chemist's for a shilling, will perform the same office. In either case, when the birds are drenched, remove the flannel (put in to absorb the wet), wipe the perches, feed the birds, and leave them again to dry; or they may after the drenching be run into a clean dry cage. We lay great stress on clean cages, since the birds begin operations at once after a cold bath of any kind, and any dust on wires or perches is at once transferred to the head near the beak, and spoils all. The cold bathing or drenching process is called "fining," and is very necessary to showing birds in good bloom. They generally look their best a day or two after washing, and ought to be covered up to keep them from knocking themselves about in the meantime.

Specimens for exhibition should be in some sense "trained"—that is, used to seeing people in front of their cages, to having those cages lifted and handled, and to be "run" from one cage into another. The last is very important and easily taught, and its use is to save unnecessary catching, which soils the birds, often damages their plumage, and we believe, by the fright it causes, often lays the foundation of disease of the heart—all of which might be avoided by training the birds from the first to run from one cage to the other of their own accord.

Show-cages are of many patterns—too many by half; and their diversity has led to prizes being offered for better designs. Most of the new inventions thus called forth have, however, missed the mark, seeking elaborate but useless contrivances for seed and water, or in other ways missing one very essential point, that of cheapness. That some progress has been made will, however, appear from the annexed diagrams. Fig. 66 is the cage formerly used for showing Norwich and similar birds. It is a plain cage, with open front and bevelled top, thirteen or fourteen inches across the front, and five and a half inches from front to back—the standard depth of all such cages—measured outside. This cage was at first always made with ends bevelled to the back as well as the top, in order to give (as was supposed) more light; but this was awkward for packing end to end in canvas, as will be easily seen. The square end was therefore the first improvement. The next step was to make the top square also, but with a *bevelled lid inside*, and thus we have what is known as the Coventry cage, shown in Fig. 67. This is a most useful cage, the inside

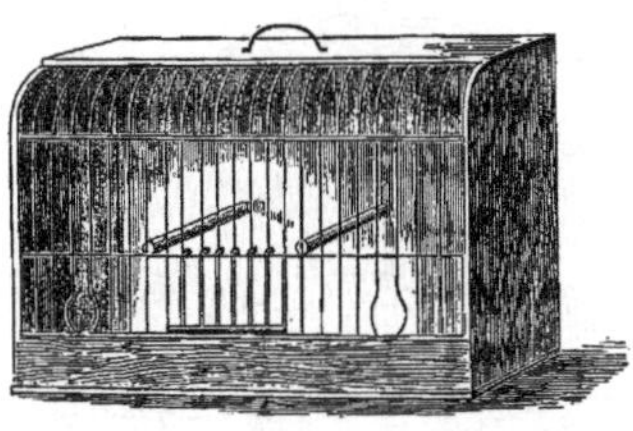

Fig. 68.

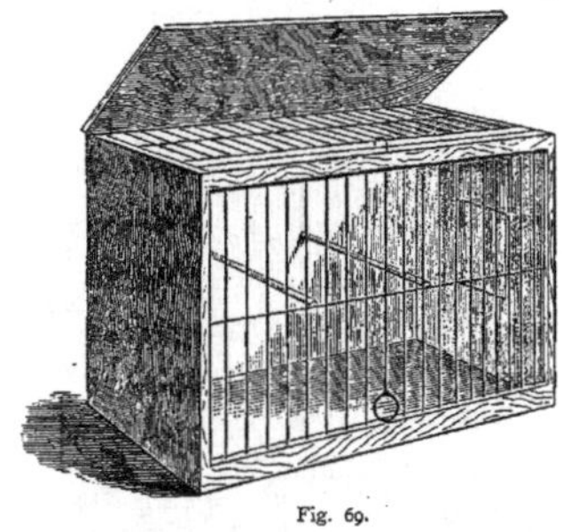

Fig. 69.

being the same as the other, while the square box top enables it either to be packed in canvas or staged in two tiers—a great advantage. It should be twelve and a half or thirteen inches from top to bottom outside, and is one of the cheapest cages made, being obtainable for 16s. 6d. per dozen. Some exhibitors, however, prefer the bevelled top, as less likely, when packed gable-fashion in the way presently explained, to have other parcels placed on top in railway transit. We consider this danger, however, more apparent than real. Fig. 68 represents a cage designed by Mr. Alden, the peculiarity of which is the half-open top, which throws more light on the birds, and hence makes such cages suitable for birds of marking; also for Lizards and crested birds. We believe, however, that *all* these various objects may be secured by the cage shown in Fig. 69, which represents a simple square cage, with a *lifting lid*, wired underneath. The lid can be lifted to throw light on the bird, or even kept propped up at an angle when another cage has not to be placed on the top, while it can be made as cheaply as the Coventry cage, and if made higher would, we believe, suit even Coppies and Belgians.

Coppies and Yorkshires are generally shown in open cages like Fig. 70; and the same cage is not unfrequently used for Belgians; but the proper Belgian cage is that shown in Fig. 71, with a domed top of open wire. We have seen a perceptible difference in what could be got out of the same Belgian in a domed cage, to what it had shown in a Coppy cage; but probably this was partly owing to habit, and partly to the greater *height* of the domed cage we saw employed for the experiment. That height or room *above the bird* is important we have been quite certain of, and hence no doubt the large and cumbrous cages described in the chapter on that variety. It is, however, usual to hold a Belgian cage against the wall, partially covered with a pocket-handkerchief; and hence we have every reason to believe that our "general purpose" cage of Fig. 69, with the top open, would, *if made high enough*, perfectly suit even the Belgian bird. We mention this point, and the reasons for our conclusions, because more uniformity of appearance at Canary shows is very desirable. For such purposes we should advise the cage being eighteen inches high, and not less than eight inches from front to back, no Belgian or Yorkshire standing well in a small space; for all other birds, twelve or thirteen inches in height, thirteen inches width, and five and a half inches depth, may be given as standard sizes.

The construction, use, and packing of Scotch Fancy cages have been described in the chapter upon that variety.

To have the cages clean and well painted is important, and the following directions on this

Fig. 70.

Fig. 71.

subject are kindly supplied by Mr. Legge, who combines a knowledge of Canaries *and* painting at Boden Street, Derby. Fancy open cages, framed with mahogany or other good wood, should first have a coat of what is sold at the colour-shops as "gold-size;" and when this is dry, apply two coats of what is known by the name of oak varnish. This will look equal to polishing, and preserve the cage. The gold-size first is necessary to make the varnish dry properly, and its omission is the cause of failure in varnishing by many amateurs. Cages such as those shown in Figs. 66 to 69 are generally blacked outside, and flatted with pale blue inside. For the outside nothing can be better than a bottle of Brunswick black; it has a good body, and will cover the bright wires, dries quickly, and is hard. The inside may be done in two ways. For the first, dissolve one ounce of Colman's white starch in a little cold water, and add boiling water in the usual manner so as to make it tolerably stiff. Then add to this one pound of whiting, powdered very fine, and a little *ultramarine* blue, of which one ounce will last for a good many paintings. Lay on with a small tool, or a good shaving-brush will answer very well, laying the colour on downwards. Care should be taken to get the real ultramarine blue and not common whitewash blue, which latter gives a greenish shade very prejudicial to the colour of the birds, especially if cayenne-fed. The starch makes this distemper wash nice and stiff, and also prevents the colour coming off. Dry in front of the fire. That is one way; but sometimes the cages are painted, and then, when they become dirty, they can be washed, and will do for several shows. Take one pound of white-lead, one ounce of "dryers," and a little blue (it will be about as much as will cover a shilling). Mix the whole up with turpentine, *without any oil;* it will then dry dead or flat, which is so necessary to give effect. Care is needed not to have the colour too blue or too light, and it is best to try a little on a piece of wood, as it looks much lighter when dry than it did in the basin. Before being done either way, new cages painted for the first time should have a coat of size, made by dissolving two ounces of glue in a pint of boiling water, and adding about a quarter of a pound of whiting. With this the cage should be first "sized" inside and out; and, when dried, sandpaper the surface smooth: the wood will not then absorb the paint or whitewash. Cages which are first given two or three coats will last several seasons, washing the inside gently with a little warm water, and the outside with a bit of rag and a drop of linseed oil; but this presumes that when done with they are wrapped in paper and packed away, so as to be kept clean for the next show. Too many put their cages away in any corner, where they have to be

Fig. 72.

hunted up, and are found more or less dusty, to the great detriment of the birds. When a cage wants a thorough cleaning, the front or back must be taken off.

The show-cages being clean and ready, the birds are transferred to them, and water-tins hung on outside. Seed-vessels are useless, a better plan being to throw about equal quantities of seed and sand on the floor of the cage: a little egg-food and maw-seed in addition help to secure a good feed before starting. Carefully see also, now, while time permits, that the labels are properly fixed to the top of each cage, checking all by the schedule; and then leave the birds, if you can, for a couple of hours to settle down. You are then ready for packing, the mode of which will depend upon the cages. Belgian and Coppy cages are often put in a bag of coarse linen made to fit, and drawn with a string round the top; then a stick is placed through the rings on the top, which are tied to the stick, say four in a row, and make a handy package. The Norwich, Coventry, or similar cages are often packed in wrappering. They are first put face to face in pairs, with two pieces of paper between them (the paper being large enough to turn over a bit and thus prevent draught), each pair being tied round the middle with string. Then three pairs, like Fig. 66, may be placed end to end on the wrapper, which is sewed up tightly by the aid of a packing-needle, leaving a corner or ear to carry by. The square-topped cages can be similarly packed in *two* tiers, thus getting as many as eight or even twelve cages together. A much better plan, however, for all such cages is a frame like that shown in Fig. 72, the cages fitting end to end in the double tray along the bottom, and resting against the centre rails *b*,*b* and *c c*. Through the bottom and end rails holes are bored for ventilation, and canvas is tacked along the bottom *a a*, projecting somewhat at the ends. This, being laced up tightly at the top and both ends, makes an admirable package. Square light boxes, or baskets like poultry baskets lined with unbleached linen, made square instead of round, also make capital packages; and such appliances save secretaries much trouble, as well as being far more secure for the birds than mere canvas. When Belgian or other open cages are sent with ordinary cages, some discretion is necessary, the lighter and weaker open cages being packed on the top. In any case, before fastening up finally, see that the water-tins, packed in flannel, are put inside the package, and also that a good supply of the proper food is included.

The words "LIVE BIRDS" should be painted as conspicuously as *possible* on the canvas or other package, independently of the show label. This last is now sent reversible by all the best-conducted shows; but it is as well to have the owner's address legibly *painted* on the box, basket, or wrapper, with a small reversible label bearing "FROM" on one side and "TO" on the other. Besides other uses, this tends to prevent loss of wrappers; which, being usually fitted to so many cages, with proper lacings, are valuable.

The exhibitor has now done with his birds; but a few hints respecting the show-room may be of use. In large shows regular staging is often erected; but a capital effect may be produced with the ordinary furniture of a school-room, or any similar hall furnished with backed seats. Raise these up on anything handy—empty barrels will do very well if nothing better offers—to the right height, back to back, and you have two rows of staging ready; and if you *can* afford the hire or otherwise of some baize or other cheap stuff, any suitable colour, and hang it over the seats, backs and all, you have an effect which cannot be surpassed, for almost nothing in the way of cost. Again, the seats being all one length, and the number of cages for each being easily calculated, the officer in charge will be able to tell almost exactly where any cage is to go as soon as the number is called out. For unpacking, a place must be selected free from draught; and as each cage is taken out of its package the operator should call out the number to the secretary, or other superintendent in charge, who will check it off his list and direct what part of the room it is to be taken to. In this way one person as checker can keep several operators at work without confusion, and save a lot of time. As soon as the package is emptied, if it is a canvas it should be folded neatly, with the *exhibitor's address outside*, and put away in the appointed place; and if food is sent, another person ought at once to see that the cages are supplied.

We paragragh one hint separately as very important. Some exhibitors send a bit of sponge in each water-tin to avoid mischief; but if not, care should be taken only to fill up the tins at first so that the birds can *just* dip their beaks in. If more is allowed, the chances are that they will begin to splash and drench themselves, and probably not be dry when the judge comes round. Many a prize has been lost through this precaution being neglected, and in particular we remember the beautiful bird known as the "Queen of Crests" being once thrown out at Coventry in this way. As soon as the class is judged, the tins may be filled up fully.

When all are staged, the secretary will of course see if any are missing, and institute inquiries accordingly; but we need not here discuss the ordinary clerical work which is common to all fancy-stock exhibitions, of whatever kind.

CHAPTER XXXII.

THE DISEASES OF CANARIES.

BY W. GORDON STABLES, M.D., CH.M., R.N.

THE ailments to which Canaries are subject are happily very few. Indeed, when properly attended to, these birds are among the healthiest and hardiest we possess; while, on the other hand, it may be safely stated that quite nine-tenths of their illnesses are induced by neglect of some kind or by over-pampering. The most common causes of disease are (1) exposure to currents of cold air; (2) the want of fresh air, as from the birds being placed in badly ventilated rooms, or high up where they are distressed by the hot burnt gas of sitting-rooms; (3) too much food, and an abuse of dainties; and (4) sour or unwholesome food, or bad water.

The medicines used in the treatment of Canary complaints are few and simple, yet to arrive at a correct diagnosis of any given case is sometimes far from easy, and a careful examination of the little patient and all its surroundings will be necessary. First and foremost, find out how the ailing bird has been fed, and note the presence in, or the absence from the cage, of green food; if it be present, examine its condition. Then see what state the bird's bowels are in—whether loose or constipated; and next turn your attention to the bird itself, and before you attempt to handle it, observe the position in which it sits or perches—that alone often gives a clue to internal troubles. Listen to any chest-sounds it may emit, such as coughing, panting, or wheezing. You may next handle the bird, for the purpose of examining the vent and abdomen. Canaries ought to be handled as gently as possible. Do not, if possible, alarm it, or cause it to flutter all round the cage; approach the hand gently, then seize it with one quick pounce, and hold it with the necessary degree of firmness.

The medicines you administer ought to be of the best quality procurable. There are two kinds of castor oil for example; and while the best is one of the safest and most effectual aperients we possess, the coarser kind may set up irritation of the bowels, which it will be difficult to subdue.

DISEASES OF THE RESPIRATORY ORGANS.

Consumption, the *phthisis* of medical practitioners, is probably the most surely fatal of any of these, and although it may be cured in its first stage, it always produces death if neglected. It is brought on, in the first instance, from exposure to cold or draughts, and especially damp draughts. Or the bird may have caught cold after its bath; and this is very likely to happen about the moulting season, when, being in a weakened condition, too much care can hardly be taken of a Canary. Some birds are more prone to consumption than others, and there is no doubt at all that the disease is hereditary. The illness may be confounded with asthma, but in this latter complaint the attacks are more periodic in their nature.

The symptoms of phthisis in its earlier stage are those of a common cold; and this teaches us never to neglect the trifling ailments of the chest our birds may suffer from. There is cough or wheezing in phthisis, and the bird is less lively, more languid, than usual. When such symptoms as these are observed, time should be taken by the forelock; for they cannot continue for any length of time without inducing great weakness, and a loss of flesh amounting at times to emaciation; when usually some secondary ailment, such as acute diarrhœa, supervenes and ends the life of the bird.

The treatment resolves itself into the constitutional, and that directed to the relief of the symptoms. The food should be changed, and in addition to the ordinary seeds something more nourishing should be given, such as the yolk of a hard-boiled egg, nicely grated and mixed with powdered luncheon biscuit. The bird should likewise be kept in a warm room—a room, however, that is daily and thoroughly ventilated; the cage may be partially covered up, especially that portion of it which is opposite to where any draughts might come from. A small dose of warm castor oil—say two drops, or three at most—will do good at the commencement. The water, which must be fresh every day, should have a morsel of gum-arabic dissolved in it, and a little glycerine as well. White bread, a day old, first soaked in cold water, then mixed with warm new milk, should also be given as a change of diet, never forgetting that it is apt to turn sour and derange the digestion; it should, therefore, be freshly made morning and evening.

Should this simple treatment not have the desired effect, stronger remedies must be had recourse to. The drinking-water may be turned into a kind of cough mixture, by adding thereto a little paregoric (twenty drops), or five drops of solution of muriate of morphia, a tea-spoonful of glycerine, and a morsel of gum-arablc. The bowels, if not opened sufficiently by the glycerine, should be kept moderately open, by the addition to the water of about as much carbonate of magnesia as will lie on a fourpenny-bit. In phthisis there is often an irritable or quickened action of the heart, which may be controlled by the use of tincture of digitalis, not more than ten minims in the water daily. A drop or two of cod-liver oil twice a day also does much good. Tonics, too, will be beneficial, and of these iron in some form will be found as good as any. A rusty nail, or twenty-five drops of the tincture of the perchloride of iron, may be put in the water daily. If diarrhœa sets in we fear there is little chance of saving the bird; the glycerine would in this case have to be stopped, and the ailment treated by astringents, as laid down under the heading of that disease.

We recommend *ordinary catarrh colds* and *coughs* to be treated as if they really were, as they often are, symptomatic of the first stage of consumption.

Asthma is another chest-complaint that Canaries are subject to; and as it may arise from a variety of causes, its treatment is often very unsatisfactory, and in its chronic form it may be said to be incurable. There is a hereditary tendency to this disease in many of our birds, but it is also the result oftentimes of exposure to cold or draughts. Improper feeding will likewise produce it, as well as over-feeding. It is also sometimes associated with a deranged state of the bowels, or indigestion. There is little difficulty in diagnosing this troublesome complaint; the periodic nature of the attacks, the difficulty of breathing, the wheezing and distress of the little patient are symptoms that are, alas! but too familiar to many of us.

Great care should be taken of birds liable to attacks of asthma. They should be kept in a warm atmosphere, and free from draughts and damp, and the food should be nutritious and easy of digestion, such as arrowroot biscuits and eggs, grated as recommended for consumption. The diet, too, should be frequently changed, but hemp-seed ought to be avoided—it is too stimulating in its nature. A due allowance of fresh green food should be given, and it must be changed every day, for anything that produces irritation of the digestive canal, is very likely to induce an attack of this disorder. Our whole aim and object, if we would cure asthma or prevent its return, is to improve the general health of the bird. With this end in view, the bowels should be regulated by the occasional addition to the water of a little carbonate of magnesia and from ten to fifteen drops of tincture of conium. At the commencement of an attack, in addition to opening the bowels in this gentle way, some antispasmodic expectorant should be administered. Some give the ethereal tincture of lobelia, with paregoric. We ourselves give preference to the simple tincture, ten drops to a wine-glassful of water, and double that quantity of *Spiritus ætheris compositus*, usually called Hoffman's anodyne. The addition, too, of a little glycerine can do nothing but good. Iodide of potassium, a few grains in the daily water, might do good in old-standing cases; our experience of this treatment, however, is not yet sufficient to warrant its use in all. Tonics should be given after the attack; iron in some form we especially recommend, and to it may be added a few drops—ten to fifteen, or even twenty—of the compound tincture of gentian.

This treatment is sure to do good; fresh cases it is pretty certain to cure, and chronic ones to ameliorate. Be especially careful of asthmatical birds in cold, damp, or foggy weather.

Loss of Voice.—This is a common complaint with Canaries, and in our opinion nine-tenths of the cases are caused by exposure to the cold. If they are allowed to moult in a draughty place, should nothing worse happen to them, you will often find that on attempting to resume their usual song, however much they may strain, no music will flow. We do not find such cases difficult to treat. It may be as well at first to give a drop or two of castor oil, then put a small tea-spoonful of glycerine in the water, a bit of gum-arabic as big as a large pea, and twenty drops of paregoric. Let the diet be a little more generous, giving some good German paste, with a dust of cayenne on it, and a supply of lettuce-leaf. There is nothing else required, unless some grated egg.

DISEASES OF THE DIGESTIVE ORGANS.

Diarrhœa, or looseness, is usually brought about by errors in diet, causing irritation of the digestive canal. Green food, if given in too large quantities, will produce diarrhœa. It should not be too wet either, and if it is left decaying about the cage, and thus eaten, it may cause the death of the bird. Bad, unfresh, or unwholesome water is another frequent cause of this complaint; so is stale egg, or bread-and-milk that has turned sour. Exposure to cold, by sending the blood to the internal organs, and stopping the natural perspiration, is one more source of diarrhœa; while, again, the disease is often induced from an overflow of bile, which is a laxative naturally.

The stools are generally watery, and contain shreds of half-digested food. If there is much irritation of the alimentary canal, the fæces will have an unpleasant sour odour. This disorder is very weakening, and cannot prevail long without causing emaciation, and probably death. When a Canary is attacked by diarrhœa, it ought to be at once turned into a clean dry cage, and hung in a well-ventilated room, where it may obtain warmth without being deprived of fresh wholesome air. Its food ought to be changed; luncheon or arrowroot biscuits soaked in new milk should be given, and the purity of the bird's drinking-water seen to.

As diarrhœa is so often caused by the lurking in the system of some offending matter, which the looseness is merely an effort of nature to expel, a couple of drops of pure warm castor oil should begin the treatment. When the oil has had time to operate, we must try by healing remedies gently to check the diarrhœa. To this end a little prepared chalk and some fresh vegetable charcoal should be mixed with the biscuit food, or the chalk only may be used, and a little powdered loaf sugar, while a small portion of gum may be added to the drinking-water. Should this fail to check the purging, about fifteen drops each of the elixir of vitriol and tincture of opium may be added to the drinking-water; or a portion—say two tea-spoonfuls—of any ordinary chalk-mixture. If the stools are very watery and offensive, and an inflammatory or congested state of the mucous membrane suspected, ipecacuanha and opium in conjunction will do good—say of the tincture of laudanum fifteen drops, of the wine of ipecacuanha thirty drops, with three or four grains of nitrate of potash, to a wine-glassful of drinking-water. About twenty drops of tincture of catechu, added to the bird's chalk-mixture, is often very effectual in checking the purging. Some care will be required of the bird after he is cured of the diarrhœa; add the grated yolk of hard-boiled egg to the food, and give a bitter tonic for about a week. (Gentian is extolled by some; it is an excellent bird tonic, but it should be remembered that it has a tendency to relax the bowels, and should therefore be avoided in treating *this* complaint.) We find cascarilla bark do well. The infusion is made by steeping half an ounce of it in five ounces of boiling water for an hour, and afterwards straining. The dose is a dessert-spoonful to the drinking-water. Other tonics which we have used are the dilute nitro-hydrochloric acid, ten drops to the bitter water, and Schacht's liquor of bismuth; and we should not forget calumba infusion. It is made like the infusion of cascarilla, only with cold water instead of boiling. It is a capital reinvigorating tonic.

Constipation.—This is an ailment from which Canaries sometimes suffer, resulting in loss of appetite and general dulness of the bird. It is usually caused by some error in the diet, and although in bad cases a little oil should be given to effect relief, permanent cure of the complaint should be effected through the medium of the food. Groundsel, watercress, and other green foods may be given in the summer-time; and the tender leaves of young dandelion, and in winter German paste, with a little cayenne and sugar, will do good. Give also in winter a slice of ripe apple, or a slice or two of well-boiled carrot. The water in either case ought to be sweetened with glycerine, which is an excellent tonic and laxative; and a dessert-spoonful of the infusion of gentian also added to the drink.

Inflammation of the Bowels.—This disease, which by the medical practitioner is termed *enteritis*, is one of the most serious by which a bird can be attacked. The causes most likely to produce it are over-eating, especially of too stimulating food, partaking of bread-and-milk which has become sour, or green food which is in a state of decomposition. Again, the water for drinking, which ought to be *fresh every morning*, is sometimes left for days. If it has not been very good when placed in the drinking-glass, and afterwards receives the addition of particles of green food, &c., it becomes next thing to an irritant poison, and is very likely to cause inflammation.

The symptoms are those of much suffering and acute pain in the regions affected. The bird is dull and drooping, cares little to move about, has no note, and often lies on the belly on his perch; there is loss of appetite and urgent thirst, the bowels are usually very costive; but at times this may be the reverse, and we get diarrhœa, with frequent straining at stool. An additional symptom sometimes present is frequent vomiting of the offensive products of inflammation, or of bile and mucus. Manual examination, which must be conducted very gently, will reveal a swollen and distended condition of the lower part of the abdomen, with some change of colour, varying, according to the stage of the disorder, from pale to dark red, amounting in very dangerous cases to an almost black hue.

If taken at once, inflammation of the bowels may be cured, but the treatment must be decided. As we advised in diarrhœa, let the bird be put in a clean dry cage and hung in a warm well-ventilated room, and the food changed. The latter must be entirely non-stimulating, but at the same time nourishing; arrowroot biscuit, mixed with new milk, to which may be added a little moist sugar. This should be all the bird has for a day or two. The bowels—if constipation be present, and if the case has been seen at the commencement—should be opened with two or three drops of pure oil; but if much inflammation has taken place, purgatives should not be employed.

Counter-irritation will do much good, and it cannot be applied by a better plan than that of painting the lower part of the abdomen, by means of a camel's-hair pencil, with warm turpentine. This gives relief, and should be repeated once or twice if necessary.

Opium is of great service in the treatment of this complaint. Place therefore every morning, in the fresh water, thirty drops of ipecacuanha wine, and fifteen of laudanum, along with a bit of gum-arabic, and two or three grains of nitrate of potash. But in more severe cases we prefer opium in conjunction with belladonna—say ten drops of each of the tinctures in the drinking-water—a little gum, and a little sweetening of glycerine. The food must be light—arrowroot biscuits and warm new milk, frequently changed.

If the bird exhibits a tendency to sink or collapse, there will be little chance of saving him, but a little brandy may be added to the other mixture as a last resource. If he gets better, tonics are required, and one small dose of castor oil; this latter often acts like a charm, after the inflammation has been subdued. The best tonic is the infusion of calumba, a dessert-spoonful to the water, with a few drops of tincture of iron, or simply a rusty nail. Give at the same time a little egg with the food, and before he returns to the ordinary diet, scald and bruise his rape, and also give a portion of poppy-seed.

Inflammation of the Liver.—This is the disease called *hepatitis* by medical men, and we have reason to believe that many more birds die of it every week than people are aware of. It is a very dangerous illness, and often proves speedily fatal. Prevention is far more easy than its cure when established. It is caused by keeping the bird in too hot a room or position, by giving him too little fresh air, and feeding on too nutritious and stimulating a diet, such as hemp-seed, dainties, &c. The symptoms of the chronic form are somewhat obscure, but after death dissection reveals an abnormally large liver. In the acute form of the disease there are the usual signs of inflammation. The bird is in evident distress and pain, nervous, thirsty, hot, and restless; while there is the absence of cough on the one hand that would indicate lung mischief, and the absence on the other of the dark redness always present more or less in inflammation of the bowels. This, with a knowledge of previous feeding and treatment, and a complete history of the case, makes diagnosis comparatively easy.

The treatment followed by many men who have had large experience, and stated by them to be carried out with some degree of success, is that by slight depletion of blood at the commencement by pulling out some of the tail and flight feathers, succeeded by the administration of calomel in infinitesimal doses, with or without antimonial powder. It has not in *our* hands been so successful as to cause us to recommend it. We mention it, however. On the other hand, we believe in supporting the little patient from the beginning, giving aperients to relieve the circulation through the liver, and opium to remove the pain and restlessness. As much carbonate of magnesia as will lie on a sixpence may be placed in the water, but we recommend a dose of oil to commence with—give three drops. When the bowels have been well acted on, put in the water daily fifteen drops of tincture of opium and a tea-spoonful of dandelion-juice. When the pain has subsided, you may omit the laudanum and continue the juice for some little time. The diet during the illness should be light and nourishing, such as arrowroot and the best new milk, and towards convalescence occasionally a little grated egg and stale bread-crumb may be given. Tonics—gentian and iron, or a small tea-spoonful of quinine wine in the drinking-water—will probably be needed to complete the cure.

In chronic cases the plainest food only should be allowed, the bath not being omitted, a small quantity of dandelion-juice in the water, and about twice a week a senna-leaf or two as well, and a little glycerine.

MISCELLANEOUS AILMENTS, AND ACCIDENTS.

Fits.—These are of several kinds, and depend upon different causes. Birds that are either constitutionally weak or weakened by injudicious treatment are most subject to them. Gluttony and the use of over-stimulating food predispose to fits; so, by weakening the heart, does injudicious pairing, as by keeping a male bird with too many hens during the breeding season. As the treatment we adopt is nearly the same in all cases, we need do no more here than give the symptoms of two kinds. The first is *syncope*, or fainting, during which the heart's action is all but suspended. It is nearly always caused by fright, as by attempting to catch the bird, or letting anything strike the cage. The little sufferer's cage should be held in the open air, and the bird sprinkled with cold water; that will revive it.

Another kind of fit is apoplectic in its nature, and, in addition to the usual causes, is often brought on by the thoughtless habit of hanging the cage in a hot, blistering sun. This is more dangerous and deadly, and probably smelling-salts will be needed, as well as the application of cold water, to revive the bird. But whatever the nature of the fit, the bird subject to it will require the most carefully regulated diet and the plainest of food, with now and then a drop or two of castor oil. For the fainting-fit, give bark and iron tonic; for the apoplectic, bark alone.

Surfeit is a name given to a kind of exanthematous disorder. There is irritation of the skin, and a slight eruption, and the bird gets gradually bald. The cause, so far as we yet can tell, is an error in the feeding; and a return to the natural diet, with some opening medicine (Epsom salts is best—a few grains in the water), the exhibition of green food (a little lemon-juice and three or four grains of chlorate of potash should also be placed in the drinking-water), will not fail to remove it. The head should be anointed with the purest, simplest ointment you can get.

Pip.—This is a meaningless term applied to a small swelling on the bird's rump. The tumour really is caused by the obliteration, for the time being, of the excretory canal of the lubricating gland placed there. When it is seen to contain matter, it should be opened with a new sewing-needle, and a little cold cream rubbed gently over it. Then give an aperient, and keep the cage very clean.

Cramp.—This is a common complaint among birds, especially among such as are kept in a filthy state and in small "poky" cages. It may proceed, too, from indigestion; but from whatever causes it arises, it should be looked upon as merely symptomatic. Give the bird a few drops of castor oil, and put a little laudanum in the water for a day or two. If in the limbs, it may be removed by immersing them in warm water, and afterwards hanging the cage in a comfortable place quite away from all draughts.

The *Claws* of Canaries often require attending to, and at times even the beak gets elongated, and prevents them from feeding with comfort. The cure is to shorten the claws or beak with a pair of sharp nail-scissors; but it should be done carefully, and too much should not be taken off.

Sore Feet.—Clean the feet, get rid of all source of irritation, such as a dirty cage, &c. The feet, after being carefully scraped, should be washed, and afterwards anointed with cold cream. The bird is then to be placed in a well-cleaned cage, and seen to every day until the feet are well. It is a very painful and distressing complaint.

Fractured Limbs.—Take all perches down, and fill the bottom of the cage with hay. Trust to nature to do the rest.

Accidents to the Joints.—These sometimes occur, and are followed by painful inflammation, which must be subdued by frequently bathing the parts in hot water, and afterwards applying a little tincture of opium. At the same time a little Epsom salts put in the water will help to reduce the swelling.

Wounds.—These are the result of accident, and are most common about the feet. The bird must be caught, and the feet carefully washed in warm water; the wound should then be touched with some astringent to favour healing. The sore or wound must be seen to every day, and twice a day, until it is perfectly healed. A weak solution of sulphate of zinc is a good astringent—say about five grains to the ounce of water—or the wound may be touched with wetted alum, or Friar's balsam, or with tincture of myrrh. But whichever is used, perfect cleanliness must not be neglected, and the perch and other portions of the cage kept clean.

Wounds in other parts of the body are best treated on somewhat similar principles, but for these I recommend for antiseptic purposes a wash of carbolic acid lotion and water. A couple of tea-spoonfuls of the strong lotion which chemists make should be thrown into a cupful of cold spring water, and the surface of the wound washed daily therewith. If the surface of the wound looks unhealthy, stimulation is necessary, and for this purpose the sulphate of zinc lotion, already recommended, will do, or the sulpho-carbolate of zinc may be used, in the proportion of three grains to the ounce of water.

Ulceration may be checked by a weak solution of chloride of zinc, or by this lotion: two ounces of water, twenty drops of the dilute nitric acid, and ten grains of extract of opium; this relieves the pain while it cools the surface.

While birds are suffering from wounds or any suppurating sore, they should be liberally fed and kept warm, but at the same time have plenty of pure fresh air.

Pest.—I apply this term, in lieu of a better, to a kind of fever, or plague almost, that sometimes breaks out in bird-rooms where a large quantity of Canaries are crowded together. Death often takes place very rapidly in such cases, and the feathered ranks are thinned by the dozen. The causes of this pest I attribute to the neglect of sanitation and the common laws of hygiene, the want of pure air and cleanliness, and the leaving of decayed vegetable matter about the cages or in the bird-room.

When such an outbreak takes place, no time should be lost; the cages should be at once thoroughly cleaned and disinfected, and the birds removed into another room where they can get fresh air and a moderate amount of sunshine. Some mild aperient should be given, and a tea-spoonful of good brandy placed in the drinking-water, with a few drops of paregoric. The food should be light and nutritious, and Sanitas powder should be placed in the bottom of the cage and scattered all round the room. Afterwards every cage should be thoroughly prepared with the same care as you would a breeding-cage, and the bird-room itself completely cleaned and disinfected.

In all our dealings with Canaries we should be as gentle as possible, and in their more severe illnesses regularity in giving the medicines, and sticking unflinchingly to the plan of treatment that seems necessary, will generally pull the worst cases through.

Every one who has a bird-room should possess a small box or cabinet, containing the following drugs:—Castor oil, gum-arabic, glycerine, carbonate of magnesia, cod-liver oil, prepared chalk, vegetable charcoal, nitrate of potash, gentian root, cascarilla and calumba barks, dandelion-juice, Epsom salts, vinum ipecacuanhæ, elixir of vitriol, Hoffman's anodyne; and the following tinctures —Tinctura ferri, tinctura camph. co. (paregoric), tinct. catechu, tinct. belladonnæ, tinct. opii (laudanum), tinct. conii, tinct. gentianæ, and tinct. lobeliæ. A pestle and mortar, a minim measure, and small camel's-hair brush will also be found useful.

CHAPTER XXXIII.

THE SONG CANARY.

BY LEWIS WRIGHT.

WE have seen that the development of the Canary has taken place in many totally distinct directions, which have been for the most part carried out by distinct classes or communities. Colour, marking, shape, attitude, size, and crest have all in turn been cultivated with wonderful success. It only remains to see what has been done in respect of the bird's song. To thousands of families the Canary is, after all, chiefly known as a *singing* bird; and such will like to know what has been done to develop *that* quality, and by whom. The answers to these questions will probably be found as interesting as any of the foregoing chapters.

As we have had to go to the Continent already for one of the most curious and marked varieties of the Exhibition Canary—for that triumph of attitude or "position" which is due to Belgian breeders—it will not surprise even the reader to whom the subject is new, to be told that the Song Canary in its perfection is a creation of Germany. It has been developed by generations of careful training and careful breeding, and the best specimens are almost confined to one district in the Harz Mountains. First in importance among the Harz towns as a source of supply stands St. Andreasberg; but several other places, such as Duderstadt, also breed many birds. Besides this district, however, Song Canaries are largely bred in Hesse-Cassel, Thuringia, Brunswick, Hanover, round Berlin, at Nordhausen, and in many other places; also in Baden and the Tyrol, which last localities at one time nearly took the lead. Of late some fair Song Canaries have been bred in Spain, but on the average these birds—which chiefly go to America—are decidedly inferior to the German strains. Malaga is perhaps the largest centre of the Spanish trade.

Of late years the quality of the German songsters imported into England has fallen off very seriously, and it is much more difficult than it was some time ago to obtain a really first-class bird. The reasons for this are not far to seek. According to Herr Reiche, of Hanover, the foreign demand was once confined to Russia, England, and Holland, which purchased unitedly about 7,000 birds per annum; while Germany, including Austria, took probably about 10,000 more. But since the through lines of steamers from Bremen and Hamburgh have been established, an immense traffic has sprung up with both North and South America, and these countries have been known to absorb in some years over 100,000 birds—all cocks, or presumed to be so. The consequence has been a keen competition for birds, which have been bred in larger numbers to meet the demand, and, as a consequence, with less discrimination. Still further, however, the large buyers formerly used to visit the Harz district about the month of October, when the breeders were able to select their breeding-stock with proper discrimination, and—what is of quite equal importance—choose their very best songsters to keep as teachers for the new stock. But the competition amongst buyers has gradually led these to pay their visits earlier and earlier, until now they often appear in July, when the birds have not learnt to sing, and when real selection amongst them is therefore impossible. The consequence is that many of the best singers—which would have been kept at home under the old *régime*—are allowed to depart in the crowd, and their work in keeping up the strain is lost. Still further, the difficulty of getting really good birds has made the dealers who supply Germany much more particular, so that very few but second or third-rate ones now find their way to England, the Germans being much greater connoisseurs in Canary song, and willing to pay higher prices for such birds as please them. Thus, a great Berlin dealer will purchase, say, a hundred birds of one known breeder at 9s. or 10s. a head wholesale; these he sorts and tests at leisure, selling at various prices according to the quality of the song, and obtaining for one or two of the best as much as £4 each. Few English buyers would dream of such a price, and the English market, therefore, fails to attract the better class of birds; such as do reach our shores being in almost every case brought over after private selection. It is not meant that many *good* songsters may not be found in England; but the highest German standard is *very* high. It has been, for instance, estimated by experts that amongst the 30,000 or more young cocks bred every year at St. Andreasberg, only forty or fifty stand in the very first class; and one of the most celebrated breeders in that town, Herr Trute, whilst selling a hundred birds to one Berlin dealer at 9s. per head, sold to the same dealer his best single birds—selected by himself—at 30s. to £3 each. What the dealer would sell the *best* of these for in Berlin can only be guessed.

There are supposed to be about four hundred families who breed Song Canaries in the one town of St. Andreasberg, and the money value of the trade to the town was estimated a few years since at £9,000 per annum. Only ten per cent. of the whole stock, however, have any reputation for qualities valued by the connoisseur, which obviously demand certain natural gifts, including a musical ear, to keep up. Good breeders make a tolerably certain but very moderate profit, and it is obviously a labour of love as much as a commercial undertaking. From a return given by a breeder of repute—Herr Maschke—to Herr Brandner, of Stettin, it appears that out of a hundred Canaries he sold the great bulk at 12s. to 18s. each, one or two at 30s. and 60s., and some at lower prices; and that, after calculating all expenses, his profit was about £12 on the hundred birds. This seems a very moderate return for the assiduous training, as well as care and attention required. In fact, few people have any idea of the amount of education a trained German Song Canary has gone through. The object is to get certain combinations of trills or modulated melody, with deep flute-like tones; and excellence consists, not in loudness or length of song, or even quality of mere voice, so much as in a continuous repetition of certain varied strains. Loud notes between these are not regarded as meritorious, but as decided faults, as are most short detached notes, however soft; and even the well-known nightingale notes are less valued than certain trills or passages of melody. Some birds have a compass of four octaves, and will execute various shakes in the most perfect style; but it is always desired that a bird, whatever strains it has mastered—and few good songsters have less than three or four—should *end* its song by a succession of soft, flute-like, descending tones. The most prized melodies are seldom learnt by a young bird in less than six months, and only by quiet birds; the more excitable ones bursting into those detached, powerful notes, which are held to impair the song. Of course it requires a very correct ear and immense experience to select the better performers; for only a few of the very choicest birds are ever tried separately, and the immense majority are picked out of a general chorus which would be distracting to a stranger.

The magnitude of the trade in German Canaries testifies of itself to an immense mortality, and this is the fact. There are several reasons for it. In the first place, the competition has led breeders to employ artificial warmth to hasten nesting; and Harz Canaries are now bred in a temperature ranging from 65° to 72°, and even higher. It is inevitable that the respiratory organs should become very delicate, and that when they are removed to a damper climate and a temperature averaging say 60°, many should perish of bronchitis and consumption. Dr. Karl Russ—the great German authority on all cage-birds—has again and again commented on this evil, and urged breeders to reduce the temperature of their bird-rooms, at all events after moulting; but hitherto his remonstrances have had little effect. Long before death ensues, partial or total loss of voice is of course experienced; and from this reason there is no doubt many persons have never had a good idea of what the song of a trained Canary really is—it has been already *lost* when they purchased the bird. It will be seen how important it is, in any case, to very gradually accustom a German Canary to our colder climate, and above all to keep it from draughts and *variations* of temperature. On the contrary, most people make the matter even worse, by hanging their bird high up, in or near a window. The neighbourhood of the window causes draught and cold; and in the evening, on the other hand, the hot burnt gas of the room causes an atmosphere almost insupportable. The very owner could not support it, as he or she will find if the head be kept for a few minutes close to the cage after the gas has been lit for some hours: how much less can the wretched Canary, reared in a warm but uniformly heated room. The poor bird does *not* stand it, but speedily dies; and moreover an open window is the very worst place that can be chosen to preserve the beauty of the song, as the birds have always been accustomed to be kept covered up or in the dark. Once again, the food is radically changed. The Germans depend chiefly on their *summer* rape-seed, as it is called; and are very particular in selecting certain mild qualities grown in particular districts, and not too old. The hens are almost confined to this; the cocks have, in addition, some bread-crumbs and egg. English purchasers, if they give rape at all, generally give common bitter seed, which spoils the voice; but very often they substitute the usual canary and hemp seed, and add sugar and cake, which Germans consider spoils the voice. Once more, the Song Canary requires the stimulus of competition, which should be with birds that sing the *same strains*. Unless they have this, all but a few very old birds gradually forget what they have learnt, and degenerate into ordinary singing-birds.

We have explained these matters, because the Canary song, in perfection, is a thing never to be forgotten, and not one in a thousand has ever heard it, for the reasons given. There is no doubt that birds could be trained in England as well as in the Harz districts; but there are at present not the materials. On the average, the English have not, to begin with, such a musical ear as the Germans; but chiefly, most of them have never even heard—much less possessed in perfection—the really best birds. Those they think so much of are at best only second-rate ones; and only now and then, when a *German* allows his friends to hear such as he has selected in his own country for his own private enjoyment, and preserved in perfection by German treatment, can the best German song be estimated correctly.

For the following remarks upon Song Canaries in England, we are indebted to Mr. W. Evans, of Manchester:—

"The first portion of these remarks are addressed to such as purchase a single bird for its song, knowing little more about it than that it requires seed and water. It is, perhaps, the latter end of November, and some thousands of German birds have been imported into this country, and have been spread over London, Manchester, Liverpool, Birmingham, Leeds, and other large towns. The purchaser calls upon a dealer, and selects one out of a number that are placed before him in small wooden cages with seed and water inside; and most likely the dealer sells another cage to keep the bird in upon arrival at its new home. There is joy in the household; and when it carols forth its song, it is universally admitted that there never was such a singer before.

It is put into its new cage, which has a seed-box and water-glass hanging outside, as used for our English birds. All goes well the first day; but the second morning you find the bird looks unwell, and moves about in a restless manner along the front wires of the cage. At night he is worse, and rolled up like a ball of feathers at the bottom of the cage; and the next morning they tell you that 'poor little Dickey is dead.' Dead! and all for want of one word of instruction from the dealer. These birds have always been accustomed to having their seed and water *inside the cage*, and lack the instinct necessary to put their heads through the round apertures made in front of the cage, so that your bird literally died of starvation, with seed and water before its eyes. For the first week after being changed out of the tiny cage, therefore, seed and water must be kept inside the cage, as well as hanging them at the usual places outside; and the bird should be enticed to put his head through the apertures by placing small bits of watercress part way through them, until he has acquired the habit of putting his head through and partaking of his food.

"The question of food is a very important one, and cannot be too much studied. When the birds first arrive in this country, they are, to all appearance, fed upon summer rape-seed; but the importer, anxious for them to sing well and bring a good price from the dealer, gives them once a day a plentiful supply of hard-boiled egg, finely chopped and mixed with crushed rusks; and the dealer also feeds liberally upon the egg-food. There is not sufficient support in seed and water to keep the birds up to that high state of health and song which is requisite; yet the egg is too stimulating for a general diet, and also liable to bring on constipation. As soon, therefore, as a bird is purchased, a cake should be made in the following manner:—Take one egg and beat it well up into a froth. In a separate vessel beat up a piece of fresh butter until it is quite soft and white, and then add it to the egg. Add one table-spoonful of Austrian or biscuit flour, one tea-spoonful of crushed lump sugar, one tea-spoonful of baking powder. Spare no pains in beating all up well together, and bake in a sharp oven in a shrimp-pot well greased with butter. The above should be crumbled fine, and given mixed with a good sprinkling of maw-seed.

"It is often found that a bird, a few weeks after arrival in this country, begins to show symptoms of constipation by sudden twitches at the vent. When this is observed, take a piece of soft stale bread, and drop it into a basin of milk that has stood over-night and has the cream upon it; then take it out with a tea-spoon, letting the cream adhere to it, and sprinkle a little maw-seed over it. Give a little at once, taking care to remove any that is left before going sour. This will act as a mild aperient, and leaves no ill-effects. In cases where the bird becomes hoarse, a little stale bread steeped in warm milk, and a little honey dropped upon it while warm, will be found very beneficial. Should this be found too thin, thicken it with a little crushed butter-biscuit until it forms a thick paste, and then place a little at the ends of the perches.

"So much for the ordinary household singing Canary. In many counties, but most frequently in Lancashire, singing contests take place during the winter months among *fanciers* of these birds. There are two kinds of competition: one for the bird that sings the most in a given time, called 'quantity;' the other for the bird that sings the sweetest song, pieces his song well together, and glides softly from one note to another—this is called 'quality.' For these matches the birds undergo a course of training and feeding. The mode generally adopted is to begin about a week before the intended competition takes place, and gradually exclude the light from the bird by placing cloths over the cage, or better still, by putting one cloth over the cage and placing him in a dark cupboard. All other birds should be put out of hearing, so as not to excite him to waste his song, and three times each day he should be taken out and allowed to feed and sing for a few minutes. Each evening, about the time that he will have to compete, he should be again taken out and hung up for as long a time as he will have to sing when competing (without seed and water). When the time has expired, fresh food and water should be again given to him, and he is placed in the cupboard until the next day. In addition to keeping his seed-box well supplied with mixed summer rape and canary seed, he should be fed freely upon the finely-chopped yolk of egg (the white being heavy, and not so easy of digestion), a little crushed butter-biscuit, and maw-seed, all well mixed, and an occasional sprig of water-cress. By following this method you will find the bird will soon begin to sing whilst holding the cage in your hand, and is almost sure to begin as soon as hung up for competition. After the match is over, the bird should be fed upon seed and water, a little watercress, and the cake as given above. In 'quality' singing, two birds are generally hung up together, a judge having been chosen for each side, and a referee sits between them, who, in case the judges do not agree as to the quality of a bird's song, gives the final decision. The names of the principal notes in Lancashire are peculiar, such as the call, the din, the blubber (or water-bubble), and many others. These notes should be gone through without break, the bird gliding easily from one to the other. Should a bird come off one note to chapping or chain notes he would not score, being no longer considered a 'quality' bird.

"Perhaps no kind of Canary is more easily bred than the German. The hens, as a rule, are good mothers, always active and alert to feed their young. The same system should be followed of feeding during breeding-time as given in the preceding pages for Norwich birds; but when the young are old enough to feed themselves, the cocks should be changed into small single cages, and placed so as not to see each other. Three or four of the very best last season's birds that can be got (called schoolmasters) should be placed in the room to sing, taking care to have no harsh or discordant sounds within hearing of the young birds. The schoolmasters should be covered up at night, to keep them from falling into early moult, and stopping their song at the very time when most needed. By the time the young birds have finished moult, and their voices have broken, it will be found that all sing the same song, or nearly so, as the schoolmasters. Much depends upon the training; and if the same attention was paid to song in England as in Germany, there would be a marked improvement in our English Canaries' vocal abilities. A very good cross is to pair Norwich hens and German cocks, as they produce fine plumage, a beautiful song, and much hardier birds than the pure German."

It will be seen that Mr. Evans rather differs from German authority in respect to the food, the German breeders considering sugar very injurious; but it is very possible a little of such food may be more necessary in our colder climate, and a final judgment on such points can only be formed after wider experience than any one we know in this country can afford. We should also advise the breeder to keep to the German strains rather than cross with the Norwich, which has a note any German fancier would consider unbearably harsh, though the voice of many certainly sounds very fair to English ears. If crossing at all be deemed necessary, we believe the best cross would be that with the wild type of Canary, which can always be obtained with a little trouble, and possesses a vocal organ of great vigour, yet of an agreeable quality. But we have every reason to believe that the German birds would lose their delicacy under a more natural treatment, and there is no difficulty in procuring German hens. The weaker sex is, of course, produced in about equal numbers to the cocks; and it is stated, on German authority, that about a quarter of them are passed off on the dealers as cocks. Every large dealer, almost, will therefore be able to supply hens; and not improbably the breeder may be able to obtain several cocks which have the same song, and which the marks on their cages prove have been bred by the same breeder and trained together. If he can get a hen or two whose cage bears the same mark, he has got hold probably of *one strain*, and is pretty sure to do well if it is a good one. Others select the hens first, asking for those of known breeders, and then seeking for one or more cocks whose cages bear the same mark. All the cocks whose song is good are then bred from, except one or two of the very best, which are used as tutors for the young ones, only birds of the same song being allowed in one room. A separate room should always, if possible, be provided for teaching the young birds, which may be hung up close together, but must be entirely prevented from seeing one another, which distracts their attention. It is very necessary to prevent a young one hearing any one but the tutor-bird, as bad notes may be picked up in a single day sufficient to spoil the finest song.

The tutors are only allowed to sing for a few hours every day, being covered up the rest of the time, which preserves their song. An hour at morning, mid-day, and evening is a good plan. When the young ones are caged off, they too should be gradually accustomed to be darkened, after which they should be uncovered for a short time every day while the tutor is singing. It is impossible to get a really good song in any other way, the great secret being that the bird is not allowed time to pick up rubbish; but even as it is, some of the birds will acquire bad notes, and all such should be drafted off before they can corrupt the others.

German Canaries can be readily taught to sing any wild bird's note, such as that of the Nightingale, by allowing the bird whose song is desired to be the only tutor. To some persons the song of the Nightingale from a Canary is very attractive; but German breeders care very little for this class of song, preferring what deserves to be called a really musical performance. There is little doubt that they employ in teaching, besides Canary tutors, the notes of a flute or flageolet.

On the whole, we should advise any who attempt the systematic breeding of German Song Canaries to adopt the German plan of feeding, using as the staple the best fresh German summer rape-seed, and avoiding sugar and rich food. Twice a week it is well to give a little stale bread sopped in water and squeezed dry, and now and then—say once a week—a little hard-boiled egg mixed with bread-crumb or crushed biscuit, dividing each egg and an equal quantity of bread among a dozen birds. The water must always be fresh, and a piece of cuttle-fish bone should be hung in the cage. In the breeding season the egg-food may be given more freely—say twice a day—and canary-seed, also rape-seed soaked in water, and green food—in fact, treating them very much as Canaries in general at that time; but the young ones should be gradually weaned to the rape, which long experience has proved to suit their song better than any other food. Temporary loss of voice may be treated as directed in the last chapter, and any huskiness by a little honey in the water.

In Lancashire there are evidences of a growing interest in Canary-singing; but most of the contests reported appear to be for quantity rather than quality of song. Various systems of deciding the prizes have been employed. From various reports in the *Live Stock Journal*—many of them supplied by Mr. Evans—we gather a few of the methods which have been employed. At one contest each bird was allowed six minutes, and one point counted for every ten seconds a bird sang without a break. The winner scored eighteen points. At other contests five minutes and ten minutes were allowed, a point for every ten seconds of consecutive singing being allowed as before; while at others a bird has been allowed one point for every second over six seconds in each burst during the prescribed time. We are glad to know that this kind of contest is gradually giving place to a more careful cultivation of the quality of the song, and trust that before long England may be able to approach, if not equal Germany, in the quality of her Song Canaries.

BRITISH CAGE-BIRDS.

By W. SWAYSLAND.

CHAPTER XXXIV.

THE THRUSH TRIBE.

THE THRUSH is deservedly one of the greatest favourites among British songsters, and, from its singing so cheerily long before the trees have burst into leaf, has generally been called the "herald of spring." It frequents the whole of Europe, but is found more generally towards the north, and is a very familiar inhabitant of Great Britain. There is a blithe, bluff heartiness about the song of the Thrush that carries with it a certain feeling of rusticity, which makes its song peculiarly attractive in a town, bringing as it does so forcibly remembrances of those green fields and shady hedgerows, where, beside some chattering spring, it sometimes builds its nest. When wild, one of its favourite habits is to repair in the early morning and cool eventide to the topmost branch of a tree, selecting some withered twig for its perch, and from thence pouring forth its flood of melody. It commences singing as early as January, if the season be mild, continuing through the spring and summer. The Thrush, being slightly endowed with imitative powers, has been known to "catch a tune" when whistled or played upon a wind-instrument.

The size of this bird considerably varies, the average length from the tip of the beak to the end of the tail being about eight inches, though at times reaching nine inches. It is a fine bird, neatly shaped, and pretty, though plain, in its plumage. The whole of the upper part is an olive-brown, deepening in colour on the head and neck. The breast, which is pale buff, has a darker tinge on either side, and is flecked with triangular oval spots of a very dark brown reaching from each side of the throat down to the thighs; the throat, however, is a yellowish-white, and nearly free from spots, which are more thickly spread at the sides, gathering in clusters on the breast. The wing-coverts are brown, tipped with a reddish-yellow, whilst the rest of the wing is of a dark olive-brown, the under wing-coverts being bright tawny-brown; the tail is also of dark olive-brown, rather slender and rounded at the tip. The beak is horn-brown, except the half of the lower mandible nearest the base, which is yellow. The difference between the sexes is scarcely distinguishable, except, of course, by the song, the hen being mute; she is, however, generally somewhat smaller than the male, whilst the head and upper part of the neck are lighter; the spots on the breast are larger, and the eye not so bold as in the male.

The Thrush is very fond of water, and it is in the neighbourhood of a stream or brook that the nest is generally built; but it oftentimes breeds in bushes, trees, and even furze, and where water is scarce. The nest is formed externally of green moss, fine roots, leaves, and small twigs, the inner surface being lined with mud. There are generally four or

SONG THRUSH. BLACKBIRD.

five eggs of a light greenish-blue colour, with a few black spots at the larger end. Its food when wild consists of snails, worms, insects, and, in summer, fruit; in winter it also feeds upon berries. It is particularly destructive in the gardens during the fruit season, no doubt thinking itself entitled to some remuneration for having destroyed so many insect pests. It is extremely interesting to watch with what patience and perseverance Thrushes will search the wall fruit-trees, notably the apricot, when in quest of their favourite snails, which they are also especially dexterous in extracting from their shells. When a Thrush has found a snail it generally resorts to a large stone, where, taking the snail in its beak, it dashes it with considerable force against the stone, thus breaking the shell and obtaining the cherished morsel.

The cage for a Thrush should be large. The dimensions of an ordinary-sized one are—height eighteen inches, width seventeen inches, and depth twelve inches. It should have a

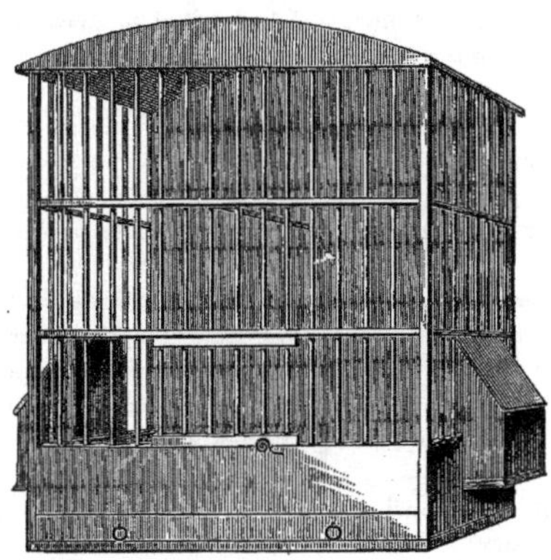

FIG. 73.—CAGE FOR THRUSH.

wooden cottage-roof and wooden back; wooden bars an inch apart are far preferable to wire; the perches should be placed from front to back, one in the centre of the cage and one other on either side near the feeding and drinking troughs, so as to obviate any necessity for the bird standing on the floor to feed. The cage must be kept dry; but supply the birds with plenty of water, both for drinking and bathing; a little gravel or sand should be sprinkled over the floor of the cage.

The best food is a mixture composed of ground oats ("fig-dust") made into a stiff dough with equal quantities of milk and water, though milk is not absolutely necessary. Two or three times a week it is advisable to add a pinch of soaked grocer's currants or a small quantity of finely-shredded raw lean beef; or some sopped bread, the crust being preferable, may be given. Of course its own natural food will always be acceptable, and a snail will be esteemed a great delicacy; not forgetting, however, with the latter treat, to also provide a stone whereon the bird may break the shell.

When wild, Thrushes will have as many as three broods during their breeding season, which oftentimes extends from April until July, and though they will not breed in cages, have been known to breed freely in an aviary if supplied with the necessary materials wherewith to build a nest; but they seldom rear more than one brood a year when in confinement. When breeding is thus attempted, they should not always be associated, but paired together in the early part of the year. The eggs are generally hatched in fourteen days, and in a fortnight the young will probably leave the nest. They should be brought up upon a paste made of crust of bread soaked in milk, with some crushed hemp-seed and a small quantity of finely-shredded raw lean beef. If strong, healthy birds, and kept warm, they may be expected to make an attempt at singing in about six or eight weeks.

The Thrush is, as a rule, a very healthy bird, and will, when care and attention are given, attain to an age of from seven to ten years. If, however, neglected, and especially allowed to get dirty, it is sometimes seized with cramp, which often ends fatally. Should such illness occur, the best remedy is change of food, substituting something more nourishing, such as ground oats made into a paste with new milk, wherein is mixed some shredded beef, hard-boiled egg chopped fine, and a little crushed hemp or maw seed; its feet may also be put in a little warm brandy and water, taking care to dry them in a warm cloth, and some hay should be spread at the bottom of the cage.

Another ailment to which the Thrush is somewhat subject is constipation, and this is chiefly occasioned by too much solid food. The disease exhibits itself in a constant drooping of the tail, while the bird will turn round and round on its perch, and show generally great uneasiness. A large spider or a mealworm dipped in olive oil is considered the best and safest remedy.

When kept in large towns this bird is subject to atrophy, a disease which occasions a wasting away of the flesh and a corresponding loss of sprightliness, whilst the feathers will become ragged and untidy. This is merely a pining for fresh air and freedom, and the only remedy, except the all-potent one of a visit to the country, is to vary the food, substituting as much as possible such natural food as the bird would obtain when in a wild state.

THE MISSEL THRUSH is a much larger bird than the preceding, being ten to eleven inches in length; its plumage is, however, somewhat similar in appearance, though lighter in colour. The upper part is of a greyish olive-brown, whilst the breast is white, slightly tinged with yellow, the belly being white; the spots on the throat are very small and faint, those on the breast being more bold and considerably rounder. When free it is rather a shy bird, though when breeding it does not scruple to approach the outskirts of towns. It finds its food—consisting of worms, slugs, insects, and the very small species of snails—out in the marshes and meadows. In the autumn it feeds also on various berries, especially the mistletoe and juniper. It is popularly credited with its name from its fondness for the mistletoe berries. The nest is generally built in the fork of a tree, sometimes at a height of thirty feet, an orchard being frequently selected. The song is of rather an inferior quality, consisting of a few notes, which are uttered in a loud wild tone, mixed with a certain strain of melancholy. From its habit of thus singing during or preceding a storm it has obtained in some districts the name of the Storm Cock; it is also known as the Holm Thrush and Screech Thrush.

Though, from its pugnacious habits and large size, it is not a desirable bird to be introduced into an aviary, the Missel Thrush will thrive in a cage, if provided with a large one; if confined in a small one it is very likely, from its restlessness, to injure its plumage and perhaps itself. It requires constant cleaning, and plenty of coarse sand. The same food holds good as for the Song Thrush; it is not, however, a dainty bird, and will even feed on wheaten

1. FIELDFARE. 2. STARLING. 3. REDWING.

bran moistened with water. A little boiled potato, or whatever may come to table, will be highly relished.

The ailments of the Song Thrush, and their treatment, apply equally to the Missel Thrush.

THE REDWING breeds in Norway, and visits these shores in the middle of October or beginning of November, staying with us until the following April or beginning of May. When it arrives it is somewhat shy, keeping to the open country, unless pressed by hunger, when it will approach human habitations in search of food. Being rather smaller in size than a Thrush, the same kind of cage is well adapted for its keeping. Its food should also be similar, adding for variety a little grated carrot. The remark as to the kind of snail eaten by the Missel Thrush applies equally to this bird, as their food when wild is very similar.

Its tameness, familiarity, patience, and appearance make the Redwing a good cage-bird; and it will also make itself at home and thoroughly agreeable when placed in an aviary. It possesses a fine song, though somewhat broken and irregular. Linnæus met with the bird several times in Lapland, and says, "Its amorous warblings from the top of the spruce-fir were delightful. Its high and varied notes rival those of the Nightingale herself." In length it is nearly eight inches, and the great distinctions between it and the Song Thrush are a large yellowish-white streak over the eyes, reaching from the upper mandible to the back of the ear, whilst the feathers on the sides of the breast and under the wings are of a bright rusty-red. The female is smaller than the male, and her colours are not so bright.

For ailments and treatment, refer to Song Thrush.

THE FIELDFARE, like the Redwing, is a visitor to these islands during the winter. Its home is principally in Norway, where it is the most common bird. The nest may there be found built in the spruce-firs.

As it is a denizen of cold countries, this bird should not be kept in a room near the fire. It should have a cage as large as a Missel Thrush's, as it is quite ten inches in length. Its plumage is somewhat different to that of the rest of the Thrush tribe. The tip of the beak is darker; and from the base, which is brown, to the eye, the feathers are black; the upper part of the head ash-grey, spotted with brown; the neck, ears, rump, and upper tail-coverts are also ash-grey; the back wings and wing-coverts are a rich chestnut-brown, towards the end of the wing slightly shaded with bluish-grey, which shows more perceptibly during flight; the throat and breast are speckled somewhat similarly to the Thrush, the ground tint being a rusty-yellow; the belly and under tail-coverts are greyish-white. The female differs slightly from the male, being rather smaller and slighter; the upper part of the beak is darker; the back less clear in colour; the throat lighter, and head browner.

Its food when wild is very similar to that of the Redwing, and, its habits being much the same, it may be fed upon the same paste, not forgetting to vary with scraped carrot. Not being much of a songster, this bird is not generally kept; but it is capable of being rendered a handsome addition to large aviaries, as it is not of a quarrelsome disposition.

For ailments and treatment, refer to Song Thrush.

THE BLACKBIRD, as its name denotes, is jet-black over the whole of his body, wings, and tail. The beak, which is an inch long, is of a brilliant yellow, showing markedly against its sable plumage; the eyelids are also of the same brilliant yellow, surrounding a bright full brown eye. The length is about ten inches. The tail is long and slightly rounded. The legs and toes are dusky brown. The beak and eyelids lose some of their brilliancy in winter. The female differs so considerably from the male as to have occasioned some naturalists to consider it a distinct species. She is darkish brown on the head, neck, and back, having the throat and breast a light rust-colour, the belly being a paler brown. The bill is brownish-yellow, sometimes with age becoming quite yellow. The young are blackish-brown on the upper parts, each feather being streaked with reddish-brown in the centre, the male being darker than the female; the under parts are a light reddish-brown, tipped with dark spots, which are clearer in the males. When in the nest the sexes of the young may be distinguished by the males having blackish-brown wings and tails, the female's being a lighter brown. When wild this bird is of a shy and restless disposition, and quickly detects the approach of strangers. It frequents hedgerows, furze, and copses, and may be found in thick shrubberies. It has a peculiar habit, when disturbed, of lying close until the interruption is past, when it

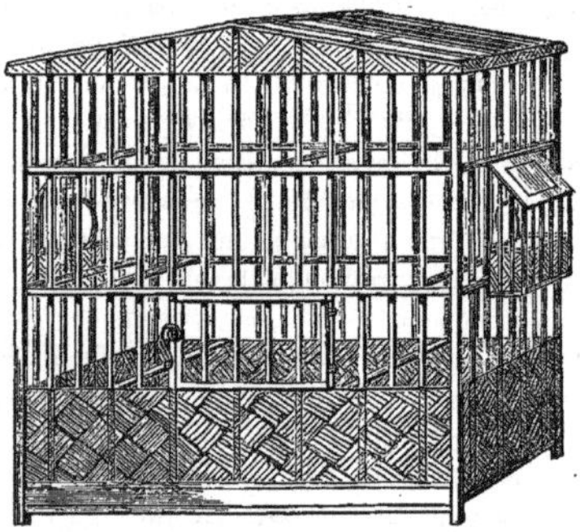

FIG. 74.—CAGE FOR BLACKBIRD.

will suddenly rise with a frightened screaming clatter, and take refuge in the nearest available thicket.

The food of the Blackbird consists chiefly of worms, slugs, caterpillars, beetles, and such-like insects; it is also fond of fruit and berries, according to the season of the year. It is particularly destructive amongst cherries, strawberries, currants, gooseberries, and apples; the blackberry, too, furnishes the Blackbird with many a meal.

Blackbirds pair and breed early in the spring. Their nest is composed of coarse roots and grasses with the mud still adhering, which form a strong fabric; it is then lined inside with finer grasses. It may be found in a variety of situations, as the builders are very erratic in their choice; a hedgerow bordering a copse or wood appears to be a favourite position, but they will sometimes build on the stump of a tree, or even on the ground. The eggs are also very erratic in their colouring, there being seldom two nests alike. The ordinary colour is a light greenish-blue, speckled and streaked with pale reddish-brown, sometimes gathered in a ring towards the larger end, the rest of the egg being faintly covered, or else distributed in an irregular manner over the whole. They are generally four or five in number.

As these birds seldom congregate in flocks, being generally found singly or in pairs, and as they possess a domineering disposition, they are very apt to be somewhat unruly in an aviary. It is better to keep a Blackbird in a large wicker cage, where it will behave itself uncommonly well. It is advisable to cover the top with canvas during the hot summer months, so as to keep it cool when placed in the sun. The food in confinement should be somewhat similar to that provided for the Thrush, adding, by way of a treat, a few garden worms, caterpillars, or any fruit that may be in season, which the bird will greedily devour. These little attentions will tend to keep the bird in good health, as it requires something more nourishing than mere sopped bread or bran. It should be provided with *plenty* of water, and, above all, be sure to provide your bird with plenty of gravel, which he will pick up to assist in digesting his food.

When reared by hand from the nest, the Blackbird is capable of forming strong attachments, and, from his wonderful imitative powers, will make himself a great favourite. He will, if trained when young, learn to whistle almost any tune that may be taught him. The best, and perhaps the quickest way, is to take him, when about six weeks or not later than two months old, to a quiet room away from any other bird, and in the evening and the first thing in the morning give him his lesson. The tune may be played on a flute or other wind-instrument. It is advisable to feed him *before* commencing operations; and some bribe or other, as, for instance, a lively worm, should be placed in his sight. Play over a portion of the tune you wish him to learn, and he will evidently pay particular attention to it. Repeat it, with precisely the same time and expression, say twenty times; then give the bird a little quiet, so that he may, if he will, have an opportunity of imitating it. If he should make any attempt, instantly give him his reward, coaxing and caressing him meanwhile. Being, for a bird, possessed of strong reasoning powers, he will soon discover why the worm or other bribe is given him, and will before long understand how to earn it. When once learnt, the tune or tunes will never be forgotten, but pass, as it were, into its song. It is rather a tedious undertaking, but the result is invariably satisfactory.

A Blackbird will also imitate other birds very minutely, and though there is little variety in his natural song, it is made up for by its pure flute-like tone and full volume. It most readily imitates the Thrush, but it will catch many notes from the Nightingale, to which bird its tone has most resemblance, were it not for the introduction of several harsh notes. When kept in confinement, it is always advisable to bring it up when young near to some good singing bird, as it will thereby learn its neighbour's song, and, intermixing the notes with its own, make a most agreeable songster. Whenever the weather permits, place the bird out in the sun, and he will repay all the care bestowed upon him by his keeper. He is not dismayed, however, by damp weather, as it is invariably after a shower that his song is blithest, and during the hottest days of summer he should be well shaded and kept cool, as in very dry weather his song seems to depart. He will begin to sing early in the year—say the end of February or in March—and will continue until the autumn, if the summer be not too hot. He is sometimes rather eccentric in his choice of subjects for imitation, one having been known to imitate very correctly the crowing of a cock, which he would mix up in his song in rather a ludicrous manner.

Many anecdotes are related of this bird. Mr. Jesse says:—"A very young Blackbird was put into a cage, which was hung up under the porch of a lodge. After the bird had become reconciled to its confinement, and had begun to feed, an older Blackbird was caught and put into the same cage. This old bird moped, and refused to feed itself, and would probably have died, had not the younger brought it food in its bill, and in every respect treated it as if it had been its mother, nourishing it with the greatest perseverance for some time." Another individual is recorded to have formed a very strong attachment to a dog. Blackbirds are very devoted to their young, and when attacked by any animal will defend their nest most valiantly. A tale is related of a pair that had built a nest near a paled fence, which a cat, by crawling along the paling, endeavoured to approach; thereupon the hen left the nest, flew to meet her in a state of great alarm, and placed herself almost within her reach, uttering the most piteous screams of wildness and despair. The cock-bird, on perceiving the danger, showed the greatest distress, and uttered loud screams and outcries, sometimes settling on the fence just before the cat, who was unable to make a spring in consequence of the narrowness of its footing. After a little time the cock flew at the cat, and succeeded in driving her away. A second time the same scene occurred; but the Blackbird was again victorious, and the cat became so intimidated at the attacks made upon her that she gave over her attempts to get at the young ones. After each battle the Blackbird celebrated his victory with a song, and for several days afterwards he would hunt the cat about the garden whenever she left the house.

The ailments of the Blackbird greatly resemble those of the Thrush, and should be treated accordingly. He is, however, subject to another painful disease, caused by the obstruction of the rump gland, which is situated immediately over the tail. This very often swells up in the form of a pimple, and should be, directly it is perceived, anointed with a little fresh butter, which must be free from salt, mixed up with a small quantity of sugar. If necessary, make an incision in the pimple with a needle or small sharp penknife. Bechstein mentions, and particularly recommends, an ointment made of litharge, white-lead, wine, and olive oil. If possible to save the bird without, an incision should only be made as a last resort, as it may destroy the gland, and consequently deprive the bird of the oily matter secreted there, which is used to moisten and plume the feathers, such oil being particularly missed during the moulting season.

THE RING OUSEL, unlike the Redwing and Fieldfare, visits these islands in exactly contrary seasons, arriving in the month of April and departing in October. It is a very shy, wild bird, preferring mountainous or open country, only approaching enclosed lands when the fruit is ripe. It is more common in Scotland and the west and north of England, where heather abounds. In its habits it somewhat resembles the Blackbird, and is, therefore, in some districts designated the "Mountain Blackbird." Its food also is similar, and it may be treated much the same when kept in confinement, not forgetting to supply it freely with elderberries, of which fruit it is very fond. In winter, soak a few dried elderberries or grocer's currants, and mix with its ordinary food.

The cage should be large, as it is a fine handsome bird, measuring about eleven inches. The bird is almost uniformly blackish-brown, with the exception of a crescent-shaped band of greyish-white across the breast; the female being rather lighter, whilst the band is narrower and not so distinctly marked. The song is composed of only a few notes, which are loud and sonorous.

For treatment of ailments, refer to Blackbird.

BLACK-CAP. WHITE-THROA

NIGHTINGALE.

THE NIGHTINGALE, the
pretending, but its form
beak, like that of all
insects), is straight and
size; the upper one dark
whole of the upper pa
brighter; the tail reddish
slightly tinged with brow
brownish-white; the
smaller than the male.
and we would recommen
been held by some auth
it may therefore be advi

The stay of the Nig
birds begin to arrive, th
even a fortnight. An ex
is that they invariably, b
only the young of the
must choose a fresh sit
as they more readily ta
the 20th April—the bird
and dies. Almost direc
attract their mates. If
are scarcely ever kept a

The Nightingale's
bits of bark and fibro
placed in some hollow
hedgerow. During th
always been a subject of
having often been heard
by the comparatively
shady copses, groves,
it favours us with varied
peculiarly beautiful
tion, and is directly
monotonous duties. T
contest, and all others

CHAPTER XXXV.

WARBLERS.

THE NIGHTINGALE, though possessed of so sweet a song, is in plumage exceedingly unpretending, but its form is very graceful. In length it is about six and a half inches. The beak, like that of all birds of this class (*i.e.*, of those whose principal food consists of insects), is straight and oval-shaped, thin and pointed, with both mandibles of nearly equal size; the upper one dark brown and the lower yellowish-brown, but darker at the tip. The whole of the upper part of the bird is a rich chestnut-brown, the wings being slightly brighter; the tail reddish-brown, rather long and rounded; the breast is a dull whitish-grey, slightly tinged with brown; the throat and belly pale whitish-grey; the under tail-coverts pale brownish-white; the legs (which are rather long) a greyish-brown. The female is somewhat smaller than the male, but the difference between the sexes is very difficult to distinguish, and we would recommend any purchaser to choose a large bird with a bold eye. It has also been held by some authorities that the throat of the male is lighter than that of the female; it may therefore be advisable to keep that point in view.

The stay of the Nightingale in this country is but short. In the early part of April the birds begin to arrive, the males preceding the females sometimes by as many as ten days or even a fortnight. An extraordinary feature in these birds, and one worthy of particular notice, is that they invariably, by some inscrutable instinct, fly direct to their last year's nesting-place; only the young of the preceding year straying from the old familiar spot, since they necessarily must choose a fresh situation wherein to build their nest. This is the best time to catch them, as they more readily take food, and you are sure of procuring a male; later on—say after about the 20th April—the bird is much wilder, very often refuses food, and in a short time pines away and dies. Almost directly after the arrival of the males they begin to sing, by which means they attract their mates. If taken during the pairing season they will become absolutely mute, and are scarcely ever kept alive.

The Nightingale's nest is built of a variety of materials, such as leaves, dried stalks of grasses, bits of bark and fibrous roots, lined with finer grasses and horsehair, loosely put together and placed in some hollow in the ground, in the roots or stump of a tree, or towards the bottom of a hedgerow. During the building the male bird puts forth the whole volume of its song. It has always been a subject of surprise that so small a bird should possess such extraordinary power, it having often been heard in the stillness of night at a distance of a mile; but the fact is explained by the comparatively great strength of the muscles of the throat. The favourite haunts are small shady copses, groves, plantations, woods, quiet gardens, and thick hedgerows. From such retreats it favours us with varied and beautiful lays, which are full of the richest melodies, and end with a peculiarly beautiful "scale" that sounds almost like harmonics. This continues during incubation, and is directly inspired by love for the mate, who so quietly and patiently performs her monotonous duties. The answering song of some neighbour challenges it, as it were, to a vocal contest, and all others in the neighbourhood, taking up the strain, will fill the whole valley with floods of song of a most enchanting description. These remarks are more particularly applicable to the night-time, but it is not only when darkness covers the earth that we are favoured with the Nightingale's sweet and flute-like strains, for they will sing all day long, making themselves distinctly heard above the chorus of the surrounding sharers of the copse. Some naturalists contend that these day songsters are a distinct species, and only sing by daylight, whereas the nocturnal bird invariably chooses darkness; but we have known many birds that would sing both day and night, and from experience cannot coincide with those opinions. It would, however, be advisable to hold this idea in view when choosing a place to hang the cage, some birds preferring light, while others will sing better in the shade.

The eggs are generally five in number, and of an olive-brown colour. As soon as the young are hatched, the song almost ceases, generally in June, unless the first nest has been taken or destroyed, in which case they immediately commence another, and the singing is continued until the eggs are hatched. The whole time of the parents is then employed in providing their young with food, which is principally composed of small green caterpillars. The food of the adult bird consists of insects, such as caterpillars, small worms, beetles, moths, and flies, though it is particularly fond of the larvæ of ants.

The cage in which a Nightingale is confined may be of various kinds, but we recommend one made of the following shape and dimensions:—Eighteen inches long, eight inches deep, and thirteen inches high, rising to fifteen inches in the centre; the top and back of wood, the bottom of osiers, with bars also of osier or wood, the floor being formed by a wooden drawer, which may be strewed with sand or covered by a piece of blotting-paper, the sand being then provided in a pan. The feeding-trough should be placed at the side, and if the cage can be so constructed as to have a semi-circular projection to contain the water-vessel, which must be cleaned and filled daily, it will help to keep the cage and perches dry. Two perches should be placed near the feeding and drinking vessel, and another in the centre of the cage, which perches it is advisable to cover with soft green cloth; the roof should be also covered inside with the same material, to prevent the bird from injuring itself. The cage also had better be painted, taking care that it be thoroughly dry before placing the bird in it. This cage will be darker than if of wire, and will consequently give the bird more privacy.

Fanciers have a peculiar recipe for inducing the freshly-caught birds to take food, which is called "meating off." It is managed in the following ingenious manner:—Some fresh raw beef or bullock's heart is scraped, and, being divested of all fibrous substance, is mixed into a soft paste with hard-boiled yolk of egg; and for the first day or two a few mealworms or beetles, cut up, are placed among it. This mixture is placed in a large bird-pan. In the middle of this food is placed a large deep watch-glass, or, if that is not obtainable, a very small inverted liqueur-glass with the stem broken off. Under this glass are introduced three or four lively mealworms, whose oft-repeated endeavours to break out of prison attract the attention of the Nightingale. Not understanding how these worms are placed beyond his reach, he continues to peck at them, until by degrees he tastes the beef and egg, which is artfully rubbed over the sides of the glass. This being palatable, the bird satiates its appetite and soon feels a zest for it, particularly as his attempts to get at the mealworms always prove abortive. He will soon eat regularly; in fact, he is "meated off." It is advisable, however, so as to be assured that the bird gets something, to cram it with the mixture, giving two small pieces three times a day; this will whet its appetite without satiating it, and will also accustom the bird to the flavour of its new food. The writer has tried this recipe with unvarying success.

In the aviary, if a Nightingale be allowed to fly about freely with the other birds, it will possibly miss the more delicate food to which it has been accustomed in the cage, and its song will not be so good or so frequent. If it should show any sign of ailing, at once place it in a separate cage and feed it as before. This bird is seldom known to breed in confinement, yet instances are on record of such a circumstance. The birds thus reared do not attain to so beautiful a song as when wild.

The size of the Nightingale, as well as the tone and power of its song, may be greatly increased by the use of carefully-selected food; and when young it should be placed near a bird of acknowledged singing powers, as it will thereby add its neighbour's notes to its own natural repertory. This habit of imitating its fellows holds good even when wild, and the birds of one district will consequently far exceed in the brilliancy and variety of their song those of another; for instance, the birds of Surrey are acknowledged to be better than those of Middlesex. This may, perhaps, be accounted for by the formation of the country, which supplies a more plentiful and beneficial stock of insects and larvæ; certain it is, however, that these increased powers are transmitted to the progeny.

The food is capable of great variation, and should be selected according to the individual tastes of the birds. The most successful is scraped bullock's heart or raw beef mixed with chopped egg, bread-crumbs, German paste, and some ants' eggs, adding a few mealworms or beetles as a treat; when obtainable, it may be given a few gentles, which will be thoroughly enjoyed. In summer fresh ants' eggs would undoubtedly prove the best food, together with two or three mealworms daily. During the seasons when fresh ants' eggs are not to be procured, dried ones may be substituted mixed with boiled bullock's heart dried and grated small, with a little scraped Swedish turnip to assist in digestion. These turnips keep fresh through the winter if placed in a cellar, or can be readily procured. A little cooked lean mutton, chopped finely, will make a healthy change. Should the scraped beef tend to become stale and putrid in the summer-time, by *scalding* before scraping the putrefaction is stayed, and the beef still retains its feeding properties.

Young birds should be taken when about ten days old, and placed in a basket for three or four days; then put into a cage with some soft hay strewed upon the bottom; give them plenty of perches. The best food to rear them upon is scraped beef, boiled yolk of egg, sopped bread, and a small quantity of crushed soaked hemp and maw seed mixed into a paste with a little water, adding some ants' eggs and some mealworms or beetles cut up small. In handling the young it is best to take them in a soft dry cloth or handkerchief, being especially careful not to touch the feet or legs, which are very delicate. These birds are very liable to cramp; if they are attacked with this malady, the best remedy is to place their feet in brandy and water for a few moments, then dry them carefully, and feed them on scraped beef, boiled yolk of egg, and mealworms.

The following method of propagating mealworms may be carried out with great advantage:—Fill a half-gallon jar with wheat bran, barley, or oatmeal, and a few pieces of sugar-paper or old shoe-leather. In this half a pint of mealworms may be placed, and if allowed to remain for three months, being occasionally moistened with a cloth soaked in beer, will become beetles, which again lay eggs, and propagate their species with great rapidity. One such jar will supply a Nightingale.

The rule holds good particularly with this bird, that the nearer the food assimilates to that it would obtain when wild, the more healthy the bird will be, and the better his song. In such circumstances a Nightingale will live as long as fifteen years; indeed, one has been stated to have attained the age of twenty-five years.

The following recipe to make German paste may be recommended:—Three-quarters of a pound of peameal, a quarter of a pound of coarse Scotch oatmeal, one ounce of moist sugar, one ounce of olive oil, two ounces of honey, half a pint of well-crushed hemp-seed, half a gill of maw-seed. The meal and sugar should be well rubbed in, then add the oil and honey, which has been first well mixed. Stir the whole together so that there be no lumps, then add the hemp and maw seed.

The moulting season is particularly dangerous to this delicate bird. If it shows signs of ailing, give some good nourishing food and a large spider or two, taking especial care to keep the bird out of any draught. Should the stomach be out of order, the bird will show it by puffing up its feathers, half closing its eyes, and putting its head under its wings, continuing thus for a long time. This will be best relieved by a diet of ants' eggs, a spider, or just sufficient saffron in the drinking-water to give it an orange tinge. A good tonic in case of raggedness or loss of flesh may be found in a finely-chopped fig mixed up in its ordinary food, also placing a rusty nail in the water.

The Blackcap, like the Nightingale, arrives in England towards the end of March and beginning of April, leaving again in August or September; the males also precede the females. The song of this bird is so agreeable that it is called the "Mock Nightingale." Its tones are loud, sweet, and especially flute-like. It is a small bird, considering the fulness of its song, being smaller even than the Nightingale; the average length is about five and three-quarter inches. The beak is shaped similarly to the Nightingale's, its colour dark horn-brown, paler beneath, the edges yellowish-grey, the inside of the mouth bluish-grey. Its distinguishing characteristic is a jet-black cap or hood on the crown of its head, which has earned for it in Germany the name of the "Monk." The cheeks and nape of the neck are grey; the back and wing-coverts are ash-grey, shaded with olive-brown; the pinions and tail are dark brown, edged with the same colour as the back; the breast is light grey, paler towards the throat and belly. The female differs from her mate, inasmuch as she is a trifle *larger*, while the cap on the head is a chocolate-brown, the other parts of the body being slightly tinged with brown.

Like the Nightingale, this bird chooses its dwelling in some secluded copse or undergrowth or orchard; it is shy, timid, and rather restless, also somewhat pugnacious when wild, hardly ever breeding very near to another pair. It feeds on caterpillars, spiders, flies, and other insects; and berries and fruits, such as elderberries, currants, raspberries, and green figs. Its nest is generally found in a bramble or amongst honeysuckle, and it has been known to build in gooseberry and currant bushes. The nest is built exceedingly lightly of thin bents of dry grass and fibrous roots, scantily lined with horsehair. The eggs are usually five in number, of a dull white, lightly tinged with green, mottled with grey and light brown, mingled with a few spots of darker brown. The male bird assists in the duties of incubation. They sit very closely, and will even risk capture rather than forsake their nest; the writer having once thus caught a very fine male bird, which was successfully "meated off," and proved to be a first-class songster. The plumage of the young is very similar to that of the adult female, the distinctive features of the male bird only showing after the first moult.

The cage for a Blackcap should resemble that of the Nightingale, not forgetting the green baize for the perches; the bird is very fond of bathing, and should be provided with *plenty* of water, care being taken to prevent him from wetting his perches. It is rather wasteful with its food, unless the troughs be placed outside the cage and covered in to prevent scattering. As it does not care much for sunlight, preferring shade, it is as well to cover the cage with green gauze to take off the glare of the sun. It is a quiet, sociable bird in an aviary, but its song is not so frequent. It is somewhat delicate, but if care be bestowed and proper food supplied it will live to a good age. The writer has successfully kept them in an open aviary during severe winters, but if a greenhouse be available would advise that they be placed there.

An esteemed correspondent (Mr. J. Young) writes us:—"I kept a pair for over four years in perfect health; the cock was at length carried off by an epidemic which decimated my aviary. This pair of Blackcaps had the migratory fever regularly every September and March, and occasionally during the winter months. The cock-bird began to show its symptoms about a week or ten days before the hen; as the time approached, the hen, who at other times lived on good terms with her mate, would drive him fiercely about the cage. They were fed on the general food of the aviary, viz., bread-crumbs, egg, ants' eggs, and German paste mixed; occasionally mealworms or gentles. Fruit of some kind was always in the cage, such as apples, pears, currants, elderberries, &c. The cock warbled inwardly during the autumn and winter and early spring, but in April, as soon as the migratory fever was over, he suddenly broke out into loud song. They moulted in August. The cock was very tame, and would take flies or mealworms from my hand, or catch them as I dropped them from the roof of the cage; the hen never became tame. They lived in an all-wire cage, four feet by two feet, and three feet high, with other birds, in a room without a fire."

The food should resemble that recommended for the Nightingale. The bird must, however, be supplied with soft garden fruit, such as currants and raspberries, when in season. Elderberries and green figs will be eaten with great satisfaction, whilst as a treat a ripe pear may be given. In order to supply the bird with elderberries in winter, a stock of dried fruit should be set aside; when given to the bird, they should be soaked in water until soft. If the elderberries be exhausted, grocer's currants will make a very fair substitute; also split a fig, and place it against the bars for the bird to peck. A few flies or spiders will be greedily devoured. Some finely-chopped walnuts, or any other kind of nuts similarly treated, will make an agreeable change.

The usual ailments are much the same as a Nightingale's, and must be so treated.

THE WHITETHROAT.—This bird is of all the warblers the most common in England; it is also known in some parts by the name of the Nettle Creeper. It generally frequents hedgerows, gardens, the edges of woods or plantations, thickets, or any brushwood, where it may be seen sitting on a spray of the bramble, its delicately tinted breast shining in the sunlight, whence it will rise in the air, fluttering at a height of about thirty feet and singing its merry little song, then suddenly dropping to the bush in silence. It is very sprightly in its habits, of elegant shape, rather slight in build, and about five and a half inches in length. The beak is horn-brown; the head and neck grey; the back grey, deeply tinged with brown; the tail dark brown, slightly edged with rust-colour, the two outer feathers being greyish-white, which are distinctly perceptible in flight; the wings are dark brown, each feather being edged with a light rusty brown; the throat and belly are white; the breast, sides, and vent very pale grey, delicately tinted with a beautiful rosy flesh-colour. The female is somewhat smaller than the male, and the tints on the breast lighter.

A pair which built in our garden were particularly useful in ridding some gooseberry-bushes of the small caterpillars that infested them, devoting the whole of their energies to feeding their young with this troublesome insect, which they carried off in their beaks to the expectant brood, until the caterpillars were completely destroyed. The food, when wild, is similar to that of the Blackcap, and, when kept in confinement, it should be fed on the same pastes, insects, and fruit.

Being delicate, it will require as much care and attention as are bestowed on that bird. A similar cage should also be provided. They also thrive in an aviary.

The usual time of arrival is the beginning of April, and of departure the months of September and October, but we once saw one several days together as late as the latter end of December.

The ailments and treatment are similar to those of the Nightingale.

THE LESSER WHITETHROAT.—This elegant little bird is well worth keeping, as it will become very tame and attached to the person who feeds it. Its song also, though rather weak, is full of variety and very pleasing. It is smaller in size than the preceding bird, being just over five inches in length; the plumage somewhat resembles that of the Blackcap, except that the head and neck are of ash-grey instead of black. When wild its food greatly resembles that of the Whitethroat. The Blackcap's diet will answer all its requirements.

A small Nightingale's cage will be well adapted for it, or it may be kept in an aviary, to which it will form an attractive addition. We should not omit to draw attention to its nest, which is a delicately built fabric, consisting of bents of dried grasses and a little wool, lined with hairs, the whole being dexterously clothed with spiders' webs. The usual ailments are as nearly as possible those of the Nightingale, and should be so treated.

THE GARDEN WARBLER.—This is another summer visitor, arriving in the beginning of May, and departing again in August and September. Although rather a common bird, it is not very generally known, on account of its retiring disposition; and perhaps, also, from the fact that its plumage is not very striking, it has often escaped notice. Its exceedingly fine song, however, places it next the Blackcap as a songster, the notes being especially deep and flute-like, almost rivalling those of the Blackbird in power, while the song will last for nearly half an hour almost uninterruptedly; it is somewhat irregular in time and tone, but is certainly very sweet. It is a small bird, rather stouter built than a Blackcap, but not quite so long. It frequents gardens, orchards, and woods, retiring from the latter in the autumn, and visiting the two former in quest of fruit. The whole of the upper part of the body is olive-brown; the wings and tail darker brown, slightly edged with lighter brown; the under part is grey, much paler on the throat and belly, and tinged with pale reddish-grey on the breast; the legs, toes, and claws lead-colour. The female is scarcely distinguishable from the male—a little lighter colour on the back, and a more uniformly brownish-grey on the under part, being the only difference. Its main food consists of caterpillars and insects, as well as their larvæ. In the summer they will be found in the gardens feeding upon the currants and raspberries, or such-like soft-skinned fruit; they are likewise very fond of elderberries.

Though generally avoiding observation, the Garden Warbler is not a wild bird, and will take kindly to a cage, which should be of the Nightingale pattern. It will agree well with other birds, especially those of its class. The Blackcap's food well suits this bird; a little sopped sponge-cake may be added, and, as with all the warblers, variety is a great feature in the treatment. This attention alone may add several years to their life. *All the longest-lived birds we have known received very frequent changes of diet.* If care be bestowed, this bird will not unfrequently sing, with a very slight interval, during the whole of the year. Its ailments greatly resemble those of the Blackcap, and should be treated accordingly. If the bird be found pining or ragged in its plumage, a few green caterpillars, such as may be found on cabbages, should be daily administered.

A correspondent informs us that he kept one from September, 1877, to May, 1878, which stood the winter (which, it must be remembered, was a very mild one) without a fire. It was fed

1 ROBIN. 2. WREN. 3. REDSTART. 4 WHEATEAR.

on bread, German paste
it never throve; and
their food.

THE ROBIN is un
childhood he is closely
into the childish mind
pet of the nursery;
friend? Even the scho
with a fearless confide
upon him; for it is the
mute, that Robin show
of man, certain as he
not attended to he w
and has been known
it were, a connecting
fire and those who are
naked trees. At Chris
holly that decks our wa
hopping amongst the
and nearer to the wind
the white snow, his
their faces against the
of Robins that have b

It is not a very
house, making itself th
table. A story is told
that it would peck from
bird is sometimes called
occasion, having observe
and beat himself quite
fellow, and will keep
of his own species.
rival answering it from
answered by song, unti
who will, immediately th
A most terrific conflict
They have been found
thing else, and will the
the combat.

Robins take a
spring-time tempts th
pairing season, when
topmost branch of a
trolls out his carol, wi
bowing and up-and-dow

on bread, German paste, egg, ants' eggs, mealworms, gentles, and a constant supply of fruit; but it never throve; and this gentleman gives it as his opinion that they require *meat* introduced into their food.

THE ROBIN is undoubtedly the most popular of all the feathered tribe. In our earliest childhood he is closely associated with many of those nursery rhymes which strike so deeply into the childish mind that they are never thoroughly forgotten. He is *par excellence* the pet of the nursery; and as years grow upon us, who does not look upon Robin as an old friend? Even the school-boy hesitates to take its nest. Bold he is, and appeals to our feelings with a fearless confidence, expressing by his actions the wants that wintry snows have cast upon him; for it is then, when almost all our songsters have departed, and those remaining are mute, that Robin shows his individuality, and with a sure instinct approaches the habitations of man, certain as he is to receive his full share of the crumbs that fall from the table. If not attended to he will sometimes even tap at the window until he has attracted attention, and has been known to fearlessly enter into the room if the window be opened. He is, as it were, a connecting link between the happy family seated in comfort around the yule log fire and those who are doomed to be the sport of every bleak wind that whistles through the naked trees. At Christmastide he takes a place in our thoughts almost as palpable as the holly that decks our walls; indeed, his presence would seem to be actual; for see, there he is hopping amongst the shrubs, now on the holly bough, now on the laurel, approaching nearer and nearer to the window, his brown back and bright breast showing most conspicuously against the white snow, his full bright eye looking with confidence at the children who are pressing their faces against the window to catch a glimpse of poor Cock Robin. Instances are on record of Robins that have become so tame as even to feed from the hands of their benefactors.

It is not a very uncommon occurrence for a bird to take up its winter quarters in a house, making itself thoroughly at home, and in some instances feeding from the plates upon the table. A story is told of one which had taken a partiality to a house, and became so tame that it would peck from off the very plates from which the inmates were eating. "Bob," as this bird is sometimes called, resented any intruders, and was so exceedingly jealous that on one occasion, having observed his reflection in a looking-glass, he flew at it in a most furious rage, and beat himself quite out of breath against it; for with all his virtues he is a most pugnacious fellow, and will keep the whole of his domain perfectly free of any other bird, more especially of his own species. Often will he troll forth his carol, and become most excited at hearing a rival answering it from a neighbouring post of vantage: the challenge has been given, song is answered by song, until eventually the stranger invades the territory of the Robin in possession, who will, immediately the imaginary boundary line is crossed, fly most furiously at the invader. A most terrific conflict ensues, and so furiously will they fight that they often kill one another. They have been found so engaged in their encounter as to become totally oblivious of everything else, and will then even allow themselves to be taken by the hand rather than relinquish the combat.

Robins take a liking to a certain locality, and will return to it every winter, until spring-time tempts them once more to the woods and fields. They live separately until the pairing season, when they seem most devoted partners. The cock generally selects a post or topmost branch of a tree, or the end of a wall, in fact any prominent projection, whence he trolls out his carol, which is first introduced by a sharp "tsit, tsit," accompanied by a ludicrous bowing and up-and-down motion with his tail. His song is very telling, especially in the wintertime, being necessarily more conspicuous then in consequence of the absence of any rivalry from the rest of the feathered tribe. The notes are sweet and varied, consisting of disconnected passages of considerable beauty, and these plaintive warblings he will continue for upwards of half an hour. Though seemingly so bright and cheerful, there is to some minds an inexpressible undercurrent of melancholy in his song, which sounds almost like an ode to the memory of the summer which has departed, with its accompaniment of sweet songsters; whilst others hail it as the earnest that spring will return once more; and one and all are thankful that Robin, who is totally oblivious of these speculations, comes to cheer them in the dull monotonous days of winter. Robin also sings in the summer, but his voice is often lost in the general chorus around him.

The popular idea against keeping Robins obtains even in the present day; formerly the superstition that Robins brought ill-luck to a house was very great. But many persons have caged them during the winter, and allowed them freedom in spring; and such have been known to return to their comfortable winter quarters as soon as the inclemency of the weather deprived them of the means of subsistence.

In length the Robin is about five and three-quarter inches; the beak is dark brown; the head, neck, back, tail-coverts, and tail are of a yellowish olive-brown; the greater wing-coverts are edged with buff; over the base of the beak, round the eyes, and covering the chin, throat, and upper part of the breast is an orange-red, bordered with bluish-grey down to the wings; the lower part of the breast, and the belly, are white. The female differs but slightly from her mate; most authorities give it that she is smaller and her plumage not so brightly coloured. The sex, however, is very difficult to distinguish.

The Robin feeds mostly upon worms, caterpillars, insects and their larvæ, and fruit and berries. The nest is composed of leaves, moss, dry roots, and grass, lined with hair and a few feathers, placed generally in a hole in a bank; they are, however, very capricious in their choice of situations, sometimes choosing a flower-pot, an old kettle, or a hole in a wall—in fact, there seems to be no law to guide their choice. The eggs are generally from five to seven in number, of a delicate pale reddish-white, faintly freckled with darker red, the spots being gathered more thickly at the larger end, sometimes forming a ring or zone, though specimens have been found of a pure white. The young are fed principally on worms and caterpillars; they differ totally from the adult bird, the whole of the upper part being yellowish olive-brown, mottled with orange and buff, each feather having a pale olive-brown tip; the chin, throat, and breast are dull reddish-brown, the feathers being margined with darker brown.

The Robin may be kept in any shaped cage, but perhaps it is advisable to keep him in one that is only open in front, as he is very inquisitive, and will think of nothing but watching the other occupants of the room, and while thus engaged forgets to sing. He will thrive on a Nightingale's food, giving him a little more bread. A few small garden-worms will greatly please him, and help to keep him healthy and in good plumage. Some will agree well in an aviary, but being naturally of a pugnacious disposition, will oftentimes attack the other birds, especially those of the same class; and it is *never* advisable to have two in the same aviary, as they will undoubtedly fight, and possibly kill one another; moreover, it sings better in a cage, and they are seldom trustworthy companions. They will breed in confinement, though they get very quarrelsome during the time of incubation, and if in an aviary may kill or injure the other birds; it is therefore always advisable to keep them in a breeding-cage by themselves. The young had better be provided with the same food as is recommended for young Nightingales.

They generally leave the nest in fourteen days, and in about a fortnight's time will be able to forage for themselves.

The bird is subject to much the same ailments as the Nightingale, and should be treated accordingly.

THE REDSTART is a handsome little songster. It seems alternately shy and familiar, sometimes choosing the most retired and sequestered spots, and at others even building in a hole in the wall of an inhabited house. It has a very pretty song, though composed of but few notes. It is, however, very imitative, and will sometimes acquire the song of a Garden Warbler or Lesser Whitethroat; and can be taught to pipe a tune almost as well as a Blackbird.

It becomes very tame in captivity, and will show great affection for those who feed and tend it, eating out of their hands, &c.; when wild it has a habit of darting to and from the hedgerows, showing its pretty colours in a striking manner. It is a somewhat timid bird, and readily detects the approach of danger. It is lively and graceful, though rather restless.

Its length is about five and a quarter inches. The beak is black, except at the corners, which are yellow, as is also the inside; the forehead is white; the neck and back lead-grey, slightly tinged with red; the chin and throat black, the feathers being generally slightly edged with grey; the wing-feathers are brown, with the outer edges rather lighter; the breast, sides, upper part of the belly, and the rump are a bright rust-red, the belly being clouded with white; the under part of the belly and vent are rusty yellow; the tail is rust-red, with the two centre feathers brown. The female, unlike most birds of this class, differs materially from her mate. She is a trifle smaller; the upper part of the body is a uniform greyish-brown; the chin and throat dusky white; the breast dirty rust-colour; the wings lighter than the male's, and the tail not so bright. The adult males in winter, as also the young males of the year after their autumn moult, lack the white forehead, the feathers being edged with brown; the chin, throat, and breast are variegated with whitish-grey; the upper part of the body pale reddish-brown, tinged with grey.

When wild this bird feeds principally on insects, such as ants and their larvæ, flies and moths, worms, spiders, caterpillars, and beetles. It will pursue and catch flies and moths when on the wing as well as when on the ground. They build a loosely constructed nest of roots and grasses, and a little feathers and hair; the eggs, from five to seven in number, are apple-green in colour. As soon as the tail-feathers appear, the young birds hop out of their nest on to the branches of any bush or tree that may be closely adjoining, and the parent birds may be seen feeding them there until they are old enough to forage for themselves.

The Redstart may be kept in a Nightingale cage, or if tame in a pagoda or wagon, as it will then show off its handsome plumage to more advantage. It makes a very bright and pretty addition to an aviary.

A correspondent favours us with the following:—"I kept one from April to December, during that time feeding it on scraped beef and egg, ants' eggs, mealworms, gentles, fruit, bread, and German paste. It grew very tame, and when allowed out of its cage it would pick off the flies from the walls and ceiling of the room. It was a merry bird, constantly singing. It moulted well, but always felt the cold when the thermometer fell to 40°. I regret to say that some cold weather in November sent it into a decline, of which it died. I have tried some since, but find they cannot stand the winter without a fire."

The food should be similar to that of a Nightingale, and the nestlings will thrive on the food recommended for the young of that bird. Its diseases are also very similar to those of the Nightingale, and should be treated accordingly; it is, however, also subject to dysentery, which may be traced by a chalky excrement which clings to the feathers beneath the tail. This is of so acrid a nature that it causes a severe inflammation of the adjoining parts. Clip these soiled feathers, and anoint the flesh with fresh unsalted butter; also place a rusty nail in its water, or scrape some chalk into it until it is thick; keep the bird some time without water until he is thirsty, then replace the chalky water, which should be recently stirred so as to ensure his taking the chalk, which if allowed to stand will settle to the bottom. This remedy may also be applied to the Nightingale or any of the warblers, should they be attacked by this dangerous and troublesome disease.

The Black Redstart, which is also known as the Blackstart, is a very elegant bird, neatly shaped, and of pretty plumage. It is not a common bird, but is not so rare as is generally supposed, as we have caught in past years about a dozen in the county of Sussex. It visits this country in the winter, when most of the warblers have departed. It may be distinguished from the Redstart by the sooty black on its breast and belly where the other is red. Its wings are also barred with white, except the outer feathers, which are brown. Its food and habits resemble those of the Redstart, except that it prefers stony ground or chalk cliffs; it will also be found in gardens or pig pounds; it often visits farm-yards, and may be seen on the heaps of manure placed out on the land. Care should be taken in "meating off,". and it should afterwards be provided with Nightingale's food, and otherwise be treated in a similar manner.

The Grey Redstart very nearly resembles the female of the Black Redstart. It is of an entirely greyish ashen-brown, paler beneath, especially at the throat and belly; the tail-coverts are bright rusty red, which colour extends to the tail, except the two middle feathers, which are ashen-brown. It certainly is not generally known as a British bird, but has often come to our notice, having taken several in late years. In its habits it greatly resembles the Black Redstart, and if successfully meated off we would recommend the ordinary Nightingale's food. It would undoubtedly give its possessor great trouble, but would repay everything by its rarity of plumage.

The Hedge Accentor, which is known by the various names of Hedge Sparrow, Dunnock, Hedge Warbler, and Shufflewing, is a frequenter, as its name denotes, of hawthorn hedges, where it may be heard uttering its plaintive little song, which, though not of any great variety, is very pretty, and may be heard almost all the year round. It builds very early in the year, and its nest is therefore quite exposed in the leafless hedgerows, and it is surprising that it continues so common a bird, considering that the school-boy is invariably used to boast many a string of its delicately tinted light blue eggs. It is also particularly liable to the depredations of the Cuckoo, it being notorious that as many young Cuckoos are reared by this little bird as by any other victim of that houseless robber. The manner in which the young Cuckoo obtains sole possession of the nest is peculiar. The egg is deposited in the nest by the shiftless Cuckoo, and is hatched by the Hedge Sparrow in blissful ignorance of the enemy that has been insinuated into her otherwise happy family. The young Cuckoo soon shows his superior strength, and having a peculiar hollow in its back, heaves the unfortunate nestlings one by one out of their warm abode, they of course perishing, whilst the unsuspicious parents continue their attentions to the murderer of their unfortunate offspring.

The food of the Hedge Sparrow, as it is more frequently called, consists of insects in their various stages of development, worms, and seeds, such as grasses and grains. These birds do not all migrate, and in hard weather will visit the towns and farm-yards, frequenting gutters and sinks, where they pick up crumbs and other morsels from amongst the sweepings; but in the milder weather they depend principally upon the larvæ of insects and worms, which latter may then be always seen stirring in the early morning or in the evening.

The length of the bird is about five and a half inches; its plumage is rather unpretending, the whole of the upper part, including the wings and tail, are chestnut-brown, the back being speckled with black, whilst the head and neck are shaded with bluish-grey; the under part is grey, slightly tinged with brown, and speckled on the breast and sides with chestnut-brown.

This bird may be kept in almost any cage, and will thrive in an aviary, although at times it proves unsociable. We possess one that had a most desperate encounter with a Robin which was kept in the same aviary. The Robin would undoubtedly have killed him had they not been parted. He still retains evidence of the severity of the conflict, inasmuch as the feathers upon the top of his head are raised like a crest, which gives him a ludicrously important appearance. They have always lived harmoniously since then, but the Hedge Sparrow invariably gives way to his pugnacious companion.

The Hedge Accentor should be fed on canary-seed, hemp-seed, and dry coarse oatmeal, varied with bread-crumbs and German paste; an occasional mealworm will help to keep him in good plumage and song. A small garden-worm, spider, or other insect will be a treat that may be given whenever available, and will afford him great enjoyment.

The Stonechat is a frequenter of dry heaths and commons, where it may be seen perched on a topmost spray of furze or brushwood uttering its peculiar call; from thence it will suddenly dart to the ground in pursuit of some insect, and just as suddenly return to the spray it had quitted. It also flutters in the air at a slight elevation, and there sings its pretty little song. Its length is about five and a quarter inches. The head, cheeks, and throat are black, slightly shaded with brown; the back is black, deeply edged with brown; the upper tail-coverts white, speckled with brown, and margined with a light rust-colour; the tail brown; the wings also brown, edged with greyish-brown; the tertials white; the sides of the neck white; the breast rich chestnut-brown, shading lighter until it becomes almost yellowish-white on the belly, vent, and under tail-coverts. The female has the whole of her upper part dusky brown, edged with buff; chin and throat blackish-brown, spotted with white and red; the breast light chestnut-brown, and the white space on the neck and wings of smaller extent than in the male.

Being a handsome bird, the Stonechat may, if tame enough, be kept in an open cage, but will always be a striking addition to the aviary. The food consists of insects and their larvæ, and worms, taking the former when on the wing after the manner of the Flycatchers. It is a delicate bird, and if adult when taken will seldom live; it may, however, be reared from the nest if fed upon the food recommended for the young Nightingale. A young bird of the season may sometimes be meated off if care and attention are bestowed.

The song improves in confinement, and it will sing much better in a cage than when placed in an aviary. The food of the adult should also be similar to that of the Nightingale; abundance of insects, such as flies, moths, caterpillars, worms, and small beetles, will tend to keep the bird in good health and plumage, and also add to its song.

Though a great many of these birds never migrate, it is advisable to keep them under constant supervision during the winter, as, from their delicate nature, a sharp change of weather may be fatal; if any signs of ailing be apparent, at once move the bird to a moderately warm room. If possible, it is perhaps more advisable to keep it where it will experience an equable temperature, as under these conditions it will sing nearly the whole of the year, though, of course, but weakly during the winter, and not at all while moulting, which generally occurs in autumn. In all other respects treat as for a Nightingale.

The Whinchat, though difficult to keep, repays all trouble by its handsome appearance and sweet song. It was a very favourite bird with the late Mr. Sweet, who speaks of it as the most interesting bird he possessed. It is lively and cheerful when at liberty, living on heaths, commons, railway embankments, or amongst furze, retiring from these haunts in the autumn, and visiting arable lands and cornfields, where it may be seen sitting on the sheaves or hanging to the ears of corn, from which habit it is known in some districts by the name of "Barleyear." It may often be found at that time of year in the fields of mangold wurzel or between cabbage rows, searching for insects. When first placed in confinement it is very difficult to induce the bird to partake of the ordinary food of the aviary, and it requires, therefore, especial care and attention. It should be first enticed with gentles mixed up with its food, or little beetles and flies; then give it mealworms, and in time it will take ants' eggs freely, as well as usual Nightingale's food. It should be kept as much as possible in the open air, as in confinement with an artificial atmosphere it oftentimes becomes dull and melancholy, losing its natural sprightliness, and with that its song, which has many features in common with that of the Goldfinch, being cheerful and sweet.

The Whinchat arrives in April, leaving again for a warmer climate in September; and, unlike the Stonechat, it never stays through the winter in this country. It had better be kept moderately warm during the winter, as any sudden severe frost may kill it; and though it may be possible to keep them without a fire, the risk would be great.

In length it is about five inches; the beak is black, and from its base to the eye and round to the neck is a brown streak, over which runs a stripe of white, nearly meeting at the back of the neck; the whole of the upper part is brown, the centre of the feathers darker brown, edged with a lighter shade; the chin is white, which colour runs down the sides of the throat to the shoulders; the throat and breast a reddish-buff, lighter towards the belly, which is pale buff; the principal wing-feathers are black, those nearest the body white; the spurious quills white, edged with brown; the pinion-feathers dark brown, edged with lighter brown; the tail white at the base, except the two centre feathers, which, together with the rest of the tail, are brown, edged with lighter brown.

The Wheatear is a very difficult bird to thoroughly tame if captured when of mature age, and it is therefore advisable to rear it from the nest, or procure it while quite young. It will, however, thrive in confinement, and its song seems to improve upon careful attention to food and treatment. It should be kept in a Nightingale cage, and must be carefully watched when first captured, or it will perhaps refuse food, and droop and die. After becoming accustomed to artificial food it may be turned out into the aviary, but will seldom sing so well there as in a cage. It has a pleasant song, sometimes perchance interspersed with a peculiar sort of scream, but continued both by day and night in a connected way. It should be provided with a plentiful supply of insects, none of which seem to come amiss. It is very partial to beetles and crickets, and these can be easily procured from a neighbouring baker, who would no doubt be equally delighted to find that his greatest nuisances were at last put to use.

The adult male is about six inches in length; the beak is black; from its base to the eyes, and thence to the ear-coverts, runs a band of black, over which is a similarly shaped streak of white; the forehead is also white; the head, neck, and back are a delicate light grey; the wings are blackish-brown; the upper tail-coverts white; the tail-feathers blackish-brown, those on the outside edge being white towards the roots; the chin, breast, belly, and under tail-coverts are very pale greyish-white, delicately tinted with rusty brown, which colour increases in depth towards the breast and sides. The female has the head, neck, and back brown, tinged with grey; the wings are dark brown, each feather being deeply fringed with light brown; the band on the cheek is brown, and the stripe over the eye tawny; the whole of the under part is rufous brown, paler towards the chin and belly; the tail is dark brown, tipped with light brown; all except the two centre feathers are white towards the roots. After the autumn moult the males greatly resemble the females in plumage. These birds vary very considerably according to their age and the season of year. In the old birds the grey on the back becomes more decided, the breast whiter, and the brown tints deeper in colour.

The Wheatear should be kept upon the food recommended for the Nightingale, not omitting the insects.

THE GREATER WHEATEAR, which arrives in England about the middle of April, may also be called the Bush Wheatear, as, unlike the Wheatear, it invariably settles on a bush, or even a tree. It has been strangely overlooked by most naturalists, but has often come beneath our notice. It is a larger bird than the preceding, is much wilder in its nature, and is not so docile in confinement.

Its great distinctions from the Wheatear (which it otherwise greatly resembles) are its size; the band which runs from the beak to the ear has the feathers edged with brown; the head, neck, and back are shaded with brown; the wings are dark brown, each feather being edged with lighter brown; and the legs and beak are larger even in comparison of the increased size.

THE GRASSHOPPER WARBLER, although not a very generally known bird, is not at all uncommon in some parts of England, and would seem to be pretty generally dispersed throughout the country. It is so very retiring that it manages to elude any but the most patient observer. From the colour of its plumage, and a habit of running along the bottoms of hedgerows or amongst the grass and sedge, it has often puzzled those who have heard its cricket-like song, seemingly close at hand, yet provokingly deceptive as to its real position. It may be heard singing in the evenings as well as during the day. It is about five and three-quarter inches in length; the beak is brown and thin; the head, neck, back, and wings are greenish-brown, the centre feathers darker brown, producing a spotted appearance; the tail is greenish-brown and wedge-shaped; the chin and throat yellowish-white, the latter being sprinkled with small spots of brown; the breast is yellowish-green, shading to greenish-brown on the sides. Mr. Sweet mentions that he kept one for some time, but that it unfortunately killed itself by too much bathing. It should be kept similarly to the Nightingale, and be fed upon the same food.

THE DARTFORD WARBLER, a hardy little bird, is another winter resident in England, and is found amongst furze, being principally a frequenter of the south-eastern counties. It often sings when on the wing, after the manner of the Whitethroat, and is possessed of a cheerful note, which is delivered in a collected manner, and is very soft and sweet. It has a habit of perching on a topmost spray of furze, throwing up its tail in somewhat similar style to the Magpie, and then suddenly quitting its perch, and dropping, as it were, into the bush. We once found a nest as early as the middle of May, in which were five young. Owing to unavoidable circumstances we were unable to give them all the attention they required, or we believe we should have been able to rear them.

This bird is rather difficult to obtain, but from its appearance would be a very interesting addition to the aviary. Bechstein greatly wished to have one, but never succeeded in procuring a living specimen. Could this difficulty be surmounted, no doubt many ornithologists would be delighted to keep them, in order thoroughly to investigate their nature and habits. It is about five and a quarter inches in length; the head, neck, and back are greyish-black; the wings brownish-black; the tail, which is somewhat long, is greyish-black; the chin, throat, breast, and sides are reddish-brown, shaded with purple, the chin and throat having the feathers tipped with greyish-white; the belly is grey; on the sides of the neck the grey tint is more decided.

We would recommend Nightingale's food, adding such insects as may be procurable, especially flies or moths. Although it braves the cold of winter, we would suggest that it be not placed in too chilly a situation.

THE WOOD WARBLER, which is also known as the Wood Wren, is very handsome, and may be safely recommended to any one with an aviary. It is generally to be found in plantations and woods, giving a decided preference to beech, and living almost entirely amongst the trees, being seldom seen at any great distance from them, and hardly ever upon the ground. Though brighter, it is very similar in plumage to the Chiffchaff and Willow Warbler, but is the rarest of the three. It is nearly five inches in length; the whole of the upper part is olive-green, tinged with sulphur-yellow; from the base of the beak, over the eye to the ear, runs a narrow streak of yellow, underneath this is a brownish line; the chin, throat, and breast are yellow, inclining to a silvery-white on the belly; the wings and tail are brown, each feather being edged with greenish-yellow. It arrives in this country in May. The nest is spherical, built upon the ground, sometimes under a tuft of grass or amongst beech leaves, of which the external portion of the nest is often composed.

This bird becomes exceedingly tame, and may be induced to perch on the hand and take flies or other dainty morsels. If allowed to fly about the room, its first thought is the selection of a perch; when it has satisfied itself on this point, it will show great expertness in catching the flies from off the walls and ceiling, always returning to its favourite perch to eat them. They should be fed upon scraped beef and egg, bread-crumbs, German paste, ants' eggs, gentles, and mealworms; as also any insects, such as flies, spiders, small moths, or caterpillars, that may be obtainable. They must be kept warm, and will require artificial heat in winter.

THE WILLOW WARBLER, which is also known as the Willow Wren, is not of so bright plumage as the preceding, and is best distinguished from the Chiffchaff by its legs, which are light brown. It inhabits woods, copses, plantations, shrubberies, thick hedgerows, and bushes, or furze on commons and hills, building its nest upon the ground. It is a pretty and lively bird, quite amusing in its actions, flying or hopping from branch to branch, capturing any small insect that comes in its way. It has a very soft and pleasing song, not unlike the Robin's, though not so powerful; neither does it possess much variety, yet having the advantage in its favour of being commenced in the early morning and continuing with slight intermissions until the fall of evening.

Like the preceding bird, it is capable of being easily tamed, and will then feed from the hand, or if allowed to range the room will pursue and capture the flies, or peck them off the walls and ceiling. It should be kept warm, and have artificial heat during winter; at night-time they invariably huddle close together for the sake of warmth. It should be fed and treated the same as the Wood Warbler.

The Chiffchaff, though one of our most diminutive songsters, is one of the first of the summer warblers to arrive in this country, being only preceded by the Wheatear. It may be seen early in the spring flitting about in shady woods, bushes, and hedgerows, uttering its fussy "chiff-chaff, chivvy-chavvy." It may be distinguished from the Willow Warbler by its size, being slightly smaller, and by having dark brown legs, and its nest is invariably built off the ground; it has been called by many the "Lesser Pettychaps."

Like the Willow and Wood Warblers, this bird is very sociable, and may be easily tamed so as to readily take tempting food from the hand, or will catch the flies if allowed the freedom of the room. It should be fed and treated similarly to those birds.

The Sedge Warbler has its head and neck olive-brown, each feather being tipped with brown so as to form stripes; the back olive-brown; from the base of the beak to the ear a band of brown, and over this, running from the beak over the eye, a narrow streak of white; the whole of the under part a delicate yellowish-white, deepening in colour on the sides and breast; the wings brown, each feather being edged with lighter brown, and the tail also brown.

Being very difficult to "meat off" if full-grown when caught, it is preferable to rear this bird from the nest, when it should be fed upon the same food as young Nightingale's, but otherwise the Wood Warbler's food will amply suffice. It should be given plenty of water for bathing, but must not be allowed to indulge too much in this luxury during winter, as it considerably weakens the bird. Though rather difficult to keep, the Sedge Warbler has a comparatively strong song, and is a lively and attractive bird.

The Reed Warbler is very similar in plumage to the Nightingale, but smaller in size, and having a white streak over the eye, whilst the breast is lighter, and the back and tail not so rich a brown. The nest, composed of grasses and wool, is built suspended between three or four reeds over a ditch or stream. The Wood Warbler's food is best for this bird.

The Common Wren, familiarly called Jenny or Kitty Wren, holds almost as popular a position as Robin himself, associated as both are in many a nursery tale, and also through being likewise a winter resident and a visitor to our gardens and houses during inclement weather. It is lively in its habits, hopping cheerily from place to place, seldom flying far, but keeping principally to the hedgerows or gardens, though oftentimes climbing trees, running round and round them in search of the insects or larvæ that may be secreted in the bark. It has an exceedingly pretty song, of great strength considering the size of the bird, and very nearly resembling some of the notes of the Canary.

Jenny is one of the smallest of British birds, being only about four inches in length, and of unpretending plumage unless closely inspected. The head and neck are bright rusty brown, barred with darker brown; the back reddish-brown, also marked transversely with bars of darker brown; the chin, throat, and breast dusky grey, tinged with brown towards the belly; from the base of the beak, over the eye to the back of the ear, runs a narrow streak of dusky grey; the wings are reddish-brown, each feather barred with darker brown, the outside feathers being lighter; the tail is also reddish-brown, barred in the same manner with darker brown. The nest of the Wren is extremely interesting, being built of a variety of materials, the selection of which is generally determined by the nature of its surroundings. The shape is spherical, having a dome, and a small aperture at the side. It is built in a variety of situations. I have found one that was placed in a cabbage that had run to seed; another overhanging a running stream, only a few inches above the water. Their favourite building site is, however, against the trunk of a tree.

From their merry and lively habits, Wrens are exceedingly pretty additions to the aviary, where they had better be provided with some small covered boxes, or the outside husk of a cocoa-nut, having a hole cut in them, and lined with moss, as these birds, although staying in England when wild during the winter, are very subject to cold when in confinement, and always huddle up closely together for warmth when roosting.

They had better be fed upon Nightingale's food, a few small worms, caterpillars, spiders, or flies when procurable, together with plenty of ants' eggs.

THE GOLDEN-CRESTED WREN is the most diminutive of all British birds, and may close the long list of Cage Warblers, a class of birds embracing some of the most beautiful of our songsters, but which seem to be sadly neglected, perhaps under the impression that they will not repay the trouble the nature of their food necessitates; yet beyond the question of song, their plumage is delicately tinted and their habits are extremely interesting, whilst with ordinary care and proper food they are not so difficult to keep as is generally supposed.

This little bird, which is only three and a half inches in length, is exceedingly beautiful, and may be kept in a cage or turned into the aviary, if fed and treated similarly to the Wood Warbler. Though many of them remain through the winter, they should be kept warm.

The whole of the neck and back is a greenish olive-brown; upon the crest of the head is a patch of reddish-orange; round the eye is a pale dusky ring, encircled by another of dull white; the wings are brown, double-barred with white, and edged with greenish-yellow on the pinion-feathers.

Vincent Brooks Day & Son Lith

TREE PIPIT. WOODLARK.

SKYLARK

CHAPTER XXXVI.

LARKS, PIPITS, AND WAGTAILS.

THE SKYLARK is entitled to a prominent position in the foremost ranks of our songsters, whether we contemplate its merits whilst soaring high amid the clouds of song, mellowed by distance into delicious cadences, or as the pet of some family cramped in between the walls of narrow streets in the midst of our densely-populated towns. Even under these adverse circumstances a Lark will enliven the whole neighbourhood by the clear and lively tones of its inspiring song, which is to be especially esteemed for power and brilliancy. Perhaps there is no other British bird so much kept by townsfolk; certainly none other puts forward his claims with such sturdy eloquence. Even when in its narrow cage the Lark seems constrained to use some muscular exercise during singing, for it flutters its wings and tramples the turf as if it were once more free. Excepting perhaps the Nightingale, no bird would seem to have exercised the quaint conceits of poets with more felicity than the Skylark, yet, as with most of our sweetest songsters, its plumage is most unpretending. The beak is dark brown above, pale yellow-brown at the base; the feathers on the top of the head dark brown, edged with paler brown, and rather long so as to form a crest, which the bird can elevate at pleasure; the cheeks are pale brown, the whole of the upper part is varied with three shades of brown, the centre of every feather being darkest giving the bird a streaked or spotted appearance; the tail is brown except the outside feathers, which are white; the throat and upper part of the breast pale brown, streaked with darker brown; the belly pale yellowish-white; the legs strong, and the feet especially formed for walking, the hind toe being long and straighter than with perching birds. Though it is very difficult to distinguish the difference between the sexes, the female is slightly smaller than the male, and its plumage is given by most authorities as being rather darker.

In the fallow lands, or out in the meadows amid a wealth of buttercups and cuckoo-flowers, in a slight indentation of the ground, the Skylark builds its nest, in direct antithesis, as it were, to the boldness of its flight. The nest is very simply constructed of dry bents of grass, and the eggs are from three to six in number. The young are easily reared if properly attended to, though they are inexorable in their demands to be fed early. This should be about four or five o'clock, and by no means later than six o'clock, when a few mouthfuls must be given, and so on at short intervals during the day. A little given often is far better than over-cramming. They should be given soaked bread mixed with crushed hemp-seed, and a little scraped beef and egg. The adult birds may be fed on bread-crumbs and crushed hemp-seed, varied with morsels of cheese or potato or any table scraps. A better but more expensive food is bread-crumbs and crushed hemp-seed, German paste, scraped beef and egg, varied with gentles and mealworms.

The Skylark is a strong, hardy bird, and will stand a deal of cold weather, great numbers staying through the winter in this country. The fowlers sadly decimate them during the winter months, as they are considered a dainty in the market.

Though the bird is never seen near a pond, as it drinks when wild the dew from the grass, it is very fond of dusting, and should always be provided with plenty of road gravel, such as may be found in the road-side gutters after a heavy shower of rain. No perches are required, but a piece of turf should be placed in the circular front of the cage, which should be of the ordinary Lark pattern, obtainable of any wire-worker.

As the Lark always lives upon the ground when not soaring, and seldom settles upon a tree or bush, when wild, in the aviary a piece of turf should be set aside out of the reach of the perches.

The Woodlark's song is greatly prized, and by some has been assigned a rank next in order of merit to that of the Nightingale itself. Though not so loud and piercing as the Skylark's, it possesses some brilliancy, modulated by deep pathos, being noted more for mellowness and plaintiveness than for sprightliness and execution. In confinement it sings from the perch, but when wild will sing from the bough of a tree, or, in summer, when poised in mid-air, ascending in spiral gyrations even higher than the Skylark. It is not so common a bird as the Skylark, preferring rough grass land, interspersed with trees or woods and copses. It generally commences breeding very early in the season.

The following is a plain description of a Woodlark that procured the first prize at the Crystal Palace Bird Show for two years in succession, and once also at the Alexandra Palace:—The beak is dark brown above, pale yellow-brown beneath; over the eye and ear-coverts runs a pale yellowish-brown streak; the feathers on the top of the head are of a light brown colour, streaked with dark brown, and are long, forming a crest, which can be elevated at pleasure; the whole of the upper part wood-brown, streaked on the neck and patched on the back with dark brownish-black; the tail has a very light brown feather on either side, and two pale brown in the middle, the rest being brownish-black, triangularly tipped with white; the whole of the under part pale yellowish-brown, speckled with elongated flecks of dark brown, smaller and more thinly scattered on the throat, and gathering in size and number on the breast, and not at all on the belly. It is smaller in size than the Skylark, and its tail and hind claw are shorter.

Equally to be desired in the cage or aviary, the Woodlark is a bird that we can safely recommend. Its food, whilst resembling the Nightingale's, is not quite so elaborate. The best is composed of cooked beef chopped up very fine, some hard-boiled egg (both yolk and white), also finely chopped or run through a sieve, some German paste, a little finely-pounded hemp-seed mixed with a good proportion of fine crumbs of bread.

We have found that upon this food the birds thrive better and keep their song longer; their plumage is also neater, and they invariably moult very much better than if fed without the beef and egg. An occasional mealworm should be given as a variation, and ants' eggs and gentles whenever procurable.

The Shorelark is a very handsome bird, but unfortunately very uncommon, or its finely tinted breast and prettily marked head and throat would recommend it to many. Its song is somewhat eccentric, but sweet, though comparatively short, and uttered generally when on the wing at a slight elevation. We knew one that was caught near Brighton, and which lived in an aviary for over five years. We should advise that this bird be fed and kept the same as a Woodlark.

The Tree Pipit, as may be seen upon reference to the Plate, is a very graceful bird, and, though not striking in plumage, has a pretty appearance. Its song is very pleasing, and when wild the manner in which it is delivered adds greatly to its charm. The bird generally perches upon the leafless branch of a tree in a meadow or copse, from thence ascending on quivering wings, which, with its tail, are then outspread whilst the song is uttered. At its close it again seeks its former perch. This bird, being very tamable as well as sociable, will thrive in an aviary, where also its graceful carriage will be better displayed.

The Tree Pipit, being fond of water, is often found near a pond or stream. It also bathes, not dusting itself so much as the Skylark. Its food when wild consists of insects and their larvæ, especially flies, caterpillars, and worms; and it therefore thrives best in confinement upon the food recommended for the Woodlark. The nest is generally found beneath a tuft of grass, in and about a small copse or plantation, and the young should be fed and treated similarly to young Nightingales; but we would recommend, in preference to those reared from the nest, a bird caught in the autumn.

THE MEADOW PIPIT was formerly included with the Larks, and the error still prevails in many districts—it being commonly known by the name of Titlark. This bird is much more common than the preceding, which, however, it greatly resembles in appearance, though smaller, and of a more decided olive-green colour on the back, whilst the breast is not so bright a buff. Over the whole of England this hardy bird may be found, whether on hills or in the valleys. Being docile and easily tamed, it would do well in an aviary of insect-eating birds. The food recommended for the Tree Pipit is equally good for this bird, as their food and habits when wild are somewhat similar.

THE ROCK PIPIT is very nearly allied to the Meadow and Tree Pipits in its mode of flight and song; it is, however, larger in size than those birds, and its plumage is olive-brown, lighter on the throat and breast. Though called the Rock Pipit, this bird also frequents low flat shores in the vicinity of the sea, feeding on the marine insects that are left by the receding tide.

We find from experience that it will thrive upon Woodlark's food.

THE WATER PIPIT, though supposed to be very uncommon, is often to be met with. We have taken as many as fifty in a season. It may generally be found upon the sea-shore, among the sea-weed that has been cast up by the waves; and is hardy enough to brave an English winter. It is a larger bird than either of the preceding; its plumage is slate-colour on the upper part, shaded with dark olive-brown; the wings and tail olive-brown; the under part is greyish-white, shaded on the breast with a beautiful salmon-pink, slightly streaked with grey.

When wild its food consists of flies, gnats, and aquatic insects and their larvæ; but we find it will thrive upon such food as is recommended for the Woodlark. One we have now in our aviary has been so fed for upwards of a year.

THE RICHARD'S PIPIT and TAWNY PIPIT are fine handsome birds, somewhat uncommon in these islands, but well worthy the attention of any one possessed of an aviary, when we would recommend they be fed and treated the same as Woodlarks.

THE PIED WAGTAIL is an elegant bird, but unfortunately has not much song to recommend it to notice; yet its plumage is so very striking as to always make it a prominent attraction to an aviary, whilst its light and airy carriage, combined with the eccentric motion of the tail, from which its name is derived, is very interesting. This bird is often found near water, either wading in the shallows, or, sylph-like, alighting on the lily leaves whilst in search of aquatic insects or larvæ, although not disdaining flies and gnats or such-like insects, which latter often fall victims to this pretty bird. In the cage or aviary there should be always plenty of water provided, both for drinking and bathing. They are also fond of grass lawns, where they look extremely pretty. Some of these birds stay through the winter in England, and we know a pair that were kept for more than four years in an open aviary. They stood the winter well, and bred.

The Pied Wagtail should be fed and treated as a Woodlark, not forgetting the mealworms, gentles, or small worms.

THE YELLOW WAGTAIL, which is also known as Ray's Wagtail, is the handsomest of our soft-billed birds. From a habit it has of frequenting meadows where cows are feeding, and of running around and between the legs of those animals to catch the insects aroused by their trampling, it has obtained the name of "Cowbird." It also pursues and catches insects when on the wing. A specimen in our aviary has been fed, and thrives, upon food similar to that recommended for the Woodlark, standing the winter well in an open aviary without a fire, although when wild this bird always migrates to a warmer climate. Mealworms, gentles, and ants' eggs are very favourite food of this bird.

THE GREY WAGTAIL is also one of our most handsome and elegant birds, and though possessing but little song, its plumage accords it a prominent position amongst the aviary favourites. It visits this country in the autumn, and stays through the winter, generally frequenting spring ditches and ponds, and is often a visitor to the farmyard in order to secure any insect that may be found in the gutters and puddles. Like all the Wagtail tribe, this bird is especially to be noticed for its light and airy carriage. This species should be fed as the Pied Wagtail, and may be safely kept in an out-door aviary, where it will agree well with the other birds; but it is not advisable to keep more than a pair together. We know of one that paired with a hen Pied Wagtail, and brought up a handsome brood of mules, some of which also interbred and reared their young.

THE GREY-HEADED and WHITE WAGTAILS are rather uncommon in this country, but are very handsome, and possess an elegant form and carriage in common with the rest of their tribe. We would recommend that they be fed and treated similarly to the other Wagtails.

LINNET.

GOLDFINCH. BULLFINCH.

CHAPTER XXXVII.

THE FINCHES.

THE GOLDFINCH, from various causes, is unfortunately much scarcer now than formerly. No doubt the many demands made for caging this very handsome and sweet songster have tended to lessen its numbers, for besides almost rivalling tropical birds in the beauty and variety of its plumage, the Goldfinch is possessed of an exceedingly sweet song, combining a clear metallic ring with modulated power, much softer and sweeter than the Canary's, and linked together by a continual twittering, making the song last for a long time without intermission. "Goldie" is also very sagacious, and can be taught many tricks almost without coercion, such as drawing up its water from a well and opening its seed-box. Properly constructed cages with this apparatus are easily procurable, and the bird will soon understand the management of the well chain, pulling it up with its beak, and adroitly holding it with its feet.

As may be seen upon reference to the Plate, the Goldfinch is of particularly striking plumage, the red feathers on the face and the bright golden bars across the wings being its prominent distinctions. The difference between the sexes is very difficult to distinguish; in the female the feathers immediately over the beak are lighter, the black feathers on the back of the head are edged with brownish-grey, as are also the black feathers on the shoulder, whilst the head is invariably smaller, and the eye not so bright and bold.

When wild the Goldfinch is of great service to the gardener and farmer, as in spring it feeds almost entirely upon the seeds of the groundsel and dandelion, which are then the favourite food, and the fluff from whose seeds forms the lining to its nest. In the summer, when the long thistles have run to seed, Goldie may be seen hanging to the thistle heads, and with its long beak extracting the seeds. The red feathers on its head are particularly short and strong to form a protection against the prickly thistles. In the autumn and winter the seeds of the thistle and button-weed form its staple food. It is very desirable that these seeds should be given to the bird at their proper season, as they greatly add to the bird's song and keep it in good health. It also greatly enjoys a piece of watercress or lettuce.

The nest is very ingenious and exceedingly pretty, being composed principally of moss lined with wool and the down from the thistle, groundsel, and dandelion seeds, with an outside covering of lichen; the eggs are generally from five to six in number. If intended to rear from the nest, the young should be taken when about ten days old, and fed upon soaked stale crust of bread, soaked rape and hemp-seed crushed, maw-seed, and finely-chopped hard-boiled egg; but it is better to have them taken when adult, as they very soon become tame. Those taken during the months of September and October are preferable.

From its extreme docility the Goldfinch is a great favourite in the cage. The bird is of a restless disposition, continually hopping about, clinging to the wires, and rattling its beak against them as if in order to escape. When in the aviary it sometimes acts in a dominant manner, driving the other birds from the food; but it seldom fights, although often showing ill-temper. Goldfinches will breed in the aviary or breeding-cage; they will also breed with Canaries. They have been known to breed with the Bullfinch and other Finches, the details of such hybrid breeding having been already described. If obtainable, the birds should be provided with an old nest, or the nest of a Chaffinch, in preference to the nest-bag.

The Goldfinch, in common with all the Finches, shows a very varied taste in regard to its favourite kinds of seed. The best food is composed of a selection of the following seeds:—Canary, flax (also known as linseed), oat-grits, rape, hemp, and maw-seed, generally diminishing in favour as in order named. Some birds will not eat all these seeds, therefore it is advisable to watch the general choice, and give those only, as otherwise it will scatter and waste the rest in order to obtain the favourites. Should the bird show a decided preference for hemp, it is not advisable to let it have too much, as this seed is very fattening. In order to break it of scattering when in search of the hemp, give a few—say twelve—seeds upon the top of the rest, and the bird will soon understand the arrangement, and give up its endeavours. One very important item in its treatment consists in providing plenty of road gravel or sand, the former being preferable. This gravel or sand assists digestion, and is a source of great pleasure to the bird, besides conducing to health.

The Goldfinch, particularly when in the aviary, very often suffers from diarrhœa and a wasting away of its flesh. When thus attacked, at once separate from the other birds, place in a small cage with plenty of gravel, over which strew some lettuce-seed. Feed as recommended, adding plenty of lettuce-seed, also giving some chalk in its water, first having deprived the bird until thirsty—say about an hour—not omitting to stir the mixture recently so as to ensure the bird getting its dose of chalk. If it has been previously fed on any green food, it had better be deprived of that luxury, or *vice versâ.*

THE CHEVERIL GOLDFINCH, which has the distinction of a white streak from the base of the lower mandible down the breast, is greatly admired. It should be treated in all respects as the Goldfinch, being only a variation of colour.

THE BULLFINCH is a heavily-built bird of rather inelegant shape, but very striking plumage, as may be seen depicted in the Plate; his bright red breast contrasting most forcibly with the black hood on the head and the beautiful grey on the back. The female has the breast chocolate-brown, and the grey on the back tinged with brown. These birds have been known to lose their colours and turn almost black, which freak of Nature has been generally attributed to their having fed upon too much hemp-seed; yet one caught young and reared by us is so affected, although it has never eaten any seed but canary, so that we think naturalists must search for some other reason for this curious phenomenon.

Although the Bullfinch has but a moderate song, it is possessed of imitative powers in the highest degree, and it may be taught to pipe a tune more readily than any other British bird. This may be done in a somewhat similar manner to that recommended for the Blackbird, but the tedious task is much more often successful, and the Bullfinch then attains a great value. In Germany regular piping schools are established, where the birds are taught when quite young.

The Bullfinch is a somewhat slovenly bird, and very apt to scatter its food. It should be kept clean, and be given plenty of gravel. It breeds very freely in the aviary, if provided with proper materials for building; we find that they prefer small pieces of heather and fine roots. The young should be fed upon soaked stale crust of bread, scalded rape-seed, and finely-chopped hard-boiled egg. The adult should be fed and treated as the Goldfinch.

Vincent Brooks Day & Son Lith.

GREENFINCH. MOUNTAIN FINCH.
HAW FINCH.
CHAFFINCH.

THE CHAFFINCH is one of the handsomest of the Finches, and from its compact and elegant shape, combined with lively habits and short but pretty song, is deservedly held everywhere in high estimation. It is a bold bird, and approaches the bars of the aviary with extreme confidence, chirping the while or uttering its lively call-note of "pink." Its song also has a telling ring in it, and is very cheerful and clear. In Germany, where the Chaffinch is much admired, singing matches are held to test their comparative merits.

In England also this species of sport is carried on. The song of the Chaffinch is composed of three distinct notes, each of which is uttered several times in succession, forming a short phrase or song, which, to be perfect, should consist of so many syllables, ended with a distinct "wee do" uttered in rather higher pitch; though the song of some birds has a different termination. A good songster will repeat this phrase with extreme pertinacity, and this may be stimulated by placing the young bird with an older one of acknowledged singing powers. Amongst a certain class this fact has been made the basis of matches that are managed in a business-like manner. A judge, referee, and scorers are appointed; and the rival birds, confined in small cages, are brought into the room covered; the signal is given, they are uncovered, and the match commences. Every *perfect* "song" is scored down to the respective singer until time is up, when the singer of the highest number of songs wins. The judge notifies each song to the scorer, and, in case of dispute as to the imperfections of any song, the assistance of the referee is called in. The usual betting characteristic of too many English pastimes of course prevails, and there is little doubt that the match is esteemed more as a medium for betting than from any love of the bird's song. From an erroneous idea that the bird sings better in the dark, instances have occurred of the owners cruelly putting out the eyes of the poor bird with a red-hot wire, with the intention of increasing its song. We cannot too strongly reprehend so barbarous a practice, especially as its cruelty is only equalled by its uselessness.

The Chaffinch is extremely neat and clean, and should always be provided with a bath. The nest of this bird is a very pretty structure. When wild its food consists of seeds and grains, insects, and the buds and tender leaves of plants. It is fond of groundsel, and should be provided with this favourite food of all Finches whenever possible. In the aviary it is somewhat dominant, though otherwise a good companion. If it proves quarrelsome it is advisable to cut four or five wing-feathers, as it will then be unable to fly so fast as the other birds. The Chaffinch, however, will always sing better in a cage, which should not be bell-shaped. It will breed in confinement, and should be given an old nest to breed in, feeding the young as recommended for Bullfinches. The adult birds should be fed and treated as Goldfinches, giving the bird the opportunity of selecting its favourite seeds.

THE GREENFINCH is a somewhat heavily-built bird of rather handsome plumage, but little song, and its call is a melancholy note. It is an extremely common bird, and of a hardy nature, and will become very tame in captivity, where it will breed freely, or may be mated with a Canary. They have also been known to breed with Linnets. The young should be brought up as recommended for young Goldfinches, though it is possible to rear them on soaked bread and crushed hemp-seed. The adult should be fed and treated as recommended for Goldfinches.

THE MOUNTAIN FINCH, known also as the Bramble Finch or Brambling, is another very handsome bird, as may be seen upon reference to the Plate. It is only a winter resident in England, being more common in the north. The Mountain Finch is a hardy bird, and should be fed and treated as the Goldfinch; it may be kept caged or turned into the aviary, where, however, it sometimes proves quarrelsome, and should then be treated as recommended for the Chaffinch. They will breed in confinement, and we know of one that paired with a Chaffinch, rearing a very handsome brood of young.

THE HAWFINCH is a handsome bird, with peculiarly-shaped blue feathers overlapping the wings; it is not so common as the preceding. We reared a nest of young upon the same food as is recommended for young Goldfinches, and these birds agreed very well in the aviary; but others that we had when adult caused great havoc amongst the birds with their powerful beaks, one even biting off one of the claws of another bird. We think it therefore always advisable to keep them in a separate cage. The adult birds should be fed the same as Goldfinches.

THE CITREL FINCH and SERIN FINCH are occasional visitors to England, and are very pretty additions to the aviary, or may be kept in a cage, feeding and treating the same as Goldfinches. We have been successful in keeping both these birds. The Citrel Finch was fed principally on canary-seed, and the Serin Finch at present in our aviary shows a preference for canary and rape.

THE LINNET is also known by the various names of Brown, Grey, and Rose Linnet, from the plumage varying so greatly according to age and the season of the year. When young, Linnets are lighter in colour than the one depicted in the Plate, and when wild, after the second moult, the male obtains a rose-red hue on the head and breast. It is then known as a Rose Linnet; but in the succeeding autumn it loses this colour and becomes of unpretending plumage, composed of different shades of brown. As with the Lark or Nightingale, however, the plumage is no criterion of the vocal powers, for the Linnet has an extremely pleasing song, beautifully modulated and flute-like, and so sweet as to make it an especial favourite as a cage-bird.

The Linnet is somewhat shy, but capable of being tamed, and will become exceedingly attached to those who feed and tend it. As with the rest of the Finches, it is extremely erratic in its choice of food, except that all show a preference for hemp and rape; the former seed, however, is much too fattening, and should be given sparingly, especially as the Linnet is rather a greedy bird and apt to overfeed itself. We find that the average of them prefer canary, rape, and flax; a small proportion of hemp may be given. Chickweed or groundsel should be given when obtainable, or a little watercress or lettuce. The young should be fed and treated as recommended for young Bullfinches.

THE TWITE, or MOUNTAIN LINNET, is closely allied to the preceding bird; it is, however, slightly smaller and more slender-looking; the beak is smaller and yellow instead of brown, and the whole plumage is darker. The sex is distinguishable by the male having a red rump. This bird is more often found in the north, only visiting the southern counties of England in the autumn and winter. It has a very pleasant song, though not so elaborate as the Linnet's, and its name is derived from its peculiar call-note. It should be fed and treated as recommended for the Linnet.

THE SISKIN is a very beautiful little bird of diminutive size, but prettily-marked plumage, as may be seen depicted in the Plate. Its beauty is especially displayed when seen flitting amongst the branches of the alder trees, feeding upon the seeds, and keeping up a continual twitter the while. It is very docile, and may be soon taught the accomplishments of the Goldfinch. Though Siskins have not much song, and that occasionally interspersed with harsh, jarring notes, yet they are continually twittering, and being lively, hopping from perch to perch,

Vincent Brooks Day & Son Lith

1. SISKIN.
2. WAXWING.

3. REDPOLL.
4. CROSSBILL.

they are very pretty additions to an aviary, where also their twittering may induce the more favoured songsters to sing. If reared from the nest they may be taught the songs of other birds, but can never be taught to pipe a tune.

The Siskin should be fed upon canary-seed, flax, maw-seed, and oat-grits, adding a little hemp-seed, of which the bird is very fond. This may also be used as a reward whilst teaching it tricks. It becomes exceedingly tame in confinement, taking food readily from the hand. It will also breed, and should then be provided with an old Goldfinch or Chaffinch nest, or the usual nest-bag; the young may be reared upon the food recommended for young Goldfinches. The Siskin will also mate with the Canary, and the young of this cross make very nice and handsome cage-birds.

THE COMMON or LESSER REDPOLL (as may be seen upon reference to the Plate) is a very pretty bird, and from its lively habits is a great attraction to the aviary, though it has not much song to recommend it, being merely possessed of a simple twittering note, which, however, being continually uttered, acts as an incentive to the rest of the birds, and will often cause them to sing. The Redpoll is a very affectionate bird, and may be very easily tamed and taught many tricks. Its food is similar to the Siskin's, and it should be treated accordingly.

THE MEALY REDPOLL is not so common a bird as the preceding, from which it is most distinguishable by its greater size; the breast is more distinctly spotted, and the lower part of the back, rump, and upper tail-coverts are a mealy or greyish-white. It should be fed and treated as the Siskin.

THE CROSSBILL is a handsome bird, especially noticeable for the peculiar formation of its beak, from which feature it derives its name. It is subject to great variations of plumage, being sometimes red and otherwise a yellowish-green. It is not a common bird in England, being found only in certain favoured localities, where it generally frequents fir plantations. The cage for this bird *must* be all wire, for it would soon destroy a wooden one.

It should be fed upon canary, rape, hemp, and fir-cones, giving a piece of apple or its pips occasionally, as also a few juniper-berries, of which it is very fond. The song is not pretty, as it is somewhat harsh.

THE TREE-SPARROW is a much more handsome bird if closely inspected than is supposed by those who only obtain a cursory view, the markings upon its head and throat being especially noticeable; the sex is not distinguishable. When caught, do not place immediately in an aviary, as they would then invariably sulk and behave wildly, frightening the other birds, but rather keep in a small cage until tame. It should be fed upon canary-seed and oats.

THE HOUSE SPARROW, like the preceding, is really a handsome bird, but being invariably begrimed by the smoke and dirt of towns, the plumage is completely hidden. This bird is so well known that it is unnecessary to dilate upon its habits; and though not a desirable cage-bird, if it is reared from the nest when quite young it will become a very interesting pet, and show great attachment to its keeper. It should be fed as the preceding bird, though nothing seems to come amiss to its voracious appetite.

CHAPTER XXXVIII.

TITMICE, WOODPECKERS, AND BUNTINGS.

THE GREAT TIT, the largest of its tribe, is a very striking bird, strongly marked, and of great activity and vivacity; when wild hopping from branch to branch and clinging to the trees, which it examines most minutely in search of any insects or larvæ that may be secreted in the leaves or bark. It has, however, a reputation for being extremely dangerous if placed in an aviary with other small birds, being credited with having killed its neighbours by repeated blows of its hard beak on the head of the victim, whose brains are thereupon picked out and eaten. If reared, as recommended for young Nightingales, from the nest by hand, however, these birds may be turned into the aviary with comparative safety. An aviary of Titmice is one of the most interesting of any, because of their beauty, diminutive size, and unflagging vivacity; and if given plenty of perches, or, better still, the branch of a tree with many boughs and twigs, they will be continually flitting from perch to perch, uttering their short note the while. All of the tribe are fond of water and bathing.

The Great Tit should be fed upon scraped beef and egg, German paste, soaked bread and hemp-seed, whole hemp-seed and oats, suet, and any insects that are procurable, such as meal-worms, gentles, and flies; a few shelled nuts of any description afford them especial pleasure, as will also picking a meat bone. They are capable of being easily tamed, and will in time eat out of the hand of their feeder.

THE BLUE TIT is a very diminutive bird, being only four and a half inches in length, but so common as to be little appreciated, or no doubt its beautifully marked blue head and back, combined with its grace and activity, would cause it to be much more often found in aviaries than is now the case. When in search of food, which consists principally of insects, this bird is most amusing in its actions, often assuming the most grotesque positions, hanging beneath the branches and searching with most critical eye every possible hiding-place that could shelter its prey.

This bird is perfectly safe if placed in the aviary, as it is not dangerous to the other birds. When first caught it should be placed in a cage for a few days, and fed upon any live insects and mealworms and gentles, adding whole hemp-seed and some pieces of shelled nuts, walnuts or Spanish nuts being preferable; in other respects it should be fed and treated as recommended for the Great Tit.

THE COLE TIT is another common bird about the size of the preceding, principally found in woods and small plantations; it is also particularly active and indefatigable in its search for insects. The Cole Tit is a pretty little aviary pet, and may be made exceedingly tame. One now in our aviary of Tits has been fed for the last five years upon the food recommended for the Great Tit. It is very fond of bathing.

1. BLUE TITMOUSE. 2. BEARDED TITMOUSE. 3. COLE TITMOUSE. 4. MARSH TITMOUSE.

THE MARSH TIT, though not so generally distributed as the preceding species, is still to be found plentifully in some localities, the preference, as its name implies, being given to lowlands, where are moist meadows, with brushwood and old willow trees; it is a lively, active little bird, and is continually chirping its one solitary note. Though from the amount of dusky brown in its plumage it is not so striking as the foregoing Tits, yet it is a pretty little bird, and enlivens the aviary with its continuous twittering and restless activity. The Marsh Tits at present in our aviary have been fed for the last five years in the same way as recommended for the Great Tit.

THE BEARDED TIT, unlike the rest of this tribe, generally frequents reeds and sedges, climbing up them in search of insects or the seeds. They are very handsome birds, having the whole of the upper part fawn-colour, the face and ear-coverts grey, and from the beak across the eye, down each side of the throat of the male bird runs a jet-black band, which the bird has the power of puffing out at pleasure, and from this feature its name is derived; the chin, throat, and breast are white, the tail is long and wedge-shaped, the wings dark brown, the feathers edged with fawn-colour, the primaries edged with light grey.

The Bearded Tit should be fed as the Great Tit. These birds have been known to breed in confinement. One cock and a pair of hens having been provided with some coarse rank grass, placed in a pot, built their nests, and in one season laid as many as forty-nine eggs.

THE LONGTAILED TIT has occasioned much controversy as to its proper classification. It is much more difficult to keep than any of the tribe, being somewhat similar to the Golden-crested Wren, and should be fed and treated as that bird.

THE CRESTED TIT is a very scarce bird in England, though often found in Scotland. Being a pretty bird, it is a very desirable addition to an aviary of Tits, and it will feed upon the general food recommended.

THE WOODPECKER TRIBE.

THE GREEN WOODPECKER is one of the very handsomest of British birds, as may be seen from the Plate; it is also a fine bird, and is especially conspicuous in consequence of the brightness of its plumage and peculiar habits, it being very interesting to watch clinging to a tree in search of insects, which its long beak and peculiar tongue are particularly adapted to extract from the crevices of the bark. The tail is short, strong, and pointed, being used as a support in climbing. As this bird, in common with the whole of its tribe, is not a perching bird, the bark of a tree or some virgin cork should be placed against the sides of the cage or aviary.

The Green Woodpecker will eat most insects, principally depending upon spiders and caterpillars, or ants and their eggs, which latter it digs out of the ant-hills; failing these or other insects, it will feed upon soft-skinned fruits, and sometimes nuts. In confinement the bird should be fed upon scraped beef and egg, and soaked bread and hemp-seed; it should also be given ants' eggs, mealworms, gentles, beetles, or other insects, either separately or mixed with its food. If reared from the nest it will become quite tame; at this time the males may be distinguished from the females by their crimson cheeks, which the latter do not possess.

The one in our possession, which has been greatly admired, became exceedingly tame, eating from the hand; when offered food it would approach the bars of the cage and project its marvellously prehensile tongue with great rapidity, and draw the proffered delicacy into its mouth.

It is always advisable to keep these birds separate from their own species, as they invariably fight, and will even kill one another, as we can unfortunately vouch from experience. The young had better be placed in separate baskets when about a fortnight old, feeding as recommended for the adult bird. They are moderately hardy birds, staying through the winter in this country. The "laugh" of the Woodpecker is a very peculiar sound, somewhat startling if heard unexpectedly.

THE GREAT SPOTTED WOODPECKER is another handsome bird distributed locally in England, but never in great numbers, wooded districts being obviously its favourite resorts. The dominant colours in the plumage of this bird are black and white, with a pink patch on the back of the head and on the under tail-coverts; the female, however, is not possessed of the patch upon the head. In habits it is like the preceding bird, feeding upon similar food, and in confinement it should be fed and treated in every respect the same.

THE LESSER SPOTTED WOODPECKER, though considerably smaller, is rather similar in plumage to the preceding bird, except that the whole of the top of the head is crimson, and in the female white; its habits and food are the same as the larger bird, and it should be treated in the cage accordingly.

THE WRYNECK is a summer visitor to these islands, of elegant form but plain plumage in comparison with the handsome Woodpeckers. This bird is also known as the "Cuckoo's mate," and "Snake Bird," which latter, as also its proper name, are derived from the eccentric movements of its head and neck. The young are easily tamed if brought up from the nest, but it is much more delicate than any of the Woodpeckers, and being a migratory bird will require warmth in winter. It should be fed the same as those birds, and, not being of a quarrelsome disposition, may be kept in the aviary, especially with Warblers.

THE CREEPER is a very delicate bird, requiring great care and attention; but it will become very tame, and as it is of delicately tinted though modest plumage and diminutive size, it makes a pretty addition to the aviary, where it should be fed and treated in every respect as the Wren, not omitting the boxes with holes in, lined with moss or wool for the sake of warmth.

THE NUTHATCH is a very beautiful bird, and an especial favourite of ours, being one of the most interesting in our aviary, where its incessant activity attracts every one's attention. If given a nut it is very amusing to notice with what adroitness it fixes the nut into a crack of the cork in order to break the shell more readily. When this is accomplished, however, the Tits are always ready to pounce upon any stray morsels, sometimes indeed securing the whole kernel. When wild this bird feeds upon almost every variety of nut, especially beechmast, as also berries, seeds, and insects; and in confinement it should be fed upon nuts, cracked, scraped beef and egg, German paste, soaked bread and hemp-seed, as well as hemp-seed whole, and beechmast whenever obtainable.

Vincent Brooks Day & Son Lith

1. BLACK-HEADED BUNTING. 2. CIRL BUNTING. 3. YELLOW BUNTING.

BUNTINGS.

THE YELLOW BUNTING, or Yellow-hammer, is a somewhat common bird, of handsome plumage but indifferent song, which consists of one note repeated several times; and two lower prolonged notes of not very pleasing tone. It frequents small thickets and hedgerows, generally building its nest under shelter of some small bush in a hedge-bottom or amongst the grass of a ditch. It feeds principally upon seeds, small grains, and insects, and in the summer-time is one of the most attractive of British birds, flitting from bush to bush, and displaying to marked advantage the bright lemon-yellow on its breast and head, and the rich chestnut-brown on the back and upper tail-coverts. It is certainly a desirable addition to an aviary. The one now in our own, where its very handsome plumage ranks second to none, has been kept there for three years. This one feeds upon the general food supplied, nothing seeming to come amiss to it; whilst others confined in cages invariably have shown a marked preference for canary-seed, also eating oats and grass-seed, upon which food they thrive. If they will eat other seeds, they may be given by way of variation. The particular characteristic of the Bunting tribe is the possession of a hard palatine knob or tooth in the upper mandible, which is especially adapted for breaking and shelling seeds and grain. They will breed in confinement, and in addition to the ordinary nest-bag should be given a supply of dried bents of grass and fine roots. The young are easily reared; they should be fed upon sifted ground oats ("fig-dust") mixed into a stiff paste with scraped beef and egg.

THE CIRL BUNTING is a bird that is very little known in England except to ornithologists, especially as it closely resembles the Yellow-hammer when wild. Its great distinctions from that bird are a black throat, the head and neck are shaded with bluish-grey, and the lower part of the back and upper tail-coverts are olive-green. The female, not having the black throat, has often been mistaken for the Yellow-hammer; but the latter has a chestnut-brown rump, whilst the hen of the Cirl Bunting has olive-green, by which feature they may always be distinguished. As with the Yellow-hammer, its song is not very elaborate, consisting also of one note rather more rapidly delivered and without the prolonged finishing note. The Cirl Bunting is somewhat shy, although often approaching habitations to build its nest. If in confinement it shows an inclination to build, treat as for the Yellow-hammer. When wild it frequents grass fields, the seeds of which form their staple food; when in confinement it should be fed and treated as advised for the Yellow-hammer.

THE BLACKHEADED BUNTING is another very handsome bird, having in the summer-time a jet-black head and throat, with a band or collar of white round the neck and down to the breast. In winter the plumage is less brilliant, and the hen has not these striking characteristics. This bird is generally to be found near water, and adjacent thereto builds its nest, often selecting the edge of a reed-bed or the side of a ditch. The food when wild consists of the seeds of reeds and aquatic plants, and also of insects. It is a very attractive addition to the aviary, where it should be given plenty of water, being remarkably fond of bathing. It also is a good cage-bird, and should be fed and treated as the Yellow-hammer.

THE COMMON BUNTING is a thick-set bird, rather larger than the rest of the true Buntings, of plain plumage and little song, which is harsh and unmusical. It is a common bird, feeding principally on grains and seed, for breaking or shelling which the hard knob or tooth in the upper mandible is admirably adapted. There is little difference between the plumage of the male and female. It should be fed and treated as the Yellow-hammer.

The Snow Bunting visits this country during the winter, sometimes appearing in large flocks, and at other times rarely met with. The plumage is light and handsome, but as it is a somewhat dull bird, it is not desirable for either cage or aviary. When wild it generally frequents wheat stubbles in high and open country, and is seldom found near inhabited places. It should be fed and treated as the Yellow-hammer.

The Lapland Bunting is a very handsome bird, but uncommon, as is also the Ortolan Bunting, which latter, however, is not so prettily marked, being somewhat heavy of plumage. In the aviary these birds should be fed and treated as recommended for the Yellow-hammer.

Although we have generally been in the habit of separating our seed-eating birds from the Warblers and other soft-billed birds, also devoting another small aviary to the Tits and Nuthatch, it may be well to remark that they all will thrive together, as we have proved by experience during our personal superintendence of the aviary of Mr. H. A. Jenner, which is in a garden upon the outskirts of Brighton. It is a wooden construction about five feet by six feet, with a slanting roof rising from three feet to five feet. The floor is of wood, raised about four feet from the ground; a portion of one side is of wire, one other glass, and the remainder wood; the roof is a quarter glass and the rest wood. The wooden sides are lined with virgin cork, pieces of which, in imitation of branches, are fixed as perches. In this aviary have been confined as many as forty birds at one time, which have thriven remarkably well, the greatest trouble and anxiety having been to keep the ice on the water-trough broken during the severe winter of 1878–79. Almost all the Finches and the principal Warblers and Buntings are well represented, also three species of Wagtail—a grey Wagtail being an especial feature. The Woodlark and Tree Pipits are very handsome specimens, but the most amusing of all are some Titmice, who are very daring little birds, stealing everything they can, and often purloining a mealworm from the beak of a much larger bird. These birds are given daily one hard-boiled egg chopped fine or run through a sieve, about two ounces of stale bread-crumbs, two ounces of German paste, all of which is mixed together; besides which we supply them with a mixture of canary-seed, hemp, oat-grits, linseed, rape, millet, and maw seeds, diminishing in proportion as in order named. Some scraped beef is mixed with the egg, bread-crumbs, and German paste about two or three times a week; chopped nuts of any description are given daily; also some fruit, such as grapes, currants, elderberries, strawberries, &c., and when they are not procurable, soaked grocers' currants make a fair substitute. A pear is always a treat, as is also a damped sponge-cake. Mealworms are always kept, and gentles are often given in summer, as well as groundsel for the Finches, as we find that the more natural food the birds obtain, the better their song and the handsomer their plumage.

1. JACKDAW. 2. MAGPIE.

CHAPTER XXXIX.

CROWS, HAWKS, AND OWLS.

THE RAVEN, although not strictly a cage-bird, on account of its size, is very often kept as a pet, and should always be reared from the nest, which is generally found in forests or cliffs. His proverbial glossy feathers are of the densest black, tinted with violet. This bird is the largest of the Crow tribe, and from the breadth of its tongue may be easily taught to talk, and will then repeat words and phrases with very clear enunciation, whilst its drollery is very amusing. It should be kept in a large cage, or allowed to roam the garden with clipped wings unless very tame indeed, when it may be allowed perfect freedom; however, in that case, all glittering articles of value must be kept out of sight, as the Raven has a strong propensity for thieving and hiding anything bright and shining.

The comparatively young one we have (for they live to a very great age) is now six years old, and talks freely. It has been confined in a wire-fronted, wooden cage, about three feet square, and always has a bone given it to attract its attention, as otherwise it devotes the whole of its energies to eating the wood of its cage. It is fed chiefly upon pieces of raw meat (beef and mutton being preferred), ground oats, mixed stiffly, and any table scraps (it is very fond of picking a bone); and, in fact, nothing seems to come amiss to it, being possessed of a voracious appetite and a good digestion. Whenever obtainable, give mice, birds, and small rats.

THE CARRION CROW is very similar to the Raven, only smaller in size. They generally live in pairs when wild, but are now become very scarce. The one we have we reared from the nest, which was found in a tree, and it is now five years old, having grown to be a peculiarly sagacious-looking bird, cracking its beak together and ducking its head whilst uttering its long-drawn-out "craw." It is fed the same as the Raven.

THE ROOK, although it has few good qualities to recommend it, is capable of being made a very tame pet, and should be fed and treated as the Raven.

THE JACKDAW is a very sagacious-looking bird, and from its droll antics is an especial favourite amongst boys. Jack can be easily reared, and may be taught to speak a little; its comical cry of "Jack," accompanied by its mock-serious look, will always make it a cheery companion; though, like the Raven, this bird is also, unfortunately, very fond of stealing (which circumstance has given us the laughable legend of the Jackdaw of Rheims), and should therefore have all bright articles placed beyond reach. It will become very affectionate, and may be allowed its freedom, so far as the clipping of a few wing-feathers will permit. Under these circumstances Jackdaws have been known to strike up acquaintance, and ultimately firm friendship, with a dog or cat, eating out of the same platter and reposing upon the hearthrug together, although sometimes this peaceful disposition is exactly reversed.

There is a peculiarly reverend appearance about the Jackdaw, perfectly in keeping with its habit of often selecting a church tower or old ruin wherein to build its nest, though it also builds in holes of trees and in cliffs. Instances are recorded of their sometimes even taking possession of a deserted rabbit-warren. This bird should be fed and treated as the Raven.

THE CHOUGH is another jet-black bird, with the exception of its bright-red legs and beak, which latter is long and thin. This bird is also sometimes kept as a pet, and will become very tame. It should be treated as the Raven.

THE MAGPIE is so well known as to make description superfluous, though perhaps many casual observers have little idea that the black in its plumage (which contrasts so markedly with the very pure white) is shaded, especially upon the lower part of the back and the tail, with varied rays of glistening sheen that rival the beauty of the peacock itself. Its thieving propensities have occasioned many a tale, and one naturally associates the bird with silver spoons and the "Maid and the Magpie." These pilfering habits have often occasioned the Magpie to be confined in a cage, though from its extreme liveliness and vivacity it seems a shame to have to debar it of liberty, especially when reared from the nest, as it is exceedingly tame in its disposition, and apart from its immoral notions of property, becomes a very nice pet. It is easily taught to talk, and if allowed to range the house invariably contracts either great friendship or antipathy for the dog, cat, or any other rival.

When wild the Magpie is the terror of all small birds, and as it oftentimes preys upon their young, they often band together in order to drive off the intruder, especially during the breeding season. The appetite of this bird is not at all dainty, and young rabbits, carrion, insects, fruit, and grain all serve to meet its requirements. The nest is deserving of notice, being a very elaborate specimen of architecture, generally built in a thick hedgetop or the highest branches of a tall tree, and having a canopy built over it as a protection. The Magpie should be fed similarly to the Raven.

THE JAY is an especially handsome bird, the delicate light fawn-colour of its general plumage contrasting most effectively with the bright blue, black and white bars on the wings; the feathers upon its head are long, and capable of being elevated as a crest. This bird invariably inhabits woods or the neighbouring trees, and after the young have left the nest they generally accompany the parent birds, living in bands, and then becoming a complete terror to all the small birds around, whose eggs and young often fall victims to their voracious appetite. The Jay otherwise feeds upon acorns, fruits, beechmast, worms, cockchafers, and other insects, as well as mice, frogs, and small reptiles.

Jays are of an inquisitive and garrulous disposition, and their true note is decidedly harsh; but they have great powers of mimicry, and may be taught to imitate a variety of sounds, even learning to talk slightly. A Jay may be confined in a large cage, or if very tame may be allowed to range the house. Feed as for the Raven.

THE STARLING is a very handsome bird, and is especially beautiful when the sun shines upon its glossy speckled feathers as it runs upon the lawn searching for worms or insects. It is of a very garrulous disposition, as indeed many can testify who have been awakened by its peculiar screaming (it cannot be dignified by the name of song), while in the early morning it sits perched upon a neighbouring chimney-pot. They often build in a spout on the roof of a house, or in the holes of trees, a very loosely constructed nest, with several

Vincent Brooks, Day & Son Lith

1. GREEN WOODPECKER. 2. JAY. 3. NUTHATCH.

straws protruding from the opening. From its extreme loquacity the bird always betrays its nest. The young are easily reared upon sifted ground oats and raw beef chopped fine.

Though its chattering kind of scream is not much of a recommendation, the Starling is a very nice pet, and like most of this class, from the breadth of its tongue, may be taught to whistle and talk with tolerably clear articulation. It will often form curious attachments, especially if allowed to roam the house.

The Starling should be fed and treated as the Thrush, giving a little fruit as a variation, and any garden worms will be an especial treat. A mealworm, spider, or a few flies, or other insects occasionally, will greatly add to the bird's health and enjoyment.

PEREGRINE FALCON.

THE PEREGRINE FALCON is a very handsome specimen of a class of birds that formerly were held in high estimation, when falconry was almost a science and the custom of hawking general. It is a very noble bird, and especially gifted with great powers of flight, which occasioned utilisation for that sport. When wild its food is of a very diverse character, comprising birds and small quadrupeds, especially partridges, plovers, pigeons, rabbits, and rats. It is very docile, and becomes very tame if reared from the nest, when it may be fastened by the leg to a stump, or block of wood, or an ordinary parrot-stand, unless it be kept in a large cage strewed with saw-dust. It should be fed twice during the day, and the food should be given to the bird by hand, so as to keep it tame. We feed one, which we have possessed nearly six years, upon raw beef or mutton, pieces of chicken's heads and necks (which are easily procurable from the poulterer), and a dead mouse or rat or a small bird about once or twice a week. These latter are obviously especially good for the bird, tending to keep it in health. The females are much larger than the males, and this feature holds good with the whole of the Hawk tribe.

Should the bird show indisposition, becoming weak, losing appetite, and moping, it is advisable to give it as much powdered rhubarb as may be placed upon a sixpence, put inside a small piece of meat about the size of an ordinary mouthful.

THE GER FALCON is even a handsomer bird than the foregoing, but it is rather uncommon, as is also the RED-FOOTED FALCON, or Orange-legged Hobby, as it is sometimes called. One of the latter birds we were once fortunate enough to take. These birds should be fed and treated as recommended for the Peregrine Falcon.

THE MERLIN is the smallest of the British Falcons, but is a very handsome little bird, of such great powers of flight and undaunted spirit, that it was formerly greatly used in falconry, especially by ladies, being often sent in pursuit of birds much larger than itself, but which it would easily kill by one sharp blow. Though, if required as a pet, it should be reared from the nest, yet it is easily tamed even if adult when taken, and is then more desirable for training for falconry. The form of the Merlin is the model of perfection

YOUNG SNOW OWL.

as regards hawking, as its body is compactly shaped and muscular, with great depth of chest and a clean round head. In confinement it should be fed as recommended for the Peregrine.

THE KESTREL is a more common bird than any of the preceding, being the most general of all British Hawks. It is often confused with the Sparrow-hawk by the uninformed, but it is smaller than that bird, and of a reddish-brown on the back and wings, shaded with grey on the head and neck. It also has the name of Windhover, which is obtained from its habit of remaining suspended with outstretched wings in the air, whilst anxiously watching for the slightest movement amongst the grass that may betray the presence of its prey, which principally consists of mice and beetles, except when a small bird falls a victim. A pair we kept for seven years once gave signs of breeding, but unfortunately the eggs were broken. They should be fed as the Peregrine.

THE SPARROW-HAWK is not a very tamable bird, and cannot be so well recommended as the preceding. When wild nothing in the shape of small birds seems to be safe from the ravages of this rapacious little freebooter, even partridges and chickens having good reason to fear its dreaded onslaught. In confinement it is rather dirty, and should always be reared from the nest, feeding as the rest of the tribe.

THE BARN or SCREECH OWL is the commonest of British Owls, and is often kept as a pet. It is the only one of the tribe that is in the habit of frequenting buildings, a church-tower being often selected as its home, otherwise any old building or hollow tree is chosen, and from these resorts it issues at nightfall in search of food, which consists principally of mice and beetles, the former especially suffering when the parent Owls have a nest of young to feed. We were once successful in breeding three young.

This bird should be fed upon mice, sparrows, or any small birds, raw beef or mutton, pieces of chicken's heads and necks, &c. The floor of its cage should be strewn with fresh sawdust, as by this means much of the noxious smell is obviated, a result not obtainable by sand.

THE TAWNY, BROWN, or WOOD OWL, as its latter name denotes, generally frequents woods, building in the holes of the trees. If reared from the nest it becomes very tame and docile, and should be fed and treated as the Barn Owl.

THE LONG and SHORT EARED OWLS are more uncommon than the preceding. They are smaller, and have tufts of feathers on either side of the head, which can be elevated or depressed at pleasure. The Short-eared Owl only visits the south of England during the winter, and is more difficult to keep; it must be given a mouse or bird at least three times a week. The Long-eared Owl may be fed as the Barn Owl.

THE SNOWY and EAGLE OWLS being very fine, handsome birds, are often kept in confinement, where they have both been known to breed. They should be fed as the Barn Owl, adding to their food, whenever obtainable, rats or rabbits.

CHAPTER XL.

MISCELLANEOUS BRITISH BIRDS.

THE WAXWING is a winter visitor to these islands, sometimes appearing singly, and at others in flocks. The name is derived from the waxlike appearance of the white ends of the secondary wing-feathers, and a small tip or appendage to the shafts of some of those feathers, which has been likened to red coral or sealing-wax. It is a very handsome bird, about the size of a Redwing, having a reddish-grey crest on the head, which can be raised or lowered at pleasure; this colour is almost uniform upon the body. The wings are black, barred with white and yellow, and the tail is black, tipped with yellow. It is easily tamed, and in the aviary is docile and quiet. It should be fed upon German paste, ground oats, "fig-dust" made into a stiff paste, a little hard-boiled egg, and some soft-skinned fruit; otherwise it would thrive well on the Blackcap's food.

THE GOLDEN ORIOLE is unfortunately a very scarce bird in this country, only occasionally crossing from the Continent. It is one of the handsomest birds that visit us, being of a bright lemon-yellow with black wings, as are also the two middle feathers and the base of its tail. Though it has not much natural song, its very handsome plumage accords it a very prominent position in the aviary, or it may be kept caged, and should be fed and treated as recommended for the Blackcap.

THE SPOTTED FLYCATCHER is one of the most familiar of British birds, often choosing some briar, vine, or other tree that may be trained against a house or wall, in which to build its nest. It is also known as the Beam-bird, from a habit of sometimes building on the end of a projecting beam. It is an interesting bird when feeding, as it generally selects a post or rail, or the end of a bough, from whence it watches for insects, which are pursued and captured on the wing with the greatest ease, the bird invariably returning to its perch to watch for more prey. The song is very limited.

From the nature of their food and habits, the Flycatchers are very difficult indeed to keep in confinement. We would advise that they be fed and treated as the Golden-crested Wren.

THE PIED FLYCATCHER is not so common a bird as the Spotted, being found more generally towards the north of England, and particularly the Lake districts, where it breeds in the holes of decayed oaks and pollards. This bird is, however, much more easily kept in confinement, and may be caged or placed in the aviary, especially with Warblers, as it should be fed and treated as recommended for the Nightingale. It is a very striking bird, its plumage being strongly marked black and white.

THE CUCKOO in confinement seldom, if ever, gives out the note by which it is known so well when wild, and is not very frequently caged. For the following particulars we are indebted to Mr. Joseph F. Hills, of Sudbury, Suffolk, whose experience with the bird has been considerable :—

"Although so much interesting matter has been written about the Cuckoo, there is probably no common bird about which there is still so much to be learned. Unfortunately, however, the keeping of Cuckoos in confinement throws but little light on their peculiarities in a wild state; for although I have hardly ever been without one during the last ten years, I know little more about their natural habits than do those who have never kept one. As a bird for the aviary it has but few attractions. Dull, heavy, and sluggish in its movements, it is extremely awkward on the floor. Only during its natural flight is the bird at all active; and it must have a large room to enable it to fly.

"To those who wish to keep Cuckoos, there is no difficulty; they are easily reared, and in most parts of England easily obtained. No less than thirteen young Cuckoos were brought to me during the season of 1878, and half a dozen in the following year. One was caught on the 6th September, and was not more than three weeks old; this is the latest time of the year at which I ever heard of one of that age. No bird that I know of falls so readily into the hands of boys, &c., as, when a fortnight or three weeks old, long before they can fly, they scramble out of the nest or fall out in their anxiety to be fed. When one is secured there is no trouble in getting it to take whatever in the way of food may be offered it. I have had scores, but never had one that refused its food. Certainly, if they are over three or four weeks old they will pick and fly very savagely; it is therefore better to obtain one as young as possible. The best food, I find, is raw beef chopped fine, with soaked bread and hard-boiled eggs; they will also eat earthworms, cockroaches, and snails, which latter they will partially extract from the shell without breaking it. If, however, you have an aviary in which you keep any insectivorous birds, Wagtails, Hedge Sparrows, &c., these make capital foster-parents. The easiest plan is to place the young Cuckoo in the aviary, when its plaintive cry and (I was about to say) insinuating appeals for food will soon secure for it the consideration of some of the other inmates, who will quickly commence feeding it, giving it all that it will take, which, by the way, is all that is offered to it. Instances are common enough where young birds of various species have been placed in cages and aviaries, and have been reared by some of the other inmates; but the extraordinary charm which the young Cuckoo appears to possess, of inducing other birds, many of them not a third of its size, to take compassion upon it, and attend to its wants, is something wonderful.

"The Cuckoo in confinement, if not in its wild state, will allow itself to be fed many weeks and even months after it is well able to provide for itself. It moults very late, and during the moulting period most of them die, unless they are kept warm. They cannot stand the cold so well as many of our migratory birds. A large aviary with other inmates is best for them. I have never found them quarrelsome; they are too lazy, and would rather be fed than fight. They drink a good deal, and are exceedingly dirty, but I never knew one to wash itself, and have always taken them in hand and washed them when they required it. Some writers state that they do bathe in confinement, but that has not been my experience. I never had one which gave out the peculiar call so familiar to us all."

THE NIGHTJAR, like the Cuckoo, is a very difficult bird to keep, and must also be reared from the nest. We have kept them as long as twelve months, but it is rather a dull bird, as its name denotes, becoming more lively at night than it is in the daytime, and therefore very likely to disturb the rest of the birds in the aviary. It should be fed as a Nightingale.

The Kingfisher is, of all British birds, the most beautiful, and when seen skimming the pool, as it flies straight and very swiftly, it looks like a brilliant streak of golden-green light. It is extremely interesting to see it when fishing, perched upon a twig overhanging a stream, intently watching for fish, which it dives after and captures in a very expert manner. It entirely depends upon its finny prey for its daily food, and the bones help to form its nest, or are strewn in heaps around it.

This bird is capable of being reared, although we fear most attempts hitherto have proved failures. No doubt the extreme trouble, not to mention expense, would go far to counterbalance the pleasure; but that the task is not impossible is shown by the following remarks with which we are again favoured by Mr. Joseph F. Hills, whose experience proves that the most gorgeous of our British birds is not so difficult to rear as generally supposed:—

"That a bird so lovely in its plumage, and not frequently seen (owing to its shyness), although it is not very uncommon, should have engaged the efforts of many naturalists to keep it in confinement, is not to be wondered at. There are difficulties in this, but they are not insurmountable, and I frequently see birds far *more* difficult to keep in confinement, and on which more trouble and expense must have been expended, which have not half the attractions of the Kingfisher. Such a splendid addition to our aviaries, therefore, should not be missing.

"A bird so shy as the Kingfisher should not be caught when old, as the attempt to tame it would be useless. I have read of their being tamed when old, but question their ever being really so, and such birds certainly must have a considerable quantity of fresh fish and natural food given them, which I should be sorry to recommend any one to attempt. Moreover, the natural shyness of such inmates of an aviary would go far to counterbalance the pleasure of keeping them. A nest of young ones should be obtained, which numbers from five to seven. The birds should not be allowed to remain too long in their nest, and should be taken a week at least before they can fly; if left too long there may be some difficulty in getting them to 'gape.' The nest is usually found in some hole in a bank by the water-side, probably some old water-rat's hole; the same hole being often tenanted for years. The birds will, however, make a hole themselves, which invariably runs upwards, and is about two to three feet in depth. It is a question with naturalists whether the bird builds a nest or not, some asserting that the eggs are laid on the bare ground; others that dead grass, roots, and feathers are employed in its construction; while the more common belief appears to be that the nest is built up of old fish-bones. Certainly the nest *consists* of old bones. I am, however, inclined to think these are not conveyed there for the purpose of constructing the nest, but are the accumulated pellets thrown up by the birds; as, like birds of prey, the Kingfisher has the power of disgorging the indigestible portions of its food. And as this bird lives almost exclusively on fishes, these pellets are nothing but fish-bones. The number and quantity of them found are surprising, and the disagreeable scent arising from this accumulated matter is very strong, and will often enable one to discover the nest.

"As soon as the young are obtained, and until they can fly and feed themselves, they should be put into a small cage with plenty of dry mould. This will destroy the scent and keep the birds clean. At first they should be fed with fresh-water fish, any description obtainable, such as roach, perch, bream, dace, trout, jack, minnows, &c. These must be cut up into small pieces and the bones taken out, but the older the bird gets the less care will be required in this respect. As soon as they can pick and do partly for themselves, they may be placed in the aviary or large cage, in a compartment without other occupants if possible. The plan of giving them all fish may now be discontinued, and fresh beef chopped up into small pieces and mixed with the fish may be given, also a little hard-boiled egg. This mixture should be placed in a small pan or on a plate.

1. KING-FISHER. 2. YELLOW-WAGTAIL. 3. PIED-WAGTAIL.

and the birds will pounce down upon it from their perches, often securing a piece without alighting. The pieces of fish, if fairly free from bones, need not be very small; it is astonishing what a swallow the birds have; I have seen them manage a piece, or a whole fish, which looked nearly as large as the head of the bird itself. I have frequently found that they prefer the meat to the fish. Nearly all writers recommend the food to be placed in a vessel of water, that the birds may take it as they do in their wild state. This, however, does not work well in practice, especially with young ones. They tumble into the water, get thoroughly soaked, and, unless the pan is very flat, cannot scramble out; and if they do, must be taken in hand and dried. With half a dozen birds doing this two or three times a day, one may have nothing else to do. In my early attempts to rear this bird I was particularly anxious to carry out this idea, supplying the birds as 'near to nature' as I well knew how, also constructing a small fountain with a basin beneath for the birds to feed out of. But the trouble the birds gave me through getting too wet two or three times a day, to say nothing of the annoyance of finding several dead from cold, &c., caused me to abandon the 'natural' scheme and resort to the plan above recommended.

"When the birds can do for themselves, continue to give them the same food, only by degrees substituting beef and egg in place of the fish. With a few persons the difficulty of obtaining fresh-water fish is no serious matter; and with such there is no need to persevere in the idea of weaning the birds from a fish diet; but with most people obtaining a daily supply of fresh-water fish would be a serious matter, and therefore with such the sooner the birds get accustomed to artificial food the better. In the course of a few weeks the fish may be dispensed with, and only given at such intervals as opportunities arise for obtaining it. Small earthworms and water-leeches may be given when obtainable, but the birds will live and thrive well on beef and egg. The cage or aviary must be well supplied with water for drinking and bathing, and if the vessel for bathing is placed for them in the morning, it should be withdrawn after the birds have been in it, or they will be getting wet all day long.

"All writers say that the Kingfisher is very pugnacious; but it is nothing compared to some of the inmates of the aviary. Robins, Nightingales, &c., are far worse in this respect; half a dozen Kingfishers may be kept together comfortably. It is a pretty sight, which will well repay for the trouble taken, to see half a dozen of them sitting in a row upon their perch, especially if the sun should shine on their lovely backs. When reared from the nest, the birds exhibit but little of their natural shyness, and will take the food out of your hand, especially if it should be a live minnow or any other small fish, which they immediately bolt head foremost, not waiting to kill it, as is often asserted."

THE RING DOVE is a common bird, known also as the Wood Pigeon, rather too large for the aviary, but may be kept in a special cage, when it will become very tame. These birds should be reared in pairs from the nest on soaked tares, lentils, or peas cut small, and when adult should be fed upon peas, wheat, or any other grain except oats.

THE STOCK DOVE may also be kept in confinement, in pairs, if fed and treated as the Ring Dove.

THE TURTLE DOVE, from its sentimental associations, is more often kept than either of the foregoing. It is much smaller than either of the preceding, and from its extreme docility and quiet habits may be kept in a moderately large aviary. It should be fed the same as the Ring Dove, adding canary, rape, hemp, and millet seeds.

THE RED-BACKED SHRIKE is otherwise known as the Butcher Bird, which name is derived from its fierce disposition, and from a peculiar habit it has of impaling upon the thorns of a bush the remains of the victims of its repast, which principally consists of beetles, bees, wasps, and such-like insects, and sometimes even small birds and frogs. It possesses a most voracious appetite considering its size, and is very serviceable in destroying so many garden pests. It is a handsome bird, and possessed of some song, which is pleasant and unintermittent, though occasionally mixed with some harsh notes. If taken young it may be easily reared, becoming very tame and attached to its feeder. The way in which it seizes its prey is very much after the manner of the Hawk. From the fierceness of its nature it is obvious that it should never be placed with other birds, even if of larger size, but be confined in a separate cage, feeding upon pieces of raw beef, soaked bread, and hemp seed, adding a little German paste, beetles, mealworms, or any insects whenever obtainable. A small bird or mouse may be given occasionally.

THE GREAT GREY SHRIKE is rather an uncommon bird, visiting these islands during the winter; being a handsome bird, it is a great favourite of some. Its plumage is a pretty ashen grey on the whole of the upper part, shading to white on the shoulders and under part, which is also striped with wavy lines of dark brown; the greater wing-coverts are black, the lesser ashen grey, the tail wedge-shaped, the outer feathers white, the inner black; from the beak across the face runs a broad black stripe, and there are two white spots on each wing. In the manner of taking its food it resembles the preceding bird, feeding upon the same food, and in confinement should be treated similarly.

THE GOLDEN PLOVER is a handsome bird, and may be kept in confinement in a large aviary, where it must be given plenty of water, and fed on pieces of raw meat and soaked bread; or it may be allowed the run of the garden, where it would be of great service in ridding the place of insects, especially worms and slugs.

THE REDSHANK is a wading bird that will become very tame in confinement. We had one that was taken when adult, but became very tame, agreeing well with the other birds in the aviary. It was fed upon raw beef, sopped bread, and garden worms. This bird must always have a good supply of water. There are several other birds of this class that become tame, and would be very attractive in a large aviary, especially if a good supply of water is obtainable.

THE STONE CURLEW had, perhaps, better be turned out in the garden, as it will soon clear, and keep clear, the plants of their insect pests. However, if confined in the aviary, feed as the Redshank.

THE LAND-RAIL is notorious from the habit it has of uttering its harsh "crake-crake" in the meadows during the summer evenings, from which is derived its name of Corn-crake. It will become tame, and should be fed as the Redshank.

THE WATER-RAIL is a handsome bird of dark greenish-brown plumage, shading into grey upon the neck and head; the beak is long and of a reddish flesh-colour, and the eye bright red orange. It should also be fed as the Redshank.

FOREIGN CAGE-BIRDS.

BY AUGUST F. WIENER.

CHAPTER XLI.

GENERAL MANAGEMENT OF FOREIGN BIRDS.

THE most popular foreign cage-bird is the Canary, which has been described in such detail in foregoing chapters; but the Finch of the Canary Islands has been so completely acclimatised since he became domesticated about three centuries ago, that Canaries are now commonly thought of as a kind of European bird. Such complete success should encourage further attempts in the same direction. It should, however, be observed, that a wild Canary Finch on the Canary Islands or the West Coast of Africa resembles our European Siskin, if we imagine the Siskin a trifle larger and the black marks on his feathers absent. The golden colour of our household friend of the present day is due to the influence of captivity, and the selection of stock for cage-breeding. Now besides the Canary, other foreign birds have undergone, and are undergoing, a similar great change of colour as a result of cage-breeding. The Japanese breed piebald and pure white Manikins from a little brownish-black Finch, and the Chinese breed white Java Sparrows. During the last year or two Australian undulated Grass Parrakeets (*P. undulatus*) have produced several *yellow* instead of *bright green* young; and it is not at all improbable that in ten or twenty years' time these Parrakeets may be bred regularly of a colour as different from that of their ancestors, as a bright lemon-coloured Canary is different from his wild brown and green original.

Curiously enough, the wild Canary (*Serinus canarius*) is said to have been found in England in some few cases. As these birds are not frequently imported, it is more than improbable that those found in England had escaped from captivity; consequently we must assume that a small Finch may be driven occasionally by storms, or other causes, all the way from Western Africa to the British coast. This statement may surprise many readers, but if the lighthouse keepers were to collect all the bodies of the multitude of migratory and other birds which break their skulls against the lighthouse lanterns at night, attracted by the dazzling or flashing lights to deviate from the path of their migrations, many more curious ornithological facts would probably be found. A few years ago the writer saw an African purple-headed glossy Starling (*Lamprocolius auratus*) shot that very day in Essex. A careful examination of the plumage showed feathers so perfect that the bird could scarcely have been confined in and have escaped from an aviary; and how that bird came to Essex has never been explained. The rose-coloured Starling, whose ordinary home is India, is met with in Central Europe in considerable numbers, but at intervals of many years. The distinguishing line between non-migratory European and foreign birds is therefore not quite so clearly defined as it is popularly supposed to be.

Parrots have been kept as domestic pets by the Romans since about 50 B.C., and elsewhere in Europe since the fifteenth century, when the discovery of America and the circumnavigation of the Cape of Good Hope led to their importation. The smaller foreign cage-birds were exceedingly rare in Europe as late as 1850. In 1860 a list of about sixty species would have named every foreign bird then imported into Europe for sale. Ten years later about two hundred varieties of foreign birds arrived in the course of a year in Europe, whilst at the present day a complete list of all the foreign birds imported alive would include some seven hundred names. Some of these birds arrive only in single specimens, and very rarely, whilst others are brought to this country in thousands of pairs, and as articles of commerce.

Australia supplies a large and rapidly increasing number of beautiful or brilliant birds, most of which have the advantage that they are easily kept in confinement and in our climate. Brazil, notwithstanding its wondrous bird-life, has, with the exception of Parrots, not very many birds suitable for cage-life. The mighty rivers of that country are very favourable to the development of insect life, and consequently the majority of the gorgeous Brazilian birds are entirely insectivorous, and as such not easily provided for during long voyages, or for keeping on artificial food after arrival in Europe. Africa supplies an immense number of birds to the European bird-market. Scarcely a ship leaves the African coast without a number of Parrots, and boxes containing hundreds of delicate little Waxbills, Weaver Birds, &c. These are brought to London, Liverpool, Marseilles, Bordeaux, and to other ports in tens of thousands. Notwithstanding a very large percentage of the Waxbills die on the voyage, and others arrive with the seeds of disease and soon end their existence, thousands of little African Finches are often sold in one bargain, and then find their way in dozens or hundreds to the retail dealers.

These little strangers, and, in fact, all foreign Finches, seem to make themselves more at home in their cages than our European birds ever do; they never display that restless craving for liberty, which Goldfinches and Linnets rarely forget. In keeping exotic Finches, we feel, when contemplating them, that they are entirely dependent on us, they have been brought from distant climes and entrusted to our care, and the demeanour of these little birds is such as if they knew they were entirely dependent on their keeper and felt the utmost confidence in him. It has been proved by the experience of years, and by many experiments, that it is often much easier to keep even a delicate foreign Finch in confinement than their apparently much more robust European cousins.

Few of the foreign Finches can fairly be called songsters of merit, and on the whole they cannot compare in this respect with our wild birds. There are some, however, whose song deserves to be called by that name, like the little African grey Singing Finch and the green Singing Finch, *Crithagra* (*fringilla*) *musica* and *Crithagra* (*fringilla*) *Hartlaubi*, whose notes are certainly equal, if not superior, to our Siskin's. Amongst the foreign soft-food birds there are a few of great merits as songsters.

Notwithstanding the enormous number of foreign birds annually imported into England, which to many readers would appear incredible were reliable statistics available, the "fancy" (would there were a better word) for foreign birds is really in its infancy in this country. To find its true home we must cross the Channel and go to Germany. In England a Canary is kept in the nursery, but scarcely ever in the drawing-room; a talking Parrot may be found now and then admitted into a dining-room; but of a *bird-room* we very rarely hear in an English household In Germany we find thousands of by no means wealthy people whose delight it is to keep, to rear, and to study birds. The taste for foreign birds has grown to a surprising extent in

Germany, and more foreign birds are kept and bred there than in the rest of Europe together. Almost every city or provincial town of importance in Germany has its society of amateurs,* and several excellent weekly publications and magazines are devoted entirely to ornithological matters. This is chiefly due to the unrivalled writings of Doctor Karl Russ, of Berlin, the guide and friend of all lovers of birds, and a very esteemed friend of the writer. Between the years 1867 and 1870 a series of charming articles on foreign cage-birds, written by Doctor Russ, appeared in German daily papers and periodicals, which attracted much attention at the time. In 1871 Doctor Russ published his "handbook" on foreign cage-birds, for the use of amateurs and breeders, giving a mass of valuable information and advice which no other book on the subject had previously offered. In 1872 Doctor Russ established a magazine, "Die Gefiederte Welt," or "The Feathered World," devoted *solely* to matters relating to birds; this publication appeared first fortnightly, and soon after weekly. In it all the observations communicated by correspondents were duly published and made readily available for reference hereafter by a most carefully compiled index. Meanwhile Doctor Russ was preparing for a larger work on his favourite subject. Whilst in his handbook of 1871 he could only occupy himself with about two hundred varieties of birds then imported, new species arrived every month since then. Doctor Russ was not content to write on birds from notes made on stuffed specimens in museums, but every foreign cage-bird found its way into his aviary, and was carefully watched, tended, and, if possible, reared; its habits, the nest, the eggs, the young brood, were carefully described; and as a result a magnificent German work on foreign cage-birds is now in course of publication, which forms the most reliable guide to such amateurs as are able to understand the language. The writer will frequently have to refer to Doctor Russ's work; and his own observations, experiences, and mishaps in bird-keeping and rearing have mostly been at some time published as advice or warning to other amateurs in Doctor Russ's magazine. I have kept for many years a collection of several hundred living foreign birds, natives of every clime. Their supervision and care, the contemplation and study of their life and habits, has formed, during my leisure hours, a most agreeable and valuable relief from heavy work. It was quite amusing to see the astonishment with which most beholders regarded this collection of small Finches when seeing it for the first time. "How troublesome, how difficult it must be to keep all these little beings! how difficult it must be to feed them!" was the invariable remark. "How many you must lose!" was the half-pitiful sentence next addressed to one who is supposed to be somewhat enthusiastic in the matter of birds. I can conscientiously state that the trouble is small; the difficulties as regards food are easily overcome; and as to losses, they are not more—if as much—than they would be if I had kept as many Canaries, or for that matter Barndoor Fowls.

As regards the food and general treatment of foreign cage-birds, I cannot do better than extract the following short directions, sketched by me in a paper contributed to the *Live Stock Journal Almanack* for 1879, which are based on many years' experience:—

Nobody does know, and nobody can know exactly, what a wild bird feeds on in the course of twenty-four hours. If we look around us, we find our European Finches living mainly on seeds, but in the breeding season becoming insectivorous; Starlings, Thrushes, Blackbirds, and Robins eating worms, insects, and fruit in summer, berries and who knows what in winter. Of one thing we may be certain, and that is that birds in their wild state live on an immense variety of food. Instead of laying down any hard and fast rules as to the proper

* The German *societies* of bird amateurs number about two hundred. The Crown Prince of Austria is a considerable authority on birds. Prince Ferdinand of Coburg-Gotha, residing at Vienna, has the largest private collection of living foreign birds on the Continent. The German amateurs include ladies and gentlemen of the most varied ranks.

food for foreign cage-birds, I would prefer to suggest to every amateur to think out the food question for himself; to be guided by common sense, and to endeavour to give to each bird a home and food corresponding as nearly as possible to his natural habits and tastes.

A cage-bird is, however we may gild his prison bars, more or less a prisoner. How long would a human prisoner live in solitary confinement, with nothing to do, and nothing else than beef-steaks and port wine continually placed before him in quantities which he could not possibly eat? or a horse in a loose box, with a sack of oats perpetually in his manger? Analogous mistakes do we see committed every day by bird-keepers. If we bear this in mind, the value of cages sufficiently large for exercise, and of fittings, by way of branches or shrubs in pots, to amuse and distract the birds, will be apparent, as well as the importance of some variation and limitation of food.

For seed-eating birds, canary and millet seed are the staple food. The best canary-seed comes from Spain; the grain should be large and heavy, and the seed free from admixture of other seeds. Good canary-seed can be purchased from almost any corn-chandler. Millet-seed varies much in quality, from a very small, hard, yellow, or brown seed, to the large grain white French millet. The latter is the best, but sometimes difficult to procure. Really good millet-seed is invaluable to the bird-keeper. By way of variety, a little maw-seed may be given sometimes, if it be duly remembered that maw-seed, being very rich in oil, is fat-producing. The sweepings of a hayloft contain large quantities of grass and other seeds, and a handful of such sweepings are picked over by small Finches with much delight. Most valuable of all is, however, the so-called spray millet, or millet in the ear. Whether it be that the exertion of pulling the grains from the ear gives birds an extra appetite, or that the husk of the unthreshed seed contains some peculiar virtue, the fact is that nothing is more beneficial for all seed-eating foreign cage-birds than a liberal supply of millet in the ear.

But I know few foreign cage-birds, except Rice Birds, Australian Zebra Finches, and some Parrots, which I would undertake to keep in perfect health all the year round on nothing but seeds. All birds seem to like, at times, a little extra food; and in their breeding and moulting season this becomes indispensable. There are some beautiful Australian Finches, such as the Australian Firetail and Crimson Finch, &c., which appear not to thrive altogether satisfactorily on any known bird-seeds, and for whose natural food a better substitute has yet to be found. I mean, thereby, something corresponding to the odd spider, or beetle, or butterfly our sparrow or chaffinch picks up, besides his food at the barn door, or with the fowls, or in the corn-field. Millet-seed soaked over-night in warm water, and then carefully strained, is very good for young birds or for birds of weak digestion.

I find, in the case of small foreign Finches, a morsel of common sponge-cake at breeding or moulting time a very valuable additional dish. If it is just very slightly damped with water, a trifle of maw-seed, a little hard-boiled egg, and a few ants' eggs (previously soaked and strained) are added, the mixture becomes a very good food to rear broods of young Finches with. A cold, wet, or foggy November day is more trying for small birds than any other time of year, or than severe cold. Half a sponge-cake quickly dipped in water, then pressed, and mixed with half a tea-spoonful of cayenne pepper, will at such times be very gladly eaten by most of the small foreign Finches, and will prove very beneficial if given two or three times a week. The same mixture at moulting-time will help little birds wonderfully over this trying period. It may here be remarked that at moulting-time cage-birds eat, and require to eat, much more food than at other times.

A healthy bird should be plump but not fat. To avoid fatness—which generally ends in consumption—exercise and green food are the best safeguards. Fresh chickweed or groundsel should never be absent from a bird-cage in the summer-time; but if the green-meat be wet from recent rains, it should be dried before giving it to birds. The common grass growing by the roadside, when in bloom, is of immense value for some Australian Finches.

Cuttle-fish (Latin, *ossa sepia*) is a white chalky substance, the backbone of a fish, and sometimes found on the English sea-coast, but more frequently on the coast of the Mediterranean. The pieces are of elongated elliptical shape, from six to twelve inches and more in length. A small piece of cuttle-fish, or, better still, a very thin slice, easily cut with a sharp knife, is greedily picked by birds, and helps their digestion greatly. Cuttle-fish is obtainable at most bird-shops, or from wholesale druggists. Apothecaries and chemists only keep the powdered article, which is useless for birds.

Soft-food birds are the next category of our feathered friends whose larder must be provided for. But here the difficulties of an amateur increase largely, and much judgment and forethought are required. All insectivorous birds are great eaters, if the food is always before them. In their natural state, however, these birds have to hunt and struggle for every morsel of food. On the one hand they have a vast amount of exercise while searching for food, and on the other hand only just one morsel at a time. Caged birds cannot have so much exercise, and therefore their diet must be lowered accordingly. For years past I have fed my soft-food birds with more than average success on the following diet:—First thing in the morning they receive a small quantity of sop, consisting of stale household bread soaked in water over-night; the water is pressed out by hand; with the wet bread about one-third of its volume coarse Scotch oatmeal is mixed, and a little boiled milk poured over the whole. Care should be taken that not more milk is added than the bread will completely absorb, and retain even if placed on a strainer. I have never known this mixture turn sour within the twenty-four hours. An hour or two later I give a mixture of German paste, dry bread-crumbs, ants' eggs, currants, and either fresh boiled eggs or preserved yolk of eggs; and about mid-day, Starlings, Thrushes, &c., get a few morsels of raw beef cut very fine indeed, whilst the smaller birds receive a few live meal-worms.

German paste can be bought readily and of very fair quality in most bird-shops. It consists of peameal, a little maw-seed, more or less hemp-seed crushed in a coffee-mill, mixed with a very small quantity of treacle and a little lard, the whole being gently heated in an earthenware vessel, and continually stirred until hot, when it is spread on a paper or cloth and allowed to cool. This preparation will keep for weeks, and to make or buy a week's supply at one time is quite safe.

Ants' eggs are, as is well known, not the eggs but the larvæ of the ant. They are largely collected in Germany and Russia, and dried either in kilns or bakers' ovens. Properly dried, the ants' eggs remain good for a year or more. In England there are fewer insects—ants included—than on the Continent, owing, probably, to the damp climate. The ants' eggs are collected by keepers and used fresh for the rearing of young pheasants, partridges, &c., but never, as far as I know, are English ants' eggs kiln-dried and sold in that state. The dried ants' eggs, as well as the currants, should be soaked for a couple of hours in water, and then strained previous to being mixed with the German paste.

Preserved yolk of eggs is a German preparation but lately introduced to English bird keepers and breeders. Millions of fresh fowls' eggs are broken annually for the sake of the white to manufacture albumen, an article used in printing muslins, &c. The fresh yolk being difficult to dispose of, a process to dry and preserve this yolk has been invented, and an article has resulted which is admirably adapted for bird-feeding. The white of hard-boiled eggs is not useful for birds, because highly indigestible, and therefore superfluous to bird-keepers. Instead of having the trouble of first boiling an egg, then testing whether it is fresh, breaking it up, and wasting a great part in doing so, this preparation of egg-yolk offers pure bird-food ready for use in tin canisters, a dessert-spoonful of the bright yellow flakes being equal to one boiled egg, and the price being less than one-half cf that of fresh eggs.

Live insect food, especially mealworms, are, in the hands of a beginner in bird-keeping, very much what the first sharp knife is in the hands of a small school-boy, and almost sure to lead to some trifling accident. Mealworms are extremely fattening and stimulating. One or two do no harm, and if given at the proper season they are very good, but to give them liberally makes birds forsake their other food; and whenever I tried to rear a young brood of Mocking-birds, Cardinals, Indian Starlings, Blue Nightingales, &c., by feeding the parent birds liberally on mealworms, ill-success resulted. I believe the cause to have been that mealworms are so very tempting that the old birds find it impossible to resist swallowing a good many by mistake; neglect of the young brood follows; whilst the old birds are so much stimulated that they want to build a fresh nest and lay again before their proper time.

Fresh ants' eggs are much better to rear broods of young birds on; and I owe such success as fell to my lot in breeding insectivorous birds to the substitution of these for mealworms. It is not difficult to find an ant-hill, and such a one I put bodily—earth, ants, larvæ, and all—in a bag, giving the birds a handful or two every three or four hours. The old birds will find plenty to do in collecting the ants, and scratching or picking the larvæ out of the earth. A few spiders are very healthy, whilst flies and gentles (meat-maggots) appeared to disagree with all those small birds to whom I gave such in any quantity.

But he who will try to keep or breed soft-food birds must arm himself with inexhaustible patience, and make up his mind to persevere in spite of repeated failure.

For Parrots, canary-seed should form the staple food; Parrakeets take millet also, but the larger Parrots do not care much about it. Variety of food cannot be too much recommended, and an almost endless variety can easily be offered to most kinds of the larger Parrots. Undulated or Shell Parrakeets do not care for much beside canary and millet seed. Grey Parrots, Cockatoos, Rosellas, &c., however, will take hemp, oats, barley, Indian corn, sunflower seed, and in fact almost any seed that is given to fowls or pigeons. Hemp should be given only as a delicacy; it is very heating and fat-producing. A bird may thrive on hemp in winter, and perish in consequence of too much hemp in summer, eat it ravenously for a time, and refuse it altogether some other time. Parrots once used to a free supply of hemp will often refuse other food, and necessitate the disagreeable process of semi-starvation to preserve their health. Sunflower seed contains about as much oil and is less heating than hemp seed, thus forming a relish at once safe and agreeable to the bird. Oats are liked by Parrots because they contain a good mouthful. Indian corn may be given boiled or raw; when raw it employs the beak and amuses the birds, but it is somewhat constipating, and is therefore a good food in the summer, when the birds have plenty of green food.

The greatest treat for Parrots is millet in the ear, Indian corn on the stalk, corn, oats, barley, or wheat in the ear; and a small quantity may be given, even if not ripe, instead of green-meat. Salad, groundsel, chickweed, should be given freely, but never wet; and to those Parrots who have an inclination to gnaw, a budding branch of willow or elderberry, or even a stick of firewood, will afford much amusement and some benefit. A piece of cuttle-fish to gnaw and exercise the beak upon is also to be much recommended; whilst a piece of bread-crust, biscuit, rusk, or sponge-cake may be freely given at any time, and will create a bond of affection between the Parrot and his owner. Fruit is harmless when very ripe and quite free from acid. Walnuts or filberts are useful and beneficial. Bread and milk are, at the best, fattening, and at the same time liable to give diarrhœa, and worse if they should turn sour. The practice of giving meat or chicken-bones to some Parrots I consider peculiarly unfortunate. Parrots are strict vegetarians, and any animal food seems to me opposed to their natural habits. I would as soon give meat to a Parrot as dose a dog with brandy. It can only stimulate abnormally and unhealthily, and thus produce evil effects, such as irritation of the skin, &c.

With proper food, sufficient room, and convenient opportunities, very many kinds of Parrots, when acclimatised, will breed in confinement, and most Parrots are infinitely more hardy than is generally supposed.

The Lories are a large class of Parrots—mostly of extraordinary beauty of plumage, and living, in their natural state, on flowers, from which they extract the honey by a peculiar arrangement of the tongue, and on fruit, nipping a few seeds at times. As regards keeping them in confinement, I am tempted to give *Punch's* advice to people about to marry—Don't. These birds are, without exception, costly and delicate, and to provide them with suitable food rarely succeeds. Boiled rice, with sugar and fruit, is practically almost the only food many will touch at first. If their keeper succeeds in inducing them to eat, first soaked and then dry, sponge-cake, a great step in the right direction has been gained. Canary-seed should always be in the cage, and possibly the Lories will take to it some day, in which case their chance of enduring for some years is immensely improved. Blue Mountain Lories take most readily of all Lories to canary-seed, and become fairly hardy birds if fed on seed while on board ship. But even in their case a little sponge-cake daily is almost indispensable. Blue Mountain Lories are the only kind of Lories bred so far in confinement. In one case the fortunate breeder attributed his success to a liberal supply of the soft shoots of Virginian creeper. I tried Blue Mountain Lories with the same delicacy, and they refused to touch it. About these well-known and most enduring species of Lories opinions are therefore still very much divided.

The idea that tropical birds should be kept night and day, summer and winter, in a hot-house temperature is a great error. Even in the tropics the nights are sometimes chilly, and a healthy bird can endure a great change of temperature without harm or inconvenience. What does harm to cage-birds is vitiated or foul air, draught, and absence of sunshine. Sunshine is the very elixir of life for all birds, and cages should be so placed, or aviaries so arranged, that the birds have the full benefit from early morning to afternoon of every ray of sunshine which our English climate affords. Open aviaries must be protected to the north and west, to keep out the cold northerly winds and the driving rains from the west. Garden aviaries open on all sides, through which the wind can blow from all quarters, are instruments of torture, but easily made comfortable by being boarded on the north and west sides. Black japanned wire allows the birds to be seen much better than brass wire or galvanised wire. Water should be always fresh, clean, and in sufficient quantity for bathing whenever the bird feels inclined to bathe. As a wet floor of a cage or aviary produces foul smells, and often gives the birds colds, the water is best given in a small earthenware saucer, placed inside a larger saucer of the same material. If there be two inches space between the rims of the saucers, the outer vessel will take nearly every drop of water splashed by the birds, leaving the floor of the aviary sweet and dry.

The floor of cages should always be thickly covered with dry, gritty sand,* renewed as frequently as possible, kept scrupulously clean, and no accumulation of excrement, waste seed, husks, stale green-meat, &c., should be allowed to remain in any cage or aviary. Soft-food birds digest their food very rapidly, and evacuate large quantities of excrement, and in their case especially small cages should be cleaned once a day, and aviaries twice a week. Cages should be simple, devoid of superfluous ornaments which may harbour insects, and should be easily cleaned. We cannot expect a bird to feel happy or comfortable if surrounded on all sides by open wirework, if continually observed, and deprived of a quiet nook into which he may withdraw when seeking rest or shelter from observation. But only when birds feel perfectly happy and at home in their cages can we expect them to prosper or to breed in captivity. For this reason cages with solid sides as well as solid backs are preferable to all others, and the common London canary breeding-cage is about the best model, though for many foreign birds it is better if the solid board forming the roof is replaced by wire, which arrangement admits more light and air.

Great enemies of bird-keepers are cats, rats, and mice. I have myself seen feats by cats which I would have considered incredible if told me. I used to breed Canaries in a garden aviary made of straight wire five-eighths of an inch apart. One morning, looking out of my dressing-room window, a cat sat before the aviary, and seemed innocently to watch the gambols of the Canaries, whom I thought quite safe, as, eighteen or twenty inches from the ground, the lower part of the aviary was protected by zinc plates. I saw a fine cock Canary clinging to the wires some four feet or more from the ground, and singing merrily, when, quick as lightning, puss made one huge bound, fastened her claws in the Canary and pulled his body through the wires. In this manner birds disappear unaccountably from garden aviaries.

To keep rats out of the aviary, a Portland cement floor is better than any other, and the cheapest in the long-run. Rats will undermine brick floors and gnaw through lead pipes, but iron wire and Portland cement are proof against even their teeth. Mice are the greatest difficulty, for canary-seed seems to attract them more than any other food, and at some time or other mice will get almost anywhere. The quantity of canary-seed a pair of mice will devour in one night is surprising, and what they leave is sure to be spoilt by their urine, which, by the way, rots wirework very quickly and very completely. When mice have once made their way into an aviary, many poor birds wake up in the morning to find their seed-boxes or glasses emptied over-night, and if such an occurrence be not observed at once, sad losses by starvation result. The only way to battle with this vermin is to construct the aviaries so that every part can be readily examined when necessary, and to avoid hiding-places, such as artificial rock-work or similar ornaments. If mice have access to canary-seed, you may bait your traps how you will, no mouse will go into them. Mice will climb up perpendicular wires, or jump a height not far from two feet to reach canary-seed; I have seen them running along perches, and dropping into food-dishes suspended three and four feet below the perches. When the presence of mice is suspected in an aviary, the best way to feed the birds is to place the seed in a dish on the top of two inverted flower-pots, placed one on the top of the other. Possibly you may then catch the mice in a wire trap placed on the floor and baited with canary-seed; but a better way is to carefully stop up all holes by which mice may possibly gain ingress, and to arrange a comfortable retreat for the mice in the aviary by filling a small packing-case, or such-like, with loose hay, straw, woollen rags, mixed with a few handfuls of canary-seed;

* Sea-sand containing fragments of shells is preferable to any other sand, and of very great use. I have cured many sick birds and brought damaged specimens into beautiful condition, simply by a handful of sea-sand.

fasten the lid of the box down, and cut a hole in the side just large enough to admit a mouse comfortably. In a day or two all the mice in the aviary will make themselves quite at home in this retreat. When a box thus arranged is left for a week in an aviary, and then suddenly moved—care being taken to block the small hole before removal—box and all may be put in a tub, and probably every mouse be removed and drowned at one stroke.

The model open-air aviaries exhibited at the Crystal Palace for some years past are better than anything of their kind which the writer has seen offered for sale ready made. They are practically large doll's houses, seven or eight feet high, five or six feet wide, and two to three feet deep, with a door in front. This door opens into an enclosure about six feet square, wired all over, forming a miniature garden, which may be laid out with turf and gravel, and ornamented with fountains, shrubs, &c. In this space the birds can bask in the sunshine, or enjoy a warm summer shower, retiring at night under the sheltering roof of the house, where they are protected from rain and draught. If these aviaries are placed facing south-east, a great variety of foreign birds can be kept in them without artificial heat, even during winter. For most Australian Parrakeets these open-air aviaries are infinitely better than any bird-room or in-door aviary cage.

The writer's experience would, however, suggest an improvement of this, by far the best model, viz., to raise the floor of the bird-house some two feet from the ground, and by coating the lower portion of the front with zinc-sheeting to make it next to impossible for mice to climb into the house, it being simply useless and hopeless to attempt to keep them out of the outer cage.

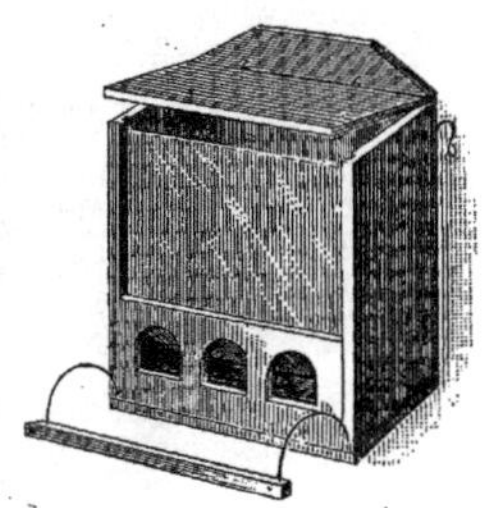
FIG. 75.—SEED-HOPPER.

The seed-hopper shown in Fig. 75 is a very valuable piece of furniture in any aviary, if used as a supplement to seed-dishes placed on the floor. If mice ever reach the dishes, the birds find a food-store in the hopper to fall back upon, and mice do not easily reach these hoppers if hung against the smooth wall of an aviary. Simple as the contrivance looks, these seed-hoppers require some daily supervision, for they sometimes become clogged by dust, cobwebs, or damp, and no seed then passes down to replace the grains abstracted from the bottom tray by the birds.

The number of beautiful foreign birds obtainable at a reasonable price increases annually, and the taste for keeping birds appears to be spreading rapidly in this country. It is much to be hoped that at an early date amateurs may undertake the management of bird shows, and make these exhibitions worth the attention of scientific ornithologists, and of real value to those who take an interest in foreign cage-birds. The popular idea of a considerable risk being incurred by exhibiting birds at a well-managed show is a mistake. I have exhibited hundreds of birds in London and abroad, and have invariably found that fairly acclimatised birds suffer not only no harm through being exhibited, but, if well cared for, come back all the better for their temporary change of surroundings, and as distinctly benefited by a week in a bird show as a human being is after a change of air and occupation. But as long as the prizes of bird shows in England remain confined to a trifling sum of money, it can scarcely be expected that amateurs will care to exhibit interesting and valuable birds as numerously as might be. Further, a foreign bird show should be held by itself, and not subordinated to Canary shows. Canaries are generally exhibited between December and March, for before December the stock bred in the previous year is not yet fit to show, and after March the best birds are wanted for breeding. A cold raw February is about the worst time of the year to send foreign birds to an exhibition, and some of the most interesting kinds, for example, Weavers, Whydah-birds, &c., are not then in colour, and would look very much like sparrows. A show of foreign birds should take place in June or July, and need not exclude Canaries, although the latter would be less numerously represented than at another time.

In purchasing foreign birds, it should be borne in mind that the first month after arrival in this country is the most trying time for the little strangers. They all suffer more or less in health and plumage during the long voyage, and frequently succumb soon after arrival to the effects of the mere change of climate and food. At the shops of the large London wholesale dealers—Joseph Abrahams, Charles Jamrach, and Charles Rice—hundreds, and sometimes thousands of the same species may be seen just as they are brought from the ship, and buyers must expect to find more or less raw birds. Experienced amateurs will derive pleasure from seeing birds, bought in an imperfect state, rapidly improving under their care; but for beginners the deaths amongst new purchases are sometimes disheartening, and they had better purchase seasoned specimens from retail dealers.

FIG. 76.—TRAVELLING-CAGE.

I would warn collectors against importing birds themselves, or having them sent over by correspondents in distant lands. Although I had kind friends in many parts of the world who were anxious to send me birds, the intended importation always ended in failure, and in much expense to somebody. A friend of mine residing in Japan had unusual opportunities of obtaining birds from parts of the country rarely visited by Europeans. He had prepared a collection of live birds at much trouble and expense, and found somebody going to Europe willing to take charge of them. At the last moment the "somebody" had to travel *viâ* San Francisco, and was therefore unable to take the birds with him; my friend had to undertake a journey in Japan, and there remained no alternative but to give the birds collected for me their liberty. Another friend sent me a wonderful Parrot from the Philippine Islands, but the Parrot escaped from on board ship and flew away, and I owe my friend many thanks for his kindness, although I never saw the Parrot. A friend in India sent me some rare Himalayan Pheasants, and to an amateur on the Continent a collection of Weaver-birds. Of the Pheasants, one was killed at Calcutta by a stoat or rats, and the three survivors arrived by a piece of rare good fortune. What was believed to be the pair of Pheasants turned out an old and a young male, and the freight, gratuities, and charges together came to three times as much money as would have bought a pair in Europe; and the collection of Weaver-birds could have been bought in London for half the money paid for them in Calcutta. Similar examples might be given *ad infinitum.*

Large dealers like Jamrach, Abrahams, and Rice of London, Cross of Liverpool, Hagenbeck of Hamburg, and Reiche of Hanover, have their collectors and agents in all parts of the world who send over birds, besides which ship captains and sailors continually bring over a number.

When large numbers of one kind arrive they are sometimes to be bought at ridiculously low prices, and the only way to collect rare specimens is to await an opportunity of buying them on the spot. I once or twice found very rare birds at Mr. Hawkins', in Bear Street, Leicester Square, and at Mr. Obermüller's, Great Portland Street, Regent's Park.

For the conveyance of small birds, Mr. Hawkins has constructed a travelling-cage which is perfection in its way, and cannot be too much recommended for all purposes of transit. As shown in Fig. 76, a piece of muslin on a sliding frame is inserted just behind the wire front of the miniature box-cage. This muslin keeps out all draught, prevents any seed being spilled by careless handling of the box, and behind this screen the most nervous bird, while having sufficient light, will feel himself perfectly secure. The square water-tin has a lid, with a round hole in it about the size of the bird's head. The lid alone will prevent the water from spilling, but the immersion of a small piece of sponge into the water will be a further safeguard against such an accident. I have sent valuable and delicate tropical Finches in these cages, per Continental Parcels Post, from London to Berlin and other distant places, and never met with an accident.* Starlings and the larger soft-food birds I prefer to send without water, fixing an orange in the cage with a circular piece, about the size of a sixpence, cut out, to enable the bird to suck the juice. Parrots can do without water, and can travel safely for a couple of days with a damp sponge-cake and some seed, but they must be sent in stronger boxes, having a screen outside the wire.

DISEASES OF BIRDS AND DIFFICULTIES IN BIRD-KEEPING.

Much has been written on the subject of diseases, and very little to any practical good purpose. The outward sign of a healthy bird is that he looks bright, and that not a feather is ruffled, out of place, or dirty. If a bird be out of sorts, my advice is to think over the probable cause, to remove it, and let nature, proper food, pure air and water, and clean sand do the rest. In some few instances castor oil may be given, and this is really the only medicine which I ever employ. Two or three drops of castor oil can easily be administered by means of a quill tooth-pick filled with oil. Parrots, being apt to resent handling, may be given castor oil by pouring just sufficient over the drinking-water to cover the surface, which will oblige them to take it with the water when thirsty. It would be superfluous to state when castor oil is requisite. Egg-binding is the cause of many deaths in the aviary, but easily overcome by the introduction with a camel-hair brush of a drop of sweet oil into the egg-passage.

Birds when just imported are mostly out of condition, and often in sad plight. Crammed in large numbers into filthy boxes, they frequently pull out each other's feathers, become dirty and sickly. With proper care they recover in a clean cage, with pure food, water, and air, in a surprisingly short time; but they should never be put into an aviary or large cage with other birds before they are fully recovered and fully able to take care of themselves, and, if need be, to resent aggression. Nor should any bird be supplied with nesting materials or be given an opportunity to nest before being in perfect health and condition. If feathers are broken, and the moulting-time be far off, one or two feathers may be carefully pulled out every other day, when nature will replace them at once. But the process, being painful to the bird, is not to be commended, and the operation ought never to be performed except by very experienced hands.

Parasites and vermin are due as often to weak health as to want of cleanliness. A

* On one occasion the judges of a bird show at Berlin were so much struck with these travelling-cages, that they awarded me a prize for using, and thus unintentionally exhibiting them.

healthy bird, with sufficient opportunities to bathe, will keep himself quite free from insects. If insects appear, sprinkling a little insect powder on the skin, between the roots of the feathers, and thoroughly cleansing the cage, will at once stop the plague, if care be taken simultaneously to improve the bird's health by suitable and generous diet.

It is useful to remember that Australians are our antipodes, that the Australian summer—*i.e.*, the breeding-time—corresponds to our winter season, and that birds brought from Australia to Europe do not change their moulting and breeding time to suit our European seasons, except in the second or third generation, when bred under European skies. Australian and some other foreign birds will breed in winter, if food and surroundings are favourable, and I have reared many broods successfully between November and March. In keeping and breeding foreign birds the temperature is not so great an obstacle as our long nights. Birds do not feed in the dark; this therefore means fifteen or sixteen hours' fast, or, in other words, an impossible existence for young or weak birds. I formerly lost many foreign Finches during a winter, but now keep small lamps burning during the long winter nights. These are hung opposite the cages, and a reflector is so arranged that the nooks and corners of the aviary are shaded, the light being thrown on the food-dishes. If a bird wakes up hungry in the dark, he can find his way to the food; and the practical result was that I lost fewer birds in winter than at any other time of the year, and that I had the pleasure of seeing broods of foreign birds leaving their nest at Christmas.

A great and common mistake, against which all amateur breeders should be warned, is the keeping of many varieties of birds in one cage, however large that cage may be. The birds are certain to disturb each other, and the separation of species cannot be too much recommended. Birds have as much individuality as other and larger animals. I have kept birds whose species is known for their gentleness, but which had to be removed from the aviary on account of their individually quarrelsome disposition; while others reputed to be unbearably combative happened to be individually very gentle. Let me especially warn the reader against the Red Cardinal, or Virginian Nightingale, the Red-headed Cardinal, and the American Mocking-bird—all valuable birds in a cage, but if introduced into an aviary, sooner or later a small bird will be the victim of their strong beaks and vicious tastes, and be found one day minus eyes and brain.

NEST-BOXES AND NESTING MATERIALS.

Foreign Finches build their nests, some in bushes or trees in the aviary, whilst most prefer boxes or some kind of solid basis for the construction of their family residence. Mr. Hawkins' improved open Canary-nest, shown in Fig. 77, affords a secure and solid nest-bottom. The well-known French artificial nests, made of wire and lambswool, with a gay, conical, calico roof, look pretty, but are utterly useless. The globular rush nests, as shown in Fig. 78, harbour insects, and teach the birds the habit of sitting all night and half the day in the nest, whilst a perch might be a much more healthy abode for them. These rush nests should therefore be used with much discrimination, and are only recommended for small birds when just arrived from hot climates with imperfect plumage, and are in want of extra warmth. For breeding I find nothing better than the common little wooden cage in which German Canaries are hawked about in the streets. These I purchase for a few halfpence, and soak in boiling water until perfectly clean, remove the little earthenware pot and the perches, and take out two or three of the wooden bars to give the birds just room to get freely in and out, as shown in Fig. 79. Such a small cage is soon filled with fibre, feathers, &c., by birds seriously intent on nesting; is easily fixed anywhere, easily removed, and easily defended by breeding birds against the intrusion of others. Another very useful nest I make out of empty cigar-boxes, by simply nailing or tying the lid down, and then sawing the lid through midway, removing the upper half, as seen in Figs. 80 and 81. Insects will rarely trouble a nest in an old cigar-box, and birds do not object to tobacco at all. Those who desire a more ornamental

FIG. 77.—OPEN NEST.

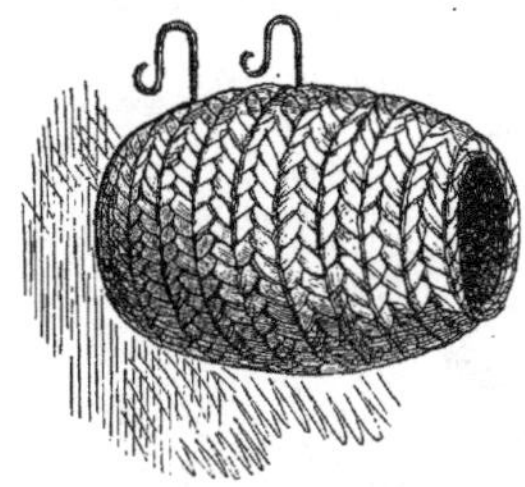

FIG. 78.—RUSH NEST.

FIG. 79.—GERMAN CAGE AS NEST-BOX.

nest-box will find the model shown in Fig. 82 very useful. These boxes are made of polished mahogany.

For nesting material, anything liable to twist round the feet should be carefully avoided; therefore wool and every kind of thread should be rejected. Soft short hay has the disadvantage that it retains moisture and becomes mouldy, and birds, bathing as freely when sitting as at other times, bring a certain amount of moisture into their nests. Manilla hemp, or the hard

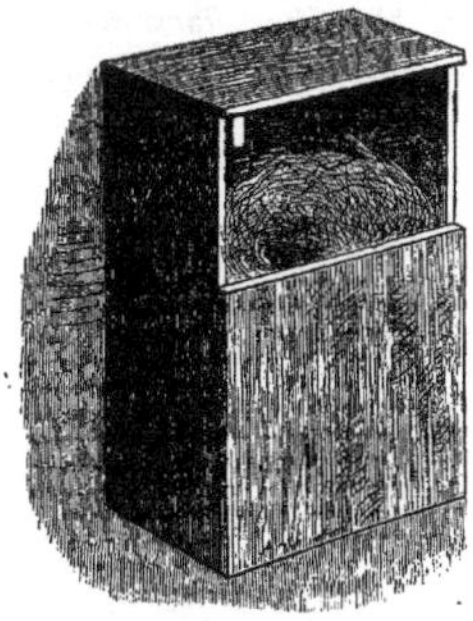

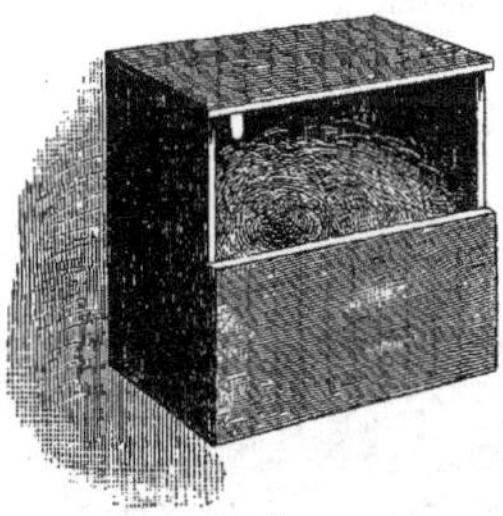

FIG. 80. FIG. 81.
NESTS MADE OF CIGAR-BOXES.

FIG. 82.—MAHOGANY NEST

straight aloe fibre used by matting makers, and sometimes as summer ornament for fire-places, cut into lengths of six to eight inches, with a few very small feathers, I find better nesting materials than any others, and suited to the wants of all my birds, from the hardiest Weaver to the most delicate Waxbill, from Starling and Cardinal to Bulbul or foreign Nightingale.

Parrots nest in hollow trees, and occupy or scoop out a round or oval mould. Some few leave a layer of particles of wood in this mould, others lay their eggs on the solid wood. To breed

Parrots or Parrakeets a very large cage or aviary is required, and then a log of wood must be scraped, or turned hollow, to imitate as nearly as can be a natural tree with a decayed branch-root (Fig. 83). A branch should be left on the trunk, or fixed to it, on which the male will sit keeping guard over the nest, which must be fixed at some height from the floor. Some Parrakeets, notably the undulated, like a cocoa-nut husk, which can be fixed as shown in Fig. 84.

FIG. 83.—TREE-NEST FOR PARRAKEET.

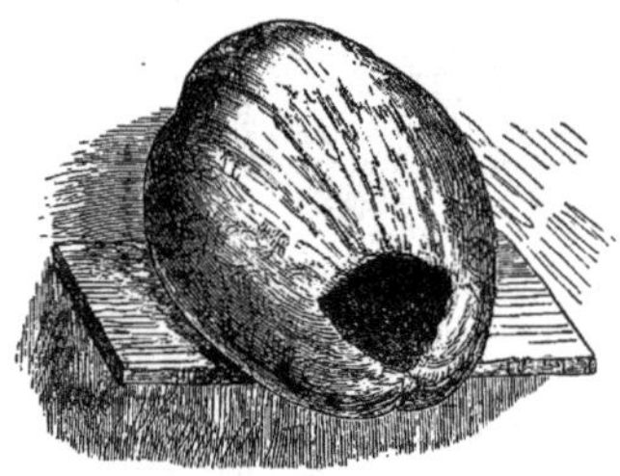

FIG. 84.—COCOA-NUT HUSK.

The illustrations to these chapters will speak for themselves. They have been drawn by Mr. William Rutledge, of Sunderland, with much talent and care, from live specimens. Miss Dyson, T. C. Marsh, Esq., Mr. J. Abrahams, Mr. Jos. Groom, Mr. Chas. Jamrach, Mr. Anton Jamrach, and Mr. Edward Hawkins have very kindly lent valuable birds, some of them very rare, for the purpose of being illustrated.

Vincent Brooks Day & Son Lith

1. NONPAREIL FINCH.
2. COMMON BLUE BIRD.
3. YELLOW BELLIED LIOTHRIX OR PEKIN NIGHTINGALE.
4. INDIGO BIRD.

CHAPTER XLII.

SOFT-FOOD BIRDS.

DR. RUSS divides the foreign cage-birds into three chief categories, viz., Seed-eating Birds, Soft-food Birds, and Parrots. This classification is, no doubt, convenient, and the temptation to follow in the same path is great, yet for the purposes of this book it seemed preferable to follow the list of the Zoological Society of London. One of the difficulties in the way of reference is the great variety of names given to each bird by different writers, scarcely two authorities agreeing as to what ought to be the Latin name of a species. I shall endeavour to give all the names under which a bird is described by scientific ornithologists, in order to enable those who wish to do so, to refer readily to scientific works.

The first foreign bird we come to in the Zoological Society's list belongs to the order *Turdidæ*, or Thrushes, therefore soft-food birds.

THE BLUE ROBIN, OR COMMON BLUE-BIRD (*Sialia Wilsonii Swainson*), NORTH AMERICA. (See Illustration.)
Sylvia sialis (Russ), *Motacilla sialis*, *Saxicola sialis*. Blue Nightingale or Blue Robin of Dealers.
German name—"Der blaue Hüttensänger." French name—"Rossignol bleu."

The popular name of Blue Nightingale is clearly a misnomer, as this charming bird is not a Nightingale, but much more nearly related to the Robins. The German name, signifying "Blue Cottage Songster," is perhaps the most happily chosen of any; for wherever a settler builds a cottage in North America, there the Blue-bird greets him, approaches his dwelling with entire confidence, and forthwith builds his nest under the thatch of the cottage, in a hole of the wall, or cavity of the nearest tree. By no means shy, the Blue-bird does not care to hide himself in leafy trees, but may be seen from morn to eve sitting on a dead branch, on a stone, on the eaves of a house or other projection, singing his melodious but unpretending song, and watching for insects, which he catches after the manner of Robins. His home extends from Mexico to Labrador; in summer he comes north, in winter he migrates southward.

In size the Blue-bird is somewhat larger than our European Robin. The back of the male Blue Robin, the wings, and tail are of a beautiful ultramarine blue tint; the breast is a pale brown. The female is similarly coloured, but the colours are much less bright.

In captivity this bird thrives well in open-air aviaries, and is easily kept for years without artificial heat in winter; he is perfectly gentle with other birds, and will prove quite as robust as any foreign insectivorous bird. His food is the ordinary Thrush's food, to which should be added a little ripe fruit, a few currants, and at times a little seed. A few meal-worms will make the Blue-bird quite tame, and in a short time he will take them from his keeper's hand. It should, however, be borne in mind that these birds are somewhat voracious, and the necessary consequence is a large amount of dirt. Large cages and scrupulous cleanliness, much sand, and plenty of water to bathe in, are indispensable for these birds.

The Blue Robins breed in confinement, building a rather slovenly nest in any hole, crevice, basket, or box which may be in the aviary, provided it is deep enough for the bird's taste. Into such a receptacle grasses and fibres of all kinds will be carried and formed into a nest; and four to six light blue eggs of large size will soon be laid. The hen-bird sits very steadily on them, being fed by the male, who will always hover near the nest, but never condescend to keep the eggs warm himself. The eggs are hatched in about thirteen days, and the young are diligently fed by their parents, but mostly by the male. Many broods are, however, forsaken after a few days, and I have also found the young birds frequently thrown out of the nest when four to eight days old. Other breeders have been more successful, and have reared broods of Blue-birds repeatedly. To do so requires much patience and perseverance, and a supply of fresh food every two or three hours from sunrise to sunset. Mealworms, fresh ants' eggs, raw beef scraped fine, and egg-food should be given in small quantities as many times per day as the young brood requires to be fed. In about twenty-five days from the date of hatching the young birds leave the nest, and their plumage resembles that of the female.

In the Zoological Gardens of London, Blue-birds were bred as long ago as 1869, and again in 1870. Since then they have been bred repeatedly by many amateurs.

MOCKING-BIRD (*Mimus polyglottus*), NORTH AMERICA.

Turdus polyglottus (Russ), *Orpheus polyglottus.* German—"Spottdrossel."

According to American writers, the Mocking-bird is, of all cage-birds, the very best songster, an opinion which is, however, not generally shared in Europe. Mocking-birds are trans-Atlantic cousins of our Song Thrush, and to me the song of our Thrush always seemed much preferable. It may be, however, that the comparison is not quite fair, nearly all the Mocking-birds arriving in Europe having been taken from the nest and brought up by hand, therefore without opportunity to learn their parents' song to perfection. Even in America the talent of individual birds varies considerably, and first-rate songsters are sometimes sold at very high prices.

The home of the Mocking-bird is North America. In the Southern States he remains summer and winter, whilst in the Northern States he disappears late in autumn and migrates south. His habits resemble closely those of our Blackbird. Quick in his movements and very intelligent, he is at first somewhat shy, and approaches human habitations warily, but once assured that no harm will befall him, he becomes bold and quite confident after a time.

The plumage is sober and yet prettily marked, the predominant colour being light grey, with black and white marks. The male is distinguished from the female by having a white band extending over all the feathers of each wing, and forming when the wing is spread almost a crescent, whilst the female has a white mark on only the outer wing-feathers.

In confinement the Mocking-bird is fed exactly like a Thrush or Blackbird, and will live a long time, say ten to fifteen years. In America he is frequently fed on boiled potatoes, mixed with boiled egg, and also on damp maw-seed meal, which is maw-seed from which the oil has been extracted. In Europe, however, he seems to thrive best on Thrush's food. As an inmate of an aviary the Mocking-bird is to be avoided, for he will boldly attack any bird of his own size, and is likely to kill birds smaller than himself.

In his wild state this bird builds his nest like our Thrushes and Blackbirds, in forks of branches, or into the crown of a bush, in gardens or small plantations. A pair will unhesitatingly build a nest in confinement when circumstances are at all favourable, and will then avail themselves of an artificial basis for a nest. In my own aviary they repeatedly built a nest of hay, grass, and fibres into a little German Canary-cage, from which the bottom was removed, and which was then hung upside down against the aviary wall. They lay from three to seven bluish-green eggs with brownish spots, and hatch them without much difficulty. But rearing the young brood is another matter; and at this stage we meet with great troubles. Mocking-birds require live food—mealworms and fresh ants' eggs—to bring up the young, and these morsels are so very tempting that the old birds sometimes swallow them, and then soon feel the stimulating effect. Instead of bringing up their young, they want to build and lay again. I once thought that the fault of repeated neglect of the young broods was due to the male enticing the hen away from her duties, and therefore removed the male as soon as the eggs were hatched. This stratagem was, however, not a success; the solitary male sang all day to his mate, distant some ten or twelve feet from his cage, and the effect of his love-song was so overpowering that madame forgot her duties altogether, allowed the young to die of starvation, built a new nest, and laid an egg whilst her lord was absent. The only way to succeed in rearing broods of such-like birds is by giving them their food in small quantities, and very often. Then the hungry cries of the little ones may keep the parents to their duty, and when the little mouths are full the dainties for the delicate digestions of the youngsters ought all to be consumed, so that the old birds are out of the way of much temptation, and bound to subsist on their more frugal and habitual diet.

Mocking-birds have been bred in the London Zoological Gardens repeatedly in 1873 and 1874. Before that time amateurs had bred them in France.

PEKIN NIGHTINGALE, OR YELLOW-BELLIED LIOTHRIX (*Liothrix luteus*), INDIA. (See Illustration.)
Leiothrix luteus, Sylvia lutea, Leiothrix sinensis, Leiothrix furcata, Tanagra sinensis, Parus furcatus.
Dealers' names—Sun-bird, Lesser Pekin Nightingale, Japanese Nightingale. German name—"Sonnenvogel."

Since the year 1866 the Parrot-house of the Zoological Gardens of London contained a pair of birds—until then quite unknown—the admiration of every beholder, and the envy of the writer. *Liothrix luteus:* I well remember how that name impressed itself on my memory whilst watching a charming pair of birds, with coral-red beaks and feet, flying merrily from perch to perch, sometimes clinging to the roof of the cage, and coming neatly with a somersault back on to the perch; then eyeing me with their large intelligent eyes, whilst singing a strangely melodious little note. When, a few years later, one pair was offered at a high price, the temptation to acquire them was irresistible. But since then hundreds of pairs arrive regularly; the bird is now readily obtainable by every amateur, and the price has ceased to be extravagant. The Liothrix has become—and deservedly so—a general favourite, and is no doubt one of the prettiest and most interesting inhabitants of an aviary. By some naturalists the Liothrix is classed amongst the Tomtits; but any one who closely observes these birds must come to the conclusion that they form a class of themselves.

The Liothrix is a trifle larger than the Cole Tit. The back is olive-brown, changing to an olive-yellowish tint at the head, and to greyish-brown at the sides. The throat and breast are ornamented by a patch of bright orange, shaded towards the border. The wings are dark; each wing-feather is edged with bright deep orange-colour. The female is very similar to the male, and only to be distinguished by the orange tints being a shade less deep and a trifle less spread over the breast.

China, Japan, and the Himalayas are the homes of this bird. In India he is seldom found at a lesser altitude than about 4,000 or 5,000 feet above the level of the sea. Hence the bird is not nearly so delicate as other Indian birds; hardy as regards climatic influences, and content with almost any food. In the aviary he will be found feeding with the Blue Robins and other soft-food birds, and again paying some attention to the seed-dishes, swallowing canary or millet seed entire. A piece of ripe fruit and a mealworm are equally welcome to him. Even a little boiled rice will not come amiss. In the cage we cannot offer the Liothrix too much variety of food. Even a few grains of hemp-seed may be given, which the birds will, if the seeds be large, carry to a perch, hold daintily with their feet, and try to break by hammering with their coral-red, soft beaks. Two or three times a day the birds will take a bath, and almost incessantly will they be busy preening and arranging their pretty feathers, until these are the very perfection of neatness and good order. Not the least of a Liothrix's merits is that he never molests any other birds, large or small, and is a model of good behaviour in the aviary, whether kept singly or in pairs. Even several pairs do not apparently molest each other.

Dr. Russ first bred the Sun-bird in captivity in 1874, and since then several successful broods have been recorded annually. The nest is rather inartistic, either in a bush, on a ledge, or in a nest-box, German cage, or any similarly suitable contrivance. It consists of hay, fibres, and grasses, with a few small feathers. About four bluish or greenish eggs, with brown or reddish spots, will be laid; the male and female sit alternately, and hatch the eggs in about twelve or thirteen days. The young appear less difficult to rear than those of other insectivorous birds, and resemble the old birds, except that the colours are faint and somewhat dull.

THE CHINESE JAY THRUSH (*Garrulax Chinensis*), CHINA.

Garrulax Sinensis (Russ), *Leucodioptron canorum.* Dealers' names—Japanese Mocking-bird, Pekin Mocking-bird. German name—"Heherdrossel."

Some readers of this book may remember a bird, exhibited at the Crystal Palace Bird Show in the original Japanese cage, in February, 1876. That specimen was one of the first of this kind ever imported, and since then these birds are frequently obtainable.

The plumage of the Chinese Jay Thrush is an unpretending brown, and the bird is rather larger than our European Thrush. One of these birds has lived in my possession for seven or eight years, and is alive now. His song is far superior to that of the American Mocking-bird, and superior to that of any other foreign songster. The specimen for so long under my daily observation was a bird of much individuality. When in full song he continued singing so long that his tongue became swollen. I treated this irregularity medicinally by applying a little honey to the tongue, and sweet oil to the mandibles, which soon put matters right, and allowed of a fresh burst of song. This Thrush used to get over the moulting-time by a very short road. Over-night the tail would fall out, and the bird then offered a very curious sight in the morning. Within less than fourteen days the tail was always renewed, and in splendid order again.

Unusual opportunities of observing this Thrush allow me to name him as an incomparable songster, a long-lived cage-bird, and one of rare intelligence. My old friend used to remind me by a peculiar call that he expected a mealworm, and would grow exceedingly angry and jealous if his neighbours were favoured with this delicacy before him. He readily took a worm from my fingers, and always sang a little stanza, with the worm wriggling in his beak, before swallowing it.

Whether females are ever imported is not known for certain, all those birds arriving being much alike; therefore no attempt at breeding has yet been made. In the aviary the bird would certainly prove quarrelsome, and might prove destructive. He is clearly fitted only for being kept for his song, in a separate cage, where he will thrive on ordinary Thrushes' food in almost any temperature, and where his song will amply repay his keeper for the trouble of his keep.

Four other varieties of *Garrulax* are named in the list of the Zoological Society, but are very rarely offered for sale, and not likely to come within reach of amateurs.

CHAPTER XLIII.

BULBULS.

THE genus *Pycnonotus*, or Bulbul, next engages our attention. These birds are found in Egypt, in India, Persia, and China, in Ceylon, and on the islands of the Eastern Archipelago. Eastern literature is full of praise of the Bulbul, the cage-bird *par excellence* of the East. In their wild state the Bulbuls live in the jungle, in small woods or bushy plantations, feeding on insects, berries, and fruit. As cage-birds they are hardy, and can be accustomed to all those kinds of food on which Thrushes and Nightingales are kept, but it must always be borne in mind that ripe and sweet fruit is to them a necessary article of diet. In India, Bulbuls are often tamed, and trained to obey the commands of their keepers; to fly abroad, to return when called, and to fight in the manner of gamecocks. In calling the Bulbuls Eastern Nightingales their vocal merits seem to be largely overrated. Their docility seems to be more remarkable than their song. A striking peculiarity of the Bulbuls is a crest, varying in size, and giving these birds a very peculiar appearance.

That the Bulbuls will ever become very popular cage-birds in Europe may be doubted. Never imported in large numbers, the birds are not often obtainable, and never cheap; and their requirements in the matter of sweet fruit make their keep expensive and somewhat troublesome. A trained Bulbul may be a pretty toy in the East, and as such highly prized by the natives, but tame Bulbuls are never exported, and the many which came under my observation were untrained and not very good songsters. As these Bulbuls were, however, kept in a large aviary, their vocal powers may have been less noticed than they deserved to be. No Bulbuls have probably been bred in captivity in Europe; but this may be owing to the few experiments made so far.* Male and female being very similar, and difficult to distinguish, makes it difficult to select a pair, and greatly increases the difficulty of the experiment. That these birds would, however, breed readily in an aviary I can affirm, having had a specimen of the Red-eared Bulbul for some years, which several times built a rather artistic nest in a bush, laid three and four pink eggs with chocolate-coloured spots, and sat on them patiently. As there was no male bird the eggs came, of course, to nothing. The nest was built after the manner of our Finches' nests, between the higher branches of a bush, roots, hay, and small branches forming the outside, soft fibres the inner lining.

In company with Blue Nightingales and Sun-birds, Bulbuls might be kept in the aviary, yet some caution may be advisable. They should not be trusted with smaller birds, nor would it be wise to allow Bulbuls in the same cage with a brood of newly-hatched birds in an exposed nest.

A description of the varieties of Bulbuls in the list of the Zoological Society is impossible within the limits of these pages. To assist readers in referring to works on natural history, all the names by which the best-known kinds of Bulbul have been described by various writers are subjoined.

THE BLACK BULBUL (*Pycnonotus pygæus*, Russ), BENGAL.

Ixos pygæus, Hæmatornis cafer, Turdus cafer, Brachypus pygæus, Pycnonotus Bengalensis. Called "Kala" in India.
German name—"Kala Bulbul," or "Rothsteissiger Bulbul."

* While these pages were in the press, a brood of young Syrian Bulbuls have been reared in Germany, from parents exhibited by me in February, 1879, at the Crystal Palace.

THE WHITE-EARED BULBUL (*Pycnonotus leucotis*, Russ), North-west India.
Ixos leucotis. German name—"Hauben Bulbul," "Weissohrige Bulbul."

THE RED-EARED BULBUL (*Pycnonotus jocosus*, Russ), India.
Lanius jocosus, Hæmatornis jocosus, Ixos jocosus, Ixos monticolus, Ixos pyrrhotis, Turdus jocosus, Otocompsa jocosa, Pycnonotus sinensis, Pyrrhotis erythrotis. German name—"Rothbäckige Bulbul," or "Schopfbulbul."

RED-VENTED BULBUL (*Pycnonotus hæmorrhous*, Russ), India.
Muscicapa hæmorrhousa, Ixos hæmorrh, Ixos cafer, Hæmatornis hæmorrh, Hæm. pusillus, Hæm. chrysorrhoides, Brachypus hæmorrhous. German name—"Rothbäuchige Bulbul."

SYRIAN BULBUL (*Pycnonotus xanthopygos*, Russ), Syria.
Pycnonotus nigricans (Russ), *Turdus capensis, Ixos nigricans, Ixos aurigaster, Ixos xanthopygos, Turdus nigricans, Pyc. aurigaster.* German name—"Arabische Bulbul," or "Goldsteissbulbul."

The list of the Zoological Society names six Bulbuls, Dr. Russ mentions eight varieties, and Dr. Brehm gives the names of no less than twenty-five.

A highly-interesting relative of the true Bulbul, or *Pycnonotus*, is the wonderfully brilliant

MALABAR GREEN BULBUL (*Phyllornis aurifrons*, Russ), India.
Chloropsis aurifrous, Merops hurryba. German name—"Goldstirn Blattvogel."

Very few cage-birds combine such a beautiful plumage with such qualities of song as this bird does. The entire body is bright golden-green; the face, round the beak, and extending half over the head, bright orange; chin and throat of a magnificent azure-blue tint, bordered by a black band.

How this bird comes to be called a Bulbul is one of those many riddles presented by the nomenclature of birds. He is evidently a honey-sucker, as his long, slender, slightly-curved beak shows, and as an examination of his peculiar brush-like long tongue will demonstrate. There are five or six varieties of this bird, varying, however, in little except in size, all natives of the enormous country extending from the Malabar coast to the Himalayas, to Assam, Burmah, and over the Eastern Archipelago.

As lately as 1874 the Zoological Gardens of London appear to have had the first live specimen, and in the same year, if not a few months earlier, the Berlin Gardens had one. In the following year the writer procured two, and since then the species has been imported more frequently. But the Green Bulbul is not a bird easily kept in captivity. Of the two I purchased in January, 1875, one died within a few weeks, having, however, enabled me to observe that two of these gentle-looking birds, when put into one cage, will fight furiously without delay. My surviving bird was exhibited in 1876 at the Crystal Palace for a day or two, and lived about eighteen months, which is perhaps as long as any other specimen has endured. It was pleasant to see a very good specimen exhibited, in fine condition, at the Crystal Palace in February, 1879.

My treatment of *Phyllornis aurifrons* was based on the observation that the bird stood midway between the Flycatcher and the Honeysucker. I gave him plenty of mealworms and fresh grapes. Into the latter he would dip his beak, sucking the juice. The staple food consisted of dried ants' eggs, soaked in water and mixed with honey, and a piece of sponge-cake soaked in water, pressed, and then well mixed with a quantity of cayenne pepper. Other amateurs have tried to keep the birds on boiled rice, much sweetened; but birds thus fed seem not to have endured very long. Nightingale food and figs have been tried with more success than rice diet.

About the beauty of their song all those who heard it are agreed.

CHAPTER XLIV.

TANAGERS.

A GROUP of gorgeously coloured South American birds are the *Tanagridæ*, or Tanagers. Every one has seen many specimens of this family, for few cases of stuffed birds prepared for drawing-room ornamentation are without one or more representatives of this wondrously brilliant genus. A few years ago it was the fashion to ornament ladies' hats and bonnets with bird-skins, many of which were Tanagers'; and the vagaries of taste caused the slaughter of millions of birds. At that time ladies' hats ornamented (?) with all kinds of birds in impossible and absurd attitudes could be seen hourly in every street of every city. Dr. Russ had the courage to protest against the thoughtless absurdity of the fashion, and the German press nobly took the part of the birds against the ladies. A little reflection convinced many ladies that there was something ridiculously incongruous in placing a stuffed Starling or Tanager on a hat, and the fashion died out. For all that, a visit to the Billiter Street warehouses in London will reveal hundreds of cases, containing many thousands of bird-skins, which are sold at periodical auctions in Mincing Lane. The magnificent plumage of the Tanagers is their worst enemy.

Our acquaintance with these birds is unfortunately not likely ever to become much more intimate than a contemplation of their stuffed skins will afford. The list of the Zoological Society of London embraces no less than twenty varieties of Tanagers, varying in size from that of a Siskin to nearly that of a Thrush. All are natives of Brazil, and all live more or less on fruit, besides insects, and some few seeds. In our northern climate it is found next to impossible to supply Tanagers with appropriate food, therefore only the skilled attendants of a zoological garden, with all the resources of such establishments, succeed in keeping them alive for any time. In the market-place of Rio de Janeiro, Bahia, or Pernambuco the most beautiful Tanagers can be bought at about 2d. per head; in England they are worth £2 each, and but rarely offered for sale. This difference in price sufficiently indicates the difficulty of bringing Tanagers to Europe. In their native country the caged Tanagers are mostly fed on "farinha de mandioca," *i.e.*, tapioca flour, damped with the juice of sweet oranges. This very meagre food seems to suffice for the birds while in Brazil, or on board ship in the tropics, but when the steamers near England the Tanagers die in ever-increasing numbers. Under the brighter sky of France their chance of life is much greater, and even in Antwerp they do better than in England.

As regards song, the Tanagers have none, and therefore it is solely the beauty of their plumage which causes them to be valued as cage-birds. Nor can the manners of these birds be called gentle; they will always remain somewhat clumsy and wild in the cage.

In England, Tanagers should be kept on Nightingale food, with a little crushed hemp-seed. Sweet over-ripe pears and bananas, or very sweet grapes, should be given as much as possible, together with a few mealworms. If their keeper succeeds in inducing them to eat figs (cut open), he may keep them over the winter, in a very warm temperature. Oranges do not agree with them, as those arriving in this country are shipped unripe, and are therefore not sweet enough. I kept many Tanagers in my time, but they never lived long, and a few foggy days in autumn or winter would cause them to die, even when placed in a hothouse with their cage surrounded by palms and tropical plants. I therefore gave up attempting to keep them, but were I to try again, I would, besides the Nightingale food, try soaked sponge-cake, mixed with a few ants' eggs, and a little cayenne pepper. The following are most likely to reach the hands of a collector:—

VIOLET TANAGER (*Euphonia violacea*), Brazil.

Tanagra violacea (Russ). "Gutturama" of the Brazilians. German—"Der gemeine Organist," or "Violette Organist."

This is a curiously-coloured little bird, the back being a dark violet-black, and the chest and abdomen bright yellow. The size of this, one of the most frequently-imported Tanagers, is only about equal to that of our Siskin, and if we can supply him with plenty of fruit, the bird will live for some time in the cage, consuming an incredible quantity of pears, bananas, &c. Some ornithologists who have observed this species in its wild state write of its song: whilst in the cage nothing beyond a peculiar gurgling but not unpleasant sound is ever heard. The Violet Tanager is comparatively harmless in the aviary, being peaceable towards other birds.

SUPERB TANAGER (*Calliste fastuosa*), Pernambuco.

Tanagra fastuosa (Russ). German—"Vielfarbige Tangara," "Prachttangara."

Some of the most brilliant colours to be met with in nature under a tropical sky seem to have been lavished on this bird, whose size equals that of our Goldfinch. His head is bluish-green, with a golden gloss, bordered on the throat, on the side of the head, and extending a little way down the back, by a band of deep shining black. From the middle of the back to the tail, bright golden-orange; whilst the chest is bright pale blue, deepening into a bright azure tint on the abdomen. The tail and wings are brilliant blue, the outer wing-feathers are bordered by a line of golden-orange. By this description one might imagine that the contrasts of brilliant colours would be somewhat harsh; yet Nature blends her colours so harmoniously, that the appearance of this gorgeous creature is simply indescribably beautiful. No wonder that the bird is imported annually, *viâ* Bordeaux and Antwerp, and that, notwithstanding his high price, he tempts some amateur to repeat the experience of the writer, to see the birds die within a few weeks, in spite of infinite care.

BRAZILIAN TANAGER (*Ramphocœlus Brasilius*), Brazil.

Tanagra Brasiliensis (Russ), *Ramphocœlus coccineus*, *Ramphocœlus Brasiliensis*, *Tanagra cardinalis*. Red-and-black Tanager. German—"Der Purpurrothe Tangara," "Purpur Tangara."

This Tanager is larger than those previously mentioned, being rather larger than a Bunting. He is more frequently imported than all the other Tanagers, and is far more hardy. The plumage is of rich purple-red hue all over, except the wings and tail, which are jet-black. The beak is black, but the lower mandible has an elongated white patch near the root. The female is reddish-brown, with dullish brown wings; but many birds sold as female Brazilian Tanagers turn out to be young males. Much less delicate than the smaller Tanagers, this beautiful bird will live for years, in a roomy cage, under favourable circumstances. He has been bred repeatedly and reared successfully by a lady in Belgium, but not as yet elsewhere. In the aviary this Tanager will be found dangerous to small birds, and inclined to kill and devour newly-hatched fancy Finches. His food is like that of the other Tanagers, but he is less dainty, and will take a little raw beef, a few seeds, boiled rice, and any kind of sweet fruit, besides Nightingale food.

CHAPTER XLV.

DWARF OR FANCY FINCHES.

THE Dwarf or Fancy Finches must be considered the foreign cage-birds *par excellence*, but it should be stated at once that very little indeed is known of the life and habits of most of these little birds in their wild state, whilst a great mass of information on their habits in the aviary has been collected by Dr. Russ, who closely observed most of them from the hour they were hatched until the young ones had again a family of their own. Next to Dr. Russ, I had probably greater opportunities than any other amateur to observe the habits of my especial favourites; but Dr. Russ devoted his *entire* time for many years to the study of foreign cage-birds, whilst I could only devote my leisure hours to the same pursuit. My own experience has corroborated many facts first observed and described by Dr. Russ, whilst in some cases I could supplement his wonderfully exact observations in consequence of my birds being kept in a slightly different climate, generally at a less temperature, and a good deal in the open air.

These diminutive Finches are found in Asia, Africa, and Australia, whilst no representative of the family has been discovered in America or Europe. In size they vary from that of our common Chaffinch down to something less than our smallest Wren. These of all birds deserve the name of Love-birds. At the dealers' shops hundreds may be seen in one cage, sitting as close together as they can, trying to keep each other warm, and lovingly arranging each other's feathers. In the aviary pairs keep together in and out of season. At night they will be found either to occupy an artificial nest, or to sit close to each other on a perch. With the approach of breeding-time there may be a little jealousy, but as a rule these little Finches are models of behaviour, and many of them, be they varieties or several pairs of the same species, can be safely kept in one cage. As regards cages, it should be remembered that some which would safely hold a Canary would allow the smallest of the foreign Finches to escape. The wires of cages for foreign Finches must not be more than five-eighths of an inch apart, and half-inch wirework is better.

The wants of foreign Finches when kept as cage-birds are easily supplied, canary and millet seed being their staple food, and only at breeding-time is extra food required as a rule. The Australian Finches deserve the foremost rank as domestic pets, as they adapt themselves most readily to our climate, and some of them breed with remarkable facility in the temperature of an ordinary sitting-room. Whether the immense importation of Australian Finches will continue permanently is another question. A good deal has been heard lately about the spread of the European rabbit in New Zealand threatening to drive the sheep off their pasture grounds. The European Sparrow, too, has been imported into Queensland, and seems to thrive so well, monopolising the best feeding-grounds and the best breeding-places, that the indigenous and weaker birds are in some districts being driven to other quarters, and some of them possibly out of existence. A sparrow, having no commercial value, is never trapped; while the beautiful little Australian Finches are caught by thousands, in order to bring hundreds to the European market.

African Finches require a certain amount of heat, and if the temperature of their abode should be permanently much below 60° Fahr. in winter, their plumage will suffer sooner or later, and there will be very little chance of breeding. They will live at a less temperature if they are protected from draught and damp, and are carefully tended as regards food, but to *breed* them an even temperature of something near 70° is needful. Insufficient temperature, like foul air or wrong food, causes the feathers to lose their lustre and to fall out; the birds will lack stamina for the development of their plumage, will remain bald for awhile, and then die of exhaustion. None of these little Finches can stand a temperature near freezing-point for any length of time. There may be a cold night even late in spring, and the thermometer may then fall low for an hour or two just before daybreak without any harm resulting to delicate birds if healthy; but they cannot endure cold for any length of time like the Canary and many larger Finches.

Ornithologists disagree in respect of the scientific classification of the Dwarf Finches almost more even than about other birds. Dr. Russ divides the large family into two groups, viz., the Small-Billed Astrilds—*Æginthinæ;* the Strong-Billed Amadinæ—*Spermestinæ.* In the list of the Zoological Society we find the generic names of *Estrelda* in place of Dr. Russ's *Ægintha*, and *Pytelia, Amadina, Munia,* and *Poëphila* instead of Dr. Russ's *Spermestes.* With the aid of this explanation and the list of Latin names the reader will be enabled to trace in scientific works all those foreign Finches named in this book.

Many years ago the merest accident made me possessor of a small cage with half a dozen of the smallest foreign Finches. At that time my knowledge of foreign birds was a blank, but the little creatures interested me more and more day by day. Passing shops where foreign birds were offered for sale, I could not help comparing the bright and happy demeanour of my little pets with that of birds lately arrived, worn and bruised by the voyage, and now and then I increased my stock. The one cage was soon followed by the purchase of others; the half-dozen birds became dozens. When a mishap occurred and a bird died, I tried to discover the cause, in order to avoid it for the survivors; and this led, step by step, to highly interesting studies, and as pleasant an occupation for leisure hours as any one can possibly wish for. All the foreign Finches usually offered for sale were soon represented in my little collection, but then came the ambition to possess and keep alive birds not often seen elsewhere. The construction of an aviary soon gave suitable quarters to my birds, and permitted the addition of many varieties. Periodical visits to the dealers on the chance of finding some rare birds proved often fruitless, but sometimes a prize fell into my hands.

In the course of ten years I had thus in my care every kind of foreign Finch named in the list of the Zoological Society, and a good many besides. Rare birds have come into my hands in the most unexpected manner imaginable. Very few museums have a skin of the beautiful Australian Painted Finch (*Emblema picta,* Gould), and there is probably no living specimen in Europe: the Zoological Garden of London never possessed one. I shall relate hereafter how I once found a pair in a hairdresser's shop in Liverpool, and bought them for a few shillings, and how on another occasion I bought three from a journeyman wireworker. I have before me now a little African Finch which had much puzzled myself and others, until it was settled beyond doubt that he was an entirely new species, strangely overlooked by all scientific ornithologists. Another fortunate accident enabled me to purchase a pair of birds of a kind I had never seen before, and which were not to be found alive in any collection. I had the good luck to breed and rear them successfully, and one such success rewards the amateur amply for many failures.

1. PARROT FINCH. 2. BICHENO'S OR DOUBLE BANDED FINCH.
3. AUSTRALIAN CRIMSON FINCH. MALE. 3a FEMALE.
4. CHESNUT-BREASTED FINCH.

The list of the Zoological Society begins with the Australian Finches, the first of which is

THE CRIMSON FINCH (*Estrelda Phaëton*, Hombr. and Jacq.), NORTH AUSTRALIA.
(Illustration painted from live birds in the Author's collection.)

Ægintha Phaëton (Russ), *Fringilla Phaëton, Neochmia Phaëton, Uræginthus Phaëton.* German—"Sonnenastrild," or "Australische Amaranth." English dealers generally call this bird Australian Fire Finch.

We have here one of the most beautiful, but hitherto rather rare, Australian Finches before us. About the size of the well-known St. Helena Waxbill, the male bird's face, cheeks, throat, chest, and the entire lower body are of brilliant dark carmine-red, the back is plain brown, the wings reddish-brown, and the dark red tail is rather long, the middle feathers being longest. The beak is bright coral-red. On the sides of the chest are small white spots, which become slightly larger as the bird grows older. The female has a pale red face and throat, the breast being greyish-brown instead of the bright red of her mate, but showing also white spots at the sides. Seen in the full light of the sun, this graceful little bird must charm every beholder. The rich red of the breast is then brightest, the white spots on the sides will appear like small pearls, and he will presently raise his head high, and swaying slowly from one leg to the other, he will sing his insignificant little song, or spread his tail somewhat like a miniature fan. With rapid, graceful flight he will visit every corner of the aviary, peering with his intelligent eyes into every food-dish, or seeing from afar the chance of a mealworm.

There is a very similar kind, the African Fire Finch, worth very much less than the Australian Crimson Finch, and in buying the latter it is as well to avoid the mistake of buying the former instead. The African Fire Finch is very much smaller, and has very minute white spots on the sides, but his inferior size alone is ample guide.

The native country of the Crimson Finch is Northern Australia, and he comes to England mostly from Port Essington. According to Gould, he lives on grassy plains, and subsists mainly on grass seeds. When we bear in mind that Northern Australia is semi-tropical, and the voyage thence to England is a long one, mostly accompanied by great changes of temperature, we cannot wonder that these little birds often arrive in Europe much exhausted, and that they frequently die soon, especially when winter sets in before they have time to recover. That, notwithstanding their considerable value, they should be imported so rarely is a curious fact which I cannot explain. Of those which do come, the females are decidedly the more delicate.

Although the Crimson Finch has been kept at the Zoological Gardens since 1861, Dr. Russ could never succeed in obtaining a pair fit for breeding, the hens generally dying; but an amateur in Hamburg succeeded in 1878 in rearing successfully a brood of five young birds hatched in his aviary.

I had never seen more than one or two of these birds at one time, and at long intervals, until I had an opportunity in July, 1878, of acquiring eighteen or nineteen newly-imported young Crimson Finches in unusually good condition. The young birds resemble the female until their second moult, and for the purpose of acclimatising and observing the habits of these interesting birds, I purchased the entire lot. Although the time of year was favourable, they required great care; but with the aid of plenty of millet in the ear, a little egg-food, and tufts of fresh grass, with the seed stalks, roots, mould and all, they prospered very well. Some live animal food was, however, indispensable, and an allowance of two or three mealworms per head daily assisted me much. The colour of the males became very bright, and by rare good fortune there were more females than males. Of the females several died in spite of all my care, and towards autumn some of the most beautiful males began to be very quarrelsome, a sure sign of the breeding season drawing near. I decided to remove the two most bellicose gentlemen, associated each with a hen, and sent one pair to Dr. Russ, the other to another friend, in hopes that one of us three would succeed in breeding. Of the pair sent to Dr. Russ the hen arrived dead; of the other pair the hen died a few days after arrival. The birds I retained proved to be rather susceptible to cold weather during the winter, but continued to thrive. In February the plumage of one pair became wonderfully brilliant. They took possession of a little German canary-cage hung against the aviary wall, and piled up a layer of leaves nearly two inches high on the bottom of the future breeding-place. The male carried henceforth aloe fibre with restless activity into this receptacle, and filled the remaining space completely with this material. The fibre carried into the little cage was turned and twisted until it formed a hollow ball. A deep mould, completely arched over, with a very small entrance at the side just large enough to admit this tiny bird, formed the nest. In the course of about as many days five pure white eggs were laid, and then began the serious business of incubation.

The birds' manners now became daily more interesting. Woe to any bird that dared approach the nest, for the male Crimson Finch would attack him furiously. But a model father of a family was he. When he thought the female wanted food or a bath, he would fly to a branch nearest the nest and wake her from her slumbers by a call. As soon as she answered he would creep through the narrow hole into the nest, and when he had fairly settled on and covered the eggs, the female crept out and flew down to take her food. The male would patiently sit on the eggs until his mate had leisurely taken her food, her bath, and an airing. When she was again ready for her maternal duties she relieved the male exactly as he relieved her. It was amusing to observe how the male crept into the nest and turned to the left, and the female evidently turned right about, for the tails of these little birds became quite twisted through sitting in the narrow nest, and the twist of each tail was the reverse way.

The successful amateur in Hamburg thought the eggs were hatched in eleven or twelve days. In my case I did not note exactly when the birds began to sit in earnest, nor when the young were hatched, as experience had taught me to be very careful not to look at nests unnecessarily. But when the birds had been sitting about three weeks, without the usual signs of broken egg-shells thrown out of the nest, I had given up the hope of a young brood. I therefore looked in, determined to destroy the nest, when I discovered that every egg had been hatched, and a remarkably strong lot of young birds were in the nest.

On the chance of such an event I had fed the birds, in addition to their usual allowance of dry seed, on millet and maw seed soaked over-night in warm water and then strained, also yolk of egg and sponge-cake mixed with dried ants' eggs soaked, and a few mealworms. The young brood prospered nicely for a week, when one day their voices became faint, and next day I found them all thrown out of the nest, and their dead bodies carried to the furthest part of the aviary. The parent birds wanted to build again. I removed the old nest, and they at once commenced a fresh one, and within a fortnight they had again five eggs, on which they are sitting while I write. It is therefore clear that when once this beautiful little bird has become fairly acclimatised there cannot be much difficulty in breeding, and a pair of cage-bred Crimson Finches being worth over £3, there is some inducement for other amateurs to try the experiment.

In the aviary the Crimson Finch is one of the most combative of small birds, especially at breeding-time. I had two pairs in a large room, and one male was nearly killed by the other, whilst one hen lost her tail in a dispute. A Crimson Finch I sent with five other Australian Finches in one travelling-cage to Berlin, has been accused of breaking a Zebra Finch's and a Diamond Sparrow's legs during the journey. No other Australian Finch is equally quarrelsome; it is therefore advisable to keep each pair of Crimson Finches in a separate cage, or at all events to watch over their behaviour towards other birds in the aviary.

BICHENO'S FINCH (*Estrelda Bichenovii*), Queensland.

(Illustration painted from live specimen kindly lent by Miss Dyson.)

Fringilla Bichenovii, Estrelda Bichenovii, Hictoptera Bichenovii. Dealers' name—Double-banded Finch. German—"Ringelastrild," or "Gitterflügel."

Compared with the brilliant hue of the Crimson Finch, the smaller Bicheno's or Double-banded Finch appears at first sight very modestly attired. A pure silvery-white is the ground colour. The feathers are delicately pencilled with fine black lines or bars, which, when seen at a distance, give the bird a light silver-grey appearance, but examined more closely, the plumage of this Finch, one of the smallest of the Australian Finches, is of great beauty and marvellous delicacy. The face, throat, breast, and the lower part of the body are white. A narrow black line, which crosses the throat, extends from ear to ear. A second black line across the lower breast runs parallel with the former, and gives the bird the name of Double-banded Finch. The wings are black, but the feathers have rows of white square spots, which on the dark ground appear something like a trellis. The Germans have named the little bird for this reason "lattice wing." The beak is of silvery-grey tint, and the tail is black. The female bird cannot be distinguished from the male; possibly the markings of the female may not be quite so sharply pencilled, but this may be due to age, just as well as to sex, and there is no certain distinguishing mark.

When these little birds arrive in this country, they are often very shy, and much care is advisable, to avoid accidents. They become, however, quite tame in a little while, and soon make themselves at home. By no means delicate, they require but little minute care. Canary and millet seed, with a little chickweed, will supply all their wants, and they will live for years in perfect health and happiness.

Although four specimens had been presented to the Zoological Gardens in 1861, Dr. Russ did not see the Double-banded Finches until the Paris Exhibition of 1867, and in London they were probably not offered for sale before 1872. In that year Dr. Russ and I acquired several Bicheno's Finches at about the same time, and since then they arrive every year, but not in very great numbers. They have been constant inmates of my aviary for years, and lived from April to the end of October in the open air. A temperature of 50° to 55° sufficed in winter. But it grieved me a long time that I could not induce these birds to build; they left every kind of nest-box and nesting material unnoticed. At last I obtained some very hard aloe fibre, and this seemed to please the Double-banded Finches, for they busied themselves at once with it, and soon built a large ball in the crest of an Arbor Vitæ. The ball was nearly as cleverly constructed as a Weaver-bird's nest, had a very small entrance at the side, and formed a capital nest, in which four or five pure white eggs were laid and hatched in the usual time of thirteen to fifteen days.

The young brood is not at all difficult to rear. Millet and maw seed soaked in hot water and strained, a little egg-food, some soaked ants' eggs, and a few mealworms are ample. The young birds resemble their parents in so far that the pencilling of the feathers is much more faint, the black tints are replaced by grey, and the white is lustreless, but at a very early period the young birds resemble the old ones so much that they cannot be distinguished. In Dr. Russ's aviary, some Double-banded Finches occupied the nest forsaken by Weaver-birds, but I am inclined to think this adoption of prepared nests due to abnormal stimulus. Healthy Double-banded Finches have evidently the desire and the instinct to build a nest of their own, similar to the Weaver-birds. Undoubtedly the Double-banded Finch is one of the prettiest, one of the most interesting, and one of the best-tempered inhabitants of the aviary.

Mr. Gould, in his celebrated work on the birds of Australia, mentions and illustrates *Estrelda Bichenovii*, and a very similar bird, *Estrelda annulosa*. Whether the latter be really a separate species seems, however, a little doubtful. I have carefully examined all the skins at the British Museum marked *Estrelda Bichenovii* and *Estrelda annulosa*, and I have also carefully examined hundreds of live birds, but have failed to observe any difference, except such as is easily accounted for by age and quite in accordance with the variations of plumage of those birds I bred myself.

AUSTRALIAN WAXBILL (*Estrelda temporalis*), AUSTRALIA.
(Illustration painted from live specimen kindly lent by T. C. Marsh, Esq.)
Fringilla temporalis, Fringilla quinticolor, Amadina temporalis, Ægintha temporalis. Dealers' name—Sydney Waxbill.
German—"Dorn Astrild."

This little bird is common enough in Australia, and yet not often met with as a cage-bird. Dealers do not like him much, as he does not fetch a high price, and is apt to die unexpectedly. With me the Australian Waxbill never attempted to build a nest, whilst Dr. Russ managed to see several broods hatched, but even he did not succeed in bringing them up.

The Sydney Waxbill is the most sober-coloured of the Australian Finches, the back being olive-green, and the throat, breast, &c., grey. The distinguishing mark of the bird is a broad scarlet line from the coral-red beak through the eye towards the region of the ear, and a few scarlet feathers at the root of the brownish-black tail. The bird is peaceable and amiable, but uninteresting in the aviary, and male and female are alike.

FIRE-TAILED FINCH (*Estrelda bella*), AUSTRALIA.
(Illustration painted from specimens in the Author's possession.)
Spermestes nitida (Russ), *Loxia bella et nitida, Loxia bella, Fringilla bella, Amadina nitida, Zonæginthus nitidus, Zonæginthus bellus.*
German—"Feuerschwanz Amandine."

The Fire-tailed Finch seems to have been a puzzle to everybody who had to do with him. Ornithologists call him *Estrelda, Loxia, Fringilla, Amadina*, and *Spermestes* in turns, and amateurs do not know what to feed the bird on. He is one of the most beautiful Australian Finches, and yet it is difficult to describe his beauty. The plumage is nearly uniform dark brownish-grey on the back, light underneath, but the whole plumage is marked by wave-like delicately-pencilled cross-lines of black. Just round the root of the beak is a little black, extending in a line towards and forming a ring round the eye. The eye again has a distinct bare bluish-white ring round it, forming a most peculiar contrast to the black feathers surrounding it. At the root of the dark brown tail is a patch of brilliant scarlet feathers.

A pair was exhibited in the Zoological Garden in 1870, and no earlier account exists of this Finch as a cage-bird. I have had many Fire-tailed Finches since then, but always found them die in the most unexpected and disappointing manner. One single bird out of many lived in my aviary for over a twelvemonth, but he was sent to a show on the Continent as a curiosity, and died there as unexpectedly as many newly-imported specimens had done.

Vincent Brooks Day & Son Li

1. CHESTNUT EARED FINCH OR AUSTRALIAN ZEBRA FINCH MALE. 3. AMADUVADE FINCH MALE.
1A Do Do Do Do FEMALE. 3A Do Do FEMALE
2. AFRICAN ZEBRA WAXBILL MALE. 4. THREE COLOURED FINCH OR NUN
2A Do Do Do FEMALE.

My own experience has been unfortunately shared by Dr. Russ, by Prinz Ferdinand, of Coburg Gotha, and all other amateurs. The bird seems to require some kind of seed or food which we have yet to discover, and without which he does not thrive in Europe as a cage-bird. I have heard that the Fire-tailed Finch is very shy when newly caught, and for this reason is often brought over in dark cages. If this be true it may well be that the birds which died so unaccountably may have perished through sheer fright in consequence of the admiration of their purchasers. One of the most intelligent London dealers, who frequently imported the Fire-tailed Finches, always placed them on the top shelves in his shop, out of reach of observation, and seemed to lose comparatively few. The first specimen Dr. Russ had in his aviary was so nervous that whenever he entered his bird-room the poor little bird flew on to his hand, and tried to hide in his coat sleeve, evidently seeking for a dark shelter. It is needless to say that the bird has never been bred in captivity.

Although it would be most tempting to continue the account of the Australian Finches, the list of the Zoological Society next names a very small and very well-known Indian bird.

THE AMADUVADE FINCH (*Estrelda amandava*), INDIA.

(Illustration painted from live specimens kindly lent by Mr. Charles Jamrach.)

Ægintha amandava (Russ), *Fringilla amandava, Amadina punctata, Amandava punctulata, Pytelia amandava, Sporæginthus amandava, Linaria amandava, Fringilla punicea, Estrelda punicea, Fringilla mystacea, Regulus Indicus, Bengalus punctulatus.* Dealers' name—Avadavat, or Averdavat. German—"Tigerfink," or "Getigerter Astrild."

Many people who never heard the name of any other foreign Finch have heard of the "Avadavat," and have possibly possessed a pair at some time, for this little bird appears to have been casually sent to Europe since long ago, and has arrived of late years in ever-increasing numbers. The Amaduvade Finch is one of the smallest foreign Finches, and is found in immense numbers in British India and Java, where he lives on seeds, building a nest in October in low bushes, or between the stems of high grasses. The nest is constructed of vegetable fibres, is completely covered over, and has an opening at the side. The eggs are white, like those of all the *Estreldæ*; their usual number seems to be four.

This dwarf Finch has been bred repeatedly by Dr. Russ and by many amateurs, but to succeed we must keep him in a high temperature. He will then propagate without loss of time if other circumstances are moderately favourable. Dr. Russ found the nests constructed by Avadavats in his aviary to differ considerably; sometimes a bundle of fibres, bits of paper and horsehair, and in another case a more elaborate structure, which, being near the food receptacles, the male bird constructed a clever sort of screen, to prevent observation of the sitting hen-bird whilst the food-vessels were replenished. In my aviary the Amaduvade Finch never attempted to build, as the low temperature—viz., 55° to 60° Fahr.—did not appear to be sufficient for the purpose. Is it worth while to breed this little Finch? He is imported in thousands, and can be bought sometimes for a couple of shillings per pair, or less than the food of a young brood would cost. The proper place of this bird in the estimation of an amateur seems to me to be that of a beautiful and amiable inmate of a little aviary-cage kept in the drawing-room or conservatory, where breeding is neither attempted nor desired, and where he will live for many years, on millet and canary seed.

The Avadavat is smaller than our smallest European Wren, of slender build, and vivacious and graceful in his movements. His plumage is dark brown, with a carmine-red tint, and covered all over with small pearl-white spots. When the breeding season arrives the red tints become more brilliant, and the little bird, with his coral-red beak and shining purple hue, is then a sight of rare beauty. The female is more sober in her appearance, the back being brown, and the chest, abdomen, &c., a brownish-yellow tint. The white spots are visible also, but less numerous. If kept for many months in the vitiated air of a wholesale dealer's over-crowded store-cages, the Avadavat will become almost black, and old birds sometimes have a few white feathers. I had one very old male with two white centre feathers in his dark brown tail. According to Dr. Russ, the Amaduvade Finches caught in large numbers in the neighbourhood of Bombay are of much brighter crimson colour than those coming from other parts of India, but do not readily breed in confinement. I found that the Avadavats, wherever they came from, did not breed in my aviary, and I could never discover a noteworthy difference. As the Austrian Lloyd mail-steamers run regularly between Bombay and Triest, it may be that Avadavats from Bombay find their way direct, *viâ* Triest, into Germany, and arrive with the bloom of newly-caught birds within three weeks of their capture; whilst the birds imported from Calcutta arrive *viâ* Marseilles or London, have a longer voyage, and remain longer in the wholesale dealers' over-crowded store-cages, thereby losing much of their colour.

Several pairs will live very peaceably together, and towards dusk they will all sit on the same perch, very close together, selecting generally the highest perch in the cage. At that time one and then another will suddenly raise itself and sing a little melodious stanza, settling down to sleep when it is done. The female will sing nearly as well as the male.

What has been stated above about the treatment, habits, and prospects of breeding the Amaduvade Finches applies to nearly all the smaller African Finches. They are most charming and amiable inmates of an aviary or aviary-cage, but their natural breeding season is our winter. Any one who sets his heart on breeding them can do so by keeping them in a summer-like temperature, providing them with the right sort of food and fair opportunities for nesting. But to improvise an approach to an African climate is not very easy, and the very low price at which most of these little birds can be bought makes the task of breeding them in the cage not only a thankless one, but the difficulty arises for the successful breeder what to do with the young birds, raised at infinite trouble and much expense.

They will live in perfect beauty of plumage and in happiness for many years in a very moderate temperature, and I would advise amateurs to content themselves with the charm of the every-day life of these little creatures. Where many birds are kept in one cage I would strongly advise the burning of a small lamp during the long winter nights, or for some hours during the evenings of midwinter, as named in the introduction in the chapter on food. In our northern climate the winter nights are too long for these little creatures to remain without food, and as they will not feed in the dark, we must shorten the long nights by artificial light, or risk that the birds are famished in the morning, and either lack strength to seek their food or are driven away from the breakfast dishes by the strongest among them.

COMMON WAXBILL (*Estrelda cinerea*), WEST AFRICA.

(Illustration painted from live specimens kindly lent by Mr. Edw. Hawkins.)

Ægintha cinerea (Russ), *Fringilla cinerea*, *Fringilla troglodytes*, *Estrelda cinerea et rubriventris*, *Estrelda melanopygia*, *Habropyga cinerea*, *Habropyga nigricanda*. Dealers' names—African Waxbill, Senegal Waxbill, Common Waxbill. German—"Graue Astrild," "Graues Fasänchen." French—"Astrild Ordinaire," "Bec de Corail Ordinaire."

This little bird is best described by referring to the excellent drawing. We have here one of the smallest, one of the most nimble, and one of the most easily obtainable foreign Finches. A cage, the wires of which are only a trifle more than half an inch apart, will rarely contain the

Common Waxbill long, and any opening for food or water glasses should be most carefully closed whenever the birds are fed. Should they once escape, it will be found most difficult to catch them in a room, and quite hopeless to recover them if they have found their way through a window.

The life of this little bird in the wild state has scarcely been observed, but of his habits in captivity we have very full informaton. The Common Waxbill has been imported into Europe since the last century, and ancient writers have mostly thought him the same bird as the larger St. Helena Waxbill. Both have a greyish-brown plumage, marked with extremely faint wave-like dark lines athwart the body. The abdomen has a very bright roseate hue, which is brightest in the centre and fainter towards the sides and chest. The beak is a bright coral-red, and a broad red line passes from the root of the beak through the eyes. The tail is dark brown, rather long, the central feathers being longest and wedge-shaped; and Dr. Russ very truly says that the tail of this and other *Estreldæ* seems to be, like the dog's tail, the organ by which they outwardly express their feelings. When the tail is at rest the bird is listless; when excited or singing the tail is spread fan-like; when in search of food, or curious, the tail moves incessantly sideways. Male and female are alike in plumage, except in autumn, when the rosy tint of the male becomes much brighter.

In captivity this bird lives very well, is always cheerful and happy, and rarely loses his feathers, even if kept at a low temperature, in which the Amaduvade Finch would become bald. His food in the cage consists of spray millet, French millet, and canary-seed.

To breed the Common Waxbill is a different matter. Dr. Russ has led the way, and a number of amateurs have succeeded after him, but it has been ascertained that the bird can scarcely be bred in a cage, although he will breed freely in a large aviary. In my experience this species never made an attempt to build a nest, because my aviary, during the breeding season of African Waxbills—viz., September to March—was kept at a temperature of 55° to 60° Fahr., which was not sufficient. Dr. Russ had several pairs breeding peaceably at the same time in one room, and found the nests constructed in all manner of ways, sometimes in shrubs, and again in nest-boxes, and even on the ground; in some cases very artistically constructed, and in others an immense accumulation of fibres. Very often they fail to bring up their young, but they have been bred often with success for all that, and have in those cases fed the young brood on dried and soaked ants' eggs and egg.

RED-BELLIED WAXBILL (*Estrelda rubriventris*), West Africa.

(Illustration painted from life.)

Loxia astrild, Fringilla astrild et rubriventris, Fringilla astrild, Estrelda astrild, Habropyga astrild, Estrelda occidentalis, Estrelda cærulescens, Estrelda or Fringilla cærulescens, Estrelda undulata, Linaria cineria orientalis, Senegalis striatus, Fringilla undulata. Dealers' name—St. Helena Waxbill. French—"Astrild de St. Hélène," "Astrild Ondulé." German—"Der Gewellte Astrild," "Fasänchen," "Wellen-Astrild," "Rothbäuchiger Astrild."

The Red-bellied or St. Helena Waxbill is annually imported in very large numbers, and is one of the most common birds on the island of St. Helena. In appearance the bird is very similar to the Common Waxbill. We find the same coral-red beak, the same red line through the eye region, the same soft brown body-colour and roseate tint on the lower body. But the wave-like cross-lines, which are mostly very faint on the plumage of the Common Waxbill, are very distinctly marked on the St. Helena Waxbill. This bird is somewhat larger than his miniature cousin, less agile, more stately in his movements, and an ever-welcome inhabitant of any aviary. His manners are peculiarly gentle, his movements very graceful, and his appearance is decidedly handsome. Neither shy nor bold, the St. Helena Waxbill quietly observes his owner, and will readily become quite confiding if properly treated and cared for. His plumage is always in perfect order. Millet and canary seed, with an occasioual mealworm in winter, and chickweed or flowering grass in summer, will satisfy all his wants. He will live many years in a cage, but to breed him requires much care, much patience, and a somewhat high temperature. The nest will be a great mass of fibres of all sorts, piled up rather loosely, and from three to five eggs will be hatched in eleven or twelve days. The young birds are fed on ants' eggs, mealworms, hard-boiled egg, and scalded seeds, but are rather difficult to rear, as the parent birds are somewhat inclined to throw them out of the nest if the food provided is not quite suitable. The beak of the young is black, and gradually changes to red four to six weeks after the birds are hatched. Male and female are alike, except that the roseate tint of the male is brighter.

The St. Helena Waxbill has no song, but a rather loud, by no means unpleasant call. When not breeding, the bird is perfectly peaceful and gentle, and even at breeding-time the male birds may quarrel about a good nesting-place, and disturb the incubating hen-birds, but never engage in mortal combat. Under ordinary conditions the St. Helena Waxbill will rarely attempt to breed, and will live in perfect peace with any number of his own species or other small Finches, delighting his owner with his sprightliness, beauty, and graceful movements.

ORANGE-CHEEKED WAXBILL (*Estrelda melpoda*), WEST AFRICA.

(Illustration painted from life specimens kindly lent by Mr. E. Hawkins.)

Ægintha melpoda (Russ), *Fringilla melpoda*, *Fringilla lippa*, *Habropyga melpoda*, *Melpoda lippa*. Dealers' name—Orange-cheek. French—"Joue Orange." German—"Orangebäckchen," "Gelbwangiger Astrild."

A pair of these very small Waxbills is frequently obtainable in London for a few shillings, and will prove a very good addition to an ornamental aviary in any conservatory. The tints of the bird are mainly light greyish-brown, whilst bright orange patches on the cheeks, extending to the root of the beak and round the eyes, are unmistakable distinguishing marks. The lower part of the body is greyish and brownish-white. On the abdomen there is a diffused patch of orange, gradually shaded towards the chest and sides. The tail is dark brown, with a reddish patch at the root; the beak coral-red. Male and female are much alike, but the orange is much more pale in the plumage of the female.

The Orange-checked Waxbills are fully as amiable inhabitants of an aviary as any of the other African Astrilds. They are very pretty, very active, and very intelligent. In fact, it has been observed that the Orange-cheeked Waxbill will constitute himself the guardian of the inhabitants of an aviary, and be the first to discover a supposed impending danger. His ever-watchful eye will at once discern the approach of a stranger or anything unusual, and should the birds just then be busy feeding on the floor of the aviary, the Orange-cheeked Waxbill will be the first to seek safety in flight, uttering a note of warning, which induces all the other little birds to follow his example.

The bird has been bred in Germany more than once or twice, but as many thousands of Orange-cheeked Waxbills are annually imported, it is really not worth the trouble to breed a little bird which can be bought at less than the cost of feeding a nest of young birds. Success in breeding the Orange-cheeked Waxbill is by no means easy, for he requires the high temperature of the other African Waxbills, and his lively and watchful disposition makes him leave the nest very easily. Intending breeders are therefore more often disappointed than rewarded by success. In the aviary the bird will endure as an ornamental inmate for many years, and retain his plumage if kept in an ordinary temperatnre. Food, &c., the same as the preceding African Waxbills.

Vincent Brooks Day & Son L

1. ORANGE-CHEEKED WAXBILL.
2. CRIMSON EARED WAXBILL, OR CORDON BLEU. A. MALE. B. FEMALE IN RUSH NEST.
3. CINEREOUS WAXBILL
4. YOUNG SAFFRONFINCH 4 MONTHS OLD.
5. COMMON AFRICAN WAXBILL.
6. AFRICAN. FIRE FINCH. A. MALE B. FEMALE.

CRIMSON-EARED WAXBILL (*Estrelda phœnicotis*), West Africa.

(Illustration painted from live specimens kindly lent by Mr. E. Hawkins.)

Fringilla Angolensis et Bengalensis, Fringilla Bengalus, Fringilla Bengalensis, Fringilla Mariposa, Estrelda Bengalus et Mariposæ, Estrelda Benghala, Estrelda Angolensis, Uræginthus phœnicotis, Mariposa phœnicotis, Pytelia phœnicotis. Dealers' name—Cordon Bleu, Blue-bellied Finch. French—"Cordon Bleu." German—"Blaue Astrild," "Schmetterlingsfink."

The Crimson-eared Waxbill, or Cordon Bleu, is annually imported in very large numbers, and hundreds of pairs may sometimes be seen at a large dealer's, where they will sit closely packed on the perches, and the drooping feathers of many will already prognosticate their early death. Although this bird is found in the greater part of Africa, and has been met with on mountains of considerable altitude, he is, when imported into Europe, one of the most delicate of all the foreign Finches. A sceptic might say he is brought over but to die, for the mortality is fearful.

According to my experience, the usual temperature of a sitting-room in England is not sufficient to keep the Cordon Bleu in health. Sometimes one bird out of many will survive and thrive for a time, but in the end, either moulting-time or an accidental change of temperature will affect the Cordon Bleu beyond recovery, and he will gradually droop and die. In Germany, where the summer sun is much more hot, and where in winter the dwelling-houses are habitually kept considerably warmer than in England, the Cordon Bleu has been bred often, and without very great difficulty. My experience may be summed up shortly as follows:—The Crimson-cared Waxbill is very beautiful, but if the reader wishes to keep him he should make up his mind to provide a temperature between 60° and 70° Fahr. in winter. If that be impracticable, the Cordon Bleu will not thrive, but vex his owner by ailing and an early death.

The bird is very prettily coloured, being pale brownish-grey on the back; the face, throat, chest, and tail being pale sky-blue; the cheeks of the male are ornamented with a patch of crimson; the beak is very dark red. The female is similar, but the sky-blue tint is much less brilliant, and the red patches on the cheeks are absent. According to Dr. Russ, the red cheeks of the young males begin to show when the birds are five to eight weeks old. I have, however, bought Crimson-cared Waxbills in London without the red patches on the cheeks, believing them to be females, which after the next moult displayed the distinguishing marks of male birds—viz., the crimson cheeks—for the first time. These were evidently very young birds at the time of shipment, and the change of climate and food had delayed the first moult of this delicate little bird for a whole year, whilst two months would have sufficed for the full development of the bird under favourable circumstances.

The Cordon Bleu has been imported into Europe since the last century, and should be fed and treated like the other Waxbills. He will rarely build his nest in a box or other contrivance, but prefers a construction of his own in a bush or among branches fixed to the wall of the aviary, selecting generally the highest suitable spot within the bird-room. The young require the same animal food as other Waxbill nestlings, but the parent birds are, perhaps, more difficult to please as regards the proper food for their progeny. Fresh ants' eggs are always the best food where obtainable, but a breeder will do well to accustom his birds to egg-food mixed with dried and soaked ants' eggs, because fresh ants' eggs may prove some day, or at some time of the year, beyond reach when wanted.

The German name signifies "Butterfly Finch," and is owing to the bird hovering often near his nesting-place, as a butterfly does near a flower. The Crimson-eared Waxbill is very well-mannered in the society of other small birds, and exceedingly loving towards his mate. Male and female will perch as near each other as possible, and frequently improve and preen each other's plumage.

AFRICAN FIRE FINCH (*Estrelda minima*), AFRICA.

(Illustration painted from live specimens kindly lent by Mr. E. Hawkins.)

Ægintha minima (Russ), *Fringilla minima, Estrelda Senegala, Lagonostica minima, L. Senegala, L. ignata, Senegalus ruber.* Dealers' name—Fire Finch. French—"Amaranthe." German—"Kleiner rother Amaranth," or "Karminfink."

What has been stated above about the delicacy of the Crimson-cared Waxbill applies as much, and perhaps even more, to the African Fire Finch. I should say that of all those Fire Finches which remain in England, not one in a thousand survives the first winter after their importation. The Zoological Society of London has never placed the bird in the collection at the Gardens, and very wisely, for he should be kept in a semi-tropical atmosphere, very uncomfortable to visitors. Being one of the very smallest of the African Finches, it may well be that his very small body cannot contain sufficient vital energy to bear much hardship or loss of heat. And yet, if the bird has once recovered from the fatigue and vicissitudes of the voyage, and has been fairly acclimatised, he will endure cage-life for years under favourable conditions.

His native country is Central Africa, and there he is as much the friend and companion of mankind as our Sparrow is in England. His nest is found in the thatch of roofs, in all sorts of holes, and sometimes in trees and bushes. In captivity he soon makes himself at home, and becomes quite fearless.

The male Fire Finch is of dark red plumage, except the back and tail, which are dark greenish-brown. On the sides there are a few minute white spots, which, however, are frequently absent in young birds. The beak is coral-red, and around the eye is a narrow straw-coloured ring. The female is dark brown, with a little red at the root of the tail, and the same minute white spot at the sides.

This bird has been bred times innumerable, and will readily build a nest, either in a nest-box, a bush, or any other suitable place, provided he feels at home and the climate of his abode reminds him of Central Africa. In a cage with other small birds, the Fire Finch is very peaceable, and probably the most confiding and most self-relying of all its inhabitants. He will find his way through the open door of a bird-room before any other bird, and find his way back again, which few other birds do. Food like that of all the other Dwarf Finches.

VIOLET-EARED FINCH (*Estrelda granatina*), AFRICA.

Fringilla granatina, Uræginthus granatinus, Mariposa granatina. Dealers' names—Grenate Finch, Brazilian Finch, and Three-coloured Mannikin. German—"Granatrother Astrild," "Granatfink."

Why this most beautiful of all the African *Estreldæ* is not in the collection of the Zoological Society is difficult to explain. And perhaps more inexplicable is the rarity of this bird in the market, considering that he has been kept alive in Paris more than a hundred years ago, has been described by most authors of works on the birds of Africa, and can be bought sometimes, though rarely. In old handbooks on cage-birds this native of Africa is called Brazilian Finch.

Dr. Russ had several live specimens; and I once purchased three heads, under the curious name of Three-coloured Mannikin, at a bird-dealer's in Liverpool. These were, unfortunately, sickly, like so many African dwarf Finches, and soon died. Subsequently I had one male, which I received in fine condition and perfect health. This bird lived in my aviary for nearly two years in a very moderate temperature, and sang merrily and sweetly last winter, with the thermometer at 50° to 55° Fahr. I parted with him to enable a friend and very successful breeder at Baden-Baden, who owned a hen-bird, to make the experiment of breeding. This bird was sent from London to Germany in February, and endured the journey without the least ill-effects, which certainly speaks well for the stamina of this Finch when once acclimatised and in perfectly healthy condition.

The Grenate Finch is of soft rich brown colour, a narrow rim round the beak and the root of the tail is bright blue of peculiar richness, a large patch on the cheeks is violet colour, and the beak is coral-red. The female is reddish-brown, somewhat lighter on the lower part of the body, and the violet on the cheeks is less brilliant. A peculiarly sweet song distinguishes this remarkably beautiful little bird, and I am informed that the female in my friend's possession sings nearly as well as the male.

The food I gave consisted of canary-seed, French millet and millet in the ear, flowering grass, and two or three mealworms per day. The movements and manners of the Violet-eared Finch are very similar to those of the Red-eared Finch.

CINEREOUS WAXBILL (*Estrelda cærulescens*), West Africa.

(Illustration painted from live specimen kindly lent by Mr. E. Hawkins.)

Ægintha cærulescens (Russ), *Fringilla cærulescens*, *Lagonostica cærulescens*, *Habropyga cærulescens et fimbricata*, *Pytelia cærulescens*, *Estrelda incana*, *Habropyga Natalensis*, *Pytelia incana*, *Fringilla Perreini*, *Estrelda melanogastra*, *Habropyga Perreini*, *Estrelda Perreini*, *Pytelia Perreini*. Dealers' name—Lavender Finch. French—"Gris Bleu." German—"Rothsihwäuziger Astrild," "Blaugranes Rothsihwäuzchen."

A beautiful small Finch is the Cinereous Waxbill, of a delicate soft lavender or pale slate-colour all over the body. The lower part of the back and the tail are purple, and the beak is crimson. A line of black runs from the beak beyond the eye. When in perfect health there is a bloom on this bird's plumage which reminds us of the delicate bloom on very ripe fruit. Male and female are alike.

The first Cinereous Waxbills reached the Zoological Gardens in 1868, and the birds are latterly often obtainable from dealers, but not nearly so often or in such numbers as many other African Waxbills. They mostly arrive with their feathers in sad disorder, and are then exceedingly delicate. But with great care they recover, and then endure for years, though many die soon after their arrival. They require the same treatment as the Amaduvade Finch, and are neither more nor less delicate than that bird.

Dr. Russ and several amateurs in Germany have succeeded in breeding the Cinereous Waxbill, but, all in all, the failures were numerous and the successes extremely rare. This Waxbill is perfectly peaceful in the aviary, and Dr. Russ found that even at breeding-time he did not quarrel with other birds, though two males would then fight gallantly.

ZEBRA WAXBILL (*Estrelda subflava*), Africa.

(Illustration painted from live specimens kindly lent by Mr. E. Hawkins.)

Ægintha sanguinolenta (Russ), *Fringilla sanguinolenta*, *Estrelda sanguinolenta*, *Fringilla subflava*, *Amadina sanguinolenta*, *Sporæginthus subflavus*, *Sporæginthus miniatus*, *Habropyga subflava*, *Pytelia subflava*. Dealers' name—African Zebra Waxbill. French—"Sénégali à ventre Orange." German—"Goldbrüstiger Astrild," "Goldbrüstchen."

The Zebra Waxbill is one of the smallest of the African Finches, and frequently found at dealers', or in ornamental aviaries. His plumage is dark greenish-brown on the back; the throat, chest, and lower body are pale yellow, with a diffused patch of bright orange about the middle of the lower body, shaded towards the sides and throat. The beak is coral-red, and a red line extends from the beak through the eye towards the ear. The female is without the orange on the lower body.

I have kept this bird many years, and yet can say very little about him. He is very pretty and very peaceful, active and intelligent; male and female are very affectionate towards each other, and with proper care the Zebra Waxbill will live and display the beauty of his plumage to perfection. But his little song is only heard at breeding-time, and to breed him successfully requires two things—high temperature and fresh ants' eggs. Dr. Russ mentions an instance of one pair of Zebra Waxbills having brought up fifty-four young in one year, sixty-seven eggs having been removed from the nests of the same pair, giving a total of one hundred and twenty-one eggs laid by one hen-bird in a twelvemonth. This shows to what degree of unnatural productiveness these little birds may be stimulated. On the other hand, most beginners in bird-keeping complain that these, like the other African dwarf Finches, die without apparent cause. I would advise these disappointed amateurs just to pluck the feathers off a dead African Waxbill, note the small size of the body of the bird, and then think of the hardships which the diminutive mechanism in this body had endured while alive, during the voyage from Africa, in the hands of wholesale and retail dealers, and in transit to his final owner. Then the bird has possibly been expected to live in a draughty corner of a room or near the ceiling, in an atmosphere heated and vitiated beyond endurance by gas during the evening, chilly at night, and with the probability of a servant opening door and windows to the raw and foggy morning air before lighting the fire. Some amateurs wonder why a poor bird dies, but if we think a little we must wonder that they endure as they do.

Food and general treatment should be like that of other African Waxbills.

With the Zebra Waxbill we should, in following the order of the list of the Zoological Society, take leave of the Astrilds, *Æginthæ*, or Waxbills, by whichever name we may please to designate the slender-billed Dwarf Finches, for next come the stronger-billed *Spermestinæ* and *Amandinæ*. But between these two families we find a few names of birds which really either belong to the Waxbill tribe, or at all events should be placed midway between the Waxbills and the stronger-billed Finches. These few birds happen to be of extraordinary beauty, but unfortunately very rare until now.

PYTELIA WIENERI, Africa.

Ægintha Wieneri (Russ). German—"Wiener's Astrild."

As an instance of the incomplete state of our knowledge of African and other foreign birds, *Pytelia Wieneri* deserves a passing notice. In the year 1877 I purchased four little birds from a dealer in London, the like of which I had never seen before, and though they reminded me of *Pytelia melba*, yet they were evidently not the same, for the wings and most of the other parts of the plumage were deep orange, shaded with olive-green, and the lower part appeared a very pale mixture of olive-green and grey with yellowish bars. The crimson face, the figure of the bird, and other details left very little doubt that the bird belonged to the class of *Pytelia*, but the British Museum contained not a skin of a bird agreeing with my four live Finches, and the British Museum Library contained not a work in which this bird was found described. In the course of time two of these birds died, and one skin is now in the British Museum, the other was sent over to Berlin. The greatest living authorities are agreed that this bird had either been overlooked altogether, or mis-described beyond recognition. Dr. Russ and Dr. Otto Finsch have been good enough to name the bird after me, because accident put me in possession of the few live specimens which may or may not be the only ones ever brought alive to Europe.

Unfortunately I could not induce the birds to breed, although they made themselves at home in a nest-box and constructed a slovenly kind of nest, in which they liked to sit for hours during the day-time. The last surviving specimen was presented to the Zoological Gardens, in order to be more accessible to scientific ornithologists and to others who take an interest in rare foreign Finches.

The food I gave was millet and canary seed and millet in the ear, and the birds lived for years very quietly with Double-banded Finches.

THE CRIMSON-WINGED WAXBILL (*Pytelia phœnicoptera*), West Africa.

Ægintha phœnicoptera (Russ), *Estrelda erythroptera*, *Zonogastris phœnicoptera*. Dealers' name—Aurora Finch. German—"Aurora fink."

The Crimson-winged Waxbill is nearly but not quite as large as a Goldfinch. Whenever obtainable, he is one of the greatest ornaments of an aviary tenanted by foreign birds. The head and back are a soft grey tint, the lower part a shade darker and prettily marked by white wave-like bars. The wings and tail are brilliant red, the beak is black. These red wings give the bird a most striking appearance, especially when basking in the hot summer sun, which he loves to do. The female is similar, but easily distinguished by the wings being much less bright.

In the London Zoological Gardens the first Crimson-winged Waxbills were received in 1874. I have had them before that date more than once, and Dr. Russ had one bird of this species in 1870. Dr. Russ succeeded in breeding the Crimson-winged Waxbill, and in my aviary one pair built a nest and laid four eggs late in autumn, which nest I had unfortunately to destroy. Whilst Dr. Russ found his *Pytelia phœnicoptera* building their nest in a nest-box, mine built theirs in a rather artistic manner in the sunniest part of their summer aviary in a bush. Cold weather coming on, I was obliged to shut the birds into their winter quarters and to separate them from their pretty little nest and four pure white eggs.

The food is the same as that of other Waxbills, but a little more additional animal food is required, and it would not be safe to keep this beautiful Finch at a less temperature than 60° Fahr. I found him by no means delicate, and it is much to be regretted that there should be but little probability of the bird ever being imported in sufficient numbers to be readily obtainable. He is found in only a small part of Africa, and his habits not being gregarious, bird-catchers will never be able to secure many at a time.

THE PAINTED FINCH (*Emblema picta*), North-western Australia.

Ægintha picta (Russ). German—"Gemalter Astrild."

The Painted Finch was considered by Mr. Gould to be the most beautiful of all the Australian Finches, but amateurs seem destined to have to wait long until this magnificent bird shall become known. The skin of the first specimen discovered was lost, and for many years the only proof of the existence of the bird was a drawing. At the present moment there is probably no zoological garden in Europe in possession of a live specimen, and very few museums have even a skin.

It will show how an amateur can render services to science by simply keeping his eyes open, if I relate how I came to be possessed of this almost mythical bird more than once. In the year 1869 I had occasion to employ a journeyman wireworker, who, seeing my interest in foreign birds, used to report to me whatever new birds he saw at bird-dealers' for whom he worked. One day he told me of "Julian Finches," and as I had never heard of such, he brought me the birds for inspection. They proved to be a pair of Painted Finches, and were probably the first ever brought alive to Europe. I purchased them as a matter of course, and kept them for a little while. Again, in 1873, I heard when in Liverpool that a hairdresser in one of the most elegant streets of the town had a number of foreign birds. This intelligence caused me to require hair-cutting at once. In the hairdresser's stock of birds I saw, to my astonishment, a pair of *Emblema picta*, which their owner was pleased to call "Australian Mountain Diamond Sparrows." I left Liverpool with the prize in my possession, and have wished ever since I had known then what I know now, about the best and safest treatment of rare Australian Finches. The Museum at Berlin was very glad to receive the skin of one of these Painted Finches.

A few years later, in 1877, I paid one of my periodical visits to Mr. Hawkins' shop in Bear Street, Leicester Square, who showed me the bodies of some birds which had died soon after their arrival from Antwerp. Among these was the body of a young male Painted Finch. Dr. Russ received one live specimen from Hamburg within the last two years, and heard of another which arrived at Trieste. It is thus abundantly clear that the Painted Finch does arrive sometimes, and in five or ten years' time he may be as easily obtainable as other Australian Finches which were almost unknown to amateurs a few years ago.

The upper part of the Painted Finch and the tail are brown; the face, the throat, and the root of the tail are scarlet; the chest and abdomen being jet-black, with white spots on the sides. On the middle of the abdomen is a crimson patch, shaded towards the chest and sides. The upper mandible of the beak is black, the lower one red. Females (and young males ?) have more of an olive-greenish tinge on the back; the scarlet of the face does not extend over the throat and chest, which are rather greyish-green, and the diffused patch of red on the abdomen is absent. Should this magnificent bird ever come into the hands of an amateur, let him give millet in the ear, flowering grass, and a few mealworms.

CHAPTER XLVI.

THICK-BILLED FINCHES.

THE stronger-billed foreign Finches, viz., the *Amadinæ, Spermestinæ*, &c., vary in size from that of our Chaffinch down to the medium-sized Waxbill, are not so slender of body as the Astrilds, and do not build such artistic nests. As regards song they have not even the small pretentions of the Waxbills. On the other hand they are more robust, and most of them endure better in our English climate, thriving very well on a diet of canary and millet seed.

According to the list of the Zoological Society, the Hooded Finch (*Spermestes cucullata*), familiarly known as the Bronze Mannikin, would come next; then the larger Mannikin, or Pied Grass Finch; and a few pages further on the Black or Two-coloured Mannikin, or Cape Palmas Finch; and again later on, with several birds intervening, the Striated Finch, and the Sharp-tailed Finch, all birds known to amateurs as Mannikins, or Manakens, and all nearly related to each other. For the purpose of this book it will be most convenient to class all those birds which are popularly known as Mannikins together. They are stout little birds, either black and white, or dark brown and white, prettily marked, and easily kept. From one of this family of birds, viz., from the Sharp-tailed Finch, the well-known White Japanese Mannikins are the descendants. But we will begin with the largest species of the group.

PIED GRASS FINCH (*Spermestes fringilloides*), WEST AFRICA. (Illustrated.)

Spermestes fringillina (Russ), *Ploceus fringilloides*, *Amadina fringilloides*, *Munia fringilloides*, *Amauresthes fringilloides*.

English dealers' name—Magpie Mannikin. German—"Grösste Elster Amandine."

On reference to the drawing of this bird* the reader will see at a glance that it is about equal in size to our European Goldfinch. The head and shoulders are black, with a greenish metallic lustre. The wings are dull black, and the back is brownish-black, while the chest and lower body is white, with a tinge of yellow towards the abdomen, and a light brown patch on the side. Male and female are alike.

Whilst the first Pied Grass Finches reached the Zoological Gardens as late as 1871, Dr. Russ obtained one specimen from a German bird-dealer in 1868, and since then they are not always—but sufficiently often—obtainable to place them within reach of every collector or amateur. In an aviary-cage, in company with the very smallest and most delicate Astrilds, the Pied Grass Finch may be a little rough, but he will live and thrive in a very moderate temperature, and be merry in winter whilst living on canary and millet seed in a temperature which would be destructive to African Astrilds. The bird is very easily bred when once an actual pair has been obtained, and after these have been induced fairly to begin to nest. The nest is built either in a box or in a bush, as may be most to the individual taste of the old birds, and the young are readily brought up on egg-food and scalded seeds. In

* "Red Grass Finch" on Plate should read "Pied Grass Finch."

my aviary the Pied Mannikins brought up a brood of young without my knowing it or seriously intending to breed this bird. Dr. Russ and many amateurs in Germany have also bred the species.

HOODED FINCH (*Spermestes cucullata*), WEST AFRICA. (Illustrated.)
Spermestes cucullata (Russ), *Amadina cucullata*, *Loxia prasipteron*, *Coccothraustes scutatus*, *Spermestes scutatus.*
English dealers' name—Bronze Mannikin. German—"Kleine Elster Amandine."

The Hooded Finch is very much smaller than his near relation, the Pied Grass Finch, and is one of the smallest of the Thick-billed Dwarf Finches. His body is short and stout, but scarcely so large as that of the St. Helena Waxbills. When imported in large numbers and first seen at a wholesale dealer's, this little Finch looks unpretending and of sombre plumage, but on closer acquaintance, and when his feathers have been re-arranged after transfer to the aviary, the Hooded Finch displays a beauty all his own. What appeared at first sight a dull black tint of head, throat, wings, and back, assumes various shades of metallic sheen. On the shoulders a few small feathers will become dark green, and on the sides under the wings a similar lustrous tint will appear. The chest is pure white. Male and female are alike.

I do not remember ever having seen this little bird with his plumage greatly disordered, and, as a rule, they arrive fairly hardy, and endure in a cage or aviary on simple canary and millet seed diet. They will become perfectly tame, and make themselves as readily at home in the smallest cage as in the largest aviary, building a nest wherever they think an opportunity favourable for this enterprise, and taking whatever materials come to hand. But they will fight courageously for the best place near the food, and in defence of their nest or favourite perch; and though one Hooded Finch in a cage containing a number of Waxbills may be harmless, the introduction of a pair might end in mischief.

Although much smaller than the Pied Grass Finch, yet the Hooded Grass Finch has been crossed with the former, also with the Cape Palmas Finch, and with the White Japanese Mannikin. One male and two female Hooded Finches bred successfully, and, in short, the little bird will bring up a number of broods in almost any favourable condition, but he is not quite so hardy in cold weather as the larger Pied Grass Finch.

CAPE PALMAS FINCH (*Amadina bicolor*), WEST AFRICA.
Spermestes bicolor (Russ). English dealers' name—Two-coloured Mannikin.
German—"Zweifarbige Elster Amandine," "Glanzelsterchen."

Very similar in size and markings of plumage to the previously-described Hooded Finch, I consider the Cape Palmas Finch far prettier. The entire upper part of the body and the head, throat, and wings are jet-black, the lower body pure white. Male and female are alike. In the Zoological Gardens only since 1872—but these last few years by no means rarely seen in bird-dealers' shops—the bird has, until now, been far more frequently bred in captivity than observed in his native country, the Gold Coast.

The Cape Palmas Finch does not breed so early nor so frequently as the Hooded Finch. His manners and his treatment should be the same, but the Cape Palmas Finch is suspected of being often individually quarrelsome, notwithstanding his diminutive size.

STRIATED FINCH (*Munia striata*), INDIA.
Spermestes striata (Russ), *Loxia striata*, *Amadina striata*, *Fringilla leuconota*, *Lonchura leuconota*, *Spermestes leuconota*, *Uroloncha striata*, *Trichogrammoptila striata*. English dealers' name—doubtful. German name—"Gestreifte Bronze Amandine." French name—"Grosbec de l'isle de Bourbon."

Vincent Brooks, Day & Son Lith

COMBASSOU OR STEEL FINCH. RED GRASS FINCH. BRONZE MANNIKIN.

SILVER-BILL. ST HELENA WAXBILL. CUT-THROAT.

SHARP-TAILED FINCH (*Munia acuticauda*), INDIA.

Spermestes acuticauda (Russ), *Munia leuconota*, *Amadina acuticauda*, *Amadina molucca*. No English dealers' name. German name—"Spitzschwänzige Bronze Amandine."

The Striated and the Sharp-tailed Finch are both natives of India, Southern China, and Japan. Both birds are so very similar that amateurs can fairly consider them as one species, the more so as our interest in this Finch is chiefly concerned with his progeny, bred in captivity by the Japanese. These little birds are a trifle larger than a Bronze Manakin, but brown on the back. The head is nearly black, the lower body dull white. The shaft of each brown feather being white, the plumage appears striated—hence the name. The beak is bluish-black. The feet are dark grey. Male and female are alike. An unpretending, amiable little bird in the aviary, sometimes—but not often—obtainable, and easily kept if fed like the Waxbills.

Keeping and breeding cage-birds as a pastime or for sale has been practised longer in Japan than in any other part of the world. Whilst our forefathers in Europe began to breed cage-birds only three hundred years ago, the Japanese living three thousand years ago knew quite as well how to breed birds in cages as we do now. Whether it was originally the Striated or the Sharp-tailed Finch from which the Japanese bred the White Bengalese has not been ascertained, and perhaps never will be determined. That it was one of the two is certain. We see the singular result of a breed of perfectly white or mottled little birds being regularly produced, descended from Brown Striated or Sharp-tailed ancestors—another example how birds through cage-breeding may change their colours in the same way as our old friend the Canary has done. Breeding these little white Finches has certainly been practised for centuries in Japan. When and how the change of colour was brought about is not known, but the birds produced may and should be considered as a distinct variety, for they are as different from their ancestors as the Norwich Canary is from his forefather of the Canary Islands. The new species, or white variety of the Striated Finch, is called

THE WHITE AND VARIEGATED BENGALESE (*Munia acuticauda* [?], *Munia striata* [?]), JAPAN. (Illustrated.)

Spermestes acuticauda (Russ). English dealers' name—White Bengalese. German name—"Japanesische Mövchen." French name—"Muscades Blanches," "Bengalis Blancs."

The Zoological Society appear to have purchased two specimens of the White Japanese variety of *Munia striata* in October, 1860. I do not remember to have met with any White Bengalese before 1869 or 1870, when I purchased, from a London dealer, the first bird of the kind I had seen. In 1871 a number of White and Variegated Bengalese were offered to amateurs by the Zoological Gardens in Antwerp, and since that time these birds have been offered for sale in increasing numbers, so that latterly they are rarely absent from a well-stocked retail bird-dealer's shop.

The white variety of Japanese Manakin must not be considered as an albino or *lusus naturæ*, like the White Blackbird, for the bird has no red eyes, and his progeny is about as certain to be white as the yellow Canary's offspring is certain to be yellow. By continuous cage-breeding, carried on by the Japanese through many generations, and during centuries, a naturally brown-black bird has become pure white, or brown-and-white piebald, or black-and-white piebald. The bill and feet of the Bengalese are pale pink, and this colour indicates, as much as the plumage, the cage-bred origin of the species, for the Striated Finch in his natural state has a bluish-black bill and dark grey feet.

When these little birds first appeared in the market they created quite a sensation, which, however, soon wore out. The White or Piebald Manakin has been bred in small cages through so many generations that very few of the original habits and manners of their ancestors remain. The first specimen I saw and possessed was believed by me to be partially blind, for the bird would allow me to handle him without stirring from his perch, and was peculiarly indifferent to the doings of the other small Finches which inhabited the same cage. He would allow any one of them to drive him from his chosen perch or from the food-dishes, and did not live long. Since then I discovered that what seemed partial blindness was only helplessness. Subsequently acquired Piebald Manakins I allowed to fly in a large aviary, but there they were completely bewildered. Through being bred by the Japanese in miniature cages, the imported White and Piebald Manakins seem to be almost unable to fly, and consequently they are nearly as helpless in a large aviary as a young bird just leaving the nest. They tumble into the water, or hide in corners, or get into all sorts of scrapes. It is therefore advisable to keep these birds, if not always, certainly for some time, in a roomy cage by themselves, and then they may please their owner by their docility and tameness.

They will readily build a sort of nest out of any suitable material in any nest-box or other receptacle, and they will, under favourable circumstances, prove wonderfully prolific. The male bird is amusing, for he will take a piece of fibre in his bill and execute a peculiar sort of dance to please his sweetheart, whilst trying hard to sing a scarcely audible song. When several Japanese Manakins are kept in one cage they will all sit at night, and a good part of the day, packed in one nest-box nearly as close as sardines are laid in a tin. Breeding, when several pairs use the same nest as a dormitory, is of course impossible. In an aviary these birds are apt to creep into other birds' nests, and thereby to destroy young broods. It is therefore advisable to keep each pair of Japanese Manakins in a cage by themselves. If they once begin to breed they will produce a very numerous progeny, and the young will breed again when four to six months old.

For nest-building these birds will avail themselves of any material and of any sheltered spot. To rear the young brood, millet and maw seed, both soaked in hot water and strained, should be given, besides either soaked or fresh ants' eggs and egg-food.

If the birds are stimulated too much they are apt to degenerate in this way: the old birds will build nest after nest, and lay eggs without number, not caring for the trouble of hatching them regularly, but sitting in the nests only for pleasure, and as many hours as it pleases them. A young bird bred by chance will inherit this undesirable habit, and the stock will become unfit for breeding purposes. The best way to breed is to place one pair only of White Manakins in a London canary breeding-cage, without nest-boxes or nesting materials, and feed them on millet and canary seed, with plenty of green food—that is, chickweed and grass-flower. When the birds are in as perfect plumage and condition as they can be, and when the weather is genial and warm, then begin by feeding them with egg-food, ants' eggs, fresh or dried and soaked, &c., and give them a nest-box and nesting materials. If the hen-bird should then prove one of those restless egg-layers, deficient in the natural instinct of sitting on and hatching the eggs, the best way is to get rid of her. There is not much difficulty in obtaining another female, and a hen-bird which will prove a good sitter and a good mother will surely be found if patiently looked for.

Thousands of these birds are now bred annually in Europe, and it is certain that, through being kept in larger cages and not being over-stimulated, a more bird-like bird than the imported Japanese Manakin will be produced. It should be stated that in the same nest may be found pure white and piebalds of various shades. The young should be removed from the breeding-cage as soon as they can feed themselves, because they will surely creep into the nest of the parent-birds when these want to sit again, and thus disturb the second sitting.

AFRICAN SILVER-BILL (*Munia cantans*), NORTH-EAST AFRICA. (Illustrated.)

Spermestes cantans (Russ), *Loxia cantans, Coccothraustes cantans, Estrelda cantans, Amadina cantans, Uroloncha cantans, Euodice cantans*. English dealers' name—African Silver-bill. German name—"Silberschnabel Amandine." French name—"Bec d'Argent."

An unpretending little bird, almost always obtainable, exceedingly amiable in the aviary, and very easily kept, bred, and reared. The upper part is fawn-colour, the wings and tail are a shade darker, and the lower body is dull white; the beak is bluish-grey. Male and female are much alike, and the surest way to select a pair is to choose two birds of different shades of bluish-grey bills. The male is very industrious in singing his pleasing little song, and when not so occupied the birds will creep with great agility through the bushes, or the pairs will nestle lovingly close to each other on the perch. They will build a nest in any cavity or large nest-box, and sometimes rear their young brood on seeds alone, although a few ants' eggs and a little egg-food are always more likely to lead to success.

INDIAN SILVER-BILL (*Munia Malabarica*), INDIA.

Spermestes Malabarica (Russ), *Loxia Malabarica, Amadina Malabarica, Euodice Malabarica, Loxia bicolor.* English dealers' name—Silver-bill. German name—"Malabar Amandine," or "Bleischnäbelchen."

The Indian Silver-bill is very similar to his African cousin, and the habits of both species are alike. The plumage is pale chocolate-brown, the head being somewhat darker; the wing-feathers and tail are nearly black-brown. The lower part is brownish-white, marked with faint spots on the sides; bill bluish-grey. This bird is not so frequently imported as the African Silver-bill, and is often mistaken for the latter. Food, &c., same as Waxbills.

NUTMEG-BIRD (*Munia undulata*), INDIA. (Illustrated.)

Spermestes punctularia (Russ), *Loxia punctularia, Munia punctularia, Fringilla punctularia, Amadina punctularia, Uroloncha punctularia, Oxycenca nisoria, Spermestes punctularia, Loxia undulata, Amadina undulata, Munia lineoventris, Lonchura nisoria, Spermestes nisoria, Spermestes undulata, Munia topela, Munia fuscans.* English dealers' name—Nutmeg-bird, or Spice-bird. German name—"Muskatvogel." French name—"Grosbec tacheté de Java."

The illustration shows a curiously-marked bird, rich chocolate-brown on the back, the lower body being marked with numerous white crescent-shaped spots on light brown feathers. The Nutmeg-bird is very common in India, on Ceylon, Java, Borneo, and all the other islands in the Indian Ocean, is annually imported in large numbers, and has been known and kept in Europe for very many years. By no means delicate, this bird will live a long time in a cage or aviary, and will not require very minute care. With the smallest Waxbills he will be invariably on good terms, and share their food and treatment.

Dr. Russ has succeeded in breeding the Nutmeg-bird with very much trouble, and undaunted by repeated failures. It is doubtful whether the bird has been bred elsewhere in captivity, and the attempt cannot be recommended, non-success being almost certain. It was for some time erroneously supposed that the White Japanese Manakin had been bred from the Nutmeg-birds. These birds are kept solely for the sake of their plumage, the only interesting feature in their manners being the attempt of the male bird to sing. He will stand almost upright on the perch, the crop will extend as if the bird were about to make a violent effort, the bill will open and shut, and scarcely a sound will be heard. If other birds happen to be chirping or singing, the performance will appear like a dumb show. Male and female of Nutmeg-birds are alike.

According to bird-dealers' phraseology, the entire hierarchy is represented in the bird-world—we have a Pope, Cardinals, Bishops, Parson Finches, and Nuns. The latter, of which there are four varieties, all natives of India or the East Indian Islands, next engage our attention. They are all very quiet birds, and no doubt called Nuns by reason of their sober but pretty colours. In size they are about equal to our Goldfinch, and in manners extremely gentle and retiring, sitting mostly in some retired corner of the aviary, except when in search of food. The song of the male bird is confined to a soft call or to a scarcely audible twitter. They endure very well, require only millet and canary seed, with a little green-meat, and perhaps, but not necessarily, an occasional mealworm or ants' egg. They very rarely breed, and failure has thus far resulted from almost every attempt to induce these birds to propagate in confinement, although crosses between Nuns and other Finches have been obtained latterly, some by accident, others by design. Male and female Nuns are alike. Their sedate habits frequently cause the claws of Nuns to grow very long, and if that is the case and remains unobserved and not remedied, accidents result by the birds becoming entangled and hung up.

MAJA FINCH (*Munia maja*), MALACCA. (Illustrated.)

Spermestes maja (Russ), *Loxia maja*, *Amadina maja*, *Fringilla maja*, *Dermophrys maja*. English dealers' name—White-headed Nun. German name—"Weissköpfige Nonnen Amandine." French name—"Nonnette à tête Blanche."

The Maja Finch is of soft chestnut-brown colour all over, except the head, which is silvery-grey, delicately shaded where the neck joins the shoulders. As the bird grows older, the grey head becomes almost white. An amateur in Hamburg has succeeded in breeding a number of young birds from a male White-headed Nun and a female Japanese Manakin in several successful broods. Some of these young birds were exhibited at the bird show in Vienna, held in May, 1878.

JAVAN MAJA FINCH (*Munia ferruginea*), JAVA.

Spermestes ferruginosa (Russ), *Loxia ferruginosa*, *Fringilla majanoïdes*, *Dermophrys ferruginea*, *Munia ferruginosa*. No English dealers' name. German name—"Schwarzbrüstige Nonnen Amandine."

Similar to the White-headed Nun in every respect, except that the lower part of the body, including chest and throat, are deep black. The Javan Maja Finch is very rare, and I have never met with the bird at any dealer's. The Zoological Society appear to have purchased four specimens in 1867, and not to have received any since then.

BLACK-HEADED FINCH (*Munia Sinensis*), INDIA. (Illustrated.)

Spermestes Sinensis (Russ), *Coccothraustes Sinensis*, *Loxia atricapilla*, *Amadina Sinensis*, *Lonchura melanocephala*, *Spermestes melanocephalus*, *Spermestes rubronigra*. English dealers' name—Black-headed Nun. German name—"Schwarzköpfige Nonnen Amandine."

The Black-headed Finch, or Two-coloured Nun, does not appear in the list of birds living at the Zoological Society's Gardens, and is (as illustrated) of a rich bright chestnut-brown colour, the head, neck, and upper part of the breast being deep black. The bird is almost always obtainable, and its habits, food, &c., are the same as the other Nuns.

BLACK-HEADED FINCH (*Munia Malacca*), INDIA.

(Illustration painted from live specimen kindly lent by Mr. E. Hawkins.)

Spermestes Malaccensis (Russ), *Loxia Malacca*, *Spermestes Malacca*, *Amadina Malacca*, *Dermophrys Malacca*, *Coccothraustes Javensis*. English dealers' name—Three-coloured Nun. German name—"Dreifarbige Nonnen Amandine." French name—"Nonnette à tête Noire," or "Nonnette à ventre Blanc et Noir."

Munia Malacca, or "Black-headed Finch," is the Three-coloured Nun, so called because

1. PIED MANNIKIN. (FAWN AND WHITE)
2. PIED MANNIKIN. (CHESTNUT AND WHITE)
3. SPOTTED SIDED FINCH OR DIAMOND SPARROW.
4. NUTMEG OR SPICE-BIRD.

the lower part is pure white, in strong contrast to the black head and rich brown back; otherwise the bird is exactly like *Munia Sinensis*—viz., rich bright chestnut-brown, with black head, neck, and shoulders. Habits and food exactly like the preceding.

CUT-THROAT FINCH (*Amadina fasciata*, Russ), WEST AFRICA. (Illustrated.)

Loxia fasciata, Loxia jugularis, Fringilla detruncata, Amadina detruncata, Sporothlastes detruncatus, Sporothlastes fasciatus.

English dealers' name—Cut-throat or Fasciated Finch. German name—"Bandamandine," "Bandfink." French name—"Cou Coupé," "Gorge Coupé."

There exists no African Finch so generally and so well known as the Cut-throat Finch, so called because the male has a red band extending from ear to ear across the throat. The female is easily recognised by the red band being absent, and there can never be any mistake about the sexes, because male fledglings leave the nest with the distinguishing red mark already perceptible. The illustration makes a description of the plumage superfluons. When in perfect health and condition the soft fawn-colour and delicate markings of the plumage are remarkably pretty, and any amateur may be recommended to acquire a pair of these inexpensive birds. To see their plumage in perfection is a pleasure worth some trouble, and besides, no other African Finch is so ready to breed in captivity. In my aviary I have bred Cut-throat Finches without knowing what was going on, until I saw the young birds after they had left the nest. Breeding this Finch has, however, this disadvantage—that imported birds are so cheap that cage-bred Cut-throat Finches have scarcely any money value; but for breeding simply as a pastime, for pleasure, or a beginning amateur's practice, the Cut-throat is to be highly recommended.

Dr. Russ mentions in his newest work that a pair began in his aviary by laying 9 eggs, which were lost through an accident. The same pair brought out of their nest 2 young on November 8th, 4 on December 25th, 3 on February 13th following, 4 on April 2nd, 5 on May 15th, and 3 on June 20th. The same pair bred in the following season in even quicker succession; and a lady in Vienna had from one pair in three years 45 broods, altogether over 240 eggs, out of which 176 were hatched! The young hen-birds were ready to breed at the early age of two to three months.

But Dr. Russ warns his friends against breeding the Cut-throat Finch in an aviary where other small Finches are breeding. He gives the bird a bad character, because he found him cowardly, a bully towards weak and small birds, and faint-hearted when a plucky little opponent showed courage. In their eagerness to breed rapidly in succession, the Cut-throat Finches are apt to take possession of other bird's nests whilst their own nest is yet fully occupied by a young brood. A separate cage is therefore to be recommended. I must say that I found the Cut-throat Finch peaceable and harmless, but I may have been fortunate with my individual birds, or I may not have noticed the disturbance they caused to other birds which might otherwise have bred successfully.

The nest is built in a nest-box, a German canary-cage, or abandoned nest of other birds and consists of any kind of fibre, grass, hay, or feathers which the birds can pick up. The male bird builds the nest, the female only interesting herself in the arrangement of the inner part of the rough structure in which the Cut-throat rears his family. The young are easily reared on soaked seeds, egg-food, and ants' eggs, and a temperature of about 60° to 70° Fahr. is sufficient to breed in midwinter. It often happens that the male bird throws the newly-hatched young brood out of the nest, in which case the brood, of course, perishes. This is due to an unnatural desire of the male bird to breed again. There are two ways of checking this evil—namely, either to separate the male bird, and to allow the female to bring up the brood alone, or to remove the first and second nests and sittings of eggs, and thereby to cool the birds.

Several Australian Finches will next deserve special notice, because they readily adapt themselves to our climate, and some of them will gratify their owner by breeding without difficulty. They are in so far indifferent to temperature that they will thrive perfectly well during winter, if kept in a room in any ordinary dwelling-house, provided the windows admit the rays of the morning or noonday sun. A temperature below freezing-point they will not endure for more than a few hours, but protected to this extent they will live on canary and millet seed, and be less subject to accidents than any other foreign Finches.

MODEST GRASS FINCH (*Amadina modesta*, Russ), AUSTRALIA.

Ægintha modesta (Russ), *Estrelda modesta, Aidemosyne modesta.* English dealers' name—Cherry Finch, or Plum-headed Finch. German name—"Ceres Astrild."

The Modest Grass Finch is the Australian Finch next following, but happens to be rarely met with, and has until now rather puzzled amateurs and students of ornithology. The Zoological Society purchased one specimen in 1862, and the next in 1872. Until 1872 the bird was almost unknown to amateurs, and even now only a few pairs arrive at a time, together with large numbers of other Australian Finches. It may be that the name of Modest Grass Finch is against the bird. Because the bird is rare, he is therefore rather expensive, but many people paying only high prices for gorgeously coloured birds with high-sounding names, there is not much inducement to catch and import the Modest Grass Finch in large numbers. His colours are modest, but, closely seen, very beautiful.

The plum or dark cherry-coloured crown of the bird has given it the name by which dealers recognise the bird. The brown bars on the nearly white lower body are very pretty, whilst a white edge of the principal wing-feathers and white spots on their dark tint mark the bird very gracefully. The male has a small black patch on the throat, just below the lower mandible, which the female has not, otherwise the sexes are alike. In size the Modest Grass Finch equals the Cut-throat or our Goldfinch.

This bird does not appear particularly susceptible to the influence of climate, and yet he will distress amateurs by dying quite unaccountably, few living very long. I incline to the opinion that in his wild state the Modest Grass Finch feeds on some kind of seed for which canary and millet seed are not quite perfect substitutes, and would advise to give millet in the ear and flowering grass very freely. Dr. Russ has bred these birds once, and no other instance is recorded of the Modest Grass Finch having bred in confinement.

CHESTNUT-EARED OR ZEBRA FINCH (*Amadina castanotis*, Russ), AUSTRALIA.

(Illustration painted from live specimen in the Author's possession.)

Spermestes castanotis (Russ), *Loxia guttata, Stagonopleura castanotis, Tæniopygia castanotis, Zonæginthus castanotis.* English dealers' name—Australian Zebra Finch. German name—"Zebra Amandine," "Zebrafink." French name—"Diamant à Moustache," "Diamant Zébré," "Zébré d'Australie."

The Chestnut-eared or Zebra Finch is the very opposite of the Modest Grass Finch, for he will live, be happy, and breed anywhere. He is as cheerful in the smallest cage as in the largest aviary, perfectly content with the most simple food, and indifferent as regards temperature, so long as he is not exposed to severe frost. In the aviary he will not interfere with other birds, and not allow others to interfere with him and his nest. Ever active and cheerful, he will always let his mate know his whereabouts by a call which reminds one of a wooden halfpenny trumpet.

The Zebra Finch is one of the smallest Australian Finches, being not larger than a European Wren. His plumage is decidedly pretty, a delicate pearl-grey being the prevailing tint. The lower body is white. A patch of chestnut colour marks the cheeks, and a band of chestnut colour, dotted with white spots, ornaments the sides. The throat is grey, shaded with black, the black forming a sharply defined collar-like mark where it borders on the white of the breast. The black tail is ornamented by white bars across each feather. The bill is brick-red; the feet also brick-red. The female is without the chestnut-coloured patches and bands on the cheeks and sides, and the lower body is a dull greyish tint.

There can be no doubt that the Zebra Finch is the best known and deservedly the most popular of all Australian Finches. He has been bred with more general success than any other foreign cage-bird. A little time since large numbers were bred regularly for sale at the Zoological Gardens in Antwerp, and by private breeders elsewhere on the Continent. Since the price of imported Zebra Finches sank to ten or eight shillings per pair, cage-breeding of Zebra Finches has, however, diminished somewhat.

A few years ago I exhibited at the Crystal Palace a cage containing thirty-five Zebra Finches, the result of one season's breeding from two pairs; and other amateurs and breeders have had success far exceeding mine. The only difficulty in breeding Zebra Finches is their sometimes prodigious reproductiveness. This is almost invariably due to their food being too stimulating, which will result in the birds building nests and laying eggs without hatching them.

If a healthy and apparently strong pair of Zebra Finches are obtained, it is advisable to keep them for a time without nesting materials, and to feed them only on dry millet and canary seed, with a little green-meat at times. When the birds have become used to their new home and surroundings, and when the perfection of their plumage denotes their perfect health, then—and not before—give them an opportunity to begin to nest. In a cage this opportunity is best given by fixing a roomy nest-box, into which the birds will forthwith carry a mass of any material they can pick up. Bits of hay and straw, moss, small twigs, pieces of green-meat, wool, fibre, feathers—nothing comes amiss to construct as slovenly a nest as any Sparrow ever built. Now is the time to give the Zebra Finches a very little extra food daily. The eighth part of a sponge-cake, the eighth part of the yolk of a hard-boiled egg or a corresponding quantity of preserved egg, a quarter of a tea-spoonful of maw-seed, and about as much soaked ants' eggs, all mixed together, will be an ample daily allowance for a pair of Zebra Finches, besides their regular dish of millet and canary seed. They will soon lay from four to seven very small white eggs, and hatch them in about eleven days. The young brood will be reared perfectly well on the above food, with a little soaked millet-seed. The young Zebra Finches will emerge from the nest as little pearl-grey birds, with *black* beaks, and mostly sit in a row on a perch or branch, waiting to be fed by their parents. When about six weeks old the black beak will gradually change to a yellowish brick-red, and the chestnut-coloured ear-marks of the males and the white lower body will become conspicuous. This is the sign that the young birds are fit for breeding, and I have myself observed that a young hen-bird, which I had placed for observation in a separate cage, laid an egg when just three months old. The young broods should be separated from their parents as soon as they are able to feed themselves, for if left in the aviary they will, unless the aviary be very large and the nesting opportunities be very many and extremely varied, almost surely interfere with the success of later broods of their parents, by either wanting to build nests in the same boxes, or laying eggs in their mother's nest, or sitting in it when they ought not to be there. When the Australian Zebra Finches have once fairly begun breeding, they will often continue to do so all the year round, not even stopping during moulting-time. A thoughtful breeder will prevent this, for exhaustion of the old birds and a weak progeny must be the result.

In the aviary the Zebra Finch will build his nest in many places—sometimes in nest-boxes, sometimes preferring German cages, and sometimes making a huge pile in a bush, in the midst of which bundle of sticks, weeds, hay, and straw there will be a very small nest, snugly housing a young family.

Very curious crosses have been bred with the Zebra Finch. A most remarkable one was a cross between the Zebra Finch and the Spotted-sided Finch, or Diamond Sparrow, bred by a celebrated German amateur, and exhibited alive by Dr. Russ at the Crystal Palace Bird Show in 1876. Whilst writing I have the opportunity of daily watching a male Zebra Finch who paired with a St. Helena Waxbill, built a nest, and the pair are now busy sitting.

SPOTTED-SIDED FINCH (*Amadina lathami*), AUSTRALIA. (Illustrated.)

Spermestes guttata (Russ), *Fringilla leucocephala, Loxia guttata, Fringilla lathami, Amadina guttata, Stagonopleura guttata, Zonæginthus guttatus.* English dealers' name—Diamond Sparrow. German name—"Diamant Amandine," or "Tropfenfink." French name—"L'Oiseau Diamant," or "Diamant Ordinaire."

The Spotted-sided Finch, or Diamond Sparrow, is the reverse of the diminutive and active Zebra Finch, for he is nearly as large a bird as our Sparrow. He has a somewhat heavy body, and his habits are not active. The plumage of the Diamond Sparrow is as splendid as the name will lead the reader to expect, but the colours are strong and the contrasts great. Silver-grey head and back, somewhat darker brownish-grey wings and tail; the lower part pure white, with a broad rich black band extending along the sides, which bands are ornamented with large irregular pure white spots; the chest is crossed by a band of velvet-like black. The end of the back and root of the tail are rich carmine-red, which gives the bird a very brilliant appearance when flying.

Male and female are so much alike that it is difficult to select a pair. Some dealers and some amateurs believe that the female has fewer or smaller spots on the sides; but these and other marks often prove misleading, and probably the best way to select a pair will be to compare the size and fulness of the heads carefully, and then to match a bird with a round and full skull, with one whose head and body seem to be a trifle smaller. The former will prove the male, the latter the female.

This Australian Finch has been known for many years, and is annually imported in very large numbers, generally arriving in a deplorable state, the majority being without any small feathers whatever. Hundreds of almost naked, shivering bird bodies, each provided with a pair of wings and little else in the way of feathers, being huddled together in a box-cage, would be a ridiculous sight, if the poor birds did not look so pitiable. But their real state is not so bad as it looks. The dealers place each bird immediately after arrival in a very small cage by himself, and in a surprisingly short time the feathers grow again. In from two to four weeks' time nobody would recognise in the full-plumaged bird the miserable naked little creature which had been shivering in the ship's cage.

Different theories have been propounded to explain why the Spotted-sided Finches pull out each other's feathers during the voyage from Australia. Some writers think that the absence of animal food causes the birds to masticate the ends of feathers; others say that the want of something to do makes the birds long to carry something about in their bill. No doubt both theories will soon be tested, for the new German egg-food will readily supply the animal substance for which the birds are supposed to crave, or a handful of canary or millet in the ear, or even of common chaff, would afford birds on the voyage something to play with. This Finch is peculiarly jealous, and I think his temperament will finally explain this mania for destroying each other's plumage during the long voyage to Europe.

In the aviary the Diamond Sparrow is fairly peaceable, but the bird lacks the agility and liveliness of the smaller Finches, and is apt to become too fat. A pair will sit for hours quietly on a branch or perch, when the male will slowly erect his body, utter a long-drawn, loud call, and then sink back into his former position. Canary and millet seed, with some millet in the ear, are really all the Spotted-sided Finches require as food; they will take a few mealworms and some soft food, but this should only be given at breeding-time. This is one of the few Finches bred at the Zoological Gardens. Amateurs have often bred the Diamond Sparrow, but with very variable success. One breeder will rear a great many, whilst others do not succeed at all.

If breeding is intended it is advisable to separate the males and females during the winter, and to keep two or more of each sex in a very large cage. Their jealousy will cause a sufficient amount of exercise. The bird is quite indifferent to temperature, and may be kept almost anywhere; in fact, some breeders maintain that very cold weather improves the plumage of the Diamond Sparrow. About March the birds may be paired, but never should more than one pair be put in a cage or aviary. Breeding Diamond Sparrows in winter is not to be recommended. These Finches will build a very rough nest, either in a high bush, or in a German cage, possibly on the top of a cage. Nest-boxes with solid sides they will not inhabit. The nest is a huge bundle of sticks, hay, green-stuff, grass, or fibre; and the pure white eggs will be hatched in about twelve days. The young brood is, however, somewhat slow in maturing, and the difficulty is to rear them and to keep the parents in order. It has been observed that in many cases the mother is so jealous of the young brood that if the male bird comes near the nest he will be persecuted so vigorously that the young brood may be forgotten, or the male parent killed by the mother of the chirping family. A separation of these veritably hen-pecked husbands from their family is then the only remedy. For feeding the young Diamond Sparrows, live insect food is absolutely necessary, and fresh ants' eggs the best; in their stead mealworms, egg-food, and scalded, soaked, and strained seeds may be used. Cage-bred Diamond Sparrows have some value, and it may be worth while to breed them with an eye to a pecuniary return for the trouble and expense. Breeders should bear in mind that their chief care must be not to allow the stock-birds to get fat, and to separate the males if, after hatching, there should be any family quarrels. A very large cage for each pair is indispensable, and the presence of other Finches will probably lead to mischief. If too comfortably housed and provided for, the Diamond Sparrow is apt, like other foreign Finches, to build a number of nests, and to shirk the trouble of hatching.

In my own aviary the Spotted-sided Finch carried a lot of grass, hay, and fibres into the crown of a small tree, and formed a pile of nesting materials, which might or might not be a nest. I found at various times eggs, but was not fortunate enough to obtain any broods of young Diamond Sparrows, whilst a friend of mine succeeded with very little trouble in rearing brood after brood in a cage about twice as large as a London-made canary breeding-cage.

BANDED GRASS FINCH (*Poëphila cincta*), QUEENSLAND.

(Illustration painted from live specimen kindly lent by J. C. Marsh, Esq.)

Spermestes cincta (Russ), *Amadina cincta*. English dealers' name—Parson Finch. German name—"Gürtel Amandine," or "Bartfink," or "Pfaffenvogel." French name—"Diamant à Bavette."

According to the list of the London Zoological Society, this handsome Australian Finch was first placed in the Gardens in 1861. Dealers began to import the Banded Grass or Parson Finch about the year 1869, and I well remember with what pleasure I purchased the first pair of Parson Finches, together with the first pair of Double-banded Finches, at a considerable price, in 1869. Since that time this Finch is imported regularly, and has deservedly become a great favourite, as much for his beauty as for his gentle manners.

In size the Banded Grass Finch is very nearly equal to the Spotted-sided Finch, or Diamond Sparrow, but his body is more slender, his habits are more lively, and his temper is decidedly less excitable than the latter's. The name of Parson Finch is probably due to a broad patch of glossy black ornamenting the throat of this beautifully coloured bird, from whose plumage, however, all glaring colours are absent. The head is of a very pretty silver-grey tint, the body a light but rich chestnut-brown, the tail is black, but the body at the root of the tail is pure white. Through the eye a black line extends from the black beak backwards. The feet are pink. Male and female are much alike, though not very difficult to distinguish by the somewhat less extent of the black patch on the female's throat. The difference is, however, so slight that only an actual and close comparison will enable a connoisseur to select a pair.

This Finch lives very much like the Diamond Sparrow, but never arrives plucked like the latter, which fact confirms to some extent my opinion that the Diamond Sparrow's jealous temper, and not the food on board ship, is the main cause of these birds pulling each other's feathers out. In Queensland the Parson Finch is found mostly on the large plains in the interior of the country, and is somewhat rare near the sea-coast. Whether this Finch is found in other parts of Australia seems as yet imperfectly ascertained. Transferred to Europe, the bird stands our climate very well indeed, although he will not bear as much cold as the Diamond Sparrow. It might be somewhat risky to keep Parson Finches in an out-door aviary during winter, though a frosty night or two in spring would not hurt a healthy bird in a properly-constructed aviary.

To amateur breeders the Parson Finch should be very strongly recommended, for he is not difficult to procure in good condition, and is easily kept on a simple diet of millet and canary seed. In the aviary he neither disturbs the smallest African Finches, nor is he easily disturbed by less well-behaved birds. With very little care the Parson Finches will proceed without delay or difficulty to breed a valuable stock of young, and rear their progeny with comparatively few mishaps. As a nesting-place they will prefer a nest-box or a German cage to an entirely self-made construction; and they have been known to lay double the usual number of five pure pinky-white eggs. In my aviary they bred quite unobserved; and Dr. Russ has collected evidence from other amateurs, according to which the Parson Finch was bred in an aviary occupied by a quarrelsome lot of Weaver-birds. A more curious instance of the strong reproductive instinct of this Finch is mentioned by Dr. Russ. A gentleman in Hamburg had a pair of Parson Finches in an aviary, together with many other small foreign Finches. The Parson Finches and a pair of Amaduvade Finches had nests and eggs in the same part of the aviary, but the Parson Finch hen, finding her own eggs clear, forsook these and her nest, drove the Amaduvade Finches from their eggs in order to hatch them, and finally hatched and reared the young brood of birds, scarcely half her own size.

1. MAGAFINCH OR WHITE-HEADED NUN. 2. BLACK-HEADED FINCH OR NUN.

3. JAVA SPARROW.

4. JAVA SPARROW. WHITE VARIETY.

As food for the young brood, egg-yolk, sponge-cake, and scalded, strained millet-seed should be given, together with some soaked or fresh ants' eggs. A very few mealworms might be given in addition whilst the brood is very young, but the stimulating effects of mealworms always involve a little risk, and fresh ants' eggs, if procurable, are safer.

CHESTNUT-BREASTED FINCH (*Donacola castaneothorax*), QUEENSLAND.

(Illustration painted from live specimen kindly lent by Mr. Charles Jamrach.)

Spermestes castaneothorax (Rùss), *Amodina castaneothorax.* English dealers' name—Chestnut Finch. German name—"Schilfamandine," or "Schilffink." French name—"Diamant Brun."

The Chestnut-breasted Finch is the last on the list of Australian Finches, and a bird of whom it is somewhat difficult to say much, although he is now regularly imported in considerable numbers. The German name means "Reed Finch," and all we know of his wild state is that he is supposed to live on marshes or in swampy districts, and to feed on the seeds of reeds and coarse grasses.

Hard dry millet and canary seed, on which this Finch is fed during the voyage to Europe and in our aviaries, are probably but a poor substitute for the bird's natural food, and consequently the Chestnut-breasted Finch often arrives sickly, though apparently in fair health, and rarely endures as long in the cage as other Australian Finches of equally robust body. I feel, however, confident that with suitable treatment and a little extra care the Chestnut-breasted Finch might be completely reconciled to our climate and the ordinary seed-food, if gradually accustomed to it. If purchased early in summer, various grasses in flower and with seed-stalks, a little millet in the ear, and a trifle of insect food added to the ordinary diet of seed-eating birds, would probably build up the constitution of the Chestnut Finch, and fit him for many years of cage-life and for breeding.

A few instances are known of the Chestnut-breasted Finch having been bred in confinement, but success has been exceedingly rare, and non-success the rule. An extraordinary cross between the Chestnut-breasted Finch and the White-headed Maja Finch is recorded by Dr. Russ, a German amateur having reared several broods of this peculiarly matched pair. It should, however, be added that the anatomy of the Chestnut-breasted Finch, and especially the form of the beak, is very similar to that of the family of "Nuns" (*Munia*).

Like the Nuns, the Chestnut Finches appear when singing to monopolise their own music, and to sing inwardly, for they will sit nearly upright, and seem to make a great effort, whilst a few scarcely audible long-drawn sounds issue.

The colours of the plumage are soft, and form agreeable contrasts of light grey on the head, cinnamon-brown on the back; the face and throat are dark brown, whilst the chest is light chestnut colour, with a broad black band across the middle of the breast, the lower part being pure white. Male and female are alike, but the black breast-band is less sharply marked in the case of the female.

JAVA SPARROW (*Padda oryzivora*), JAVA. (Illustrated.)

Spermestes oryzivora, Loxia oryzivora, Loxia Javensis, Coccothraustes oryzivora, Fringilla oryzivora, Amadina oryzivora, Oryzivora leucotis, Munia oryzivora, Oryziornis oryzivora. English dealers' names—Paddy-bird, Java Sparrow. German name—"Reisamandine," "Reisvogel." French name—"Padda."

The Java Sparrow, Paddy, or Rice-bird is a native of Java and of other East Indian islands. From thence this Finch appears to have spread, probably through the escape of cage-birds, to the Madras coast, and to Southern China. Whether the Java Sparrow was always indigenous to Japan, or has been imported there, is uncertain. In most rice-producing countries the Java Sparrow is as common as our Field Sparrow, and the immense flocks which then feed in the rice-fields do considerable damage. The natives of Java try to diminish this damage by frightening the Java Sparrows with a contrivance similar to the one used in a simplified form by English gardeners to protect seeds from the sparrows. Strings, to which pieces of paper or rags are attached, are stretched all over the field. In the midst of the rice-fields a small elevated hut is constructed with bamboo-poles, and from this hut all the strings radiate. A native placed in this hut keeps all these strings, rags, and papers continually in motion, and thus watches over the safety of his rice-crop. But the Java Sparrows fatten for all that when the rice is in the fields, and are then sometimes eaten. During that part of the year when the rice-fields are under water, the Paddy-bird lives on other seeds and a few insects.

No foreign Finch is so generally known as the Java Sparrow. When the first specimens may have reached Europe is impossible to tell, because every writer speaks of the Rice-bird as a well-known cage-bird, and very large numbers have been exported from Java ever since Europeans visited that island. In appearance the Java Sparrow is rather handsome, and especially remarkable for the very perfect condition in which the bird will always maintain his plumage. The soft slate-coloured body-feathers are ever as close as they can lay, the large white patches on the cheeks are ever clean, the black face and throat shine like new velvet, and the rather large wax-like beak is pink, like a doll's cheek, and looks as if just modelled by a wax-worker.

No foreign bird is kept as easily as the Java Sparrow, for as a rule he will touch nothing else but canary-seed, and live on that for years in perfect health and splendid condition. A cold temperature does not affect this Finch at all, an open-air aviary is as good winter quarters for him as a warm room. About equal in size to our House Sparrow, the Java Sparrow is somewhat clumsy in his movements, and notwithstanding his handsome plumage, he is devoid of the peculiar charm of the smaller foreign Finches. In the aviary Java Sparrows are only safe when the room is large, for if smaller birds should incommode this very peaceful-looking bird, he will freely use his powerful beak, and spitefully bite little legs, which sometimes get broken. When kept in a cage by themselves, Rice-birds are somewhat dull and uninteresting. To breed them is not worth while, for to do so successfully is extremely difficult, and the birds when bred are scarcely of any value.

One other quality, besides their great frugality, recommends the Java Sparrow to amateurs, and that quality is docility. One of these birds kept for some time in a sitting-room can easily be taught all sorts of little tricks, such as feigning to be dead, standing on his head, &c. To be a pet and plaything of a lady in her boudoir seems to me the proper place of the Java Sparrow amongst foreign cage-birds. But the lady must not mind being pinched sometimes in her fingers by her pet. The song of the Java Sparrow will not disturb an invalid, a few chirps and an attempt of a faint warble being the alpha and omega of his musical performances. Male and female are alike. Young birds display the pure white patches on the cheeks only after the second moult, and old writers mistook young birds with dark cheeks for females.

The white variety of the Java Sparrow is another instance of a total change of a bird's colour by cage-breeding, and due, like the production of White Manakins, to the perseverance and ability of the Chinese and Japanese. How the change of colour was brought about will perhaps never be known. Some writers relate that the Chinese keep Java Sparrows in white cages, and allow them to see no other colour but white; thereby producing a breed of white young birds. There probably is a grain of truth, but only a grain, in this story. If any breeder took ordinary Java Sparrows and tried to breed white birds in this way, his experiment would certainly end in failure. But in breeding from White Java Sparrows it frequently happens that in the same brood some of the young birds turn out speckled, or even quite blue, whilst others are pure white. No doubt the Chinese allow the white parent-birds to see no other colour but white, in the hope of obtaining a majority of valuable pure white progeny.

The Japanese seem to treat the White Java Sparrows very much like a breeding machine. Each pair is put into a small cage with only one perch and a nest. By means of very careful feeding the birds are brought to lay freely, and ingeniously contrived paper screens prevent the hen-birds being disturbed whilst sitting. As soon as the young are hatched, the Japanese breeder takes their care into his own hands, and with infinite trouble rears the brood by hand. Thereby he avoids not only the risk of the parent-birds neglecting their progeny, but also saves time, for whilst the Japanese bird-breeder is rearing the nestlings the parent-birds are hatching another brood. The visitor to a Japanese breeding establishment will see a row of small straw baskets on the floor, each provided with a lid of straw matting. An attendant will lift one lid after the other and disclose a nest of chirping Java Sparrows under each, and into each open beak a mouthful of millet-seed, scalded with some vegetable decoction, will be conveyed by a sort of spoon cut out of a thin bamboo. In the climate of Japan this purely vegetable food seems to suffice for the young White Java Sparrows. In Europe they require a slight addition of egg-food to rear young birds successfully.

The White Java Sparrow breeds very readily in confinement, and is a good-natured, though rather stupid bird. He will build a nest in any kind of deep nest-box, preferring coarse materials, such as hay, straw, fowls' feathers, and such-like. The nest is often built so slovenly that it is as well to help the bird a little when the shape of the nest seems to go wrong.

Although the value of these Finches has declined these last few years from about £4 or £6 per pair to about a sovereign, yet their breeding deserves the attention of amateurs, since from good stock-birds breeding is nearly as easy as that of Canaries, and certainly more remunerative. A careful selection of stock, and scrupulous removal of defective or speckled young birds, is the chief and almost sole requisite.

FIRE-TAILED FINCH (*Erythrura prasina*), Java and Sumatra.

Spermestes prasina (Russ), *Fringilla prasina*, *Erythrura prasina*, *Loxia prasina*, *Emberiza quadricolor*, *Fringilla sphenura*; *Lonchura quadricolor*, *Erythrura viridis*, *Amadina prasina*, *Erythrura prasina*. English dealers' name — Pin-tail Nonpareil, or Java Nonpareil. German name—"Lauchgrüne Papagei Amandine," or "Ostindischer Nonpareil."

It must be an oversight by which *Erythrura prasina* is called the Fire-tailed Finch, for a beautiful and totally different Australian Finch—*Estrelda bella*, see page 372—is also named Fire-tailed Finch according to the list of the Zoological Society of London. For once the dealers' name, "Pin-tail Nonpareil," seems much preferable, as it cannot be mistaken, and conveys some idea of the bird. The reader may note with advantage that as there are two Fire-tailed Finches, besides a Red-tailed Finch, considerable misunderstanding as regards some foreign birds can only be avoided by habitually using the Latin name as well as the English name.

This bird is one of the most beautiful Finches imported, but unfortunately absent from many collections. In former times the Pin-tail Nonpareil arrived much more frequently, and generally *viâ* Holland, but as the birds mostly died after a few weeks, they acquired a bad reputation, became difficult of sale, and were rarely imported. In the very earliest days of my keeping foreign birds, I purchased a Pin-tail Nonpareil, and it died after a very few weeks. Regretting the loss of the handsome bird, I consulted one of the most celebrated authorities on the subject of foreign birds, and received the unsatisfactory reply that the bird "never lived in confinement." Not satisfied with this negative information, I set myself the task of discovering *why* this bird should not live, and completely succeeded. It was easy to find out that the Nonpareil Pin-tail lived chiefly on rice in his native Java. Cleaned table-rice the birds do not care for; but rice with the husk on, the so-called paddy-rice, was accepted by them as their natural food, and on that, with a little canary and millet seed, the Pin-tail Nonpareils, which were supposed never to live long, endured in my aviary for six or seven years in perfect health and unimpaired beauty of plumage. With a little judicious addition of egg-food it should be possible to breed and rear this Finch; and Dr. Russ had actually a brood hatched, which however was lost, through the death of the parent-bird, whilst the nestlings were still helpless.

The Pin-tail Nonpareil is best described by reference to the well-known American Nonpareil. The arrangement of brilliant colours is very similar, but the colours are not so intense, though not less beautiful for being somewhat softened. Head and throat of the male bird are light blue, the back is olive-green, the wings dark brown, each wing-feather edged with olive-green. The lower body is bright scarlet, diffused towards the sides and chest, where the scarlet tint becomes light brownish-yellow. The tail-feathers are brown, with scarlet edges, the two middle tail-feathers are much longer than the rest (wherefore the name *Pin-tail* Nonpareil), and dark scarlet. The female is simply olive-green on the back, dull yellowish-brown underneath, and without the blue head and scarlet abdomen. In size this Finch about equals our Goldfinch, and his form is slender. In the aviary the Pin-tail Nonpareil is perfectly harmless, and, though actual experience is wanting, I should say the bird would readily winter without harm in a low temperature. Mine never showed any ill-effects from a night in which the thermometer declined to 50°.

PARROT FINCH (*Erythrura psittacea*), New Caledonia.

(Illustration painted from live specimens in the Author's possession.)

Spermestes psittacea (Russ), *Fringilla psittacea, Fringilla pulchella, Acalanthe psittacea, Estrelda psittacea.* No English dealers' name. German name—"Eigentliche Papagei Amandine."

The Parrot Finch is a near relation of the preceding Pin-tail Nonpareil Finch, though totally different in colour. The entire body of this bird is of a rich deep green tint, shining in the sun with almost golden lustre; the face and throat down to the middle of the breast are bright scarlet, and the tail is dark red, with a patch of scarlet at the root. Male and female are alike, and only to be distinguished by the scarlet on the chest being a trifle less extended in the case of the female. This exceedingly handsome Finch ought perhaps not to find a place in this book; for he can scarcely be called a cage-bird as yet, although without doubt he will soon be less rare, orders having to my knowledge been sent by London dealers to their travelling collectors to bring over this Finch at almost any price. If once imported, he will soon be bred. Whilst writing there are probably only eight live birds of this species in Europe—four in my own aviary, and four others bred by the writer are, if they are still alive, in a collection on the Continent.

In May, 1877, Mr. Charles Jamrach received and advertised three foreign Finches, which he called Green Parson Finches. I was abroad at the time, and on my return to London there was only one of the three left unsold, and this bird was blind in one eye and bald. I secured him, and found that the two others had been disposed of to a London retail dealer, and ultimately these two also came into my hands. When these three birds were located in my aviary they soon made themselves at home, and built a covered ball-shaped nest of Mexican fibre in a German canary-cage. In due course four white eggs were laid, and four young birds were hatched and safely brought up on a diet of egg, ants' eggs, maw-seed, and sponge-cake. Through a vexatious accident three of these young birds were killed, when their removal from their parents was intended. A second brood resulted in only two fully-developed young birds. Of these young Parrot Finches, I presented one to Dr. Russ, and the other two remained in my hands and bred and reared four young birds in the following year. These four cage-bred Parrot Finches, of the second generation bred by me, were exhibited in Berlin in March, 1879, and claimed by a distinguished amateur at the supposed fancy price of £20, although at that time insignificant-looking dull green fledgelings, without the bright crimson heads and throats of their parents, and minus the golden lustre body-colour of full-grown birds. If the very first attempt at breeding a newly-imported valuable bird results in successfully rearing two generations, that bird will surely soon cease to be unknown to amateurs. Whilst writing, my old stock-birds are sitting again on four eggs, after a brood of five young birds, just hatched, were destroyed a fortnight ago by a mouse taking a flying leap of fully two feet horizontal distance into the nest. The mouse was subsequently caught and met his doom, but the five newly-hatched birds were dead.

The only record of a live Parrot Finch in any European Zoological Garden is, that in 1873 one specimen was seen in the garden of the Paris Acclimatisation Society. My Parrot Finches were always perfectly amiable towards other birds, and nested within a few feet of the Double-banded Finches, without either interfering with the domestic arrangements of the other. At first they were rather shy, and left their nest whenever any one came near, but latterly they have become used to visitors. My success in breeding this rare and valuable Finch is probably due to the birds being placed in an aviary sufficiently large to leave them comparatively undisturbed. As food, canary, French millet, and millet in the ear proved sufficient, with the usual addition of animal food in the breeding season.

The beauty and the gentle graceful manners of this Finch are sure to make him a favourite whenever he becomes available. His size is about equal to that of the Goldfinch; his vocal powers, however, are only productive of a long call similar to that of the Diamond Sparrow, and a chirp reminding the hearer of the sounds emitted by crickets.

A very curious group of African Finches are the Whydah-birds, so called because they were first brought to Europe from Whydah, on the West Coast of Africa. Linné gave the genus the name of *Vidua—i.e.*, Widow; and English dealers and sailors love to talk of Widow-birds. Whether Widow-bird is a corruption of Whydah-bird, and was Latinised by Linné into *Vidua*, or whether Linné called the genus *Vidua*, Widow, by reason of the somewhat sombre plumage, cannot now be ascertained. At all events, it is better to call the birds Whydah, and not Widow birds. Although not imported in such large numbers as some of the small African Finches, the ordinary Whydah-birds are always to be had, and have been well-known cage-birds in Europe for very many years. Their very striking appearance is sure to arrest attention, and their endurance in our climate on very simple food — millet and canary seed — is a further point in their favour. But, on the other hand, they will not breed readily in captivity; very little is known of their habits in their wild state, and their great beauty is only periodical. For six months in the year, or more, the Whydah-birds are very common-looking, grey and brown, spotted and streaked Finches, and only when their breeding season commences—about midsummer—does the plumage assume the rich tints and extraordinary shape we so much admire. About midwinter the moult begins, and about the time of year when bird shows take place every Whydah-bird is again in what I might call undress; the male birds look then as insignificant as the females, and very much like a dark Linnet.

To keep the Whydah-birds in perfect condition, a bath at frequent intervals is necessary, for their desire to keep their plumage in faultless order is great, and whenever they cease to care for the beauty of their long tails, it is a sure sign of ill-health. Open-air aviaries would suit the Whydah-birds very well in summer and autumn; but their moulting-time falling into our winter months, a severe frost, or exposure to cold rain, would then probably prove fatal.

PARADISE WHYDAH-BIRD (*Vidua paradisea*), WEST AFRICA. (Illustrated.)

Vidua paradisea (Russ), *Emberiza paradisea*, *Fringilla paradisea*, *Steganura paradisea*, *Steganura sphenura*. English dealers' name—Paradise Whydah, Widah, or Widow bird. German name—"Paradies Widafink," "Paradies Wittweuvogel." French name—"Veuve à Collier d'Or."

If the reader will refer to the illustration he will agree with me that such a superb bird ought not to be absent from any aviary, especially as the Paradise Whydah-bird is not costly, not difficult to obtain, very harmless, and by no means delicate. Male and female are alike when out of colour, that is, between January and midsummer, and then resemble a dark Linnet. But when the time of year comes round which in their native country is the breeding season of Whydah-birds, viz., about June or July, a marvellous change takes place in the appearance of the cock-bird. The head and wings assume a more or less intense black colour, a broad collar of rich brown ornaments the neck, the lower body becomes nearly white, and with surprising rapidity four black tail-feathers grow to a great length; the two centre feathers being about ten inches long, and two outer feathers assuming a shape resembling that of a laurel leaf about five or six inches in length. A small cage will of course destroy the beauty of this long tail in a few hours, and to obtain a perfect bird, a male should be obtained at a very early stage of the change of plumage, and before a single feather has been ruffled in the dealers' store-cage. Placed in an aviary, and in perfect plumage, the graceful flight of the bird, with his long sweeping tail, is a sight of great beauty. At first smaller inmates will be a little frightened when the Whydah-bird swoops down among them, but about twenty-four hours reconciles even the most timid amongst the small Finches to the tail of their new friend. When feeding on the ground the male Whydah-bird carries his tail very carefully in a graceful curve, the extreme ends just touching the ground, whilst the agile feet scratch in the sand and food-dishes, after the manner of fowls.

Some years since three Paradise Whydah-birds, of rare beauty and great value, came into my hands, which I ascertained to be *Vidua verreauxi*, a local variety of *Vidua paradisea*. The brown collar was golden-yellow at the back of the neck, and the black head and throat were of a much more intense tint. The tail reached the extraordinary length of fourteen to sixteen inches. One of these birds escaped one day, and to see him floating from tree to tree in the garden was a sight of such beauty that one might almost forget the loss of the bird. The excitement of the Sparrows was amusing, and they at once mobbed their strange long-

Vincent Brooks Day, & Son Lith.

SHAFT-TAILED WYDAH.

PARADISE WYDAH

YELLOW BACKED WYDAH.

tailed visitor. It was less amusing that they drove the poor bird from the neighbourhood, beyond the reach of recapture, and probably some cat breakfasted on his valuable body before dawn of the following day. For food and treatment see the two preceding pages.

PIN-TAILED WHYDAH-BIRD (*Vidua principalis*), AFRICA. (Illustrated.)

Vidua principalis (Russ), *Emberiza principalis*, *Fringilla principalis*, *Emberiza serena*, *Vidua minor*, *Fringilla serena*, *Vidua erythrorhyncha*. English dealers' name—Pin-tailed Whydah-bird. German name—"Dominikaner Widafink." French name—"Veuve Dominicaine."

When in full plumage the Pin-tailed Whydah-bird is one of the most elegant inhabitants of our aviaries. He is a trifle smaller than the Paradise Whydah, and his plumage is less sombre, the black head, back, and wings being relieved by a coral-red beak, white breast, and a white mark on the wings. The two central jet-black tail-feathers grow to a length of eight or ten inches, but are quite narrow. In his movements and in the carriage of his tail the Pin-tailed Whydah-bird is quite as graceful as the Paradise Whydah, and it is difficult to say which of the two species is the most beautiful. The Pin-tail is a good deal more lively and excitable than his imperturbable cousin, the Paradise Whydah, and some individuals prove combative in the aviary; it is therefore as well to be a little careful at first. The change of colour in the male takes place in the same way as with the other Whydah-birds. Towards midsummer the bird's black and white garb assumes more intense tints, without the feathers falling out, and the long tail grows rapidly. About midwinter an actual change of feathers, a regular moult, occurs, and the loss of the tail-feathers is generally the first sign of the approaching change. The new feathers are of very modest brown and black colour, the same as those which distinguish the female all the year round.

It is asserted that the Pin-tailed Whydah-bird has bred in captivity, but I doubt whether complete success has been achieved, and it will certainly remain difficult to breed and rear this Finch. To begin with, it is not easy to obtain females, many of the supposed females being young males. Many writers suppose the Pin-tailed Whydah-birds with four long tail-feathers to be a variety of the ordinary Pin-tail with two feathers. I believe that I can assert that this divergence is due only to the age of the birds, for I have a splendid four-feathered Pin-tail before me as I write who had only two long tail-feathers last year and the year before. For food and treatment see pages 399 and 400.

LONG-TAILED WEAVER-BIRD (*Chera progne*), SOUTH AFRICA.

Vidua caffra (Russ), *Fringilla caffra*, *Chera caffra*, *Loxia caffra*, *Emberiza longicauda*, *Vidua phœnicoptera*. English dealers' name—Long-tailed Whydah-bird. German name—"Hahnschweifwittwe." French name—"Veuve à Epaulettes."

This is the most rare and most beautiful of the Whydah-birds, and certainly the one which has given rise to more disputes between dealers and their customers than any other variety. Somehow the bird seems never to arrive in such plumage that his identity can be determined with certainty. In undress the Long-tailed Weaver or Whydah bird resembles so closely some of the larger kinds of Weaver-birds that it is easy to mistake the one for the other. And I suspect, furthermore, that this, the king of the Whydah-birds, comes into full colour only after the third year, if not later. Many purchasers may have actually possessed young Long-tailed Weaver-birds, and disappointed that the birds did not come into colour in due course, they probably ceased to care for them, or let them fly, whilst other purchasers may have acquired hen-birds, which are exactly like males out of colour.

The Long-tailed Weaver-bird is of nearly the size of a Starling, and quite black, with the exception of scarlet shoulders, bordered by a stripe of white. The bushy tail consists of numerous feathers, each fifteen to sixteen inches long, and curved after the manner of a domestic cock. I have seen this magnificent bird in various zoological gardens, but never met with one in colour at any dealer's. It is more than probable that the scientific travellers, who assert that this Whydah-bird is a clever weaver and constructs an artistic nest, are mistaken. The males of all the Weaver-birds are the architects of their nests, and it is incomprehensible how a bird with such an enormous tail could build a nest after the manner of Weaver-birds. It may well be that this Whydah-bird inhabits the disused nests of Weaver-birds, and adapts them to his own purposes. The enormous tail becomes a source of peril to its wearer. I saw a glorious stuffed specimen, of which the owner told me he had picked up the bird alive at Natal after a heavy shower of rain. The poor bird could not fly with his tail thoroughly wet. A strong wind also impedes the flight of a male Long-tailed Weaver-bird. Would it be very surprising if many full-grown male birds in full colour became the easy prey of *Carnivoræ?*

Owing to the Zulu war and other causes it seems probable that our knowledge of the South African fauna will now be considerably added to, and that the certain improvement of the means of communication with the interior of the South African colony will cause the shipment of larger numbers of hitherto rare birds.

YELLOW-BACKED WHYDAH-BIRD (*Coliopasser macrurus*), West Africa. (Illustrated.)

Vidua macroura (Russ), *Loxia macroura, Loxia longicauda, Fringilla chrysoptera, Fringilla flavoptera, Penthetria macroura.* English dealers' name—Yellow-backed Whydah-bird. German name—"Gelbrückige Widafink," or "Trauerwida." French name—"Veuve à dos d'or," or "Veuve chrysoptère."

About the size of a full-grown, well-fed sparrow, the Yellow-backed Whydah-bird is a strong-bodied and strong-billed bird, whose gentle manners in the society of smaller birds had better be doubted. Instead of describing the beautiful velvet-black plumage of the male, I may refer the reader to the illustration. The female is pale-grey on the back; wings and tail are dark brown. On the shoulders and back each feather has a very narrow yellow edge; the breast is dull white. The beak of the female is reddish-brown, while that of the male is black. The Yellow-backed Whydah-bird is until now rather rare, and not often met with in private collections.

ULTRAMARINE OR STEEL FINCH (*Fringilla ultramarina*), Africa. (Illustrated.)

Vidua nitens (Russ), *Fringilla nitens, Fringilla ultramarina, Loxigilla nitens, Amadina nitens, Hypochera nitens, Hypochera ultramarina, Fringilla funerea, Tiaris funerea.* English dealers' name—Combasou. German name—"Stahlblaue Widafink." French name—"Combasou."

Few beholders of the Ultramarine Finch would suppose this very small and short-tailed bluish-black bird to belong to the family of Whydah-birds; and no one who happens to see a cage with fifty or a hundred of these birds in a dealer's shop would suppose that a little foreign Finch, obtainable for a few shillings, happens not to be included in the list of birds living at the London Zoological Gardens.

The Ultramarine Finch, or Combasou, is about the size of the St. Helena Waxbill, and, like the other Whydah-birds, he scratches with his feet in the sand, and the male changes the colour of his plumage completely when the breeding season arrives. On the other hand, his tail is short, like that of the common Finches. The male when out of colour, and the female, are pale brown, with reddish-brown marks over the back, and stripes over the head, very similar to the female Paradise Whydah-bird. The breeding season is between July and September, and towards this period of the year the male Cambasou changes to a uniform deep blue-black tint of considerable metallic lustre. The date of this change of colour is however somewhat uncertain, and apparently depends on circumstances. Old birds will sometimes retain their court-dress for a year or more, and I have at present a Combasou before me who to my certain knowledge was as black as now eighteen months previously, and has remained so.

In the aviary this pretty little bird is lively and bold, perhaps a little quarrelsome, but without being dangerous to even the smallest foreign Finches, except in exciting their jealousy by singing to every female. To breed him successfully would require a temperature of about 85° to 90° Fahr., but to keep the Combasou simply as an ornamental inmate of the aviary he will be found quite hardy, and ever lovely and in good condition. Abyssinia and the borders of the Nile are the Combasou's native home, where he apparently lives much after the manner of our European Sparrows. Some travellers assert that he breeds between July and September, others say between January and March; some say his nest is in trees, others found it under the thatch of roofs and in holes.

The food and treatment are the same as other Whydah-birds or Finches, *vide* pages 399, 400.

CHAPTER XLVII.

THE WEAVER-BIRDS.

ONE of the most interesting families of foreign cage-birds which reach Europe is that of the Weaver-birds. Most of them are natives of Africa, a few species are found in Asia, and none in America or Australia. The Weaver-birds are so called because their nests are constructed by a clever interlacing of fibres, roots, &c., by which a very curious and durable family mansion is formed. Instinct and necessity have made these birds wonderful architects. Natives of a land where the rays of a vertical sun alternate with tropical rains; where monkeys, serpents, and all kinds of other enemies abound, the Weaver-bird has learnt to avoid these manifold dangers for his progeny; and consequently Weaver-birds abound in many parts of Africa, delighting the eye of the traveller as soon as he sets foot on the shore of the West Coast of Africa, and are ever present wherever he may wander in the interior.

In its details the nest of each species of Weaver-bird varies, but all of them are more or less ball-shaped. The roof is always very thick, and substantial enough to keep off the heaviest downpour, as well as to protect the inmates from the tropical sun. The nest is invariably suspended from frail branches or reeds, just strong enough to bear its weight, but never strong enough to tempt any predatory animal to climb up. The entrance to the nest is invariably from underneath, a sort of ridge dividing the nest proper from the entrance, and preventing eggs or young from falling out. No bird of prey can therefore possibly see the contents of a Weaver-bird's nest, much less commit any ravages on a brood. This natural instinct the Weaver-birds never lose in confinement, and with unceasing activity the male birds will ever busy themselves with the construction of nests, the female scarcely ever sharing her mate's laborious building operations. Given a roomy cage, suitable food, a few branches, and a quantity of stiff fibre, the male of a pair of Weaver-birds will without delay begin to build nest after nest, probably pulling most of them to pieces when half finished if their construction does not entirely please the somewhat proud architect. For his own special use the male Weaver-bird loves to build a kind of half-nest, consisting of an arched roof, with a sort of rope stretched across underneath to serve as perch.

Gentle or affectionate birds the Weavers are certainly not. Their declarations of love seem to consist in the male driving the female furiously about the cage. Next, the male will offer battle to any other male Weaver-bird in the cage, and then set to work with much excitement on building nests. The birds seem then to forget everything, food included, and to be simply intent on building, which is done with incessant flapping of wings, and a continuous hoarse and grating twitter. The hen takes very little or no notice of her fussy lord. When the nest is finished she will condescend to inspect it, smooth a fibre here and there, and, if convenient, she will inhabit the nest, lay eggs, and sit on them. But now the male does not take very great care of her, beyond a great row when another bird comes near. In his turn, sitting on the eggs is not to his taste.

The Weaver-birds, notwithstanding their tropical native country, are strong and hardy

Vincent Brooks, Day & Son, Lith.

1. RED-FACED WEAVER-BIRD. 3. RED-BEAKED WEAVER-BIRD.
2. ORYX. OR GRENADIER WEAVER-BIRD. 4. BLACK-BELLIED OR NAPOLEON WEAVER-BIRD.

(THE NEST FROM MR AUG. F. WIENER'S AVIARY.)

birds in our northern climate. With judicious treatment they can be wintered without artificial heat, and will breed readily if one or two points are kept in view. Notwithstanding his restless and excited temperament, the Weaver-bird is apt to become fat when in his winter plumage. At that time he should be kept only on millet and canary seed, of which he will consume a great deal if unlimited quantities are supplied. Plenty of green-meat should be added. If kept very warm the change of plumage takes place in May; if the temperature is cool the Weavers will not come into colour until June or July. At that time a little animal food should be given, such as ants' eggs, a few mealworms, egg-food, and fine German paste, and this addition to his rations should be maintained during the breeding-season, that is, while the bird is in colour, if breeding is attempted, and until the Weavers have fairly completed moulting at the end of the season.

Like the Whydah-birds, most of the male Weavers undergo a most complete change, not of plumage, but of appearance, with the approach of their breeding season. Dr. Russ has collected some interesting facts on this point from his own and the observations of some amateurs.

The most gorgeous Weaver-birds, the Oryx, the Bishop, and the Napoleon, look in their winter undress—and the females all the year round—something like hen-sparrows. In full colour they are rich velvet-like black and orange, or black and bright yellow. This change takes place by the tips of the brown feathers changing colour, and a multitude of small tinted feathers growing between the old feathers. When the moult occurs these short tinted feathers are shed first, and subsequently the other plumage is renewed, with the sober-coloured brown winter plumage.

Whether these splendid Weaver-birds come into full colour in their second or third year has not, I think, been satisfactorily determined as yet. The females are nearly valueless, and the long period during which breeders have to wait before they can know whether young birds are male or female is a great drawback to breeding. I once bought forty Bishops out of colour just arrived, by way of experiment, at one shilling per head, to try whether the experienced dealers could pick out the males. The lot would surely have been sorted, before it was given away at such a price. In the course of the first two years about ten young male Bishops grew gradually into superb plumage, about twenty were the red-faced Weaver-birds, and the few remaining were Bishop hens.

GRENADIER WEAVER-BIRD (*Euplectes oryx*), West Africa. (Illustrated.)

Ploceus oryx (Russ), *Emberiza oryx*, *Loxia oryx*, *Coccothraustes oryx*, *Oryx oryx*, *Pyromelæna oryx*, *Euplectes Sundevalli*. English dealers' name—Oryx Weaver-bird, or Oryx Bishop, or Grenadier Bishop. German name—"Oryx Webervogel," or "Doppelter Feuerweber." French name—"Oryx," or "Le Grenadier."

The Grenadier, as well as the Crimson-crowned, the Orange, and the Black-bellied Weaver-birds are known in bird-dealers' parlance as Bishops, by reason of their plumage being a rich black and crimson, black and orange, or black and yellow, and are birds of great splendour. The name of Grenadier Weaver-bird, or Grenadier Bishop, is in so far happily chosen, as the bird so called compares in size to the other Bishop Weavers like a Grenadier to a militia-man, being perceptibly larger. His colours are better described by the illustration than by any verbal description. Besides the difference in size, the Grenadier, or Oryx, cannot be mistaken for the similarly-coloured, smaller Orange Bishop, because the entire head of the latter is black, whilst the head of the Oryx is orange-red at the top as far as the upper mandible, the sides of the head and the lower part of it being black.

The orange tint of the Grenadier Weaver is very varied, some individuals being deep orange-red, others rich bright yellowish-orange.

The female is, as already stated, much like a hen-sparrow, and smaller than the male. Of all the Bishop Weavers, the Oryx is the most valuable, and very rarely are more than a few pairs offered at a time. Dr. Russ calls the bird very excitable and combative in the aviary during breeding-time, whilst I found the Oryx less quarrelsome than the smaller Bishops. A pair of Grenadiers will without any hesitation build a nest very much like one shown in the illustration, and will breed freely if circumstances are at all favourable. A very rare local variety of Grenadier Weavers, viz., the *Euplectes Sundevalli*, bred in my aviary without my knowledge, and I was not even aware that they had been incubating until two young birds were flying about. How these young birds, almost as large as a Bullfinch, had room with their mother in the nest, I have never been able to make out.

One of the strangest sights a collection of Weaver-birds affords is the Oryx, when endeavouring to attract the notice of the hen-bird. He will gradually raise his body and blow himself out until he looks much larger than he is, and the feathers stand nearly erect, whilst he will utter sounds which seem a mixture of hissing, chirping, and the noise of scissors-grinding. Should the female remain indifferent to the charms of this music, he will chase her all over the aviary, but presently his vanity will overcome his wrath, and he will begin to blow himself out afresh. All that is needful to know about food has been said in the general remarks respecting the Weaver-birds.

ORANGE WEAVER-BIRD (*Euplectes franciscanus*), WEST AFRICA. (Illustrated.)
Ploceus franciscanus (Russ), *Loxia franciscana*, *Fringilla ignicolor*, *Euplectes ignicolor*. English dealers' name—Orange Bishop. German name—"Orange Webervogel."

The Orange Weaver-bird, or Orange Bishop, is about the size of a Goldfinch, and a most brilliant-coloured bird. The plumage of the male is bright reddish-orange and velvet-like black, and the arrangement of these colours is more readily understood by referring to the illustration than by any amount of description. The female is, like all Bishops, of a very sober brown colour. Easily, and when out of colour very cheaply obtainable, the Orange Bishop deserves a place in every aviary, and especially in open-air aviaries, as he will stand a good deal of rough weather. But amateurs must bear certain peculiarities in mind, which, if overlooked, may cause much annoyance, but if taken into consideration can be made use of. An extremely excitable, restless, and jealous bird is the Orange Bishop. Two males, when in colour, will fight terribly, and if males and females are brought together in the breeding-time, the poor hens will be worried and driven all over the cage or aviary without cessation. The best plan will be found to be, to secure a male bird and two or three females, before the male is in colour, and to turn them together into an aviary. As the breeding season approaches, the male bird will divide his attention between the females, and not interfere with other birds in any way, provided they are not Weavers. With unceasing activity he will build a number of nests, and possibly one of the hens may take up her abode in one of them. The presence of several hens will so stimulate the activity of the male that he will not waste time on pulling unused nests to pieces, and these are often made use of by small African Finches in preference to any artificial contrivance we can give them for nesting. For food and treatment see general remarks on Weaver-birds, pages 404, 405.

Vincent Brooks, Day & Son, Lith.

1. CRIMSON-CROWNED WEAVER-BIRD, OR ORANGE BISHOP.. 2. RED-HEADED OR MADAGASCAR WEAVER-BIRD.

3. SAFFRON FINCH.

CRIMSON-CROWNED WEAVER-BIRD (*Euplectes flammiceps*), WEST AFRICA.

Ploceus flammiceps (Russ), *Euplectes flaviceps*, *Euplectes pyrrhozona*, *Hyphantornis flammiceps*, *Pyromelæna flammiceps*. English dealers' name—Red Orange Bishop. German name—"Flammen Webervogel."

A very rare species of Bishop is the Crimson-crowned Weaver-bird, and when a few specimens arrive now and then they are probably mistaken for Orange Bishops. The difference is, however, considerable to the close observer. All Bishops vary considerably in the shades of their bright colours, but the Crimson-crowned Weaver-bird has a distinct crimson tint without a trace of orange, and besides, the tint of the upper part of the head is not black like the Orange Weavers, but crimson. With these exceptions, this bird resembles the Orange Weaver-bird so much as to be easily mistaken. I once bought a few specimens under the name of Brazilian Bishops, and I need not add that this description was totally wrong, though it showed the keen perception of the seller, who had discovered that the birds were not quite like the Orange Bishops, although the orange tints of these latter vary a good deal between crimson and yellow. I fancy this Weaver-bird is rather more delicate than the other Bishops; at all events, mine proved less enduring, although I had received them in splendid condition.

NAPOLEON OR BLACK-BELLIED WEAVER-BIRD (*Euplectes afer*), WEST AFRICA. (Illustrated.)

Ploceus melanogaster (Russ), *Loxia melanogastra*, *Loxia Abyssina*, *Fringilla ranunculacea*, *Euplectes ranunculaceus*, *Euplectes melanogaster*, *Ploceus Abyssinicus et afer*, *Euplectes Abyssinicus*, *Paha Abyssinica*. English dealers' name—Napoleon Weaver-bird, or Napoleon Bishop. German name—"Napoleonsweber." French name—"Le Worabée."

Why this Weaver, whose colours are those of the Austrian Monarchy—intensely bright yellow and brilliant black—has been called Napoleon Weaver, is difficult to explain. Dr. Russ hazards the opinion that the bird, being one of the most brilliant Weavers imported, and happening to arrive for the first time in large numbers when Napoleon III. was in the zenith of his power, enterprising dealers popularised this Weaver-bird by giving it what was then a popular name. Be that as it may, the name of Napoleon Weaver is preferable to that of Black-bellied Weaver-bird.

Like all the Bishops, the Napoleon, too, reaches Europe from the West Coast of Africa, but is believed to be indigenous to the greater part of the African Continent, with the exception of the extreme south.

His habits and manners in the cage, and his food, are identical with those of the other Bishops, the same restless activity characterising all. He will take possession of a suitable branch of a shrub in the aviary, and selecting a couple of twigs he will weave and interlace pieces of fibre until a stout, upright ring rests on the twigs. Sitting in this ring, the male bird will gradually fix in it the ends of fibres, each one forming a semi-circle, and in this way a globular nest is formed, an entrance-hole being left low down in the side of the structure. Many nests will be begun and abandoned when half finished, and the male bird's excited and unsteady activity is the chief difficulty in the way of obtaining nests fit to breed in.

RED-HEADED OR MADAGASCAR WEAVER-BIRD (*Foudia Madagascariensis*), ISLE OF FRANCE. (Illustrated.)

Ploceus Madagascariensis (Russ), *Loxia Madagascariensis*, *Cardinalis Madagascar*, *Ploceus Madagascar*, *Euplectes ruber*, *Calyphantria Madagascar*. English dealers' name—Madagascar Weaver-bird. German name—"Madagascar Webervogel." French name—"Le Foudi."

The Red-headed Weaver-bird is best known as Madagascar Weaver, the former name having the disadvantage of been easily confounded with that of the Red-faced Weaver-bird. As the name signifies, the Madagascar Weaver is a native of that island. Imported to St. Helena, this Weaver-bird has increased there with such rapidity, that he is blamed for doing damage to crops. The Madagascar Weavers arriving in England from beyond the seas come mostly from St. Helena, those from Isle of France being, as a rule, shipped to Bordeaux, Marseilles, or other French ports. According to the latitude under which the Madagascar Weavers are born, they will assume their magnificent plumage towards the end of our summer or the beginning of our winter. This Weaver does not display the strong contrasts of intense black and bright orange, or crimson, or yellow, like the Bishops; but his prevailing colour is perhaps even more striking, and its effect is increased by the greater part of the bird being of the brightest tint—that is, intense scarlet. The brown wings and tail, each feather slightly shaded with faint olive-green, do not heighten the beauty of the bird much.

In the aviary the Madagascar Weaver, when in colour, is as inclined to fight other male Weaver-birds as any Bishop, but his mode of attack is different. Whilst the Bishops erect their feathers and raise their bodies into an almost upright position, the Madagascar will lean his head and body forward, and dart with head well down and drooping wings straight upon his enemy. When the room is very large, the disputes arising when several pairs of various Weaver-birds are kept together will not matter very much, because after a time each pair will establish itself supreme in some part of the room, and will only resent intrusion; but in a cage or small aviary fatal consequences are but too likely to result from such struggles.

The nest of the Madagascar Weaver-bird is entered from below, and consists of an elongated ball with a short tube bent downwards attached to its side. A remarkable feature in all the Weaver-birds' nests is that whilst the top is so very thick, the bottom and sides are so thin that the eggs can be seen through the interstices of the material composing the nest. Dr. Russ first bred Madagascar Weaver-birds in 1869, and since then others have been equally successful; but to wait two or three years until cage-bred Weavers come into colour is a long time. As regards food and treatment, precisely the same applies that has been written about the Weaver-birds in general.

RED-BEAKED WEAVER-BIRD (*Quelea sanguinirostris*), WEST AFRICA. (Illustrated.)

Ploceus sanguinirostris (Russ), *Loxia sanguinirostris*, *Emberiza quelea*, *Passer Senegalensis erythrorrhynchus*, *Fringilla queléa*, *Ploceus Lathami*, *Euplectes sanguinirostris*, *Quelea occidentalis*, *Hyphantica sanguinirostris*, *Quelea Lathami*, *Quelea oricutalis*, *Coccothraustes sanguinirostris*, *Euplectes gregarius*, *Loxia Africana et quelea socia*, *Emberiza quelea*, *Ploceus Æthiopicus*. English dealers' name—Red-beaked Weaver-bird. German name—"Rothschuäbeliger Webervogel," or "Dioeh," or "Blutschnabelweber." French name—"Le Travailleur."

The Red-beaked Weaver is the most common and cheapest of all the Weaver-birds, but for all that one to be strongly recommended to amateurs, and especially to beginners, for the bird is very hardy, can be kept almost anywhere and in any numbers, and will amuse his owner by his industry in weaving, for which reason the French have named him "Travailleur." This Weaver, whose appearance is much like that of a hen-sparrow, with a red beak, can generally be bought for the small sum of five shillings per pair, and though his plumage when in full colour cannot be compared with that of the magnificent Bishops, it is yet rather pretty, for the face of the male will become black, and the head, throat, and chest will be suffused with a pretty roseate tint. The hen-bird will, like all Weaver-birds, retain the former colour of her plumage, but her beak will in the breeding season become of a wax-like yellow colour.

In a small cage these Weavers will interlace bits of Berlin wool between the bars of their cages; but to appreciate these interesting birds several pairs should be placed in an open-air aviary, which should be plentifully studded with shrubs, and additional branches should be fixed in convenient positions. Lively scenes of great industry will then ensue, and perfect colonies of nests will be constructed as if by magic. The birds will scarcely allow themselves the time to quarrel, and will peaceably build any number of nests close to each other. A variety of Finches might be kept in the same aviary without absolute risk of life or limb, for the Red-beaked Weaver-bird is not spiteful, but the other inhabitants of the aviary would scarcely lead a happy life. In his restless anxiety to weave nests, anything comes handy to the Red-beaked Weaver-bird, and a small Finch coming near him would at once find himself minus a wing or tail feather, a friendly pecking at the neighbour's plumage being more convenient to the Red-beaked Weaver than a search after a bit of fibre.

To breed these birds in captivity has been shown by experience to be more difficult than the breeding of more valuable kinds, but for the purpose of observing his strange constructive cleverness, and with the object of gaining experience in the way to treat Weaver-birds, the Red-beaked Weaver is invaluable. Seeds are the principal food of this and all Weavers, to which a very little animal food should be added whilst the birds are in full colour.

YELLOW-SHOULDERED WEAVER-BIRD (*Euplectes capensis*), AFRICA.

Ploceus capensis (Russ), *Loxia capensis*, *Coccothraustes capensis*, *Loxia phalerata*, *Oryx capensis*, *Pyromelæna capensis*. English dealers' name—Caffre Finch. German name—"Sammtwebervogel."

Considerably larger than the preceding Weavers, the Yellow-shouldered Weaver-bird, or Caffre Finch, is nearly the size of a Starling—a strong-beaked and strong-limbed bird, which I found quarrelsome beyond endurance, though Dr. Russ gives him a better character. This Weaver-bird—*i.e.*, the male—is of very rich velvet-like black all over, except the wings, which are dark brown, but a bright yellow back will be displayed whenever the bird droops the wings. The female, and when out of colour the male bird, are dark brown, with light brown markings. For the aviary the bird is unsuitable, except perhaps if kept amongst Starlings; but then the probability is that he will neglect the seed-food and live entirely on soft food, whereby the Yellow-shouldered, like any other Weaver-bird, will get out of condition. According to Dr. Russ the Caffre Finches breed more easily than other Weaver-birds, but most amateurs will get rid of this clumsy and hard-biting specimen of his tribe after a short time. Among the shrubs planted in the aviary they will commit havoc from sheer mischief.

RED-FACED WEAVER-BIRD (*Foudia erythrops*), WEST AFRICA. (Illustrated.)

Ploceus erythrops (Russ), *Euplectes erythrops*, *Quelea capitata*, *Quelea erythrops*, *Calyphantria erythrops*. English dealers' name—Red-headed or Red-faced Weaver-bird. German name—"Rothköpfiger Webervogel." French name—"Dioch à tête rouge."

All the preceding Weavers had long been well known to amateurs and collectors of live foreign birds before the Red-faced Weaver-bird appeared in the market. Even the Zoological Society of London did not obtain a specimen until 1871. Since then the bird has arrived in considerable numbers, but somehow he has not found much favour. As shown in the illustration, the head of this Weaver assumes a bright blood-red colour in the breeding season, the female bird of course showing no trace of such a change. All that need be said about this bird is that he does not build as industriously as the Red-beaked Weaver, and that he is extremely difficult to breed. He is neither as beautiful as a Bishop nor as interesting as the Red-beaked Weaver, and therefore in the somewhat unfortunate predicament of missing his mark in the estimation of his would-be friends. In the aviary he is comparatively peaceful.

There are a number of other Weaver-birds, but they are not as frequently imported as those named and described.

52

CHAPTER XLVIII.

TRUE FINCHES.

THE next family of birds, that of the *Fringillidæ*, or True Finches, will require and deserve all the space the limit of these pages affords. Amongst these the two first are natives of North America, and they are birds which deserve to be as popular as they are. To me they always seemed to be the American representatives of our Linnet and of our Chaffinch, but their plumage is infinitely more brilliant.

INDIGO-BIRD (*Cyanospiza cyanea*), NORTH AMERICA. (Illustrated.)

Fringilla cyanea (Russ), *Tanagra cyanea*, *Emberiza cyanea*, *cærulea et cyanella*, *Passerina cyanea*, *Spiza cyanea*. English dealers' name—Indigo-bird. German name—"Indigofink." French name—"Le Ministre."

In size and in his winter plumage the Indigo-bird resembles somewhat our Linnet. But about March or April the unpretending brown plumage of the male will change to a deep blue, and this colour the bird will retain until autumn. The female retains her modest brown garb all the year round. Large numbers of Indigo-birds are brought to Europe every summer, and mostly by German Canary dealers, who go out to America with German Canaries and Bullfinches, and bring back Indigo-birds and Nonpareil Finches. This will explain why these American Finches are, as a rule, offered for sale in German canary-cages. But among every hundred males imported there are only a very few females, and it is by no means easy to obtain a hen-bird when such a one happens to be wanted.

In the cage the Indigo-bird will sing during the summer months, and though his song is not equal to that of a Linnet, yet it is agreeable enough. In the aviary, however, he will live in silence and peace. To introduce a hen-bird is not advisable, as the chances of breeding the Indigo-bird are very small indeed, and the probability of quarrels arising is increased.

Although the Indigo-bird is generally fed on seeds only, every bird-keeper will soon find out that this is a mistake, for the bird will neither remain healthy nor endure long on such a diet. A little animal food, in the shape of a few mealworms, flies, or spiders, is indispensable to him, and giving these regularly, the Indigo-bird will soon become so tame that he will take insects from between the fingers. During the summer months the Indigo-bird is plentiful in the northern parts of the United States of America, but in the autumn he migrates southwards towards the Mississippi region. With proper treatment the bird is well able to live all the year round in an English open-air aviary, displaying only a little restlessness at the period of migration. Cross-breeding with Canaries has been attempted, but with very little success. In the very rare cases where young cross-breeds resulted, their colours were disappointing.

NONPAREIL FINCH (*Cyanospiza ciris*), NORTH AMERICA. (Illustrated.)

Fringilla ciris (Russ), *Emberiza ciris*, *Passerina ciris*, *Spiza ciris*. English dealers' name—Nonpareil. German name—"Papstfink." French name—"Le Pape," or "Nonpareil."

Surely this Finch is the American cousin of our Chaffinch. The colours and their arrangement are very similar, only infinitely more bright in the case of the American Nonpareil. The slate colour of our Chaffinch's head is bright blue on the Nonpareil; the dull brown-red of the Chaffinch's breast we see as vermilion on his American relative; and the brown back is represented by a pretty olive colour. Few cage-birds will arrest the attention of any one who sees them for the first time as certainly as this beautiful Finch is sure to do. His song is agreeable, though not as remarkable as his beauty of plumage. Like the Indigo-bird, the Nonpareil is imported in considerable numbers, but hen-birds, whose plumage is of dull olive colour, darker on the back than underneath, are rarely brought over.

The young male Nonpareil Finches resemble their mothers, and assume a highly ornate plumage only in the third summer. It is therefore as likely as not that birds believed to be hens, and bought for breeding, are found to be young males. In the wild state the habits of the Nonpareil Finch are described as being very similar to those of the Chaffinch, whilst in the cage he should be fed exactly like the Indigo-bird—viz., on seeds and a little insect food. Breeding Nonpareils is not difficult, but scarcely to be recommended to amateurs. Three years is a long time to wait until the young male birds are in full colour, and even then cage-bred Nonpareils would never be as bright and beautiful as the imported specimens. It is, in fact, difficult to preserve the bright colours of old birds for a great length of time when kept in confinement. The crimson breast becomes but too often orange or yellow. To retain his beauty the Nonpareil requires, more than many other cage-birds, sunshine, pure water, shady growing bushes where to seek repose at pleasure, besides suitable food.

MELODIOUS FINCH (*Phonipara canora*), CUBA.

Fringilla canora (Russ), *Loxia canora*, *Pyrrhula collaris*, *Passerina collaris*, *Euethia canora*. English dealers' name—Cuba Finch. German name—"Kubafink," or "Gelbkragen." French name—"Chanteur de Cuba."

A charming, lively, but bold and quarrelsome little bird is the Melodious or Cuba Finch, a native of Cuba, where he lives on seeds, and loves to nip a little honey off flowers, or to feast on spilled sugar near the plantations. His song is over-praised in calling the bird Melodious Finch, and the French name, Chanteur de Cuba, can only be justified by the absence of better songsters from Cuba. The Melodious Finch is one of the very smallest Finches, and about the size of the Amaduvade. His prevailing colour is olive-green, the face, cheeks, and throat are black, and round the throat is a broad collar of yellow tint. The breast is black, gradually fading to grey and dull white over the abdomen. The female is similar, but the yellow collar in her case is dull, and looks as if washed out; the breast is dull grey instead of black.

In the aviary these tiny Finches are extremely lively and interesting, but veritable fighting cocks. They live very well on seeds, and require no extra care in winter. The facility with which the Cuba Finches breed has raised them so much in the estimation of amateurs that they command now prices about four times as high as ten years ago. And to breed them is very amusing, for they will build a nest nearly as cleverly as any Weaver-bird, and very similarly constructed. Branches of Arbor Vitæ or firs are most to their taste, and to these they will fix a nest about the size and shape of a goose's egg, with a tube opening downwards attached to the side, which serves as a door. The eggs are found to vary in colour from white, with small green spots at the thick end, to greenish or bluish white, with minute black, red, and brown spots. Male and female are frequently found sitting together; and Dr. Russ, as well as many amateurs, brought up many broods of this Finch in the cage and in the aviary. The young birds leave the nest very early and when scarcely fledged, but must be removed for their protection as soon as their parents build again, otherwise it is quite likely that their father may kill them.

OLIVE FINCH (*Phonipara olivacea*), JAMAICA.

Fringilla lepida (Russ), *Emberiza olivacea, Emberiza dominicensis, Passerina lepida, Passerina olivacea, Spermophila olivacea, Euethia lepida.* English dealers' name—Olive Cuba Finch. German name—"Grössere Kubafink." French name—"Grand Chanteur de Cuba."

The Olive Finch is also found in Cuba, and although called larger, he is very similar in size to his cousin, the Melodious Cuba Finch. This bird is not as often met with as the former, and then frequently mistaken for and sold as the female of the Melodious Finch, although it is easy to distinguish the two species. The Olive Finch has not the yellow collar which marks the last-named bird, but only a very small yellow mark from the eye downwards, and a minute patch of yellow where the upper throat meets the lower mandible. These yellow markings are bordered by broader bands of black, and the rest of the bird is olive-green, the lower part more greyish-green. The female is similar, but the yellow marks are pale and faint. Habits and food of the Olive Finch are the same as those of the Melodious Finch.

CARDINALS.

We next come to a group of well-known birds of brilliant plumage and some pretensions as songsters, viz., the "Cardinals." True Finches they are, but considerably larger than any Finches thus far described, for they are about the size of a European Grosbeak. All are natives of South America, and prove very hardy, easily kept, and easily bred cage-birds. Seeds, with the addition of a little animal or soft food, will maintain them for many years, and if they are kept singly or in pairs, they are sure to please by their song and by their enduring beauty. But let me warn the reader always to keep Cardinals singly or in pairs, and never with birds of their own kind, or with smaller Finches. Peace and happiness there may be for a time in an aviary containing Cardinals, but some day during the Cardinal's breeding season a smaller bird will be found minus legs or eyes or brain; or the owner of the aviary may watch how some unlucky little bird is mercilessly driven about until he falls down exhausted, or with fractured skull, or frightened to death.

RED-CRESTED CARDINAL (*Paroaria cucullata*), SOUTH AMERICA. (Illustrated.)

Coccothraustes cucullatus (Russ), *Loxia cucullata, Fringilla cucullata, Spiza cucullata, Calytrophorus cucullatus, Cardinalis cucullatus.* English dealers' name—Red-crested Cardinal. German name—"Gehäubter grauer Kardinal." French name—"Cardinal huppé," or "Paroare huppé."

The Red-crested Cardinal is the Cardinal *par excellence*, and is meant when dealers speak of Cardinals without specifying which kind they refer to. This sleek bird, prettily marked grey, white and black, with his crimson head and crest, is sure to attract the notice of every beholder. His great activity, more than his considerable size, requires a roomy cage, wherein with fair treatment a Cardinal will keep his plumage in perfect condition, entirely indifferent as to the temperature in which he is kept. Some amateurs speak highly of the Red-crested Cardinal's song, which I found composed of rather shrill and loud, short notes; however, tastes differ. It is not difficult to breed this bird in an aviary, where he will build his nest in a bush, something after the manner of Thrushes. Live ants' eggs are undoubtedly the best food for bringing up the young brood, but too often the parent birds vex their owners by braining their young. The female is exactly like the male bird, in some cases a very little smaller. For food and treatment see above.

Vincent Brooks Day & Son Lith.

1. BLACK-CRESTED OR GREEN CARDINAL. 3. RED-CRESTED CARDINAL.

RED-HEADED CARDINAL (*Paroaria larvata*), BRAZIL.

Coccothraustes dominicanus (Russ), *Loxia dominicana, Spiza dominicana, Spiza larvata, Fringilla dominicana, Paroaria dominicana, Calyptrophorus dominicanus, Cardinalis larvatus.* English dealers' name—Pope-bird, or Dominican Cardinal. German name—"Dominikaner Kardinal." French name—"Cardinal Dominiquain."

The Red-headed or Dominican Cardinal, often called Pope by the dealers, completes a curious list of popular bird names, in which nearly all the dignities of the hierarchy are represented. We have a Pope, several Cardinals, Bishops, a Parson Finch, and a variety of Nuns.

The Red-headed Cardinal is very similar to the Red-crested Cardinal in every respect, except that the crest is absent, and that his size is a trifle inferior. The feathers of this bird's head are all short, as in the case of other Finches, but the scarlet colour is the same as the Red-crested Cardinals. Years ago the Crestless or Dominican Cardinal used to be frequently obtainable, but for some time past the birds have been very rare, and I have seen none offered for sale for years. Dealers have been accused of selling Red-headed Cardinals as the female of the Red-crested species; but such accusations are easily and far too freely made. And it may here be mentioned that some amateurs too often suspect intentions of fraud where none has been attempted. When dealing in foreign birds, mistakes must and will occur; but the buyers are more frequently at fault than the experienced dealers. In the whole course of my considerable experience I have not once found myself wilfully deceived, although as regards many birds the dealers as well as myself have been mistaken at the time of sale. Respecting food, &c., see page 412.

YELLOW-BILLED CARDINAL (*Paroaria capitata*), CHILI.

Coccothraustes capitatus (Russ), *Tachyphonus capitatus, Cardinalis capitata.* Dealers' name—Brown-throated or Yellow-billed Cardinal. German name—"Mantel Kardinal." French name—"Cardinal à gorge brune."

In 1873 the Zoological Gardens purchased a pair of Yellow-billed Cardinals, which about that time were imported now and then, but have lately disappeared again from the market. This species is smaller than the Dominican Cardinal, and not much larger than a Bullfinch. It is, like the Red-headed or Dominican Cardinal, crestless. The bill is wax-like yellowish-brown, wherefore the name; but the German name, signifying "Cloaked Cardinal," seems preferable, for the back and wings of this bird are darker than those of the other Cardinals. The head down to the breast is crimson, a brown patch marking the throat. I would venture to place this rare Cardinal in an aviary with small birds, but not to winter him out of doors, for he seemed to me to have less stamina than the others.

BLACK-CRESTED CARDINAL (*Gubernatrix cristatella*), SOUTH AMERICA. (Illustrated.)

Coccothraustes cristatellus (Russ), *Emberiza cristatella, Emberiza gubernatrix, Gubernatrix cristata, Lophocorythus gubernatrix, Cardinalis cristatella.* English dealers' name—Green Cardinal. German name—"Grüner Kardinal." French name—"Cardinal vert."

The Black-crested or Green Cardinal is, as the illustration shows, a very pretty though not brilliantly coloured bird. I confess to a special predilection in his favour, for I found him the most gentle of Cardinals, and every pair I had bred without difficulty. The cigar nest-box illustrated in the introduction was one containing a Green Cardinal's nest, in which young were hatched and successfully reared. Old birds will live on canary, millet, and hemp seed, to which a few oats may be added with advantage, and a mealworm at times will prove very acceptable. The Green Cardinals always built their nests in my aviary without the least shyness, constructing a very fair nest in a cigar-box. Three or four light blue eggs, with dark brown spots, were laid and assiduously hatched by the hen, the tip of whose bill could just be seen projecting over the edge of the front part of the improvised nest-box. About fourteen or sixteen days matured the eggs, and the young birds were well nurtured by both their parents. But a liberal supply of mealworms generally doomed the young brood to an early death, and stimulated the old birds to lay again. Cautioned by experience, I avoided mealworms, and by the substitution of fresh ants' eggs, egg-food mixed with soaked ants' eggs, and Thrushes' food, succeeded in bringing up several broods.

It is a curious fact that several books on foreign cage-birds say the female of the Green Cardinal resembles the male closely. Surely those writers have never seen a pair, for every child could tell the difference at a glance. If the reader will look at the illustration of the male Green Cardinal, and imagine all the bright green colour removed, and a light grey with just a greenish tint at edges substituted, he will have a fair picture of the female. Young males resemble the female on leaving the nest, but assume a marked green tinge in a few weeks, and cannot be distinguished from old birds when twelve months old.

CARDINAL GROSBEAK (*Cardinalis Virginianus*), NORTH AMERICA. (Illustrated.)

Coccothraustes Virginianus (Russ), *Loxia cardinalis*, *Coccothraustes cardinalis*, *Fringilla cardinalis*, *Pitylus cardinalis*. English dealers' name—Virginian Nightingale, or Red Cardinal. German name—"Rother Cardinal." French name—"Cardinal de Virginie."

Enthusiastic American writers have named the Cardinal Grosbeak "Virginian Nightingale," and have described his song as equal or superior to that of the European Nightingale. Tastes differ. According to American taste the Mocking-bird "beats all creation" in song, whilst most people on this side of the Atlantic prefer the Thrush's song. I have heard frogs called Dutch nightingales, and the poor Nightingale must lend her name to all sorts of musicians. However, the Cardinal Grosbeak, or Red Cardinal, is certainly a diligent and melodious songster, though to my taste the song is too loud. Dr. Russ frequently heard the Red Cardinal sing in his bird-room after dark; and other observers, who kept hen-birds in separate cages, state that they also sing. In their wild state the Red Cardinals will probably sleep silently at night, and the female will probably be too busy with her progeny to practise singing. At all events, those Virginian Cardinals which I kept in an open-air aviary sang only in broad daylight, and preferred to display their musical talents perched on the top of a bush or clinging to the wires.

The bird is one of great beauty, and deserves all his popularity. Whether we overpraise his vocal merits or not, his song surpasses in richness that of most other foreign birds, and with moderate care the Red Cardinal is one of the most hardy and enduring cage-birds. His plumage is of a uniform brilliant red tint, excepting the face, which is black. The head is ornamented by a red crest, which the bird can erect at pleasure. The beak is strong and red like the plumage, and if I had had to name the bird, I should have felt inclined to call him Mephistopheles. The hen is rusty brown. Contrasted with green foliage, the Red Cardinal looks very beautiful indeed, and he retains his beauty all the year round, and with proper treatment for many years. If improperly fed, or deprived of sunshine, fresh air, and plenty of water to bathe in, the red plumage will become dull.

Seeds—*i.e.*, canary, millet, oats, hemp-seed—and Indian corn are the staple food of this Cardinal, but a little egg-food, ants' eggs, chopped meat, a few mealworms, spiders, flies, or beetles should be given in small quantities, if not daily yet several times per week. Ripe fruit, green peas, and elderberries he is very fond of. Few foreign birds are as indifferent to changes in temperature as the Red Cardinal, and he may be seen in open-air aviaries as cheerful and happy during a severe frost as on the warmest summer day.

To breed him is not difficult, for he will build his nest in a box, a German canary-cage, or after the manner of Thrushes and Blackbirds in a bush, and rear his brood with very fair success, unless too many mealworms be given, which the old birds would find irresistible to swallow, and the effects of which would probably make them lay again and neglect their young. The hen sits alone on the eggs, guarded and fed by her husband. The eggs are hatched in about a fortnight, and both parents feed the young. In the aviary I cannot praise the Red Cardinal, and though some amateurs have kept the bird without evil consequences with small Finches, I do not trust his temper nor his disposition. During the breeding season two pairs in the same aviary would mean death to one and probably damage to the other, whilst during autumn and winter old and young Red Cardinals roam in flocks through orchards in North America, and are sent to Europe in cages containing several dozen heads.

The Red Cardinal could easily be acclimatised in Europe, for Dr. Russ relates an authentic instance of a pair having escaped in Germany during autumn which was re-captured next spring after a very severe winter, through the accidental discovery of their nest containing a young brood, in a wood several miles away from the place where the birds escaped. The old birds were recaptured by means of bird-lime, and the young were successfully brought up. Newly-imported birds are mostly shy, and should be slowly accustomed to their new surroundings. Box-cages with canvas tops are very useful for the purpose, and preserve the bird from damage. They should be placed in such a position that the inmates are not exposed to being frightened by the near approach of human beings; their feeder the Red Cardinals will soon learn to know. It is curious that these American birds should still be comparatively dear. A pair of Virginian Nightingales costs as much as several pairs of Australian Undulated Parrakeets, and more than a fresh imported Grey Parrot or White Cockatoo.

GENUS SPERMOPHILA.

Under the generic name of *Spermophila* the list of the Zoological Society of London contains the names of seven little Finches, viz.:—

SPECTACLED FINCH.

Spermophila ophthalmica (Russ), *Coccothraustes ophthalmicus*; *Brillen Pfäffchen.*

LINED FINCH.

Spermophila lineola (Russ), *Coccothraustes lineola*; *Weiss stirniges Pfäffchen.*

BLUISH FINCH.

Spermophila cærulescens (Russ), *Coccothraustes cærulescens*; *Blaupfäffchen.*

WHITE-THROATED FINCH.

Spermophila albagularis (Russ), *Coccothraustes albagularis*; *Weisskehliges Pfäffchen.*

REDDISH FINCH.

Spermophila nigro-aurantia (Russ), *Coccothraustes aurantius*; *Pomeranzengelbes Pfäffchen.*

PLUMBEOUS FINCH.

Spermophila plumbea (Russ), *Coccothraustes plumbeus*; *Bleigraues Pfäffchen.*

HALF-WHITE FINCH.

Spermophila hipoleuca (Russ), *Coccothraustes hypoleucus*; *Rothschnabeliges Pfäffchen.*

These little Finches are all natives of South America, and vary in size from that of the Amaduvade Finch to that of a Siskin. They are distinguished by a singularly thick and arched beak, which gives them a peculiar appearance. Their plumage is unpretending, and their song quite insignificant; but they are funny-looking, amiable little beings, who are content to lead a perfectly harmless existence in the aviary munching millet and canary seed. In the course of years I have kept all those named above without discovering anything specially interesting in any one of them. As a rule these Spermophila Finches are only met with in single specimens by chance. Their value is uncertain. If a dealer wanted to dispose of any, a few shillings might buy them; if any one wanted some kind specially, the offer of several sovereigns might not bring any for sale. But as only a very few collectors would buy these birds at present, and a larger number could scarcely be sold at all, these little Finches are, and are likely to remain rare.

One of the most frequent and prettiest is the Lined Finch, a bird about the size of a Siskin. The head and back are black, with a greenish gloss. Right down over the forehead is a white stripe, and across each cheek is another white stripe, giving the bird the appearance as if his black forehead were marked with a white cross. On each black wing is a white spot, and underneath the bird is white, but the beak is black. Dr. Russ mentions no less than twenty-seven varieties of Spermophila Finches.

The food of these little Finches consists of millet and canary seed, and I found them by no means delicate.

SAFFRON FINCH (*Sycalis flaveola*), BRAZIL. (Illustrated.)

Fringilla Brasiliensis (Russ), *Emberiza Brasiliensis*, *Passerina flava*, *Linaria Aurifrons*, *Sycalis Brasiliensis*, *Crithagra Brasiliensis*, *Sycalis flaveola*. English dealers' name—Saffron Finch. German name—"Safranfink." French name—"Chardonneret à front d'or."

The Saffron Finch, sometimes called Brazilian Canary, is a wonderfully hardy bird considering the climate of the land of his birth. I found him thrive on very simple food, and have seen broods of young Saffron Finches leave the nest at Christmas, as well as in spring, summer, and autumn; in fact, they seemed to breed all the year round in my aviary. As shown in the illustration, the Saffron Finch is of bright yellow colour, with a shade of orange marking the face of the male. The female is similar, but the yellow body-colour is not quite so bright as the males, and the orange tint on the face is very faint. Young Saffron Finches attain their adult plumage only after the second year has been completed; and very often young birds are mistaken for hen-birds. For this reason a young Saffron Finch about four months old has also been illustrated. The sexes cannot be distinguished until the plumage has fully arrived at maturity. The greenish-brown young Saffron Finches may be males or females; no one can tell for certain which they are. In size the Saffron Finch equals a Norwich Canary, but as regards song he does not take a high rank; though not unpleasant, his song is insignificant.

The love-making of a pair of Saffron Finches is a very peculiar affair, consisting in either the male bird persecuting the hen and punishing her severely if she be not quite ready to receive his advances, or if the male should happen to be of a retiring disposition, the female may be seen pursuing him vigorously. Thus there is sure to be a family quarrel before the beginning of each brood, and these domestic feuds frequently become so inveterate as to upset the equanimity of all the other smaller inhabitants of an aviary. Presently, again, the male Saffron Finch may be seen pouring out his love-song to his mate, with head bent back, wings drooping and trembling, and the tail spread like a fan. Even a large cage is too small for these lively birds to breed in, but in a roomy aviary occupied by Weaver-birds, Java Sparrows, and such-like birds, the Saffron Finches will do well.

In their wild state the Saffron Finches nestle in holes of walls or of decayed trees, or in the old nests of other birds. In the aviary they seem to prefer a cigar-box (as

Vincent Brooks Day & Son Lith

1. ST. HELENA SEED-EATER OR GREEN SINGING FINCH.
2. GREY SINGING FINCH.
3. AUSTRALIAN FIRE-TAILED FINCH.
4. BANDED GRASS FINCH.
5. AUSTRALIAN WAXBILL.

illustrated in the introduction) to every other contrivance. In such a nest-box they form a rough mould with fibres, grasses, and whatever else is to hand, in which four or five eggs, closely resembling those of a Sparrow, will be laid in as many days. Male and female sit alternately on the eggs, and in about fourteen days the young Saffron Finches will be hatched. These, like the eggs, might be taken for a brood of Sparrows, but before leaving the nest a greenish tint will begin to show on the nest-feathers of the brood.

Any kind of soft food seems to do equally well for rearing Saffron Finches. A mixture of egg, bread-crumbs, and scalded seeds will be found quite sufficient, but a few mealworms or ants' eggs will also be readily accepted by the parent-birds, who when not breeding will take little else than canary and millet seed.

SINGING FINCH (*Crithagra musica*).

(Illustration drawn from live specimen in the Author's possession.)

Fringilla musica (Russ), *Estrilda musica*, *Hypochera musica*, *Fringilla leucopygos*, *Dryospiza leucopygos*, *Serinus leucopygos*, *Crithagra leucopygia*, *Pholidocoma musica*, *Serinus musicus*. English dealers' name—Grey Singing Finch. German name—"Weiss bürzeliger Grauer Sänger." French name—"Chanteur d'Afrique."

However unpretending the grey and white plumage of the African Singing Finch may be, and though the bird is absent from the list of the London Zoological Gardens, every amateur should endeavour to obtain this little songster, for his musical talents are of a very high class indeed. It seems marvellous that a little Finch, about as large as an Australian Zebra Finch, should be able to sing so loudly and yet so sweetly, and no stranger entering a bird-room in which the Grey Singing Finch was just pouring forth his melodies would suspect that the very small bird sitting on the top of some branch was capable of such a song as was just then heard.

All amateurs of song-birds owe a debt of gratitude to Dr. Russ for having practically discovered the merits of this bird. Vieillot described a Grey Singing Finch bred in captivity as long ago as 1790, but subsequently the bird seems to have disappeared from the market, and to some extent from the cognisance of subsequent authors. When the demand for foreign cage-birds increased, about the years 1860 to 1865, dealers often mistook the Grey Singing Finch for the female of the Ultramarine Finch or Combasou. Few of these unpretending grey birds arrived, fewer still were sold, dealers and amateurs left them unnoticed; and so they might have remained if Dr. Russ had not made this Finch, like every other available foreign cage-bird, a subject of careful study in his aviary. The rich music of the Grey Singing Finch's song, which would scarcely be uttered in a bird-dealer's store-cages, could not escape the Doctor's notice, and the attention of amateurs was soon drawn to him, with the result of, for a time, increasing the demand and price. When imported in larger numbers, the Grey Singing Finches often arrive sickly, and many die during the voyage or soon after, whereby the cost of the survivors becomes considerable. Brilliant and gaudy-coloured birds sell rapidly, and dealers find that the sober-coloured little songsters are, after all, only known to that minority of amateurs who study books. Thus, a dealer who imports these songsters may sell a few at a remunerative price, and find the others dying in his hands. The importation, therefore, decreased of late years to an extent much to be regretted. When once fairly recovered from the fatigue of the voyage, the Grey Singing Finches live very well, in a moderately warm temperature, on a diet of millet and canary seed, with green-meat, and a very little egg-food now and then. They breed without difficulty, but best in a roomy cage, building an open nest much like that of a Canary. The young birds are reared on scalded or soaked millet-seed and egg-food, or fresh ants' eggs, and the pairs live in great affection for each other. The plumage of the female resembles closely that of the male, but the brown marks are a trifle less distinct.

YELLOW-RUMPED SEED-EATER (*Crithagra Angolensis*), SOUTH-WESTERN AFRICA.

Fringilla Angolensis (Russ), *Fringilla tobaca, Linaria Angolensis, Linaria atrogularis, Fringilla uropygialis, Polvspiza Angolensis.* English dealers' name—Angola Singing Finch. German name—"Angolahäufling," or "Gelbbürzeliger grauer Girlitz." French name—"Chanteur d'Angola."

The Angola Singing Finch, or Yellow-rumped Seed-eater, is very similar to the Grey Singing Finch, but has a yellow patch on the rump, whilst the latter is white on the same part. The quality of his song is much inferior to that of his near relation. In other respects the birds are nearly identical.

ST. HELENA SEED-EATER (*Crithagra butyracea*), SOUTH AFRICA.

(Illustration drawn from a live specimen in the Author's possession.)

Fringilla butyracea—Hartlaubi—(Russ), *Fringilla ictera, Crithagra chrysopyga, Serinus chrysopygus, Serinus ictera, Crithagra Hartlaubii, Fringilla flavifrons* (?), *Crithagra Mossambica.* English dealers' name—Green Singing Finch. German name—"Hartlaubszeisig." French name—"Chanteur Vert," or "Chanteur de Mozambique."

Next to the Grey Singing Finch, the St. Helena Seed-eater—for which bird I prefer the name of Green Singing Finch—is the best songster among the small foreign Finches. Mr. Rutledge's brush renders a description of his plumage superfluous.

I cannot resist quoting verbatim Dr. Russ's charming and graphic description of this little favourite of mine, as an example of my enthusiastic friend's powers of observation and description :—

"From afar we hear a clear melodious note. Repeated again and again, we fancy the same song is faintly echoed. Attentively listening and watching, we observe that the hen answers each warble of the male. But great becomes our surprise that the two birds, evidently a pair, should worry each other in the liveliest manner. From early morn to late in the evening the male pursues the hen-bird, without giving her a moment's rest through the whole long day.

"When, at the beginning of my experiments in breeding, I was not yet sufficiently acquainted with this bird, I had almost become convinced that I had an old and a young male instead of a pair, the more so as the colours of the latter were nearly as bright as those of the former, and as his song was loud and powerful. Just as I was on the point of separating the birds, I luckily discovered the first preparations for nesting.

"It is a very frolicsome life which a pair of these birds lead in their honeymoon. Their constant disputes and quarrels had at first prejudiced me considerably against them, but I soon found that roguish and wanton teazing alternated with effusions of graceful tenderness. Their tenderness for each other is not so fervent as that of the Astrilds, but is displayed rather in graceful gambols, culminating in dove-like caresses, the male feeding the female from the crop, and immediately afterwards again chasing and pursuing her."

I found the Green Singing Finch enduring for many years, and breeding without difficulty in a moderately warm aviary, in which he did not in the least inconvenience a large number of other small Finches. This species is much more frequently offered for sale than the Grey Singing Finch, and less delicate than the latter.

CANARY FINCH (*Serinus Canarius*), Canary Islands.

Fringilla Canaria (Russ), *Crithagra Canaria, Dryospiza Canaria.* English dealers' name—Canary Finch. German name—"Wilder Kanarienvogel." French name—"Serin des Canaries."

The wild Canary, the progenitor of our household friend, ought to be one of the best known foreign birds, but the fact is that we know very little indeed about him. It may be taken for granted that the Canary-bird is the descendant of a green Siskin-like Finch brought from the Canary Islands three hundred years ago. At present Canary-birds are sent from Europe to the Canary Islands, and unfortunately very few wild Canaries are sent back. And even as regards these I find the authorities disagree, for the African coast opposite the Canary Islands produces several kinds of Finches belonging to the same family which are so similar that it seems difficult to determine which should be considered the true Canary Finch. A further difficulty arises from the fact that bird-catching and the export of live birds is a trade on the African coast, but little practised in the Canary Islands; wherefore birds arriving from the islands may, after all, be caught in Africa.

There are many so-called Green Canaries bred now and priced by breeders for producing high-coloured or curiously marked progeny, which resemble very much the wild Canary, who looks much like a cross between a Greenfinch and Siskin. Those who have heard the Canary's song on his native islands have praised it, but as a cage-bird the wild Canary is but a poor songster, delicate of constitution, and of unpretending plumage. When, where, and how the transmutation of colour was brought about is unfortunately not known.

The Spaniards took possession of the Canary Islands first in 1311, and again in 1478, and by them Canaries were first brought to Europe, and the birds became highly-prized pets of noble Spanish ladies. About the year 1550 a number of Canaries are said to have escaped in the Mediterranean in consequence of a Spanish vessel being shipwrecked, and these birds are supposed to have flown to the Isle of Elba. But this story seems somewhat doubtful. What chance of escape have small birds in cages on board a ship when it is being wrecked? And the Spaniards were about the last people in the world to take compassion on the little prisoners by opening their cage-doors in the excitement of a shipwreck. So much is certain, that a book published in Germany in 1669 mentions that at that time Canaries were already bred there in cages, and before the beginning of this century Canaries bred in Germany were exported in considerable numbers to England. Since then the cage-bred Canary has thrown his wild ancestor so entirely into the background, that in speaking of Canaries we never think of the little green finch to be found wild on Teneriffe and the other islands of the Canary group, but of our household friend whose plumage has been so completely altered by cage-breeding.

CHAPTER XLIX.

STARLINGS.

THE family of Starlings has a large number of representatives in America, some in Asia, and a few in Africa. If the space at my disposal were less limited, many interesting facts about foreign Starlings might be stated, but I am compelled to be brief about birds which, after all, do not come very often into the hands of amateurs.

Respecting their treatment in captivity, the importance of extreme cleanliness and plenty of bathing water cannot be over-rated. As regards food, it must be borne in mind that Starlings are insectivorous, but live also largely on fruit, and do not disdain seed if hungry. The great danger for Starlings in captivity is over-feeding, which invariably ends in fits and premature death. Their food cannot be too varied. The soft food mentioned in the introductory chapter should be given in small quantities at a time, and varied with ripe fruit—apples, pears, grapes, berries, currants, oranges, in fact any fruit which is ripe and sweet—supplemented by a few mealworms, maggots, or, best of all, spiders, and if these are not available three or four morsels of raw beef.

The Starlings are amusing, good-tempered, and sociable birds. To keep them in an aviary with other birds may do for a time, but never for long. They are very voracious, and if kept with other soft-food birds they would gorge themselves and die from over-feeding, whilst the other birds would starve, and the society of small birds would tempt Starlings sooner or later to eat one of them with perfect equanimity, long after his owner had become perfectly convinced that his particular Starling was quite free from any such desires. If kept in an aviary at all, Starlings should have one to themselves. The different species will agree, as a rule, very well; and an aviary devoted only to Starlings is very pretty, besides having the advantage that artificial heat may be entirely dispensed with.

All the Starlings love to walk on the ground, and do so with a peculiar rolling gait, closely inspecting everything. A fallen leaf they will turn over, a piece of turf will be probed by their long beak, and when they come to the food-dish their closed bill will be dipped to the very bottom, and then jerked open. In this way the contents of the dishes are turned over and minutely examined, and the richest bits will be extracted with wonderful dexterity. After a few Starlings have examined a food-dish, other soft-food birds would find only the crumbs left.

I deem it very important that Starlings should have something to exercise their beaks upon—say a piece of turf, or a deep saucerful of mould or gravel, in which to dig. For want of such exercise I have seen pitiable deformations of the beak of valuable foreign Starlings when kept in cages.

As a natural consequence of their greediness, it is very difficult to breed and rear Starlings in captivity. The young brood requires an enormous amount of food, and if we place the same without limit at the disposal of the old birds, they will either neglect their young and lay again, or over-feed themselves. I have used a little stratagem successfully. By covering their food with a layer of a quarter of an inch of fresh garden-mould, I made the old birds work for every morsel they carried to their ever-hungry young brood, and the tempting food was thus withdrawn from being constantly before their eyes. In this way I have repeatedly reared Malabar Mynahs, which have not, so far as I know, been bred anywhere else, and other Starlings could probably be reared as successfully.

RED-SHOULDERED STARLING (*Agelæus phœniceus*), NORTH AMERICA.

Sturnus phœniceus (Russ), *Oriolus phœniceus*, *Icterus phœniceus*, *Psarocolius phœniceus*, *Sturnus prædatorius.*
English dealers' name—Red-shouldered Starling. German name—"Epauletten Star."

A black bird, about the size of our European Starling, ornamented on the shoulders with a bright scarlet patch, bordered with yellow. When the bird is at rest but very little of this scarlet shoulder-patch is visible, but with outspread wings the bird is very beautiful. The female of this Starling is dark brown on the back, greyish-brown underneath.

Immense flocks of Red-shouldered Starlings appear in the Northern States of America in spring, and sometimes damage the corn-fields considerably. When the birds are paired they withdraw to swampy or marshy districts, and build their nests among reeds; at the end of the breeding season old and young birds re-assemble and roam over the fields in flights. For food see general remarks on Starlings.

Of another family of Starlings, the Trupials—*Icterus*—only two need be mentioned here, although Brehm describes no less than twenty-three varieties, all natives of North and South America. The Trupials are called Hang-nests, because they suspend their artfully-woven nests from the branches of trees. Their food consists of insects and fruit in about equal parts, and oranges they are very fond of. In the cage they may be kept on oranges and other fruit, soft-food mixture, and a few mealworms or other insects. They will endure for years, pleasing their owner by the brightness of their plumage and the quaintness of their song. Their intelligence is equal to that of our European Starling.

BALTIMORE HANG-NEST (*Icterus Baltimore*), NORTH AMERICA.

Sturnus Baltimorensis (Russ), *Oriolus Baltimore*, *Yphantes Baltimore*, *Psarocolius Baltimore.* English dealers' name—Yellow Trupial, or Baltimore Oriole. German name—"Baltimore Trupial."

The Baltimore Hang-nest, Trupial, or Oriole is somewhat smaller than a European Starling. The head, wings, and upper part of the back are black, the lower body and lower back bright reddish-orange; a white bar ornaments the wings. Most scientific writers have erroneously described the plumage of young birds, believing them to be females, whilst Mr. C. W. Gedney, of Bromley, had the best possible proof of the female being identical in colour and markings with the male, for he obtained eggs, and thereby the sex of his birds was placed beyond controversy. North America, including the eastern part of Canada, is the Baltimore Oriole's breeding-place; with the approach of autumn he migrates south as far as Central America.

BRAZILIAN HANG-NEST (*Icterus Jamacaii*), BRAZIL.

Sturnus Jamaicensis (Russ), *Oriolus Jamacaii*, *Oriolus aurantius*, *Pendulinus Jamaicensis*, *Psarocolius Jamaicensis*, *Icterus aurantius*, *Xanthornus aurantius.* English dealers' name—Jamaica Oriole. German name—"Jamaica Trupial."

The Brazilian or Jamaica Oriole is considerably larger than the Baltimore Hang-nest, and rather larger than a common European Starling. Like the Baltimore, his head and wings are deep black, but the orange of the lower body and the lower part of the back is brighter and less reddish than the Baltimore's.

MILITARY STARLING (*Sturnia militaris*), Chili.

Sturnus militaris (Russ), *Trupialis militaris*, *Pezites loica*, *Sturnella militaris*. English dealers' name—Rose-breasted Starling. German names—"Soldatenstar," "Lerchenstar," "Rosenbrüstiger Lerchenstar."

Although I have seen as many as fifty of these interesting birds at one time in a dealer's warehouse, the list of the London Zoological Gardens does not contain the bird. During the last few years I have seen no Military Starlings offered for sale, which is remarkable, because they command a high price when imported, and deserve the favour of amateurs. These birds resemble in size and shape a Thrush, and their rose-coloured breast gives these Starlings a striking appearance. The back looks like mottled light brown, each feather being black, with a pale brown rim. A red line extends from the dark brown upper beak through the eye. The female is similar, but the rose-colour on the breast is much more faint.

As regards food, see general remarks on Starlings. For a week or two the Military Starling can live on hemp-seed alone. I kept these birds in a separate cage. Dr. Russ says that he had a pair for a long time in his bird-room; they were exceedingly peaceable, only now and then the male broke a small sickly bird's skull and ate his brain.

The most brilliant of all Starlings are the *Lamprotornithinæ*, or Glossy Starlings, whose beauty words would fail to describe, and the painter's art cannot adequately represent. When these birds are basking in the sunshine, their plumage reflects the rays of light like a mass of highly burnished metal, and no cage-bird which came under my observation can compare in beauty with these Starlings. But in strong contrast to the beauty of their plumage are the execrable sounds which the Glossy Starlings utter.

In a large aviary they are not difficult to breed, and a number of the short-tailed kinds will live peaceably together. In a cage the Glossy Starlings will scarcely develop their beauty to the fullest extent, and their harsh, hoarse voice may become disagreeable. I found these birds very hardy, and kept several for over six years without any one ever showing a trace of any ailing, and at the end of this long time these old birds were as beautiful, or more so, than they were when I received them

Their food may be advantageously varied with small pieces of meat, spiders, crickets, grasshoppers, beetles, worms, and all kinds of fruit.

GREEN GLOSSY STARLING (*Lamprocolius chalybeus*), North-east Africa.

(Illustrated from live specimen lent by Mr. Charles Jamrach.)

Sturnus chalybæus (Russ), *Lamprotornis chalybæa*, *Lamprotornis niteus et chalybæus*, *Lamprotornis guttatus*, *Lamprocolius cyanotis*, *Lamprocolius Abyssinicus*. English dealers' name—Green Glossy Starling. German name—"Grünschwänziger Glanzstar."

This Glossy Starling is of the same size as our European Starling, of dark bluish-green or greenish-blue colour, according to the light in which the shining plumage is seen. A spot on the cheeks and one on the wings are of bluish tint, and the lower parts appear purple if seen in a strong light. Male and female are alike. Food, like other Starlings. The first specimen of this bird was presented to the Zoological Gardens as long ago as 1850, and in 1872 some were bred there. The nest is built in hollow trees or large nest-boxes.

1. GREEN GLOSSY STARLING. 2. MALABAR MYNAH.
3. PURPLE-HEADED GLOSSY STARLING. 4. LONG-TAILED GLOSSY STARLING.

PURPLE-HEADED GLOSSY STARLING (*Lamprocolius auratus*), West Africa.

(Illustrated from live specimen kindly lent by J. C. Marsh, Esq.)

Sturnus auratus (Russ), *Turdus auratus*, *Lamprotornis lucida*, *Lamprotornis ptilonorhynchus*, *Lamprotornis aurata*, *Juida aurata*. English dealers' name—Purple-headed Glossy Starling. French dealers' name—"Merle resplendissante." German name—"Gold Glanzstar."

The Purple-headed Glossy Starling is slightly larger than the Green Glossy Starling and his European relative, and the most brilliant of his family. The head and lower body are purply violet-blue, the throat is somewhat more violet, the back of the neck more blue. Wings and back are metallic green, and the tail purple. All the Glossy Starlings have a peculiarly flat head, but in this species the flat shape of the skull is remarkable, and the large bright yellow eye adds to the bird's peculiar appearance. The first specimen was purchased by the Zoological Gardens in 1856, and young were hatched there in 1871 and 1874.

LONG-TAILED GLOSSY STARLING (*Lamprotornis aeneus*), West Africa.

(Illustration from live specimen kindly lent by J. C. Marsh, Esq.)

Sturnus aeneus (Russ), *Turdus aeneus*, *Corvus aeneus viridis*, *Juida aenea*, *Urauges aeneus*, *Lamprotornis Eytoni*. English dealers' name—Long-tailed Glossy Starling. French name—"Merle resplendissante à Longue Quene." German name—"Bronze Glanzstar," or "Erzglanzstar," or "Glanzelster," or "Langschwänzige Glanzdrossel."

The manners of the Long-tailed Glossy Starling resemble—like his form, size, and tail—much more those of a Magpie than of a Starling. In size the bird is considerably larger than all other Starlings, and the form of his long tail, as well as the manner of carrying it, is similar to our Magpies.

A peculiar feature of this Starling's plumage is the black head, with a sheen on the black feathers like burnished brass. The body-feathers lie not quite as close as those of the Purple-headed Starling, and do not therefore reflect the light from as large a surface, although the purple and blue colours are fully as rich, and the long purple-violet tail, with very faint wave-like bars, renders the appearance of the bird even more remarkable than that of any other Glossy Starling. Some naturalists, who have observed the Long-tailed Glossy Starling in his native woods, write of a song which is said to be heard at times. I have kept this Starling for years, and never heard anything but a hoarse, piercing, and disagreeable call.

Male and female are said to resemble each other closely, but the female is believed to be smaller. I found one day a Long-tailed Glossy Starling in a bird-shop at Brighton, and purchased him because he was smaller than my old friend at home, thinking that I had secured a hen-bird. When the two Long-tailed Starlings were brought together, all seemed to be well as long as I was present, but I had scarcely turned my back when the smaller bird was killed outright. The murderous survivor subsequently came into the possession of Mr. Marsh, who, contrary to my advice, turned him loose in a bird-room occupied by all kinds of birds, from Parrots to fancy Finches. There this same Starling proved quite peaceful and harmless; but, for all that, I should as soon keep a cat in an aviary with other birds as a Long-tailed Glossy Starling.

Their food consists, in their wild state, of insects and fruit, the proportions depending on the seasons. In confinement they will eat almost anything, from raw beef to boiled potatoes, and from mealworms and crickets to pears and grapes.

MALABAR MYNAH (*Sturnia Malabarica*), HINDOSTAN.

(The illustration was drawn from live specimens bred by the Author.)

Sturnus Malabaricus (Russ), *Turdus Malabaricus*, *Sturnia Malabarica*, *Gracula Malabarica*, *Pastor pagodarum*, *Acridotheres Malab.*, *Pastor Malab. et caniceps*, *Blythi Malab. et cinereus*, *Pastor rufocinereus*, *Hetaerornis Malab.*, *Maina affinis*, *Temenechus Malab.* English dealers' name—Grey-headed Pagoda Starling. German name—"Grauköpfiger Mainastar."

A dwarf among the Starlings is the Malabar Mynah, for he is but slightly larger than a Chaffinch. The soft brown of his body and the grey colour of the head and neck harmonise well. In the aviary the bird is extremely gentle, and his short but frequently repeated song is not disagreeable. Undoubtedly the best-tempered and most amiable of all the foreign Starlings, this species should be made welcome to any aviary. I possessed a pair for more than six years, and had the opportunity of watching how these intelligent birds educated themselves until they learnt the serious business of bringing up a family, which they did without interfering with other birds.

Their first attempt at nesting consisted of a few dry leaves dropped into a small parrot-box. In the following year they made a slovenly nest of leaves, hay, and fibres, and laid two blue eggs with dark brown spots. These they left often, preferring to creep in and out of the box to the slow work of incubating. A subsequent laying they hatched; but as soon as the young made their entry into the world, the old birds threw them out of the nest. The broods of the following year shared a similar fate, but by that time the old birds fed them for a few days. At last they brought up one young, and the year after the Starlings took possession of a cigar nest-box, and went to work steadily, building a very fair nest, in which they hatched three eggs, and brought up the brood with great care. I followed the plan of never giving much food at a time, and making the birds work for it. Their food-dish, containing egg, bread-crumbs, German paste, and ants' eggs, I partly covered with a thin layer of garden-mould, and thus taught them to dig out the richer bits. One hour I gave them a few mealworms, another some spiders, or little morsels of raw beef, or a handful of live ants, mould, and larvæ, and so on, until the young birds were able to take care of themselves.

ROSE-COLOURED PASTOR (*Pastor roseus*), INDIA.

Sturnus roseus (Russ), *Turdus roseus*, *Turdus Seleucis et suratensis*, *Merula rosea*, *Acridotheres roseus*, *Gracula rosea*. Dealers' name—Rose Starling. German name—"Rosenstar," "Star Amsel," "Heuschreckenstar."

The Rose-coloured Pastor is a native of India, but sometimes considerable numbers of this bird visit Southern Europe, and periodically he is met with in Central and even in Northern Europe. His wanderings seem to depend on the fruitfulness of grasshoppers. I doubted the accounts I had read of Starlings waging a war of extermination against locusts and grasshoppers; till seeing one day a Rose-coloured Pastor offered for sale, I remembered that I had a hot-pit over-run with crickets, and resolved to try an experiment. The Pastor was placed in an aviary, and I proceeded to catch crickets by placing balls of crumpled brown paper into the warmest corners of the pit. Hundreds of lively crickets could be shaken out of the papers in the morning, and I could thus produce at pleasure something like a swarm of grasshoppers. A well-bred terrier will face any number of his natural enemies—rats; but his zeal is nothing compared to the Pastor's powers of methodical destruction of grasshoppers and crickets. The crickets covered the ground on which the bird stood; they ran up his legs and over his body, and coolly would he peck away, devouring one after the other, until none were left. Where he put all the insects seemed incomprehensible; but the immense services which such insectivorous birds, with endless appetites, can render to the agriculturist, are palpable.

The Rose-coloured Pastor is a pretty bird, about the size of our common Starling. The head is ornamented with a tuft of jet-black feathers reaching down to the nape of the neck; the throat and part of the breast, as well as the wings and tail, are bluish or brownish-black; the rest of the body is a pale rose-colour. Unfortunately this pink tint becomes dingy in confinement.

SMALL HILL MYNAH (*Gracula religiosa*), SOUTHERN INDIA.

Sturnus religiosus (Russ); *Gracula minor, Gracula musica, Gracula Indica, Pastor musicus, Mainatus, Mainatus Javanus, Eulabes Indicus, Eulabes religiosa.* German name—"Meina," or "Gemeiner Beo."

This Mynah, sometimes called Mino, is the talking cage-bird of India and China, and combines power of song with a great talent for learning tunes, and of imitating the human voice. Talking or singing Mynahs are highly prized in the East, and for those specimens which reach Europe sufficiently high prices are asked to make most amateurs pause.

I once purchased a Hill Mynah, and though I have much patience in matters concerning the aviary, I soon got rid of him again at any price. The appetite of these birds seems insatiable, and they will feed as long as any food is left in the dish. The amount of dirt is correspondingly great. To obviate over-feeding, a Mynah should be fed about three times a day, in small quantities at a time, and to keep his cage tolerably clean would necessitate cleaning twice a day. In the East, where servants cost little and do not grumble, such attention is more practicable than in Europe, and without such minute attention Mynahs will become offensive or die.

These birds may be kept on Thrushes' food, but will soon become accustomed to eat almost anything. Small pieces of raw beef, plenty of ripe fruit, and a little boiled rice are very good additions to their diet.

The Hill Mynah is a little larger than a European Starling, but much stouter. His plumage is black, with a white bar on the wings. The feet and the rather short beak are yellow. A ring of the same tint surrounds the eye. Yellow patches on the sides of the head, and collar-like appendages of bare orange-coloured skin extending from the ears backwards, distinguish the Hill Mynah beyond the possibility of mistake.

CHAPTER L.

PARROTS AND PARRAKEETS.

THE docility of the Parrots, the facility with which most kinds can be accustomed to cage-life, and the talent of some species for imitating the human voice and pronouncing words or sentences, have made Parrots favourite cage-birds, and sufficiently explain that, when America was first discovered, they were found domesticated by the natives, and that tame Parrots have been kept as pets by the natives of India from time immemorial.

According to Dr. Finsch, Parrots were unknown to the ancient Israelites. The earliest mention of Parrots to be found in ancient history occurs in the description of a festival which took place in Alexandria, in Egypt, 284 B.C. In the time of Alexander the Great the first Parrots were brought to Greece by a general returning from India. But Aristotle, classing the "*Psittace*" with the birds of prey, evidently never saw a Parrot, and derived his scant information from hearsay. Fifty years before Christ, Parrots were known to the Romans, for Parrots are mentioned in writings of that date as brought from Syria. Pliny, A.D. 50, gave the first description of some Parrots found by the emissaries of the Emperor Nero on the banks of the Nile, and evidently *Palæornis torquatus*, or the Ring-necked Parrakeet, is meant. Other early writers mention India as the native country of Parrots, and say that the birds were not eaten in India, but were held sacred on account of their ability to imitate the human voice.

In Rome, Parrots became articles of luxury at an early date, and the price of a Parrot often exceeded that of a slave. During the feasts of the Emperor Antonius Heliogabalus, dishes of cooked Parrot-heads were served,* and the same Emperor's lions were sometimes fed with Peacocks and Parrots. It is nearly certain that the Romans knew no other kind than the Ring-necked Parrakeet. From the first century of the Christian era, history is almost silent on the subject of Parrots during 1,400 years. The Eastern trade had come into the hands of the Venetians and of the Portuguese, and Parrots appear not to have been transported by the tedious trade routes of the Middle Ages. In 1455 a Senegal Parrot was first heard of in Europe. Towards the end of the fifteenth century (1498) the Portuguese circumnavigated the Cape, and acquired during the next years a part of India, where tame Parrots were found by them in many houses of natives. Columbus, too, had returned from his voyage of discovery to America, and had brought Parrots with him when he held his solemn entry in Seville on March 31, 1493. In England the first Parrots were shown as a great curiosity in 1504. A book of birds published in Zurich in 1557 mentions fourteen kinds of Parrots, of which seven can be now recognised by the description published 342 years ago. As a curiosity it may be mentioned that in 1707 a description and illustration of the great black

* In Cuba and some West Indian Islands, parrot soup is at the present day a much-prized dish.

1. COCKATEEL MALE 2. ROSEATE COCKATOO

1A Do FEMALE 3. SCALY BREASTED PARRAKEET

4. LEADBEATERS COCKATOO

Cockatoo of New Guinea (*Microglossa aterrima*) were published at Amsterdam, whilst up to the present day this bird is so rare that a live specimen sells in London at from £15 to £25.

In 1747 to 1764 "A Natural History of Uncommon Birds," by Edwards, was published in London, which depicted 37 species of Parrots; Brisson's "Ornithologia," published 1760, more than doubled the number of known Parrots; and Latham's "General Synopsis of Birds" (1781) added 45 new Parrots to those described by the former author, 25 of these new species being Parrots from Australia and the South Sea Islands. Buffon's "Natural History of Birds" (Paris, 1783) contains drawings of 82 species of Parrots. Shaw, in the "Zoology of New Holland" (1794), first mentions the Undulated Parrakeet, or Budgerigar, of which many thousands are now imported annually into Europe. In the beginning of this century about 120 varieties of Parrots were known. Wagler's work on Parrots, published in Munich, 1832, contained a description of nearly 200 varieties of the Parrot family, which number had grown to 350 by 1867, when Dr. Finsch published his exhaustive monograph on Parrots. Of these 350 Parrots, 142 species are indigenous to America, 23 to Africa, 18 to Asia and Sunda Islands, 83 to the Moluccas, 59 to Australia, and 29 to Polynesia. Not a single species of Parrot is, or ever has been, indigenous to Europe. In view of the distribution of Parrots over the warm and temperate zones of all the rest of the world, the absence of Parrots from Europe is curious. The climate alone cannot be the cause, for we find in North America the Carolina Parrakeet as far north as 43° northern latitude, and in Polynesia we find the New Zealand Parrakeet as far south as 55° southern latitude. On the Himalayas, Parrots are found 4,000 feet above sea-level, and on the Andes close to the snow region. It is abundantly proved that very many Parrots would thrive perfectly well in our climate. Some years since, the owner of an estate in England practically tried to acclimatise Parrots by turning out a number of Cockatoos and other, mostly Australian Parrots. The experiment succeeded beyond expectation, as far as the climate was concerned; but it seems few men with a gun in their hands can see a strange bird without shooting it, and the expensive Parrots let loose by an enthusiastic ornithologist were all wantonly shot.

In size the Parrots vary from that of a Linnet to that of the well-known Macaw and large Cockatoo. Their intelligence and docility vary as much as their size. The best talkers are the African Grey Parrots, and next to them the Brazilian Amazons, the Cockatoo from the Moluccas, and the Indian Ring-necked Parrakeet. Australian Parrots do not as readily learn to talk, but please the eye by their brilliant plumage.

No other birds become so entirely domesticated and so much attached to their keepers as Parrots, and none are so long-lived. But many Parrots utter distracting screams, which may become quite unbearable. It is well to know, however, that most Parrots only scream from fear, and quite forget this bad habit when they become thoroughly tame. Their powerful beaks render Parrots very destructive, and their keeper should therefore provide the strongest possible cages. Experience shows that the larger Parrots, and especially the tame ones, thrive best when kept singly in cages. Tame Parrots are extremely jealous, and to place these in an aviary will cause them often to pine, or to become exceedingly quarrelsome; in the latter case they will inflict fearful injury on each other. Almost all Parrots possess very much individuality, and form strong attachments and equally strong antipathies.

The limits of space at my disposal will oblige me to be much shorter than I had intended to be in my remarks on the various species of Parrots.

CRESTED GROUND PARRAKEET (*Calopsitha Novæ-Hollandiæ*), AUSTRALIA.

(Illustration drawn from living specimens in the possession of, and kindly lent by, Mr. Anton Jamrach.)

Psittacus Novæ-Hollandiæ (Russ), *Palæornis Novæ-Hollandiæ*, *Leptolophus auricomis*, *Nymphicus Novæ-Hollandiæ*, *Cacatua Novæ-Hollandiæ*, *Calipsittacus Novæ-Hollandiæ*. English dealers' name—Cockateel. German name—"Nymfensittich," or "Korella."

The sober-coloured Cockateel is the most gentle and amiable of all Parrots, and if closely scanned, a very pretty bird withal. Very frugal in his food, which consists of canary and a very little millet seed, equally at home in an in-door cage as in an out-door aviary, the Crested Ground Parrakeet deserves to be one of the most popular cage-birds. Never noisy, and not destructive, a pair of these birds may be kept in any roomy, ornamental cage in any sitting-room, or be safely associated with the smallest Finches. Few birds breed more readily in captivity, some pairs laying in a hollow log of wood, whilst others prefer to breed on the ground. They lay from three to seven or even nine white eggs, which are hatched in about three weeks, and the newly-hatched young look like a little yellow bundle of fluff. Cage-bred Cockateels will sometimes learn to talk, male birds proving most teachable. The female, when in fear or angry, indulges in a cat-like hissing. When breeding, my Cockateels ate a little scalded bread mixed with milk and oatmeal, in addition to canary-seed; but I believe dry seeds will be found sufficient to rear these birds with. When very young, scalded canary and millet seed might be added with advantage.

COCKATOOS.

Virtually the genus Cockatoo is confined to Australasia. South of the Australian continent we find Cookatoos in Tasmania, but none in New Zealand. Several species inhabit New Guinea and the Moluccas, including Celebes, but west of Celebes no Cockatoos exist. Towards the east the Solomon Islands appear to be the limit of their zone, and north of the Equator only the Philippine Islands are inhabited by Cockatoos (and by one species only—*Cacatua Philippinarum*, Red-vented Cockatoo). In this comparatively limited zone a large number of species of Cockatoos exist, varying in size from that of a European Jay to that of a Raven. Most Cockatoos are of white plumage, and their feathers have the peculiarity that a fine white dust adheres to them which may be rubbed off, and which will adhere to a coat-sleeve like flour. The distinguishing feature of Cockatoos is the crest, which the birds can erect at pleasure by a contraction of the skin covering their skull. The shape of the crest varies in the different species.

Cockatoos are easily tamed, and very easily kept. Canary, hemp-seed, oats, and Indian corn are their staple food, which may be supplemented by biscuits, green-meat, and any kind of fruit. Boiled rice and boiled Indian corn must be added in the case of Cockatoos newly imported from the Moluccas or from New Guinea. The Molucca Cockatoos reach Europe mostly *viâ* Holland, and show much aptitude for learning to talk.

Within the last ten or fifteen years the large numbers of Cockatoos arriving in England from Australia have almost supplanted the more expensive and much more delicate Cockatoos from the Moluccas. The Australian Cockatoos are, as a rule, so hardy that no limit can be stated as to the number of years they may endure in captivity; but they have much less talent for learning to talk than their cousins from the Moluccas.

All Cockatoos are, when tame, very affectionate, but also very jealous, and long remember and resent an injury. The tremendous power of their beaks should never be lost sight of, and makes the handling of Cockatoos a dangerous operation, to be avoided by any one who is not

MEALY ROSELLA PARAKEET.
HEN.

ROSELLA PARAKEET

practised in taking a Parrot round the neck and holding him firm. If Cockatoos are kept in cages, these should be made of the very strongest iron wire, no ordinary woodwork withstanding their beaks. If kept chained to stands, the chain must be very strong, and the perch of the very hardest wood. Metal perches are liable to cause cramp, colds, and inflammation of the abdomen.

A number of Cockatoos will live peaceably together, and there is no reason why these birds should not breed freely in captivity, provided they were placed in an aviary specially constructed, and so designed that the birds could not succeed in wrecking it. But only a deaf amateur, or one without nerves, should keep a number of Cockatoos, for their screams are simply distracting.

The list of the London Zoological Gardens contains ten Australian Cockatoos, of which the following are the best known:—

THE GREATER SULPHUR-CRESTED COCKATOO (*Cacatua galerita*), Australia.
Psittacus galeritus (Russ), *Plyctolophus galeritus* (Finsch). English dealers' name—Great White Cockatoo. German name—"Grosser gelbgehäubter Kakadu."

A large bird, nearly the size of a Raven, of pure white colour, with pointed crest of bright yellow, hated by Australian farmers, in whose fields of maize he does much damage. If obtained young, this Cockatoo becomes exceedingly tame.

LEADBEATER'S COCKATOO (*Cacatua Leadbeateri*), Australia.
(Illustration drawn from live specimen kindly lent by Mr. Chas. Jamrach.)
Psittacus Leadbeateri (Russ), *Plyctolophus Leadbeateri* (Finsch). English dealers' name—Leadbeater Cockatoo. German name—"Inka Kakadu."

A magnificent native of New South Wales, and the most beautiful of all Cockatoos, but not very docile. The feathers of the pointed crest are red at the base, then an inch or so yellow, then red again, and tipped with white. The body of the bird is white, the head, neck, and underside being delicately tinged with pink.

ROSEATE COCKATOO (*Cacatua roseicapilla*), Australia.
(Illustration drawn from live specimen lent by Mr. Charles Jamrach.)
Psittacus roseicapillus (Russ), *Eolophus roseus*, *Eolophus roseicapilla*, *Plictolophus roseicapillus*. English dealers' name—Rosy Cockatoo. German name—"Rosenrother Kakadu."

This Cockatoo must have been one of the very earliest acquisitions of the London Zoological Society, for we find a specimen presented to the Gardens in 1843. The Roseate Cockatoo is now very frequently imported, and if kept in pairs the screeching propensities will be less than when kept singly. I found the Rosy Cockatoo stupid and uninteresting; others may think differently. Mr. C. W. Gedney has successfully bred this Cockatoo, a success which until now remains unique. Male and female are alike; the crest is very short, and consists of rounded feathers.

Of the Molucca Cockatoos three species are very well known:—

THE LESSER SULPHUR-CRESTED COCKATOO (*Cacatua sulphurea*), Moluccas.
Psittacus sulfureus (Russ), *Psittacus albus galeritus*, *Cacatua luteo cristata*, *Plictolophus sulphureus*. English dealers' name—Lesser Yellow-crested Cockatoo. German name—"Kleiner gelbgehäubter Kakadu."

A small cousin of his big relative, the Greater Sulphur-crested Cockatoo of Australia. Size about that of a Jay, crest pointed, large pale yellow patches on the cheeks, otherwise pure white. This Cockatoo becomes very tame and affectionate, is quite hardy, but not as good a talker as the two following, although a much better linguist than all the preceding species.

THE ROSE-CRESTED COCKATOO (*Cacatua Moluccensis*), MOLUCCAS.

Psittacus Moluccensis (Russ), *Cacatua rubri cristata, Cacatua rosacea, Cacatua erytrolaphus, Plictolophus Moluccensis.* English dealers' name—Rose-crested Cockatoo. German name—"Rothhaubiger Kakadu."

THE GREATER WHITE-CRESTED COCKATOO (*Cacatua cristata*), MOLUCCAS.

Psittacus leucolophus (Russ), *Cacatua leucolophus, Cacatua alba cristata, Cacatua cristatella, Psittaca alba cristata, Plictolophus leucolophus.* English dealers' name—White-crested Cockatoo. German name—"Weissgehäubter Kakadu," "Weisshauben Kakadu."

The Rose-crested and White-crested Cockatoos are very large birds, and almost too big to be kept in an amateur's cage. Their crests are not pointed, the feathers being rounded at the ends. As the names denote, the crests differ in colour. These two species are very clever talkers, but also very loud screamers when untamed.

THE MACAWS,

I may dismiss with a very few words. I tried a Red-and-yellow Macaw (*Ara chloroptera*) and a Blue-and-yellow Macaw (*Ara ararauna*). A couple of expensive cages were demolished very quickly, and before a pair of stands could be finished by the maker. The destruction of the hard wood perches and mahogany uprights of their new stands afforded about two days' amusement to the birds, who next peeled off the wall-paper within reach, and gnawed the corner of a billiard-table. This mischief was accompanied by such deafening screams that a couple of weeks' possession had quite settled my determination to get rid of the magnificent Macaws on any terms, and never to buy one again at any price. Their huge size, brilliant feathers, and loud screams are a very good advertisement for a travelling menagerie, to whom amateurs had better abandon these birds, unless some one would care to construct a wrought-iron in-door aviary (I doubt whether bricks and mortar would be proof against their beaks) to make an attempt at breeding. A pair of Blue-and-yellow Macaws exhibited some years since at the Crystal Palace were said to have laid eggs in confinement; and as Macaws always arrive in Europe quite tame, it ought to be possible to breed them.

Of the American Conures, three kinds will interest the amateur:—

THE CAROLINA CONURE (*Conurus Carolinensis*), NORTH AMERICA.

Psittacus Carolinensis (Russ), *Psittacus luteocapillus, Psittacus ludovicianus, Aratinga ludoviciana et Carolinensis, Conurus ludovicianus.* English dealers' name—Carolina Parrakeet. German name—"Karolina Sittich."

The Carolina Conure is the only Parrot to be found in North America, and lives in higher latitudes than any other kind of Parrot. During a hard winter the Carolina Conure may frequently be seen in the snow, whilst in summer he is the unwelcome guest of farmers in Arkansas, Missouri, and Maryland, doing much damage to fields of Indian corn. Those Carolina Parrakeets which arrive in Europe are almost without exception wild birds caught when fully grown, and are stupidly shy in a cage, screaming terribly at the approach of a human being. When left to themselves they will quickly demolish all but the strongest cages. On the other hand, they will breed freely when placed in a room by themselves; and Dr. Russ reared several broods in his aviary. As these birds are used to very great heat and severe cold in their native country, they may safely be exposed to the vicissitudes of the English climate in an

RING-NECKED PARAKEET. PLUM-HEADED PARAKEET.

open-air aviary during winter. The plumage is green, except a bright yellow head and orange face. Male and female are alike. Food, Indian corn, hemp and canary seed.

THE BLACK-HEADED CONURE (*Conurus nanday*), PARAGUAY.

Psittacus nanday (Russ). English dealers' name—Nanday Parrot. German name—"Schwarzköpfiger Sittich."

This Conure was very rare until lately, but is now frequently obtainable. I found a pair of these birds both hardy and amusing. Their green plumage and black face are in pretty contrast. My pets used to begin to scream terribly when they saw me, and boldly darted at my fingers whenever I put a hand in their cage; but for all that I liked the saucy, bold, noisy birds much. My hopes of breeding them were disappointed by their gnawing the hollow log intended for a nest into minute particles. Food, canary, hemp-seed, Indian corn, millet in the ear, and a little sponge-cake.

THE WHITE-EARED CONURE (*Conurus leucotis*), BRAZIL.

(Illustration drawn from live specimens lent by Mr. Charles Jamrach.)

Psittacus leucotis (Russ), *Aratinga ninus*, *Sittace leucotis*, *Psittacara leucotis*. English dealers' name—White-eared Conure. German name—"Weissbäckiger Sittich."

This small Conure is only a little larger than the Australian Undulated Parrakeet, and was very rare until a year or two ago, but latterly the birds are frequently offered for sale. I believe no other Conure will afford his owner as much pleasure as this one. A pair I kept for a long time proved very intelligent, lively, and hardy, and were quite free from the destructive mania of other Conures, and never indulged in screaming. The food I gave consisted of millet, canary, and a little hemp-seed, with about a quarter of a sponge-cake daily. On this diet my pair of White-eared Conures grew daily prettier.

THE RING-NECKED PARRAKEET (*Palæornis torquatus*), INDIA.

THE ROSE-RINGED PARRAKEET (*Palæornis docilis*), WEST AFRICA. (Illustrated.)

Psittacus torquatus (Russ), *Psittacus Alexandri*, *Psittacus manillensis*, *Psittacus docilis*. English dealers' name—Ring-necked Parrakeet. German name—"Kleiner Alexandersittich."

These are practically the same birds. This Parrot is the only species indigenous to both Africa and Asia, and, as mentioned in the introductory remarks, the Rose-ringed Parrakeet is the Parrot which the Romans brought from Africa in Nero's time, and which is mentioned in the writings of Aristotle, and described by Pliny. The only difference between the Indian and African Ring-necked Parrakeet is that the former have red and the latter black beaks. In Calcutta and in Ceylon these Parrakeets are found wild in every garden, and tame specimens are so common throughout India that sailors bring them over on almost every ship coming home from the East. No other Parrot is more docile, and though slow to learn to talk, the Ring-necked Parrakeet acquires a very clear pronunciation. When first imported, care is requisite to avoid colds, but with judicious treatment these birds become very hardy, and will live many years on a mixture of all kinds of seeds. The female and young birds have no ring round the neck.

PLUM OR BLOSSOM-HEADED PARRAKEET (*Palæornis cyanocephalus*), HINDOSTAN. (Illustrated.)

Psittacus cyanocephalus (Russ), *Psittacus erythrocephalus*, *Psittacus ginginianus*, *Psittacus Bengalensis*, *Palæornis Bengalensis*, *Psittacus annulatus*. English dealers' name—Plum-headed Parrakeet. German name—"Pflaumenkopfsittich."

The Zoological Society's catalogue mentions Hindostan as the habitat of this beautiful Parrakeet, but it is found also on the Madras Coast and in Ceylon. When first imported this species is very delicate, the natives in India feeding the birds mostly on rice in the husk, and the sudden change to canary-seed, together with the change of climate, frequently proves fatal. But if paddy-rice is procured, and these Parrakeets are gradually accustomed to eat canary-seed, millet, Indian corn, and a little sponge-cake, besides rice, they will become very hardy. Dr. Russ not only bred the Plum-headed Parrakeets once, but actually in three generations. In 1877 Dr. Russ exhibited at the Crystal Palace a young pair of these Parrakeets, together with their parents, all of which had been bred in his aviary. Gentle, but not particularly talented, is all that can be said of the characteristic qualities of this bird, whose name is derived from the delicate plum-colour of the head.

MALABAR PARRAKEET (*Palæornis columboides*), SOUTH INDIA.
(Illustration drawn from specimen many years in Author's possession.)
Psittacus peristerodes (Russ), *Psittacus melanorhynchus*. No English dealers' name. German name—"Taubensittich."

Young Malabar Parrakeets are very insignificant-looking bluish-grey and green birds, which few would care to buy, wherefore dealers do not pay a price which tempts sailors and others to import this Parrakeet. But any one becoming possessed of a young Malabar Parrakeet will find himself owner of a treasure, for these gentle birds become year after year more beautiful, until, in the course of three or four years, their plumage attains the perfection shown in the illustration. I found the bird extremely gentle when by himself, but jealous in the society or even within sight of other Parrakeets.

UNDULATED GRASS PARRAKEET (*Melopsittacus undulatus*), AUSTRALIA. (Illustrated.)
Psittacus undulatus (Russ), *Nanodes undulatus*, *Euphema undulata*, *Sagittifer minor undulatus*. English dealers' names—Budgerigar, or Shell Parrot, or Zebra Grass Parrakeet. In Australia the birds are called: Budgerigar—a corruption of the native name—also Shell Parrot, Canary Parrot, or Warbling Grass Parrakeet. German name—"Wellen Sittich," or "Wellenstreifiger Sittich." French name—"Perruche Ondulé."

The Undulated Grass Parrakeet, Shell Parrot, or Budgerigar is so well known that a detailed description of his plumage is superfluous. This miniature Parrot is about the size of our Sparrow, but slender and of elegant shape, vivacious in his movements, and very intelligent, yet good-tempered, and of great beauty. No wonder that this Parrakeet has become a universal favourite, and the most popular foreign bird.

In their native country the Undulated Grass Parrakeets are found in ordinary seasons spread over immense districts, if sufficient rains favour the growth of grass, on the seeds of which the birds live chiefly. Their favourite breeding-places are the southern parts of the Australian Continent, and to these the birds flock in countless numbers, if plentiful spring rains in September—October produce a sufficient crop of grass seeds towards the end of October. If these rains do not occur, and drought should leave the ground bare of vegetation, the Grass Parrakeets migrate north, where tropical rains and thunder-storms invariably produce some amount of grass and seeds. It thus happens that in districts where one year thousands of Grass Parrakeets are caught, not one is even seen in another year if drought occurs.

Of late these birds are chiefly caught at the period of their migration, and I am informed that, as is the case with many other birds, the males arrive first at the place selected for breeding, the females following a little later. Immense flocks thus appear suddenly in certain localities during October or November, and this is the time when the bird-catchers are chiefly at work. Hundreds of Undulated Parrakeets will perch upon one tree, and dozens of pairs may be found to nest in various holes, or even between the roots of the same old stump.

1. WHITE-EARED CONURE. 2. MALABAR PARRAKEET.
1A Do Do Do 3. BLUE-BONNET PARRAKEET.

Bird-catchers have no difficulty when in the midst of these migrating flocks in capturing large numbers. But then in one week they take nothing but males, a few weeks later mostly females, and thus it happens that sometimes large shipments consist mostly of one sex.

As already stated, the first work mentioning these birds was published in 1794. Mr. Gould brought the first pair of live Undulated Grass Parrakeets to England in the year 1840. Between 1840 and 1850 a pair of these little birds were worth £20 or £25. About the years 1850 to 1855 a pair would cost about £5. Between 1855 and 1858 larger numbers of Undulated Parrakeets reached Europe, and their price sank to a couple of sovereigns. Within the last five years the importation of this one species of Parrakeet has increased enormously. About three years ago they could be had in London for about seven shillings per pair, but drought in Australia, and dearth of canary-seed combined, stopped the supplies for a season, and their price rose again to twenty-five and even thirty-five shillings per pair. Previous importations, however, had stocked so many aviaries, and the prices then obtainable were such an incentive to cage-breeding, that Dr. Russ estimates from 10,000 to 25,000 Undulated Grass Parrakeets to be now bred annually in Europe. A few years ago I have myself seen an aviary in Belgium where from 500 to 800 Budgerigars had been bred every year in one enclosure.

The largest importation of Undulated Parrakeets which ever took place was that from January to July, 1879. One ship, the *Hesperus*, brought as many as 4,000 pairs, say 8,000 Undulated Parrakeets, safely and alive to London, and one London dealer sold in four months 14,800 pairs of these birds. The total importation of Budgerigars in London was, in the first six months of 1879, over 50,000 pairs, and they all found buyers. Prices certainly declined, until a dozen birds could be bought retail for a guinea, and captains of Australian ships sold wholesale at one shilling, and even for less, per pair.

In the year 1862 the first specimen of this Parrakeet was deposited in the Zoological Gardens, and in 1879 this bird is nearly as common a cage-bird as the Canary. And a most charming creature the little chattering, chirping, nimble, bright-green fellow is. If we look closely at his plumage we find the yellow markings and black pencilling most delicate and of rare beauty. And if an Undulated Parrakeet should happen to escape us, the pretty sight of seeing his graceful flight from tree to tree almost reconciles us to the loss of the bird.

Surely no other cage-bird is equally frugal as the Budgerigar. A little canary-seed is all he requires, and even the accidental absence of water will not inconvenience him in the least. The organism of these birds is adapted to live in the oftentimes waterless plains of Australia. Thousands of Undulated Grass Parrakeets are brought to Europe annually without receiving a drop of water during the three or four months' voyage, and, strange to say, fewer birds die on the voyage when kept without water, than of those which are supplied with water. After arrival the case may be different; and I more than suspect that of those birds who have made the voyage from Australia to England without tasting water, a good many die soon after arrival. It cannot be natural that a bird should live very long on hard, dry seed without any moisture whatever; and though his organism may be so arranged that he can endure dry food without water for some time, yet a permanent existence under such conditions can scarcely be possible.

From one hundred to five hundred Undulated Parrakeets are put, in Australia, into an old packing-case provided with a shelving row of perches, and over one side of the case wire netting is nailed. It stands to reason that the water-supply in these crowded cages would become very dirty, and that no water at all may be safer during the voyage than contaminated water; but when the poor little birds come afterwards within reach of a drink, they are apt to injure themselves by taking too great a quantity too suddenly. With very little care and thought this danger can easily be avoided, by giving the birds only a few drops of water at first, and *ad libitum* afterwards.

Sometimes a shipment arrives with a loss of only two to five per cent., and in another season the mortality during the voyage may be fifty per cent. and even more. There have been seasons when disease became epidemic, and nearly all Undulated Grass Parrakeets died during the voyage or soon after; and a quite unusual mortality was then observed among Budgerigars of former seasons, and beyond the reach of direct infection. This, as well as the fluctuating import, accounts for the rapid fluctuations in the price of this favourite bird during one season. In the early part of 1879 Budgerigars could be bought retail at three shillings per pair, but sold readily a little later for ten shillings. One would have thought that dealers would hasten to buy every shipment offered at the low prices—for the Undulated Parrakeets only arrive between January and July—and would have kept them until their price rose again. But the experience of former years had taught dealers that it is far better to sell rapidly at a small profit in preference to risking an epidemic and consequent total loss of the capital invested. The birds imported in 1879 proved unusually healthy, and any one buying them might have re-sold them within three months at treble the amount paid for them. Notwithstanding the immense importation, few imported Budgerigars can be bought in the autumn, and the market is then supplied with young cage-bred birds.

On the plains of Australia the Undulated Grass Parrakeets live on grass-seed, and in confinement they care for little else than canary-seed, and nothing agrees with them so well. To tame Undulated Parrakeets is a difficult task, for the simple reason that the birds are entirely indifferent to dainties, and we have no means to tempt their confidence or reward them for their meeting our overtures half-way. They will not touch sugar, they are not very greedy after green-meat; we may withhold water, and they do not mind it in the least; the only thing they absolutely want, and which we cannot leave them without, is canary-seed, to which we may, if we please, add a little millet and some oats. The only way to tame the bird, therefore, is by perseverance in regular feeding by the same hand, accompanied with a little coaxing. Talent for learning to talk the bird has none, but one or two authenticated cases are recorded of Budgerigars learning to say a word or two, probably about as well as the talking seal (called talking fish) once exhibited in London. Not unfrequently the Undulated Parrakeets will, however, learn to imitate the song of a Canary or of other birds.

It is very easy to breed the Grass Parrakeets in confinement. In their natural state they breed in holes of old trees or any other cavity, and all that is required is an appropriate nesting-place. Some like the husk of a cocoa-nut, others a hollowed log of wood. They will lay four to seven white eggs on the bare wood or on a few chips of wood, and hatch them in about twenty days, the young remaining about five weeks in the nest. If the nests are not quite to their taste, the Budgerigars will lay their eggs on the floor of the cage, and there hatch them.

Various breeders have recommended the most heterogenous kinds of food for rearing young Budgerigars. Some recommend bread and milk, others ants' eggs; others, again, egg-food, &c. I believe that healthy Budgerigars require no such, to them, unnatural food, for I consider the birds as strictly seed-eating, and believe they will best bring up their young on canary-seed. Intending breeders should be warned against a few obstacles to success. Single pairs

Vincent Brooks Day & Son Lith

AMAZON PARROT. GREY PARROT.

of Undulated Grass Parrakeets are apt to become too fat for breeding successfully. If a few pairs are kept together, some spiteful individual amongst them frequently destroys the eggs, and the evil-doer is difficult to discover and to remove. These mischief-makers are always unmated hen-birds. But if a room be stocked with fifty, one hundred, or two hundred Budgerigars, supplied with more than sufficient amount of nest accommodation, no such accidents will arise, and all the birds, which in their wild state are eminently gregarious, will select the chosen habitations without difficulty, and nest without trouble. The newly-hatched young are queer-looking grey-brown bodies, and become green only when the feathers begin fully to develop. When hatched in nests of hard wood which happen to be too deep, there is danger of the young birds over-straining their legs when endeavouring to leave the nest, and thereby becoming cripples.

Cage-bred Undulated Parrakeets never fully acquire the bright green of their imported parents, and are found to breed less freely. Male and female are easily distinguished by the male having what the dealers call a blue nose, viz., the hue of the nostrils is blue, while that of the female is pale brown. The birds breed freely almost all the year round after having once begun.

The Undulated Parrakeets are utterly indifferent to warmth, and may safely be kept in a dry open-air aviary during the coldest winter. In fact, they might easily be acclimatised in this country; and a pair of escaped Budgerigars lived for several years in the trees of one of the West-End squares. I kept a pair in an open-air aviary during the severe winter 1878—1879, and no birds could be healthier than they were. It was a curious sight to see these birds flying about merrily whilst thick snow covered the wire roof above them. They were exhibited at the Crystal Palace in February, 1879, and their transfer to the warmer temperature of the show-tent caused them to lay eggs on the floor of their cage, and to begin the serious business of incubation regardless of the thousands of daily spectators.

Budgerigars, when once fairly settled in an aviary or cage, are not likely to fall ill, but many females are lost through egg-binding, the premonitory symptoms of which are drooping wings and a distended abdomen. In such cases I administer a few drops of castor oil with a tooth-pick, and introduce a little sweet oil into the egg-passage by means of a small feather.

A very wide-spread idea is that the Undulated Parrakeets are such affectionate love-birds that if one of a pair happens to die, the other will speedily die from grief; but the fact is that, although these merry little Parrakeets are happiest when kept in pairs, or happier still if kept in large numbers, yet they will live for years singly. No bird that I could name is as harmless towards other birds and as peaceful at all times with his own fellows. In their matrimonial relations these birds are very affectionate. The male bird devotes the whole of his attention to his own mate and the young, and jealously guards the entrance to the nest. Even surplus males are not quarrelsome, but quite the contrary, for unattached male birds often assist in feeding young broods, whilst only unmated females—possibly from disappointment—have often proved destructive to eggs, and had to be removed.

Of late years varieties of the Undulated Parrakeet have been bred with increasing frequency. More or less pure yellow birds have been bred, mostly in Belgium. Even a blue variety has occurred, and at least one breeder has, through careful selection of stock, produced a breed of unusual size. Without doubt another ten or twenty years will witness as great results of intelligent breeding of varieties of the Budgerigar as has been witnessed in the case of the Canary.

TURQUOISINE PARRAKEET (*Euphema pulchella*), NEW SOUTH WALES.

(Illustration drawn from specimens lent by J. C. Marsh, Esq.)

Psittacus pulchellus (Russ), *Psittacus Edwardsii*, *Nanodes pulchellus*, *Lathamus azureus*. English dealers' name—Turquoisine. German name—"Schön Sittich."

This handsome Parrakeet is very little larger than the Undulated Parrakeet, and quite as lively and interesting. Unfortunately most of them arrive in poor condition and minus part of their plumage, in which state the birds are delicate; but if quietly housed in a clean cage and supplied with good canary-seed, the Turquoisine Parrakeets recover in a few weeks, and are then perfectly hardy birds, which may safely be placed in any out-door aviary, and which will breed freely, laying from four to eight eggs. In the London Zoological Gardens some were first bred in 1860, and since that time thousands have been bred elsewhere. Their treatment should be like that of the Undulated Parrakeets.

BOURKE'S PARRAKEET (*Euphema Bourkii*), AUSTRALIA.

(Illustration drawn from specimen in the possession of Mr. Joseph Groom.)

Psittacus Bourki (Russ), *Nanodes Bourkii*, *Platycercus Bourki*. English dealers' name—Bourke's Parrakeet. German name—"Bourk Sittich."

This delicately tinted Australian Grass Parrakeet is one of the most gentle birds of the Parrot tribe. It is much to be regretted that the Bourke's Parrakeet is so rarely imported, and therefore very dear to buy. If once acclimatised the birds are very hardy and breed freely. Mr. Groom, of Camden Town, London, had the best pair which I ever saw, and kept them summer and winter in one of the open-air aviaries of his own construction, where the birds hatched a brood of young. I quote Mr. Groom's report verbatim:—"The egg of the Bourkii is about the size of a Turquoisine's egg, of roundish shape. The male bird assists in the incubation. Time, about seventeen days. Nest in wood log hollowed out for them, as they do not appear to have the power to cut away the wood like most Parrakeets do."

The three next Australian Parrakeets are considerably larger than the Grass Parrakeets, and of very gorgeous plumage. Their colours are, if anything, too loud to please all tastes, but the illustrations will speak for themselves.

They are easily obtainable at moderate prices (fifteen to thirty shillings each), and are kept solely on account of their great beauty. Gentle and confiding creatures, they are not very intelligent. Being very hardy, they may be kept easily on all kinds of seed, and are best fed on a mixture of oats, hemp, canary-seed, and Indian corn. Some writers assert that Pennants, Rose-bill, and other Parrakeets feed partly on insects; but I consider this assertion, for many reasons, open to doubt. Be that as it may, during breeding-time—viz., January to April—some soaked bread, oatmeal, and milk, and a little egg may be given with advantage, and it will be found that all these Parrakeets are not difficult to breed. Male and female are so much alike that no absolute distinguishing marks can be named.

PENNANT'S PARRAKEET (*Platycercus Pennanti*), NEW SOUTH WALES. (Illustrated.)

Psittacus Pennanti (Russ), *Psittacus gloriosus*, *Psittacus splendidus*. English dealers' name—Pennantes, or Pennant's Parrot. German name—"Pennant's Sittich."

ROSE-BILL PARRAKEET (*Platycercus eximius*), NEW SOUTH WALES. (Illustrated.)

Psittacus eximius (Russ), *Psittacus capitatus*, *Psittacus omnicolor*. English dealers' name—Rosella. German name—"Bunt-sittich."

PALE-HEADED PARRAKEET (*Platycercus pallidiceps*), NORTH-EAST AUSTRALIA. (Illustrated.)

Psittacus palliceps (Russ), *Platycercus palliceps*, *Platycercus cœlestis*, *Conurus palliceps*. English dealers' name—Blue Rosella. German name—"Blassköpfiger Buntsittich."

VII

1. TURQUOISINE PARRAKEET.
2A. MANY COLOURED PARRAKEET, MALE.
2B. Do FEMALE.

A very interesting and charming bird is the next:

THE BLUE-BONNET PARRAKEET (*Psephotus hæmatogaster*), Australia.

(Illustration drawn from live specimen at the Zoological Gardens, London.)

Psittacus hæmatogaster (Russ), *Platycercus hæmatogaster*, *Psephotus hæmatorrhous*, *Euphema hæmatogaster*. English dealers' name—Blue-bonnet Parrakeet. German name—" Blutbauchsittich."

I do not know a more pleasing Parrakeet than the Blue Bonnet, whom I used to consider the clown of a collection of Parrakeets I had at one time. A pair of these birds used to play together like kittens, rolling over and over in the sand, or sitting on the perches and cawing to each other in the most amusing manner. Whenever their cage was fresh sanded, they picked out all the small stones, and cleverly arranged them in a row on a ledge in their cage. This rare Parrakeet is probably one of the most intelligent of all Australian Parrots, although I have not heard that any have learned to talk, nor do any appear to have been bred.

Their food consists chiefly of canary-seed, millet, oats, and Indian corn. Mine were exceedingly fond of oats. Male and female very similar; the plumage of the female is supposed to be less bright.

BLOOD-RUMPED PARRAKEET (*Psephotus hæmatonotus*), Australia.

(Illustration drawn from specimens lent by Mr. Jas. Abrahams and Mr. Chas. Jamrach.)

Psittacus hæmatnotus (Russ), *Euphema hæmatonota*. English dealers' name—Blood-rump. German name—" Rothrumpf," or " Blutrumpf," or " Singsittich."

This Parrakeet is also one of those imported in very large numbers—very hardy and very easily bred. Undulated Parrakeets, Turquoisines, Cockateels, and Blood-rumps breed about equally well, and much in the same manner. A peculiarity of the Blood-rump is his song, which is quite surprisingly agreeable, and by which he endeavours to attract the attention and gain the affections of his mate. Food, same as other Parrakeets.

The two next species are well named the Many-coloured and the Beautiful Parrakeet, but they have caused more disappointment and loss to amateurs than all the other Parrakeets together. To begin with, these birds are rarely obtainable for less than £5 a pair, but their wondrous plumage attracts one amateur after another to try his luck, and the result is generally the same—either early death or a quite unexpected fit just when their owner believes he has achieved a triumph in keeping the bird for a time.

I have been informed that these Parrakeets live for part of the year on grass and other seeds, but that when the so-called "wattle shrub" is in flower they chiefly feed on its blooms, and that birds caught when feeding on seeds will live, whilst those caught during the flower season will not endure. What may be the European substitute of the Australian wattle shrub blooms has yet to be found out, and will no doubt be discovered; meanwhile blooming groundsel does duty, and a plentiful daily supply certainly prolongs the life of these splendid Parrakeets in a very extraordinary manner. The Australian wattle shrub is a kind of acacia, and bears a white ball-shaped flower.

MANY-COLOURED PARRAKEET (*Psephotus multicolor*), Australia.

(Illustration drawn from live specimens, the male in the possession of J. C. Marsh, Esq., the female in that of the Author.)

Psittacus multicolor (Russ), *Platycercus multicolor*, *Euphema multicolor*. English dealers' name—Many-coloured Parrakeet. German name—" Vielfarbiger Sittich."

A glance at the illustration will convince the reader that the Many-coloured Parrakeet is one of the most beautiful birds of his tribe. The female in my possession happens to have endured for years, but I feel sure that some day she will be so unreasonable as to die, without any palpable reason, as several of her mates did long ago. Meantime she feeds on canary-seed and millet, with a little sponge-cake daily.

BEAUTIFUL PARRAKEET (*Psephotus pulcherrimus*), AUSTRALIA.

(Illustration drawn from specimens belonging to Mr. Jas. Abrahams.)

Psittacus pulcherrimus (Russ), *Platycercus pulcherrimus*, *Euphema pulcherrima*. English dealers' name—Paradise Parrakeet. German name—"Paradies Sittich."

There cannot be two opinions that the Paradise Parrakeet is the most beautiful of all the Parrakeets, and it would be difficult to describe in words the splendour and variety of colours displayed in his plumage. As a male bird only attains perfection in his third year, and young males are often mistaken for hen-birds, Mr. Rutledge has drawn a pair of old Paradise Parrakeets and a half mature male, about one and a half or two years old. It will be seen that the female can be readily distinguished.

Beyond referring to what I have stated on page 437, I cannot, in spite of many years' observation, give any useful hints as to their keep. Once I had what I thought to be the most beautiful pair which could be seen, and I was anxious to procure a second hen, as the pair did not seem inclined to breed. In course of time I picked a good hen out of a number just arrived. The excitement of the male was great when I introduced the new hen. He spread his wings, and called and bowed, and all at once fell dead off his perch. Another time I introduced a male very slowly and cautiously, bringing his cage a little nearer each day; but he presently declined his food, and soon died of exhaustion. An opportunity to buy a pair very cheap led me to try an open-air aviary, but the first chilly night was the death of that pair. I could give numerous other examples, and yet one female lived in my aviary for years. Dr. Russ had a pair during four years, and a friend of mine at Baden-Baden is determined to be the first to breed these Parrakeets at some future time. So far my friend has succeeded only in obtaining eggs; which anyhow is more than any one else has achieved.

Dr. Russ observed in his aviary that the Paradise Parrakeets were fond of hemp-seed, and ate fresh ants' eggs, mealworms, and egg-food, eating but little canary and millet, whilst I fed mine on canary-seed, millet in the ear, and groundsel. An Australian bird-catcher informs me that the Beautiful Parrakeets build their nests in forsaken ant-hills, into which they burrow a hole. Can this be correct?

BARRABAND'S PARRAKEET (*Polytelis Barrabandi*), NEW SOUTH WALES.

Psittacus Barrabandi or *rosaceus* (Russ), *Palæornis Barrabandi*, *Palæornis ro.aceus*, *Platycercus rosaceus*, *Platycercus Barrabandi*, *Barrabandius rosaceus*. English dealers' name—Cut-throat Parrakeet, or Green-leek Parrakeet. German name—"Schild Sittich."

This Parrakeet, like the two preceding, is said to live on the bloom of the wattle shrub during part of the year, but he does not appear to be quite as delicate as the Paradise or Many-coloured, although I have gathered costly experience by seeing Barrabands fall in fits from their perch for very trivial causes. A fit means either immediate death or partial paralysis, and I can only suggest a constant supply of green food and a great variety of seeds as a preventive. The bird will endure a low temperature without harm or inconvenience, but no amateur has yet come near breeding this species. Bright green body-colour, orange-yellow face and throat, the latter encircled by a broad band of crimson, are the leading characteristics of the male Green-leek's plumage. The female is simply green, without orange or crimson. In size the birds exceed that of the well-known common Ring-necked Parrakeet.

1. BOURKE'S PARRAKEET. 2. RED-WINGED PARRAKEET.
3. BLOOD-RUMPED PARRAKEET (A) MALE. 3B FEMALE.

RED-WINGED PARRAKEET (*Aprosmictus erythropterus*), Australia.
(Illustration painted from live specimen lent by Mr. Chas. Jamrach.)
Psittacus erythropterus (Russ), *Psittacus melanotus*, *Platycercus erythropterus*, *Ptistes erythropterus et coccineopterus*. English dealers' name—Blood-wing Parrakeet, or Crimson-wing Parrakeet. German name—"Rothflügeliger Sittich."

The Red-winged or Crimson-winged Parrakeet is a timid, rare, and very beautiful bird, very nearly as large as a Grey Parrot, and well adapted for cage-life. Though the Crimson-wing may not learn to talk, neither will he scream; and his gentle manners, together with his brilliant plumage, will recommend him as a pet. I once possessed what I believed to be the most perfect specimen of a male Crimson-wing, and took much trouble to find him a wife. When I at last succeeded in obtaining a female, the result was a great fight and considerable danger to life and limb. Although kept for a year in cages standing within a few inches of each other, the two birds never became even reconciled, and yet if the books are correct (?), according to which the plumage of the female is less bright, and the red on the wing less extensive, I had an undoubted pair.* The Crimson-wing has never been bred in confinement, but an amateur in Germany had a solitary hen which laid a few eggs.

KING PARRAKEET (*Aprosmictus scapulatus*), New South Wales. (Illustrated.)
Psittacus cyanopygus (Russ), *Psittacus scapulatus*, *Psittacus tabuensis*, *Platycercus scapulatus*, *Platyc. scapularis*, *Platyc. cyanopygus*. English dealers' name—King Parrot. German name—"Kœnigs Sittich."

The largest, one of the best known, and most brilliant of the Australian Parrakeets is the very sedate and amiable King Parrakeet. Whilst European amateurs pay high prices for these birds, Australian settlers have good reason to wish the whole species eradicated or transferred to some other part of the world, for they do much damage to crops of grain. King Parrakeets require much water. Drought in the interior of the Australian continent forces large numbers to visit the coast settlements, where they are caught whilst bathing and drinking. Newly-caught birds will at once take to their food in a cage, and thrive on Indian corn, hemp-seed, canary-seed, oats, wheat, and almost any other seeds. Artificial heat in winter seems not to agree with King Parrakeets at all, and provided they are wintered in a room without a fire, no difficulty will be experienced in keeping these Parrakeets for years. Notwithstanding detailed "instructions" for breeding King Parrakeets invented by various authors and published in due course, I do not think that this Parrakeet has yet been bred and reared successfully, although there really exists no reason why it should be difficult or impossible. Until the birds are over two years old, male and female are very difficult to distinguish, but subsequently the bright crimson of the breast and lower body will spread over the head and neck of the male, whilst the head of the female remains green.

GREY PARROT (*Psittacus erithacus*), West Africa. (Illustrated).
Psittacus erithacus (Russ), *Psittacus Guineensis cinereus*, *Psittacus ruber*. English dealers' name—Grey Parrot. German name—"Grau Papagei," or "Jako."

The best-known and most popular Parrot is our domestic pet "Polly," the Grey Parrot from Africa. Whether the Romans had already learnt to esteem this bird is doubtful, but

* Since the above was written I parted with my unloving pair of Blood-wings. They came into the possession of a very intelligent amateur in Germany, and vexed him, as they had vexed me, by furiously fighting when placed in one cage. A simple expedient succeeded in making the birds agree, and is worth knowing. The partiality of pigeons for aniseed oil is well known. A few drops of this oil were spread on the plumage of the Blood-wing hen, and the effect was beyond all expectation, for instead of quarrelling and biting, the birds at once displayed great affection for each other, and there is every prospect of a successful brood resulting.

he, or "she" (as Parrots are usually called "she"), is certainly well known in Europe since the Middle Ages. Volumes of anecdotes about the cleverness, sagacity, linguistic and musical talents of Grey Parrots might be collected. The French explorer and ornithologist, Levaillant, describes a Grey Parrot he found at the house of a lady at Amsterdam at the end of the last century, which bird not only fetched his master's slippers and nightcap at the word of command, but also called the servant and spoke Dutch fluently, which language, according to Levaillant, the Grey Parrot has a special aptitude to learn. Since Levaillant's time Grey Parrots have, however, learnt every European language about equally well, and as every mother's baby is the prettiest darling ever seen, so every pet Grey Parrot is a perfect wonder in the eyes of his owner. There can be no doubt, however, that the Grey Parrot is the most intelligent of all Parrots, and a being gifted with an extraordinary memory and a wonderful talent for mimicking any kind or almost any number of sounds.

About his life in the wild state we know very little. His nest is supposed to be in the holes of trees in forests difficult of access, and the natives are said to believe that the nests are so hot that any one putting a hand into a nest would burn his fingers. The burnt fingers probably mean a very sharp bite, and read in this way, it becomes perfectly plain that nobody would care to put his hand into a Grey Parrot's nest.

Those Parrots brought to Europe are generally young birds caught soon after leaving their nest. Until accustomed to captivity and to human society they make a fearful noise, consisting of a continuous grating hoarse scream, which they forget gradually when becoming tame. In times gone by, sailors used to bring one or two Grey Parrots to Europe, which were petted and tamed during the long sea-voyage of sailing-ships. Now, dozens of Grey Parrots are packed like merchandise into any old box and stowed away anywhere on board the steamers without much regard to ventilation or health. As a result, Grey Parrots can be bought in hundreds for less than a sovereign each, but these birds are almost without exception tainted by blood-poisoning, and will regularly die within a few months. I have tried half a dozen apparently healthy young Grey Parrots with every kind of treatment I could think of, and the result has invariably been death within three to six months; and several German doctors have tried batches of fifty Grey Parrots, applying all known remedies against blood-poisoning without satisfactory results. An acclimatised tame Grey Parrot at the price of £5 is cheaper than a raw young bird at so many shillings. Young Grey Parrots can easily be distinguished by their grey eyes, the eye of old birds being straw-coloured. Male and female are alike, and both sexes are equally gifted.

Buffon (who died in 1788) wrote that some one had bred Grey Parrots in confinement, but beyond this rather vague account of a tame Grey Parrot's propagation, I have heard of no modern instance of success in breeding. Considering the frequent instances of Grey Parrots laying eggs, although kept singly, it ought to be easy to breed them, and cage-bred Grey Parrots would fairly be worth any price in reason. It is marvellous that cage-breeding of foreign birds has never yet been taken up as a business in England. Dozens of aquaria have sprung into existence, where people may see soles and codfish disporting themselves in their native element. The habits of fish are not nearly so interesting as those of birds, and for one private aquarium there are hundreds of private aviaries. A large well-arranged aviary, in which the life and habits of birds in their natural state could be observed, would be one of the prettiest sights, and would interest thousands. Breeding and acclimatising foreign cage-birds for sale would afford a source of large profits if properly managed. Zoological gardens can scarcely be expected to do much in this direction,

Vincent Brooks Day & Son Lith

KING PARROT. PENNANT'S PARAKEET.

as visitors of these establishments expect to see a general collection of animals, and thereby the minute care of any special department becomes difficult. In the Zoological Garden of Antwerp, birds have been bred and dealt in as a business, and the enormous success of this splendid garden has been largely due to its traffic in foreign birds.

But to return to Grey Parrots. It is certain that some have lived for over fifty years, and no limit to their endurance, if once acclimatised, can be stated. Their food should be hemp, canary-seed, oats, wheat, and Indian corn. They will become accustomed to almost anything which human beings eat. Ripe fruit, nuts, and biscuits are a welcome occasional addition to their diet. Bathing is very beneficial, and if Parrots do not bathe of their own free will, exposure to a warm shower in summer, or a warm shower bath, so applied by a garden syringe that the bird does not become frightened, improves the condition and plumage.

BLUE-FRONTED AMAZON (*Chrysotis æstiva*), South America. (Illustrated.)

Psittacus æstivus (Russ). English dealers' name—Amazon Parrot. German name—"Rothbug-amazone."

The Amazon is, next to the Grey Parrot, the best talking bird in existence. Considering the enormous mortality of newly-imported Grey Parrots, I should recommend the Amazon in preference to the Grey Parrot to any one intending to train or teach a Parrot. Young Amazons may be recognised hy the brown colour of the eye, which with age changes to orange. Food and treatment of Amazons should be exactly like that of Grey Parrots.

The varieties of Amazon Parrots are very numerous, the list of the Zoological Gardens containing no less than twenty-five species, all natives of South America, Central America, and the West Indies. Opinions differ greatly about the talents of the various kinds, which, if fairly compared, are probably about equal. The Blue-fronted Amazon is the most frequently imported.

From the large short-tailed Grey and Amazon Parrot we now turn our attention to the smallest members of the Parrot family, the Love-birds. It may be stated at once that a great deal of trash has been written about these birds. They are neither more nor less loving than many other birds; and as to their dying if the mate happens to die, it is simply a myth, for a single bird will live very well. The truth is that thoughtless bird-keepers have often treated those birds wrongly, and the same improper food or draught caused both birds to fall ill, only not quite at the same time. Number One is then supposed to have died because he was home-sick, and Number Two from grief for Number One; while in reality both birds together, or either singly, might have done very well, if it had either arrived free from disease and been properly treated.

RED-HEADED LOVE-BIRD, OR LOVE-BIRD PARRAKEET (*Agapornis pullaria*), West Africa. (Illustrated.)

Psittacus pullarius (Russ), *P. minimus*, *P. Guineensis*, *Psittacula pullaria*. English dealers' name—Red-headed or Abyssinian Love-bird. German name—"Unzertrennliche," or "Inseparable."

This Parrakeet is not larger than a Sparrow, and the little green fellow with his crimson face is a very pretty sight. When many are seen together, as at a wholesale dealer's, they will be found sitting together on the same perch as closely as possible. Male and female are much alike; the face of the hen-bird is believed to be less red, but as the intensity of the red tint depends as much on age as on sex, this is not a sure guide. A certain distinguishing mark is that the male bird is black on the inner side of the wings, the female green.

No Red-headed Love-birds have been bred in captivity as yet, and therefore it does not matter very much whether amateurs obtain a real pair or two birds of the same sex, which will agree quite as well as a pair does. Food, canary, millet, Indian corn, and oats.

ROSY-FACED PARRAKEET (*Agapornis roseicollis*), SOUTH AFRICA.

Psittacus roseicollis (Russ), *Psittaculus roseicollis.* No English dealers' name. German name—"Rosen-papagei."

Somewhat larger than the Red-headed Love-bird, with red forehead and rose-coloured throat. This Parrakeet is remarkable for having been bred repeatedly by Dr. Russ, and by at least two other amateurs. The species is so rare that I have never seen any specimens at a dealer's; as I missed seeing the few arrivals which took place during the last ten years, before the birds were sent abroad.

MADAGASCAR LOVE-BIRD, OR GREY-HEADED PARRAKEET (*Agapornis cana*), MADAGASCAR. (Illustrated.)

Psittacus canus (Russ), *Psittacus polyocar, Polyopsitta cana, Psittacula Madagascarensis.* English dealers' name—Grey-headed Love-bird Madagascar Love-bird. German name—"Graukōpfiger Zwerg-papagei."

Until about five years ago the Grey-headed Love-birds were rare, but notwithstanding their considerable price these charming little Parrakeets found willing purchasers, and as a consequence they are now imported in large numbers.

The Madagascar Love-bird is not larger than a Sparrow, of green body-colour, and the male has a pale silver-grey head; the female is uniformly green. These birds bear a moderately low temperature very well, and breed freely in our climate. They, as well as the Rosy-faced Parrakeet, construct a kind of nest in a curious way, for they will tear wood into strips, and, placing these strips between the feathers of their back, will carry them into the hole selected for a nest. As these bits of wood mostly fall to the ground during their flight or in entering the nest, extraordinary assiduity and patience are shown by the quantity of splinters which a hen Grey-headed Love-bird accumulates in her nest. Although I have not been fortunate enough to breed this Parrakeet successfully, I obtained from various pairs numerous eggs, and other amateurs have bred them freely. Food, canary-seed and millet.

PASSERINE PARRAKEET (*Psittacula passerina*), SOUTH AMERICA.

Psittacus passerinus (Russ), *Psittaculus passerinus, Agapornis cyanopterus, Conurus passerinus, Psittacula Brasiliensis, Uropygio cyaneo, Psittacula passerina gregaria et modesta.* English dealers' name—Brazilian Love-bird. German name—"Sperlings-papagei," or "Blauflügeliger Zwerg-papagei."

The Passerine Parrakeet is if anything a trifle smaller than his red-faced and grey-headed relatives from Africa and Madagascar. His plumage is bright green, but underneath the wings, and at the root of the tail, brilliant blue. When newly arrived the Brazilian Love-bird is rather delicate, but with a little care the species becomes quite hardy and a highly-esteemed and pretty cage-bird. Dr. Russ has bred these Parrakeets repeatedly; elsewhere such success has been very rare. Food, like that of the other dwarf Parrakeets, millet and canary seed.

Vincent Brooks Day & Son

BLUE STRIPED LORY. BLUE MOUNTAIN LORY.

BLUE-CROWNED HANGING PARRAKEET (*Loriculus galgulus*), MALACCA.

Psittacus galgulus (Russ), *Psittacus flavigulus*, *Psittacus pumilius*, *Psittacula galgulus*, *Psittacula galgula*, *Psittacula cyaneo-pileata*, *Loriculus pumilis*, *Coryllis galgulus*. English dealers' name—Malacca Hanging Parrakeet. German name—"Blauscheiteliges Papageichen," or "Blauscheiteliger Fledermans-papagei."

The most beautiful of these small Parrakeets is the gorgeous Blue-crowned Hanging Parrakeet (*Loriculus galgulus*), from Malacca, a miniature Parrot not larger than a Goldfinch, of bright green colour, a bright blue spot on the top of his head, and a large patch of brilliant vermilion on his throat and tail. This little bird loves to hang head downwards in his cage. If we could but keep this charming little bird! I have tried it, and *Loriculus galgulus* would not live: the English climate does not appear to agree with this delicate Parrakeet. In France and Germany amateurs have been much more successful. Boiled rice well sweetened, very ripe fruit, and canary-seed are the only things these dainty dwarfs will touch.

BLUE MOUNTAIN LORY, OR SWAINSON'S LORIKEET (*Trichoglossus Novæ-Hollandiæ*), AUSTRALIA. (Illustrated.)

Psittacus Swainsonii (Russ), *Psittacus Novæ-Hollandiæ*, *Psittacus hæmatodus*, *Psittacus cyanogaster*, *Trychoglossus hæmatodus*, *Tr. multicolor*, *Tr. Swainsonii*. English dealers' name—Blue Mountain Lory. German name—"Lori von den Blauen Bergen."

In 1868 the Zoological Society of London purchased a pair of Blue Mountain Lories, and about 1870 these brilliant birds first began to make their appearance in bird-dealers' shops. Since then they have been frequently imported, and are now readily obtainable by any amateur willing to spend £4 or £5 on a pair of such very gorgeous Parrots.

Of all known Lories the Blue Mountain Lory most readily takes to a diet of seeds, eating chiefly canary-seed. I would advise to feed these birds on a mixture of canary-seed, oats, millet, Indian corn, and hemp-seed, giving daily in addition either a piece of sponge-cake, a little sweetened boiled rice, a couple of dates or figs, or some ripe fresh fruit.

Some writers on cage-birds have called Swainson's Lorikeet a very delicate bird. This assertion is contradicted by the fact that I have kept these birds for years without difficulty. I presented one bird of this kind to a friend in the autumn of 1870, and this bird lived over six years in my friend's study, laying several eggs, although kept singly. Besides canary-seed and maize, this Blue Mountain Lory was fed on a little sugar, with occasionally a morsel of raw beef scraped very fine and mixed with scraped carrot. I have before me the names of four amateurs who have successfully bred this Parrot.

Male and female of Swainson's Lorikeet are very difficult to distinguish, the only difference being that the blue head of the female is a trifle less bright. Whether the sometimes more orange, sometimes more scarlet tint of the breast is due to sex or age has not yet been determined.

Like most Parrots, the Blue Mountain Lory can only be kept with other Parrots at considerable risk, and I had to learn that two males put in one cage under the impression of being a pair can kill each other. On the whole the bird is amiable, but rather shy. His noise, however, is nearly as disagreeable as his plumage is beautiful.

BLUE-STRIPED LORY (*Eos reticulata*), TIMORHAUT. (Illustrated.)

Psittacus reticulatus (Russ), *Domicella reticulata*, *Lorius Corneus*, *Eos cyanostriata*. English dealers' name—Blue-striped, Blue-streaked, or Blue-necked Lory. German name—"Blaugestrichelter Lory," or "Gestreifter Lory."

A highly ornate bird, but very difficult to acclimatise. As stated above, the Blue Mountain Lory is really the only Lory, many specimens of which endure cage-life in Europe. The only way to treat Lories successfully is to feed them on boiled rice, sponge-cake, and fruit (currants in winter are a good makeshift), and to accustom them gradually to canary-seed and Indian corn, by keeping a dish of seeds continually in the cage. If they once take to eating dry seed, the daily allowance of boiled rice, &c., may be very gradually reduced, and the sponge-cake may then be given dry. The choice of beautiful and enduring Parrots is so large that amateurs may well leave these costly and delicate Lories to the zoological gardens.

SCALY-BREASTED PARRAKEET (*Trichoglossus chlorolepidotus*), NEW SOUTH WALES.
(Illustration drawn from stuffed specimen shot and preserved by Mr. Anton Jamrach.)
Psittacus chlorolepidotus (Russ), *Trichoglossus matoni*. English dealers' name—Scaly-breasted Lory. German name—"Gelbgeschuppter Lori."

It would scarcely interest the reader if I expressed my doubts whether those ornithologists are right who class this Parrakeet amongst the Lories. Mr. Gould says that the Scaly-breasted Parrakeet in New South Wales lives almost entirely on the flower of the Eucalypti. The six or more of these lively and charming little Parrakeets which I possessed at various times ate canary-seed and a morsel of dry sponge-cake very cheerfully, and prospered on this diet as well as any cage-bird can do, and as Lories unfortunately do not.

It is much to be regretted that this very handsome Parrakeet is so very rarely obtainable, for other amateurs would no doubt be as much pleased with this gentle and beautiful Parrakeet as I was.

SWIFT LORIKEET (*Lathamus discolor*), TASMANIA.
(Illustration painted from stuffed specimen, in the Author's possession when alive.)
Psittacus discolor (Russ), *Ps. humeralis*, *Ps. Lathami*, *Ps. Australis*, *Ps. Banksianus*, *Nanodes discolor*, *Euphema discolor*, *Trichoglossus discolor*. English dealers' name—Latham's or Swift Lorikeet. German name—"Schwalben Lori," or "Lori mit rosenrothem Gesicht."

The brilliant Swift Lorikeet, which I consider one of the most beautiful Australian Parrakeets, is a migratory bird, breeding in Southern Australia, and migrating north in the winter, His very rapid flight has caused it to be named Swift Parrakeet. Though not rare in Australia. it is not often brought to Europe, where high prices are readily obtained for the species. Immediately after arrival these birds are delicate, and require careful feeding on millet and canary seed, and soaked bread or sponge-cake, to both of which a little honey may be added with advantage. I have, however, been credibly informed that this Parrakeet, like many other Australians, becomes so hardy when fairly acclimatised, that Swift Parrakeets have been wintered in perfect health in out-door aviaries.

Every connoisseur will see at a glance that many birds of which the reader might wish to have had some account have not even been mentioned; but the limits of the foregoing chapters had been fixed before I was requested to write them, and the chief difficulty was to compress the material into the allotted space. Should the interest in foreign cage-birds extend as much as seems probable, a future edition may enable me to add matter necessarily excised now, and meanwhile other amateurs will no doubt gather fresh experience of interest to keepers of foreign birds. The communication of any fresh discoveries or observations relating to foreign cage-birds, addressed to the care of Messrs. Cassell, Petter, Galpin & Co., will much oblige

THE AUTHOR.

Vincent Brooks Day & Son Lith.

1A. BEAUTIFUL PARRAKEET. MALE.
B. Do. Do FEMALE.
1AA " " YOUNG MALE.
2. SWIFT LORIKEET

INDEX.

CANARIES.

BRITISH CAGE-BIRDS.

FOREIGN CAGE-BIRDS,

INCLUDING GERMAN, FRENCH, AND LATIN SYNONYMS.

ÇASSELL, PETTER, GALPIN & CO., BELLE SAUVAGE WORKS, LONDON, E.C.

SD - #0002 - 050923 - C0 - 229/152/37 - PB - 9780259462897 - Gloss Lamination